Politics **USA**

Politics USA

Robert J. McKeever

Philip Davies

Harlow, England • London • New York • Boston • San Francisco • Toronto • Sydney • Auckland • Singapore • Hong Kong
Tokyo • Seoul • Taipei • New Delhi • Cape Town • São Paulo • Mexico City • Madrid • Amsterdam • Munich • Paris • Milan

Pearson Education Limited
Edinburgh Gate
Harlow
Essex CM20 2JE
England

and Associated Companies throughout the world

Visit us on the World Wide Web at:
www.pearson.com/uk

First published in Great Britain in 1999
Second edition published 2006
This edition published 2012

ISBN 978-1-4082-0450-4

British Library Cataloguing-in-Publication Data
A catalogue record for this book is available from the British Library

Library of Congress Cataloguing-in-Publication Data
McKeever, Robert J., 1951-
Politics USA / Robert J. McKeever and Philip Davies. -- 3rd ed.
p. cm
Includes bibliographical references and index.
ISBN 978-1-4082-0450-4
1. United States--Politics and government--Textbooks. I. Davies, Philip, 1948- II. Title.
JK276.M35 2012
320.473--dc23
2012008797

10 9 8 7 6 5 4 3 2 1
16 15 14 13 12

Typeset in 10/12.5pt ITC Century by 35
Printed and bound in China
EPC/01

Contents

Preface to the third edition

Much has happened in the United States since the second edition of this book was published in 2006 – and little of it has been positive. The American economy has experienced its deepest recession since the Great Depression of the 1930s and while some signs of recovery have appeared, these are partial and slow. American foreign and defence policy has also seen serious disappointments, despite huge levels of expenditure and significant combat casualties. President Obama has withdrawn all US troops from Iraq, but it is far from clear what benefits have accrued from the war launched by President George W. Bush in 2003. President Obama has also announced the date for the final withdrawal of US troops from Afghanistan, but if anything, this war is widely perceived as even less successful than that in Iraq.

Unsurprisingly, these major setbacks have had a deep impact on American politics. In this third edition, we set out to analyse these contemporary developments and place them in the context of the enduring structures and themes of the American political system. We aim to provide our readers with a comprehensive, lucid and stimulating account of the origins and development of the American system of government. It is for this reason that we look at the economic and social roots of the system as well as its constitutional and political dimensions. For it is only when the interactions of all these elements is understood that students of politics in the United States can not only appreciate the past and present but also readily understand future events as they occur.

We have received many kind comments about the first two editions of *Politics USA* and also some helpful suggestions for improvement. We have tried to incorporate these, most notably in the area of US foreign policy. We are delighted that Andrew Moran has joined us to add a new chapter on this subject, which strengthens the theoretical analysis of America's international relations.

Finally, we would like to thank the team at Pearson for their encouragement to undertake a third edition. Particular thanks go to Kate Ahl and Sarah Turpie for their unflagging enthusiasm and support during what turned out to be a longer process than it should have been.

Bob McKeever
Phil Davies

We dedicate this book to our children, Jack, Elise and Anthony McKeever; Andrew and Carolyn Davies.

Contributor

Dr Andrew D. Moran is Course Leader for International Relations and International Development and is a Senior Lecturer in International Relations at London Metropolitan University.

He has contributed to scholarly journals such as *Presidential Studies Quarterly*, *Political Studies*, *Party Politics* and *The Amicus Journal* and is the Book Reviews Editor for *Democratization*. He has also been interviewed on US and British television. He is currently co-authoring a book on Security Studies to be published by Pearson.

Acknowledgements

We are grateful to the following for permission to reproduce copyright material:

Figures

Figure 8.5 from http://elections.gmu.edu, Michael P. McDonald; Figure 14.1 from *Parties, Politics, and Public Policy in America*, 9th edition, CQ Press (Keefe, W. J. and Hetherington, M. J. 2003) p. 157.

Tables

Table 4.1 from *The Proud Decades: America in war and peace, 1941–1960*, Norton (Diggins, J. 1988) 186; Table 6.1 from *American Women since 1945*, Palgrave Macmillan (Gatlin, R. 1987); Table 9.2 from *Mass Media and American Politics*, 6th edition, CQ Press (Graber, D. 2002) 246.

Text

Box 19.2 from Guttmacher Institute

Photographs

The publisher would like to thank the following for their kind permission to reproduce their photographs:

(Key: b-bottom; c-centre; l-left; r-right; t-top)

Alamy Images: flab 194; **Kirk Anderson:** 185; **Archiving Early America:** 13, 14; **Daryl Cagle:** 351; **Corbis:** Bettmann 84, 149, Bettmann 84, 149, Ann Johansson 37, Miroslav Zajic 352, Reuters 202, Reuters/Win McNamee 361, Ron Sachs 146; **www.eyevine.com:** Terry Schmitt 130; **Flickr:** US Government Work 195; **Getty Images:** 374, Jewel Samad 270, NY Daily News 205; **Bob Gorrell:** 266; **National Archives and Records Administration (NARA):** 119; **Picture History:** 47; **Press Association Images:** AP 74, AP/Dave Martin 29, AP/David Adame 92, AP/Nam Y Huh 103, AP/Rob Carr 3, Ed Reinke 83I, Robert F Bukaty 93; **Reuters:** John Gress 122, Molly Riley 83; **Steve Sack:** 214, 217; **Shutterstock.com:** kovacsf 6.

Cover images: *Front:* **Getty Images**

Every effort has been made to trace the copyright holders and we apologise in advance for any unintentional omissions. We would be pleased to insert the appropriate acknowledgement in any subsequent edition of this publication.

Chapter 1

Introduction – A troubled nation

The first decade of the twentieth century was a traumatic one for the United States. The terrorist attacks of 11 September 2001 led to two major wars in Afghanistan and Iraq and a global 'War on Terror'. These proved difficult and costly conflicts, which often appeared to lack clear focus and purpose. Even the killing of Osama bin Laden in May 2011 provided only a temporary lift to the war-weariness that seemed common among politicians, the military and citizens alike. When Secretary of Defense Robert Gates addressed the graduating class of cadets at the West Point military academy in February 2011, he told them '. . . you will be joining a force that has been decisively engaged for nearly a decade. And while it is resilient, it is also stressed and tired.' A few months later, in a speech delivered in Brussels, Gates warned America's European allies that the United States was tired of bearing what it considered to be a disproportionate share of the West's military burden: 'The blunt reality is that there will be dwindling appetite and patience in the US Congress, and in the American body politic writ large, to expend increasingly precious funds on behalf of nations that are apparently unwilling to devote the necessary resources . . . to be serious and capable partners in their own defense.' While Gates' speeches stopped well short of advocating a new era of American isolationism, they did indicate that the time was ripe for a fundamental review of when and how the United States should engage in military adventures abroad.

If a decade of war left the American people in a gloomy, introspective mood, the deep economic recession that began in December 2007 left them angry. The recession was the longest in duration since the Great Depression of the 1930s and began with the collapse of the housing market and the banking sector. Although the country officially came out of the recession in June 2009, the economy continued to be sluggish, with unemployment levels stuck around 9 per cent. Moreover, many of the new jobs created after the recession are lower-paying than those lost earlier. A further consequence of the recession was the record number of house repossessions that occurred as homeowners were unable to meet their mortgage payments. Add to this a bitter fight between Democrats and Republicans over the soaring budget deficit and it comes as no surprise that many Americans are pessimistic about the country's economic prospects. According to a Gallup Poll taken in June 2011, 65 per cent of Americans believed that the economy was getting worse, while only 31 per cent thought it was getting better. Logically enough, when Gallup asked people in May 2011 what they considered were the most pressing problems facing the country, 74 per cent nominated economic concerns, while only 4 per cent mentioned foreign policy issues and 5 per cent health care and education problems.

This context provided the setting for both the congressional elections of 2010 and the early stages of the 2012 presidential election. The upsurge of hope that had propelled Barack Obama to victory in 2008 had long disappeared. In November 2008, Obama had captured 53 per cent of the popular vote in the presidential election. His approval ratings soared in the first few weeks in office, but soon began to decline steadily, roughly in line with the deteriorating economy. By the spring of 2011, those who disapproved of his performance as president outnumbered those who approved by 48 per cent to 43 per cent. The problem for the president was that his successes attracted strong condemnation from his opponents and often only lukewarm praise from his supporters. Despite his historic achievement in securing passage of his health care bill in March 2010, opinion polls showed that a clear majority of the public were opposed to it. While Democrats in particular were delighted with President Obama's announcement in August 2010 that US combat missions in Iraq had ended, others were critical of his failure to keep his pledge to close the notorious Guantanamo Bay prison for suspected 'enemy combatants'. Above all, however, it was the perceived failure of the president's high-cost economic stimulus package to bring about recovery that underpinned the Republican triumph in the 2010 mid-term elections. The plan had involved $787 billion and was described by the president as 'the most sweeping recovery package in our history'. While the plan prevented the recession from becoming a full-blown depression, Americans were disappointed with its results – and the president's party felt the electorate's wrath.

In the elections for the House of Representatives, the Republicans gained 63 seats from the Democrats and took control of the chamber. In the Senate, the Republicans made some important gains but the Democrats retained their majority, albeit a significantly reduced one. The voters had once again returned the country to 'divided government', a familiar phenomenon in modern American politics. With a Democrat in the White House, a solid Republican majority in the House of Representatives and a slim Democrat majority in the Senate, the scene was set for either a period of bipartisan cooperation or an increasingly bitter political stalemate. As is usually the case, it was the latter that occurred as the parties took up position in preparation for the 2012 presidential election.

The Tea Party movement

However, the dynamics of party politics have been rocked in recent years by the rise of the so-called 'Tea Party' movement. Taking its name from the Boston Tea Party of 1773, when Americans protested against colonial taxes by dumping tea from British ships into Boston harbour, it is essentially a populist movement vehemently opposed to high federal spending, high taxes and the federal government in general. Its ideology is libertarian in economics and its anti-Washington stance resonates strongly with American political culture. In sociomoral matters, however, it owes much to evangelical religious values.

Opinion is divided as to whether the Tea Party movement represents a new force in American politics or rather a re-energised but familiar conservative grouping. Noting the spontaneity with which the various elements of the Tea Party arose, some see it as a force exterior to and independent of the two-party system. There is some evidence to support this view. Although its ideology is perfectly compatible with conservative strands within the Republican Party, Tea Party-backed candidates have attacked and defeated well-established Republican politicians. In the 2010 federal election round, as many as eight 'establishment' Republican candidates were defeated in primary elections by candidates strongly identified with and funded by the Tea Party.

However, closer inspection suggests that the Tea Party movement is better understood as an insurgency within the broader Republican tent. It seeks to remove moderate Republicans and replace them with passionate, populist advocates of economic libertarianism and social and moral conservatism. Take, for example, the candidacy of Christine O'Donnell for the vacant Senate seat in Delaware in 2010. The Republican Party establishment in the state had backed Mike Castle, a moderate Republican considered capable of winning the seat in a traditionally Democrat state. O'Donnell, however, launched a vigorous and heavily publicised campaign appealing to Tea Party sentiments. When she won the primary, the media heralded the Tea Party as a powerful new force in American politics. Yet O'Donnell was a life-long Republican who had run for the Delaware Senate seat before. What was different this time was that she had latched onto the Tea Party movement for political and financial support and this took her to victory in the primary. More generally, a variety of studies have shown that there is a great deal of overlap between Tea Party activists and supporters and conservative Republicans. In elections, Tea Party supporters and conservative Republican candidates have sought each other out in an effort to move the Republican Party – and the Congress – to the right.

This new energy in conservative politics is not necessarily a boon to the Republican Party. The key to winning elections in the United States is

Figure 1.1 Christine O'Donnell, Tea Party candidate, during the 2010 Senate Republican primary campaign in Delaware.
Source: © AP/Rob Carr

attracting the votes of moderates in both parties and those who are often labelled 'Independents'. The more extreme statements and positions of Tea Party candidates tend to alienate such voters, particularly when they have been subject to derision in the media. This was precisely the fate of O'Donnell in Delaware in 2010. Having won the Republican primary, she then lost by a margin of 57 per cent to 40 per cent to her Democrat opponent, Chris Coons. One analysis suggests that some 18 per cent of Republicans deserted their party and voted for Coons.

Nevertheless, the conservative insurgency took another step forward when the Congressional Tea Party caucus was formed in 2010. Some 60 Republicans joined it, mostly members of the House of Representatives. Its leader, Michele Bachmann, a congresswoman from Minnesota, launched her bid in 2011 for the Republican presidential nomination. Other Republicans also saw the potential in using the Tea Party movement as a springboard to the White House. These included Sarah Palin, the Republican vice-presidential nominee in 2008 and Congressman Ron Paul of Texas, whose libertarian views are held to have inspired the Tea Party activists.

It may be that the Tea Party is not much more than re-branded conservative Republicanism, but that does not deny that it has touched a nerve with a significant section of the American people. What has made conservatives so angry? The short answer is: the Obama administration's policies and Obama himself.

President Obama inherited the worst economic crisis since the Great Depression of the 1930s. His response was broadly similar to that of President Franklin D. Roosevelt some 80 years earlier. Obama accepted that it was the federal government's responsibility to lead the country out of recession, rather than simply waiting for business and industry to recover. He therefore embarked upon an ambitious stimulus package that injected some $787 billion into the economy in the form of government spending programmes and tax cuts. Inevitably, this sent the level of American debt soaring to unprecedented heights, although it should be emphasised that the national debt had been rising steadily since the early 1980s. Nevertheless, with the national debt now within touching distance of gross domestic product, alarm bells were ringing for many conservatives. There was a real concern that Obama was creating a dominant federal government that betrayed America's political traditions.

This fear was fuelled by President Obama's health care law, the Patient Protection and Affordable Care Act of 2010. Health care had been a bone of contention for many decades in the United States. With no national health system on the European model, Americans were responsible for securing their own private health insurance. For the economically comfortable this was no problem. Moreover, many employers offered private insurance to their workforce, so most Americans were covered. However, in 2008, some 46 million Americans were thought to have no health insurance because they could not afford it. Democrat presidents going back to Harry Truman (1945–53) had tried – but largely failed – to address this problem of health care for the poorest fifth of Americans.

In securing the passage of his health bill, President Obama achieved a cherished dream of many Democrats. However, a majority of the public oppose it, especially Republicans and Independents. First, critics charge that it is too expensive and that it will increase the budget deficit and the national debt. Second, they oppose the bill because it forces all Americans to take out health insurance, whether they wish to or not. 'Obamacare', as its opponents like to call it, therefore combines perhaps the three things that conservatives dislike most – federal expenditures, federal taxes and federal compulsion.

Some Americans see the Obama administration's policies as 'un-American'. Many of these go further and believe, literally, that Barack Obama is not an American. Barack Hussein Obama II, to give the President his full name, was born on 4 August 1961, in the state of Hawaii, to an American mother and a Kenyan father. His parents divorced in 1964 and his mother later married an Indonesian citizen. That was how the young Barack Obama came to spend four years in Indonesia from the age of six until he was ten, whereupon he returned to Hawaii.

This personal profile led a significant number of Americans to believe that Obama was not really born in Hawaii or anywhere else in the United States. This in turn meant that Obama was ineligible to be president, since the Constitution requires the holder of that office to be a 'natural born citizen'. In 2008 the Obama campaign released the short form of his birth certificate. The so-called 'Birther' Movement, however, campaigned to force Obama to release the full or long-form version of his birth certificate. When he eventually yielded in April 2011, it was immediately condemned by Birthers as a forgery, although polls suggest that the release of the long-form certificate halved the number of Americans who are convinced he was not born in the United States, from 20 per cent to 10 per cent.

Another thread of conspiracy about Obama is that, although a professed Christian, he is secretly a Muslim. An opinion poll in 2010 revealed that while 34 per cent of respondents believed he was indeed a Christian, 18 per cent believed he was a Muslim and 43 per cent said they didn't know. It seems that Obama's middle name – Hussein – is the inspiration for the idea that Obama is a Muslim, though the four years he spent in Indonesia, a Muslim country, is also a factor.

For the most part, those who believe that Obama is not an American and is a Muslim are critical of his policies and align themselves with the Republican Party. In that sense, the conspiracies can be dismissed as the desperate tactics of those who have lost a political contest. On the other hand, the strangeness – not to say craziness – of the beliefs that underpin these conspiracy theories, together with the relatively large number of people who subscribe to them, tells us something about politics in the contemporary United States. It tells us that there is a bitterness and polarisation of politics in some sections of the population. It may also tell us that while most Americans are comfortable with an African-American as president, a minority are disturbed by what they see as an alien presence in the White House.

This bitterness and polarisation is also demonstrated in another feature of contemporary American politics: the decline in the standard of public discourse. Few would deny that the language used by some public figures has become much harsher over the last decade, as have the accusations they make against their opponents. Radio and TV 'shock jocks', such as Glenn Beck and Rush Limbaugh, attract large audiences with their blend of outrage and verbal aggression against all things liberal and Obama. Beck, who appeared on the conservative Fox News Channel, condemned President Obama in the following terms: 'This President, I think, has exposed himself over and over again as a guy who has a deep-seated hatred for white people or the white culture . . . This guy is, I believe, a racist.' Beck eventually went too far even for his employer when he began to promote nakedly anti-Semitic conspiracy theories and was taken off air. Rush Limbaugh has been the leading conservative shock jock since the late 1980s. He attacks, among others, liberals, feminists, environmentalists, gays and those who favour abortion rights. However, it is the attacks on President Obama that are perhaps the most shocking. There has been a tradition in the United States of showing respect for the president, even if one disagrees passionately with his policies. Limbaugh and others have ignored this tradition. On several occasions, Limbaugh has said that Obama was only elected president because he was black and traded on white guilt over the history of slavery. Gone, too, is any notion that the president is even patriotic. As Limbaugh put it: 'Our nation was created in ways that allow human potential to prosper, and it created the greatest nation for people in the history of humanity. Now Obama is dismantling it, because he has no appreciation for our greatness. In fact, he resents it. He blames this country for whatever evils he sees around the world.'

It is one thing for media controversialists to engage in such discourses, but in recent years politicians have been following suit. Concerns over the deterioration in the standards of political discourse came under the spotlight following the shooting of Democrat Congresswoman Gabrielle Giffords of Arizona, in January 2011. Giffords was seriously wounded when a gunman started shooting at a public meeting she had called at a supermarket in Tucson. While Giffords was the target, the gunman killed six people and wounded many more.

The veteran local sheriff expressed the view that the vitriolic language used by some public figures

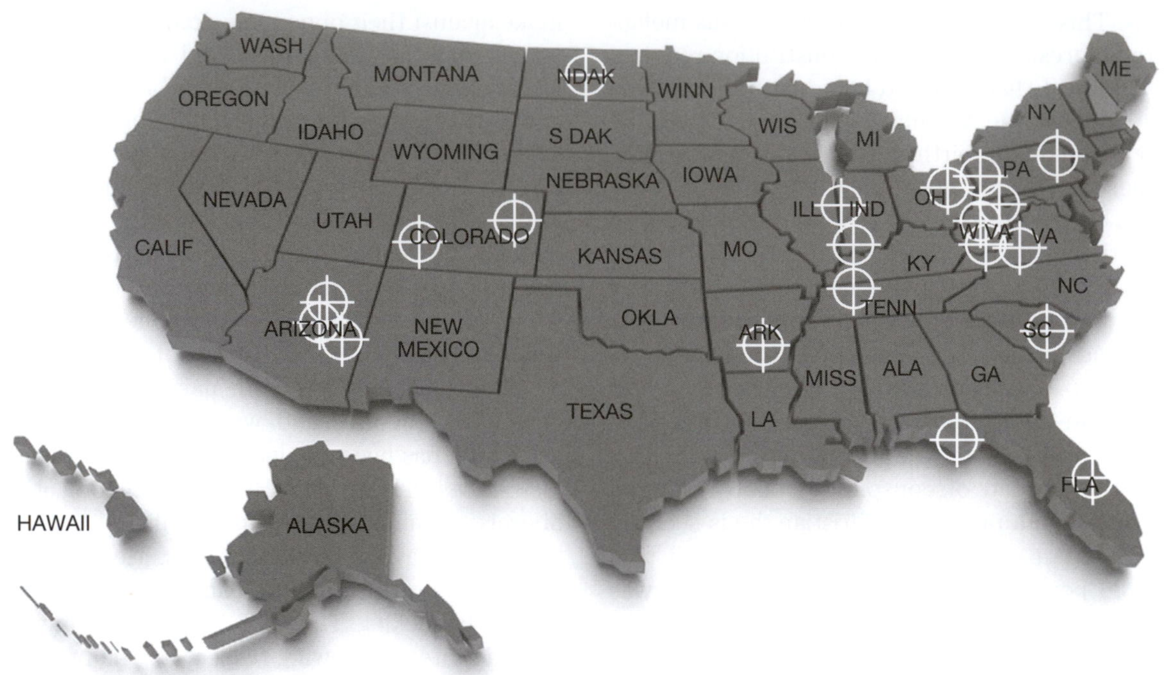

Figure 1.2 Sarah Palin website identifying 20 members of Congress who voted for President Obama's health care bill. Their constituencies were marked by the cross-hairs of a rifle site.
Source: © Shutterstock/Covascf

was responsible for creating a climate of bigotry and hatred in the country. And it emerged that Giffords had recently complained about being targeted by Tea Party favourite Sarah Palin on her website. Palin called for the recapture of 20 congressional districts whose Democrat members had supported President Obama's health care bill. She identified them with the cross-hairs of a rifle sight. Palin had also commented: 'Commonsense conservatives and lovers of America: Don't Retreat, Instead – RELOAD.' Palin's use of such violent imagery was widely condemned and the offending item was quickly removed from the website. Palin issued a statement condemning the shooting and sending her condolences to Congresswoman Giffords and the other victims.

Eventually, the man arrested for the shooting, Jared Loughner, was deemed mentally unfit to plead and it was unlikely that he had any rational political motive. Yet the response to the shootings brought home to many Americans the dangers of a political discourse that overstepped the boundaries of acceptable debate and political disagreements. One symbol of that growing concern was the creation in February 2011 of the National Institute for Civil Discourse at the University of Arizona, based in Tucson. Its co-directors are former presidents George H. Bush (1989–93) and Bill Clinton (1993–2001). The goal of the institute, a bi-partisan organisation, is to promote 'civility in public discourse' and return the country to a time when political differences were expressed in respectful language.

The concerns about the state of public discourse are yet another sign that the United States is struggling to come to terms with the range of challenges that it faces. While, as already noted, Americans are most concerned about their economic circumstances, some threats to the economy have their origins beyond America's borders. Immigration is one such issue, with anti-immigration feeling at its strongest in the southern border states, such as Arizona and Texas. In 2010, Arizona passed a controversial law, aimed at cracking down on illegal immigration. It requires all immigrants to carry documentation proving they are in the country legally and empowers the police to stop anyone they think might be an illegal immigrant and demand to see those papers. While the Arizona law is considered the toughest immigration bill in decades, it is actually only the tip of the iceberg. According to the National Conference of State Legislatures, in 2010 alone, 48 states enacted some 222 laws and passed 131 resolutions on the subject of immigration reform. There is every prospect of illegal immigration becoming a national issue, as Democrats seek to appeal to Hispanic voters and conservative Republicans to white voters in the states that border Mexico. President Obama has publicly criticised the Arizona law, while Senator John McCain of Arizona, his 2008 Republican opponent, took a step to the right in coming out in favour of it. He did so under pressure from a fiercely conservative opponent of immigration in the 2010 Republican primary for his Senate seat.

Opponents of current immigration laws in the US express concerns about jobs, welfare dependency and terrorism. Supporters of the laws stress the fact that the United States has always been a nation of immigrants and that immigration should be seen as a strength rather than a threat. President Obama has recognised the sharp divide in the country over immigration and has backed a plan that gives something to both sides: stronger border controls on the one hand, but a process for the 'Americanisation' of illegal immigrants on the other. The coming years will see whether such a compromise can defuse the issue.

If ordinary Americans are vexed about illegal immigration, elites speculate anxiously about the rising rivals to American economic power. Primarily, this concerns the rapid ascendance of China, but other countries experiencing rapid growth include Brazil, Russia and India. Together they make up the so-called BRIC countries and while the American economy limps along with a growth rate of 2.5 per cent, the BRIC countries are experiencing double, triple or, in China's case, quadruple the American rate. Moreover, China is the United States' greatest creditor. Like all other governments, the United States finances its debt by issuing Treasury bonds which are bought by other countries and institutions. As of October 2010, China was the largest holder of US bonds, owning over $900 billion's worth. While this situation is of no immediate threat to the USA, it does symbolise an extraordinary turnaround in the relative economic power of the two countries in the last 20 years. In 2010, China overtook Japan as the world's second-largest economy and many believe that it will overtake the United States at some point in the next 20 years. Moreover, some ask whether China's growing economic power will one day be translated into military power and thus undermine the United States' position as the world's lone superpower.

For most Americans, however, America's place in the global pecking order is not a major issue right now. In June 2011, President Obama announced the phased withdrawal from Afghanistan of the 33,000 US troops who were sent there in 2009 as part the of the US 'surge' to defeat the Taliban. In so doing, he signalled his intention to concentrate on domestic affairs. 'America', he said, 'it is time to focus on nation-building here at home.' Few Americans would disagree that this should be the national priority over the coming years. It will also, therefore, be the battleground of politics in the USA for the foreseeable future.

Part 1

The constitutional dimension of American politics

It is no exaggeration to say that Americans view their Constitution with the kind of reverence usually reserved for religious texts. This is not so surprising once we recall that the US Constitution was effectively the founding text of the newly independent country and that it has served the nation for over 200 years. In a very real sense, then, the Constitution is synonymous with the American people as well as their government. It is the source of the people's rights and it has enabled them to stand up to their government when it has sought to oppress them. More prosaically, but equally important, the Constitution provides the framework for the key institutions and processes of national politics and for the relationship between the federal government and the governments of the 50 states. Any study of the government and politics of the United States must, therefore, begin with an examination of the Constitution. In Chapter 2, we analyse the origins of the Constitution: its genesis in the political flux created by the successful war for independence, the principles upon which it was based and the institutions and political processes it established. In Chapter 3, we examine in detail the operation of federalism in the United States: in particular, we analyse the historical development of the division of powers between the federal government and the states and assess the importance of federalism in contemporary government.

Contents

Chapter 2

The Constitution and constitutionalism

This chapter examines the origins, development and impact of the single most important document in American politics – the Constitution of the United States. The Constitution provides not only a framework for government in America, but also a way of thinking about government. For inseparable from the Constitution is the idea of constitutionalism – the belief that all things governmental and political must comply with the principles set out in that document. The US Constitution was drafted in 1787 and came into force in 1789. Yet it is no mere historical relic. Because it has been regarded as a 'living document', subject to new interpretations as well as formal amendment, it has developed in line with the socio-economic and political transformation of America from a rural, eastern seaboard nation to a post-industrial, continental power that dominates the world in so many respects. As you might expect, just as America has not achieved this transformation without struggle and contention, so too the Constitution has been fought over and its development has been far from smooth. Nevertheless, it remains the keystone of American government and any understanding of American politics must begin with an appreciation of the Constitution and constitutionalism.

The origins of the Constitution of 1787

The Constitution of 1787 has philosophical roots in the progressive European thought of the eighteenth century, but its driving force was a distinctly practical consideration: how to replace British colonial rule with a government that was effective but not oppressive. The United States had been wrestling with this problem since the Declaration of Independence in 1776, but even after the successful conclusion of the War of Independence in 1783, it still had not found a solution. Part of the difficulty lay in the fact that achieving independence and implementing self-government were distinctly different projects, and Americans took some time to make the transition from the one to the other. It was also the case that the people who provided the momentum for independence were not the same as those who seized the initiative to write a new constitution in 1787: they had not only different goals, but, to some extent, different interests and ideologies too. The outcome was that the more radical thought behind the Declaration of Independence was, in part, replaced by the more pragmatic conservatism of the Founding Fathers. As a consequence, the Constitution emerged as an innovative document that combined radicalism, conservatism and sheer pragmatism. That combination is still evident today and each element needs to be understood by any student of contemporary American politics and government.

The Declaration of Independence and the American Revolution

Historians disagree over the causes of the American Revolution. Some argue that economic rivalry between American and British merchants fanned the flames of revolution, while others point to American resentment of new taxes being imposed on them without consultation. A third view is that Americans were simply developing a national self-consciousness that led naturally to the desire to rule themselves. All of these probably played their part. Certainly the period from the end of the Seven Years War between Britain and France (1756–63) until the Declaration of Independence in 1776 saw rising tensions over clashes of economic interests. The British tried to tax Americans more heavily and to control trade more strictly in the interests of British merchants, both with the aim of recuperating some of the expenses of the war with France. It is also logical that such clashes would increase awareness that British and American interests were not identical and that greater self-rule was desirable in order to nurture America's distinctive needs.

Where there is broad agreement among historians is that most Americans were reluctant revolutionaries. Indeed, many of those who felt obliged to back the movement for independence saw themselves as fighting to restore the rights of Englishmen, rather than to abandon the political traditions of the Mother Country. In effect, the independence activists were immersed in a political debate between Whigs and Tories in Britain that dated back to the English Civil War. The Whigs took their cue from the writings of the English philosopher, John Locke. Accordingly, they opposed the notion of the divine right of kings to rule as they see fit and believed that each man has natural rights, granted to him by God, that no king or parliament may take away. They also accepted Locke's belief that governments depend ultimately on the consent of the people: if a government violates the social contract between the ruler and the ruled, then the people have the right to change their government.

Only when they finally concluded that they could never persuade George III to accept their Whig agenda did the Americans turn to independence. As Michael Heale put it, 'The only course left was rebellion, a rebellion which was begun . . . not so much against the British constitution as on behalf of it' (Heale, 1977, p. 34). In this sense, it can be misleading to think of the independence movement as *revolutionary*. Certainly there was no intention to overthrow the economic or social order that prevailed in the colonies. On the other hand, the mere act of overthrowing an established monarchy through a popular uprising was a radical step. Indeed, the main purpose of the Declaration of Independence was less to announce independence than to justify it. Moreover, the act of fighting for independence did bring forth more radical thinking.

One manifestation of this was the contrast between the new state constitutions that followed in the wake of the Declaration of Independence and the colonial systems of government that preceded them. While the War of Independence was emphatically not fought to create a democracy in America, it did inspire a strengthening of democratic elements in the new constitutions. For example, while no state formally abolished property qualifications for the franchise, states such as New

Box 2.1

The Declaration of Independence (1776) and equality

Jefferson's Declaration consists for the most part of a long list of somewhat contentious accusations levelled at King George III. However, it is best remembered and celebrated for its ringing proclamation of the equality of all men, their possession of unalienable rights, and popular consent and sovereignty as the legitimate basis of government:

'We hold these truths to be self-evident, that all men are created equal, that they are endowed by their Creator with certain unalienable rights, that among these are Life, Liberty and the pursuit of Happiness.

That to secure these rights, Governments are instituted among Men, deriving their just powers from the consent of the governed, That whenever any Form of Government becomes destructive of these ends, it is the Right of the People to alter or abolish it, and to institute a new Government . . .'

Source: © Archiving Early America

Much debate surrounds Jefferson's claim that 'all men are created equal', given the existence of slavery in the American colonies. Indeed, Jefferson himself was a slave-owner. How can this contradiction be explained, if not by sheer hypocrisy or unconscious racism? In terms of political theory, Jefferson was simply restating John Locke's premise that, in the state of nature prior to the formation of society, all men are created equal by God. At the same time, Jefferson and some others were clearly aware that slavery was wrong and could do untold harm to America at some point in the future. Of course, they were proved right as a bitter conflict soon developed over the abolition of slavery, which culminated in the Civil War (1861–65). The Declaration's statement of equality was at odds with slavery and, for that reason, it became a rallying cry for abolitionists. Other groups, most prominently women, have also invoked the Declaration of Independence in their struggles for liberty and equality. It has thus proved an invaluable tool for those determined to make American practice match the promise of the American Revolution.

Hampshire, Pennsylvania and Georgia eased them to the point where there was near-universal white male suffrage. Another democratic spurt came in the form of frequent elections to state legislatures, something which increased popular control of political elites.

At the national level, however, the most obvious radical development was the decision to replace a monarchy with a republic. Whig theory allowed for both monarchical and republican systems of government, but even in the years immediately prior to independence, most Americans thought of republicanism in pejorative terms. It was a close relative of the even more alarming concept of democracy, which was equated with 'mob rule'. Yet practical considerations pushed Americans into republicanism, including the impossibility of finding an American royal family to replace the British one. Embracing a republic, however, required a deliberate and careful attempt to distinguish it from democracy. As a result, American constitutionalism after independence was based on incorporating democratic elements of government, while ensuring that they were contained by elitist counterbalances.

While most of those who led the independence movement retained aristocratic or even monarchist leanings, there were more radical voices, such as that of Thomas Paine, the English pamphleteer, and Sam Adams, the Massachusetts politician. These radicals pushed hard in the direction of popular control of government. Between 1776 and 1789 they were engaged in something of a political struggle with the conservatives to control America's political destiny. The historian Donald Lutz argues that the radicals had the upper hand at first, but had

Box 2.2

Thomas Paine's *Common Sense*
The rule of law should replace the rule of kings

In his famous work, *Common Sense*, published on the eve of the War of Independence in 1776, Paine sought to reassure those who feared the vacuum that would be left by the overthrow of the monarchy. The rule of the king, he said, would be replaced by the rule of law.

'But where says some is the King of America? I'll tell you Friend, he reigns above, and doth not make havoc of mankind like the Royal of Britain. Yet that we may not appear to be defective even in earthly honors, let a day be solemnly set apart for proclaiming the charter; let it be brought forth placed on the divine law, the word of God; let a crown be placed thereon, by which the world may know, that so far as we approve of monarchy, that in America THE LAW IS KING. For as in absolute governments the King is law, so in free countries the law ought to be King; and there ought to be no other.'

Source: © Archiving Early America

Paine was considered a dangerous radical by the British and, indeed, by many Americans. With hindsight, however, Paine was simply in the vanguard of the movement for American democracy and his ideas came to be embraced by most Americans.

lost their grip by 1787. As a result, '. . . the political theory underlying the Declaration of Independence of 1776 is not the same as that underlying the Constitution of 1787. The theory of consent implicit in the Declaration not only does not naturally evolve into the Constitution but in some important respects is contradictory to it' (Lutz, in Graham and Graham, 1977, p. 61).

Whatever the nuances of political theory and the clash of interests and factions, there remains a common core to American politics in the period 1776–87. The most important element was a commitment to republicanism and a government based on popular consent. This embraced political ideas and rhetoric that, over time, facilitated the emergence of a modern democracy. In short, while the War of Independence was not fought to create a democracy and while the Constitution did not produce one, both contained seeds of democracy that were to germinate and flourish in time.

The Articles of Confederation 1781–89

The Articles were America's first constitution and they embodied the spirit of 1776. The Americans had fought to overthrow a distant, centralised government. It was logical, then, to replace it with government close to the people and that meant government at the state level. As a result, the Articles provided only for the very weakest of national governments. There was no national executive or judiciary at all. Moreover, the national legislature – the Congress – was so constituted that it was, as Merrill Jensen put it, 'the creature of the state governments and thus, ultimately, of the electorate of the states' (in Latham, 1956, p. 16). Each state, regardless of size, had one vote in the Congress. And, without any effective means of ensuring compliance with such decisions as were agreed, states could simply renege on their commitments. The Congress had no independent power to raise revenue and, as the end of the war came into view, the states were even less inclined than before to attend to national issues.

There were those in the country who believed that a stronger national government was both necessary and desirable. Becoming known as the Federalists, they were alarmed by certain developments in the post-independence years. For example, the Congress was showing few signs of being willing to honour the national debt that had grown up to pay for the war. If the United States failed to repay this, it was unlikely that bankers would be willing to invest further in America. This would undermine economic development and prosperity. Another problem was the growing tendency of states to behave as economic rivals, imposing trade barriers on each other's goods. Yet another major problem was defence and social order. Federalists feared that a weak United States might yet fall prey to the colonial designs of European powers still present on the continent. Moreover, there was alarm at internal unrest, such as the so-called Shay's Rebellion in Massachusetts in 1786–87.

These issues prompted the Federalists to call for the amendment of the Articles of Confederation. Delegates from the states were asked to gather in Philadelphia in 1787 to discuss proposed changes. However, once the Constitutional Convention was in place, it staged a political coup. Rather than working on amendments to the Articles, it called instead for a new constitution to be drafted along Federalist lines. Supporters of the Articles of Confederation, the Anti-Federalists, had shown themselves fatally complacent by not attending in sufficient numbers at Philadelphia. When a new constitution was duly produced, the Anti-Federalists were already on the back foot and never recovered. The Constitution of 1787 was ratified by the required nine states and came into operation in 1789.

The philosophy and design of the Constitution

The differences between the philosophy of the Declaration of Independence and that of the Constitution of 1787 can, to a significant degree, be explained by differences in purpose. The Declaration was a justification for an anti-colonial war. The Constitution was intended to produce a government that would consolidate independence and take the country forward. The Founding Fathers therefore took the core philosophy of the Declaration but applied it to the practical task of gaining agreement on a new and more effective national government system. Political principle was combined with pragmatism to produce a unique document. At the heart of the new Constitution lay a number of key features that embodied both pragmatism and principle.

Federalism

It was noted above that, under the Articles of Confederation, the national government was 'the creature of the states'. One major problem for the Philadelphia Convention, therefore, was how to transfer enough power from the states to the national government to make it effective, without transferring so much that the states would never allow it. This was solved by compromises in two key respects. First, the powers of the national or *federal* government would be specified or *enumerated*. The logic was that any power not specifically granted to the federal government remained in the possession of the state governments. This logic was later reinforced by the Tenth Amendment to the Constitution (see Bill of Rights below). Secondly, the states were given control of the upper chamber of the Congress, the United States Senate. This was achieved in two ways. First, the states were given equal representation in the Senate: two senators per state, regardless of population. Secondly, the state legislatures were given control over the selection of their senators. Since no national legislation could be approved without the consent of the Senate, the states could use their power base there to block any unwanted expansion by the federal government.

Popular consent and representation

While all the Founding Fathers agreed that the legitimacy of government depended ultimately upon popular consent, they did not agree on how much direct involvement the people should have in government. Some, like James Madison, were convinced that the lower chamber of the Congress, the House of Representatives, must be directly elected by the citizenry. He believed that the stability of the government would depend considerably on whether the people had faith in its ability to reflect their moods and demands. Others, like Elbridge Gerry, thought this unwise. His experience in his home state of Massachusetts had convinced him that the people were often misinformed and too easily misled by 'designing men'. However, with the people shut out of the selection of the president, the senators and the justices of the Supreme Court, the more democratically minded delegates carried the day on the House of Representatives. This was to be the major democratic element in the new Constitution.

The separation of powers

The principle of the separation of powers was a familiar one by 1787. As expounded by the French political thinker, Baron de Montesquieu, in his book *On the Spirit of Laws* (1748), the separation of powers in government would help to prevent despotism. And while Montesquieu thought the British government was based on such a separation, Americans believed that they had been in danger of tyranny because of George III's attempt to subvert it. For the Founding Fathers, then, the separation of powers into legislative, executive and judicial branches of government came quite naturally.

The problem at Philadelphia was how to turn the separation of powers into functioning government institutions. And while it was important to ensure that none of these institutions would become too powerful, it was also important that all three of them should be able to function effectively together. The Convention devoted considerable time to the construction of the three institutions and all three required compromise between the delegates. One of the thorniest issues was the process of selecting the various office-holders. If, as was at first suggested, the president (executive) was to be chosen by the Congress (legislative), would

Box 2.3

The separation of powers and the selection process

Executive branch	**The president** Chosen by the electoral college, composed of state delegations whose members are selected in a manner determined by each state legislature
Legislative branch	**The Congress:** *The House of Representatives* Members chosen directly by the voters in each state district *The Senate* Members chosen by state legislatures in any manner they wish
Judicial branch	**The Supreme Court** Justices chosen jointly by the president and the Senate. The president nominates Supreme Court justices and the Senate confirms or rejects them.

this not undermine the separation of powers by allowing the control of one office by another?

In the end, the Convention came up with selection systems that differed for each institution and that avoided placing selection in the hands of another institution acting alone.

Checks and balances

The separation of powers was complicated, however, by the further imposition of checks and balances on each institution. The president was given a veto over any bill passed by Congress, although this could be overridden by a two-thirds majority of both the House and the Senate. The Congress, for its part, could restrain the activities of the president through its control of finances, *the power of the purse*. Each chamber of Congress checked the other, because all bills have to be passed in identical form by both the Senate and the House before they become law. This ability to intervene in the powers exercised by other branches of government had both negative and positive aspects for the exercise of federal power. As already noted, it made it difficult for any branch to become dominant to the point of tyranny. Moreover, because representatives of many different interests and viewpoints could influence national policy-making, the system was highly consensual. However, the other side of that coin was that the system would prove difficult to coordinate and allowed entrenched minorities to block action that might benefit the majority. This tension between majority and minority power is a major feature of American government to this day.

Ratification of the Constitution

The Convention decided that each state should be given the opportunity to debate and approve the new Constitution. It would come into force once nine of the thirteen states had ratified it. As a result, there was a national debate over the new Constitution, featuring the Federalists, who supported it, and the Anti-Federalists who opposed it. Both sides produced some thoughtful and persuasive pamphlets. Most famously, for the Federalists, James Madison, Alexander Hamilton and John Jay authored the *Federalist Papers*. Intended principally to persuade the voters of New York State to ratify the Constitution, they have come to be regarded as an authoritative explication of the constitutional design. However, for all the insight they yield into the minds of the framers, it should not be

Box 2.4 The Federalists v. the Anti-Federalists, i

The Federalist Papers **No. 10**

In the 10th *Federalist*, James Madison famously argued that a large republic, as opposed to either a small republic or a democracy, would prevent any faction from seizing control of the government and using its power to abuse the rights of citizens. The dangerous faction could be a majority or a minority of the people.

'AMONG the numerous advantages promised by a well-constructed Union, none deserves to be more accurately developed than its tendency to break and control the violence of faction. The friend of popular governments never finds himself so much alarmed for their character and fate, as when he contemplates their propensity to this dangerous vice. He will not fail, therefore, to set a due value on any plan which, without violating the principles to which he is attached, provides a proper cure for it. . . .

By a faction, I understand a number of citizens, whether amounting to a majority or a minority of the whole, who are united and actuated by some common impulse of passion, or of interest, adversed to the rights of other citizens, or to the permanent and aggregate interests of the community . . . A republic, by which I mean a government in which the scheme of representation takes place . . . promises the cure for which we are seeking. Let us examine the points in which it varies from pure democracy, and we shall comprehend both the nature of the cure and the efficacy which it must derive from the Union.

The two great points of difference between a democracy and a republic are: first, the delegation of the government, in the latter, to a small number of citizens elected by the rest; secondly, the greater number of citizens, and greater sphere of country, over which the latter may be extended.

The effect of the first difference is, on the one hand, to refine and enlarge the public views, by passing them through the medium of a chosen body of citizens, whose wisdom may best discern the true interest of their country, and whose patriotism and love of justice will be least likely to sacrifice it to temporary or partial considerations.'

However, Madison conceded, this might not be enough to prevent scheming men from acquiring the power of government and using it for malevolent purposes. The critical safeguard, he argues, is to have a large republic in which the multiplicity of interests, groups and individuals makes it difficult for a majority to form; and even if it does, it makes it more difficult for that majority to act.

'The smaller the society, the fewer probably will be the distinct parties and interests composing it; the fewer the distinct parties and interests, the more frequently will a majority be found of the same party; and the smaller the number of individuals composing a majority, and the smaller the compass within which they are placed, the more easily will they concert and execute their plans of oppression. Extend the sphere, and you take in a greater variety of parties and interests; you make it less probable that a majority of the whole will have a common motive to invade the rights of other citizens; or if such a common motive exists, it will be more difficult for all who feel it to discover their own strength, and to act in unison with each other. Besides other impediments, it may be remarked that, where there is a consciousness of unjust or dishonorable purposes, communication is always checked by distrust in proportion to the number whose concurrence is necessary.'

In effect, Madison was arguing for *a pluralist republic*. That theme of pluralism has run throughout American political history ever since.

forgotten that they are as much propaganda as an objective analysis of the Constitution. Nevertheless, certain of the *Federalist Papers* are rightly viewed as authoritative statements of the philosophy and hopes of the Founding Fathers, as they set about persuading their fellow citizens of the merits of the new Constitution.

The Anti-Federalists also put their case to the people of the several states through pamphlets and newspapers. One such Anti-Federalist critique of the new Constitution was published as *Letters from the Federal Farmer*, written by either Richard Henry Lee of Virginia or Melancton Smith of New York, or possibly by both. Another anonymous Anti-Federalist was 'Brutus', thought to be Judge Robert Yates of New York. Brutus did not simply disagree with the Federalists over such issues as the merits of a large republic, he was quite prophetic in seeing how the federal government would acquire increasing powers at the expense of the states.

The Anti-Federalists feared a centralised and distant government. They cherished the independent powers of the states and believed that the new Constitution would erode the autonomy of the states. They also feared that there were those who harboured aristocratic or even monarchist sentiments and who would try to use the powers of the federal government for the benefit of the social and economic elite. Unsurprisingly, such fears were widespread and the Federalists only narrowly won the ratification campaign. Even then, they had to promise to enact a Bill of Rights that, in the main, emphasised the limits of the new federal government. Moreover, the Anti-Federalist current remained powerful in the new political system, and does so even to this day. Not for nothing do contemporary candidates for national office campaign 'against Washington' and promise to make the federal government hear the voice of the 'ordinary folks' back home.

Box 2.5 The Federalists v. the Anti-Federalists, ii: the Anti-Federalists

'Brutus', Letter in the *New York Journal*, 18 October 1787

Article I, Section 8 of the proposed Constitution was, at first glance, an unobjectionable statement allowing Congress to use its specified powers through 'all necessary and proper' laws. Brutus, however, correctly foresaw that Article I, Section 8 could be later interpreted to allow Congress a wide array of powers going well beyond those enumerated in the Constitution. Sure enough, in the case of *McCulloch* v. *Maryland* (1819), the US Supreme Court did precisely that and thereby endowed the Congress with an indeterminate number of 'implied powers'. The outcome today is that there is hardly any subject on which Congress may not legislate if it wishes to.

'How far the clause in the 8th section of the 1st article may operate to do away all idea of confederated states, and to effect an entire consolidation of the whole into one general government, it is impossible to say. The powers given by this article are very general and comprehensive, and it may receive a construction to justify the passing of almost any law. A power to make all laws, which shall be *necessary and proper*, for carrying into execution, all powers vested by the constitution in the government of the United States, or any department or officer thereof, is a power very comprehensive and definite [indefinite?], and may, for ought I know, be exercised in a such manner as entirely to abolish the state legislatures . . .

It is not meant, by stating this case, to insinuate that the constitution would warrant a law of this kind; or unnecessarily to alarm the fears of the people, by suggesting, that the federal legislature would be more likely to pass the limits assigned them by the constitution, than that of an individual state, further than they are less responsible to the people. But what is meant is, that the legislature of the

Box 2.5 continued

United States are vested with the great and uncontroulable powers, of laying and collecting taxes, duties, imposts, and excises; of regulating trade, raising and supporting armies, organizing, arming, and disciplining the militia, instituting courts, and other general powers. And are by this clause invested with the power of making all laws, *proper and necessary*, for carrying all these into execution; and they may so exercise this power as entirely to annihilate all the state governments, and reduce this country to one single government. And if they may do it, it is pretty certain they will; for it will be found that the power retained by individual states, small as it is, will be a clog upon the wheels of the government of the United States; the latter therefore will be naturally inclined to remove it out of the way. Besides, it is a truth confirmed by the unerring experience of ages, that every man, and every body of men, invested with power, are ever disposed to increase it, and to acquire a superiority over every thing that stands in their way. This disposition, which is implanted in human nature, will operate in the federal legislature to lessen and ultimately to subvert the state authority, and having such advantages, will most certainly succeed, if the federal government succeeds at all. It must be very evident then, that what this constitution wants of being a complete consolidation of the several parts of the union into one complete government, possessed of perfect legislative, judicial, and executive powers, to all intents and purposes, it will necessarily acquire in its exercise and operation.'

Box 2.6

The Bill of Rights

The idea of a Bill of Rights had been raised at the Philadelphia Convention, but had been rejected. Many believed that the structure of government, characterised by separation of powers, federalism and checks and balances, provided sufficient protection for basic rights. However, during the ratification campaigns, Federalists were forced to concede on this point and promised to begin enactment of the Bill of Rights as soon as Congress met. The Bill's ten amendments to the Constitution were duly enacted and ratified in 1791. Many of the rights protected in the first ten amendments now apply to the states as well as to the federal government. However, it should be emphasised that, as originally conceived, they were designed to limit the power of the federal government and preserve state power and citizens' rights. This is most evident in the wording of the First and Tenth Amendments.

The First Amendment

'Congress shall make no law respecting an establishment of religion, or prohibiting the free exercise thereof; or abridging the freedom of speech, or of the press; or the right of the people to assemble, and to petition the government for a redress of grievances.'

The Tenth Amendment

'The powers not delegated to the United States by the Constitution, nor prohibited to it by the states, are reserved to the states respectively, or to the people.'

The development of the Constitution

The fact of agreeing a new Constitution did not mean that the system would necessarily work. Indeed, the sheer novelty of the framers' design was enough to cast doubt on its viability. However, the first generation of national office-holders included many such as Presidents George Washington, Thomas Jefferson and James Madison who honoured the terms of the Constitution while implementing it with flexibility and intelligence. Some clauses of the Constitution were quietly dropped. Thus, President Washington at first applied literally the requirement that treaties be ratified with the 'advice and consent' of the Senate. When he asked for advice on a treaty, the Senate took so long to study it that Washington lost patience. Thereafter, he and other presidents simply sent agreed treaties to the Senate for approval: consent was still required, but not necessarily advice.

Two developments that were to prove of enormous importance were the advent of political parties and a power of judicial review vested in the Supreme Court.

Political parties

Madison and many other framers disapproved of parties. They were factions within the meaning of *The Federalist* no. 10 and thus likely to be selfish and harmful to the general welfare. The Constitution was designed to inhibit their emergence, yet they became a feature of national government during the very first presidential administration, that of George Washington (1789–97). Based on the Federalist/Anti-Federalist division, President Washington found it preferable to surround himself with those who shared his Federalist philosophy. President Thomas Jefferson (1801–9), who garnered the support of the Anti-Federalist current in forming the Democratic-Republican party, took things further by his strategic collaboration with fellow party members in Congress. Although parties briefly disappeared during the so-called 'Era of Good Feelings' (1812–24), they soon re-emerged and remain to this day. Parties are virtually unavoidable in a system with free elections. It is testimony to the Constitution of 1787 that, although it was not designed to cater for them, it has easily been able to encompass their activities. Moreover, if the Constitution did not prevent the rise of parties, as Madison had wished, it did help to ensure that American parties would be weaker than in comparable political systems.

Judicial review of the Constitution

The most important development in the history of the Constitution was the emergence of the United States Supreme Court as its sole, ultimate interpreter. This occurred in the landmark case of *Marbury* v. *Madison* (1803). The Constitution had failed to make clear which institution or group of institutions should have authority to interpret the Constitution. Federalists strongly believed that the Supreme Court should have this power, but Jeffersonians believed that each of the three branches of government had the right to interpret the Constitution. However, for reasons explained in Chapter 16, the Supreme Court successfully claimed a monopoly of the right to declare state and federal laws unconstitutional in 1803. Thereafter, the Court usually took a flexible approach to constitutional questions and, in particular, often showed a shrewd awareness of when statesmanship should trump strict principle in the interpretation of the words of the Constitution. Chief Justice Marshall gave voice to the need for flexibility in his famous dictum in *McCulloch* v. *Maryland* (1819). He said that the Constitution was intended to endure through the ages '. . . and consequently, to be adapted to the various crises of human affairs'. The notion of adapability in the Constitution is crucial to the success of the United States. Its society, economy and international role have undergone several transformations since 1789, and only a constitution adaptable to such change could survive.

One of the most important developments in constitutional interpretation involves the First Amendment to the Constitution. Originally viewed as a restriction only on the federal government, its clauses were gradually interpreted by the Supreme

Box 2.7

Substantive due process: the magic of constitutional interpretation

The Fifth Amendment to the Constitution reads in part:

'[no person shall] be deprived of life, liberty, or property, without due process of law'

The Fourteenth Amendment has a similar clause, restricting the state governments from doing the same. The wording implies that a certain legal *process* has to be observed by government before citizens can have basic rights taken away. Starting in the nineteenth century and then gathering pace in the twentieth century, the Supreme Court began to interpret the clause as meaning that there were some rights that were so fundamental to a citizen's liberty that governments could not take them away even if they observed the proper procedures. This new judicial doctrine was called 'substantive due process'. In the contemporary era it has become a subject of sharp debate between the justices of the Supreme Court and has caused considerable controversy outside the Court. This is because 'liberty' has no fixed meaning except that which the justices choose to give it. And in recent decades, a majority of justices have held that it includes a woman's freedom to choose an abortion or a homosexual's freedom to engage in sexual acts with others of the same sex. Substantive due process thus provides a striking example of how judicial interpretation of the Constitution can change to fit the emergence of new societal values and conceptions of liberty.

Court in the twentieth century to restrict state governments as well. As a result, neither states nor the federal government may abridge freedom of speech and the press. In the modern era, this means, for example, that there are few government limits on political or artistic expression. The Supreme Court gradually applied other restrictions on the federal government to the state governments, giving rise to the concept of the '*nationalisation of the Bill of Rights*'.

Even more controversially, the 'due process' clauses of the Fifth and Fourteenth Amendments have been expanded to cover more than the procedural rights they originally guaranteed, and are now held to protect rights that were far from the minds of the Founding Fathers.

Sometimes, however, the Court has not proved adaptable enough in its application of the Constitution, with disastrous consequences. Most important, in the case of *Dred Scott* v. *Sandford* (1857), the Court refused to allow Congress a last chance at finding a compromise on slavery. Instead, the Court came down wholly on the side of slave-owners' property rights and thereby helped to cause the Civil War (1861–65). Again, in the first third of the twentieth century, the Court upheld a notion of property rights that was probably similar to that held by the framers themselves. When the Great Depression (1929–39) arrived, however, the government needed new powers to deal with the emergency, and some of those new powers infringed that traditional understanding of property rights. As a result, the Court clashed with President Roosevelt's New Deal and only saved its independence when it finally recognised the need to adapt to a new concept of government power to regulate property rights.

Constitutional amendment

As well as flexibility of interpretation and adaptation by the Supreme Court, the Constitution has also endured thanks to formal amendment. There have been relatively few amendments – 27, including the 10 that make up the Bill of Rights. Some have been of relatively minor importance, such as the most recent regulating the salaries of members of Congress. Many, however, have been of monumental importance, such as the so-called Civil War amendments (Thirteenth, Fourteenth and Fifteenth) that abolished slavery and advanced equality for black Americans. Others have fundamentally altered the country's political institutions by changing the way the Senate is elected (Seventeenth) and limiting the terms of office of the president (Twenty-second). Still others have extended the right to vote to women (Nineteenth) and 18-year-olds (Twenty-sixth).

The process of constitutional amendment is, however, very cumbersome. Proposed amendments first have to be approved by either a two-thirds majority of both houses of Congress or two-thirds of the state legislatures. That is, in itself, difficult to achieve. However, the proposed amendments must then be ratified by three-quarters of the state legislatures. These 'super-majoritarian' requirements empower minorities to defeat even popular proposed amendments. As a result, the difficulty of amending the Constitution serves the legitimate purpose of ensuring that the founding principles of American government cannot easily be altered. Only measures acceptable to the great majority of citizens and states will pass muster.

On the other hand, the formal amendment process is often too rigid a method of responding to those crises and fundamental changes that all nations may endure over the centuries. The Supreme Court, through flexible interpretation of the Constitution, has thus become an informal constitutional convention. While there is not a hint in the Constitution that the Court was intended to play such a role, the fact that it has emerged to do so is testimony to the pragmatism of American constitutionalism. And it is precisely that pragmatism which has permitted the Constitution not only to survive the transformation of the United States since 1787, but to become the most revered document in American politics.

Chapter summary

The Constitution of 1787 was inspired by the desire 'to form a more perfect union'. The chief goal of the framers was to strengthen the national government so that the United States could become safe and prosperous. At the same time, it sought to preserve the philosophical principles of the War of Independence, especially the notion that all government was dependent upon the consent of the governed. This synthesis was achieved by introducing a national legislature, executive and judiciary, while controlling their behaviour through the separation of powers and a system of checks and balances. Although it created a republic rather than a democracy, there were sufficient democratic elements to secure the consent of the governed and for a democracy to emerge with the passage of time. One of the main reasons that the Constitution endures to this day is that it has been applied flexibly, in order to incorporate the new demands that arise from changing times and circumstances.

Discussion points

1. Was the War of Independence a revolutionary movement?
2. Did the framers get the balance right between preventing tyranny and constructing an effective national government?
3. What were the main purposes behind the demand for a Bill of Rights?
4. What are the major sources of flexibility in the Constitution?
5. Were the framers right to make the amendment of the Constitution so difficult?

Further reading

On the ideas and events behind the movement for independence and the Constitution of 1787, see, for example, Gordon S. Wood's *The Creation of the American Republic*, 1776–1787 (Chapel Hill: University of North Carolina Press, 1969); Michael Heale's *The Making of American Politics*, 1750–1850 (London: Longman, 1977); Ray Raphael's *The American Revolution: A People's History* (London: Profile, 2001); Jack P. Greene's *Understanding the American Revolution: Issues and Actors* (Charlottesville: University of Virginia Press, 1995). An edited version of the Federalist Papers is Charles Kesler (ed.) *The Federalist Papers* (New York: Signet, 2000).

On the Constitution, see Robert A. Dahl's *How Democratic is the US Constitution?* (2nd edn, New Haven: Yale UP, 2003); Larry J. Sabato's *A More Perfect Constitution* (London: Walker & Co., 2007); Page Smith's *The Constitution: A Documentary and Narrative History* (New York: Morrow Quill, 1980); Jack Rakove's *Original Meanings: Politics and Ideas in the Making of the Constitution* (New York: Vintage Books, 1997).

A useful website for teachers is www.besthistorysites.net

References

Heale, M. (1977) The *Making of American Politics, 1750–1850* (London: Longman).

Jensen, M. (1956) 'The Articles of Confederation', in Latham, E. (ed.) *The Declaration of Independence and the Constitution* (Boston: D.C. Heath).

Lutz, D. (1977) 'Popular consent and popular control, 1776–1789', in Graham, G.J. and Graham, S.G. (eds) *Founding Principles of American Government* (Bloomington: Indiana University Press), p. 61.

Chapter 3

Federalism

The politically minded citizens of the United States felt competing pressures in the late eighteenth century. They were the proud defenders of a new nation, established in a spectacular stand against the imperial might of Great Britain, but still vulnerable to predation by strong European powers. The requirement to establish a government system with strength enough to build and maintain the nation's presence on a difficult international scene suggested that a strongly centralised authority was needed. America's population had also developed significantly differing political cultures within the boundaries of distinct colonies and this varied heritage militated against governmental centralisation.

American federalism attempts to answer these competing demands on the system. The structure has proven so resilient that the original states and those added since have retained their individuality in many ways into the third century of America's history as an independent nation. Functions are performed separately and in combination by states, and by the nation, in a way that adds complexity to the American polity, but that provides a flexibility that continues to lie at the core of policy-making and implementation in the United States.

The states were there from the start

The USA has always been a nation of variety. Even the 13 states that made up the nation in the late eighteenth century already contained populations that were different in their origins and ancestry, in their religious beliefs, in their business interests and their commercial motivations. To some degree the original states had been founded, and had grown and developed, around these differences, and competition and separation between states was clearly evident in the early days of American independence. This was in tension with the generally accepted wish to cooperate within a national structure.

The Articles of Confederation recognised the force of state feeling, speaking of a 'Perpetual Union', but pointing out that 'Each state retains its sovereignty, freedom and independence.' This union was clearly made up of states that were in some way seen as equal entities, regardless of size. In the Continental Congress the states had delegations of different sizes, but when decisions were called for they were made on the basis of one vote per state. When the Continental Congress was not sitting, authority was passed to a Committee of the States, on which each state had one delegate.

While this initial form of central government for the United States of America had an impressive list of powers delegated to it by the states, it remained a relatively weak authority in what was, even in its original form, a fairly large nation for its time. Conscious of their different origins, and different traditions, the states were not eager to surrender power to the centre, and at times their actions did not meet even the limited obligations that they agreed in support of the central administration. The Continental Congress found national authority difficult to progress in these circumstances.

While some defended the loose confederation as a vibrant environment in which the states could develop their individual responses to their populations' individual needs, other opinions were voiced, concerned that the balance of authority was too much dispersed from the centre. Some political opinion at state level was resistant to moves towards the Philadelphia Convention of 1787, but opinion within several of the states was becoming sympathetic to the need for greater cooperation at the centre to be somehow sanctioned within the United States.

Box 3.1

The position of the states in 'The Articles of Confederation and Perpetual Union'

This original instrument of American government was constructed to be very conscious of state power. While this probably helped speed the evolution of the United States of America, it also limited the strength of its national authority. Federalism scholar Joseph Zimmerman (1992) argues that, under the Articles of Confederation, the Continental Congress had five major defects:

1. States failed to honour their obligation to fund the national treasury. Congress could not levy taxes. States were expected to contribute, but many of them failed to do so, leaving the national government finances in a critical state.
2. States did not feel obliged to honour nationally initiated legislation or agreements, and Congress had no authority to enforce laws and treaties, or any sanction against those individual states that ignored them.
3. States moved quickly to establish trade tariffs. Business across state boundaries was hampered by barriers of taxes and fees, and Congress had no authority over commerce between states.
4. States could not rely on the support of national armed forces for common defence. In spite of a continuing threat from European forces in North America, and from disharmony within the states, the weak national treasury did not provide the resource for reliable military response.
5. States could dissolve the Union.

The states in the Constitution

Given the significance of the individual states in the early history of the nation, it is not surprising that the tension between the states and central authority should surface in several ways, and feature in some of the major compromises that were negotiated on the way to a ratified US Constitution.

Led by James Madison, the delegates to the Philadelphia Convention from Virginia proposed that states be represented in the new national government according to their population. This did not find favour with the smaller states, which felt that

Box 3.2

National powers and state powers in US federalism

The US Constitution delegates many powers expressly to the US federal government, particularly in Article I, Section 8, where the powers of Congress are enumerated. The constitution also allows the federal government 'to make all laws which are necessary and proper . . . in the Government of the United States', an 'elastic clause' that broadens central government authority. At the same time, the Constitution reserves to the states those powers not specifically given to the federal government, or denied to the states. The boundaries between state and federal authority remain negotiable, and through US history many decisions in the federal courts have contributed to the shifting nature of federalism.

The powers of the US federal government include those:

- to lay and collect national taxes, duties, imposts and excises;
- to provide for the common defence and general welfare of the United States;
- to conduct foreign affairs through diplomacy, and to maintain the armed forces;
- to regulate commerce with foreign nations, and between the states;
- to borrow, print and coin money;
- to enforce federal laws;
- to declare and conduct war.

The powers of the state governments include those:

- to establish local governments;
- to provide important services such as education;
- to conduct elections;
- to pass laws on marriage, divorce, wills and domestic relations;
- to exercise state-level police power in support of the public welfare.

Powers held concurrently by federal and state governments include those:

- to borrow money, spend money and impose taxes;
- to establish courts;
- to charter and regulate banks;
- to pass, enforce, and interpret laws.

their interests would not properly be protected in a system that could be dominated by those states with large populations.

In the compromises that emerged from a summer of debate in Philadelphia, state rights were embedded in a number of ways into the proposed constitution. The US Senate, one of the two chambers of the US Congress, was to be made up of two senators from each state, regardless of size, and the senators were to be appointed by the states, through their legislatures. The members of the Electoral College, the vehicle for electing the president of the United States, were also to be appointed in a manner chosen by the state legislatures, and the members were only to meet in their separate state capitals. The number of Electoral College members allocated to each state was made equal to the state's total numerical representation in the US House and the US Senate, building in the weighting towards small states that equal representation in Senate affords.

While representation in the House of Representatives was designed to be distributed according to the census record of population, the integrity of state borders was protected. No congressional constituency border was allowed to cross a state border, and the states retained the authority to draw the boundaries of the congressional districts within their state borders. The integrity of those state borders was also protected within the Constitution, and cannot be altered without the approval of the state.

The Tenth Amendment of the US Constitution makes it clear that powers not expressly granted to the national government, or prohibited to the states, were 'reserved to the states respectively, or to the people'. In this arcane phraseology we find the constitutional foundation stone of the federal system in the United States. Finally, all of these protections for state authority and participation are protected by a system of constitutional amendment that requires massive state input.

Dealing with differences

Federalism emerges from the US Constitution as one of the core concepts of US government and politics. In a federal system there is a central government and a layer of sub-national governments. Both elements derive their power directly from the citizens and exercise authority directly over the population that elected them.

The central national government (the federal government) consists of those separated, checked and balanced branches – the presidency, Congress, judiciary – established by the US Constitution, and now headquartered in Washington DC. The various governments of the individual states, their position in the system also guaranteed by the US Constitution, meet in each of the capital cities of America's 50 states.

The US Constitution embeds history into any understanding of contemporary America. Constitutional provisions have been amended, and reinterpreted, but the core documentary foundation of the USA remains intact to a large extent as it was over two centuries ago. The success of governance in twenty-first century America owes a great deal to the strength and the versatility of this historic document.

Federalism institutionalises the states and the federal governments in a relationship that has to be worked at in order to succeed. The working out of that relationship is important in the defining of an active federal system that can operate to satisfy the various needs of its citizens at national, state and local level.

Federalism also works to create spaces within which the historical variety that has contributed to the nation can still have impact. Waves of immigration from different parts of the world have introduced ethnic variety to the United States throughout its history. A feature of this immigration is that different periods were characterised by the dominance of particular ethnic, national and racial groups, whose settlement patterns have had long-term impact within the federal system.

The early immigrant communities congregated in geographically defined areas, often settling where the experience of the first migrants of that nationality signalled the existence of opportunities. Scandinavian farmers, for example, colonised mid-western agricultural states such as Minnesota and Wisconsin. German brewers also ended up in the

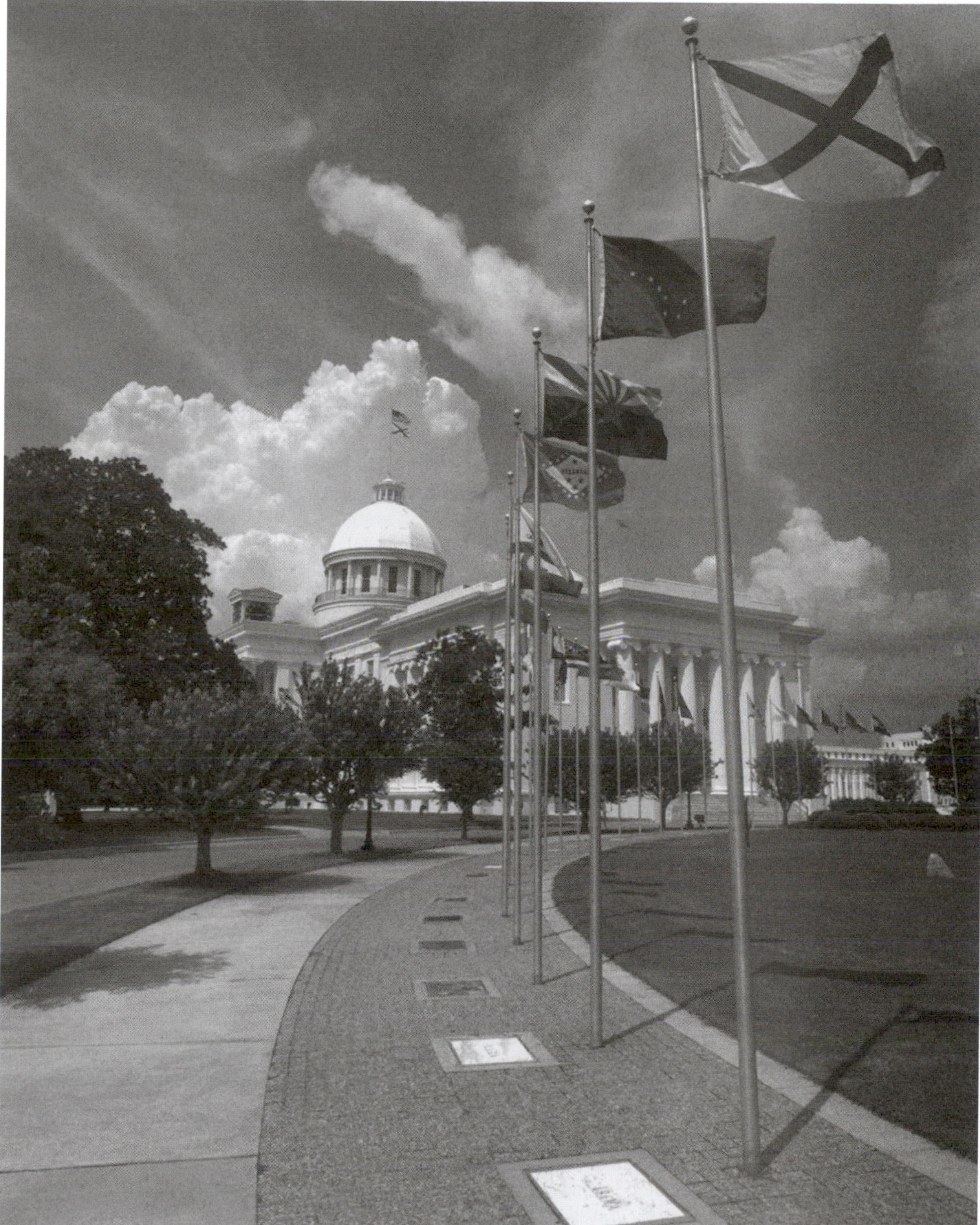

Figure 3.1 Flags of the individual states grace the south lawn of the Alabama Capitol in Montgomery, which flies the American and state flags over the dome.
Source: © Press Association Images

Midwest. Irish and Italian communities made use of opportunities in the nation's major cities, which were growing rapidly when these groups were entering the country. Other national groups who moved to the USA in large numbers in the late nineteenth and early twentieth centuries, such as Polish immigrants, were attracted to the then burgeoning areas of heavy industrial production. Geographical proximity can also be important, and in recent decades there have been increasing concentrations of Asian populations on the West Coast, of Latin American groups in the South and Southwest, and of Cubans in Florida.

Immigrant groups old and new often remain identified at least in part by the variety of their ethnic and religious heritage. The celebration of these differences, whether by Italian-Americans, Cuban-Americans, Irish-Americans, Vietnamese-Americans or other hyphenated-Americans has become almost perversely a definition of a community's 'Americanness' – partly a nostalgic statement about the nations left behind, but primarily a witness to the community's place in pluralist America.

This web of historic and contemporary demography is laid over a nation where resources – natural, social, and fabricated – are not evenly distributed. For example, traditional heavy industries developed in the nineteenth and twentieth centuries around areas where raw materials could be extracted; similarly, oil extraction has prompted related business in Alaska and in the southern states; the concentration of prestigious universities, for example in Massachusetts and in California, has aided the development of modern, research-based industries in these states; agribusiness regimes of various kinds are dependent on particular predictabilities of weather, water and soil.

The characteristics of America's states and localities continue to reflect the amalgamation of interrelated ethnic, commercial, historical and geographical factors such as these. State boundaries give a political shape and context which can act to maintain these cultural and economic diversities, along with related differences in social and religious organisation, in the face of all homogenising pressures. The protective borders of the states create the environment in which state political cultures and local government political cultures can develop, sensitive to these important differences. State and local politics reflects this rich variety, and the federal system of government affords these differences a continuing and active place.

Dual federalism

In the scholarship on federalism there are a number of concepts that compete to encapsulate the relationship between the federal and state governments. A distinction is commonly drawn between 'dual federalism', a model said to apply to the whole period from America's founding to the early twentieth century, and 'cooperative federalism', covering roughly the last century, and sometimes subdivided into shorter periods. Some scholars are uncomfortable with the apparent concreteness of these categories, and prefer to consider federalism as a steadily evolving system of intergovernmental relations.

The model of dual federalism posits that the national and state governments operate as equals, with authority in separate spheres that do not overlap. The theory assumes that the national government does not stray from the list of powers enumerated in the Constitution, since to do so would breach the boundary of its proper sphere of influence. More prosaically, this is sometimes called 'layer cake' federalism, envisioning the federal and state government structures as layers that might touch but remain identifiably separated and independent within their jurisdictions.

Some scholars have challenged this image, pointing out that even in the early days of federalism there were interventions by the federal government into areas that might be considered reserved to the states – for example, as the federal government intervened to support transport and communications developments that promoted the spread of settlement into the land mass of North America. Nevertheless, it is fair to say that, throughout the nineteenth century, most domestic affairs were considered to be the concern of state and local governments.

Dual federalism did not necessarily equate with weak central government. The history of the Supreme Court has been peppered with cases that deal with a variety of content, but revolve on the relationship between states and the federal government. For example, in 1819 the case of *McCulloch* v. *Maryland* considered the authority of the US Congress to charter a national bank. The Supreme Court's decision in support of the Congress meant much more than the establishment of a new financial institution, since it used the 'elastic', or 'necessary and proper', clause to find the 'implied powers' that gave Congress this authority, and simultaneously underlined that federal law was the supreme law of the land.

Throughout the nineteenth century, different challenges came through the courts, creating a body of precedent and helping define the scope of national government power. However, by 1860, a wholly different and more tangible challenge was emerging, with the approach of a civil war between the states of the Union. The differences between northern and southern states had already produced major legal battles, but tensions simmered on. Southern states argued that they had the authority to nullify federal law in order to protect their way of life and its culture of slavery. With the election of Abraham Lincoln to the presidency, southern states began to declare their secession from the Union. Under President Lincoln, the North refused to accept that union was a mere creature of the states. The victory of the North was a practical confirmation that the states owed a duty of loyalty to the nation.

Cooperative federalism

Crises such as the US Civil War can have a lasting impact on the structure of government. In the USA they have often been associated with a temporary centralising of authority, some aspects of which have not always faded away when the crisis itself has declined in significance. In the first half of the twentieth century, the pace of technological, industrial and demographic changes might have been enough to provoke a sense of crisis in some. The Wall Street Crash and the subsequent Great Depression made many feel that unusual responses were needed to face these unusual times, and President Franklin D. Roosevelt responded with a battery of programmes in the New Deal that helped shift federalism into a new form.

The economic burdens of unemployment, the collapse of business confidence, the failure of industrial investment, and the need for social welfare responses in the 1930s were beyond the experience or resource base of the states. The federal government role in domestic policy expanded dramatically as it moved in to initiate and support domestic welfare, job creation, and price and production control in the commercial, financial, industrial and agricultural sectors, all in the name of solving the economic crisis that had fallen upon the United States.

One of the key features of this increased federal government involvement is the federal 'grant-in-aid'. This is a distribution of national funds to states for specific policy purposes. This form of transfer was used first in the late nineteenth century, but it was the Sixteenth Amendment to the US Constitution, passed in 1913, and authorising the federal government's right to collect income tax, that significantly altered the ability of the federal government to use this facility. The national income tax gave federal government a resource much greater than had existed before – a foundation on which a more cooperative relationship could be built between levels of government, and in which the voice of the federal government could be heard clearly stating policy objectives.

Fiscal federalism – spending (and raising) the revenue

It is clear that state and local government cannot be disregarded as small or parochial. For example, the general expenditure by the US federal government in 2008 was estimated by the government to be $2,931.2 billion. Almost 21 per cent of this ($607.3 billion) was spent on defence. A further $1,486.6 billion (50.7 per cent) was reserved for nationally paid pensions, income support, veterans' benefits and Medicare, and a net amount of $243.9 billion went on interest payments. Of the total federal outlay, around $600 billion was left for other spending, some of which went into domestic programmes. In 2005 (the last year for which figures are currently available), combined state and local spending, all on domestic programmes, amounted to $2,368.8 billion – substantially more than the direct spending on domestic policy that could be made by the federal government. This is the consistent pattern of government spending in the USA.

In individual domestic policy areas, states regularly spend more than the federal government. On higher education, state and local governments spent almost six times more in 2005 than the federal government. Highways, and police, prisons and probation services are other policy areas supported primarily by state and local governments. In some policy areas, state and local governments are especially important. For example, state and local government spent $473.4 billion on primary and secondary education in 2005, almost 99 per cent of which was spent by local governments. The federal government outlay on primary, secondary and vocational education in the same year was just $38.3 billion. Given this commitment to schools at the local level, it is perhaps not surprising that education expenditure is the single largest item in local government budgets, amounting to 36 per cent of direct expenditure in 2005.

In addition to the policy areas already discussed, fire protection, policing, sanitation and a wide variety of other functions are dealt with at this level. It is clear that, within the federal system, state and local government is critical in the provision of public services that have a direct effect on the day-to-day lives of Americans. The state and local control of such a wide spectrum of areas provides the opportunity for different communities to design policy agendas suitable to their needs and their political culture. It also allows the possibility of different local and state governments confronting similar issues in alternative and different ways. Forums exist for state governors, state attorneys-general, city mayors, and many other government officers to discuss the issues that they have in common in the search for innovative and successful policies. This is one significant way in which the states and localities continue to perform a role encapsulated in Supreme Court Justice Louis Brandeis's description of the states as America's 'laboratories of democracy'.

The federal grant-in-aid support of states and their local governments has grown over the past generation, both in terms of dollars and as a percentage of total federal outlays, but looks relatively constant when expressed as a percentage of gross domestic product, and as a proportion of expenditure from state and local sources. This provides further evidence for the growth of state and local governments as the focus of domestic policy spending, though only a proportion of that money is raised directly by state and local governments.

It was estimated by the US government that, in 2008, the largest single element within the estimated $466,568 million total federal grants-in-aid was $220,432 million, or over 47 per cent of the total, for health policy expenditure, most of which was to help underwrite the states' Medicaid programme expenditure. Other large elements were $94,232 million (20 per cent) for income security programmes such as food stamps and child nutrition; $59,596 million (12.8 per cent) for education and employment services; and $52,880 million (11.3 per cent) for transportation. Smaller elements went to support policies such as natural resources, agriculture, community development, justice and veterans' benefits.

The federal government gains influence through the grant-in-aid programme since, as the collector and distributor of these funds, it is in a position to demand terms and conditions for their receipt. Decisions on the distribution of grants will be affected by government priorities, and funding may be designed to satisfy multiple aims. The federal government is in this happy position since it collects the majority of the tax revenue collected by governments in the USA. In 2007, federal income, corporation and excise taxes raised $1,598.8 billion, with another $869.6 billion coming from social insurance and retirement contributions. In the same year, combined tax receipts for all state and local governments amounted to $1,292.7 billion, with an additional $25.9 billion from social insurance contributions. The federal government has a particular revenue advantage in its domination of income tax collection. In 2007, the federal government collected 80 per cent of the nation's income tax deductions.

State and local governments do not have the same relatively easy access to tax revenues. State and local income taxes raise only a fraction of the

Table 3.1 Federal grants-in-aid, 1970–2008

	Total grant ($ million)	As percentage of state/local govt. expenditures from own sources	As percentage of all federal outlays	As percentage of GDP
1970	24,065	29.1	12.3	2.4
1975	49,791	34.8	15.0	3.2
1980	91,385	39.9	15.5	3.3
1985	105,852	29.6	11.2	2.6
1990	135,325	25.2	10.8	2.4
1995	224,991	31.5	14.8	3.1
2000	285,874	27.4	16.0	2.9
2005	428,018	31.0	17.3	3.5
2010 (est.)	653,665	(n/a)	17.9	4.5

Source: Constructed from data on US Bureau of the Census website: http://www.census.gov

national take, and are supplemented by sales taxes (most important to states), property taxes (providing almost three-quarters of local government tax revenue), and an increasingly wide range of other revenue streams.

With only one exception, the states are required to balance their budgets, and while there are ways to finesse this limitation, they certainly cannot plan to run constant, and even growing, deficits, as happens regularly at the federal level. Their own-sourced revenue is therefore particularly subject to broader changes in economic conditions. Periods of economic growth and decline can have differing regional implications. The 1990s saw a period of economic growth in the USA, and some states, such as California, did particularly well.

The sharp reversal of the stock exchange boom, accelerated by economic anxieties in the wake of 11 September, 2001, hit state governments particularly hard. Reported state government reserves fell by more than 75 per cent in the three years to 2003, leaving many states in considerable fiscal stress. New York raised taxes in 2003, while California cut spending, for example by halting planned road construction. Kentucky saw a decline in child care provision, while Michigan cut its budget for environmental enforcement by one-third.

The end of a speculative boom in the 'dot.com' sector, early in the twenty-first century, was a shock to California and other states with considerable high-technology industries, although more steady growth in that economic sector was soon re-established. By the middle of the first decade in the new century, growth was again the touchstone of most economic predictions, contributing to a speculative bubble that began sharply to deflate during the late stages of the George W. Bush presidency.

The international economic crisis provoked widespread problems at state level from the outset. This was true especially in those states with a high dependency on manufacturing industries, where the economic downturn produced high unemployment rates. In the boom years, banks had been happy to

Table 3.2 Grants-in-aid by policy area, 2010 (government estimates)

	Total grant ($ million)
Energy	5,927
Natural resources and environment	8,836
Agriculture	1,231
Transportation	72,249
Community and regional development	21,221
Homeland Security	10,353
Education, employment, training, social services	111,715
Health	294,613
Income security	121,818
Veterans' benefits and services	938
Administration of justice	5,783

Source: Constructed from data on US Bureau of the Census website: http://www.census.gov

Table 3.3 State and local government general revenue sources, 2007

	$ million	$ million
Property tax	389,573	
Sales tax	439,586	
Individual income taxes	289,827	
Corporation income taxes	60,592	
Other taxes	103,705	
Total other charges	584,662	
Other own revenue	736,750	
Own-source revenue		2,604,695
Intergovernmental revenue (inc. grants-in-aid)		467,949
Total general revenue		3,072,645

Source: Constructed from data on US Bureau of the Census website: http://www.census.gov

lend to customers with less economic security, on properties that turned out to be over-valued. When this housing market proved unsustainable, the states were faced with substantial increases in their welfare responsibilities. Federalism does not solve such problems, but it does create a context in which the states may be able to show flexibility, individuality and innovation in their various responses.

Table 3.4 State and local government combined general expenditures, 2007

	$ million
Elementary and secondary education	534,905
Public welfare	384,769
Higher education	204,706
Health and hospitals	193,072
Police	84,088
Fire protection	36,828
Housing & community development	45,937
Highways	124,604
Sanitation and sewerage	67,016
Natural resources	28,717
Parks & recreation	37,526
Utility & liquor store expenditures	189,330
Insurance trust expenditure	213,652
Financial administration	39,631
Interest on debt	93,586
Government administration	108,874
Other	376,446
Total direct expenditure	2,661,210

Source: Constructed from data on US Bureau of the Census website: http://www.census.gov

The states and their local governments in US federalism

Fixing the parameters of the balance of power and authority between federal and state governments has occupied a good deal of political and legal energy ever since the nation was founded. Washington DC is the hub of the federal political structure, and politics at the national level often dominates political discourse. The undoubted significance of the national government should not, however, mask the considerable importance of state and local government in the United States.

For the most part, state government structures follow the national style. Forty-nine of the states have bicameral legislatures, modelled on the example of the two chambers of the US Congress, the House of Representatives and the Senate, although sometimes in the states these chambers have been given different appellations. Nebraska is the sole exception, with a single-chamber (unicameral) state legislature, where all the members are state senators. Nebraska also has the distinction of being the only state where the legislature is nominally non-partisan. Unlike the situation in all the other 49 states, candidates for election to the state legislature in Nebraska do not stand as political party nominees. Elsewhere in the country, the state political parties are key to the election process, and the state legislative bodies are organised along party lines after the election.

State governors and lieutenant governors fill the leading executive positions in each state, but many states elect other members of the executive branch too. Various state-level ballots offer the opportunity to vote for state treasurer, attorney-general, secretary of state and other statewide offices. In about half the states, members of the state judiciary are also subject to election.

The design of local government is very much up to individual states. This allows for regional decision-making, and consequently there is considerable variation in sub-state government patterns across the nation. There is a tendency to reflect the federal model in the practical operation of state–local relations, although the constitutional guarantees that exist for states in the federal system are absent at the local level.

Eighty-nine thousand governments

Counties, cities and other general purpose governments are common, but among local governments the most numerous perform specified functions. There are over 52,000 school districts and special districts set up to serve purposes such as the running of schools, and the organisation and administration of drainage and irrigation districts, power authorities and public housing authorities.

General purpose local governments make up over 39,000 more units – counties, municipalities, towns and townships. In 2007, the US Bureau of the Census counted 89,527 separate governments in the United States. The national government in Washington is one of these and the individual state governments constituted 50 more. The rest of these government units consisted of the immense variety of local governments throughout the nation.

With such considerable governmental diversity, accurate generalisations are inevitably rare. American federalism preserves the opportunity for local communities, within the parameters of the US Constitution and inside their own political boundaries, to take local responsibility for differentiations in local politics and policy implementation. The result is a system of domestic politics and government containing myriad variations between states, and between other governments within states.

There has been a trend over the last generation towards greater activity at state and local level, and this has continued into the twenty-first century. At local government level, there has been a growth in the number of governments as well as the number of employees within local government, but these recorded very different rates of expansion. In the 30 years up to 2007 the number of local governments grew by 12 per cent and, while growth has been slower in recent years, it still reached 2.3 per cent in the final decade of this period. Over the whole 30-year period, the number of general purpose local governments remained almost static, but the number of schools districts has declined by 14 per cent, while the number of special districts with other functions has increased by 44 per cent. This expansion in the use of special districts accounts for the growth in the number of local governments in the past three decades.

Employment trends in state and local government confirm the shift towards the significance of states and localities in the American federal system. While the number of federal (central) government employees fell over the generation to 2006, and showed a dramatic fall of 326,000 (10.7 per cent) in the period 1992–2006, both state and local government employment grew steadily and considerably throughout this time.

In the 34 years between 1972 and 2006, the number of employees at state government level rose by 73.4 per cent. While the greatest growth came in the middle of this period, there was still a rise of 12.2 per cent in the number of state employees in the decade to 2002, followed by only 1.1 per cent growth in the four years to 2006. At local government level, over 6.2 million new jobs were created between 1972 and the early years of the twenty-first century, showing a 78.2 per cent growth over the whole period and continuing to grow strongly up to 2006. In the 1970s, state and local governments employed almost 11 million people, less than four times the workforce of the central government. By the early twenty-first century, state and local governments paid over 19 million employees, over seven times as many employees as the central government had on its payroll.

Table 3.5 Federal, state and local governments

	Federal	State	Local
1972			
Number of units	1	50	78,218
Employees	2,832,000	2,957,000	7,970,000
1982			
Number of units	1	50	81,780
Employees	2,848,000	3,744,000	9,249,000
1992			
Number of units	1	50	86,692
Employees	3,047,000	4,595,000	11,103,000
2002			
Number of units	1	50	87,525
Employees	2,690,000	5,072,000	13,099,000
2006/7*			
Number of units	1	50	89,476
Employees	2,721,000	5,128,000	14,199,000

* Government units, 2007 figures. Employees, 2006 figures
Source: Constructed from data on US Bureau of the Census website: http://www.census.gov

Table 3.6 US local governments come in many forms (2007)

Counties	3,033	
Municipalities	19,492	
Townships	16,519	
Sub-total – General purpose local governments		39,044
School districts	13,051	
Special districts	37,381	
Sub-total – Special purpose governments		50,432
Total – Local governments		89,476

Source: Constructed from data on US Bureau of the Census website: http://www.census.gov

Local government can be 'special', local democracy may be 'direct'

The structure of local government offers a particular way in which differences across the nation can be expressed within the governmental structure. County governments are almost ubiquitous in the states, excepting only Rhode Island and Connecticut, although not all county governments have exactly the same range of functions. Towns and township governments exist in a total of 20 states, concentrated in the Northeast and Midwest United States, but only some of the New England states maintain the tradition of annual town meetings, a general meeting of local citizens to take the town's major political decisions, and make its major political appointments.

Across the USA there is a patchwork of thousands of local governments designed to undertake particular functions. Special districts have a certain degree of administrative and financial independence, and come in many forms. More than 90 per cent of special districts have been created to perform single functions. The biggest sub-group of special districts is devoted to delivering elementary and secondary education. While amalgamation has reduced the number of school districts considerably over the past generation, there were still 13,506 in 2002.

Many other special districts are dedicated to functions such as the provision and management of drainage, flood control, irrigation, and soil and water conservation. Fire protection, housing and community development, and water and sewerage provision are also often dealt with by special district governments, and in some states they might deal with cemetery upkeep, or mosquito control. Some states put particular faith in this form of local government, and over half of the nation's special districts are accounted for by only eleven states.

Some states provide another form of citizen access to their political system, through the 'direct democracy' of initiative, referendum and recall elections. The forms of participation differ, but over half the states, the District of Columbia, and a number of sub-state governments give the voters an opportunity to comment directly on legislative measures through initiative propositions and/or referenda which are included on the election day ballot.

In many states these political forms have been dormant or used only occasionally since they were first introduced, early in the twentieth century, but there have been high-profile examples of their use, and the popular use of initiative propositions has increased over the past generation. For example, in California, Massachusetts, Colorado, Michigan and Oregon propositions have been used in single-issue

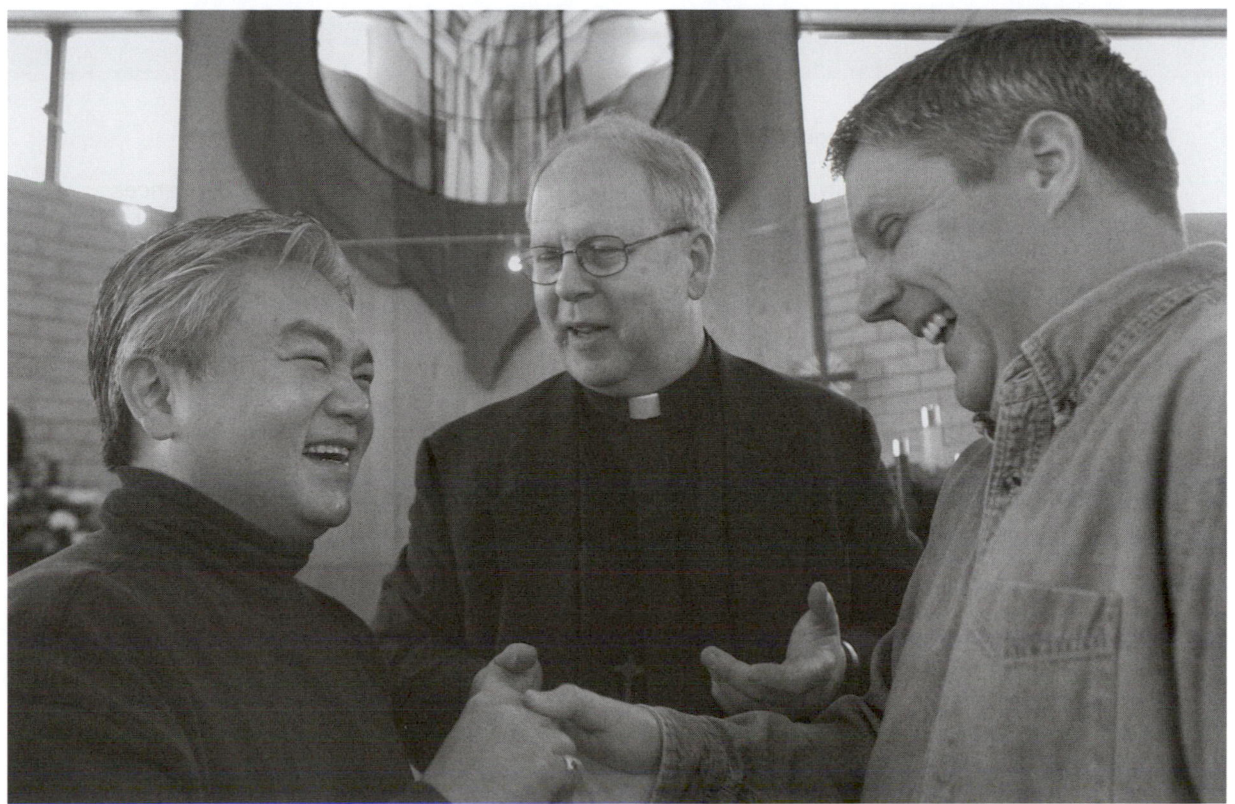

Figure 3.2 Whether gay marriage should be formally recognised has been a contentious issue in recent elections at state and federal level.
Source: © Ann Johansson/Corbis

campaigns to cap local taxation rates, legalise the medical use of marijuana, abolish bilingual education in schools, attempt to limit the size of hog farms, and try to introduce an assisted suicide law. State-level democracy has, on occasion, been used to increase the profile of an issue nationally, as was startlingly evident on election day 2004, when voters in 11 states were presented with ballot questions on gay marriage.

In addition, in about one-third of states, a public petition can force a special recall election. The single question put in a recall election is whether the current incumbent in an office should be confirmed in that position for a full term, or be removed from the position before the term of office has ended. This rarely used mechanism claimed its highest-profile victim in recent years when, in 2003, Governor Gray Davis of California was removed from office by a very high-profile recall election, and replaced by Arnold Schwarzenegger.

Table 3.7 Special district government by function (not including school districts): 2002

	Percentage
Natural resources (drainage, flood control, irrigation, soil and water conservation)	19.9
Fire protection	16.2
Water supply	9.7
Housing and community development	9.7
Sewerage	5.7
Cemeteries	4.7
Libraries	4.4
Parks and recreation	3.7
Highways	2.2
Health	2.1
Hospitals	2.1
Education (school buildings)	1.5
Airports	1.4
Utilities (electric, gas, public transport)	1.4
Other single-function districts	6.2
Multiple-function districts	9.0

Source: Constructed from data on US Bureau of the Census website: http://www.census.gov

Box 3.3

The fifty states and gay marriage

The states have the responsibility for the details of marriage and divorce law. There are differences between states regarding such details as minimum ages and periods of notice, and the state of Nevada in particular has become known for the lack of bureaucracy surrounding the marriage ceremony. These differences notwithstanding, individual states recognise marriages performed in other states.

This comity has been strained in the growing debate over gay marriage. In 1996, the US Congress passed the federal Defense of Marriage Act, which prohibits federal recognition of same-sex marriages, and which allows states to refuse recognition to gay marriages performed in other states.

As well as the emotional value that a formal marriage might provide to a couple, the institution of marriage is associated with all kinds of rights and responsibilities. Taxation, inheritance and pensions may all be affected by marital status. The right to be involved when a 'next of kin' is needed to make a decision does not automatically transfer to a life partner of the same sex.

The Massachusetts Supreme Judicial Court ruled in 2003 that the state's constitution guaranteed equal rights to gay couples, and from May 2004 same-sex marriages were performed in that state. There were others around the nation who felt that their local laws were gender-neutral. Decisions made locally in San Francisco, California, and by county officials in Portland, Oregon and Multnomah County, New Mexico also allowed the issue of marriage licences to some gay couples.

Gay marriage became a major issue in the 2004 election, when various groups of local state legislators and conservative citizen activists inserted questions on the ballot in 11 states: Arkansas, Georgia, Kentucky, Michigan, Mississippi, Montana, North Dakota, Oklahoma, Ohio, Oregon and Utah. In all of those states, the vote favoured amendments to the state constitutions to define marriage as applying only to heterosexual couples. The highest-profile ballot defeat for same-sex marriage came in California, when a November 2008 Proposition vote stopped further same-sex marriages in a state which had previously been performing this form of marriage.

This issue will continue to engage some states for the foreseeable future. By 2012 same-sex marriages were legally performed in Massachusetts, Connecticut, Iowa, New York, New Hampshire, the District of Columbia and Vermont. In all these states, except Vermont, the availability of gay marriage has come about through action in the courts. Some states recognised same-sex marriages performed elsewhere, but did not legalise their performance in-state. However, most states had laws prohibiting gay and lesbian marriages. Some states introduced further legislation, or state constitutional amendments, to reinforce marriage as a heterosexual institution. Anti-gay marriage activists indicated that the issue would continue to be pursued in state legislatures and that initiatives would appear on more state ballots, while gay and lesbian advocate groups took their case to the courts in a number of states, maintaining this as a highly contested policy area in the states.

The states face a difficult situation. Most Americans oppose gay marriage, but only a minority of the public support a US constitutional amendment on the topic, and a solid majority of citizens are in favour of some legal recognition of the civil union of same-sex couples. Civil unions that encompass the same or similar rights to those of marriage are available in a handful of states.

In general, the position of homosexuals in the USA has improved in recent decades but, as in many earlier civil rights battles, this is a slow and uneven process. As the states confront the gay marriage issue, the pattern of responses will reflect the differing political cultures of the 50 states.

Table 3.8 States making greatest, and least, use of special districts: 2002

	Number
Illinois	3,145
California	2,830
Texas	2,245
Pennsylvania	1,885
Kansas	1,533
Missouri	1,514
Colorado	1,414
Washington	1,173
Nebraska	1,146
New York	1,135
Indiana	1,125
Louisiana	45
Hawaii	15
Alaska	14

Source: Constructed from data on US Bureau of the Census website: http://www.census.gov

Has federalism stopped being cooperative?

While federalism allows for regional adaptation and change, the continued existence into the 1960s of apparently unassailable racist regimes in some southern states threatened to bring this devolutionary system into disrepute. This served to underscore that state governments generally had, at that time, failed to adapt to modern political needs. Many state legislatures met only briefly, relied wholly on amateur politicians, and restricted their governors to single, short terms in office. Sometimes individual regimes were corrupt, and the local political environment often limited, rather than encouraged, change.

States found themselves under pressure from the federal government and the federal courts to confront the social and political problems of the late twentieth century. Many resisted, but over time the nation's states responded appropriately.

State legislatures now meet regularly and take a creative approach to policy development. A broader tax base has provided a more solid fiscal foundation. State policy initiatives in education, environmental policy, health care and employment training have increasingly served as models for the national agenda.

Evidence of the increased respect for modernised state government can be found in the number of state governors who have been presidential candidates in recent years. President Obama's route via the US Senate is a rarity, while Governors Carter, Reagan, Clinton and Bush have all made the transition to the White House, and other governors have challenged for it.

The period since this modernisation of state governments began has been interpreted by some as a time when states have come back into their own. President Reagan's 'New Federalism' plans sought to thrust many programmes into the hands of the states, and to increase state autonomy in the implementation of programmes funded by federal grants. While the federal funding stream declined in these years, these moves increased the states' experience in policy-making and implementation.

At the same time, the Supreme Court's 1985 decision in *Garcia* v. *San Antonio Metropolitan Transit Authority* appeared to weaken the ability of state and local governments to resist federal government legislative pre-emption – in this case, the imposition of the Fair Labor Standards Act on state and local governments, with its contingent costs.

In the 1990s, the leaders of America's subnational governments became increasingly vocal in their dismay at the number and expense of federal legal requirements for which there was no equivalent federal funding stream. These 'unfunded mandates' give the national government effective control over part of the state and local budget, by determining part of the policy agenda, and demanding that it be underwritten from state and local budgets. After the Republican congressional election successes of 1994, the US Congress passed the Unfunded Mandate Reform Act (1995), requiring more careful consideration of any legislation that would impose an unfunded mandate totalling more than $50 million. The legislation may have imposed extra steps but it has not outlawed the unfunded mandate, and pressing issues, such as increased security concerns, can still result in costs legislated in Washington DC, but falling on subnational governments.

The turn of the century saw an apparent shift in the Supreme Court towards a more vigorous consideration of federalism. The Court's 1995 decision in *United States* v. *Lopez* declared unconstitutional the Gun-Free School Zones Act (1990). This legislation had made possession of a gun within 1,000 feet of a school into a federal crime. Advocates of states' rights believed that the Act interfered with states' law enforcement authority. Other decisions in similar vein have followed, as Pickerill and Clayton say, 'invalidating a series of federal statutes, ranging from the Violence Against Women Act to the Gun-Free School Zones Act to the Brady Bill to the Age Discrimination in Employment Act'. These authors go on to point out that, while the Court seems to have 'rediscovered constitutional doctrines and limitations on federal power . . . not used since the New Deal', the decisions have generally been by the tightest of Supreme Court margins, five votes to four (Pickerill and Clayton, 2004, p. 233).

The debate over the nature of American federalism continues to be live and lively, affected by the contexts of local, state and national politics, the pragmatic requirements of funding in any political system, and decisions made in every branch of the national government. Voices are regularly raised in concern that the defences for state autonomy are eroding. Certainly, as technology and communications become increasingly fast, there may be a growing sense of national agendas taking precedence. On the other hand, there remain considerable differences between the states. A few moments of thought would suffice to compose a simple list of economic, geographic, environmental and demographic reasons why the citizenry of, say, Alaska, Florida, New Mexico or Idaho are likely to have different policy questions high on their agendas. It is a commonplace to point out that California's gross domestic product would put it among the top nations in the world, but it is no less true that other states also have 'nation-sized' economies. All of these are run by state governments that will continue to press the value of their place in the US federal system.

Chapter summary

In the federal system of the United States of America, the national government and the state governments each have a direct relationship with the electorate. If the move from the Articles of Confederation to the US Constitution shifted the balance of authority somewhat to the national government, the states have always retained considerable autonomy. The position of the states is protected constitutionally, and the continuing role of federalism is encapsulated especially in the Tenth Amendment.

The USA is a large and heterogeneous nation. The history of immigration and American national development is imprinted in the differences between states. The variety of natural resources, weather patterns and geographical features is reflected in the industries, businesses and agricultural enterprises of the different states. The states allow the development of local and regional politics in response to these differences within the nation.

The relationship of the states to the national government has changed over time, with closer intergovernmental relationships evolving in recent decades. The federal government has the most effective fund-raising source, in the shape of income tax, and federal grants to state and local governments have a huge impact on domestic policies. It is still true, though, that most domestic policy spending is accomplished at state and local government levels.

The states devolve some authority to local governments, and altogether there are about 89,000 government units in the USA, some of which operate within very specific policy areas. Many states also offer their citizens the opportunity to vote directly on issues through various forms of referenda that appear on the ballot.

Federalism continues to adapt. The system allows local political and economic reaction to local pressures. At best, this encourages the sharing of good practice between local governments, but it can also provide the opportunity for locally dominant groups to reject cultural and political progress. It is not unusual for federal principles to be tested in the Supreme Court, and recent decisions have maintained an emphasis on the rights and individuality of the states.

Discussion points

1. How would you test the extent to which American states have maintained their political autonomy?
2. Is the existence of multiple local government units, including special districts, likely to bring more benefits in terms of local decision-making, or more difficulties in terms of adding complex layers of government?
3. Can the states really act as 'laboratories for democracy'?

Further reading

Joseph Zimmerman's *Contemporary American Federalism: The Growth of National Power* (Leicester: Leicester University Press, 1992) remains an authoritative introduction, and is complemented in detail by other books from the same author, including *Interstate Relations: The Neglected Dimension of Federalism* (Westport, Conn.: Praeger, 1996), and *State–Local Relations: A Partnership Approach* (2nd edn, Westport, Conn.: Praeger, 1995).

Another well-respected review comes in Daniel Elazar's *American Federalism: A View from the States* (3rd edn, New York: Harper & Row, 1984). David Walker's *The Rebirth of Federalism* (2nd edn, Chatham, NJ: Chatham House, 2001) provides an impressive history and analysis of American federalism. Federal relationships are examined in terms of costs and benefits in Paul E. Peterson's *The Price of Federalism* (Washington DC: Brookings Institution, 1995). John C. Teaford makes the case for the recent renaissance of the states within the federal system in *The Rise of the States: Evolution of American State Government* (Baltimore: The Johns Hopkins University Press, 2002).

The author found Alan Grant's essay 'Devolution and the reshaping of American federalism', in Grant's own edited collection, *American Politics: 2000 and Beyond* (Ashgate: Aldershot, 2000) a useful source for this chapter. Also helpful were Robert F. Nagel, *The Implosion of American Federalism* (New York: Oxford University Press, 2001) and Robert P. Sutton, *Federalism* (Westport, Conn.: Greenwood Press, 2002).

Useful information can be found at the Center for the Study of Federalism (http://www.temple.com/federalism), and from the Council of State Governments (http://.statesnews.org). The US Bureau of the Census offers a great deal of relevant data at http://www.census.gov.

In *Real Democracy: The New England Town Meeting and How It Works* (Chicago: University of Chicago Press, 2004), author Frank M. Bryan provides an extraordinarily detailed aggregation of case studies, giving a unique insight into local democratic practice in New England, and especially in Vermont.

References

Pickerill, J. Mitchell and Clayton, Cornell W. (2004) 'The Rehnquist Court and the political dynamics of federalism', *Perspectives on Politics*, vol. 2, no. 2 (June), pp. 233–48.

Zimmerman, Joseph F. (1992) *Contemporary American Federalism: The Growth of National Power* (Leicester: Leicester University Press).

http://www.census.gov

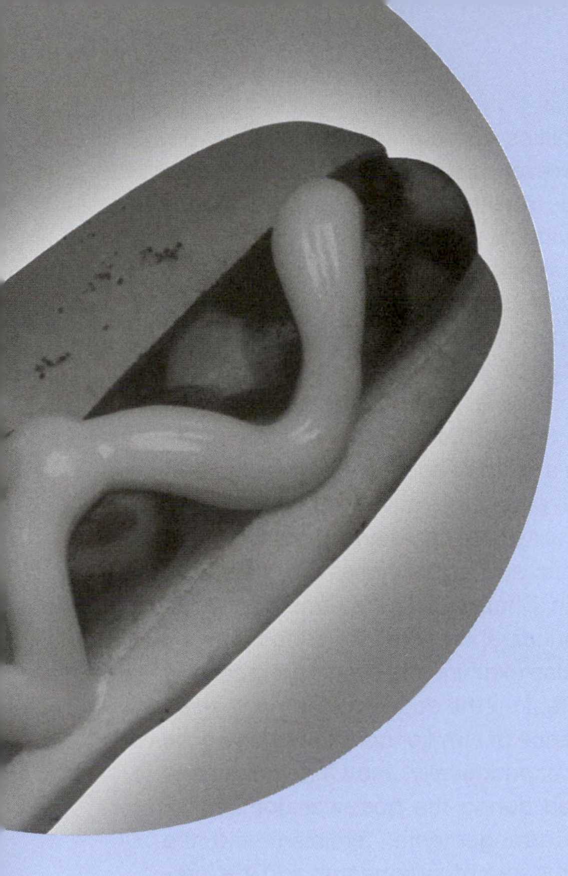

Part 2
The socio-economic contexts

We saw in Part 1 that American government and politics operate within the framework provided by the Constitution. Equally important, however, are the social and economic frameworks. In the first place, social and economic realities give life and substance to the constitutional system, as institutions and individuals seek to put into practice the abstract framework bequeathed to them by the Founding Fathers. Moreover, the very agenda of American politics is determined largely by the social and economic problems and opportunities which present themselves in any particular historical era. In this part, therefore, we examine in detail some of the key socio-economic contexts of American politics. In Chapter 4, we analyse the economic and social roots of the political consensus which characterised American politics from the end of the Second World War until the mid-1960s. For many, this is now viewed as a 'golden age' when American preeminence in prosperity and power made the political process relatively straightforward. In that sense, it established a model of how the political system could and should operate. It did not last, however, largely because its economic and social bases were severely dislocated by domestic and international change. In Chapter 5, we examine how the American economy began to decline relative to its principal competitor nations until, by the 1980s, it was considered to be in deep crisis. We also examine the economic recession that began in 2007 and which will have a powerful effect on the economy for many years to come. In Chapter 6, we analyse the rise to prominence of a major contemporary social issue, that of gender relations. Socially, as well as economically, the United States is a markedly different country from that which existed during the post-war consensus. Among the many challenges to traditional social arrangements, feminism and the campaign for greater gender equality stands out as the most fundamental: and it is precisely for this reason that it has generated some of the fiercest debates in contemporary American politics. In Chapter 7, we look at some new aspects of an old issue in American history: immigration and the ethnic and racial composition of American society. The diversity of its people is one of the country's greatest strengths, yet it also creates tensions and problems that at times seem insoluble.

The four chapters which make up Part 2 by no means paint a complete social and economic portrait of the contemporary United States. They do, however, make clear that the political process in the contemporary United States is constrained and shaped by continuing socio-economic structures and tensions.

Contents

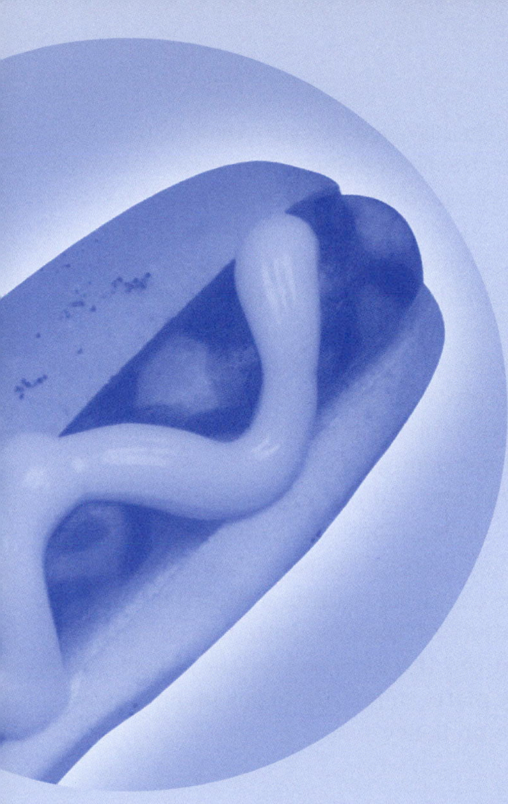

Chapter 4

The rise and fall of consensus since 1945

This chapter examines the political consensus which underpinned both domestic and foreign policy in the decades following the Second World War. From the perspective of the early twenty-first century, many Americans regard this as a great period in their history: one when social and ideological cohesion promoted affluence and stability at home and American power abroad.

In 1945, the United States was indisputably the world's greatest economic and military power. Indeed, it had no serious rival in either sphere of activity. Its economy had recovered from the Great Depression of the 1930s, thanks mainly to war contracts; yet unlike the other belligerents, its cities, factories and farms had suffered no devastation during the Second World War. Thus, despite four years at war in Europe and Asia, the American economy was not merely intact, but was ready to expand around the world. The American military machine possessed the same capability. Its troops and weapons had been the decisive factor in defeating both Germany and Japan and, most important of all, the United States alone possessed the awesome power of the atomic bomb.

Such economic and military prowess, however, was by no means an unproblematic source of joy to Americans and their political leaders. On the economic front, the spectre of recession or even depression loomed. After all, if war contracts had ended the Great Depression, it was by no means unreasonable to suppose that the disappearing stimulus of war would throw the economy into reverse. Most immediately, there was also the problem of how to reintegrate some 15 million service men and women, all clamouring for rapid demobilisation, back into the civilian economy.

It must be remembered that the pre-war years had witnessed considerable political strife over fundamental socio-economic issues. The Democratic party had largely united behind President Franklin D. Roosevelt's New Deal, of which the central feature was the acceptance of responsibility by the federal government for the general health of the economy and the welfare of the people. This, in turn, had entailed much experimentation in both governmental process and policy. There had been, for example, a shift in political power from the states to the federal government, and to the presidency in particular; government intervention in the economy on an unprecedented scale; government promotion of worker power through pro-union legislation; and the creation of a fledgling welfare state.

These departures from traditional laissez-faire, pro-business American practice had incurred the wrath of most Republicans and, increasingly, of conservative Democrats. Thus, while the electorate continued to send Roosevelt to the White House and a Democratic majority to the Congress, New Deal innovation had all but come to a halt by 1938. It was by no means clear, therefore, whether the New Deal philosophy would be sustained in post-war America.

On the foreign policy front, the debate had been equally fierce during the inter-war years. A bitter struggle over American participation in the League of Nations after the First World War had been followed by retrenchment and a strong tendency towards isolationism. This persisted right up until Pearl Harbor, even though by then President Roosevelt and other political leaders had become convinced of the need for the United States to enter the Second World War (see Chapter 20). Most Americans therefore entered the global conflict reluctantly and, with the war over in 1945, assumed their country would once again turn inwards.

On the other hand, both economic and national security factors counselled against any such 'neo-isolationism'. The health of the American economy depended in part upon access to overseas markets and raw materials. Yet, by the end of the war, there were very few countries with the wealth to import the goods that the United States had to offer. Furthermore, the policy of American neo-isolationists to terminate the loans which had been extended to European allies to fight the war would only make this situation worse.

As for access to raw materials, this depended upon ensuring global stability in general, and the freedom of the high seas in particular. With respect to the latter, the United States had always been able to count upon the protection afforded by the British navy. The old imperial order, however, had been put under terrible strain by the costs of defeating Germany and the capacity of Britain to continue playing its role of policing the world was in doubt. In addition, should Britain prove unable to resume its pre-war role, who but the United States was in a position to take up the mantle on behalf of western capitalism and democracy?

On the evidence of pre-war political conflicts in the United States, these dilemmas over post-war domestic and foreign policy might easily have plunged the country into turmoil after 1945. Instead, a combination of unprecedented economic prosperity and the threat posed by the Soviet Union produced a platform for consensus on both domestic and foreign policy.

Post-war prosperity

Rather than lapsing into recession, the post-war American economy boomed. As a result of wartime prosperity, American gross national product (GNP, the value of all goods and services produced in the country) stood at a healthy $212 billion in 1945. Yet, by 1960, that figure had more than doubled and, by 1971, had reached over $1 trillion. This wealth was, as Carl Degler put it, 'the first big fact of the postwar economy' (Degler, 1975, p. 165).

The failure of the anticipated recession to materialise was due in part to pent-up consumer demand. Americans had relatively few opportunities to buy consumer goods during the wartime austerity and had therefore saved considerable sums which they were now eager to spend. However, the key factor in sustaining the post-war boom was government expenditure: on defence, highways, education and housing, in particular. By the mid-1950s, purchases by government were more than one-fifth of total national purchases (Degler, 1975, p. 167). Government commitment to high defence and other expenditures encouraged American industry to invest in research and the development of new techniques and products. In consequence, manufacturing became increasingly automated and computerised, and ever more efficient at producing goods, either for the government or for consumers.

Despite periodic recessions, consumer purchasing power increased enormously in the post-war decades. The proportion of Americans with an annual income (in real terms) of $10,000 or more rose from 9 per cent in 1947 to 33 per cent in 1968; during the same period, the proportion of those with an income of less than $3,000 fell from 34 per cent to 19 per cent. Thus, 'the distribution of income gave the American social structure the shape less of a pyramid than of a diamond, with a vastly expanded middle class' (Leuchtenburg, 1983, p. 48).

As well as being newly affluent, this burgeoning middle class had more leisure time, as hours of work were reduced and paid vacations increased. On top of this came a credit boom, with short-term consumer credit rising from $8.4 billion in 1946 to almost $45 billion in 1958. To facilitate this further, Diners Card introduced the first credit card in 1950, soon to be followed by American Express and others (Leuchtenburg, 1983, p. 43).

The result of all this was a mass consumer society. The first steps towards this had been taken in the 1920s, but those gains had been wiped out by the Depression. Now, in the post-war years, the great majority of Americans could purchase cars, televisions, refrigerators, washing machines and so on (see Table 4.1). They also consumed increasing quantities of convenience foods and patronised 'fast-food' restaurants: in 1954, the first McDonald's was opened in San Bernadino, California. In 1956, in Minneapolis, came the first of another great symbol of modern American consumerism, the enclosed shopping mall.

Figure 4.1 A 1950s family watches television.

Source: © Picture History

Table 4.1 Distribution of durable consumer goods in American families, 1946–56

	Percentage of families owning						
Year	**Car**	**TV**	**Fridge**	**Freezer**	**Vacuum cleaner**	**Washing machine**	**Air conditioner**
1946	n/a	–	69.1	–	48.8	50.5	0.2
1947	n/a	–	71.2	–	49.5	63.0	0.2
1948	54	2.9	76.6	4.3	51.7	67.4	0.3
1949	56	10.1	79.2	5.2	52.8	68.6	0.4
1950	60	26.4	86.4	7.2	56.5	71.9	0.6
1951	65	38.5	86.7	9.3	57.7	73.5	0.8
1952	65	50.2	89.2	11.5	59.4	76.2	1.4
1953	65	63.5	90.4	13.4	60.5	78.5	2.6
1954	70	74.1	92.5	15.1	62.2	81.3	4.0
1955	71	76.1	94.1	16.8	64.3	84.1	5.6
1956	73	81.0	96.0	18.0	66.7	86.8	7.6

Source: from *The Proud Decades: America in War and Peace, 1941–1960*, by John Patrick Diggins. Copyright © 1988 by John Patrick Diggins. Used by permission of W. W. Norton & Company, Inc.

Along with the consumer and leisure boom came the baby boom, the housing boom and the rapid expansion of suburbia. The birth rate in the post-war years was remarkable, owing perhaps to a combination of rising prosperity, optimism and improvements in medical care. Whatever the reason, there were one-third more Americans in 1960 than there had been in 1940 (Dubofsky and Theoharis, 1983, p. 105). The population growth was especially pronounced in western states: by 1963, California had overtaken New York as the most populous state.

Wherever the population increased, however, it lived increasingly in suburbia. In the immediate post-war years, the federal government guaranteed the mortgages of millions of first-time home buyers. Many of these found the affordable homes they sought in the new, prefabricated suburban developments, such as those built by William Levitt in Pennsylvania and New York. These 'Levittowns', although later derided as 'little boxes on a hillside', had enormous appeal for those seeking a stable family life away from the noisy, dirty cities. Highway construction and automobiles made commuting relatively easy.

For many Americans, then, post-war affluence meant a better material life, with work, family and home at the heart of a consumer-oriented society. It also meant that Americans were becoming more like each other in their lifestyles, with mass culture diminishing regional, ethnic and class differences. Regrettably, 'commentators found the United States not only homogenous but homogenized. The typical American, social analysts complained, had become both conformist and bland. Each morning Mr Jones put on a standard uniform of button-down shirt, sincere tie, and charcoal-grey flannel suit, and adjusted his perpetual smile' (Leuchtenburg, 1983, p. 70). The rest of the Jones family seemed equally uninspiring. While Mr Jones set his sights upon climbing the corporate ladder, Mrs Jones was apparently content to aim for perfection as a homemaker. As for their children, even the college students were conformist and apolitical.

Of course, millions of Americans – black and white, young and old – did not share in the post-war economic boom or the lifestyle that went with it: and not everyone who did was willing to conform, as the 'Beats' and bikers of the 1950s attest. Yet even the Beats were disengaged rather than challenging, while other sections of America's youth were 'rebels without a cause'. The prevailing cultural mood of the post-war years, then, was one of contentment and, inevitably, this was reflected in the politics of the day.

Political consensus

The New Deal had lost much of its impetus by 1938. Moreover, when Roosevelt died in April 1945, he was succeeded by a man whom few believed capable of reviving the liberal legacy of the 1930s. Harry Truman was a relatively unknown Missouri senator, who had been chosen as his running-mate by Roosevelt in 1944 because of his solid, if unspectacular, record. Many leading Democrats did not think him worthy of Roosevelt's mantle and the Republicans were confident that he could not beat them in a presidential election. These assessments seemed borne out by the 1946 mid-term elections, when the Republicans won a crushing victory, capturing both the House and the Senate for the first time since 1928.

Yet, in 1948, Harry Truman caused the greatest upset in American electoral history by winning the presidency in his own right. To be sure, this was partly due to his growing reputation as a tough, decisive and plain-speaking leader. The underlying reason for his victory, however, was the fact that he grasped better than his rival what a majority of Americans desired and feared: 'Truman appealed to both lower-class Americans eager for housing and welfare legislation and to an emergent middle class still too insecure of its own status to turn against the New Deal' (Diggins, 1988, p. 109). In other words, Truman's campaign promise to protect and extend the New Deal legacy touched a political consensus that had its roots in the 'affluence and anxiety' of the post-war years (Degler, 1975).

At the heart of this continuing adherence to New Deal liberalism was the belief that the federal government must be active in helping to produce a healthy economy and in protecting the people from the worst depredations of recession. This was the political lesson that a majority of Americans had learned from the experience of the Great Depression. In concrete policy terms, this meant maintaining high levels of federal expenditure, the minimum wage, agricultural subsidies and the safety-net of the welfare state. As long as the Republican party threatened the economic security of a majority of Americans by attacking these basic elements of the New Deal, the Democrats seemed assured of political dominance.

So it proved until the New Deal consensus began to crumble in the late 1960s. Between 1932 and 1964, the Republicans won just two presidential elections out of nine. Moreover, their two victories, in 1952 and 1956, were gained at the cost of explicit acceptance of some key elements of New Deal liberalism. Thus, during the 1952 campaign, the Democrats reminded the electorate time and again of the disastrous, ineffectual record of the last Republican president, Herbert Hoover, during the Depression. The response of Dwight D. Eisenhower, the Republican candidate, was to pledge repeatedly that he would use the resources of the federal government to combat recession, should it arise. In the 1956 campaign, Eisenhower implicitly disowned his party's past by referring to his own philosophy as 'Modern Republicanism'. This he defined as 'the political philosophy that recognises clearly the responsibility of the Federal Government to take the lead in making certain that the productivity of our great economic machine is distributed so that no one will suffer disaster, privation, through no fault of his own' (Alexander, 1975, p. 191).

The Eisenhower Equilibrium

Eisenhower's philosophy of modern and moderate Republicanism was an astute blend of the most popular aspects of the New Deal and traditional conservative American values. Combined with his considerable personal popularity, this enabled him to construct what historians have termed 'the Eisenhower Equilibrium'. On the one hand, Eisenhower not only promised to use the resources of the federal government during recession, but he acquiesced in an extension of social security coverage and an increase in the minimum wage. On the other hand, he insisted that private enterprise should be free from government controls, that the budget should be balanced and that Americans should not expect their education or housing to be directly subsidised by the federal government. In short, he advocated traditional individualism, backed by a federal government guarantee of support if times became hard.

For a while in the mid-1950s it seemed that the Eisenhower Equilibrium had taken America beyond the political divisions and strife generated by the Great Depression. Americans at this time 'appeared generally satisfied with their economic system, their political system, and themselves. They seemed scarcely interested in ideological controversy, in searching analyses of social ills, or in seeking alternatives to the status quo' (Alexander, 1975, pp. 147–8).

This complacency would be challenged on both the domestic and international fronts before the decade was out. There was, however, more to the apolitical mood of the 1950s than affluence and self-satisfaction for, owing largely to the perceived threat of communism both at home and abroad, political criticism and dissent became difficult, and even downright dangerous, to express. This suppression of radical politics has its origins in the Cold War consensus in foreign policy.

Foreign policy consensus

There had been considerable disagreement over foreign policy in the inter-war period, and even during the war 'there had been only a fitful semblance of bipartisanship in foreign policy' (Barnet, 1990, p. 272). Yet, between 1945 and 1950, not only did a bipartisan foreign policy emerge, but it was one based on a radical departure from certain fundamental precepts that had held good since 1789.

We shall examine the traditions of American foreign policy in greater detail in Chapter 20. Suffice it to say at this point that the foreign policy of the United States had always been based upon the desire to avoid involvement in European conflicts. Americans generally considered European interstate politics to be corrupt and corrupting. Above all, therefore, the United States should steer clear of 'entangling alliances', as Thomas Jefferson put it, for these would surely drag America down to the level of the Old World. When the United States defied this tradition and belatedly entered the First World War, the experience proved so bitter that it served only to intensify distaste for involvement in Europe.

It is truly remarkable, then, that by 1950 the United States had entered into a series of military alliances with western European states and more generally accepted the political, economic and military burden of 'leader of the free world'. It is even more remarkable that this should have come about by a broad and deep bipartisan consensus.

It has been suggested that there were three main aspects to the foreign policy consensus that emerged in the United States after 1945: cultural cohesion, policy itself and procedural aspects (Melanson, 1991, p. 3). Cultural cohesion is important to foreign policy because it strengthens the sense of national identity. This, in turn, embraces values which may be considered worth not only defending, but also exporting for the 'benefit' of other peoples. American culture had always been based on both these estimates of its own worth, and the post-war economic boom served only to enhance them. While some considered American life to be 'homogenised', most ordinary Americans fervently subscribed to 'normal' and 'respectable' values such as stable nuclear families, community, religion, home ownership and the pursuit of prosperity (Melanson, 1991, pp. 8–9). While Americanism and its antithesis, un-Americanism, elude precise definition, most Americans in the post-war years thought of their national culture in these terms. It was these values which inspired a fierce patriotism, and even more so when they were threatened by 'atheistic communism'.

Policy itself is concerned with the grand design, strategies and tactics by which the nation should defend itself and its interests. In the post-war years, consensus on these was achieved on the basis of certain widely accepted propositions.

While there were specific areas of foreign policy on which there was sharp disagreement, there was little dissent from these fundamental foreign policy precepts, among either the general population or the foreign policy elites. Together they impelled the United States towards a central and global role in the post-war international system.

The procedural aspects of foreign policy concern the process by which policy is formulated and implemented. Here again, there was a marked change after 1945, but one which received bipartisan approval. The central feature of this procedural consensus was the primacy of the presidency in foreign policy-making. Both the Constitution and

Box 4.1

The post-war foreign policy consensus: some fundamental precepts

- The United States was uniquely positioned materially and morally to create a just and stable international order.
- The interests of the United States were global.
- Soviet Communist aggression was the main threat to world peace.
- Containment was the best means of preventing this aggression.
- Nuclear weapons were essential to deterring Soviet expansion.
- A stable, open world economy required American leadership.
- The United States must assume leadership of international organisations, such as the United Nations.

Source: Melanson, 1991, pp. 4–7

traditional practice had always promoted presidential leadership in the making of foreign policy. Now, however, Congress tacitly yielded to the president even its most fundamental constitutional powers, such as authority over war-making. Not one of the wars, conflicts or interventions in which the United States has been involved since 1945 has been accompanied by a formal declaration of war by Congress.

The reasons for this accrual of foreign policy-making powers to the executive branch are numerous (see Chapter 20), but none was more important than the common perception that, at a time of permanent crisis and threat, the presidency was better equipped to discern and protect the national interest than Congress. The presidential branch included the expertise of the foreign policy-making bureaucracy, the intelligence services and the armed forces. Moreover, as a unitary branch of government, it was better equipped to maintain secrecy and to take decisive action, particularly in a crisis. Underpinning these presidential advantages over Congress were the other two aspects of the foreign policy consensus. Because fundamental cultural values and policy precepts were shared by most Americans, Congress was unusually willing to entrust the safety of the nation to the president.

It should not be assumed, however, that the post-war foreign policy consensus came about effortlessly. Indeed, there was considerable political calculation behind it by those who believed that US foreign policy must be actively internationalist. The most famous instance concerns President Truman's request for aid to anti-communist forces in Greece and Turkey in 1947. Meeting with a bipartisan congressional leadership delegation, Truman and his secretary of state, Dean Acheson, asked how Congress could be persuaded to vote the funds. The Republican chairman of the Senate Foreign Relations Committee, Arthur H. Vandenberg, told him that the only way to produce the necessary consensus was to exaggerate the communist threat and 'scare the hell out of the country'.

Others emphasise the political deal between Democrats and Republicans that supported the consensus, with each side hoping to reap electoral gains from the show of unity. And yet another slant on the consensus draws attention to the advantages that bipartisanship offers to the president, in a system of 'separate institutions sharing powers' and where the opposition party may control the Congress. Secretary of State Acheson himself expressed this bluntly:

Box 4.2

Politics and the post-war foreign policy consensus

'The myth of the postwar bipartisan consensus is that the same lightning struck Democratic and Republican statesmen at the same time, causing them to put aside partisan quarrels in the face of an overwhelming external threat. What actually happened is less miraculous but more interesting. In return for a share of the credit key Republican leaders offered qualified support for the critical provisions of the foreign policy consensus taking shape within the Truman administration. In turn the rhetoric of the new foreign policy was carefully crafted to please not only Republican politicians whose votes were needed on foreign aid, loans and military appropriations, but also to win over their constituents to the Democratic Party in the 1948 election.'

Source: Barnet, 1990, p. 272

Bipartisanship in foreign policy is ideal for the Executive because you cannot run this damned country any other way except by fixing the whole organization so it doesn't work the way it's supposed to work. Now the only way to do that is to say politics stops at the seaboard – and anyone who denies that postulate is a son-of-a-bitch or a crook and not a true patriot. Now, if people will swallow that then you're off to the races.

Rourke, 1983, p. 81

For all the cynical exploitation of bipartisanship, however, there was real substance to the new foreign policy consensus: a shared fear of communism, the perception of a global threat and the determination to contain Soviet expansion. Indeed, where significant disagreements over foreign policy occurred, they were usually provoked by charges that measures against communism were too mild, lenient or limited. Even here, however, consensus often eventually triumphed. Thus, when out of office in the early 1950s, some Republicans, like the future secretary of state John Foster Dulles, wanted the country to go beyond containment and to 'roll back' communism from the gains it had already made in Europe and Asia. Once in office under Eisenhower, however, the Republicans practised containment: thus, they made no attempt to roll back communism in North Korea, nor would they come to the aid of Hungary in 1956 when the Soviet army crushed a popular uprising.

A consensus developed behind containment because roll-back was simply unfeasible in the nuclear age. Containment, therefore, met a felt need to combat communism vigorously without embarking upon a 'hot war' with the Soviet Union. In short, there was no credible alternative to containment, for if roll-back was too dangerous, both isolationism and appeasement of the Soviet Union seemed incapable of defending America's interests.

There was, however, still one further element that promoted and sustained the post-war foreign policy consensus: the crude suppression of dissenting voices and views.

McCarthyism

The infamous post-war 'witch-hunt' against alleged communist subversion in the United States is often given the blanket label of McCarthyism. The eponymous junior senator from Wisconsin rampaged through American politics from 1950 to 1954, making reckless and unsubstantiated accusations of disloyalty. While he ruined the lives and careers of thousands of innocent Americans, not once did he uncover any real spies or examples of espionage. At his peak, Joe McCarthy held the nation in thrall with his spectacular displays of macho interrogation of 'witnesses'; he also intimidated his fellow politicians to the point where few were openly willing to challenge either his methods or his mendacity. Even presidential candidate Eisenhower was anxious not to offend McCarthy. He dropped approving references to his great military friend and statesman General George C. Marshall from his 1952 campaign speeches after McCarthy had questioned Marshall's patriotism.

For all his notoriety and power, however, McCarthy was not the instigator of the anti-communist hysteria of the 1940s and 1950s. He merely exploited to great personal advantage a collective paranoia that others had already brought to the fore by the time he rose to prominence in 1950. For example, the House Un-American Activities Committee (HUAC) had begun its work as a temporary committee of the House of Representatives in 1938, and had been made a permanent standing committee in 1945.

HUAC achieved considerable publicity in the immediate post-war years by conducting investigations into the influence of communists and communist sympathisers – dubbed fellow-travellers or pinkos – in a variety of professions. Most profitably, HUAC went to Hollywood to investigate communist influence in the movie industry: there were indeed some communists and former communist actors, directors and screenwriters, but there was no evidence of any subversive activity. In fact, the main purpose of HUAC's trips to Hollywood was to gain valuable publicity for the committee's members, through the televised hearings featuring Hollywood stars as 'witnesses' and as they posed for the photographers with the idols of the silver screen.

There was actually little evidence of communist subversion generally in the United States at that time. Certainly it was revealed in 1950 that a British scientist, Klaus Fuchs, had passed atomic secrets to the Soviets when he had worked on the bomb project in Los Alamos during the war, and that he had been abetted by members of the American Communist party, including Julius and Ethel Rosenberg, who were later executed. Beyond that, however, there was little of substance. Ironically, this was demonstrated by the enormous publicity given to relatively insignificant cases. For example, Richard Nixon launched his national political career by using his seat on HUAC to pursue Alger Hiss, a former State Department official who had attended the Yalta conference. Hiss was accused by Whittaker Chambers, a former communist giving evidence to HUAC, of being a member of the Communist party in the 1930s and a spy. Hiss himself appeared before HUAC to deny the allegations, whereupon he was indicted for perjury. His first trial in 1949 ended in a hung jury; but after a second trial in 1950, he was convicted. The evidence against Hiss was, at best, flimsy and circumstantial, and he was never indicted for espionage, let alone convicted. Nevertheless, a man hesitantly convicted of lying to a congressional committee became the object of a national drama and a debate which continues even to this day. Such was the power of the anti-communist paranoia in the United States in the post-war years to transform a non-event into headline news.

What, then, really lay behind 'the Great Fear'? (Caute, 1978). The Communist party had never been strong in the United States, even in the 1930s. No rational person could conceivably consider it a threat of such magnitude as to justify mass public hysteria. Historians have suggested a variety of explanations, some of which go deep into the psyche of a nation troubled by sudden changes in its domestic and international environment.

Earl Latham, however, suggests a more prosaic, political explanation. At heart, anti-communism was a weapon employed by conservatives to suppress liberal and radical thought. It was used by Republicans to attack Democrats, and by conservative Democrats to attack liberal elements of their own party coalition. If communist subversion was the rallying cry, the real target was the New Deal. Whether it was Alger Hiss, Dean Acheson or Harry Truman himself; whether it was labour unions, the State Department or the Office of Price Administration; whether it was schoolteachers, screenwriters or state employees, the aim and the effect was to put New Deal liberalism on the defensive and its more radical elements beyond the pale.

As we saw above, the concrete policies of the New Deal were too popular to be assailed directly. However, indirect attack through allegations of red or pink sympathies had the desired effect in two most important respects. First, in 1952 the Republicans recaptured both the White House and the Congress after 22 years of almost complete Democratic ascendancy. Secondly, the anti-communist witch-hunt reinforced both the domestic and foreign policy aspects of the post-war consensus. The mere suspicion of disloyalty, or even of harbouring un-American ideas, was often enough to lose people their job, their passport and their friends. Criticism of government policy from the left was grounds for suspicion, especially if it coincided with 'the communist line'. Thus, to argue on economic grounds for a reduction in the budget of the Voice of America (VOA) was enough to raise Senator McCarthy's suspicions, since the Kremlin also wished to see VOA broadcasts curtailed.

In the 1940s and 1950s, then, the United States experienced a domestic and foreign policy consensus that had both natural and contrived roots. Unprecedented and widespread prosperity bred both contentment and anxiety that it might all end and, naturally enough, led to support for the status quo. Soviet expansion into eastern Europe after the war, combined with the weakness of western Europe, led to unsurprising agreement in many quarters on the need for 'containment'; and although no artificial reinforcement was needed, McCarthyism bolted these bases of the post-war consensus into place by eliminating the contemplation of alternatives.

The existence of such a consensus does not mean that there was no political debate in the United States in the post-war years, or that the two main parties did not compete vigorously, but politics was confined within a narrow and rigid framework. If the more liberal Democratic party strove to prove that it was not 'soft on communism', the Republicans had to demonstrate that they were not unsympathetic to the less fortunate in America. In that sense, there was a considerable degree of 'me-tooism' in both parties. This playing to the consensus continued into the 1960s. Around the middle of that decade, however, the fundamental weaknesses inherent in the domestic and foreign policy consensus forced their way to the surface of American politics with dramatic and enduring consequences.

The Kennedy/Johnson years

The administrations of John F. Kennedy and Lyndon B. Johnson (1961–69) witnessed both the apogee of the post-war consensus and the developments which led to its demise. This is true for both domestic and foreign policy.

In the first half of the 1960s, the consensus that the federal government could ensure economic growth and social justice was manifested in ambitious new policies. President Kennedy, for example, overcame the cautious economic orthodoxies of the business community as he pioneered the 'new economics'. This involved, for example, the implementation of tax cuts and budget deficits to stimulate economic growth, even when there was no recession to justify what were previously considered emergency measures (Morgan, 1994, pp. 35–40). More generally, the 'new economics' symbolised the belief that the government now had the knowledge and power to iron out the traditional ups and downs of the business cycle, and ensure steady, continuous expansion and prosperity.

Moreover, the Johnson administration in particular had ambitions to produce not just a wealthier America, but a Great Society. This was a vision of an America in which there was no poverty, squalor, ignorance, fear or hatred, and where the quality of life opened the door for all Americans to fulfil their human potential. The rhetoric of the vision far outstripped the practical implementation. Nevertheless, an impressive array of legislation was enacted. In 1964, the self-styled 'War on Poverty' was launched through the passage of the Economic Opportunity Act: this involved a number of programmes designed to improve the education, training and job opportunities of the poor. Later measures included Medicare and Medicaid, designed to improve medical provision for the aged and the poor, respectively. Welfare programmes like Social Security and Aid to Families with Dependent Children (AFDC) were greatly expanded to provide the poor with a minimum standard of living, and there were measures to improve housing and the environment in the run-down inner cities.

Box 4.3

Lyndon B. Johnson and the Great Society

'For a century we labored to settle and to subdue a continent. For half a century we called upon unbounded invention and untiring industry to create an order of plenty for all our people.

The challenge of the next half century is whether we have the wisdom to use that wealth to enrich and elevate our national life, and to advance the quality of our American civilization.

. . . For in your time we have the opportunity to move not only toward the rich society and the powerful society, but upward to the Great Society.

The Great Society rests on abundance and liberty for all. It demands an end to poverty and racial injustice, to which we are totally committed in our time. But that is just the beginning.

The Great Society is a place where every child can find knowledge to enrich his mind and to enlarge his talents. It is a place where leisure is a welcome chance to build and reflect, not a feared cause of boredom and restlessness. It is a place where the city of man serves not only the needs of the body and the demands of commerce but the desire for beauty and the hunger for community.

It is a place where man can renew contact with nature. It is a place which honours creation for its own sake and for what it adds to the understanding of the race. It is a place where men are more concerned with the quality of their goals than the quantity of their goods.

But most of all, the Great Society is not a safe harbor, a resting place, a final objective, a finished work. It is a challenge constantly renewed, beckoning us toward a destiny where the meaning of our lives matches the marvellous products of our labor.'

President Lyndon B. Johnson, remarks to the Graduating Class, University of Michigan, 22 May 1964, often referred to as the Great Society Speech

'We stand at the edge of the greatest era in the life of any nation. For the first time in world history, we have the abundance and the ability to free every man from hopeless want, and to free every person to find fulfilment in the works of his mind or the labor of his hands.

Even the greatest of all past civilizations existed on the exploitation of the misery of the many.

This nation, this people, this generation, has man's first chance to create a Great Society: a society of success without squalor, beauty without barrenness, works of genius without the wretchedness of poverty. We can open the doors of learning. We can open the doors of fruitful labor and rewarding leisure, of open opportunity and close community – not just to the privileged few, but to everyone.'

President Lyndon B. Johnson, fund-raising dinner, Detroit, 26 June 1964

The extent to which the War on Poverty and the Great Society achieved their goals, or even how seriously the Johnson administration took them in terms of financial provision, are matters which are still hotly disputed. Yet, regardless of the successes or failures, it is important to recognise that there was a political consensus in the United States at this time that deemed such measures desirable and feasible. This was indicated by the landslide presidential election victory of Johnson over the arch-conservative Barry Goldwater in 1964. While it would be a mistake to interpret this victory as evidence of popular enthusiasm for the Great Society, it did at least demonstrate that Americans were far more comfortable with the idea of extending the philosophy of New Deal liberalism than they were with the prospect of its demise.

The domestic political consensus of the early 1960s also encompassed that historically most divisive of American issues, race relations. Outside of the South, there was a growing recognition among whites that full political and legal equality for black Americans was long overdue. In the 1950s, the civil rights movement had gathered great momentum, as it campaigned to end the racial segregation and discrimination that was endemic in the South and some border states. However, despite winning the moral argument, and having achieved a symbolic victory with the Supreme Court's 1954 decision declaring school segregation unconstitutional, there had been no legislation with the muscle to turn theoretical rights into practical realities. As Kennedy took office, most southern schools were still segregated, and so too were restaurants, hotels, swimming pools, transportation and other public facilities. In addition, despite having been guaranteed the vote by the Fifteenth Amendment in 1870, most southern blacks were still unable to exercise this basic political right.

One of the main obstacles to effective federal legislation on civil rights had always been the power of the white South in presidential elections and in Congress. Even liberals such as Kennedy were fearful of offending the white South by pushing meaningful reform. In 1964, however, a combination of factors brought about a consensus on the need for action that overwhelmed southern resistance. The most important of these was the moral and political pressures brought to bear by the civil rights movement. This forced Kennedy to introduce a major civil rights bill into Congress in 1963. The bill was subjected to the usual blocking tactics by southern members, but the emotional aftermath of the assassination of President Kennedy in Dallas enabled President Johnson to obtain its passage.

The Civil Rights Act of 1964 demolished the legal edifice of racial discrimination and provided the basis for later remedial measures under the banner of 'affirmative action'. The following year, Congress passed the Voting Rights Act which obliged southern states to cease their discrimination against black voters.

It is clear, then, that the period from 1961 to 1965 saw a consensus behind the most ambitious programme of federal government responsibility and action in the history of the United States. While there were, of course, many Americans who deplored these developments, most were willing to give the federal government its head in attempting to solve the economic, social and political problems that remained. Behind the consensus, then, lay not only a basic contentment, but also optimism and confidence that things could get better still. In a very short time, however, both the mood and the consensus were to be shattered.

The end of the post-war consensus

The collapse of the post-war consensus is a complex phenomenon, but, on both the domestic and foreign policy fronts, it involved a sharp and sometimes radical challenge to traditionalism. The roots of the collapse lie partly in the perceived policy failures of the 1960s and partly in fundamental socio-economic changes that had been transforming the United States from an industrial to a post-industrial society.

These developments themselves owed much to the changing socio-economic structure of the United States. The transformation from an industrial to a post-industrial economy and society, and later the impact of globalisation upon the economy, brought about an era of reduced opportunity for many Americans. It also created a new division between those well-educated Americans who could easily adapt and prosper in the new economic context, and less-educated Americans who were tied to 'old' industries and who struggled to maintain their living standards. Unsurprisingly, this division was reflected in the realm of policy, both social and economic. The successful 'new class' of post-industrial society tended to favour policies which stressed the autonomy of individuals from governmental and societal control, while those who were losing out tended to look to the recent past as a moral and social compass.

Of course, this is an oversimplified picture. However, it serves to illustrate the deep-rooted strains that have been present in American society since the 1960s. Just as stability, prosperity and consensus left their mark upon the political process of the immediate post-war decades, so fundamental change, economic difficulty and lack of consensus have also affected the conduct of politics in significant ways.

Post-industrial politics

The government and politics of the United States today are characterised by a considerable lack of faith in government by comparison with the mid-twentieth century and an inability to produce a new consensus to replace the old one. One obvious manifestation of the latter is the tendency towards 'divided government' since 1968, where one party captures the White House but cannot gain control of Congress. There has been great speculation on the exact causes of divided government, but it seems that the inability of either party to unite the country around a political philosophy or programme encourages the electorate to ensure that neither of them exercises much control. Even when one party does control both Congress and the presidency, as in the case of the Republicans under George W. Bush, their majorities are thin.

The most distinctive change of the post-industrial political era, however, is the loss of faith in government. Both liberals and conservatives became critical of many policies in the 1960s and 1970s, as the old centre-ground of politics became unacceptable to both. Precisely because government was accorded so much of the blame for policy failure, the capacity of government to solve problems was thrown into doubt for most Americans. While the precise level of faith in the government fluctuates, the downward trajectory continues in the Obama era. In 2010, the Pew Center asked respondents if they trusted the federal government to do the right thing most or all of the time. Only 22 per cent responded affirmatively.

As he entered office in January, 2009, President Obama was faced with the worst economic crisis since the Great Depression of the 1930s. The banking system was in danger of collapse, the economy was in deep recession and unemployment was rising rapidly. As in the Great Depression, banks,

Table 4.2 Public attitudes towards government

***Question*: Is the federal government too powerful?**

	Yes %	No %	Don't know %
1941 Do you think there is too much power in the hands of the government in Washington?	32	56	12
1960 Do the activities of the national government tend to improve conditions in this country?	78	22	–
1996 Is government trying to do too much in solving national problems?	62	28	10
2003 When something is run by the government is it usually inefficient and wasteful?	57	39	4
2010 Does the federal government have a positive effect on the way things are going in the country?	25	65	9

Source: Adapted from Ladd, 1997, pp. 6 and 24, and the Pew Center's *The 2004 Political Landscape* (2003) and the Pew Center's *The People and Their Government* (2010)

businesses and individual Americans looked to the federal government to lead a recovery. On 13 February 2009, just weeks after taking office, Obama secured congressional passage of his American Recovery and Reinvestment Act (ARRA). The package, worth a staggering $787 billion, was a combination of public spending and tax cuts designed to protect and create jobs by improving services such as education and health care and investing in infrastructure projects. The tax cuts were designed to persuade consumers to spend, thus stimulating the production of goods and services.

The Obama recovery programme was created in the same spirit as Roosevelt's New Deal: government activity and government expenditure were the appropriate means of leading the country out of the major economic crisis. Yet while, in 2011, public opinion was evenly divided over how well President Obama was doing his job, a large majority of the American public had little faith in the capacity of the federal government to solve the country's problems.

The post-war consensus and the prosperity that underpinned it seem like a lost 'golden age' today. Such nostalgia probably involves a mistaken belief that things were 'simple' in the post-war halcyon years: whatever problems there were could be solved by government on the basis of compromise and consensus. At the start of the twenty-first century, however, it is impossible for most Americans to believe that problems have simple solutions or that the federal government and the political process can be relied upon to devise satisfactory policies. In other words, one major casualty of the breakdown in the post-war consensus is faith in government and politics.

Chapter summary

The post-war consensus in the United States was based on a widely shared set of both fears and hopes. The major fears were of a return to economic depression and communist expansion. The optimism was based upon America's economic and military pre-eminence. Even when problems such as poverty and race discrimination came to the fore, there was a 'can do' attitude that suggested that solutions could be found. All this added up to a reasonably contented, if conformist, society that was willing to entrust unprecedented power to the federal government in peacetime. In turn, the political process worked satisfactorily, with bipartisan agreement on the fundamentals of both domestic and foreign policy. The consensus, however, lasted only a couple of decades, overtaken by structural change at both national and international level. In its wake emerged a political process far more fractured and less inclined to optimism and grand visions.

References

Alexander, C. (1975) *Holding the Line: The Eisenhower Era, 1952–61* (Bloomington: Indiana University Press).

Barnet, R. (1990) *The Rockets' Red Glare: When America Goes to War* (New York: Simon & Schuster).

Caute, D. (1978) *The Great Fear* (London: Secker & Warburg).

Degler, C. (1975) *Affluence and Anxiety: America Since 1945* (2nd edn, Glenview, Ill.: Scott, Foresman).

Diggins, J. (1988) *The Proud Decades: America in War and Peace, 1941–1960* (New York: Norton).

Dubofsky, M. and Theoharis, A. (1983) *Imperial Democracy: The United States Since 1945* (Hemel Hempstead: Prentice Hall).

Ladd, E. (1997) '1996 vote: the "no majority" realignment continues', *Political Science Quarterly*, vol. 112, pp. 1–28.

Leuchtenburg, W. (1983) *A Troubled Feast: American Society Since 1945* (rev. edn, Boston: Little, Brown).

Melanson, R. (1991) *Reconstructing Consensus: American Foreign Policy Since the Vietnam War* (New York: St Martin's Press).

Morgan, I. (1994) *Beyond the Liberal Consensus: A Political History of the United States Since 1965* (London: Hurst).

Rourke, J. (1983) *Congress and the Presidency in US Foreign Policymaking: A Study of Interaction and Influence, 1945–1982* (Boulder, Col.: Westview).

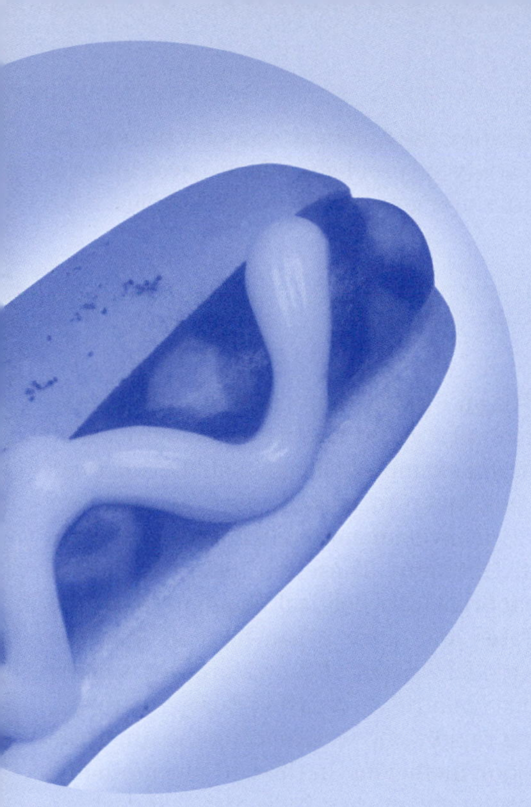

Chapter 5

Economy and society

The American economy is a vital factor in American politics. Most obviously, the state of the economy goes a long way towards defining the political agenda and the range of possible policy choices in relation to both problems and opportunities. Equally important, however, is that the 'American dream' is premised upon the ability of American capitalism to generate ever more wealth to satisfy the aspirations of an ambitious people. In this chapter, therefore, we examine the current state of the American economy and the anxieties that have arisen as a result of its perceived weaknesses.

The United States is probably the greatest economic success story in human history. Measured in terms of economic production and personal wealth, the United States transformed itself in the nineteenth century from an economic minnow into an agrarian and industrial superpower. Already in the 1920s, Americans could experience a level of material consumption undreamed of by earlier civilisations and generations, and, for much of the twentieth century, the United States was the unchallenged leader of the world economy.

To be sure, this economic success was in part based upon appalling and ruthless practices such as slavery and harsh exploitation of wage labourers. Moreover, the United States has experienced some severe economic recessions such as that which began in late 2007 and, of course, the Great Depression of the 1930s. Nevertheless, for the successive generations of immigrants who went to America to pursue 'life, liberty, and happiness', the economic system gave them the opportunity to rise far above the material station of their counterparts in Europe and elsewhere. Thus the American economy always seemed to offer the hope – and usually the reality – that each generation of Americans would be richer than the last. American capitalism appeared to be capable of infinite expansion, of producing ever-higher standards of living and of dominating the global economy.

This was never truer than in the years following the Second World War. With economic rivals like Germany, Japan and Great Britain exhausted, if not destroyed, by the war, the United States built upon superior technological and managerial methods developed before the war to become peerless in economic power. As a result, the United States was virtually able to write the rules of international trade: for only the United States had the capacity and the will to become the engine that would drive the world's economy, thereby bringing new life to the economies of war-torn Europe and Asia. The greatest symbol of American economic predominance was the almighty dollar, which the Bretton Woods agreement of 1944 made as good as gold for the purposes of international exchange.

At home, more and more Americans enjoyed a rapidly improving standard of living that was the envy of the rest of the world (see Chapter 4). While the United States certainly exported goods to the rest of the world, it was the vast, rich domestic market of consumers that was the focus of American economic output. The American economy used most of the world's raw materials and produced most of the world's goods – and the American population consumed most of those resources and goods.

The success of post-war American capitalism was the foundation stone of a political consensus that lasted for 25 years. Most Americans were content with their political system and their government and were prepared to accept the expenditure of vast sums of money on the nation's military capacity in order to defend capitalism and democracy. When problems were 'discovered' at home – race discrimination in the 1950s and poverty in the 1960s – the economy was sufficiently productive to allow the government to fund relatively ambitious attempts to solve them. As long as the majority could see themselves getting better off in their own and in their children's lifetimes, Americans avoided serious internal dispute and gave the government a free hand within the limits of the consensus. In short, for most Americans, a successful economy made for a successful political system.

This picture of the American economy, still valid in the mid-1960s, no longer holds true. In the ensuing decades, the American economy has experienced a variety of problems which have, in turn, made politics and government more complex.

Relative decline

In the 1970s and 1980s, the United States began to suffer from what is called 'relative economic decline'. This means, for example, that although the American economy continued to grow, it did so at a slower rate than its main economic competitors, especially Japan and Germany. These two countries had a different approach to political economy from the United States and some began to think that the American model was out of date. Moreover, smaller but dynamic countries in Asia and Europe were also progressing rapidly and were making the American economy look inefficient. In the late twentieth and early twenty-first centuries, India, Brazil and, above all, China emerged as dynamic economies.

Relative decline: the statistics

Economic performance can be measured in numerous ways and even experts often disagree about which statistics give the truest picture of the American economy. Nevertheless, the relative economic decline of the United States from 1960 to 1980 is beyond serious dispute. The official government figures on perhaps the most important indicator, US economic productivity, show that the growth rate of US manufacturing productivity (output per hour) was already below that of its main competitors in the otherwise satisfactory period 1960–73. Following the huge oil price increase of 1973, however, US productivity growth dipped to a very poor annual rate of 1.7 per cent for the rest of the decade.

The situation deteriorated significantly in the 1980s, with an average annual figure of just 1.2 per cent. This permits the US standard of living to double only every 58 years, compared with every 21 years in the period 1947–67, when annual productivity growth averaged 3.3 per cent (Thurow, 1994, p. 165).

Recovery in the 1990s?

The economic situation in 1992 appeared so bad that President George H. Bush failed to secure a second term of office. While his predecessor, Ronald Reagan, had created a feel-good factor with big tax cuts and optimistic speeches, his failure to curb total government spending led to unprecedented budget deficits. This, in turn, led to pressure to increase taxes in order to reduce the deficit. President Bush had promised in the 1988 election that he would not yield to this pressure, famously declaring, 'Read my lips – no new taxes.' When finally forced to renege on his pledge, he all but sealed his fate as a one-term president.

What then followed, however, was the longest economic boom in American history. How much credit for this should be given to President Clinton is debatable, but the figures are not. For not only did economic growth pick up in the 1990s, it saw American productivity once again outstrip many of its major competitors. Even the shallow recession in 2001 proved to be short-lived and productivity growth resumed a healthy rate. However, as Table 5.1 indicates, other measures of growth suggest that the long boom in the United States only allowed it to make up ground that had been lost. The United States has lost the lead it possessed back in the period 1945–70 and its productivity is merely on a par with that of its competitors.

The resurgence of the American economy in the 1990s was partial in its effects on ordinary Americans, however. For under both Presidents Clinton and George W. Bush, the average American saw only a modest rise in the standard of living, while the rich

Table 5.1 Manufacturing productivity 1990–2008*

	1990 %	1995 %	2000 %	2005 %	2008 %
United States	57.0	69.9	91.2	115.2	128.9
Japan	76.9	84.7	99.4	123.5	127.6
Germany	72.0	84.9	98.5	114.2	128.1
South Korea	36.3	56.2	93.3	122.5	147.8
UK	70.8	83.1	94.2	117.2	125.9

* Output per employed person in manufacturing
Source: US Bureau of Labor Statistics, 2010

benefited significantly. In short, the gap between rich and poor in America is growing (Table 5.2). Moreover, although the boom of the 1990s produced a marked fall in unemployment, the recovery from the 2001 recession has engendered relatively few new jobs. And whereas the Clinton administration turned the budget deficit into surplus, the major tax cuts of 2001 pushed the budget back into the red. Yet another potential problem is the US trade deficit. This is the gap between America's imports and exports, and in 2008 the deficit had reached $458.6 billion. In short, a situation exists in the early twenty-first century where the American economy is still the biggest in the world and productivity has improved since the 1980s. However, even before the deep recession of 2007–9, there remained significant problems in the US economy that dimmed the prospects of prosperity for many Americans.

The role of government

The various economic concerns of the past 40 years have spawned a sharp debate over the role of government in promoting economic prosperity. While both the major parties – and the vast majority of Americans – are staunch supporters of liberal capitalism, they disagree over some key aspects of economic policy.

Generally speaking, conservatives and Republicans believe that the United States has encountered problems because it has abandoned its traditional values and practices. On the economic front, they accuse the federal government of too much meddling in the free market. They believe that entrepreneurs have been saddled with regulations and obligations towards their workforce and the public that cause inefficiencies in their businesses.

They also reject the Keynesian economic policy of successive administrations from the 1930s to the 1970s, which involved the federal government in stimulating and managing consumer demand so as to produce constant economic growth and full employment. Instead, they advocate 'supply-side economics', which emphasises reducing the costs – including wages and taxation – of producing goods and services. At the risk of oversimplification, conservatives believe that the 'golden age' of American economic success was based on free market capitalism and minimal government involvement; a return to those practices should therefore involve a return to American economic pre-eminence. However, the low-tax policy of the Reagan administration produced soaring budget deficits, as did a similar policy adopted by George W. Bush. Between 1981 and 2005, Republicans held the presidency for 16 out of 24 years without solving some of America's key economic problems.

On the liberal side of politics, advocates of old-style Keynesianism are few and far between. Liberals do, however, believe that government must be active in producing an economic infrastructure, a skilled and educated workforce and a socially just society. Whereas supply-siders tend to think that, once free enterprise is relieved of burdensome taxes and regulation, the market will produce prosperity for all, liberals believe that government must temper, if not control, certain aspects of the market economy. Thus liberals tend to oppose tax cuts, because this usually results in a reduction of welfare programmes designed to help the poorest citizens. And if there is liberal support for tax cuts, then they support cuts that benefit the average American, rather than the rich and the corporations.

The so-called 'Great Recession' of 2007–9 and the response to it of the Obama administration brought the differing views of liberals and conservatives into sharp relief (see Box 5.1).

The differences between American liberals and conservatives should not, however, be exaggerated. Regardless of ideology and rhetoric, any president is severely constrained in economic policy by forces largely beyond his control. Take, for example, the growing gap between the incomes of the well-off minority and the majority of Americans (see Table 5.2). While taxation policy can exacerbate this, the underlying cause is mainly to be found in two major developments in the American and, indeed, world economy: post-industrialism and globalisation.

Box 5.1

The Great Recession of 2007–2009

Economists dispute how exactly to define a recession. Some refer to consecutive quarterly falls in gross domestic production, while others emphasise indicators such as unemployment and income. However, there is a wide consensus that between late 2007 and 2009, the United States suffered its most serious economic downturn since the Great Depression of the 1930s. The problem began when the housing bubble burst in 2006. Individual homeowners who had borrowed too much and banks which had lent too much began to suffer. Investment banks had invented some obscure financial instruments to make risky loans and investments. Some major institutions went bankrupt, like Lehman Brothers, while others, like Merrill Lynch, were sold for a tiny fraction of their pre-recession value.

When Barack Obama entered the White House in January 2009, he was faced with a full-blown economic crisis. The response of the private sector was to batten down the hatches and severely restrict the flow of money to businesses and individuals. This threatened to turn the recession into a depression. Unemployment had reached 7.2 per cent and was rising rapidly: in 2008, some 2.6 million jobs had been lost from the economy. The value of houses had fallen by about 20 per cent compared with 12 months before. Convinced that only the federal government was both willing and able to launch a recovery, President Obama responded with a massive injection of federal money, some $787 billion in total. Although the stimulus package was passed by the Democrat-controlled Congress, not a single House Republican and only three Republican senators voted for it. As well as pure partisanship, the vote reflects a sharp difference in ideology over the appropriate role of government in American capitalism.

Table 5.2 The growing gap between rich and poor

	Share of aggregate income received by families (percentages)			
	Lowest 5th	**Third 5th**	**Highest 5th**	**Top 5%**
1980	4.2	16.8	44.1	16.5
1990	3.8	15.9	46.6	18.5
2000	3.6	14.8	49.8	22.1
2007	3.4	14.8	49.7	21.2

Source: US Bureau of the Census, 2010

Post-industrialism

The United States has been transformed in recent decades into a post-industrial economy and society. Whereas an industrial economy relies mainly on the extraction and processing of raw materials, a post-industrial economic system centres upon the provision of services. For example, instead of the predominance of coal and steel production, or the manufacture of relatively simple goods, the emphasis is upon telecommunications, financial services or high value-added products such as pharmaceuticals or computers. By 2009, some 77 per cent of US gross domestic production (GDP) derived from the service sector, with just 22 per cent from industry and 1.2 per cent from agriculture (CIA World Factbook, 2010).

A post-industrial economy requires a more educated workforce than an industrial economy. Unsurprisingly therefore, it is those Americans with the most education and skills who have fared well in the past 20 years, while those without college education have fared worst. The American workforce has become much better educated in recent years, with almost two-thirds now having had some college education. Moreover, the likelihood of being unemployed is much greater for the less educated, and the gap between the employability of the least- and most-educated Americans has grown in recent decades. This reflects the decrease in the number of unskilled jobs in the American economy.

Table 5.3 Composition of the workforce by educational attainment, 1970–2006

	Less than high school diploma %	**High school graduate %**	**Some college %**	**Graduate %**
1970	36.0	38.0	12.0	14.0
2006	10.0	30.0	28.0	33.0

Source: US Bureau of Labor Statistics, 2010

Globalisation

Along with post-industrialism has come the globalisation of the American economy. In 1960, the United States had few serious rivals as a producer of goods that the rest of the world, or indeed Americans, wanted. Today, however, the United States must compete both at home and abroad with an ever-increasing range of rivals. Included in these are low-wage economies which specialise in producing industrial goods. This means that Americans still working in unskilled or semi-skilled jobs in the industrial sector find themselves in competition with Chinese or Indian employees who are willing to work for much lower wages.

Globalisation is thus forcing a levelling down of American industrial wages and the wages of the underskilled in general. This transformation of the economy heralds the end of the American dream for many, since even an expanding economy no longer promises a higher standard of living. As one analyst put it:

> **In an isolated national economy, President Kennedy could talk in 1960 about how a rising economic tide would raise all boats. In an American economy floating in a world economy, his famous dictum no longer holds. The general economic tides [the per capita GNP] have been rising, but a majority of the boats [individual wages] have been sinking.**
>
> Thurow, 1994, p. 53

Table 5.4 Median earnings of full-time workers by educational attainment, 2007 ($)

Not high school graduate	**High school graduate**	**Some college**	**Bachelor's degree**	**Advanced degree**
24,964	32,862	40,769	56,118	75,140

Source: US Bureau of the Census, 2010

Box 5.2

The North American Free Trade Agreement 1993

The North American Free Trade Agreement (NAFTA) treaty was negotiated by President George H. Bush. It formed a free trading block of the United States, Canada and Mexico. It eliminated high tariffs on goods traded between the three nations and allowed each to have access to the others' energy sources at prices paid by home companies. For those who supported it – including President Clinton, most Republicans and most leaders of big business – it was a timely move in the process of globalising the economy and emulating the expansion of the European Union as a free-trade bloc. American companies would benefit by being able to export more advanced and high-value goods and services to Mexico and Canada. In due course, other nations in the western hemisphere might join NAFTA.

Opponents of the treaty feared it would entail the loss of blue-collar jobs to companies in Mexico. Companies operating there could produce some kinds of goods – textiles and steel, for example – much more cheaply than those operating in the United States, for not only were wages much lower, but companies were not required to meet American standards on matters such as workers' health and safety and environmental protection. Thus, billionaire businessman and independent presidential candidate H. Ross Perot predicted that NAFTA would cause 'a great sucking sound' as thousands of American jobs were drawn to Mexico. Unsurprisingly, many union leaders and their political allies in the Democratic party also opposed the treaty. When President Clinton asked for congressional approval of NAFTA, one of his leading opponents was the then House majority leader, and fellow Democrat, Dick Gephardt.

In many ways, the debate over NAFTA epitomised the divisions in the economy and in politics caused by post-industrialism and globalisation.

The twin deficits

Two of the greatest indicators of American economic decline are the trade and the budget deficits.

The balance of trade deficit

The balance of trade is the difference between the value of what a country exports and what it imports. As befits the world's leading economy, the United States had a balance of trade surplus every year from 1893 to 1971, when its first deficit of the twentieth century occurred. The surplus was then restored for a decade, but then virtually collapsed after 1983 (Thompson, 1994, p. 112). In 2008, the United States trade deficit reached a staggering $816.42 billion – almost double the figure at the beginning of the decade. The deficit with China alone stood at $268.0 billion, up from a mere $10.4 billion in 1990. This is compounded by the fact that America's biggest creditor is its erstwhile enemy, the People's Republic of China. Surprisingly, perhaps, there is no agreement on whether or not the huge trade deficit is a bad thing. Some worry that the trade deficit makes the US economy more vulnerable. Because the trade deficit makes the United States more dependent upon inflows of foreign capital and requires a high level of interest to be paid on the debt it entails, it is argued that the American economy could be thrown into chaos by a loss of confidence among foreign investors. Others,

Table 5.5 The budget deficit, selected years, 1950–2010

	Deficit/surplus $ billions
1960	+0.3
1970	–2.8
1975	–53.2
1980	–73.8
1985	–212.5
1990	–221.2
1995	–164.0
1998	+69.2
2000	+236.4
2001	+127.4
2002	–157.8
2003	–375.3
2008	–458.6
2010 est.	–1300.0

Source: US Bureau of the Census, 2010; Congressional Budget Office

however, argue that the trade deficit is a healthy sign. As Daniel T. Griswold of the libertarian Cato Institute put it in testifying before Congress, 'The trade deficit is not a sign of economic distress, but of rising domestic demand and investment . . . I would urge Congress to ignore the trade deficit.' Others argue that China and the United States are so mutually dependent for their economic prosperity that there is little danger that China will cease to fund American debt.

The budget deficit

The budget deficit is a different matter. There have been few more politically contentious issues in recent years than what to do about the budget deficit. For while budget deficits are nothing new in the United States, in the 1980s and early 1990s it appeared to be spiralling out of control. And after a period of recovery under President Clinton, the first administration of President George W. Bush saw a return to budget deficits with a vengeance. The recession of 2008–9 and the Obama Recovery Plan then sent the budget deficit to unprecedented levels in peacetime.

The politics of the budget

The policies of the first Reagan administration (1981–5) turned the deficit into a major political issue which deeply divided the two main parties. Generally speaking, Republicans wanted to increase spending on defence, cut taxation and compensate for these measures by reducing expenditure on social welfare and other domestic programmes. Democrats, on the other hand, refused to cut those domestic programmes significantly and, since they controlled the House of Representatives, they could not be ignored. Ultimately, both Democrats and Republicans got much of what they wanted, but the result was that the budget deficit went into orbit.

Equally important was the fact that for economic conservatives, a balanced budget became an article of political faith. The perceived need to spend no more than the government received in revenue transcended economics and became almost a moral crusade for some. It was for them yet another symbol of the nation's abandonment of what were believed to be sound, traditional economic principles.

Congress did pass the Balanced Budget and Emergency Deficit Control Act of 1985 (the Gramm–Rudman–Hollings Act), which empowered the Comptroller General to make necessary cuts in budget legislation where the politicians could not come to an agreement. This, however, was declared unconstitutional by the Supreme Court.

Virtually every year since then has witnessed a major political battle over the budget between a president and Congress controlled by different parties. In some years, such as 1995, no budget at all was passed in time to prevent a shutdown of government offices due to a lack of funding. Meanwhile, Republicans and some conservative Democrats turned to an effort to pass a balanced budget amendment to the Constitution. This came within a whisker of being passed in March 1997, when the Senate voted 66–34 in favour – just one vote short of the required two-thirds majority. The House of Representatives had voted overwhelmingly for the amendment in the previous Congress and would certainly have done so again.

This failure, however, soon seemed to be of little significance. For, in August 1997, President Clinton signed budget bills that promised to eliminate the deficit altogether by 2002. Clinton heralded the legislation as a milestone for the nation and a symbol of America's ability to restore its economic strength:

It wasn't very long ago that some people looked at our nation and saw a setting sun . . . The sun is rising on America again. For too long, it seemed as if America would not be ready for the new century, that we would be too divided, too wedded to old arrangements and ideas . . . After years in which too many people doubted whether our nation would ever come together again . . . we set off on a new economic course.

Back in the red

The respite from deficit proved to be short-lived. In 2001, President George W. Bush returned to Reaganomics and pushed through a huge tax cut of $1.35 trillion, slanted towards wealthier Americans. Shortly afterwards, the terrorist attacks of 11 September caused a downturn in the economy, while the War on Terror required a much-increased defence budget. The result was alarming, if predictable: the budget was plunged back into the red and would remain so for years to come. While President Bush promised to reduce the deficit in his second term, he was equally determined to make the 2001 tax cuts permanent and to pursue the War on Terror with no less vigour than during his first administration. In the final year of his second term, the economy went into an alarming recession. In 2009, the new Obama administration concluded that only federal government spending could prevent the recession from becoming a depression. The result was almost to triple the budget deficit. Moreover, forecasters predicted that the deficit would remain at 'unsustainable' levels until at least 2020.

By the summer of 2011, the politics of the budget deficit once again brought the issue to crisis point. The federal government had reached its borrowing limit, as it has more than 70 times since the 1960s. However, only the Congress has the authority to raise the borrowing limit and this time the Republican-controlled House of Representatives tried to exploit the situation. The Republicans refused to raise the limit unless President Obama drastically cut back on government spending. With the president willing to compromise on spending cuts but also demanding tax increases, the Republicans threatened to allow a federal government shutdown rather than support tax increases.

Economic growth

The US economy endured a sustained crisis from 1973 until the early 1990s, then recovered – only to slip backwards again in the first decade of the twenty-first century. Nevertheless, despite the relative decline noted above and the impact of the recession of 2007–9, the United States remains by some distance the largest single economy in the world. Economic growth in the United States now compares favourably with its competitor developed nations, such as Japan and the countries of the European Union, but unfavourably with rising economic powers such as the BRIC countries – Brazil, Russia, India and, above all, China. Many predict that China will overtake the United States as the world's largest economy within a few decades. Many Americans feel uncertain about their economic prospects. They are seriously worried that their children will be worse off than themselves and that the American Dream is over. Above all, there is little faith in the ability of either government or big business to ensure growing prosperity for all.

Chapter summary

From the early 1970s to the early 1990s, the United States was in relative economic decline. Other nations in Europe and Asia rivalled or even surpassed the performance of the American economy. Consequently, the country engaged in a heated debate about what had gone wrong with its economy and how it could be restored to its former glory. Inevitably, this debate has taken centre-stage in American politics, as Americans have argued over taxes, welfare, defence expenditures and the very role of government itself in promoting economic strength. Although the economy had recaptured some of its old vigour by the early twenty-first century, the United States has not and cannot recapture the level of its former predominance. While it is still the most powerful single nation, many Americans are learning to live with lower expectations than previous generations. Moreover, in an era of relatively scarce government resources, the political fight over the distribution of those resources will continue to be fierce.

References

Thompson, G. (1994) 'From the long boom to recession and stagnation? The post-war American economy', in Thompson, G. (ed.) *The United States in the Twentieth Century: Markets* (London: Hodder & Stoughton).

Thurow, L. (1994) *Head to Head: The Coming Economic Battle Among Japan, Europe and America* (London: Nicholas Brealey).

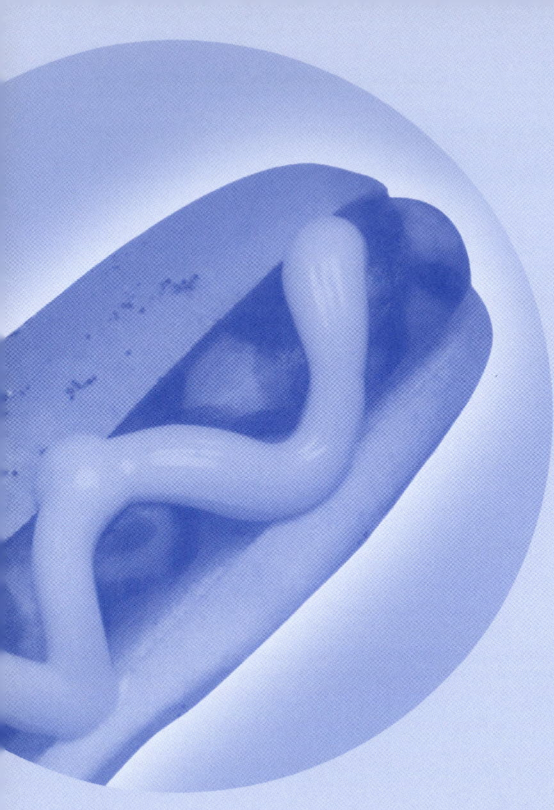

Chapter 6

Gender and American politics

The struggle to achieve equality of the sexes goes back a long way in American history. Yet still today the political system reverberates with impassioned debate over what such equality demands of public policy. In this chapter we shall see that, despite great progress in the achievement of formal political and legal equality, women remain disadvantaged in important respects compared with men. We shall examine different views on why these inequalities persist and how they have dramatically expanded the political agenda in the contemporary United States.

Sex, gender and politics

What exactly do people mean when they talk about 'gender politics'? The key to understanding this issue is to appreciate the distinction between sex and gender. Sex is a biological given: men and women are physically different by nature. Gender, by contrast, refers not to these biological differences, but to the social construction of roles based upon them (Barnard, 1971, p. 16).

Thus, while no one disputes the fact that men are generally physically stronger than women, there are wide disagreements over the political and social consequences of that biological fact. Does it mean, for example, that men and women should be employed in different jobs and, furthermore, that 'men's jobs' should be better paid than 'women's jobs'?

While that particular aspect of gender politics is now less contentious than it once was, there remains a fundamental disagreement over the political, economic and social implications of the reproductive differences between men and women. For example, does the fact that women bear children mean that they should also assume primary responsibility for raising them? Moreover, if it is accepted that women should perform that role, does it further justify the segregation of women and men into 'separate spheres': men assuming responsibility for the public sphere of economics and politics, while women take responsibility for the private sphere of the home and especially the kitchen and the children?

The link between sex and gender, then, is the question of whether physical differences between men and women are accompanied by attitudinal and behavioural differences which are also determined by nature. Thus, it has traditionally been argued that men are, by nature, more aggressive and rational than women: characteristics that make them better suited to the world of work and politics. On the other hand, traditionalists say that women are less selfish and more nurturing than men and that these traits determine that they should be preoccupied with supporting and caring for other members of their household.

Patriarchy and feminism

Traditionalists believe that such differences as just described are natural and therefore unchangeable. Their opponents – often labelled feminists – argue that they are neither natural nor unchangeable. Rather, these attitudes and roles are ascribed to men and women by a culture which systematically privileges men to the disadvantage of women. This is the cultural system known as patriarchy.

Patriarchy, say feminists, is based on the belief that men are superior to women. It permeates all facets of society and always with the same result: the roles played by men are deemed superior to and more important than those played by women. This is reflected in the fact that men are generally better paid than women and in the fact that 'men's characteristics' are accorded a higher status than 'women's characteristics'. Thus, patriarchal society has traditionally assumed a distinction between, say, 'male rationality' and 'female intuition' and placed a higher value on the former. Feminists believe that this assumption is simply false and that it can and should be changed.

Unsurprisingly, these debates have given rise to a raft of questions about the appropriate public policies to deal with them. Throughout American history, both traditionalists and feminists have fought for policies which reflect and support their view of gender. Because feminists have challenged the established social order, they have taken the political initiative. The history of American gender politics, therefore, can be profitably viewed through the successes and failures of the so-called women's movement.

The women's movement, 1789–1920

Women's rights in the early republic

For much of American history, the women's movement concentrated on the struggle to achieve formal legal and political equality with men. Although there was some discussion over the nature and extent of 'real differences' between men and women, the focus was upon whether men and women should have the same formal rights, regardless of any such differences. This is quite understandable, given the gross formal inequalities that existed well into the twentieth century.

The law discriminated against women in many ways. Upon marriage, for example, all a woman's possessions became her husband's property. If the marriage ended in divorce, the husband retained this property and custody of any children. This was true, even where the husband was responsible for the breakdown of the marriage. Thus, as Barbara Deckard wrote, 'Married women did not exist as legal entities apart from their husbands' (Deckard, 1983, p. 259).

The notion of separate spheres determined that women should not generally seek employment outside the home, and hence they were excluded from educational opportunities and entrance to many professions and occupations.

Most important of all, women were denied the right to vote. When the new Constitution came into force in 1789, it allowed the individual states to determine for themselves the extent of the franchise. However, with the exception of New Jersey, no state deemed it appropriate for women to vote. In New Jersey, female suffrage had been granted in 1776 and thus New Jersey women became the first in western history to be placed on an equal voting basis with men. However, in 1807, New Jersey fell into line with the rest of the United States and deprived women of the franchise.

Box 6.1

Marriage and patriarchal power

In 1855 Lucy Stone married her fellow abolitionist activist, Henry Blackwell. Both were feminists and objected to the marriage laws as they affected women's rights. Upon their marriage, therefore, they jointly published the following statement:

PROTEST

While acknowledging our mutual affection by publicly assuming the relationship of husband and wife, yet in justice to ourselves and a great principle, we deem it a duty to declare that this act on our part implies no sanction of, nor promise of voluntary obedience to such of the present laws of marriage, as refuse to recognise the wife as an independent, rational being, while they confer upon the husband an injurious and unnatural superiority, investing him with legal powers that no honourable man would exercise, and which no man should possess. We protest especially against the laws which give to the husband:

1. The custody of the wife's person.
2. The exclusive control and guardianship of their children.
3. The sole ownership of her personal property, and use of her real estate, unless previously settled upon her, or placed in the hands of trustees, as in the case of minors, lunatics, and idiots.
4. The absolute right to the product of her industry.
5. Also against laws which give to the widower so much larger and more permanent an interest in the property of his deceased wife, than they give to the widow in that of the deceased husband.
6. Finally, against the whole system by which 'the legal existence of the wife is suspended during marriage', so that in most States, she neither has a legal part in the choice of her residence, nor can she make a will, nor sue or be sued in her own name, nor inherit property.

We believe that personal independence and equal human rights can never be forfeited, except for crime; that marriage should be an equal and permanent partnership, and so recognised by law; that until it is so recognised, married partners should provide against the radical injustice of the present laws, by every means in their power.

We believe that where domestic difficulties arise, no appeal should be made to legal tribunals under existing laws, but that all difficulties should be submitted to the equitable adjustment of arbitrators mutually chosen.

Thus reverencing law, we enter our protest against rules and customs which are unworthy of the name, since they violate justice, the essence of law.

Feminist activism

While there is plenty of evidence to suggest that women did not happily acquiesce in this discrimination, it was some years before a determined political campaign was launched to challenge it. As was often to prove the case, feminist political activism was inspired by women's involvement in other reformist movements. The first such movement was that to emancipate America's slaves, a campaign that had achieved great political significance by the mid-nineteenth century.

Women played a major role in the abolitionist movement. There were up to 100 women's anti-slavery societies in the 1830s and women provided over half the signatures on anti-slavery petitions to Congress (O'Neill, 1969, p. 20). Moreover, some of those who were to become leaders of the movement for women's rights were very active abolitionists – women such as Lucy Stone, Elizabeth Cady Stanton, Angelina and Sarah Grimké, Lucretia Mott and Susan B. Anthony.

The Seneca Falls Convention

Despite the fact that many male abolitionists sympathised with the cause of women's rights, there was a tension between the two movements. The anti-slavery campaign was highly controversial and most male activists did not wish to attract further hostility by being associated with the even more radical cause of women's rights. As a result, feminist abolitionists were advised to keep quiet about women's rights and were even denied platform seats at some anti-slavery meetings.

Women responded by deciding to hold their own convention, dedicated solely to the cause of gender equality. In 1848, they organised the Women's Rights Convention, at Seneca Falls, New York. The convention resulted in the first manifesto for women's rights in the United States, the Seneca Falls Declaration.

The declaration made five demands in particular:

First, equal educational opportunities
Second, entry into the professions
Third, equal property rights
Fourth, an end to double standards of morality
Fifth, the vote

Banner, 1974, p. 4

These demands were cleverly justified by appropriating Jefferson's Declaration of Independence for the purposes of women's rights. Thus, the Seneca Falls Declaration began, 'We hold these truths to be self-evident: that all men and women are created equal . . .' It further paraphrased Jefferson when it substituted his protest at King George III's goal of tyranny over Americans with that of men over women: 'The history of mankind is a history of repeated injuries and usurpations on the part of man toward woman, having in direct object the establishment of an absolute tyranny over her' (O'Neill, 1969, pp. 108–11).

Women's suffrage

The fact that women could so easily justify their cause in terms of American political philosophy did not mean that government would act swiftly upon the Seneca Falls agenda. It would, in fact, be over 70 years before the most important demand – the vote – was achieved.

The principal obstacle for women was patriarchy, an even more deeply rooted ideology than Jefferson's vision of equal rights. Indeed, many women activists themselves were not wholly convinced that 'women's nature' was compatible with the vote. This was indicated by the fact that, of all the demands made at Seneca Falls, only the franchise was disputed by the delegates and failed to pass unanimously.

As a result, the campaign for the vote was often couched paradoxically in terms of fundamental differences in men's and women's natures and even the notion of separate spheres. In effect, many women claimed that their special capacity for nurturing, moral education and decency made it imperative that they should be able to influence public policy through the ballot box.

Nevertheless, this argument worked against women rather than for them throughout the

Box 6.2

The law and gender relations

The following is an extract from Justice Bradley's concurring opinion in the *Bradwell* v. *Illinois* (1873) case.

'. . . the civil law, as well as nature herself, has always recognised a wide difference in the respective spheres and destinies of man and woman. Man is, or should be, woman's protector and defender. The natural and proper timidity and delicacy which belongs to the female sex evidently unfits it for many of the occupations of civil life. The constitution of the family organization, which is founded in the divine ordinance, as well as in the nature of things, indicates the domestic sphere as that which properly belongs to the domain and functions of womanhood. The harmony, not to say identity, of interests and views which belong or should belong to the family institution, is repugnant to the idea of a woman adopting a distinct and independent career from that of her husband. . . .

It is true that many women are unmarried and not affected by any of the duties, complications, and incapacities arising out of the marital state, but these are exceptions to the general rule. The paramount destiny and mission of woman are to fulfill the noble and benign offices of wife and mother. This is the law of the Creator.'

nineteenth century, on both the suffrage question and others. For example, in 1873, in the case of *Bradwell* v. *Illinois*, the Supreme Court upheld the right of the state to exclude Myra Bradwell from the legal profession simply because of her sex. While the Court's opinion turned on a technical issue, Justice Joseph Bradley wrote a concurring opinion which was based on very crude patriarchal thought.

Just two years later, in *Minor* v. *Happersett*, the Court applied similar logic in denying that women had a constitutional right to vote under the Fourteenth Amendment.

Having failed to obtain a constitutional ruling in their favour, women turned to a state-by-state campaign for the franchise. This produced meagre results, however. By 1910, only four states had responded positively – Colorado, Utah, Wyoming and Idaho. Part of the problem was that suffragist organisations found their efforts countered by other groups which adhered to the view that it was 'unnatural' for women to vote. Thus the National American Woman's Suffrage Association was opposed by the National Association Opposed to the Further Extension of Suffrage to Women. This group believed that the entry of women into the public sphere of politics would lead to the break-up of the home and undermine family values.

However, a variety of factors soon combined to secure the vote for women. First, the early twentieth century in the United States saw a widespread movement for reform, known as Progressivism. Women active in a variety of Progressive causes drew upon the opportunities provided by the reformist ferment to advance the suffragist cause.

Secondly, the entry of the United States into the First World War in 1917 entailed many women replacing men in the workforce. This experience not only enhanced women's own ambitions, but also helped to convince some doubters that women were the equals of men.

Thirdly, women exploited growing nativist fears in the country. The late nineteenth and early twentieth centuries saw a dramatic increase in the number of immigrants from southern and eastern Europe – Italy, Russia and the lands of the Austro-Hungarian Empire. Anglo-Saxon Americans feared that this influx threatened their cultural and political dominance and sought to introduce strict new immigration laws. Suffragists argued that the enfranchisement of American women would help to counter what was seen as the harmful political and cultural effects of the new immigration.

In 1919, Congress passed the Nineteenth Amendment and the following year it was ratified by the states. It read: 'The right of citizens of the United States to vote shall not be denied or abridged by the United States or by any State on account of sex.'

Women had won their greatest political battle: yet it had been achieved with considerable help from an essentially patriarchal ideology. Although women and men were now politically equal, the notion of separate spheres still pervaded most facets of American culture and society. As a result, for all its potential for transforming the status of American women, the franchise in fact changed relatively little. Socially and economically, women were still greatly disadvantaged compared with men.

Gender politics today

The period from 1920 to 1960 promised much but achieved little of substance in the cause of gender equality. Having won the right to vote on the basis of the distinctive contribution women could make to politics, women behaved politically more or less like men.

Moreover, in the 1920s, many women, like men, lost interest in reformist politics. This decade was followed by the Great Depression of the 1930s, a period in which the sheer struggle for survival took political precedence over all.

The Equal Rights Amendment

There were some important feminist initiatives in the inter-war years, however – none more so than the introduction into Congress of the Equal Rights Amendment (ERA) to the Constitution in 1923. In its original form it read: 'Men and women shall have equal rights throughout the United States and every place subject to its jurisdiction.'

The ERA was the work of the radical Woman's Party, founded by Alice Paul in 1916. Although it would be subject to judicial interpretation, it appeared to call for an end to all legal distinctions on the basis of sex. For this very reason, however, it was opposed not only by traditionalists, but also by other women activists who wanted to preserve so-called 'protective legislation' for women.

Chief among these opponents were women's trade unions. They argued that, whatever the desirability of the ERA in theory, the practical reality for most women in the workplace was that they were more vulnerable to exploitation by employers than were men. Without current legislation that fixed maximum hours and other conditions of work for women, though not men, the economic position of women workers would deteriorate.

The debate over the ERA illustrates one of the most difficult dilemmas for contemporary feminism. Should the movement seek absolute formal legal equality of the sexes, in which no legal distinctions are permitted, or should it acknowledge the real disadvantages women suffer and campaign for laws which discriminate *in their favour*? As we shall see later, any answer to this question must in part depend on the extent and origins of the socio-economic inequalities which have persisted until today.

The contemporary women's movement

The period 1920–60 saw few substantial gains in the cause of gender equality. Indeed, there is some evidence to suggest that the cause suffered some reverses. For example, in 1920 male college students outnumbered females two to one, but by 1958 it was three to one; and in 1940 women held 45 per cent of jobs classed as professional but in 1967 only 37 per cent (Banner, 1974, p. 226).

Some progress had been made towards better pay for women, but women still lagged far behind men, even within the same professional categories. Thus, among professional workers, women's earnings were 61 per cent of men's earnings in 1939 and just 64 per cent in 1960. Among clerical workers,

Table 6.1 Women's wages as a percentage of men's

Category	1939	1960
Professional	60.8	64.0
Managerial	54.0	57.6
Clerical	68.5	68.3
Sales	51.3	42.2
Service	59.6	59.1

Source: Gatlin, R., *American Women since 1945*, 1987, Palgrave Macmillan, reproduced with permission of Palgrave Macmillan

women earned 68.5 per cent of men's wages in 1939 and 68.3 per cent in 1960.

Why had so little progress been made since the 1920s? This is puzzling, especially when we remember that, during the Second World War, women entered the workforce in huge numbers in order to compensate for the mass mobilisation of men into the armed forces. Moreover, while many of these women were obliged to give up their jobs at the end of the war, a large number soon returned to the workforce. The reason was simple: the American economy was producing a vast array of consumer goods, but most families required more than one wage to afford them.

Thus, by 1960, some 38 per cent of women aged 16 and over were employed outside the home. This compared with a figure of 25 per cent in 1940. Moreover, the profile of women in the workforce was also changing significantly. Before the

Figure 6.1 An unidentified woman is tending to 1,000-pound bomb cases at Nebraska Ordnance Plant in Omaha during the Second World War.
Source: © Press Association Images

war, the typical female worker was single and in her early twenties. After the war, she was married and more likely to be in her late forties (Gatlin, 1987, p. 25). In short, the long-standing tradition that women should work outside the home only until they married was disappearing.

The 'feminine mystique'

Despite this basic fact of life, the notion of separate spheres stubbornly persisted. While ideological change usually lags behind material change, it is also true that the post-war years witnessed an intense reaffirmation of patriarchy. Psychologists, sociologists, fashion designers and the media all placed renewed emphasis on traditional concepts of femininity, beauty and, above all, women's vocation as wife and mother. In 1963, Betty Friedan coined the term 'the feminine mystique' to describe what was, in effect, a neo-Victorian concept of women (Friedan, 1963).

Friedan vigorously challenged the idea that women should or could be satisfied by the model of domestic bliss conjured up by the feminine mystique. Rather, she argued, it alienated women in the most destructive fashion by denying the reality of their modern social and economic roles. Moreover, self-fulfilment for women lay not in some traditionalist fantasy of a woman's sphere, but in allowing them to share the male sphere of education, career and public life.

The 'new' feminism

By the early 1960s, economic changes in women's lives were clearly leading to new feminist perspectives on gender politics. Unlike previous feminist waves, the 'new' feminism of the 1960s demanded more than political, legal or even economic equality. It also urged a fundamental reassessment of gender relations that left virtually no aspect of American culture and practice untouched. As we shall see below, contemporary feminist thought is truly revolutionary in that it suggests that the whole of private and public life is gendered along patriarchal lines. Consequently, it is not merely the obvious forms of sex discrimination that have been challenged, but also 'apolitical' issues such as language, personal relations, sexuality and portrayals of women in the arts and media.

First, however, it is important to note how economic and philosophical change were translated in political action.

Feminist political organisation

As in previous eras, feminist political activism was boosted by a wider spirit of radical reform. The decade of the 1960s was one of the most turbulent in American history. The civil rights movement increasingly turned to direct, mass political action and the Black Power movement denounced American society as irredeemably racist. The anti-Vietnam War movement took to the streets in massive numbers and its more radical activists denounced American foreign policy as both racist and imperialist. Meanwhile, American youth was pioneering a new personal lifestyle that rejected the values of their parents: traditional dress codes were abandoned, a relaxed attitude to sex and drug use was prevalent and hippies advised young Americans to drop out of mainstream society and to experiment with alternative ways of living. In short, the cultural and political consensus that had long commanded respectful observance was torn apart.

Under these circumstances, it is hardly surprising that feminists should seek to add their own demands to the nation's political agenda. Moreover, just as feminists in the nineteenth-century abolitionist movement had been urged to adopt a low profile in order not to damage 'more important' causes, contemporary feminists found 1960s reformers and radicals unwilling to address their issues. As a result, feminists broke away to establish their own organisations, dedicated to action on an agenda of gender politics.

Two distinct strands have been identified in the contemporary women's movement, corresponding to what can be called the reformist (or liberal) and radical tendencies.

Reformist groups are those whose goals are, in essence, to obtain for women equal status and opportunities within the present system. Their methods are those used by other mainstream interest groups – lobbying legislatures, litigating in the courts, working in elections, building up membership and publicising issues through group literature and the media.

The leading reformist group is undoubtedly the National Organization for Women (NOW). It was founded in 1966 by women attending a convention of state commissions on the status of women. When the convention refused to accept a resolution which equated sexism with racism, its proponents quit the meeting and decided to establish NOW.

NOW was soon followed by the establishment of other groups, dedicated to furthering some aspect of what was being dubbed 'women's liberation'. The Women's Equity Action League (WEAL) was formed to campaign on economic and educational issues. The National Women's Political Caucus (NWPC) was created to bring more women into politics (Gatlin, 1987, pp. 117–18). These and other groups have achieved many notable successes. Their victories, according to some, have been due in no small part to the very fact that they have worked within the system, both in methods and in goals (Gelb and Palley, 1982, p. 7). Thus, they have been able to maximise support from non-feminist organisations through an appeal to familiar American values of egalitarianism and individual rights.

Radical feminists have attracted more hostility. Although far less organised than reformist groups, they have often been on the 'front line' of the contemporary women's movement. They have pioneered debate on certain issues and placed those issues on the political agenda, with the more moderate groups embracing them at a later stage. This was true, for example, of such issues as violence against women (especially rape), pornography and lesbian rights.

Whereas liberal feminists tend to de-emphasise the differences between men and women, radicals highlight them and incorporate them into their strategies and policies. Thus, they have been separatist, excluding men from their groups and activities, as well as advocating social and living arrangements excluding men (Gatlin, 1987, pp. 130–7). Above all, perhaps, radical feminists have been famous for their attack upon the traditional family, which they see as fundamentally patriarchal and a prime source of the oppression of women.

In short, radical feminists call for the overthrow of what they see as a thoroughly patriarchal society, while liberal feminists seek to improve current society by eliminating its patriarchal aspects. Despite these differences of policy, strategy and rhetoric, however, it is worth emphasising that the two strands of the contemporary women's movement have a great deal in common. Radical feminists support equal rights for women and liberal feminists support lesbian rights and campaigns against sexual harassment and violence against women. Indeed, it is precisely because women of varied ideological persuasions have identified a common agenda of previously ignored issues that feminism has become a powerful political force today.

The success of modern feminism

While contemporary feminism has its determined opponents, it has nevertheless achieved some notable successes since the 1960s. As measured by the acquisition of equal rights with men and the establishment of a political agenda that reflects feminist concerns, it can be argued that the women's movement has made a fundamental breakthrough. Exploiting the numerous points of access provided by the American political system, the movement has persuaded all the major institutions of the federal government to respond to its demands. As we now go on to examine some of those successes, however, it will be obvious that the victories are far from complete.

Equality in the workplace

By the late 1950s, it was becoming clear that the recent shift of women into the workplace in large numbers was a permanent phenomenon. As noted above, a booming economy based on mass consumerism required both more workers and more purchasers. Women formed a large pool of untapped labour and their wages provided additional consumer power.

Box 6.3

Landmarks in the campaign for equality of the sexes

1848 The Seneca Falls Declaration

The first manifesto of the women's movement, demanding, among other things, the right to vote.

1873 *Bradwell* v. *Illinois*

The Supreme Court denies that women have a constitutional right to enter the legal profession.

1875 *Minor* v. *Happersett*

The Supreme Court denies that women have a constitutional right to vote.

1920 The Nineteenth Amendment ratified

Women acquire the constitutional right to vote.

1963 Equal Pay Act

For the first time, the federal government requires women to be paid the same as men for doing the same job.

1964 Civil Rights Act

Title VII of the Act outlaws sex discrimination in employment.

1971 *Reed* v. *Reed*

For the first time, the Supreme Court rules that a state law favouring men over women violates the Equal Protection Clause of the Fourteenth Amendment.

1972 Education Amendments Act

Title IX of the Act prohibits most sex discrimination in education establishments and programmes receiving federal government finance.

1973 *Roe* v. *Wade*

The Supreme Court announces that a woman has a constitutional right to an abortion.

1974 Equal Credit Opportunity Act

Women acquire the same right to obtain credit as men.

1978 Pregnancy Discrimination Act

Congress reverses a Supreme Court decision and forbids discrimination against women employees on grounds of pregnancy-related absence from work.

Box 6.3 continued

1981 Supreme Court justice

Sandra Day O'Connor becomes the first female justice of the US Supreme Court.

1984 Presidential elections

Geraldine Ferraro, Democratic vice-presidential candidate, becomes the first woman to be nominated by a major party in a presidential election.

1986 *Meritor Savings Bank* v. *Vinson*

The Supreme Court rules that sexual harassment in the workplace is a form of discrimination forbidden by Title VII of the Civil Rights Act of 1964.

1987 *Johnson* v. *Transportation Agency*

For the first time, the Supreme Court upholds an affirmative action plan that discriminates in favour of women.

The federal government recognised these new economic facts of life and President Kennedy set up the Presidential Commission on the Status of Women. When it reported in 1963, the Commission recommended action to eliminate discrimination in the workplace and the first concrete result was the Equal Pay Act of 1963. Although limited in the occupations covered, it was nevertheless a landmark because it was the first attempt by the federal government to promote greater economic equality of the sexes. Furthermore, its coverage was extended in 1972 to cover executive, administrative and professional workers, and again in 1974 to cover federal, state and municipal employees (Mezey, 1992, p. 92).

The Equal Pay Act did end the most obvious form of discrimination against working women, but it has not equalised the earnings of men and women. Why women still lag so far behind men in income is a complex and disputed question.

The Equal Pay Act applied only to women doing virtually the same jobs as men. It did not therefore address the fact that many occupations are, to a considerable extent, segregated by sex. Moreover, those occupations dominated by men tend to be much better paid than those dominated by women. In short, women earn less than men in large part because 'women's work' is deemed less valuable than 'men's work'. Moreover, as Table 6.2 indicates, whatever the occupation, the median earnings of women lag significantly behind those of men.

It can also be seen from Table 6.3 that many occupations still reveal the impact of traditional gender roles. Thus, for example, women predominate heavily in nursing, elementary education, restaurant service and cleaning. Feminists believe that this pattern stems from patriarchal conditioning: society permits and encourages women to aim for these careers and discourages them from seeking employment as, say, engineers or car mechanics. Anti-feminists disagree, asserting that women choose these occupations because they involve the type of work that appeals to them. In other words, the debate turns yet again on the issue of whether men and women have fundamentally different natures, values and priorities.

Table 6.2 Women in contemporary America: the basic statistics

	Women %	Men %
Population, 2008	50.7	49.3
Electorate, 2008		
Voting-age population	52.0	48.0
Reporting registered	72.8	69.1
Reporting voted	65.7	61.5
Participation in workforce, 2003		
Never married	59.8	62.2
Married	59.2	74.2
Divorced	65.4	67.9
Median earnings, 2008	**% of women in occupation**	**Women's income as % of men's**
Chief executives	23.4	80.2
Lawyers	34.4	80.5
Accountants & auditors	61.1	77.1
Registered nurses	91.7	86.6
Secretaries & administrative assistants	96.1	83.4

Source: US Bureau of the Census, 2010; US Bureau of Labor, 2010

Table 6.3 Selected occupations by sex (percentage of women)

	1992	2003	2008
Education			
Elementary	85.4	81.7	81.2
Secondary	55.5	55.2	56.0
Engineers			
Civil	7.9	8.7	10.4
Electrical	8.4	7.1	7.7
Industrial	14.0	19.2	14.9
Mechanical	5.3	5.5	6.7
Managers			
Financial	46.3	52.7	54.8
Human resources	58.9	68.6	66.3
Purchasing	33.2	39.1	40.4
Marketing/sales	33.6	39.7	42.0
Health			
Dentists	8.5	23.7	27.2
Physicians/surgeons	20.4	29.9	30.5
Registered nurses	94.3	91.1	91.7
Pharmacists	37.8	51.5	51.8
Other professions			
Architects	15.3	22.1	24.8
Accountants/auditors	51.2	58.6	61.1
Computer scientists	33.5	30.4	27.5
Lawyers	21.4	27.6	34.4
Service			
Cleaners	94.8	88.4	89.8
Waiters/waitresses	79.6	74.3	73.2
Manual			
Car mechanics	0.8	1.3	1.6
Construction	1.9	2.8	3.1
Textile	76.4	74.9	79.2

Source: US Bureau of the Census, 1993; 2005; Bureau of Labor Statistics, 2010

One attempt to overcome the financial consequences of job segregation has been to advance the policy of 'comparable worth'. This is based on the premise that different jobs can be objectively rated according to the skills and responsibility they involve. Once measured, its proponents argue, jobs making comparable demands should be paid the same. In this way, it might be possible to argue that a nurse, say, is required to have qualities comparable to those of a skilled industrial worker and should therefore receive the same pay.

Opponents dismiss the comparable worth approach on a number of grounds: but most importantly, they argue that employee pay is in essence a market decision, based on the supply of and demand for the particular skills involved. Moreover, the 1985 Civil Rights Commission on unequal pay denied that it was the result of discrimination and instead pointed to three main characteristics of working women: lower job expectations, educational and job choices which accommodate child-rearing and interrupted participation in the workforce.

Feminists counter that these findings are not supported by statistical evidence measuring the relation between occupation and parental or marital status. So far, however, they have been unable to persuade either courts or legislatures that segregation and unequal pay result from discrimination (Mezey, 1992, p. 98). There is little sign, therefore, that government will endorse comparable worth in the near future.

It should be noted that one thing that women in America do not lack is voting power. As Table 6.2 shows, women not only outnumber men in the voting-age population, they actually register and vote at higher rates than men.

Reproductive issues

The basic biological fact that women, not men, bear children looms large in gender politics. As we have seen, traditionalists believe that this makes women's nature, values and social roles different from those of men. Even leaving aside that debate, however, there are important political questions concerning the extent to which public policy should accommodate reproductive facts.

First, there is the controversial matter of the reproductive autonomy of women. To what extent should women be allowed to determine for themselves whether to bear children and, if so, how many and when?

Contraception

Great advances in contraceptive science in the second half of the twentieth century have dramatically improved women's reproductive autonomy. By the 1960s, most states had repealed their restrictive nineteenth-century laws banning artificial contraceptives, and in 1965, when the state of Connecticut persisted in restricting the availability of contraceptives, the Supreme Court declared its law unconstitutional in the case of *Griswold* v. *Connecticut*.

Abortion

However, as we shall see in Chapter 19, the issue of abortion rights has proved far more controversial. Feminists regard easily available abortion as a precondition not merely of reproductive autonomy but also of many other aspects of gender equality. For if women do not have ultimate control over their childbearing, how can they compete with men in the workplace? Quite simply, a woman's educational or career goals may be delayed or sabotaged altogether by unwanted pregnancies.

Those opposed to abortion generally place what they see as the rights of the foetus above those of the mother. Suffice it to say at this point that, while it has been unable to ban abortions altogether, the anti-abortion movement has succeeded in making public policy hostile to abortion in important respects. Thus, for example, with few exceptions, the federal government does not permit public health funds to pay for abortions for poor women, even though it does pay for all other medical treatments, including childbirth costs. Furthermore, many states do not permit public hospitals or their staff to perform abortions.

Pregnancy disability

A further major reproductive issue in contemporary American politics is that of the rights of pregnant employees. Until the 1970s, it was assumed that pregnancy was a private matter and that neither employers nor government had any responsibility for its impact upon women workers. As a result, women employees who became pregnant were not entitled to either paid or unpaid sick leave, could be dismissed merely for being pregnant, had no rights to return to their job following birth and, when they did return, found that they had lost benefits such as seniority rights. Underlying these practices were further assumptions that pregnant women and mothers of young children could not, and probably should not, be in the workforce. However, the increasing participation of women of childbearing age in the workforce invited a change of policy.

The first major attempt came in 1972, when the Equal Employment Opportunity Commission (EEOC) issued guidelines with three main stipulations. First, employers should not refuse to hire women because they are or might become pregnant. Secondly, employers should treat pregnancy disability the same as other temporary health reasons for absence. Thirdly, employers should not single out pregnancy-related absences as a cause for dismissal (Mezey, 1992, p. 113).

However, the Supreme Court took a less sympathetic position on pregnancy disability. Two decisions were particularly worthy of note, *Gedulig* v. *Aiello* (1974) and *GEC* v. *Gilbert* (1976). In these cases, the Court determined that the exclusion of pregnancy disability from insurance programmes protecting employees against other temporary disabilities did not constitute sex discrimination. The Court's reasoning was somewhat bizarre, in that it said such programmes did not distinguish between women and men, but rather between 'pregnant women and non-pregnant persons'. In effect, the Court held that pregnancy-based discrimination was not sex-based discrimination (McKeever, 1995, p. 201).

These decisions prompted a coalition of more than 50 women's and other interest groups to launch the Campaign to End Discrimination Against Pregnant Workers. It achieved its main goal in 1978 when Congress passed the Pregnancy Discrimination (or Disability) Act. This explicitly included distinctions based on pregnancy within the meaning of sex discrimination in Title VII of the Civil Rights Act of 1964.

Many feminists do not believe, however, that it is sufficient to treat pregnancy disability as any other temporary disability. Rather, they argue that pregnancy has such a disadvantageous effect on women's careers that it requires *preferential treatment* compared with other disabilities. This is just one facet of a wider feminist view that a focus on equal treatment with men ignores the real disadvantages that women face even when formal equality is required. Thus both the short-term and long-term consequences of bearing children are far more significant than those resulting from other, truly temporary disabilities.

In the 1990s, legislative efforts on behalf of pregnancy rights focused upon the Family and Medical Leave Act, eventually passed in 1993. In its various forms, this bill sought to mandate employers to give unpaid leave to pregnant women and unpaid parental leave for men and women to care for their sick children. Although it first passed Congress in 1990, President George Bush vetoed the bill on the grounds that such leave, while desirable, should be a voluntary decision for employers.

The underlying reason for the president's veto was the fear of the business community that it would prove too costly in financial terms. According to government estimates, the Act would cost employers about $200 million a year. However, a change of administration in 1992 saw the last political barrier removed and President Clinton signed the bill into law in 1993.

Sexual harassment

Yet another issue to appear on the nation's political agenda because of feminist campaigning is that of sexual harassment in the workplace. The definition of sexual harassment can include a range of behaviour, from unwanted physical advances to sexual comments. Typically, sexual harassment is practised by a senior employee upon a junior. Sometimes such harassment is accompanied by offers to advance the victim's career or threats to wreck it. Even in the absence of such inducements, sexual harassment can create a hostile working atmosphere that causes much personal distress and serious damage to an employee's efficiency.

Like many issues in the new 'sexual politics', sexual harassment is an age-old practice, yet until the 1970s it drew little public or political attention. Many people believed that it was a more or less natural and inevitable aspect of human behaviour and therefore to be tolerated. Those who were its victims tended to keep quiet about it, or change job, fearing the embarrassment that would follow a public complaint. In essence, men had defined the workplace culture for so long that neither women nor the law challenged sexual harassment. As one writer observed, 'What men often experience as fun or flirtation, women often experience as degrading and demanding. And it is male experience that has shaped the law's traditional responses to sexual harassment' (Rhode, 1989, p. 233).

It was the combination of the increasing number of women in the workforce, their rising ambition and confidence and the perspectives offered by the new wave of feminism that identified sexual harassment as a major problem.

In 1976, the feminist magazine *Redbook* published a study of 9,000 working women: some nine out of ten reported being the object of sexual harassment of one kind or another (Gatlin, 1987, p. 229). Other studies followed and, while the incidence of reported harassment varied, the

Box 6.4

Equal Employment Opportunity Commission guidelines on sexual harassment, 1980

'Unwelcome sexual advances, requests for sexual favours, and other verbal or physical conduct of a sexual nature constitute sexual harassment when (1) submission to such conduct is made either explicitly or implicitly a term or condition of an individual's employment, (2) submission to or rejection of such conduct by an individual is used as a basis for employment decisions affecting such individual, or (3) such conduct has the purpose or effect of unreasonably interfering with an individual's work performance or creating an intimidating, hostile, or offensive working environment.'

evidence pointed unmistakably to the fact that it was a widespread phenomenon. Thus, in the 1980s, the United States Merit Protection Board found that 42 per cent of women had been harassed in their present job; it further estimated that 85 per cent of women could expect sexual harassment at some point in their working lives. Of course, men are also sometimes the victim of sexual harassment, but far less so than women (Rhode, 1989, p. 232).

Although there was no law against sexual harassment itself, political efforts focused on the attempt to persuade courts that it came within the definition of sex discrimination contained in Title VII of the Civil Rights Act of 1964. Early cases were unsuccessful, but the federal government took a decisive step in 1980 when the Equal Employment Opportunity Commission issued new guidelines on the subject. The EEOC declared that sexual harassment was sex discrimination whether it was tied to other offers or threats or simply created a hostile working environment.

Even more important was the 1986 decision of the Supreme Court in *Meritor Savings Bank* v. *Vinson*. Despite the fact that the justices were frequently in disagreement on gender issues, here the Court was unanimous in declaring that sexual harassment was a form of sex discrimination within the meaning of Title VII. Then, in 1993, in *Harris* v. *Forklift Systems, Inc.*, the Court made it easier to sue for damages in alleged cases of sexual harassment. Whereas a lower court had ruled that a person could only sue employers for sexual harassment when she had suffered severe psychological damage, the Supreme Court unanimously decided that a victim need only show that a 'reasonable person' would have found the workplace environment a hostile one.

Together, these Supreme Court decisions constitute a major legal victory. Moreover, they have spurred many employers to adopt sexual harassment policies and complaint procedures. Thus, a practice which had been the accepted norm less than 20 years earlier has been stigmatised and outlawed by the political efforts of the contemporary feminist movement.

Equality in politics

Despite enfranchisement by the Nineteenth Amendment in 1920, the number of women holding high political office was almost negligible for much of the twentieth century. This is particularly true at the federal level. Thus, there has never been a woman president or vice-president, nor even a female major party presidential nominee. Two women have been vice-presidential nominees: Geraldine Ferraro, for the Democratic party in 1984, and Sarah Palin, for the Republican party in 2008 (see Box 6.5).

Box 6.5

Influential Women in American Politics 1: Sarah Palin

Sarah Palin, the former governor of the State of Alaska, was a surprise choice as running-mate to John McCain, the Republican candidate for the presidency in 2008. A polarising figure, Palin has since emerged as a leading spokesperson for the American right. Here she is seen addressing the Tea Party, a grass roots conservative movement, in February 2010.

Source: © AP photo/Ed Reinke

Box 6.6

Influential Women in American Politics 2: Hillary Clinton

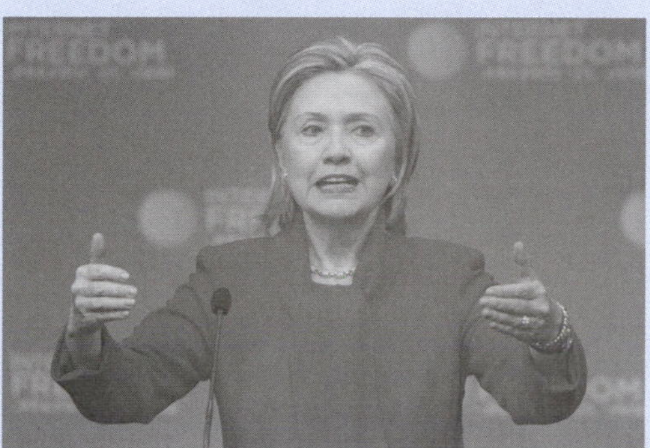

Hillary Rodham Clinton became secretary of state in January 2009. Prior to that, she had been a senator from the state of New York and First Lady to President Bill Clinton. She ran for the Democratic presidential nomination in 2008, but despite starting the campaign as the strong favourite, she was defeated by Barack Obama. Here she addresses a conference on global internet freedom in Washington, DC, in 2010.

Source: © Reuters/Molly Riley

Considering that Congress has 435 House seats and 100 Senate seats, the record there has been equally disappointing until quite recently. Before the 1992 elections, the Senate had never had more than two women members at the same time and the House had never had more than 30.

As for the Supreme Court, the first woman justice was not appointed until 1981, when Sandra Day O'Connor took her seat. It was not until 1993 that the second was appointed, Ruth Bader Ginsburg.

Nevertheless, the recent wave of feminism has at least given rise to greater expectations of increased numbers of women holding high political office. This became clear when journalists, looking ahead to the forthcoming electoral cycle, dubbed 1992 'The Year of the Women'. This was not the first time that a breakthrough by women candidates had been anticipated. For example, in 1990 eight women

Figure 6.2 In 1984 Geraldine Ferraro becomes the first woman to be nominated by a major party as its candidate for the vice-presidency.
Source: © Bettmann/Corbis

had contested Senate seats, but only one – Nancy Kassebaum (R – Kansas) – was elected and she was an incumbent.

However, 1992 did produce evidence of a marked shift in favour of women candidates. Of 106 women candidates for the House, 47 were successful; and 5 of the 11 women candidates for the Senate were elected. In one election cycle, then, the number of women representatives rose from 28 to 47. With the victory of Kay Bailey Hutchison in the Texas seat vacated by new treasury secretary Lloyd Bentsen, the number of women senators rose to 7, compared with 2 in 1990.

This progress continued, and by 2010 there were a record 96 women in the House of Representatives and 17 in the Senate. Moreover, at the state level, there were in 2010 some 1,788 women state legislators – that is, some 24.2 per cent of all state legislators.

It would seem, therefore, that the American electorate is becoming increasingly comfortable with the idea of voting for women candidates. However, given that women constitute over 50 per cent of the American population, there is still a considerable underrepresentation of women within the country's political elite.

Anti-feminism

Although the women's movement has not achieved all its aims, it has undeniably made significant progress. Even where concrete results have been disappointing, there have been important changes in public attitudes. For example, although there are still relatively few women holding high electoral office, it is no longer regarded as unnatural or undesirable that women should aspire to such positions.

Almost inevitably, the changes brought about by modern feminism have provoked opposition and resistance. Some criticism of feminism is simply reactionary in its desire to resist any change to the privileges afforded by the status quo. Others, however, while originally sympathetic to feminist goals, contend that the movement has either failed to produce the desired results or been so successful that it is no longer relevant to contemporary society. This latter group is sometimes labelled post-feminist. Inasmuch as it opposes the values and policies espoused by the contemporary women's movement, however, post-feminism may be regarded as one facet of a broader anti-feminist backlash (Faludi, 1992).

Anti-feminism is nothing new. Every historical phase of feminism has provoked a reaction from those, both men and women, who have viewed the new ideas as inimical to society. Its contemporary political strength is most obviously manifested in the movement known as the New Right. This first came to prominence in the 1970s and advocated a mixture of conservative values in economics, foreign policy and social issues.

With regard to social issues, the New Right, and especially the evangelical New Christian Right, celebrates what it sees as traditional family values. The New Right believes the traditional nuclear family to be the most important pillar of a moral and successful society. It explicitly endorses the notion of separate spheres, in the belief that men and women are biologically destined to play different, but complementary roles in society. Thus man should be the breadwinner, working outside the home to provide for the material needs of his family. Woman, by contrast, is best suited to the role of wife and mother, catering especially to the moral, spiritual and emotional needs of her family.

George Gilder is a leading exponent of such traditional views. In the early 1980s, he argued that 'separate spheres' were the natural and desirable consequence of biological differences. Moreover, any attempt to merge or abolish the two spheres entailed serious damage to both the economic and social fabric of the United States. Men are naturally more aggressive than women, says Gilder, and more suited to leadership roles: 'Because of the long evolutionary experience of the race in hunting societies, the provider role accords with the deepest instincts of men' (Gilder, 1981, p. 136). Feminism undermines this natural domination of women by men, leaving men without a socially productive focus for their aggressions. The result is social, familial and economic disruption.

The Equal Rights Amendment

The power of anti-feminism was demonstrated in the battle for ratification of the Equal Rights Amendment (ERA) to the Constitution. The ERA had first been introduced into Congress in 1923. It was not until the contemporary wave of feminism arrived, however, that it looked set for success.

The modern version of the amendment reads: 'Equality of Rights under the law shall not be denied or abridged by the United States or by any State on account of sex.' The House of Representatives passed it in 1971 by a vote of 354–23. The following year, the Senate voted 84–8 in favour. It only remained for three-quarters of the state legislatures to pass it and women would have a constitutional right to equal treatment with men. This appeared little more than a formality, as by early 1973, 30 states had already voted for ratification.

From this highly unpromising situation, anti-feminists organised a successful rearguard action. Their campaign against ratification of the ERA demonstrated both the disquiet about gender equality that a significant minority of Americans still felt and the difficulties involved in trying to amend the Constitution. The anti-feminist coalition was led by Phyllis Schlafly and her organisation, STOP-ERA.

Her strategy was to represent the ERA as a radical measure that went well beyond what most Americans would find acceptable. Thus, among the most frequent allegations were that the ERA would make unisex toilets compulsory; would force women to be drafted into combat roles in the armed services; and would force states to recognise homosexual marriages.

STOP-ERA was instrumental in persuading a sufficient number of states to reject ratification, thereby blocking the ERA. Requiring the approval of 38 states by 1982 for passage, the amendment got stuck on 35. According to many commentators, the failure of the ERA suggested that, lurking beneath the surface of the widespread acceptance of gender equality, lies a deep anxiety about any truly fundamental shift in gender roles. Thus, as one wrote:

> **The campaign against the ERA succeeded because it shifted debate away from equal rights and focused it on the possibility that the ERA might bring substantive changes in women's roles and behaviour. In this era, the American public, though changing its outlook, still objected to any major changes in traditional roles of men and women.**
>
> Mansbridge, 1986, p. 20

As the failure of the ERA suggests, the momentum behind contemporary feminism has slowed considerably since the 1970s. Partly this is because the early gains, involving decisive changes in the law, seem spectacular compared with the more piecemeal translation of those abstract rights into everyday reality. It is also due, however, to rising doubts about their movement from some erstwhile feminists. As Susan Faludi noted, 'By the mid-1980s, the voices of feminist recantation became a din' (Faludi, 1992, p. 352). No less a modern feminist pioneer than Betty Friedan alleged that the movement had been misguided in its attempts to achieve equality without regard to biological differences (Friedan, 1981).

What explains this anti-feminist and post-feminist backlash is not possible to say with certainty. A combination of factors may be responsible: the greater social conservatism generally since the late 1970s; a measure of disillusionment within the feminist movement, as anticipated gains have not been fully achieved; continuing resistance from a political and social culture imbued with patriarchy; and a generational shift, involving young women less politically attuned than their mothers.

Nevertheless, none of this should be taken as signalling the end of gender politics as a major political, social and cultural issue. In the first place, there are now enough women in most occupations to ensure that continuing areas of inequality do not go unchallenged. Moreover, women's organisations are now deeply entrenched within the political process and are therefore well placed to defend the gains that have been made and to press for others. The 'gender revolution' is by no means complete, but the women's movement may increasingly be seen as part of the political status quo.

Chapter summary

The campaign for gender equality has deep roots in American history and its progress has at times been painfully slow. The main reason for this has been the fundamentally patriarchal nature of American society, which conditioned both men and women to think of themselves as so different as to justify widely disparate treatment by law. The contemporary women's movement has challenged patriarchy and has undermined much of its influence on public policy. This represents a profound change in American society and politics and has come about only after years of controversial political struggle. This political and cultural transformation has its origins in the changing economic role of women in the workforce, the broad breakdown in cultural consensus in the 1960s and the efforts of women to organise themselves politically.

References

Banner, L. (1974) *Women in Modern America: A Brief History* (New York: Harcourt Brace Jovanovich).

Barnard, J. (1971) *Women and the Public Interest* (Chicago: Aldine Atherton).

Deckard, B. (1983) *The Women's Movement* (New York: Harper & Row).

Faludi, S. (1992) *Backlash: The Undeclared War against Women* (London: Chatto & Windus).

Friedan, B. (1963) *The Feminine Mystique* (London: Gollancz).

Friedan, B. (1981) *The Second Stage* (New York: Summit Books).

Gatlin, R. (1987) *American Women Since 1945* (Basingstoke: Macmillan).

Gelb, J. and Palley, M. (1982) *Women and Public Policies* (Princeton: Princeton University Press).

Gilder, G. (1981) *Wealth and Poverty* (New York: Basic Books).

Mansbridge, J. (1986) *Why We Lost the ERA* (Chicago: University of Chicago Press).

McKeever, R. (1995) *Raw Judicial Power? The Supreme Court and American Society* (Manchester: Manchester University Press).

Mezey, S. (1992) *In Pursuit of Equality: Women, Public Policy, and the Federal Courts* (New York: St Martin's Press).

O'Neill, W. (1969) *The Woman Movement* (London: Allen & Unwin).

Rhode, D. (1989) *Justice and Gender* (Cambridge, Mass.: Harvard University Press).

US Bureau of the Census (1993) *Statistical Abstract of the United States* (113th edn, Washington, DC).

US Bureau of the Census (2005) *Statistical Abstract of the United States* (Washington, DC).

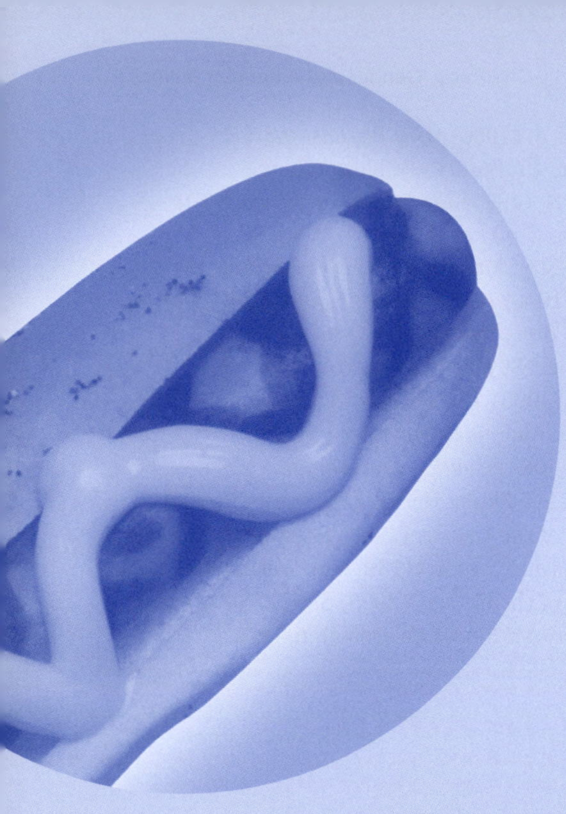

Chapter 7

Race, ethnicity and immigration in the USA

The Great Seal of the United States of America shows an American eagle carrying in its talons the arrows of war and the olive branch of peace. In its beak the eagle holds a ribbon on which are the words 'E pluribus unum' – 'One out of many'. In the 1780s, when this design was approved by Congress, it may have been seen as symbolising the uniting both of the several states and of their populations into one nation. In the more than two centuries that have passed since the Seal was adopted, the same slogan can be thought of as a continuing visible metaphor for the need by the nation to adapt to the racial and ethnic make-up of its population, and the changes brought by migration. American citizens often refer proudly to their home as a nation of immigrants, and race and ethnicity often lie at the centre of community celebrations; nevertheless, this demographic variety has not always been accompanied by equal opportunities or by unequivocal tolerance for every group. The United States may justifiably draw attention to its diversity, and it has maintained social data about its population for almost as long as it has been an independent nation.

Multiracial America: the first census

The USA recognised from its very beginnings the importance of having an accurate record of its population. The national commitment to count the people appears in Section 2 of the very first Article of the US Constitution. There it is declared that the first 'Enumeration shall be made within three years after the first meeting of the Congress of the United States, and within every subsequent term of ten years.' The first US census duly took place in 1800.

In committing the nation to this headcount, the authors of the Constitution indicated their understanding that representative government in the United States could not be expected to emerge out of rhetoric alone. Administrative tools would be needed to collect the data on which a fair representative system could be built. Without the census, there would be no way of distributing seats in the US House of Representatives between states. The same figures were needed in order to construct the electoral college for presidential elections as the Constitution required.

If the requirement to count the population came out of a commitment to make sure that the terms of the US Constitution were applied properly and accurately, the need to categorise the population count in terms of race was prompted by less noble stimuli.

A number of compromises were made between states on the way to the ratification of the Constitution. Slaves had been introduced to North America early in the colonial period, but in the South slavery had become embedded in the agricultural economy and cultural life in a way that had not happened in the rest of the colonies. When the young states came to compose their shared foundation document, this issue emerged as very contentious.

Slavery was preserved in the young United States of America. The Constitution prevented any abolition of the importation of slaves until at least 1808. There were probably some at the Constitutional Convention who thought that slavery in the USA was likely to fade out naturally once the trade in slaves could be abolished. A number of developments unforeseen in 1787 reduced the chances of matters evolving in that direction. Technological advantages in agricultural machinery, especially the introduction of the cotton gin – an efficient mechanism for removing the seeds from raw cotton – made labour-intensive plantation farming much more remunerative for the owners of properties in the South, where cotton could be grown. The continued demand for cheap labour encouraged an internal market in slaves that grew to fill the gap left when the importation of slaves was banned.

At the Constitutional Convention, delegates from the slave states were concerned to defend their economic and cultural structure. The other states were eager to maintain the allegiance of all states to a federal nation encompassing all states. One consequence of this was that the US Constitution, as agreed by the delegates in Philadelphia, had written into it a statistical devaluation of the worth of America's slave population, and of American Indians. When using the population count for purposes of distributing congressional seats, the constitution declared that free persons and indentured servants were to be counted in whole numbers, that 'Indians not taxed' be not counted at all, and that 'all other persons' (the slave population) be counted at three-fifths of their actual number. In this way, representation of slave states in national government was enhanced and firmly placed in the hands of the white population of those states, since, while black slaves might be 'worth' 60 per cent of a free person for the purposes of calculating representation, they nowhere had the right to exercise even a discounted fraction of a vote. Not until slavery was abolished in the wake of the US Civil War did this use of the census become redundant. It took almost a century more, and the civil rights legislation, before the full census count of African-Americans began to attract something like the political representation that numbers alone justified. The enslavement of so many people from one racial group has had an impact in the USA lasting long after abolition.

The US census has taken place every decade since 1800, creating a remarkable and detailed data resource about the history and development of the United States. Census data provide an intricate picture of the population of the USA, its economic and social activities, its growth, movement and the complexity of its make-up. Motivations for the initial count may have been mixed, but successive censuses have recorded the changing racial mixture of the country as it abandoned slavery, and the ethnic diversity of a nation that has throughout its history been a destination for changing migrant populations.

Multiracial America: the millennial census

America's mix of racial and ethnic population groups can be traced through census figures, and in 1980 the US Bureau of the Census introduced a question asking for each respondent's 'ancestry or ethnic origin'. There are subjective elements in the answers given to an open-ended question of this kind. Many American family trees branch into a number of different nations, ethnicities and races, as members of different waves of migration to the USA have met and intermarried. Nevertheless, the new census question, allowing everyone to give one or two attributions of ancestry or ethnic origin, gives the most accurate picture of where modern Americans perceive their roots to be.

In 2008, the US Census Bureau's American Community Survey indicated the ancestry or ethnic origins of almost 90 per cent of the US population. The largest single group – over 16.5 per cent, or nearly 50 million Americans – named German or part-German ancestry as being a significant part of their roots. The British Isles featured strongly, with a total of 13.1 per cent (almost 40 million respondents) mentioning English, British, Scottish, Scotch-Irish or Welsh ancestry. A further 11.9 per cent (over 36 million people) indicated Irish heritage.

Other large-scale contributors to the sense of American ancestry in the 2008 survey were a clutch of other European ethnicities, such as Italian (5.8 per cent), Polish (3.3 per cent), Dutch (1.6 per cent), Norwegian (1.5 per cent) and Swedish (1.4 per cent). Not all census data are reviewed annually, but in 2000 Latin America was represented among the 15 largest groups by Mexican ancestry, claimed by 6.5 per cent of respondents. African-American ancestry was indicated by 8.8 per cent. This last figure, while it is the third-largest group, appears to under-report the number of African-Americans in the USA, but this effect is caused by the subtlety of the question, which does not aggregate the many responses that mentioned individual African and West Indian national ethnicities.

In the 2000 census, 92 different ancestries were indicated by at least 100,000 persons each. The pattern of responses gives a contemporary picture of the lasting effect of the waves of migration that have entered the USA from other parts of the world. Long-standing European immigration is clear in the top-listed ethnicities. Long-standing, and still growing, Latin American immigration is also there. Other groups new to American in-migration, but important in recent years, such as Asian Indian immigrants, feature lower down the table.

At the millennium, American Indian ancestry was claimed by 2.8 per cent, or just under 8 million Americans – the tenth most popular ethnic origin indicated by census respondents. A fierce debate has raged between archaeologists about the probable size of the pre-Colombian North American native population. For many years, a population around 14 million was accepted, but recent works have expanded this estimate. With approximately 600 autonomous native groups identified in pre-European America, speaking more than 170 languages, estimates of the total population at the beginning of the sixteenth century have been placed as high as 50 million. All experts agree that thereafter there came a catastrophic collapse in the numbers of the native population, accelerated in large part by the importation of diseases common in Europe, but to which the North American population had no immunity. Measles, smallpox and typhus rapidly killed huge populations. The indifference, or positive malevolence, of the immigrant population to the indigenous population did nothing to slow this decline. Only in recent decades has the population claiming American Indian descent begun to show signs of stabilisation and, in some areas, growth.

The millennial census introduced the opportunity in a different question for respondents to identify themselves as 'multiracial', rather than under a number of discrete categories such as 'black', 'white' or 'American Indian'. The changed category provoked some debate, including a prediction that only about 2 per cent of Americans would use such a category. The argument that discrete categories preserve the notion of racial exclusivity, while a multiracial category gives recognition and dignity to those who choose to recognise and celebrate their parentage, won the day, and approximately 2.4 per cent of the population, or 6.8 million Americans, chose to identify with more than one race. While the total choosing this option was only one in every 40 Americans, the answer shed light on the nation. Among the states, in Hawaii almost a quarter of residents indicated their multiracial heritage, with

Alaska in distant second place on 5.6 per cent. Four of the five least multiracial states – Mississippi, West Virginia, Alabama, and South Carolina, each with multiracial populations lower than 1 per cent – were southern states. With a history tainted by slavery, in these communities substantial white and black populations have lived side by side for hundreds of years without the apparent development of multiracial bonds at anywhere near even the very modest national rate. Early data from the 2010 census indicate that the proportion of the America population self-identifying as multiracial is increasing, especially among young people.

Finding a place in America

Even if it can be argued that there may be some shift towards an undifferentiated American nation, the census results make it clear that the United States of America remains for now a nation of many populations. In-migration by various European groups, as well as the forced migration of slaves, began in the colonial period. As this era was followed by the establishment of an independent USA, different migrant populations at different times were prompted to make their way to the country.

Particularly as the country was opening up to settlement, into the late nineteenth century, migration patterns made a lasting impression on the human geography of the nation. British migration remained high, but by the 1850s, and through to the end of the nineteenth century, German and Irish migration to North America was also consistently high. There were many pressures on European populations. Mid-nineteenth-century social and political unrest affected many countries. Decline in demand for skilled crafts was common in areas going through the revolutionary industrial shift to large-scale factory manufacture. Labour gluts reduced wages and opportunity and tragic crises such as the Irish potato famine made escape look more like an imperative than an option. Simultaneously, transatlantic passage was becoming relatively cheap, if dangerous and uncomfortable, and American industrialisation and growth offered a burgeoning market in which labour could be valuable.

Immigrant groups tended to settle in specific areas. One successful transition would encourage others to chance their future in America. A community of those with similar heritage offered a point of stability in the threatening adventure that migration involved. Irish communities were typically in manufacturing cities and ports of entry. Germans often settled in midwestern industrial centres and farming communities. Scandinavian migration to the agricultural upper Midwest states stamped those places with a particular cultural pattern, and Italian settlement in some major cities was large enough that, even generations later, these national communities are easy to identify and self-consciously proud of their heritage.

North-west European migration streams were joined by a greater flow from Italy, Russia, and eastern European and Mediterranean communities after 1890. Once again, 'push' factors can be identified in the social and political problems being suffered from the Baltics to the Balkans, and further east, in this period. Methods of production in agriculture and industry were disrupting many countries, and population growth was increasing the pressure on resources.

At the beginning of the twentieth century, immigration to the USA was reaching record levels. Some individual years during this period saw over 1 million new migrants to the USA, and almost 20 million in total are recorded as entering the country between 1890 and 1920. By this time, 14.8 per cent of the US population was foreign-born, a figure that was to remain constant for roughly a generation, as millions of immigrants entered the country. By 1920, a majority of the population lived in cities, with migrants from outside and inside the country contributing to the industrial might that was powering the country's strength. Existing ethnic communities continued and were renewed by later immigrants in North American cities, joined by growing new communities from east European and Scandinavian countries.

At the time, there was increasing concern expressed by some about the flow of immigration. Efforts were made to ensure that the incoming

Figure 7.1 Citizenship is eagerly sought by many migrants who wish to stay in the USA, and is solemnised in a formal ceremony for those who qualify.

Source: © Press Association Images

communities were 'Americanised', and introduced to American democratic and cultural values. Populations of 'hyphenated-Americans' celebrated their origins as Irish-, Italian-, Polish-, but simultaneously asserted their common investment in being American.

While these actions confirmed the existence of the USA as a nation with increasingly varied immigrant underpinnings, the existing political community was worried enough by the pace of change that in 1924 the National Origins Act was passed to constrain and define the US acceptance of incomers. Immigration never stopped, but it slowed considerably through to the last quarter of the twentieth century, and by 1970 only 4.7 per cent of the population was foreign-born.

The foreign-born population

In addition to the decennial census, which is as inclusive as possible, the US Census Bureau also keeps abreast of any rapid or unforeseen demographic changes by maintaining a constant programme of surveys. The Bureau estimates that, by March 2007, the foreign-born population of the USA numbered 37.3 million persons, or 12.6 per cent of the population. This was almost treble the proportion of foreign-born over the period of one generation, indicating the increased significance of overseas migration to America in the late twentieth century, continuing into the early years of the twenty-first.

Throughout the 1980s and 1990s, there were only two years when the number of movers from abroad was recorded as fewer than 1 million a year; in 1999–2000 the figure was 1,745,000, and 10.3 million entered the USA between the beginning of the millennium and early 2007. Many of these are temporarily resident in the USA, and others are returning citizens who have been overseas for a time, so that the net gain from international migration is probably about half of the raw figure. Nevertheless, that still represents a steady and substantial cumulative impact, similar in numbers, if not quite in percentage of population, to the tide of immigration around the turn of the previous century.

At the beginning of the twenty-first century, the foreign-born population looks very different from that of 100 years previously. In 1900, 86 per cent of the foreign-born were from Europe, 1.2 per cent were from Asia, and 1.3 per cent from Latin America. A swing from European to Asian and Latin American migration was a strong feature of the late twentieth century. As late as 1960, European-born migrants made up 75 per cent of the USA foreign-born population, with Asia contributing only 5.1 per cent and Latin America 9.4 per cent. But by 2007, the European-born share had fallen to 12.4 per cent, while the Asian-born constituted 26.1 per cent and the Latin American-born dominated, forming 54.4 per cent of the US foreign-born population. In 2007, more than

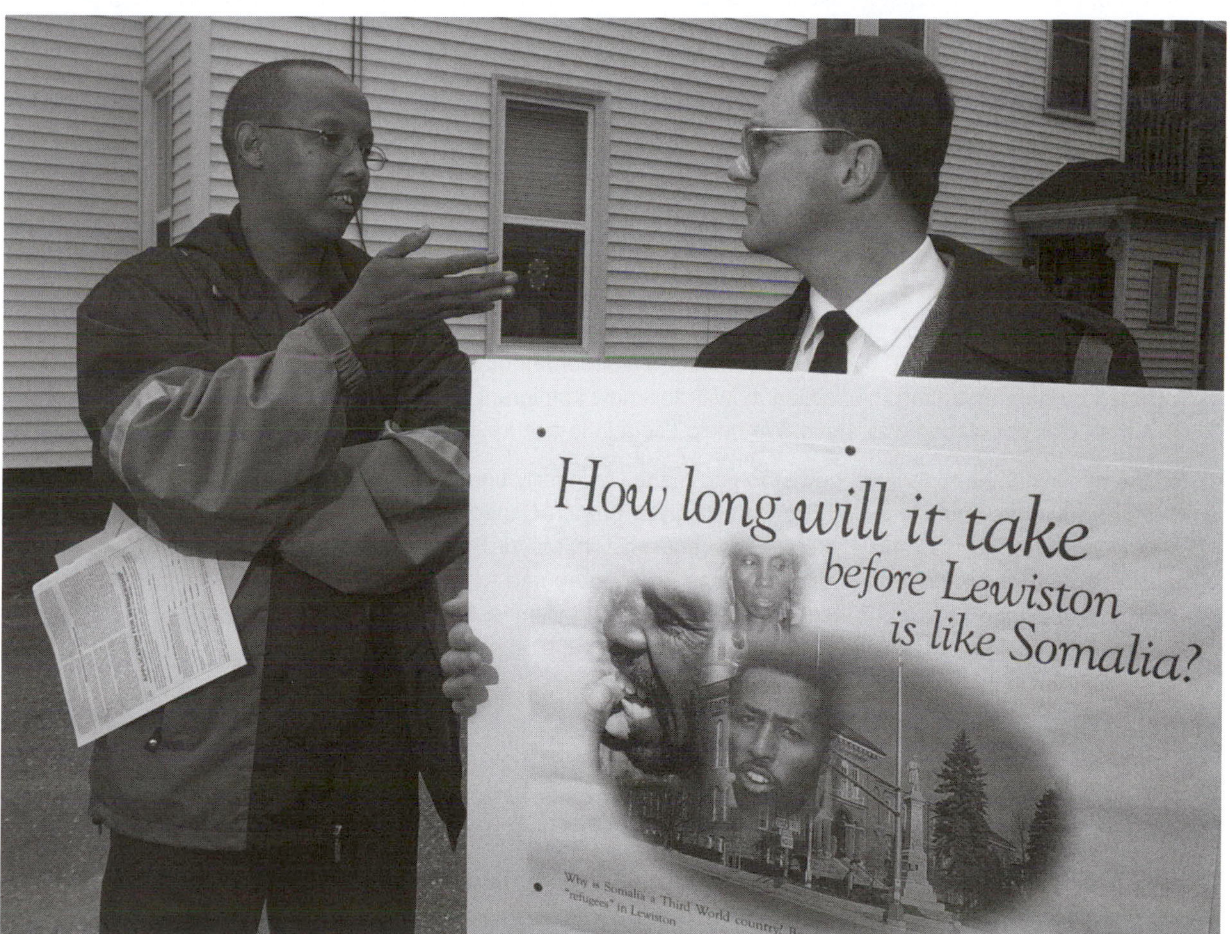

Figure 7.2 Somalian Ismail Ahmed, left, argues with Jeff Thorsvali, of Portland, prior to a march of support for the Somali community in Lewiston, Maine, 2002. Thorsvali represented the pro-white organisation National Alliance.
Source: © Press Association Images

Box 7.1

Somali immigrants in Maine

The USA is often referred to as a 'nation of immigrants', but successive waves of immigration have not always received an unequivocal welcome. In the nineteenth century, new European immigrants sometimes found that the jobs or accommodation that they were looking for were denied to them. Signs saying 'No Irish need apply' were not uncommon, and other ethnic groups also faced similar open discrimination. In the West, where immigration across the Pacific brought different groups to America, anti-Chinese and anti-Japanese sentiments and racist stereotypes were open. Tightly knit communities helped their own, and some ethnic groups found assimilation easier than others, but few groups met with no resistance.

Early in the twenty-first century, the social pressures of population change continue to have an impact. In 2000, the town of Lewiston, like the rest of the state of Maine, numbered few non-whites among its citizens. In less than two years, around 1,500 Somali immigrants arrived, approaching 5 per cent of the city's 35,000 population.

In a move that reflected the concerns of many earlier communities when faced by periods of change, Mayor Laurier T. Raymond of Lewiston called publicly for 'the Somali community to exercise discipline' to stem the flow of migration. 'This large number of new arrivals cannot continue without negative results for all,' wrote the mayor. 'We have been overwhelmed . . . our city is maxed out financially, physically and emotionally.'

The mayor's open letter sparked a vigorous response. Some defended his reaction, pointing to the impact of this immigration on welfare, health care and education budgets, and on competition for local employment, and the $450,000 city expenditure on accommodation for some of the Somalis. Others reacted by demonstrating their solidarity with this new immigrant group. One city councillor pointed out that 'Our population was static. We could use a little cultural diversity.'

In the mid-nineteenth century, Lewiston had made life initially uneasy for Irish immigrants, when a mob burned down the city's first Catholic Church. Later French-Canadian immigrants for a long time led a relatively self-contained and segregated life in Lewiston. Mayor Raymond is from French-Canadian stock. Both of these communities assimilated and contributed to the town that attracted the Somalis precisely because its low crime, good employment opportunities, and apparently strong family structures paralleled their own community values.

The authorities introduced English language training requirements for applicants for state welfare in an attempt to improve employment possibilities and integration. As the Somali community in Lewiston became larger, it began to include different groups from Somalia, and could no longer be seen as a homogeneous population bloc. In January 2009, a *Newsweek* journalist's article on 'The Refugees who Saved Lewiston' (Ellison, 2009) contributed further to the ongoing debate.

This town has engaged its various communities in its own contribution to the nation's ongoing immigration debate for almost a decade, and the effort continues. Lewiston has been tackling issues of cultural mixing and assimilation that have formed part of American development throughout the nation's history.

7 out of every 10 of the US-domiciled, Latin American-born people came from Central America, one-sixth from the Caribbean, and about one-eighth from South America.

At the start of the twenty-first century, the foreign-born population of the USA shows some differences in distribution from native-born Americans. They are proportionately more heavily concentrated in the West and the Northeast, which together hold 62.5 per cent of the foreign-born, as opposed to 39.4 per cent of native-born. The Central American-born concentrate most heavily in the South (32.6 per cent) and West (42.1 per cent). The Caribbean-born and South American-born are also heavily represented in the South (48.7 per cent and 35.3 per cent), but are also substantially domiciled in the Northeast (45.5 per cent and 46 per cent). The West is home to almost half of the Asian-born population.

According to 2006 census figures, family households with five or more people constitute 8.3 per cent of the native-born population, but 19.1 per cent of the total foreign-born population. The 2000 census figures showed the largest proportion of large families among those born in Central America (42.1 per cent). In 2006 the foreign-born were recorded as having a higher poverty rate (15.2 per cent) than the native-born (11.9 per cent), and a lower proportion of persons over 25 years of age with high school education or better (68 per cent as opposed to 89 per cent). The evidence of the 2000 census is that these characteristics vary according to area of origin, with those from Central America and the Caribbean showing most indications of deprivation, while South American, European, Asian and other groups more closely resemble native-born American population patterns. Only 5.1 per cent of the foreign-born were at that time living in non-metropolitan areas, as opposed to 20.7 per cent of the native-born. While only 27.5 per cent of the native population were living in central cities, 45.1 per cent of the foreign-born lived there. America's cities have, throughout the nation's history, often been the initial location for immigrants, and a large proportion of the foreign-born population continues to be drawn to urban communities to make their start in their new home.

Population mobility and diversity

Regionally, within the United States, the southern and western states dominated in population growth terms in the late twentieth century, and this trend has continued into the twenty-first. Regional population mobility has also followed distinct patterns over time. The US Census Bureau has calculated the geographical position of the 'mean centre of population' for the USA for each census since the first was taken in 1790, when the centre was judged to be near Chestertown, Maryland. This notional centre moved steadily west through the nineteenth and the first half of the twentieth centuries. In 1800, the US population was centred on Baltimore, Maryland. Moving through Virginia, and what is now West Virginia in the first half of the nineteenth century, by 1850 it had shifted 250 miles west, to Petersburg. Carrying on through Ohio and Kentucky, the centre of population reached Greenburg, Indiana in 1890. By 1900, and in part driven by the wave of foreign in-migration, the centre of population had travelled west about another 250 miles in the previous 50 years, and was located in Columbus, Indiana.

The rate of the westward shift of the centre of population slowed by about one-half in the next half-century, but it continued to edge across Indiana and, by 1950, on to Olney, Illinois. Since 1950, the population centre has resumed something of its nineteenth-century westward pace, and the trend has, in addition, developed a distinct tendency towards the south, so that by 1990 the population was centred on a point in Crawford County, Missouri, some 10 miles south-east of Steelville, Missouri. Continuing its south-westerly transit, by 2010 the centre had moved a further 58 miles, to a position near Plato, in Texas County, Missouri. This single, cumulative indicator has moved more than 1,000 miles over the 220 years of US census returns, travelling steadily westwards, and bending increasingly south in a way that traces the growing significance of the West and, more recently, the South in attracting settlement. These regions have shown relatively strong growth, and have been the location of some of the nation's fastest-growing metropolitan areas.

While the attraction of these areas appears to be levelling off, the 2010 census showed the slowest population growth in the first decade of the twenty-first century was concentrated in Northeastern and industrial Midwestern states. The population of Michigan fell in that decade. The largest growth took place in states such as Nevada and Arizona in the Southwest, Texas in the South, and the southeast coastal states from Florida to North Carolina. There are local differences too. While the South and West generally have leading growth rates, some individual states in those regions – for example, Louisiana and Mississippi – have not done so well.

As immigrant groups settle and have families, the long-term ethnic shape of the nation is affected. It is projected that by halfway through the twenty-first century, about 25 per cent of the US population will be from Hispanic roots, 14 per cent black, and 8 per cent Asian, although marriage patterns and a greater willingness to self-identify as multiracial may make such distinctions less relevant. The new diversity of the USA was already clear in 2000 census results from California. Less than half of the state's 33.9 million population were non-Hispanic whites (46.7 per cent), a further 32.4 per cent identified themselves as Hispanics, 11.1 per cent as Asians or Pacific Islanders, 6.4 per cent black, 2.7 per cent multiracial, and 0.5 per cent American Indian.

While at the national level in 2000 there were already 2.8 per cent of Americans claiming some American Indian ancestry, only 0.74 per cent of the population classified themselves racially as American Indian. This probably indicates individuals with complex ancestries who nevertheless usually identify themselves (and probably are recognised by others) as white, black, or Hispanic. Nevertheless, the American Indian community is growing, and one long-term projection suggests that the number of American Indians may increase threefold by 2100.

America's cities continue to be major gateways to America for immigrant and ethnic communities searching for new opportunities, even though many major urban centres have been in decline for decades. The central cities of the USA lost around 2.4 million of their population to domestic migration in every year of the 1990s. People are moving to the suburbs of their own metropolis, but the figures also suggest that those moving to other cities and other regions are more likely to choose a suburban location for their new home. Nevertheless, these net measures of population movement are made up of complex and overlapping shifts to and from every area. Places are not just losing or gaining people, they are exchanging people. In the year 1999/2000, for example, the metropolitan areas of the USA received 845,000 migrants from abroad to central cities, and 794,000 to suburbs. These figures include American citizens returning to the USA. If these millions of people form significantly different sectors of the population, then the apparently marginal net change may in fact disguise a significant shift in the character of the populations of both living environments.

It is difficult to assess the precise social and economic characteristics of these exchanging populations, but it would appear that urban migration has been economically and racially selective. The replacement in central cities of exiting affluent families with incoming less affluent people has a consequent dramatic effect on purchasing power within the cities. In spite of the fact that 'gentrification' has certainly attracted professional households into some city neighbourhoods, cities are losing more household income than they are gaining from current migration. The attraction of the central cities is still more likely to be that of concentrated service provision for the poor, as in many East Coast cities, or dangerous, difficult and unpopular jobs for the unemployed, as in the big meat-packing cities of the Midwest, than an environment for the more affluent sectors of American society. Urban migration has also been racially and ethnically selective, and in the mid-1990s, while the black population of the nation was around 12.5 per cent, and the Hispanic population was 10 per cent, the median black and Hispanic populations in the nation's 21 largest cities were respectively 28.1 per cent and 13.9 per cent.

The twenty-first century: towards a nation of minorities

In 2006, the US Census Bureau announced that the nation's population had become one-third minority

– that is, made up of residents other than the single-race, non-Hispanic whites who continue to make up a majority of the American population. The United States has become increasingly diverse in recent decades, and that trend is set to continue and possibly accelerate. Initial reports from the 2010 census indicate that, of the 27.3 million growth in the US population over the previous 10 years, just 9 per cent came from the non-Hispanic white communities. Hispanic and Asian groups showed the greatest expansion.

At the mid-point of the first decade of the new century, Hispanics were clearly the largest minority group, making up around 14.4 per cent of the population. The black population was recorded as 13.4 per cent, Asians as 4.9 per cent, American Indians and Alaska natives as 1.5 per cent and native Hawaiians and Pacific Islanders as 0.3 per cent. There is some overlap in these figures, accounted for by those who report more than one race.

The differences in rates of population growth are significant. The nation's overall population growth rate for the year July 2004–July 2005 was just under 1 per cent, but different groups showed very different patterns. The fastest-growing group were Hispanics, with a growth rate of 3.3 per cent, and the growth rate for the Asian population was 3 per cent. The black population grew by 1.3 per cent, American Indians by 1 per cent, Pacific Islanders by 1.5 per cent, and non-Hispanic whites by about 0.25 per cent. In 2004–5 the Hispanic population growth rate was over 13 times higher than that for non-Hispanic whites, and a similar ratio has been typical in the early twenty-first century. Hispanics accounted for almost half of the nation's population growth, and while immigration continued to be an important source of this increase, over 60 per cent was due to natural growth – the total of births, minus deaths.

The Hispanic population accounted for the largest number of immigrants of any of the groups. It also had the lowest median age of any of the groups – at 27.2 years, this makes an especially startling comparison with the 40.3 year median age for the majority non-Hispanic whites. While figures for 2008 show the Hispanic population growing older, with a 27.7 year median age, the increase for non-Hispanic whites had been even larger, to 41.1 years. This age difference indicates that the Hispanic population is a much more fertile group, and that in the foreseeable future it will continue to grow more quickly than the other groups, regardless of immigration figures. Estimates made by the Census Bureau for 2008 found that 47 per cent of America's children under the age of 5 years in 2008 came from a minority group, and 25 per cent were Hispanic. These were slightly higher than the figures for children under 18 years old, where 44 per cent were minorities and 22 per cent Hispanic.

Foreign-born minorities may often be non-English speakers, but some minority populations maintain a language other than English through succeeding generations, and large communities may have a critical mass which makes it easier to do this. In 2007, the US Census Bureau estimated that about 19.7 per cent of the population aged over 5 years spoke a language other than English at home. In almost two-thirds of these cases the language spoken was Spanish. The total who spoke a language other than English at home had increased from 17.9 per cent in 2000 and 13.8 per cent in 1990. By 2007, more than half of the Los Angeles population over 5, and almost half the similar population in Miami spoke a language other than English at home. Figures from the previous year show 39 per cent of persons over 5 years of age spoke a language other than English at home in the USA's 25 largest cities.

Minorities in the nation can still form substantial population groups on a regional basis. Census figures from 2008 show that 309 of the USA's 3,142 counties at that time had populations that were more than 50 per cent made up of minority population groups. Fifty-six had become 'majority–minority' counties since 2000. The states of Hawaii, New Mexico, California and Texas, plus the District of Columbia, were all 'majority–minority' in 2008.

Birth rates, population structures and migration all suggest that this diversity will grow through the first half of the twenty-first century. Projections based on the current trends indicate that non-white Hispanics will themselves become the largest minority within the US population around the year 2042, and that by the mid-point of the twenty-first century the United States will clearly be a nation of minorities.

Populations and politics

In the election results of the early twenty-first century, there have been swings towards stronger Republican control, then sharply in the direction of the Democrats. Election nights always have their emotional moments, but few have been more affecting than November 2008, when the USA elected its first non-white president. Nevertheless, while one party or the other was able to gain temporary advantage, political opinion in the nation was closely and evenly divided in ideological terms.

The supporters of each of the major parties will have hoped that they were the ones with the foundation for growth, perhaps by having a firm foothold within those sectors of the population experiencing substantial growth in the foreseeable future. Certainly, there might be policy implications if the electoral foundation of the nation's government were to be significantly influenced by the different rates of growth of the emerging populations in the USA.

Census data covering the decade to the end of 2004 show that non-Hispanic whites on average received weekly earnings around 25 per cent higher than those for non-Hispanic blacks and for native-born Hispanics, and well over 50 per cent higher than foreign-born Hispanics, and that these ratios remained fairly constant throughout this period. At the same time, poverty rates fell for Hispanics and blacks but, even at their best, they were more than double those for non-Hispanic whites. The highly reputable Pew Research Center reports the net worth of non-Hispanic white US households as almost $89,000 in 2002, an increase from over $75,000 just six years previously. Over the same period, non-Hispanic black households had seen their average net worth fall by $1,000 to just under $6,000, and though Hispanic households had seen an increase of about $1,000, this had expanded their average net worth to only just under $8,000.

Clearly, many of these economic differences reflect the different structures of the population. The older populations of non-Hispanic whites contain more workers with seniority and salaries to match. The younger and more fertile populations are likely to have more dependants, and fewer workers in established positions. While some aspects of minority experience may be shared, others will not be. Foreign-born members of the USA population on average have a lower income than the native-born, but while some foreign-born will be low-income workers looking for a better life, maybe even refugees displaced by forces beyond their control, others are highly educated and skilled, migrating to exploit their skills. About three-quarters of all American residents born in India have a bachelor's degree or higher, and they attract a median household income well above the national average and almost double that of the average foreign-born person in the USA.

Minorities are not always evenly represented in the political structure. Some established minorities may feel disengaged from and let down by the political system. Immigrant communities are likely to contain a large proportion of non-citizens. Communities with a large proportion of young people will, by definition, have a larger than usual proportion below the minimum voting age. But the history of the USA is one of immigrant communities embracing their Americanness, including its political aspects; young members of all populations become mature and the most disengaged populations can rise to the political challenge if there is cause to do so. It is plausible to conjecture that the US electorate will continue to reflect America's growing demographic diversity, and that this will bring the potential for a clash of differing political agendas generated by different groups. Policy debates of all kinds have the potential to acquire racial or ethnic dimensions. It is already clear that an ageing population presents twenty-first century society with difficult policy choices. For example, the government's pension and health care costs will increase as demands grow on the Social Security, Medicare and Medicaid systems, but in the foreseeable future an increasing proportion of the older, whiter population will need these benefits, while an increasing proportion of the younger, productive, and tax-contributing population will not be white. The traditions embedded in a country that perceives itself proudly as a 'nation of immigrants' are likely to moderate the policy debates that ensue. Skilful leadership, involving all the groups, will help.

In the elections of the early twenty-first century, indicators such as income and education showed some explanatory differences between party support, but other population identifiers, such as gender, religion and race, were much more important. The voting behaviour of different racial groups shows conclusively that, even if the country as a whole was balanced on a knife-edge of political indecision, some identifiable populations within the citizenry had no doubt about their political preferences.

While the aggregate population figures suggested a population evenly divided in their political affiliations, it was evident even before the election of President Obama in 2008 that America's black voters were inclined to opt for Democrats rather than Republicans as their chosen office-holders. Around 88 per cent had chosen the Democrat John Kerry over his Republican opponent, George W. Bush, almost the same as the 90 per cent of black voters who had chosen the Democrat Al Gore in 2000. In 2008, Barack Obama attracted around 96 per cent of the black vote, and his presence on the ballot persuaded many more black voters to the polls than in previous elections. In 2008, blacks made up 13 per cent of the total voters, up from 11 per cent in 2004 and 10 per cent in 2000. In a polity where ideological choices are fairly evenly balanced, a shift of 2 or 3 per cent of the vote can have earth-shaking electoral repercussions, and the perception of that important effect may help to undermine some of the factors that lead to political disengagement.

About two-thirds of Hispanic voters supported the Democrats' presidential candidate in 2008, a return to the proportions attracted by Democratic President Clinton, after a decline in 2004, when the level of support for Democrat John Kerry fell to 56 per cent. The importance of the strong Democratic showing among Hispanics is magnified by the fact that, while Hispanics formed 4 per cent of the electorate who turned out in 2000, eight years later they were 9 per cent of those who voted. The Asian vote has been shifting away from the Republicans since the early 1990s. Only 31 per cent of this group voted for Bill Clinton in the three-cornered election of 1992, but the percentage has increased in each election since, reaching 63 per cent in 2008. Again, the increase in this group – from 2 per cent of voters in 2000 to 4 per cent in 2008 – adds to the growing significance of diverse groups in the American electorate.

Balanced against the Democratic candidate's lead among these minority groups in the 2008 election, the Republican John McCain held an advantage among white voters of 14 per cent, only a slight decline from the Bush lead of 17 per cent in his re-election year of 2004, and a little more than the 12 per cent lead Bush had in 2000. Obama's appeal to all groups was very impressive in 2008, but his ability to attract the white vote did not match that of previous Democratic president Bill Clinton, possibly demonstrating a continuing racial effect on voting patterns.

Broadly speaking, this pattern of support has been relatively consistent over time. Variations can be caused by the changing salience of significant issues during different elections, and by the positive or negative image of a particular candidate with some racial and ethnic groups, but in recent years the Democratic party has drawn support from a more varied racial community than has the Republican party, and the Republican party has maintained a steady lead among white, non-Hispanic voters. These patterns are crucial to party political strategists. These groups are likely to have different issue agendas, requiring differing party appeals to different groups. The Republican successes in the 2010 mid-term elections indicated strongly the value to political parties of being able to energise population groups around their agenda. With many voters disappointed by the policy outcomes since 2008, and without Obama on the ballot to give an extra pull to non-white voters and young voters, the electorate who turned out to vote altered, and the Republican party was able to take full advantage of the situation and to make considerable gains. Being able to pinpoint the groups and the relevant issues gives candidates and their support teams the opportunity, should they wish, to stress and adapt those parts of their message and their appeal most relevant to the various voting communities in order to garner more support.

Hispanic Americans

Ethnically related patterns of political behaviour can themselves be deceptive, as sharp sub-divisions sometimes exist within ethnic groups. America's Hispanics are themselves a complex mix of people. There has been a Hispanic population in the territories that now form the United States for centuries, but this has grown considerably in recent generations. Over the past century, about 60 per cent of Hispanic migration to the USA has been from Mexico. Migrants from other countries of Central and South America have contributed another 13 per cent. The other largest single Hispanic communities have entered the USA from the islands of Puerto Rico and Cuba.

These national groups have distinctive backgrounds, and their political activity can also reflect their assimilation into different parts of America. Cuban-Americans, while only about one in 20 of America's Hispanics, are concentrated in Florida, adjacent to their country of origin, and their strong community antagonism to Fidel Castro's regime in Cuba gives them a strong affinity with the Republican party.

Many other Hispanic groups enter the USA as relatively poor migrants. Like immigrants through American history, many tend to enter the United States through urban gateways, often living first in city centres or economically depressed inner suburbs, and working in poorly paid jobs. Others move across the southern border of the USA to enter the low-wage agricultural labour pool. Also like earlier groups of non-affluent immigrants, these Hispanics are likely to appreciate the Democrats' commitment to social support programmes and, once citizens, to support this policy agenda. Other elements can give varying contexts to the political opinions of sub-groups within ethnic categories. Protestant and Catholic Hispanics alike tend to give greater support to Democrats, but traditionally the Catholic group has leaned more strongly in that political direction. Republicans have hoped that they may be able to gain votes in this community, in part by appealing to social values shared by some Catholics and the conservative Protestant Republicans. There is nothing automatic about coalitions or antagonisms between minorities. An abiding belief among some strategists that Hispanics would be unlikely to rally behind black candidates seemed to bite the dust with the election of Barack Obama.

As the established Hispanic community develops to contain a more middle-class element, different economic motivations come into play. The Republicans can also appeal to this population. Ronald Reagan received 40 per cent of the Hispanic vote in his 1984 re-election, when he was performing very well in every part of the electorate. Part of the later success of George W. Bush was founded on his ability to speak Spanish, his success with the Hispanic voters in Texas when he was governor of that state, and the marriage of his son Jeb Bush to Mexican-born Columba, giving the former president a family of multi-ethnic grandchildren. Important though they are, such factors in the long run take second place to policy.

In 1996 Robert K. Dornan, a right-wing Republican California congressman, was defeated in a very tight race by Democrat Loretta Sanchez. Angry in defeat, Dornan complained that Sanchez was 'voted in by non-Americans . . . voting into office someone who gives them benefits and raises taxes on the rest of us'. Even at the time it was startling to hear such intemperate language from an office-holder. Since then, Loretta Sanchez's sister Linda has won a different California seat in the US Congress, and a pair of Republican Hispanic siblings, Mario and Lincoln Diaz-Balart, hold House seats in Florida.

The 112th Congress opened in 2011, containing 24 Hispanics among its 435 representatives and 2 Hispanics in the US Senate. While one of the Hispanic senators is from each of the main parties, most Hispanics in Congress are Democrats, with 7 Hispanic Republicans in the House of Representatives in 2011. States with Hispanic representation in Congress in 2011 were Arizona, California, Colorado, Florida, Idaho, Illinois, New Mexico, New Jersey, Texas, New York and Washington. Most of these representatives sat in constituencies where the local population was predominantly non-white.

At the beginning of the twenty-first century, just over 60 of the 435 House constituencies had populations in which the majority were non-white.

Most non-white representatives are elected from these seats. While a few non-white candidates have been elected from majority-white districts, race does retain an impact in elections, and most minority race candidates have needed the platform of a geographically concentrated population group to get their career going. There has been some recognition of this when the opportunity to redraw district boundaries has arisen in recent years, with some conscious creation of districts that are likely to increase the chance of minority representation.

The political impact of Hispanics is lagging behind their representation in the American population. Continuing waves of immigration mean that a large proportion of Hispanics resident in the USA are still moving towards citizenship, and, given the tendency for migrant populations to be heavily drawn from young and fertile sectors of the population, a large proportion of Hispanics are below voting age, or in those young electoral groups that turn out to vote less often than more mature citizens. Problems of poverty and social exclusion are more common among Hispanics than in the general population, and these too are factors in depressing political participation. They are, however, well placed to maximise their group impact in the near future.

Hispanics make up more than one-third of the population in California, and are heavily settled in Texas and Florida – all large, powerful states with a critical role to play in presidential elections. Hispanic representation in local and state office continues to grow, expanding the talent pool and feeding the demand for Hispanic representation in senior posisions. While there is no guarantee that this group will develop as a politically united bloc through forthcoming generations, the growing political impact excites great interest among political activists, both within the Hispanic community and across the political spectrum.

African-Americans

The authors of the US Constitution worked towards uneasy compromises that they thought would minimise the chances of regional political breakdown in the new nation. Unwilling to abolish black slavery at the end of the eighteenth century, these leaders left America with the heritage of entrenched racial divisions. Those southern states with the largest black population were also those with the most entrenched pro-slavery cultures. For decades, the nation's leaders fudged their way from one attempted solution to another until the American Civil War. The war between the states was founded on more issues than slavery alone, but, once the conflict had begun, it was inevitable that the position of slavery in the southern states and in the nation would have to be resolved. Only with the defeat of the southern Confederacy, and the abolition of slavery in 1865, was the African-American community able to claim even the pretence of the rights guaranteed to citizens of the USA.

Even after the Constitution was amended to abolish slavery, black Americans found their economic, educational, social and political ambitions constrained by legalised racial segregation, common discriminatory practices and, in some cases, physical intimidation. Black political leaders and their allies tried in many ways to move US society to a more egalitarian basis. Standard political routes were difficult to utilise, given that non-white voters were effectively disenfranchised in those states where they were most thickly settled. Repeated pursuit of cases through the courts finally began to show promise at precisely the moment when some members of the black community adopted non-violent direct action – demonstrations, marches, silent protests – as a dignified mass movement challenge to the white power structure. The undignified and violent reaction of state and local politicians and officials in the southern states prompted a sympathetic response in favour of the black victims among others in the US population at just about the time that the US Supreme Court voted unanimously to declare racial segregation unconstitutional, in the 1954 case of *Brown* v. *Board of Education*. The extended battle for civil rights that was forced on African-Americans has provided models and precedents for other groups in society.

Having waited so long for the legal acceptance of their equality with other men and women, the black American population remains disadvantaged compared to the average American population on most social and political indices. Educational attainment rates have been converging, but in 2007 over 17 per cent of the black adult population had less than a full high school education, 4 per cent more than the proportion of whites with the same educational background. At the other end of the educational spectrum, black women, 19 per cent of whom have a bachelor's degree or higher, are closer to the figure for white women (28.3 per cent) than black men, at 18 per cent, are to white men (29.9 per cent). The unemployment rate for blacks was double that for whites in 2007, a ratio of disadvantage that has been relatively consistent for many years. Disadvantage emerges in many other ways. For example, in 1997 over one-third of blacks reported experiencing food or housing hardship, compared to just over 18 per cent of whites. In the same survey, 16 per cent of blacks reported their health status as poor or at best fair, compared with 10 per cent of whites. In confronting this health disparity, the resources are also uneven. In 2005/6, nearly 21 per cent of blacks had no health insurance coverage, and almost 23 per cent were reliant on Medicaid, as opposed to 14.9 per cent of whites uninsured and 11.1 per cent on Medicaid.

Over time, the black population has found employment in a wider variety of jobs, and their distribution between employment sectors has shifted closer to that of the white population. Breakthrough into managerial and professional-level employment is nevertheless coming only slowly, and employment in service occupations is higher than for whites. The positive economic development of the black community must be noted. At the start of the twenty-first century, over half (52.4 per cent) of black families where both parents are present have total incomes in excess of $50,000 – a figure relatively close to the 63.6 per cent of white families in the same position. However, just 29 per cent of African-American families were two-parent units, as opposed to 71 per cent of white non-Hispanic families. In total, 24.3 per cent of US blacks lived below the poverty level in 2006, compared with 12.3 per cent of the US population as a whole, and more than twice as high as the 10.3 per cent poverty rate for non-Hispanic whites.

The African-American population is not distributed randomly in the United States. Other immigrant groups might have come to America for a combination of reasons pushing them from their home countries and attracting them to America, but most African-Americans can trace their migration to the forcible importation of black slaves to serve the economic purposes of white owners. Still reflecting that heritage, over half of black Americans live in the former slave areas of the South. At the 2000 census, almost 80 per cent of southern blacks, and almost all blacks in other states, were metropolitan dwellers, with over half of the black population living in the central cities. This makes the black population substantially more concentrated in the urban core, less suburban and less rural than is the average in the USA.

Since the erosion of many major barriers to African-American political development, these areas of black population concentration have, naturally, been the locations of those political breakthroughs. The vast majority of the 44 African-Americans in the US House of Representatives in the 112th Congress (2011–13) were from majority non-white constituencies. Two of these representatives were Republicans, Tim Scott of South Carolina and Allen West of Florida, both elected for the first time in 2010. There were no black members of the US Senate. At the federal level, the number of black office-holders increased steadily, if slowly, from 10 in 1970, to 38 in 1992, since when the figure has changed only a little, to the 44 in the 112th Congress. These political gains notwithstanding, in recent years blacks, with about 12 per cent of the national population, have formed only about 9 per cent of the US House of Representatives and, only occasionally, 1 per cent of the US Senate.

Political opportunities for African-Americans have expanded. An annual survey conducted over the past generation has shown the number of black elected officials in the USA to have increased from 1,469 in 1970 to more than 10,500 by 2011. Regional disparities in black political gains remain, but large gains in states such as Georgia, Louisiana, Mississippi, South Carolina and Texas suggest that long-lasting regional differences may be converging. Differences remain, nevertheless, even within regions. The 2000 total of 897 black elected officials in Mississippi represented 18.9 per cent of the total office-holders

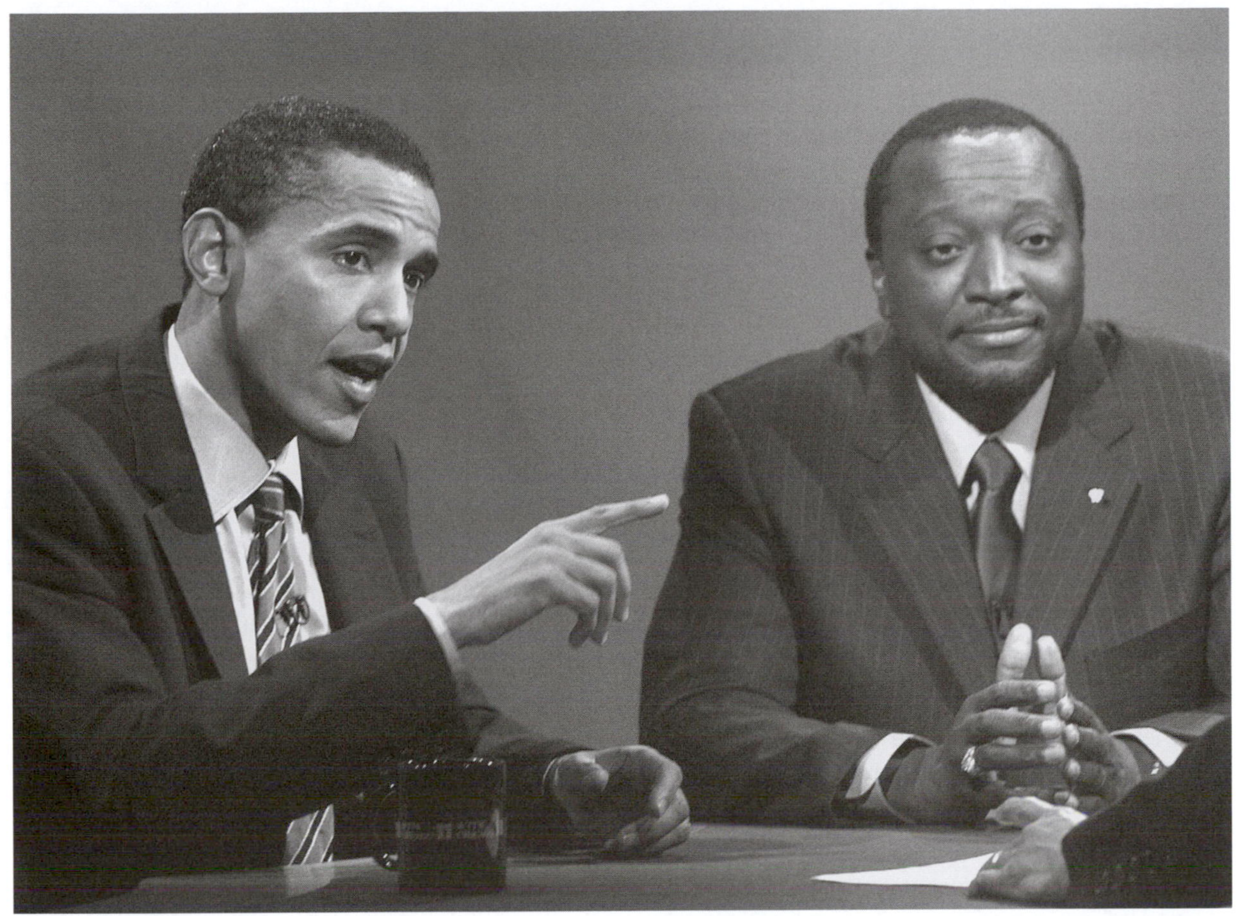

Figure 7.3 Democrat Barack Obama, left, and Republican Alan Keyes taking part in the final debate in the race for the Senate seat for Illinois, 2004.
Source: © Press Association Images

in that state, and Alabama (731 and 16.7 per cent) has also seen great advances in both numbers and proportions of black office-holders. The 475 black elected officials in Texas still represented only 1.7 per cent of all office-holders in that state.

The US political system claims to sustain about half a million elected offices, most of which are low-level community offices in special districts, local education boards, and the like. Inevitably, most of the offices held by blacks fall into the essential, but relatively mundane areas of low-level community politics, but senior office-holders are also being elected from the black community. Black mayors numbered 451 in 2001. These were elected mainly in relatively small communities, but 47 black mayors were from cities with populations of 50,000 or more. Statewide office is a more difficult challenge for candidates from any group, but 33 African-Americans occupied such positions in 2001, about two-thirds of them serving as justices in the senior courts of their states. The number of black elected officials has not only grown over the last generation, it is clearly being replenished as young candidates replace those who have reached the end of their political careers, or who retire to move on to other pursuits. A turnover of about 25 per cent of black office-holders in the three-year period up to 2000 suggested the existence of a healthy pool of political talent in the African-American population.

President Obama's route to becoming the first non-white major party nominee for the presidency, and then the first non-white president of the USA,

Box 7.2

A ground-breaking election: Illinois 2004 and the road to the White House

November 2004 saw the first contest for the United States Senate in which both the Republican and Democratic parties nominated black candidates for office.

Barack Obama, an Illinois state senator, was the nominee of the Democratic party, winning 53 per cent of the primary vote when the campaign of his major opponent within the Democratic party, a white candidate, collapsed after allegations of domestic violence emerged during a divorce case. Obama jumped to national prominence when he gave a powerful speech at the 2004 Democratic National Convention.

The Republican candidate, Alan Keyes, a religious conservative and former US ambassador to UNESCO, also benefited from a divorce case, when revelations in court papers prompted the Republicans' earlier favourite to drop out of the race.

Obama took the seat with a convincing majority in November 2004, to become only the third African-American ever to be elected to the US Senate. Edward W. Brooke (Republican) represented Massachusetts from 1966 to 1978. Carol Mosely-Braun (Democrat) represented Illinois from 1992 to 1998.

The first-ever survey of the number of black elected officials in the USA was conducted in 1970. In the 30 years between then and the first twenty-first century survey of African-American office-holding, the number of black Americans in political office increased sixfold. Over 9,000 elected offices in the USA are now held by African-Americans.

Four years later, former state Senator Obama became former US Senator Obama, after a barnstorming and brilliant campaign took him to the Democratic nomination and then to the White House. This exciting election prompted the largest non-white voter turnout ever and might well be expected to encourage a more diverse range of candidates and office-holders to emerge.

made good use of this developing training ground for minority group politicians. After graduating from college, he worked for a Public Interest Research Group in New York, followed by a community organisation in Illinois. He was a highly regarded student at Harvard Law School, after which he continued to work in community organisation, this time in a directly political, but nonpartisan way, with Project Vote. He combined further involvement in community organisations with his post as a university lecturer in law, and in 1996 was elected to the Illinois state senate. From here, he launched an attempt to enter the US House of Representatives in 2000, but failed to win the Democratic primary. His organisational skills were evident when he took Illinois' US senate seat in 2004, and once again in the exceptionally skilful presidential campaign of 2008.

American dreamers

Ethnic and racial groups in America may have criticisms of the polity and its policies as regards their own groups, but it rarely prompts them to see themselves as anything other than American. African-Americans now, as in earlier eras, such as the period of the civil rights movement, point to equality of opportunity rather than discrimination as being the necessary outcome of policy. However, there can be heated debate on whether this is best achieved by trusting in the benign, if circuitous, route of history, or intervening with affirmative action.

Role models emerge regularly from America's immigrant and ethnic communities, not always typical, and not always expected, but often showing a shared understanding of the opportunities that exist in the USA. Governor Arnold Schwarzenegger of California, white, European-born and Republican, might be seen as an untypical minority representative, but he roused his party's National Convention in 2004 with his own tale of his success as an immigrant to the United States, saying, 'an immigrant's dream. It is the American dream'. Speaking in Iowa a year before his election, Barack Obama spoke of reclaiming the American dream. This is not uncommon rhetoric in American election campaigns, but Obama's journey to the White House was exhilarating, and as an atypical African-American, from a mixed race marriage and with a father from Kenya, he can be claimed by many groups and communities. These expressions of an American dream resonate across the boundaries of groups that might be separated by race, ethnicity, native birth and immigrant status.

Chapter summary

It was the fate of the United States of America to build a nation founded on the mixed heritage of many nations, ethnicities and races. This has not always been a comfortable melding of communities under one flag, as indicated by the fact that the southern enslavement of African-Americans was initially protected in the US Constitution. Resources are not evenly distributed between America's racial and ethnic communities, and new migrant groups can still find it difficult to find a place in American society.

The history of the USA can be drawn in terms of waves of immigration coinciding with the opening of different regions and spaces within the country, so that the contribution of some ethnic communities in America can in part be seen in long-term settlement patterns. More than two centuries after the signing of the Constitution, the US census recorded that the country had 92 ancestries reported by more than 100,000 persons each, and a range of ethnicities so diverse that no one could claim to be dominant. Racial and ethnic diversity in the United States appears to be expanding and becoming more complex, as migration becomes more global and as intermarriage between groups becomes more common.

Both old-established, and newly migrating, ethnic and racial groups do nevertheless maintain identifiable characteristics. One way in which these differences are displayed is in different patterns of voting associated with the groups. Political campaigns draw heavily on these characteristics in making their appeal to voters. Racial and ethnic differences notwithstanding, there remains a firm and widespread belief in America as a nation of opportunity for its diverse population.

Discussion points

1. In what ways might the heritage of slavery put African-Americans in a different position from other racial and ethnic groups in America?
2. How important is it that racial and ethnic groups organise to gain political recognition?
3. In multi-ethnic and multiracial America is it likely to be more important that people recognise their ethnicity, or that they stress their 'Americanness'?
4. What effects will developments in ethnic and racial communities have on America in the foreseeable future?

Further reading

The work of the Migration Policy Institute (http://www.migrationinformation.org) and of the Center for Immigration Studies (http://www.cis.org) provides a great deal of useful information. The extensive research of the Joint Center for Political and Economic Studies (http://www.jointcenter.org) concentrates on African-American affairs.

Greg Oswald's *Race and Ethnic Relations in Today's America* (Aldershot: Ashgate, 2001) provides a straightforward overview, and *Remaking the American Mainstream: Assimilation and Contemporary Immigration* by Richard Alba and Victor Nee (Cambridge, Mass.: Harvard University Press, 2003) examines changes and continuities in the nature of immigration and assimilation.

Kenneth Verney's *African American and US Popular Culture* (London: Routledge, 2003) offers a different lens on racial identity in America. In *Arab-American Faces and Voices: The Origins of an Immigrant Community* (Austin: University of Texas Press, 2003), Elizabeth Boosahda offers a case study of a little-researched ethnic community.

The author consulted a number of sources that are regularly updated, including Michael Barone and Richard E. Cohen with Charles E. Cook, Jr., *The Almanac of American Politics 2002* (Washington DC: National Journal, 2001); Harold W. Stanley and Richard G. Niemi, *Vital Statistics on American Politics, 1999–2000* (Washington DC: CQ Press, 2000); and Jacqueline West (ed.), *The USA and Canada 2009* (London: Europa, 2009).

Many of the statistics came from *Statistical Abstract of the United States of America*, generously made available by the US government at http://www.census.gov/compendia/statab/. The National Exit poll at http://edition.cnn.com/ELECTION/2008/results/polls/#val=USP00p1 was very useful, as was Gerald Pomper's analysis of it in Michael Nelson's edited collection *The Elections of 2008* (Washington DC: CQ Press, 2010).

Informative studies from government and think-tanks that provided information for this chapter include David A. Bositis, *Black Elected Officials: A Statistical Summary 2000* (Washington DC: Joint Center for Political and Economic Studies, 2002); Nancy Rytina, 'Estimates of the legal permanent resident population and population eligible to naturalize in 2002' (Washington DC: US Department of Homeland Security, 2004); Audrey Singer, 'The rise of new immigrant gateways' (Washington DC: Brookings Institution (The Living City Census Series), February 2004); Sarah Staveteig and Alyssa Wigton, 'Racial and ethnic disparities: key findings from the national survey of America's families' (Washington DC: The Urban Institute, February 2000). Interest in the case of Somali migrants in Maine was stimulated by Michael Powell, 'A Maine town's immigrant blues', *The Washington Post National Weekly Edition*, 28 October–3 November, 2002, p. 31; and William Finnegan, 'The Somalis of Lewiston', *New Yorker*, 11 December 2006, pp. 46–58. Jessie Ellison's article in *Newsweek* (26 January 2009), 'The refugees who saved Lewiston', as well as many responses, can be found at http://www.newsweek.com/id/180035.

More general background came from Philip Davies, David Ryan, David Brown and Ron Mendel, *The History Atlas of North America* (New York: Macmillan, 1998), and Kenneth Morgan, *Slavery and Servitude in North America, 1607–1800* (Edinburgh: Edinburgh University Press, 2000).

References

Ellison, J. (2009) 'The refugees who saved Lewiston', *Newsweek*, 26 January.

Part 3
The representative process

The importance of political representation has been stressed throughout American history. The rallying cry of the American revolutionaries in 1776 was 'No taxation without representation'. When Abraham Lincoln sought to justify the bloodshed of the Civil War and the preservation of the Union in his Gettysburg Address of 1863, he spoke of preserving 'government of the people, by the people and for the people'. Even the most casual observer of American politics cannot fail to notice the pronounced populism of both political practice and rhetoric in the United States. In Part 3, we examine the detailed attention paid by the framers of the Constitution to notions of popular representation and the modes of election designed to give them effect. In analysing American elections today, we examine how voters respond at the polls and why. Particular attention is paid to the role of the media, especially television, and its power and influence over the conduct and outcome of elections. We also examine the spontaneous growth and development of other institutions of political representation, especially parties and interest groups. Throughout Part 3, we will be addressing the major criticism aimed at American elections today: for all the rhetoric, do they actually deliver on the promise of representative democracy?

Contents

Chapter 8

Elections and voting behaviour

This chapter begins with an examination of the complex arrangements made by the framers of the Constitution for the election of the president and members of Congress. We shall see how these arrangements have changed over time and how they translate into political practice in the modern day. We then turn to an analysis of how American voters respond to election campaigns.

The constitutional framework of elections

The Constitution of 1787 was founded upon the principle of popular sovereignty, the notion that government ultimately derives its authority from the consent of the people. This did not mean, however, that the framers were committed to democracy as we understand it today. Whilst they favoured a *republic*, they were opposed to creating a *democracy*, which many of them equated with mob rule. The constitutional framework for elections, therefore, attempted to blend the principle of popular sovereignty with a desire to restrict the power of the people to actually govern the country.

You are already familiar with the idea that the Constitution's 'separation of powers' and 'checks and balances' were intended as anti-majoritarian devices. To reinforce these restraints on democracy yet further, the framers decided that separate institutions would be elected by separate constituencies, operating separate electoral procedures. In other words, the president, the Senate and the House of Representatives would be chosen in different ways, by different people and at different times. Rival institutions would thus check each other by representing the interests of rival constituencies.

The House of Representatives

The House was intended to be the popular, democratic institution of the federal government. Consequently, its members would be kept close to the people in the following ways:

1. By being directly elected by the voters.
2. By frequent elections – every two years.
3. By representing relatively small, local constituencies, apportioned by population.

Originally, the Constitution envisaged the House containing one representative for every 30,000 people. The subsequent growth in population, however, has made this apportionment redundant: on the basis of the US Census Bureau's assessment that the nation's population reached a figure of over 308 million in 2010, constituencies of 30,000 would create a House with 10,292 representatives. Congress has therefore fixed the number of representatives at 435 and growth in population simply means that the size of House constituencies, or *districts*, increases accordingly. Today, the average population of a House district approaches 700,000 persons.

Apportionment by population means that some states send many more members to the House of Representatives than others. Every state is entitled to at least one representative, and this is the case with Wyoming (population 564,000) and Vermont (population 626,000), for example. The largest states fare much better: California (population 37,254,000) has 53 representatives and Illinois (population 12,831,000) has 18. Population change varies between states, and some shifts in the distribution of House seats take place after the results of each census are confirmed.

Members of the House, however, are not intended primarily to represent state interests, but rather the interests of their district – and these can vary considerably, even within the same state. For example, the New York inner-city voters of Harlem have very different needs and concerns from rural constituents in upper New York state.

Members of the House, both individually and collectively, are obliged to keep in close touch with constituency opinion by virtue of serving for only two years before facing re-election. With such a short period between elections, voters are unlikely to forgive or forget any representative who has seriously offended public opinion on a salient issue. As a result, representatives keep in constant touch with constituency opinion by, for example, making frequent trips back home from Washington and conducting polls in their district on major issues.

Some critics argue that two-year terms make representatives virtual 'slaves' to public opinion and have advocated replacing them with four-year terms. They also argue that it means that representatives spend too much of their time on electioneering in one form or another, and too little of their time on government duties. Whatever the merits of these criticisms, however, the present system does help fulfil the framers' aim of subjecting the House of Representatives to more popular influence than any other branch of the federal government.

The Senate

The representative functions of the Senate were intended to be significantly different from those of the House. First, instead of representing the voters per se, the Senate was to represent the states. As such, every state is entitled to two senators, regardless of population. Thus, while we saw above that Wyoming has one representative and California 53, both these states have two senators. This system was a concession to the least-populous states, who feared being swamped in the national legislature by the largest states. In line with this representative function, senators are elected by the voters of the whole state.

The second major representative difference is that, whereas the House was designed to be the popular chamber, the Senate was designed to be a more 'aristocratic' chamber which checked the popular will. In fact, as many historians have pointed out, the framers thought of the Senate's relationship to the House as somewhat similar to that between the British House of Lords and House of Commons. In line with this aristocratic bent, senators were not originally to be elected directly by the voters. Instead, the legislatures of the states would each decide for themselves how to elect or appoint US senators. At quite an early stage, the states began to introduce elections to advise this appointment system, but it formally remained in operation until replaced by the Seventeenth Amendment, ratified in 1913, which instituted the direct election of senators by the voters.

The Constitution further distances senators from popular control by giving them a six-year term of office. This enables senators to take a more long-term and independent view of issues than representatives. If a senator goes against his or her constituents' views on an issue, the chances are that, by the time the next elections come around, the voters' memories will have faded and their political passions cooled.

Nevertheless, the framers established yet another device that protects the Senate as a whole from the popular political pressures of the moment: *staggered elections*. While all senators serve six-year terms, they are not all elected at the same time: one-third of senators come up for re-election every two years. This means that, even if a ferocious political wind should blow in any election year, fully two-thirds of the senators will be electorally unaffected by it. While the House can change direction radically as a result of one year's election results, the Senate is much more resistant to sudden change – hence, its ability to act as a brake upon the House.

The presidency

The president and the vice-president are the only politicians in the United States who are elected by a national constituency. Logically enough, then, they were intended primarily to advocate and represent the national interest, as opposed to state interests (Senate) or local interests (House of Representatives).

Just as the presidency's representative function is different from those of the Senate and House, so too are its terms of office and its mode of election. The president serves a four-year term and, since the passage of the Twenty-second Amendment in 1951, is restricted by the Constitution to a maximum of two terms of office. In fact, however, the very first president, George Washington, had established the custom of not seeking a third term and the Constitution was only amended in the wake of Franklin D. Roosevelt's break with this precedent. The fear which lies behind the two-term limit is of a president who can combine executive power with personal electoral popularity and thereby gain unhealthy control over the rest of the political system.

As a result of the different terms of office for president, Senate and House, it takes four years and three successive elections to complete a full electoral cycle for the federal government.

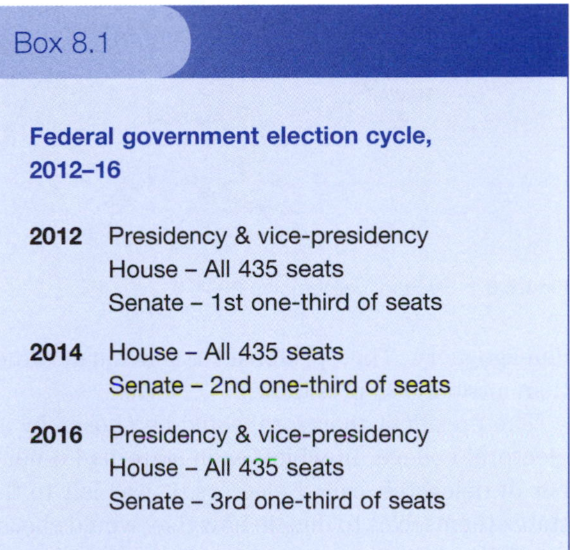
Box 8.1

Federal government election cycle, 2012–16

2012	Presidency & vice-presidency House – All 435 seats Senate – 1st one-third of seats
2014	House – All 435 seats Senate – 2nd one-third of seats
2016	Presidency & vice-presidency House – All 435 seats Senate – 3rd one-third of seats

The electoral college

The method of electing the president is again different from anything else. The first thing to note is that Article II, Section 1(ii) of the Constitution established an indirect method of election, once again taking the direct choice of president out of the hands of the ordinary voters. The framers had several reasons for this. First, the least populous states feared that the most populous would always supply the president. Secondly, the framers did not believe that, in such a large country, the ordinary people would have sufficient knowledge of the qualities of presidential candidates. Thirdly, the framers were wary of too much popular control over the choice of president, fearing that this would encourage

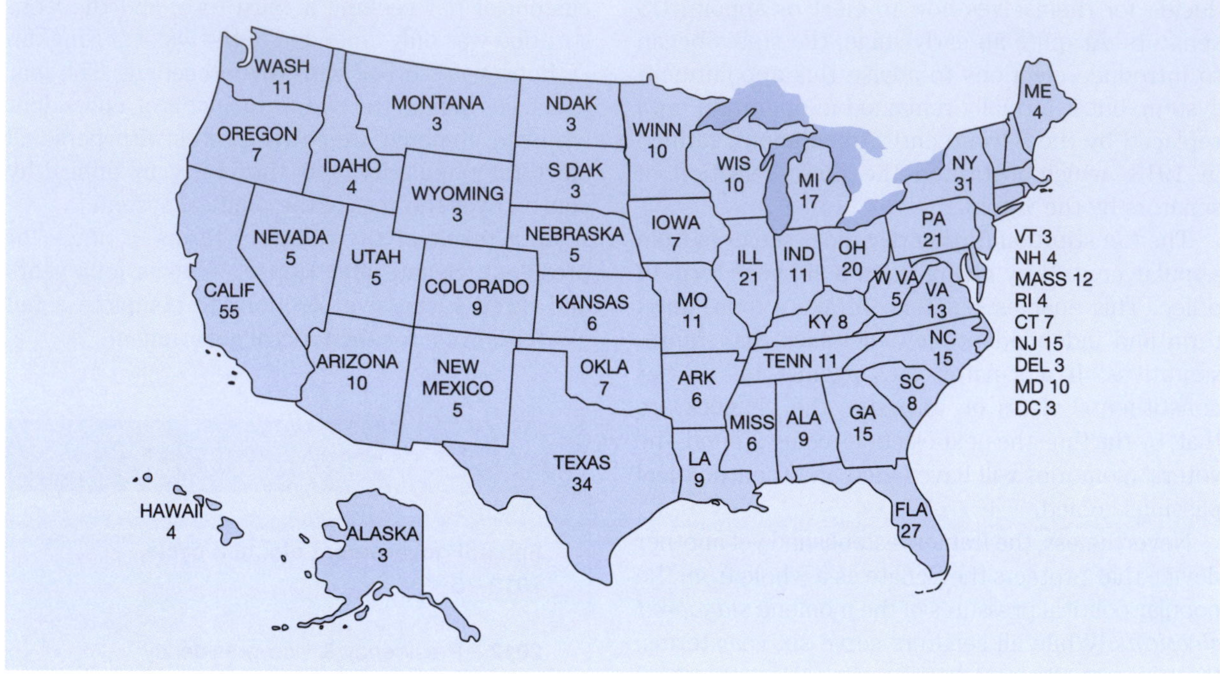

Figure 8.1 Electoral college map 2004–8.

Source: www.electoral-vote.com

demagoguery. They preferred a statesman rather than a tribune as president.

The president therefore would be chosen by an electoral college, in which each state had a number of delegates, called electors. It was left to the states themselves to decide how they would choose their electors. Originally, most state legislatures simply appointed them, but the practice quickly developed of holding some kind of popular vote on the question. By 1832, only South Carolina did not permit a popular vote. Even so, electors were not bound to vote for any particular candidate in the electoral college; rather, they were supposed to use their wisdom and experience to select the best potential president. Today, however, with the exception of the odd maverick, electors cast their vote for the candidate who has won the popular election in their state.

Electoral college arithmetic

The number of electors for each state is fixed by adding the number of its representatives to the number of its senators. To calculate the number of electors from any state, then, is easy. For example, as we saw above, Illinois has two senators, like every other state, and 18 members in the House. Therefore the number of delegates in the electoral college from Illinois is 20. Wyoming, one of the least populous states, with just one representative, has three votes in the electoral college; and California, the most populous, has 53 representatives and therefore 55 electoral college votes.

The total number of electors in the electoral college, then, is equal to the number of representatives and senators in the Congress, plus three from the federal District of Columbia: that is, 538 altogether.

Any presidential candidate must win over half the electoral college votes and therefore the minimum number required for victory is 270.

Electoral strategy

In an important sense, the American presidential election is not just one single election but rather

51 separate elections in the states and the District of Columbia. What determines victory is not the percentage of votes won in the national popular ballot, but the number of electoral college votes obtained by winning the elections in the states. For example, a candidate who takes California by a single popular vote bags all its 55 electoral college votes. The same candidate then loses, say, Illinois (20 electoral college votes) by 1,000,001 popular votes. Although he is now 1 million down on his opponent in the national popular vote, he is nevertheless ahead 55–20 in the vote that counts, the electoral college vote.

It is thus not necessary to win 50 per cent of the *popular* vote in order to win the presidency. In 1996, Bill Clinton's re-election was the sixteenth race in which the person to become president of the USA failed to reach the 50 per cent mark. Indeed, on four occasions, most recently in 2000, it has not even proved necessary to win more of the popular vote than one's chief opponent. Of the two-party vote, George W. Bush won 49.7 per cent, compared with 50.3 per cent for Al Gore: yet despite winning more than half a million more popular votes than Bush, Gore lost the electoral college battle by four votes, 267–271.

Table 8.1 Minority presidents

Percentage of popular vote	President	Year of election
49.72	Kennedy	1960
49.54	Polk	1844
49.52	Truman	1948
49.24	Wilson	1916
48.50	Cleveland	1884
48.27	Garfield	1880
48.14	Bush[a]	2000
47.95	Hayes[a]	1876
47.82	Harrison[a]	1888
47.28	Taylor	1848
46.05	Cleveland	1892
45.28	Buchanan	1856
43.42	Nixon	1968
43.29	Clinton	1992
41.84	Wilson	1912
39.82	Lincoln	1860
30.92	Adams[a]	1824

[a] Fewer popular votes than main opponent
Source: *National Journal*, 5 November 1992, p. A40; figures for 2000 calculated from Pomper *et al.*, 2001, pp. 133–4

Moreover, even where a candidate wins both the popular vote and the electoral college vote, the margin of victory in the latter is often a gross

Table 8.2 Distortion of winning popular vote margin by the electoral college system since 1960

Winner	Year	States won	Percentage of popular vote[a]	Electoral college votes	Percentage of electoral college
Kennedy	1960	27	50	303	56
Johnson	1964	44	61	484	90
Nixon	1968	32	43	301	56
Nixon	1972	37	61	520	97
Carter	1976	26	50	297	55
Reagan	1980	44	51	489	91
Reagan	1984	49	59	525	98
Bush	1988	40	53	426	79
Clinton	1992	32	43	370	69
Clinton	1996	31	50	379	70
Bush	2000	30	48	271	50
Bush	2004	31	51	286	53
Obama	2008	28[b]	53	365	68

[a] Figures are rounded; [b] The District of Columbia has consistently voted Democratic since it first had 3 electoral college votes in the election of 1964. In 2008 Nebraska for the first time split its electoral college votes, giving one to Obama, four to McCain.
Sources: Adapted from *National Journal*, 5 November 1992, p. A40; Pomper *et al.*, 1997, pp. 176–8; Pomper *et al.*, 2001, p. 134; www.cnn.com

Table 8.3 Third party candidates in recent elections

Candidate	Year	Party	Percentage of popular vote	Electoral college	Percentage of electoral college
Ralph Nader	2008	Independent	0.56	0	0
Ralph Nader	2004	Independent	0.35	0	0
Ralph Nader	2000	Green Party	2.7	0	0
Ross Perot	1996	Reform	8.5	0	0
Ross Perot	1992	None	19	0	0
John Anderson	1980	National Unity	6	0	0
George Wallace	1968	American Independent	13	46	8

Sources: Adapted from *National Journal*, 5 November 1992, p. A40; Pomper *et al.*, 1997, p. 178; Pomper *et al.*, 2001, p. 133; Federal Election Commission report of results available at http://www.fec.gov/pubrec/fe2008/2008presgeresults.pdf

distortion of the former. Thus, a candidate who appears to have won a landslide in the electoral college may only have won the popular vote by a relatively narrow margin.

Thus, it can be seen that, in 1988, George H. Bush took just over half the popular votes, but because he won the contests in 40 states he took nearly four-fifths of the electoral college vote. In 1992, Bill Clinton took only just over two-fifths of the popular vote, but more than two-thirds of the electoral college vote. It is important to bear this in mind when considering how much of a mandate a winning presidential candidate can claim.

Presidential candidates must therefore adopt the electoral strategy of winning states, rather than the national popular vote per se – and, of course, they must seek above all to win the states with the most electoral college votes. In theory, a candidate could win the presidency by carrying just the 11 largest states, including California, New York, Illinois, Texas and Florida. In practice, such a clean sweep of the big states is achieved only in the greatest of landslides. Bill Clinton, for example, had to carry the twentieth-largest state before he secured victory in 1992. In 1996, however, he needed victory in only 14 states to garner enough votes to win re-election. In 2000, Al Gore carried only 20 states, plus the District of Columbia. However, because his victories included six of the nine largest states, he came within a whisker of winning the presidency. Barack Obama did well in the large states in 2008, and the largest 13 of the states he won would have given him victory in the electoral college.

Third-party candidates

The electoral college, combined with the simple majority voting system in nearly all states (first past the post, winner takes all), not only exaggerates the mandate of the victorious candidate, it seriously disadvantages any third-party candidate. In 1992, for example, Ross Perot took almost 19 per cent of the national popular vote, yet because he failed to come first in any state, he received no electoral college votes at all. Other third-party candidates have fared little better.

The difference between Ross Perot in 1992 and George Wallace in 1968 was that, although Perot had broader appeal nationally, Wallace had a strong base in the South which enabled him actually to win some states.

Strong third-party candidates, however, pose a significant potential problem under the electoral college. If the contest between the Democratic and Republican candidates is close, then a third candidate with some electoral college votes could hold the balance of power. The framers of the Constitution did anticipate this and they provided that, where no candidate has a majority of electoral college votes, the election shall be decided in the House of Representatives. For this purpose only, however, each state delegation in the House, rather than each representative, is entitled to one vote. Although this mechanism has not been invoked for over a century, the mere possibility that a 'maverick' candidacy could throw the electoral process into confusion generates periodic calls for the reform of the electoral college system. Until a crisis actually materialises, however, nothing is likely to be done. Meanwhile, the United States continues with this arcane method of choosing its president.

Presidential nominations

The presidential election itself always takes place on the Tuesday after the first Monday in November, but the campaign for the presidency begins long before that. The first task of anyone seeking the presidency is to secure the nomination of one of the major political parties. Both the Democratic and Republican parties hold a *nominating convention* in the summer prior to the November election. The delegates at these conventions choose who shall be the party's nominee for the November general election. For the candidates, then, the goal is to ensure that a majority of the convention delegates are committed to support them. This is achieved by winning votes in pre-convention elections.

The primary campaign

There are two methods prevalent today for selecting convention delegates: the *primary election* and the *caucus election*. The rules governing these elections vary somewhat between states and between the Democratic and Republican parties, but the broad outlines are as follows. In the period between February and June of election year, each state holds either a primary or a caucus election for each of the parties. Since 1968, more and more states have opted to hold primaries, mainly because these elections make it easier to meet the technical rules governing issues such as the gender and racial composition of state delegations to the convention. Whereas in 1968 there were just 17 primaries, in 2008 the Democrats held caucuses in only 13 states, including in Texas, where the unique 'Texas two-step' involved a combination of caucus and primary selection processes. The Republicans use a more varied range of selection processes, but the domination of primary elections is no less evident.

In a primary election, participants simply enter the polling booth and cast their vote for the delegate or presidential candidate of their choice. Caucuses are more time-consuming. Voters physically gather in rooms and may spend several hours determining whom they will support. Caucuses may also be part of a more complex system, with voters indicating their preferences between potential nominees, but simultaneously electing delegates to other meetings and conventions who will make the final choice.

Both primaries and caucuses may be either 'closed' or 'open'. If it is 'closed', then only those voters officially registered as Democrats may vote in the Democratic primary or caucus, and the same for the Republicans. If the election is open, however, officially registered independents, or even members of the other party, may opt to vote in either the Democratic or Republican choice.

The number of convention delegates from each state is not purely a function of its population or even size of electorate. Rather, it depends to a significant degree on the number of those who voted for the party in recent elections. As a result, the number of delegates from a state is different for the Democratic and Republican conventions. Nevertheless, it is still the most populous states that send the most delegates to the convention, so, as in the November election, candidates must try to win primaries and caucuses in the larger states.

Although candidates will not campaign hard in every state primary, serious contenders will try to collect a winning number of delegates to take to the convention. This means that the campaign must be planned well before the first primaries and caucuses take place. This has become even more true of recent elections, because of the tendency towards 'frontloading' the primaries and caucuses. Traditionally, the presidential selection season opens formally with the first primary, in New Hampshire, and the first caucus, in Iowa. As a result of being the 'starting gates' for the race to the White House these two states have gained enormous media attention, and there has been a sense that these and other states featuring early in the process have also gained in political significance. Other states have been tempted to move their primaries and caucuses earlier in the primary season to catch some of this attention, and the phenomenon of 'frontloading' has resulted.

The impact of frontloading is debatable. Some believe it favours candidates who are already well known and those who can raise very large campaign funds in the pre-primary season. Others believe it enables a relatively unknown candidate to make a dramatic breakthrough and leave the front-runner without sufficient time to recover. Aspects of recent campaigns appear to support the former theory. In 1996, the millionaire businessman Steve Forbes and the combative populist Pat Buchanan did steal an early march on Bob Dole, the front-runner. Yet Dole's bedrock support among party stalwarts, and the huge campaign chest he had been able to amass, saw him overcome his initial setbacks and move decisively ahead by the beginning of March. Similarly in 2000, George W. Bush was able to recover from an early defeat in New Hampshire thanks to a superiority in campaign funds and support among the party establishment. In the 2004 Democratic race, Vermont Governor Howard Dean went into the Iowa caucuses as the front-runner. However, Iowa was taken by Massachusetts Senator John Kerry and Dean never had time to recover. Kerry had effectively sewn up the nomination by 3 March when his leading opponent (and soon-to-be vice-presidential candidate), John Edwards, withdrew from the race. Dean lacked the party establishment support that Dole and Bush had enjoyed in 1996 and 2000, and the highly condensed primary format of 2004 gave him too little time to rebuild his candidacy.

In 2008, so many states wished to have an early place in the process that Iowa moved its caucus to 3 January and there was very significant action right from the start. The presidential primary season provides a hard test for any campaign organisation, and the field of candidates tends to reduce as the weaker campaigns run out of resources. In 2008, Joe Biden and Chris Dodd pulled out of the Democratic race for the presidency immediately after the first caucus, and the trail was littered with expired candidacies from that point. There were expectations that the senator from New York and former First Lady, Hillary Clinton, would be the Democrat front-runner, albeit hampered by controversies that dogged the Clinton presidency. Senator Clinton's second-place finish in Iowa behind the 'freshman' US senator from Illinois, Barack Obama, came as a shock to her campaign. The Obama camp, which in the run-up to the election had already proved itself a surprisingly successful operation, gained publicity, and a substantial fund-raising boost, from its success. The Clinton campaign regrouped and went on to a slim victory in the 8 January New Hampshire primary, followed by Obama wins in Nevada and South Carolina later in the month. John Edwards remained in the race briefly, but it rapidly became clear that he was firmly in third place. This campaign's 'Super Tuesday' came on 5 February, when 23 states and districts held their primaries and caucuses. Obama took 13 of these and Clinton won 10, indicating that the Democrats were hosting a tough two-horse contest. However, Obama came out of the first stage of the primary season with a small lead over Clinton and, while Clinton had significant state victories through the spring, Obama always remained slightly in the lead. It was not clear until the final primaries on 3 June, and with super delegates increasingly declaring their voting intentions, that Obama would take the nomination at the Democratic National Convention. After the tightly fought Democratic party primary race, Hillary Clinton conceded the nomination to Obama in early June 2008.

There was no clear front-runner in the Republican camp as the primary season opened. John McCain had been thought the strongest in 2007, but his campaign appeared to falter as the formal stage began. Iowa was not natural territory for McCain, and his camp had carefully reduced any expectation of him featuring there at all, so that his 12 per cent of the vote seemed quite a reasonable result. Mike Huckabee came first in the Republican race in Iowa, supported by a strong conservative and Christian fundamentalist vote that would be unlikely to propel him to the nomination or to general election victory. McCain won in New Hampshire, then a third Republican hopeful, Mitt Romney, took a couple of states. Rudy Giuliani never recovered from delaying his formal entry into the race until after these initial contests, and the three other leaders, McCain, Huckabee and Romney, looked set for a long season of contests. However, while Super Tuesday gave victories to all three, it indicated broadest support for McCain. He may not have been most liked by a majority of Republican voters, but he appeared to incite less negative reaction than either of the others, and Republicans seemed ready to compromise on him as a candidate whom they thought might win the election, even in an unpromising year for Republicans. Romney withdrew from the contest on 9 February and Huckabee followed suit on 4 March, leaving the nomination open for Senator McCain.

Frontloading did not reduce the length of the battle for the Democratic presidential nomination in 2008. Two evenly matched and very well-funded candidates fought a gruelling campaign through the long schedule of primaries and caucuses. The Republican nomination race was over more quickly as a larger field of candidates, which looked capable of engaging in a long and brutal campaign, was in fact winnowed fairly quickly to one acceptable nominee. Whichever theory is correct, frontloading has one undeniable effect: it means that the unofficial campaign for the presidency must begin earlier than ever.

Advantages and disadvantages of the primary system

Primaries were introduced in the early twentieth century as a means of democratising the selection of presidential nominees by removing the corrupt control of the process by party bosses. Today, that democratisation can be criticised both as having gone too far and as not having gone far enough.

In regard to the former, critics argue that the elimination of party boss control has gone so far that the parties have lost almost any real say in who gets their nomination. In 1968, the Democratic party establishment was able to impose the nomination of Hubert Humphrey, the incumbent vice-president, even though he had not entered a single primary. The outcry against this led to the rule changes which encouraged more primaries and required any serious candidate for the nomination to enter at least some of them.

The results of these changes were, however, unsatisfactory to many Democrats. Candidates could now appeal directly to the voters in primaries, thus bypassing the need for support from the party establishment. This led to the nomination of candidates such as George McGovern (1972) and Jimmy Carter (1976), men who were in significant ways at odds with traditional Democratic policies. McGovern lost heavily to his Republican opponent; Carter won the presidential election but the lack of enthusiasm he generated among other Democrats, particularly in Congress, hampered his ability to govern and contributed to his defeat by Ronald Reagan in 1980.

The Democrats in particular, then, have fiddled with the rules governing primaries and nominating conventions continuously since 1968, in an attempt to produce a popular, winning nominee and a subsequently successful president. For example, the Democrats insist on a form of proportional distribution of convention delegates to reflect the votes in the states, while the Republicans are more comfortable with a 'first past the post' system giving a state's delegates to the leader in the popular vote. This difference certainly helped to extend the Democratic primary battle in 2008, and to curtail the Republican race. The Democrats also use 'super-delegates' – certain categories of elected office holders, such as governors, US senators, members of the US House of Representatives and party leaders, such as members of the Democratic National Committee, who in 2008 numbered over 800 – about 20 per cent of all delegates.

Despite these rule changes, it can be argued that the nomination process is not very democratic in practice. Most obviously, voter turnout in both primaries and caucuses is low. Caucuses, requiring people to attend a meeting at a set time and place, attract especially low turnout. Closely contested elections generally increase turnout, but in 2000 only about 15 per cent of the voting age population voted in the primaries of both major parties, with a turnout of only 4 per cent in the opening Iowa caucus (Wayne, 2001, p. 113). In 2008, the close-run Democratic race especially brought a boost in enthusiasm for the primaries and caucuses. Rhodes Cook reports that 57.7 million people turned out to vote in the primaries of both parties, and Michael McDonald's US Elections Project reports turnout figures of 16.1 per cent in the Iowa caucus, and 53.6 per cent in the opening primary in New Hampshire, though all the later caucuses had turnout lower than 10 per cent, and the other state primaries were

Box 8.2

Buchanan hijacks the 1992 Republican convention

In the 1992 Republican primary elections, the right-wing populist Pat Buchanan secured enough support to make his presence felt at the nominating convention. Not wishing to alienate Buchanan and his supporters, the victorious Bush campaign agreed to give Buchanan a prime-time speech slot. As it turned out, Buchanan's intemperate speech left the Republican party – and the Bush candidacy – tainted with extremism.

'It began with a mistake – a deal making Pat Buchanan the *de facto* keynote speaker for a slash-and-burn appeal to the hard right. . . . For four nights in Houston, it was as if the melancholy state of the union counted for little as against the scarlet sins of liberals, lesbians, gays, Democrats, feminists, Congress, Greens, trial lawyers, women who aborted babies. . . . The die had been cast with the decision, after the primaries, that Buchanan had to be appeased, that he and his brigades could wreck the convention if they were not made part of it.'

Source: *Newsweek*, 16 November 1992, p. 35

most commonly in the 20 and 30 per cent ranges. (Cook, 2008, p. 4, McDonald.)

Primary and caucus voters may include a higher proportion of committed partisans of both parties than the electorate at large, and they have certainly been known to send exceptionally partisan delegates to the national convention. The risk is that the party will find itself with a relatively extreme nominee who has pleased the activists but who alienates the more typical voter at the general election in November. This was the case with George McGovern in 1972. Even where such a radical candidate fails to win the nomination, he or she may command enough delegates to force the party towards a more extreme platform (manifesto) than it would otherwise have chosen. This happened to the Republicans in 1992.

Perhaps the greatest disadvantage of the primary system, however, is the danger of self-inflicted damage upon the party's eventual nominee. In a long and fiercely fought nomination campaign, candidates will seek not only to enhance their own image and prospects, but also to undermine those of their competitors. This can sometimes erupt into bitter conflict between candidates from the same party, bordering on political fratricide. Even incumbent presidents seeking renomination do not always emerge from this phase of the campaign unscathed. Pat Buchanan launched damaging attacks upon President Bush in 1992, just as Senator Edward Kennedy had against President Carter in the Democratic nomination struggle in 1980. In both cases, the eventual nominee was already in a weakened state by the time the 'real' campaign began in September. This experience would lead to the expectation that the long Democratic nomination campaign in 2008 might fatally wound their nominee. The campaign put a huge effort into very public reconciliation, with Hillary Clinton casting the Illinois votes to give Barack Obama the nomination at the Democratic National Convention, and both Senator and former President Clinton visible on the campaign trail for Obama in the general election campaign.

Presidential election campaigns

By custom, the general election campaign begins after the Labor Day holiday in September. The two-month campaign, however, rarely determines who shall become president, since 'for the vast majority of citizens in America, campaigns do not function so much to change minds as to reinforce previous convictions' (Polsby and Wildavsky, 1995, p. 162). Thus, candidates who trail their opponent in the opinion polls on Labor Day usually trail in the real poll on election day. The last surprise result in this respect occurred in 1948, when Harry Truman defeated Thomas Dewey against all the pundits' expectations (see Figure 8.2): but that was in the days when opinion polling was much less accurate than it is today. In 2008, Obama's slim lead in the polls on Labor Day was derailed temporarily a few days later, when the Republican National Convention and McCain's startling choice of the relatively unknown Governor Sarah Palin of Alaska as his running-mate helped give the Republican ticket a boost, but later in the month the Obama lead was re-established and carried through to election day. In close elections, the final weeks of the campaign may be important,

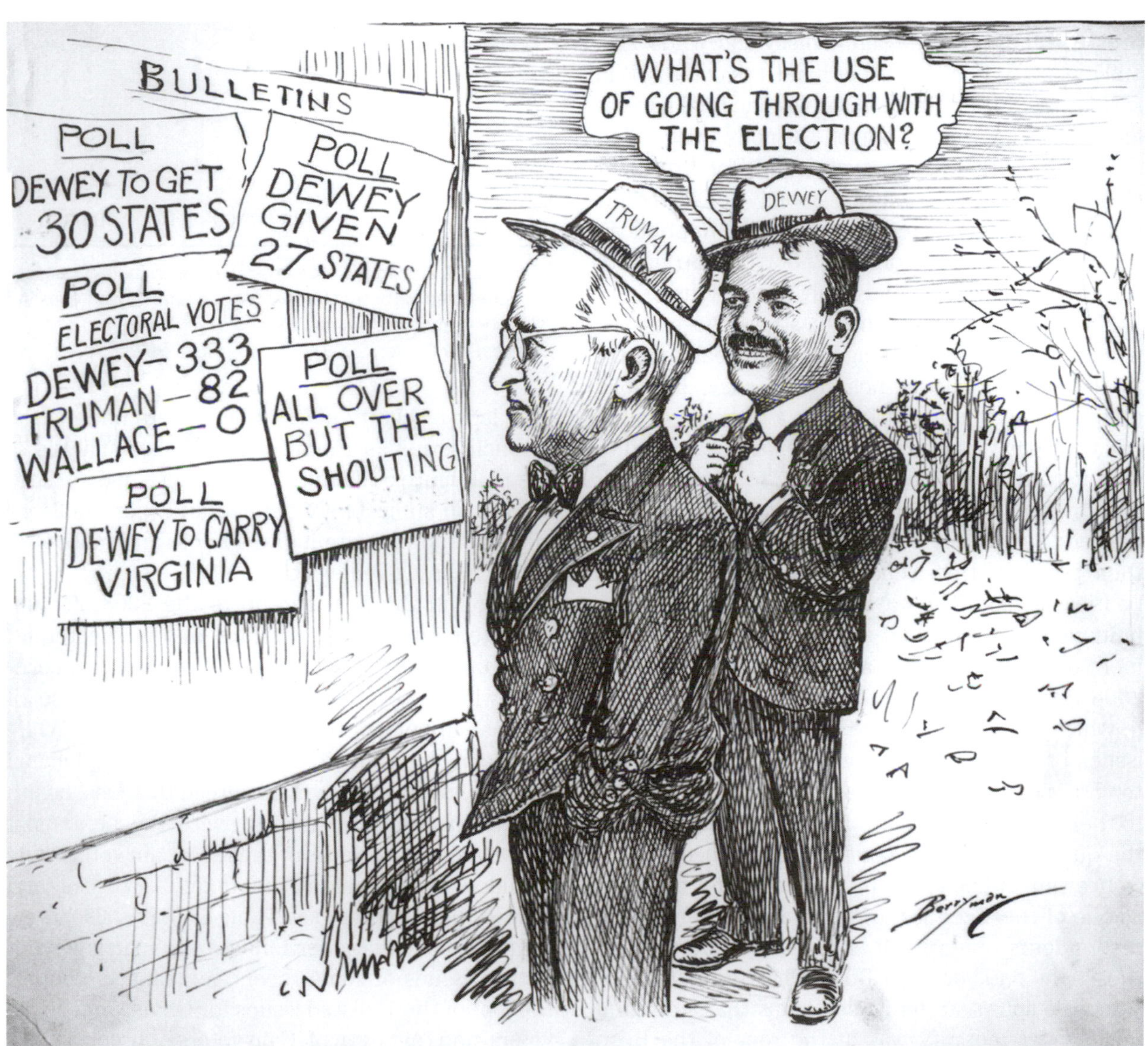

Figure 8.2 In 1948 the polls gave Truman no chance of winning re-election, but he pulled off the greatest surprise in the history of presidential elections. Source: From the US Senate Collection, Center for Legislative Archives

since even a very small switch of voter allegiance can make a difference.

The fact is, then, that most people have already made up their minds by Labor Day. While the campaign is by no means irrelevant, it is rarely decisive. This is not surprising once we appreciate that Americans engage in what is sometimes called *retrospective voting*. This means simply that the election tends to be a referendum on the past four years. If the nation has experienced both peace and economic prosperity, the party currently in power is likely to be re-elected, especially if an incumbent president is standing again (Polsby and Wildavsky, 1995, p. 166). If, on the other hand, the country is in serious trouble at home or abroad, the rival party is likely to win. Even though he was not on the ballot, the historically low approval ratings for President George W. Bush were a real liability for his fellow Republican John McCain, and the Republican nominee put a good deal of effort into trying to distance himself from the Bush White House.

The candidates try hard to stress those issues which are both on their agenda and really matter to the voters. This is not always easy. If public opinion at that moment leans in a direction that is not your party's natural territory, then it is hard to shift position and simultaneously to remain credible. In fact, most political leaders prefer to work harder to convince the electorate of the value of their positions than bend so freely to the whim of political fashion. The way questions are put can also influence the response, and therefore the assessment of the weight to attach to particular issues. A 2008 Pew Research Center survey compared polls in which voters were asked to choose from a list of issues presented to them with one which left it up to voters to volunteer the issue that mattered most to them. As can be seen from Table 8.4, the form of the question makes a significant difference.

In a similar 2004 poll, 'moral values' was included as one of the 'fixed list' options, and 27 per cent of respondents opted for it, including 44 per cent of those who had voted for Bush. This prompted considerable soul-searching and claims that a cultural divide over morality was at the root of the Bush victory. The unprompted figure was 14 per cent, which is much more in line with the 2008 figure.

Table 8.4 Voters and issues in the 2008 election

	What mattered most in your vote?	
	Fixed List* %	**Open-end**** %
The economy	58	35
War in Iraq	10	5
Terrorism	8	6
Health care	8	4
Energy policy	6	–
Other	8	43
Candidate mentions	–	9
Moral values/social issues^	–	7
Taxes/distribution of income	–	7
Other issues	–	5
Other political mentions	–	3
Change	–	3
Other	–	9
Don't know	2	7
	100	100

* First choice among the six items provided on the exit poll list
** Unprompted verbatim first response to open-ended question
^ Including abortion, gay marriage
Source: Pew Center, 2008

This lack of clarity about what voters understand by such terms as 'moral values' makes analysis of the poll figures difficult. Nevertheless, most issues are not so subjectively defined and these polls do yield an approximate indication of what motivated voters in any given election.

A poll in the final run-up to the 2008 election indicated interesting divisions in the electorate. Importantly for both campaigns, the issues concerning swing voters matched more closely those of Obama supporters than McCain supporters. While the economy ranked top for all groups, Obama supporters and swing voters agreed that jobs, health care, education and energy were the next most important issues, while of these McCain voters only included energy, alongside taxes, terrorism and Iraq, in their top five (see Table 8.5). It is also interesting to note that abortion and gay marriage, 'hot button' issues of some recent campaigns, stood at the foot of the 13 listed issues for Obama and swing voters, and that even McCain voters only considered one issue of lower significance. The position of the environment at the bottom of the McCain voters'

Table 8.5 Differences over the issues that matter

Voting priorities		
Certain McCain* %	**Certain Obama*** %	**Swing voters*** %
85 Economy	94 Economy	94 Economy
81 Taxes	88 Health care	85 Jobs
79 Terrorism	84 Jobs	79 Health care
76 Energy	82 Education	79 Education
72 Iraq	79 Energy	77 Energy
72 Jobs	73 Iraq	73 Taxes
62 Immigration	69 Environment	70 Terrorism
60 Health care	63 Taxes	68 Iraq
59 Education	59 Terrorism	60 Environment
49 Trade policy	51 Trade policy	48 Immigration
48 Abortion	39 Immigration	47 Trade policy
41 Gay marriage	38 Abortion	39 Abortion
36 Environment	22 Gay marriage	20 Gay marriage
N = 454	549	297

* Percent ranking each issue as very important to their vote.
Source: Pew Center, 2008

priority list is another indicator of the distance in 2008 between many Republicans and the mainstream position of America's voters. The low position of the 'moral values' issues does not mean that these are about to disappear from the agenda. The context changes the salience of issues to voters, and the significant minority of people who consider them very important would be the cadre of any campaign that had the opportunity to bring them back to the fore.

Usually, the state of the economy is the most important single factor in elections. For all his foreign policy problems in 1980, the main cause of President Carter's defeat was dissatisfaction with the economy. The importance of the economic issue was again clearly illustrated in 1992 when, despite a wide perception of his foreign policy record as excellent, President Bush was defeated by an equally wide perception that the economy was stagnant and unlikely to improve under his guidance. His opponent, Bill Clinton, had learned the lesson of past elections. In order to ensure that his campaign team never lost sight of the issue that could bring him victory, he had a sign prominently displayed at campaign headquarters which said simply, 'It's the economy, stupid!'

Certainly, the economy emerged as a critical issue in 2008. It was not the only issue, and its significance grew in the later stages of the campaign. With the retrospective vision that is common to most voters, the issues of the Bush administration's mismanagement of its domestic and foreign policy portfolio were seen as paramount. The memory of the administration's delayed and stumbling response in 2005 to Hurricane Katrina cannot be said to have gone away, and concerns over the consequences of the invasion of Iraq had increased. Furthermore, American voters have adopted the habit of changing the party in the White House very regularly. It may once have been common for incumbent presidential parties to have an advantage in elections, but that time has long passed. Since the election of President Eisenhower in 1952, only once has the same political party held the White House for more than eight years. With approval of the Bush administration at an all-time low, the Republican campaign for John McCain could hardly expect to buck that trend. A banking crisis of historic proportions eliminated whatever chances the Republican campaign may have had.

There were indications of growing financial instability in summer 2008, but in September the bankruptcy of Lehmann Brothers, the need for rapid and massive emergency government intervention to protect other financial institutions, and the startling fall in the value of the Stock Market sharpened the focus on financial and economic matters. Throughout the campaign, John McCain had appeared less confident with economic matters than on other, notably foreign policy-related, issues, and polls recorded that Obama consistently inspired more confidence that he could handle the economic situation better than his opponent. As this issue became more salient, overshadowing areas such as terrorism and defence, where McCain's experience resonated with the electorate, so Obama's attraction waxed, and McCain's waned.

McCain's reaction to the economic crisis also managed to associate him more closely with the Bush administration. He spoke on the health of the economy while the evidence of its decline was growing. When its critical state became obvious, he sought to suspend the campaign and rushed to

Washington in an ill-judged move that only served to demonstrate his impotence with regard to this issue. Meanwhile, Governor Palin may have proved attractive to the conservatives in the party, but was not standing up well to the rigours of a national campaign, casting further doubt on McCain's judgement.

If the economy provides the main issue context of presidential elections, that does not mean that other issues are irrelevant. As noted above, foreign policy has sometimes been very important to the outcome of elections, and it was certainly significant in 2008, especially in the Democratic primaries, where Obama's long-term opposition to the war in Iraq was contrasted to Clinton's support for President Bush's initiative. Since 1968, a cluster of issues – sometimes referred to simply as 'the social issue' or 'values' – has been of continuing, though variable influence. The social issue brings into electoral play attitudes on matters such as abortion, affirmative action for racial minorities and women, the death penalty, gay rights, and the place of religion in public life.

Beyond the policy issues that determine the outcome of presidential elections, there is also the matter of the personal characteristics of the candidates. We should not be surprised that personal character is important in presidential elections, since the voters are choosing an individual, rather than a party. The president, moreover, represents the nation as 'head of state', as well as being expected to provide able political leadership.

Precisely how much influence personal character has in elections is difficult to assess. Some presidential candidates, such as Ronald Reagan, are so well liked by a majority of voters that they are forgiven for unpopular policies. Reagan was dubbed 'the Teflon president', because the public seemed

Figure 8.3 Presidential candidates can achieve star quality, and the chance to meet them inspires enthusiasm among their followers.

Source: © Eyevine

unwilling to attach blame to him for his administration's faults. George H. Bush, on the other hand, won in 1988 and lost in 1992 without his character being of major importance in either election, while Bill Clinton, although not particularly well liked in 1996, was more popular than his opponent, Bob Dole (Pomper *et al.*, 1997, p. 193).

In 2000, on the other hand, Al Gore not only failed to benefit from the economic issue, he also suffered from the character flaws the public perceived in President Clinton. While Clinton was widely regarded as an able president, in the wake of the Lewinsky and other scandals, his morality was less respected. This could not help but tarnish his Democrat successor and create a mood for change.

In 2004, the Bush campaign damaged his Democratic opponent by attacking his character and leadership qualities. Although George W. Bush had avoided service in the Vietnam War and John Kerry was a decorated veteran of that war, the Bush campaign and its allies alleged that Kerry's military record was exaggerated, even untruthful. Kerry was also hurt by being portrayed as someone who flip-flopped on various issues, including the war in Iraq.

In 2008, both McCain and Obama were generally seen as characters of moral integrity. This campaign year was unusual in that neither a previous president nor vice-president was standing for election. The public had a lengthy period over which to develop its image of the contenders, one of whom was very little known previously, while the other had achieved limited visibility. Some of McCain's attraction, especially in a year when his own party's president was performing so poorly in the polls, was his reputation as a maverick, not necessarily bound by traditional political expectations. However, there is a point where maverick behaviour shifts from endearing to worrying, and some of McCain's decisions in the campaign brought him close to that line – for example, his indecision over whether or not to accept government funding for his primary campaign under a law that he had steered through Congress; his attempt to suspend the campaign and the presidential debates in the wake of the Lehman bankruptcy; his choice of Sarah Palin as his running mate. The advantage that McCain had through much of the campaign in being seen as the stronger leader had effectively been wiped out by October, while only two-thirds as many felt that McCain had 'a clear plan for solving the country's problems' as had the same expectation of Obama (Gallup). Obama's message that he embodied a more dramatic and more reliable hope for change than did McCain resonated more strongly with the electorate.

In short, while any presidential election may have distinctive features, voters are usually mostly concerned with the economy and associated issues, and with the character of the candidates they must choose from.

Congressional elections

Divided government in modern America

When the framers of the Constitution opted for different procedures for electing the president, the House of Representatives and the Senate, they created the possibility of divided party control of the federal government. In other words, in today's terms, it is possible for the Republicans to control the presidency but for the Democrats to control the Congress, and vice versa. This clearly presents problems of governance, since the president is expected to provide policy *leadership*, but only the Congress can actually *pass* the legislation necessary to implement his policies.

Despite the obvious problems created by divided government, this situation has become the rule rather than the exception in contemporary America. Even when the president's party controls both chambers of Congress, the narrow majorities it enjoys there may make party government difficult.

Two things stand out in Table 8.6. First, out of the 26 elections involved, 11 resulted in fully divided control of the presidency and the Congress. On a further three occasions under President Reagan, and one under Obama, one chamber of the Congress was controlled by the non-presidential party. Divided government is thus very much a political reality in the United States. President George W. Bush first had Republican control in the Senate and then

Table 8.6 Divided party control of the federal government, 1960–2010

Election year[a]	President	Senate majority	House majority
1960	**Kennedy (Dem.)**	**Dem.**	**Dem.**
1962		Dem.	Dem.
1964	**Johnson (Dem.)**	**Dem.**	**Dem.**
1966		Dem.	Dem.
1968	**Nixon (Rep.)**	**Dem.**	**Dem.**
1970		Dem.	Dem.
1972	**Nixon (Rep.)**	**Dem.**	**Dem.**
1974	Ford (Rep.)[b]	Dem.	Dem.
1976	**Carter (Dem.)**	**Dem.**	**Dem.**
1978		Dem.	Dem.
1980	**Reagan (Rep.)**	**Rep.**	**Dem.**
1982		Rep.	Dem.
1984	**Reagan (Rep.)**	**Rep.**	**Dem**
1986		Dem.	Dem.
1988	**Bush (Rep.)**	**Dem.**	**Dem**
1990		Dem.	Dem.
1992	**Clinton (Dem.)**	**Dem.**	**Dem.**
1994		Rep.	Rep.
1996	**Clinton (Dem.)**	**Rep.**	**Rep.**
1998		Rep.	Rep.
2000	**Bush (Rep.)**	**Dem./Rep.**[c]	**Rep.**
2002		Rep.	Rep.
2004	**Bush (Rep.)**	**Rep.**	**Rep.**
2006		Dem.	Dem.
2008	**Obama (Dem.)**	**Dem.**	**Dem.**
2010		Dem.	Rep.

[a] Bold type indicates presidential election year, light type indicates mid-term elections.

[b] President Nixon resigned in August 1974 over the Watergate scandal and was replaced by Vice-president Gerald Ford.

[c] After the November 2000 election, the Democrats and Republicans each had 50 seats. Until May, the vice-president's casting vote gave control to the Republicans. In May 2002, Republican Senator James Jeffords changed his status to Independent and caucused with the Democrats, giving them a 50–49–1 majority. The November 2002 elections saw the Republicans regain a 50–48–2 majority.

saw it disappear when one member of the party defected. Even when the Republicans consolidated their control in the 2002 elections, they only had a two-seat majority over the opposition.

Secondly, until 1994, the pattern of divided government was for a Republican president to be faced with a Democratic Congress. However, the 1994, 1996 and 1998 elections saw President Clinton become the first Democratic president to be faced with a Republican Congress since President Truman (1946–48).

The reasons for divided government will be explored more fully in Chapter 10. For the moment, it is enough to note that American voters clearly have different political criteria for choosing a president from those which determine their choice of senator or representative.

We have seen that economic policy, foreign policy and social issues, as well as character, can all influence the vote for the president. What then are the different factors which appear to operate in congressional elections?

Constituency service

Beyond anything else, voters in congressional elections value the local and personal services rendered by their representatives and senators. If a member of Congress is perceived as having served the constituency well, he or she will almost certainly be re-elected. The notion of constituency service includes, for example, ensuring that a slice of federal job or construction schemes, or grants for education and social services, are brought back home to the member's district or state. Representatives, in particular, may also act as a kind of ombudsman, intervening in government bureaucracy to help constituents secure benefits or disentangle them from red tape.

Senators have a higher profile than representatives and may be more associated with national political issues. Occasionally, such associations can hurt them. This was the case in 1978 – a strong conservative wind was blowing that year and, partly as a result, a number of well-known liberal Democrat senators lost their seats. In 2008, the national tide saw more Republican senators fall than might have been expected. On the whole, however, the same golden rule applies to Senate elections as to the House: those who serve their constituents well can expect to gain re-election, regardless of party affiliation or ideological disposition.

Incumbency advantage

Sitting members of Congress are well placed to ensure that the benefits of federal largesse reach their constituents. Not only do they draft the legislation concerned, but they benefit from congressional perks which enable them to publicise the good they have done. For example, they exploit the 'franking privilege', which gives them free use of the US Mail to send letters to constituents, including mass mailings detailing members' achievements and local appearances. Although there are rules against using the franking privilege for blatant electioneering, there is always room for interpretation. Representative Dennis Hastert (R – Illinois) managed 48 references to himself in just four pages, and Representative Newt Gingrich (R – Georgia) reached 54. Self-promotion did not harm their careers, since both went on to serve as Speaker of the US House of Representatives (Davies, 1999, p. 178). Challengers to incumbents also suffer other disadvantages, such as lack of access to inexpensive institutional facilities for making videos to circulate back home. Above all, incumbent members of Congress benefit from their ability to attract far greater campaign donations from interest groups than do their challengers (see Chapter 11).

These advantages contribute to high incumbency re-election rates. Members of the House of Representatives seeking re-election had a success rate of well over 90 per cent in all but the most exceptional years. According to the Center for Responsive Politics, between the elections of 1976 and 2008, the re-election rate fell below that figure only in 1992, to a dizzying low of 88 per cent.

Incumbency re-election rates for the Senate are historically neither as high nor as consistent as those for the House. Since 1964, the rate has varied from 55 per cent to 96 per cent, with the median of 85 per cent. As noted above, senators are more associated with national issues than representatives, and the larger size of their constituencies means they do not have quite the same personal identification with their voters as do House members.

It is clear that congressional elections have a life of their own parallel to, but not necessarily subsumed within presidential elections today. Neither President Clinton in 1992 and 1996, nor President Bush in 2000 and 2004, had any presidential 'coat-tails' which benefited their parties in Congress. The same can be said of President Obama. While both he and the Democrats who took former Republican seats in Congress may have benefited from the national mood for change, there were few constituencies where his vote ran ahead of the local Democratic winner. Since the Second World War, only twice has the capture of the White House by the out-party been accompanied by a similar breakthrough in the congressional elections: President Eisenhower in 1952 (House and Senate) and President Reagan in 1980 (Senate only).

Term limits

Notwithstanding the high rate of re-election, members of Congress can take nothing for granted. In addition to the dangers of an election where the voters are inclined to 'throw the rascals out', the anti-incumbency mood of the 1990s produced a significant movement to limit the number of terms of office for representatives and senators. This movement was driven by the feeling that if politicians spend too long in Washington, they may become part of a professional, self-serving governing class that is ignorant of and indifferent to the views of the people.

The movement got under way in 1990 when a referendum in Colorado produced a 71 per cent vote in favour of term limits. In the next two years alone, a further 14 states followed suit. The movement experienced a major setback in 1995, however, when the Supreme Court ruled that the only constitutionally permissible method of imposing term limits on members of Congress was by passing a constitutional amendment (*US Term Limits* v. *Thornton*). Unsurprisingly, a constitutional amendment imposing term limits was duly introduced into Congress (see Box 8.3). Because constitutional amendment involves a notoriously difficult and protracted political campaign, it is unlikely to succeed. Yet the attempt serves as a reminder of the American electorate's belief that centralised political authority needs to be curtailed.

Box 8.3

Constitutional amendment imposing term limits

H.J. Res. 42
IN THE HOUSE OF REPRESENTATIVES
February 5, 1997

Mr. BLUNT (for himself and Mr. TALENT) introduced the following joint resolution; which was referred to the Committee on the Judiciary.

JOINT RESOLUTION

Proposing an amendment to the Constitution of the United States to limit the number of terms a Member of Congress may serve, and to authorize a State to provide longer or shorter term limits for a Member of Congress from that State.

Resolved by the Senate and House of Representatives of the United States of America in Congress assembled (two-thirds of each House concurring therein), That the following article is proposed as an amendment to the Constitution of the United States, which shall be valid to all intents and purposes as part of the Constitution when ratified by the legislatures of three-fourths of the several States:

Article–
Section 1. A Representative shall be limited to three terms in such office, and a Senator shall be limited to two terms in such office . . .

Section 2. A Senator or Representative who has served one or more terms in such office as of the date of the ratification of this article, or a part of such term or terms, is deemed to have served one term in such office after the date of ratification for purposes of section 1.

Section 3. A State may, by amendment of the Constitution of that State, provide for term limits with respect to a Representative or Senator representing that State that are longer or shorter than the limits provided in section 1.

Section 4. There shall be no time limit within which this article must be ratified by the legislatures of three-fourths of the several States to become valid as part of the Constitution . . .

Voting behaviour

The franchise

The right of citizens to vote for their leaders lies at the heart of the democratic political process. Indeed, in assessing the democratic quality of any political system, one of the first questions to be asked is: 'Who is entitled to vote?'

As in most western democracies, the franchise in the United States has been greatly expanded since the eighteenth century. Early property and religious requirements imposed by some states had largely disappeared by the 1830s. Yet two great historical struggles for the right to vote remained: the enfranchisement of blacks and of women.

An organised women's movement first claimed the right to vote in the manifesto known as the Seneca Falls Declaration, issued in 1848. Yet it was not until the ratification of the Nineteenth Amendment to the Constitution, in 1920, that women were finally permitted to vote throughout the United States. While both proponents and opponents of women's suffrage predicted new, radical departures in voting behaviour as a result, these have largely failed to materialise. As we shall see shortly, however, some significant differences in the way men and women vote have emerged in recent elections.

In terms of possessing the legal right to vote, African-Americans were successful much earlier than women. Following the abolition of slavery after the Civil War, the Fifteenth Amendment to the Constitution was ratified in 1870. This declares, 'The right of citizens of the United States to vote shall not be denied or abridged by the United States or by any State on account of race, color, or previous condition of servitude.'

Despite this categorical assertion, many southern states proceeded to disenfranchise blacks by a variety of devices. For example, a 'literacy test' was often used, whereby would-be voters were required to read and explain a written passage, such as part of the Constitution, before being permitted to vote. With little or no education for African-Americans at the time, it was relatively easy for white election officials to deem them unqualified. Payment of a poll tax was also made a condition of voting, something which hit blacks in particular because of their economic subordination. Yet another device was the 'grandfather clause', which gave the vote only to those whose grandfathers had possessed the same right. Since the first post-Civil War generation of black voters in the South had grandfathers who had been slaves, they were debarred from voting. Furthermore, this was a self-perpetuating condition inherited by each subsequent generation of blacks.

A less obviously illegal ruse used by southern governments to deprive African-Americans of their electoral power was the white primary. The South was a one-party region before the Second World War: Democrats won virtually all elections at every level of government. The real election in southern states, therefore, was the Democratic primary: whoever won that was all but guaranteed victory in the general election. As a *private* organisation, the party believed it could ban blacks from participation in its primaries, without infringing the Fifteenth Amendment's prohibition on *state* discrimination against them. The Supreme Court did not rule otherwise until 1944, in the case of *Smith* v. *Allwright*.

Box 8.4

Constitutional milestones in the expansion of the franchise

1787 The Constitution leaves it to the individual states to determine who is qualified to vote.

1870 The Fifteenth Amendment is ratified, making it unconstitutional to deprive a person of the right to vote on grounds of race or colour.

1913 The Seventeenth Amendment is ratified, requiring the direct election of US senators.

1920 The Nineteenth Amendment is ratified, making it unconstitutional to deprive a person of the right to vote on grounds of sex.

1964 The Twenty-fourth Amendment is ratified, outlawing the imposition of a poll tax as a qualification for voting in federal elections.

1971 The Twenty-sixth Amendment is ratified, lowering the voting age for both federal and state elections from 21 to 18.

Box 8.5

Measuring the turnout

The traditional method of measuring turnout in the United States is to ask how many people of voting age actually voted in the election. More recently, some scholars have challenged the validity of this measure, arguing that the voting-age population (VAP) includes a significant number of people who are not entitled to vote: non-citizens, convicted felons and prison inmates, for example. Instead, it is argued, a more accurate measurement can be based on the voting-eligible population (VEP) which includes only those who are entitled to vote. Although the argument is technically more complicated than this, it is logical to count as non-voters only those who could have voted if they wanted to. We can see from the graph the difference it makes when we measure turnout by VEP rather than the traditional VAP. Whichever measure is used, the figures remain low compared with most other advanced societies. The decline in turnout after the 1960s is lower than reported by other measures, and in 2008 turnout is back near its 1960s heights. The difference between the changes indicated by these measures is explained by a rise in the number of ineligible voters in the VAP, rather than a decline in voting among those who could vote if they chose to do so.

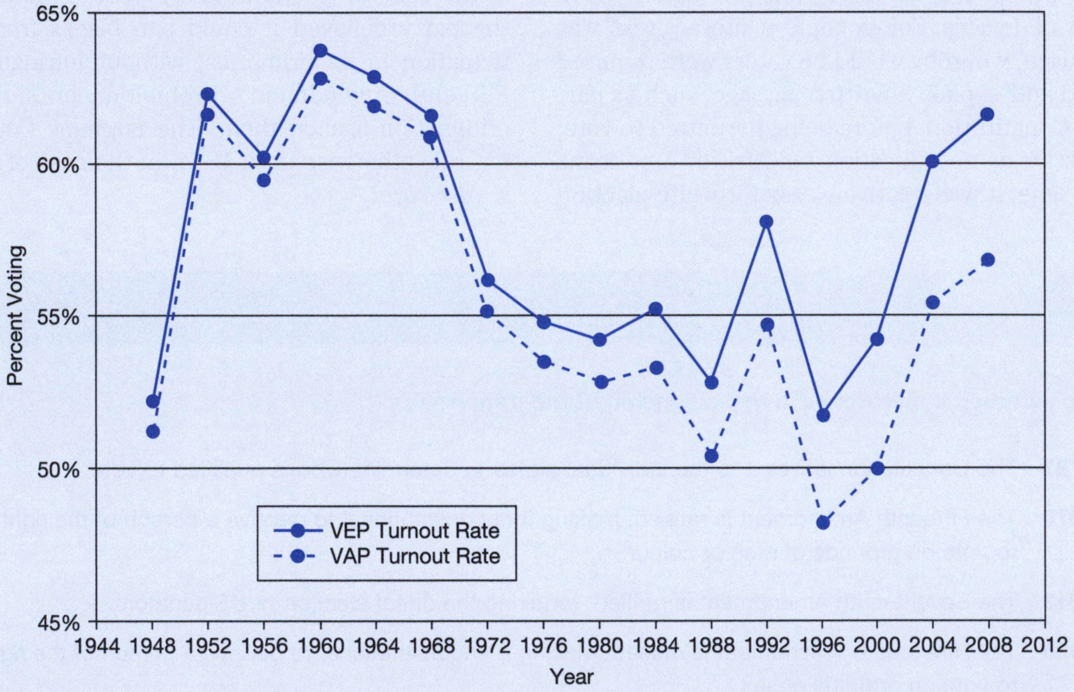

Presidential turnout rates for voting-age population (VAP) and voting-eligible population (VEP), 1948–2008.
Source: McDonald, US Elections Project, 2008

It was not until the great civil rights movement of the 1950s and 1960s that the legal right of African-Americans to vote became a practical reality in the South. With the passage of the Voting Rights Act of 1965, the federal government was empowered to take over the administration of elections in any state where racial discrimination in voting rights was detected. It is now safe to say that, in the United States, with a few exceptions such as the imprisoned and the insane, all citizens over the age of 18 can vote – if they want to.

Non-voting

Despite the constant rhetorical celebration of America's democracy and these heroic struggles to extend the franchise, many Americans do not exercise the right to vote. The United States has a lower voter turnout than almost any comparable democracy. Whereas countries such as Germany and Sweden experience around 90 per cent turnout, only rarely do more than 60 per cent of eligible Americans turn out to vote in presidential elections. In the mid-term congressional elections, the figures are significantly lower still, with rarely more than four out of ten eligible voters casting a ballot.

The relative lack of interest in voting would appear to be a less than healthy aspect of the American polity. For many Americans, voting is their primary, if not sole, means of participation in the political process. Those who do not vote, therefore, may play no role at all in the democratic process. When the proportion of such non-voters nears 50 per cent, one may reasonably ask if there is not a malaise affecting popular democracy in the United States.

Another problem created by low voter turnout concerns the mandate to govern that any president can claim. Consider the position of President Ronald Reagan, the clear winner of the 1984 election, having taken 59 per cent of the popular vote. Once we take into account the fact that the turnout that year was 57.2 per cent, we see that President Reagan was

Box 8.6

The National Voter Registration Act 1993

Popularly known as the 'motor voter' law, the National Voter Registration Act (NVRA) was passed in an attempt to overcome practical barriers to registering to vote. The key elements of the law are:

- Citizens must be allowed to register to vote at the same time as they apply for, renew or change their address on a driving licence. This facility alone can reach 90 per cent of all eligible voters.
- Citizens must be allowed to register at specified government agencies, including those that deal with people considered least likely to possess a driving licence: for example, agencies dealing with the disabled and those receiving public assistance.
- Citizens must be permitted to register by mail, rather than having to visit an office.
- States are obliged to verify the accuracy of voter registration lists on a four-yearly basis.

The NVRA works in terms of increased voter registration. It is estimated that some 20 million voters registered under the Act prior to the 1996 elections. However, the fact that those elections saw a marked decline in actual voting gives support to the argument that practical registration obstacles no longer account for Americans' disinclination to use their most basic democratic right.

Source: League of Women Voters, *The NVRA Factsheet*, 2 January 1997

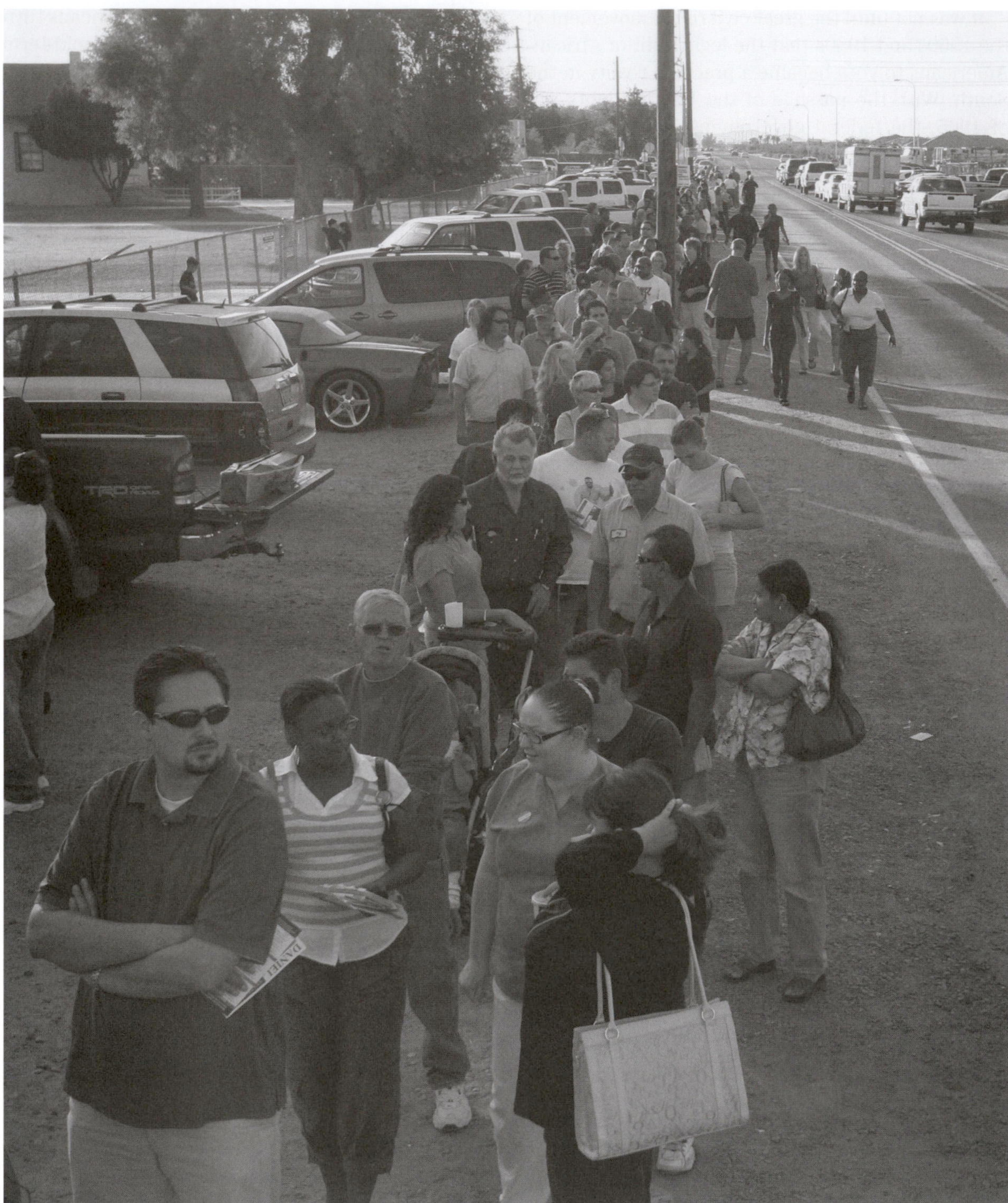

Figure 8.4 Voter turnout rose sharply in the 2008 elections, causing long delays at polling stations.
Source: © Eyevine Jervy/Schmitt

supported by just one-third of those eligible to vote. Even the Reagan 'landslide' looks far from impressive from this perspective. And more ordinary victories by other presidents begin to look rather modest.

It is hardly surprising, then, that there have been many studies which have attempted to identify the causes of this worrying phenomenon. Arthur Hadley found evidence to contradict the widespread belief that the typical non-voter was a figure whom he dubbed 'Boobus Americanus' (Hadley, 1978). This stereotype was poor, ill-educated, disproportionately southern, female and black. While some non-voters in Hadley's study did correspond to stereotype, many did not. Ruy Teixeira pointed out that a decline in the number of such stereotypical non-voters in the period since 1960 was to be expected: educational levels have risen, southern blacks have become freer to vote, and both women and blacks have become more equal citizens to white males in important respects (Teixeira, 1987). There must therefore be other reasons for low turnout in addition to the traditional ones of poverty and lack of education.

Another factor often cited in such studies is the relative difficulty of voter registration in some states. This is exacerbated by the fact that Americans are an unusually and increasingly mobile people, who move state frequently and therefore must re-register frequently under unfamiliar state laws. Unlike in Britain, where government actively solicits citizens to register by sending forms to their homes, many states require individuals to take the initiative, usually by visiting the local registration office. The extra effort thus required undoubtedly deters some eligible voters. Yet, as Hadley pointed out, turnout has been falling even in states where registration is easiest. Moreover, the introduction of the 'motor voter' law in 1993 did not prevent a drop in the 1996 turnout over 1992.

Underpinning all these contributory factors is what researchers call the issue of political efficacy. 'The basic idea of *political efficacy* is that it taps the extent to which an individual feels that he or she has any power over governmental actions' (Teixeira, 1987, pp. 18–19). In other words, political efficacy concerns the degree to which potential voters believe there is any point in voting. Those who, for one reason or another, believe it makes no difference to them who wins the election will obviously be less likely to vote. On the basis of the turnout figures quoted above, then, some 40–50 per cent of eligible voters in the United States believe elections are, in essence, unimportant to them – if not wholly meaningless. By definition, this constitutes a challenge to American democracy.

Even if the VEP scholars are right and there is a 'myth of the vanishing voter', there are still large numbers who do not vote. In 2008, when there was a concerted effort by both major parties to get their supporters out, when the election was predicted to be both close and critical, and when the emergence of Barack Obama as a candidate prompted unusually high enthusiasm at least in one political party, still only fractionally over six out of ten voters made the effort to use their franchise. Given the historic barriers to voting that have been removed, it is hard to avoid the conclusion that a very large minority of Americans simply do not think it is worth the effort.

The voters

We now come to one of the most important and interesting questions about voting behaviour in the United States: what factors determine which voters support which candidates? This is a complex question, which must take into account a variety of cultural, ideological and socio-economic factors.

In Europe, for example, we expect social class to be the most powerful, though not the sole, determinant of the way people vote. And while the notion of social class is of some use in analysing voting behaviour in the United States, the greater heterogeneity of American society by comparison with Europe brings many other factors into play. Race, region and religion, for example, are more varied in the United States than in most European societies, and American historical and cultural experience is different from European in significant ways.

Ballots, polls and voters

Article 2, Section 1, Clause 3 of the US Constitution gives Congress the authority to 'determine the time of choosing' the nation's president, and Congress opted for the Tuesday after the first Monday in November as its preference for Election Day. Election administration is the responsibility of the states, and some have introduced simplified postal voting and extended voting periods, but for most of the nation, as well as the candidate campaigns, Election Day is a fixture that can be pinpointed years in advance.

In 2008 the major parties' nominees for president were accompanied on the ballots by a number of candidates from other parties. The rules on ballot access are established at the state level, so that even at the presidential level, there is not a common ballot choice in all parts of the USA. In addition, the ballot will offer choices in the federal congressional elections, and states and localities simultaneously run a variety of races for other offices.

The voters of the township of Leicester, Vermont, for example, had, along with their compatriots, plenty of warning about the date of the election, ample time to realise that in this election they would have to choose a president and some other officeholders, and had been subjected to a goodly amount of expensive campaigning to promote the various candidates. Nevertheless, those voters, regardless of their attentiveness to political affairs, may well have had some surprises when faced with the ballot.

The 2008 presidential election in Leicester was not a simple run-off between Republican John McCain and his running mate Sarah Palin and Democrats Barack Obama and Joe Biden. Alternatives included Chuck Baldwin and Darrell Castle of the Constitution Party, Libertarians Bob Barr and Wayne Root, Roger Calero and Alyson Kennedy (Socialist Workers), Gloria LaRiva and Eugene Puryear (Socialism and Liberation), Brian Moore and Stewart Alexander (Liberty Union) and Ralph Nader and Matt Gonzalez (Independent). In addition, Vermont allows voters to write in names when they do not like the look of any of the candidates printed on the ballot.

Neither of Vermont's two US Senate seats was up for election in 2008, but there were six candidates for the state's House seat, including Peter Welch, a Democrat who had also managed to win the Republican nomination, and candidates listing themselves as Progressive, and Energy Independence candidates. Seven candidates were on the ballot competing for Governor, four for Lieutenant Governor, and other choices were available for State Treasurer, Secretary of State, Auditor of Accounts, Attorney General, State Senator, State Representative and for High Bailiff, whose duty is to arrest the sheriff, should that ever become necessary, and to serve as interim sheriff until the problem is resolved.

Not counting any other very localised offices, our Leicester voter was asked to exercise her vote up to 11 times, choosing between 44 candidates representing a total of 10 named political parties alongside several Independents. If unhappy with the choices presented, our voter could write in her choice. The formidable ballot has the potential to imbue the voter with a genuine sense of drama and occasion. Had our Leicester voter used all her votes, at no point abstaining or using the write-in option, she could have combined her choice of government personnel in 774,144 different ways.

Not surprisingly, voters tend to simplify their choices. In addition to deciding on the basis of the campaign messages they have received, and their own assessment of candidates they may know to some degree, they use cues such as party affiliation to guide their choice. However, for some the interrogation is not finished when they have registered their vote and pulled back the voting booth curtain.

At every election, thousands of voters are approached by interviewers to take part in the exit polls that help give a picture of the demographic, personal and political structure of the voting public. Co-operative voters, having already contributed potentially momentous decisions, are persuaded to provide the interviewers with details of their education, income, beliefs, affiliations, family situation and more.

The history of such polls is well established. Informal polls sometimes provided the background for interesting news articles by the early twentieth century. The effort by some pollsters, such as George Gallup and Elmo Roper, to develop scientific methods of polling were boosted when in 1936 a well-respected informal poll in the *Literary Digest* predicted a result diametrically opposed to the Franklin Roosevelt landslide of that year, while their smaller, carefully sampled polls, proved to be an accurate guide.

Exit polls developed later, in part as an effort by television companies to be able to predict results to their election night audiences without waiting for the formal count. They too have had their embarrassing moments. In 2000 a modest sampling error and a tightly fought election combined to fault the television companies into predicting on election night that Florida had fallen to Democratic presidential candidate Al Gore, while the truth was very different, and the winner in Florida, and in the nation, was not known until some weeks later.

The polls show that in the twenty-first century, women form a larger part of the voting public (53–47 per cent in 2008), and that they vote differently from men. Obama had a 56–43 per cent lead among women voters, as compared with a 49–48 per cent lead among men. Cross-cutting factors also have an influence – white men (36 per cent of the voters) favoured McCain by 57–41 per cent, white women (39% of voters) also favoured McCain by 53–46 per cent. This was counterbalanced by Obama's vote in the other 25 per cent of the voting population – reaching over 95 per cent among black men and women, and around 65 per cent of Hispanics and other races.

These polls also show us that electorates vote differently according to the office they are considering. Male voters in 2008 preferred Democrat candidates for the US House of Representatives above Republicans by 52–46 per cent, showing a 3 per cent preference for House Democrats rather than for the Democratic presidential candidate. In addition, electorates vary between elections. In the 2010 mid-term elections, the Republicans made considerable gains from the Democrats. This reflects a genuine swing in public opinion, but voter turnout fell from around 62 per cent of eligible voters in 2008 to around 42 per cent in 2010.

Among the smaller voting population in 2010, the proportion of white voters increased from 74 to 77 per cent as the African-Americans and Hispanics who had turned out in record numbers for Obama failed to return to vote for generic Democrat congressional candidates. Voters aged up to 29 fell from 18 per cent of the electorate in 2008 to 12 per cent in 2010. White Protestants made up 44 per cent of the 2010 electorate, an increase of 2 per cent, and those who reported weekly church attendance, traditionally a very conservative-leaning group, made up 48 per cent of the electorate, an increase of 8 per cent on the 2008 figure. A different electorate defeated the Democrats in 2010 than the one that elected Obama in 2008.

The extensive exit polls published by reliable news organisations, such as the *New York Times* and CNN, provide a portrait of the American electorate unparalleled in details and subtlety and deserve careful consideration.

New York Times National Exit Poll 2008. Available from:
http://elections.nytimes.com/2008/results/president/national-exit-polls.html

CNN Exit Poll 2008 Available from:
http://edition.cnn.com/ELECTION/2008/results/polls/

CNN Exit Poll 2010 Available from:
http://edition.cnn.com/ELECTION/2010/results/polls/

Social class and socio-economic status

We noted above that, in European societies, social class is expected to be a major determinant of the way people vote. Yet, for historical reasons, class is a difficult concept to employ in the context of the United States. Initially, divisions of class were far less marked in the United States than in, say, Great Britain. To this was added a greater degree of social mobility and an unwillingness on the part of many Americans to define themselves in terms of traditional classes.

Yet many of the characteristics associated with social class – income, education, occupation – *do* significantly affect the way Americans vote. Academics refer jointly to these factors as 'socio-economic status' (SES).

As the portrait of the electorate in 2008 shows, income is a good guide to explaining the way that Americans vote. Obama did well across the board, but still did substantially better among lower-income groups, while those with incomes above $50,000 provided more fertile opportunity for the Republican party. Of course, this does not mean that all wealthy people vote Republican and all poor people vote

Democrat. Thus, while the higher-income groups in 2008 divided roughly half and half between the major party candidates, John McCain won only 25 per cent of the votes of the poorest group.

Educational attainment is one of the keys to gaining a well-paid job, and also provides some indications of likely voting choice. Once again, Obama's appeal to many groups of voters is evident in the 2008 figures, but his margins are highest among the least and the most educated. The relatively high proportion of postgraduates who vote Democrat is perhaps explained by the fact that this group includes a large number of teachers, social workers and other similar professionals who tend to hold values which incline them to support the party of the 'have-nots'. More generally, it may be that education has a liberalising effect on some issues and this moderates the effect of income differences.

Other studies reveal that a higher job status means a tendency to vote Republican. Those whose occupations are classed as professional/business are more Republican than those classed as white collar, and those classed as white-collar workers are more Republican than blue-collar workers (Polsby and Wildavsky, 1995, pp. 303–5; Pomper *et al.*, 1989, p. 133).

Thus, socio-economic status provides a good guide to voting behaviour in the United States. Nevertheless other factors must come into play too.

Ideology

While American political parties are not as clearly defined by ideology as British parties, it is reasonable to describe the Democrats as a moderate-liberal party and the Republicans as a conservative party. A voter's ideological leanings may therefore signal his or her voting behaviour. Quite predictably, the 2008 voting data show that those who classify themselves as liberals are strongly Democrat, and those who classify themselves as conservatives are strongly Republican. It is worth emphasising, however, that the largest ideological group are those who call themselves moderates, and their vote is less predictable. Obama's victory in 2008 was to a great extent due to his success in attracting voters from this middle ground. In 2010, the mid-term election defeats for the Democratic party were accompanied by a switch of support among moderates away from the Democrats, as well as a large drop in turnout by some Democratic voting groups – especially young voters and black voters – who had been strongly attracted by the 2008 Obama campaign, but felt no such pull to a campaign without him on the ticket.

Sex and age

It is not difficult to understand why wealthy conservatives vote Republican, given that party's tendency in the twenty-first century to favour low taxes, unfettered free enterprise and traditional morality. Similarly, lower-income, blue-collar workers have a natural affinity with a Democratic party that has championed labour union rights, the welfare state and government regulation of employers. Or, to take another example, voters from ethnic minority groups logically gravitate towards the Democratic party, which has led the fight for civil rights.

It is not quite so clear, however, why men should be more Republican than women, or why unmarried voters should be more Democratic than married ones. Here we must speculate more than usual. A gender gap of some kind has been present in most elections since 1952. In 1952, 1956 and 1960, women showed a greater preference for Republicans than men did. The next three elections all but saw this gender gap disappear, only for it to reassert itself in the election of 1976. Beginning in 1980, however, the gender gap reversed itself: women were now clearly more favourable to Democrats than men were. In 2008, women voters favoured Barack Obama by 13 per cent, but men were almost evenly divided in their opinions, favouring Obama by a single percentage point.

Why should there be any gender gap at all, and why should the direction of the gap have changed in the 1980s? The answer to the first question may lie in biological and/or cultural factors. Men are seen as more aggressive than women and this may be reflected in attitudes towards certain policies, such as defence and law and order. The answer to the second might be connected to a change in emphasis in the agenda of issues in the 1980s. In particular, the Republican party under Ronald Reagan and the New Right called for a vast increase in military expenditure, perhaps thereby increasing its attraction for men. The Republicans simultaneously called for a return to 'traditional' or 'family' values, which was seen by some as a threat to gender equality and abortion rights: this may have caused a slippage of women's votes to the Democrats. Perhaps the issue of family values also explains the tendency of married people, with their more conventional lifestyles, to vote disproportionately for the Republican party.

Is it possible to identify a typical Democratic or Republican voter? Yes, but some caution is required. The various groupings in 2008 cut across each other: for example, better-off voters are more likely to vote Republican, while women lean towards the Democrats. It remains a matter of conjecture, then, which way a well-off woman will vote. When we take into account all the other factors which can affect voting behaviour, the permutations make generalisations difficult.

Nevertheless, on the evidence of recent elections, a wealthy, Protestant, married, southern white male, with a college degree, is very likely to vote Republican. Conversely, an unmarried, black, female union member of modest financial means, and without a high-school diploma, is very likely to vote Democrat.

We must remember, however, that voting behaviour, like most aspects of politics, is a dynamic phenomenon. Historically, group voting tendencies have changed (as we shall see in more detail in Chapter 11). In each election, parties and candidates must seek to renew their bonds with their traditional supporters and attempt to woo those who are not. Whatever the failings of American voters, politicians may pay a high price for taking them for granted.

Chapter summary

The complex system of elections in the United States has its origins in the Founding Fathers' desire to base the federal government upon popular sovereignty, without instituting a fully fledged democracy or simple majoritarianism. It also reflects their need to mollify the states, particularly the less populous of them, which feared an overweening federal government. Developments since 1787 have increased the democratic qualities of the American electoral system, both by expanding the franchise and by making more federal politicians directly rather than indirectly elected. Nevertheless, the electorate's faith in the federal government, as measured by the low numbers of those actually voting, is worrying. This raises questions about the mandate and representativeness of those who win federal office. It is ironic that a system which gives voters several modes of democratic representation at the federal level should engender such low levels of popular enthusiasm and electoral participation.

Discussion points

1. Why did the framers of the Constitution establish different electoral systems for the presidency, the Senate and the House of Representatives?
2. What are the advantages and disadvantages of imposing term limits on federal office-holders?
3. Is it important that so few Americans exercise their right to vote?
4. What are the main determinants of voting behaviour in presidential elections?
5. Are American presidential campaigns too long?

Further reading

Books providing a general introduction to elections and voting behaviour include W. Flanigan and N. Zingale, *Political Behaviour of the American Electorate* (11th edn, Washington, DC: CQ Press, 2009); Philip J. Davies, *US Elections Today* (Manchester: Manchester University Press, 1999); N. Polsby and A. Wildavsky, *Presidential Elections: Strategies and Structures of American Politics* (11th edn, New York: Rowan & Littlefield, 2003); S. Wayne, *The Road to the White House 2008*

(Boston: Wadsworth, 2007) and S.K. Medvic, *Campaigns and Elections: Players and Processes* (Boston: Wadsworth, 2010). For an analysis of the 2008 elections, see M. Nelson, *The Elections of 2008* (Washington, DC: CQ Press, 2009). On congressional elections, see P. Herrnson, *Congressional Elections: Campaigning at Home and in Washington* (4th edn, Washington, DC: CQ Press, 2003). On the issue of voter turnout, see M. McDonald and S. Popkin, 'The Myth of the Vanishing Voter', *American Political Science Review*, vol. 95, no. 4, December 2001, pp. 963–74.

Websites

http://www.lib.umich.edu
http://www.archives.gov/federal_register/electoral_college/
http://usinfo.state.gov/dhr/democracy/elections.html

References

Bailey, C. (1989) *The US Congress* (Oxford: Basil Blackwell).

Center for Responsive Politics, 'Reelection rates over the years', available at: http://www.opensecrets.org/bigpicture/reelect.php.

Cook, R. (1991) 'New primaries, new rules mark road to nomination', *CQ Weekly Report,* 7 September, pp. 2411–16.

Cook, R. (2008) *The Rhodes Cook Letter*, August 2008.

Davies, P. (1999) *US Elections Today* (Manchester: Manchester University Press).

Gallup, 'Election 2008 topics and trends,' available at: http://www.gallup.com/poll/17785/Election-2008.aspx#3

Hadley, A. (1978) *The Empty Polling Booth* (Englewood Cliffs, NJ: Prentice Hall).

McDonald, Michael *The US Elections Project* accessed at http://elections.gmu.edu/Turnout_2008P.html

Polsby, N. and Wildavsky, A. (1995) *Presidential Elections: Strategies and Structures of American Politics* (Chatham, NJ: Chatham House).

Pomper, G. *et al.* (1989) *The Elections of 1988: Reports and Interpretations* (Chatham, NJ: Chatham House).

Pomper, G., Burnham, W., Corrado, A., Hershey, M., Just, M., Keefer, S., McWilliams, W., Mayer, W. (1997) *The Elections of 1996: Reports and Interpretations* (Chatham, NJ: Chatham House).

Pomper, G. *et al.* (2001) *The Elections of 2000: Reports and Interpretations* (Chatham, NJ: Chatham House).

Teixeira, R. (1987) *Why Americans Don't Vote* (New York: Greenwood).

Wayne, S. (2001) *The Road to the White House, 2000* (New York: Palgrave Macmillan).

Chapter 9

The mass media and politics

This chapter analyses the impact of the media, especially television, on elections and politics in general. American politics without television is unthinkable. Not only do voters gain most of their knowledge about politics from television, but candidates gear their campaigns almost entirely to the demands of this particular medium. Moreover, presidents regard the media as a critical element in the art of political persuasion. Unsurprisingly, then, great controversy surrounds the power of the media in politics.

Gerry Rafshoon, a leading media consultant in American politics, tells an amusing story from the 1952 presidential election. Political television was still in its infancy. The Democrats decided for the first time to give their candidate, Adlai Stevenson, a television adviser – a man called Bill Wilson. Stevenson had been introduced to Wilson at the Democratic Convention yet, weeks into the campaign, the candidate had not once called upon his new assistant for advice. Finally, however, in a hotel at a campaign stop, Wilson received a call to come up to Stevenson's suite. Excited at the prospect of getting down to work at last, Wilson hurried to the candidate's room. Stevenson greeted him by pointing to the television in the corner and saying, 'Ah yes, the television man. Can you fix that thing? I can't get a picture' (White and McCarthy, 1985).

A few elections further on, however, no candidate or campaign would be so naive or ignorant about the enormous potential for the use of television in elections. Today, according to one expert, 'Media coverage is the very lifeblood of politics because it shapes the perceptions that form the reality on which political action is based. Media do more than depict the political environment; they *are* the political environment' (Graber, 1989, p. 238).

Box 9.1

Key dates in the history of television and politics

1947 First live television broadcast of State of the Union address (President Truman)

1952 First television advertisements for a presidential candidate

First use of television consultants in campaigns

First politically significant use of television. Vice-presidential candidate Richard Nixon is threatened with removal from the Republican ticket, after allegations that he had used a secret slush fund for personal gain. Nixon decides to appeal to the public through television. He makes the 'Checkers' speech, confessing that he had received one gift: his children had been given a little dog called Checkers. His children loved the dog and Nixon vowed that they were going to keep him, whatever the critics said. He then asks viewers to contact Republican headquarters if they want him to stay on the ticket. Viewers respond positively and Nixon is saved

1960 First televised presidential debate, between John F. Kennedy and Richard Nixon

1961 President Kennedy gives first live televised presidential press conference

1963 Network television news programmes extended to 30 minutes

1964 First controversial political advertisement on television: the 'Daisy Commercial' on behalf of President Johnson. Without mentioning his opponent by name, the advertisement implies that Barry Goldwater could launch a nuclear war, if elected

1965 US involvement in Vietnam leads to first 'televised war'

1968 Richard Nixon turns to television advertising specialists to change his negative image: they create the 'new Nixon'

The American press

When we speak of the media we mean television, radio, internet, newspapers and magazines. Although television is undoubtedly the pre-eminent form of the media in the United States, this does not mean that the others are not important. Although the *New York Times* newspaper, for example, is seen by far fewer people than network television, it is both read and taken very seriously by the political elite.

As in most democracies, the written press in the United States is privately owned. However, three characteristics distinguish it from the press in, say, Great Britain.

Circulation

First, virtually all newspapers are local rather than national publications. Most importantly, the circulation of even the 'quality press' (*New York Times*, *LA Times* and *Washington Post*, for example) is substantially limited to the city or region of origin. This means that there is a very large number of daily newspapers in total: according to the Newspaper Association of America, in 2003 there were 1,456 daily newspapers and 917 Sunday newspapers published in the United States. On the other hand, precisely because they are restricted in area of circulation, there is far less competition between papers than there is in, say, Britain. Some cities do

Table 9.1 Leading print media in the United States, 2010

Newspapers	Largest reported circulation
Wall Street Journal	2,061,142
USA Today	1,830,594
New York Times	876,638
Los Angeles Times	600,449
Washington Post	545,345

Source: Audit Bureau of Circulations, 2010

have more than one newspaper: thus New York has the *Wall Street Journal*, the *New York Times*, the *Daily News* and the *Post*; and Chicago has the *Tribune* and the *Sun-Times*. Most cities, however, have only one paper of any significance. Newspaper circulations have been falling. Betweeen 2005 and 2010, the aggregate circulation of the five leading newspapers listed in Table 9.1 fell by one-third, with some individual reductions being even more dramatic, such as the collapse of *Los Angeles Times* sales by more than 50 per cent. Young Americans are less likely to be readers of traditional newspapers, but the sharp growth in the use of newspaper internet sites and of reading newspapers on tablet-style mobile computers is bringing newspaper content to a proportion of the young audience.

Censorship

The second distinguishing aspect is that the American press is much less subject to legal restraint than the British press. This is due in large part to the protection provided by the First Amendment to the Constitution, which provides that 'Congress shall make no law . . . abridging the freedom of speech, or of the press'. Although originally the amendment restricted only the federal legislature, the Supreme Court has applied it to state legislatures as well since 1931 (*Near* v. *Minnesota*).

Moreover, the Court has generally interpreted the First Amendment in a fashion that makes it difficult to gag the press. In 1964, in the case of *New York Times Co.* v. *Sullivan*, the Court held that a newspaper could not be convicted of libel merely because it published a false story. It was further necessary to prove that the story had been published with actual malice: that is, that the paper knew it was false. This makes it extremely difficult for public officials to intimidate the press with threats of libel suits.

Even where national security is involved, the Court has granted the press wide latitude. Thus, in *New York Times* v. *United States* (1971), the Court permitted the *Times* to go ahead with publication of the so-called Pentagon Papers, a leaked Defense Department secret history of government policy-making on the Vietnam War. The Court held that publication could only be prevented in situations where it would otherwise create immediate and irreparable harm to the nation.

The Supreme Court has also interpreted the First Amendment to give strong protection to political satire. A notable case in this regard occurred in 1988, in *Flynt* v. *Falwell*. The Reverend Jerry Falwell, the leader of the Moral Majority, a politically conservative Christian group, had been parodied in the most lewd manner by the scurrilous, pornographic magazine *Hustler*. The magazine was owned by Larry Flynt, and Falwell sued him for libel. Despite the fact that the parody contained utterly and maliciously false statements about Falwell's sex life, the Supreme Court ruled unanimously that he could not seek damages from Flynt. They reasoned that since no one could have taken *Hustler*'s portrayal of the reverend's sex life seriously, Falwell could not have been libelled.

These decisions on the First Amendment pay testament to Americans' belief that a free press is indispensable to open and democratic government. They help to ensure that the press, and indeed other media, can speak with a powerful voice in American politics, both by challenging official versions of the truth and by exposing the wrongdoing of government.

Objective journalism

The third distinctive feature of the American press is that, despite the opportunities for irresponsible bias that local exclusivity and First Amendment freedoms create, the major newspapers are far less overtly partisan than those in, say, Great Britain. The journalistic profession in the United States is imbued with a norm of 'factual reporting' and political 'objectivity'. One writer described this norm as follows:

> **Objectivity rules contain two primary requirements. *Depersonalisation* demands that reporters refrain from inserting into the news their own ideological or substantive evaluations of officials, ideas, or groups. *Balance* aims for neutrality. It requires that reporters present the views of legitimate spokespersons of the conflicting sides in any significant dispute, and provide both sides with roughly equivalent attention.**
>
> Entman, 1989, p. 30

Another analyst likened the model of objective journalists to that of medical doctors: 'white-coated specialists describing pathologies as if through microscopes' (Diamond, 1980, p. 235).

Total objectivity is clearly not possible, since the very selection of the items that constitute the news involves judgements which are in part subjective. As we shall see below, many politicians and academics do believe that the American media are politically biased. Nevertheless, it remains true that American newspapers are generally much less inclined to play the role of cheerleader for a politician or political party than are their British counterparts.

Television

Television is by far the most important medium in American politics. Not only do most Americans get the bulk of their information about politics from television, but they trust it more than any other medium. Adult Americans spend a lot of time watching television. Nielsen, a company that records media use for those in the communications and advertising business, reported in 2009 that Americans watch around 5 hours per day. A growing share of this usage is through cable and satellite channels, and there is an accelerating technological shift to internet delivery of television.

Unsurprisingly, very few of these hours are spent watching news or other programmes about politics. Most Americans watch television as a leisure activity and seek entertainment, not political enlightenment from their television sets. Furthermore, even the main political programmes, such as the prime-time network news, actually convey little information compared with a newspaper. As Robert Spero pointed out, 'The word-count of a half-hour news programme would not fill up much more than one column of one page of the *New York Times*' (Spero, 1980, p. 177).

Table 9.2 Voters' main sources of campaign news

Source	1992 %	1996 %	2000 %	2004 %	2008 %
Television	82	72	70	76	72
Newspapers	57	60	39	28	29
Radio	12	19	15	15	21
Internet	–	3	11	10	33
Magazines	9	11	4	2	3

Source: Graber, 2002, p. 246; Pew Research Center, 2008

That said, television is critical to most Americans' knowledge of political affairs. If we take as an example the sources from which Americans gain knowledge of presidential elections, we still find a clear predominance of television.

The reliance of the American public upon television for political information, together with the importance attached to television by politicians themselves, raises several critical questions about the power of television in American politics. Who owns and runs television stations? How does television cover political news? Is television coverage of politics biased? And, perhaps most important of all, how much impact does television have on viewers' political opinions and behaviour? Each of these questions is examined in turn below.

Television ownership and control

Ownership of television in the United States is in private, commercial hands. There is no equivalent of the BBC. There is a small non-commercial television channel (Public Broadcasting Service – PBS) supported financially by a mixture of grants and viewer subscriptions. PBS audiences are very small, however, with a quality political programme such as the MacNeil/Lehrer *NewsHour* attracting about 1 per cent of the nation's viewers.

Television broadcasting is thus largely the preserve of private business, and especially of the four main network television companies – the Columbia Broadcasting System (CBS), the American Broadcasting Company (ABC), the National Broadcasting Company (NBC) and the Fox Broadcasting System (FBS) – and, as noted above, cable and satellite stations. The four main corporations sell their programmes to the hundreds of local television stations across the country and are estimated to dominate the programming for about one-third of the nation's television households (Graber, 1989, p. 45). They are also responsible for producing the main national evening news programmes.

American television companies are, in many respects, just like any other business enterprise. They are owned by even larger corporations or by rich tycoons and the main task of the executives who run them is to make profits. Like other businesses, television companies seek to expand their markets, something which may involve buying up other broadcasting companies.

Here, however, there is a degree of governmental regulation. Broadcasting licences are issued by the Federal Communications Commission (FCC), the members of which are appointed by the president, subject to approval by the Senate. In order to ensure that no owner or television company acquires too much media power, the FCC limits the number of media outlets that any one company can own. There is, however, a constant debate over ownership caps, with the FCC coming under considerable pressure from large corporations and their political allies to relax the regulations. The Telecommunications Act of 1996 and subsequent revisions of regulations by the FCC have allowed for a much greater concentration of corporate ownership. A handful of corporations, including AOL Time Warner, Viacom and the News Corporation, now dominate television and other media outlets. Although there has been fierce criticism of this process of consolidation, a deal agreed by President George W. Bush and the Congress in 2003 allowed a further increase that permitted Viacom and the News Corporation to keep all their stations. Whether these commercial developments have any significance for media coverage of politics, however, is the subject of much debate.

Television coverage of politics

The principal way that a television corporation seeks to maximise its profits is to increase the number of viewers who tune into its programmes. The more viewers who watch a programme, the more the television company can charge advertisers who wish to reach that audience. Inevitably, then, virtually all television programmes, including news and current affairs programmes, are designed to pull in the largest audience possible. This has significant consequences for the way in which politics is packaged for television.

Television is a visual medium that most people watch for entertainment. These are two of the principal factors which constrain the coverage of politics on television. Most viewers want visual images which entertain them, whether they are watching an election campaign item or a report of urban rioting. The main ingredients of visual entertainment are movement, drama, emotion and conflict.

Because Americans are relatively uninterested in politics and television therefore devotes relatively little time to it, news items must also be brief and simplified. Finally, because the aim of the company is to maximise its audience, news items should not unnecessarily antagonise any section of the viewing public.

One can immediately see that such constraints raise considerable problems for television coverage of the complex issues which lie at the heart of American politics – the budget deficit, health care, civil rights and foreign affairs, for example. Television takes these important political issues and, in rendering them palatable for viewers, distorts them. Distortion should not be confused with bias: while the latter slants coverage towards a particular political viewpoint, distortion involves misrepresenting events in order to meet journalistic needs.

The result of meeting these needs, say critics, is a diet of trivialised, simplified, emotion-laden items which do little or nothing to develop an informed public. An example of this occurred in the early summer of 1993, when President Clinton went to

California as part of his campaign to build political support for his budget proposal. The main story to arise from that tour, however, was not whether the president's plan was a good one, or even whether he had sold the plan well; rather, it was the fact that, while aboard *Air Force One* at Los Angeles Airport, waiting to take off for Washington, he had his hair cut by a fashionable stylist. Since all airport traffic is routinely halted when *Air Force One* is in the vicinity, the president's haircut caused a long delay to other travellers. Moreover, the haircut cost $200. The president was pilloried for his alleged indifference to other travellers and his vanity. Moreover, it later emerged that most, if not all, of the story was actually untrue.

The story, however, was entertaining, simple to tell and amenable to visual representation by pictures of the president's hair, *Air Force One* and the backlog of air traffic at the airport. On the other hand, its political significance is minuscule, except for the irony that it showed Clinton, a master of the political arts, as having been naive about the ability of the media to turn a trivial episode into one that is politically damaging.

On a more serious matter, television coverage of the Vietnam War has frequently been attacked for distorting the nature of the conflict. Television allegedly concentrated on dramatic scenes involving combat, destruction and refugees, even though such scenes were comparatively rare and not typical of the realities of life in South Vietnam. The simple fact is, however, that combat is emotionally and visually exciting, while peasants peacefully tending their rice-paddies is not.

Television bias

As well as being accused of distortion, journalists covering the Vietnam War were also accused of straightforward political bias. Robert Elegant, for example, claimed that many journalists were opposed to the war on political grounds and therefore their reports were negative and damaging to the American cause (Elegant, 1981).

Although the Vietnam War is an outstanding illustration, accusations of political bias in television and press reporting are routine in American politics. Politicians are notoriously thin-skinned and they are quick to attribute media criticism of their actions or policies to political bias. Richard Nixon made such accusations an ongoing feature of his political career. When defeated for the governorship of California in 1962, just two years after he lost the presidential election to John F. Kennedy, Nixon retired from politics, telling journalists at a press conference, 'You won't have me to kick around any more.'

Even after his successful comeback in the presidential election of 1968, Nixon was convinced that the media were out to get him. Among other things, he had his vice-president, Spiro T. Agnew, conduct an aggressive public campaign accusing the media of liberal bias. The names of many journalists also featured on President Nixon's secret political enemies list that was discovered during the Watergate scandal.

Beyond Richard Nixon's personal feelings, however, it is almost a staple of conservative politics in the United States to accuse the media of liberal bias. At first glance, this may seem an unconvincing allegation. Most obviously, as already noted, television is a commercial business and one would expect those who run it to share the pro-business values of much of the rest of corporate America. Indeed, it is on precisely these lines that the left usually accuses the media of *conservative* bias.

Nevertheless, the allegation of liberal bias is not altogether without foundation. Most obviously, the four major television networks are based in New York city, the centre of American liberal culture. Moreover, those who work in television are part of an intellectual and cultural liberalism which is strong among the artistic and entertainments community (Dye, 1995; Graber, 1989).

There is also some empirical evidence to support this view. Those who work in television, as opposed to the actual owners of television companies, are far more likely to identify themselves as Democrats or Independents, than as Republicans. One study of executive media personnel in the 1980s found that 33 per cent were Democrats, 58 per cent were Independents and just 9 per cent were Republicans. This led Doris Graber to conclude that 'owners of prominent media hire Democrats and liberal Independents to operate their media properties, although they themselves usually share the Republican leanings of the big business community' (Graber, 1989, p. 62).

Allegations of bias are easy to make and there is clearly some truth to them. Few seriously doubt that Fox News is conservative, while other stations lean towards the liberal side of politics. On the other hand, other factors can be mistaken for bias. Take the CBS scandal of 2004/5, which resulted in the retirement of superstar news anchorman Dan Rather and the firing of several top executives at CBS. The scandal stemmed from a CBS news report in September 2004, claiming that George W. Bush had received preferential treatment during the Vietnam War era by being admitted to the Texas National Guard. Not only did this mean that Bush did not have to serve in Vietnam, but CBS further claimed that he did not fulfil even his obligations to the National Guard. The basis of the CBS story was some newly discovered documents of the era. When the story was challenged, however, CBS were unable to demonstrate the authenticity of the documents or the truth of the allegations. Many conservatives believed that Rather and the CBS team had been motivated by their political opposition to Bush. An enquiry that reported in early 2005 dismissed this charge and found instead that CBS had been so determined to beat its rivals and be the first to run the story that it neglected its usual procedures for verifying the facts.

It is one thing, then, to identify media personnel as liberal, but quite another to show that their political persuasion results in slanted news coverage. Thomas Dye believes that the liberal bias of the media is most strongly reflected in the actual selection of items that are included in the news:

> **Topics selected weeks in advance for coverage reflect, or create . . . current liberal issues: concern for poor and blacks, women's liberation, opposition to defense spending, and the CIA, ecology, migrant farm labor, tax loopholes and Indian rights and, for nearly two years, Watergate.**
>
> Dye, 1995, p. 107

This argument is countered by journalists who claim that television news coverage mirrors society and the public's concerns. This view is buttressed by the point made earlier that, ultimately, television news is an entertainment designed to attract as many viewers as possible, in order to maximise advertising revenue. Content, like other aspects of journalistic coverage, is constrained by the need to please the maximum number of viewers. Any programme which ignored this, and instead pursued an agenda of issues that interested only liberals, would soon fall behind in the ratings war.

The liberal bias of the media certainly did not spare President Clinton when he became embroiled in yet another sexual scandal in 1998. Despite the fact that conservative groups had been using such scandal to undermine the Clinton presidency from its inception in 1993, liberal newspapers like the *Washington Post* took the lead in exposing the president's alleged intimate relationship with a White House employee. Moreover, broadcast and print media alike repeated unsubstantiated stories, sometimes from anonymous sources, in their rush to beat their competitors with 'breaking news'.

As the spectrum of television delivery services has expanded, space has been created for greater diversity of ideological approach. In the 2008 presidential campaign, the Pew Center's research (Pew Center, 2008a) found MSNBC, a satellite and cable station, broadcast a significantly higher proportion of negative news items on Republican John McCain, and a higher proportion favourable to Obama than the average for all channels. The Fox News channel was more critical of Obama than the average. The nightly newscasts of the three major channels, NBC, ABC and CBS, were more neutral and less negative than other news outlets. To a considerable extent, these channels are reflecting the ideological convictions of their audiences. At the time of the 2008 election, the Pew Center (Pew Center, 2008b) found that three times more Fox News viewers identified themselves as Republicans than as Democrats, with the MSNBC audience being a near-mirror image of this. The traditional major channel news programmes drew audiences more typical of the broad political divisions in American society.

A further factor which undermines the theory of liberal bias in the American media is the simple fact that reporters are heavily dependent upon government for stories and information. Daniel Hallin disputed the myth of liberal bias in reporting on the Vietnam War by showing not only that government was the major source of information relayed by the media, but also that such information was reported largely unchallenged (Hallin, 1986). What was true of Vietnam coverage is also true of political news in general (Graber, 1989, p. 78). If there is any structural bias in media coverage of politics, it is bias in favour of the government of the day, whatever its political colour.

Impact of television

There is a passionate debate in most countries about the impact of television on people's attitudes and behaviour. It is typically argued that exposure to a heavy diet of explicit television violence or sex leads to antisocial or criminal behaviour in viewers. Evidence to support this is said to be the number of criminal offenders who cite television programmes as the inspiration for their crime.

On the other hand, it can be plausibly argued that television does not cause violence in people, but rather that people prone to violence are attracted to programmes which portray it graphically. Thus the causal relationship between television and behaviour is in dispute.

The same debate exists in regard to television's coverage of politics. Don Hewitt, the executive producer of the popular politics programme *60 Minutes*, tells of a woman who told him that television violence was to blame for John Hinckley's attempt to assassinate President Reagan in 1981. Hewitt responded by asking her how much television John Wilkes Booth had watched before assassinating Abraham Lincoln (White and McCarthy, 1985).

Social scientists have, of course, investigated the impact of television on political behaviour, especially voting behaviour. These studies have failed to produce any evidence that what people see on television affects the way they vote: 'the persistent finding of almost three decades of research has been that the mass media have minimal effects in changing voters' attitudes' (Arterton, 1984, p. 4).

As another analyst pointed out, this conclusion presents us with something of a paradox: 'The public believes that the media have an important impact on the conduct of politics and on public thinking. Politicians act and behave on the basis of the same assumption. But many studies conducted by social scientists fail to show substantial impact' (Graber, 1989, p. 12).

These findings are troubling because common sense tells us that if Americans get most of their political information from television, and if they place a great deal of faith in the reliability of that information, then surely they *must* be influenced by television.

Selective attention

Here as elsewhere, however, common sense may not be right, for media researchers agree that human beings are adept at controlling what information they accept. The most important phenomenon in this respect is selective perception, also known as selective exposure or *selective attention*. Quite simply, viewers will screen out political messages which make them psychologically uncomfortable by contradicting their existing beliefs. Selective attention is thus a defence mechanism against disturbing political information. It can take a variety of forms in practice – the television can be turned off or the channel switched; the viewer can 'challenge' the unwelcome message by drawing upon different, contradictory evidence or disputing the validity of the source of the message; or the viewer may simply ignore the message.

The importance of selective attention will vary from one individual to the next. Viewers with deeply held political convictions or strong party loyalties are extremely unlikely to be affected by news or propaganda which contradicts their existing opinions. The weaker their knowledge or political beliefs, however, the less they are likely to be discomforted by new political information and the less, therefore, they are likely to invoke the defensive shield of selective attention. Consequently, this section of the population is most vulnerable to the impact of television and any political bias which operates.

It is probable, then, that the main impact of television on the substance of Americans' political beliefs stems from its power to help set the political agenda. By definition, news is what is reported in the media. Selecting newsworthy items from the mass of stories and issues available is a subjective process. However, as noted above, such judgements are likely to be guided at least as much by professional and commercial considerations as by the political bias of the television or newspaper.

It is therefore difficult to avoid the conclusion that the power of the media to influence Americans' political attitudes is frequently exaggerated by those who mistake its pervasiveness for persuasiveness. Nevertheless, as we shall now see, that very pervasiveness is a critical ingredient of the representative process.

The media and elections

Media strategy

In effect, elections take place on television in the United States. Since most Americans get most of their political information from television, candidates for office spend most of their time, effort and money on developing an effective media strategy. To be successful, the first thing they need is exposure: they need to be seen on television as often as possible. The second major condition of a successful media strategy is that this exposure must cast the candidate in a positive light.

Fulfilling both of these demands can be problematic. Take, for example, the relatively unknown politician in a large field of primary candidates. This politician needs to do something that brings favourable publicity onto herself, but the media will prefer to concentrate their attention upon the front-runners in the election. Moreover, those front-runners are likely to be better financed than she is and therefore able to buy more advertising time on television.

The front-runners too, however, may face difficulties in presenting themselves to the public via television. The most obvious problem that may arise is that the media may cover them *too* closely and expose things that they would rather keep hidden. Such was the experience of Senator Gary Hart, the leading candidate for the Democratic party presidential nomination in 1988. When rumours began to circulate about Hart's extramarital affair with model Donna Rice, Hart denied them and challenged the media to produce proof. In hindsight, this was a foolish act of bravado, as evidence soon showed the rumours to be true. The Hart campaign never recovered.

There are ultimately two kinds of media attention with which a candidate has to deal. There is coverage by others – journalists and critics – which only leaves the candidate with limited opportunities to respond, but there are situations in which the initiative and control are mainly with the candidate. Particularly important among the latter are the campaign's promotion of a preferred public image for the candidate through television advertisements and similar formats which the campaign pays to have broadcast.

Candidate image

How a candidate looks on television is crucial to his overall strategy of establishing his image in the minds of the electorate. The most basic aspect of this is literally the physical appearance of the candidate. Academics and political consultants agree that it is becoming increasingly difficult for physically unattractive candidates to get elected. They also agree that even great politicians from the past who were not physically blessed, such as Abraham Lincoln, would find it difficult today to pursue a successful political career. Professor Larry Sabato believes that, in effect, candidates are now preselected by physical appearance, with their model being good-looking television presenters: 'We've had a convergence among three types of people. Anchor-persons on television, politicians and gameshow hosts all look very much alike today. And that's the effect of television' (Rees, 1992).

The most famous example of the impact of the physical appearance of candidates on television occurred during the 1960 presidential election. In the first televised debate between John Kennedy and Richard Nixon, viewers were presented with a strong contrast between the two candidates. Kennedy was tanned, youthful and dressed in a dark suit which gave him a crisp outline against the pale studio background. Nixon was pale following a recent illness, perspiring and had a dark 'five o'clock shadow'; he also wore a light grey suit which merged his figure with the background. Analysis later showed that those who heard the debate on radio believed that Nixon had won, but those who had watched on television thought Kennedy had won.

Candidate image depends upon more than raw physical appearance, however. Politicians present themselves so as visually to symbolise their character and politics. Jimmy Carter, for example, both as candidate in 1976 and then as president, would sometimes dress casually on television in order to try to project an image of being an informal, approachable 'man of the people'.

Figure 9.1 In the first 2004 presidential debate President George W. Bush reacted with impatience to his opponent's criticisms. This counted against Bush as it was deemed 'conduct unbecoming'. Source: © Ron Sachs/Corbis

On the other hand, during the 1980 presidential election, when Carter was under severe public pressure from perceived domestic and foreign policy failures, he sought to emphasise his presidential character by adopting a 'Rose Garden strategy'. This is when an incumbent president invites the cameras in to witness him signing important bills or meeting foreign dignitaries in presidential surroundings, such as the White House Rose Garden. The object is to appeal to the respect that the voters hold for the office, in the hope that this will compensate for any lack of respect for the man or his policies.

The 2004 presidential election provided some interesting insights into the image issue. President George W. Bush chose a strategy that presented him as clear and determined in his ideas and policies. It was less important whether people actually agreed with those ideas and policies. What counted was clarity, not content. This strategy was reinforced by the attacks on his opponent, Senator John Kerry, for being indecisive and 'flip-flopping' on issues.

The 2008 election was an unusual race in having neither an incumbent nor a previous vice-president in the running. In a race of more or less well-known outsiders, the expectation might be of a vigorous and multi-member campaign. This was true – though the most eye-watering battles that developed were between Hillary Clinton and Barack Obama for the Democratic nomination, and then between the two major party nominees, Obama and McCain, for the presidency. Both Clinton and McCain attacked Obama on the grounds of his alleged inexperience, and they attempted to link him with unsavoury political allies. Obama fought back with a campaign comparing 'Hope' and 'Change' with the failures of past politicians, stressing endorsements from established trusted public figures, and linking McCain especially with the economic crisis that hit the USA during the latter stages of the Bush second term.

Political advertisements

Undoubtedly, the main opportunity for a candidate to define himself with the public is the paid television advertisement. Here the candidate, or rather his television consultant, has almost total control over the presentation.

Advertisements may try to establish a candidate's position on certain policy issues, but they are more likely to try to project his image and character. As with commercial advertising, political advertisements seek to entertain and to produce a favourable response to the 'product-candidate', by evoking an emotional rather than a rational response. Thus advertisements have very little to do with conveying information upon which a viewer can base a reasoned voting decision. Rather, advertisements try to make the viewer like the candidate for other, even irrational, reasons. Advertisements hope to make viewers prefer a candidate for the same reasons that they prefer a news presenter or game-show host.

Not surprisingly, then, political advertisements have come in for a great deal of criticism for their failure to convey the kind of information that rational voting requires. Critics claim that political advertisements present either false information about candidates or no information at all.

Robert Spero's analysis of political advertisements by presidential candidates adds weight to these criticisms (Spero, 1980). He discovered that these advertisements regularly violated the codes of truthfulness that regulate commercial advertising. They contained both demonstrable lies and seriously misleading statements. Thus, in 1976, the Jimmy Carter campaign ran commercials proclaiming its candidate to be a peanut farmer and a political outsider, who started out on his quest for the presidency with no organisation, no influential contacts and no money. In fact, Carter was a millionaire owner of a peanut-processing corporation, who had put his campaign organisation into place some three years before the election. He had also served on the Trilateral Commission, where he had established good contacts with leading politicians, academics and businesspeople.

Nevertheless, while such distortion of the truth may be morally reprehensible, it is not clear that it seriously misleads many voters. As Doris Graber says, 'Commercials are perceiver-determined. People see in them pretty much what they want to see – attractive images for their favourite candidates and unattractive ones for their opponents' (Graber, 1989, p. 196). As with political news, then, viewers are very good at screening out information which contradicts their existing beliefs, while accepting that which confirms them.

What advertisements can achieve, however, is a crystallisation of a latent feeling that the viewer has about a candidate. This is particularly important in the case of negative advertising, an increasingly common and controversial feature of American election campaigns.

Negative advertising

In terms of political impact, it seems more profitable to attack your opponent than to promote yourself. Typically, campaign consultants will interview a selected panel of voters to find out what they dislike most about the opposing candidate. Advertisements are then produced which attack the opponent on these issues, often in a crude, vicious and misleading manner. At their worst, they attack an opponent's character or distort his or her political record or position.

The first major negative political advertisement was Tony Schwartz's 'daisy commercial', screened on behalf of President Johnson during the 1964 presidential campaign. It depicted a little girl counting as she pulls the petals off a flower. Suddenly a male voice is superimposed, counting down from ten to one as if in preparation for a rocket launch. The camera zooms into the eye of the girl, and as the voice reaches zero, a nuclear explosion is heard and the mushroom cloud appears. President Johnson's voice is now heard warning of the dangers of nuclear war.

His opponent, Barry Goldwater, is never mentioned in the commercial. However, the right-wing Goldwater had a well-deserved reputation as a hard-line anti-communist, and the daisy commercial played on this to suggest that, if elected, he might be willing to risk a nuclear war. The commercial was scaremongering, but its effectiveness depended upon the fact that Goldwater's extremism was already an issue in the public's perception. It was thus a classic example of the power of advertising to sharpen and define an opponent's negative characteristics.

By the late 1980s, negative advertising had become a regular feature of elections at all levels of office and even of primary elections. For example, the 1990 Democratic primary for governor of Texas featured a Jim Mattox advertisement accusing Ann Richards of having used drugs; meanwhile, a Richards advertisement mentioned an earlier indictment of Mattox for bribery, even though he had been acquitted (Davies, 1992, p. 95).

The 1988 presidential election was particularly noted for the use of negative advertising by Republicans against the Democratic candidate, Governor Michael Dukakis of Massachusetts. In particular, they played on the fact that a convicted murderer in Massachusetts, Willie Horton, had committed rape while out of prison on a weekend pass. Although many states had such furlough systems, Dukakis was attacked for being 'soft on crime'. Other advertisements attacked him for being unpatriotic, because he had vetoed a state bill requiring schoolchildren to begin the day by reciting the Pledge of Allegiance. The advertisements failed to mention that the bill was clearly unconstitutional under well-known Supreme Court decisions.

Such advertising may lower the tone of elections and increase the cynicism of the public about politics and politicians in general. Candidates are also aware that the public condemns negative advertising and this may have helped both the Clinton and Dole campaigns in 1996 decide to avoid the worst excesses of character attacks on their opponent. The Clinton campaign concentrated on so-called comparative advertisements, which criticise the opponent's record (Just, 1997, pp. 92–3). This may still be thought of as negative in the sense that it does not concentrate on the candidate's own virtues, but it is also entirely legitimate in a contest between two individuals presenting two different programmes for the public's endorsement.

Ultimately, however, negative advertising can have a significant effect on voter choice. It seems that it is more effective to focus on your opponent's negative features than merely to emphasise your own positive features. In other words, it is sometimes more effective to play on the electorate's fears than its hopes. This is nothing new in electoral politics. It becomes a problem, however, when it is so widespread that voters are presented with a campaign which is almost wholly negative in tone. The danger is that it will simply turn people off politics altogether. However, the evidence of the 2004 presidential campaign suggests otherwise. There was a sharp rise in voter turnout, despite the fact that much of the advertising was negative. A classic example was the advertisement broadcast on behalf of the so-called Swift Boat Veterans, attacking the Vietnam War record of Senator John Kerry. Although a supposedly independent group, it was later discovered that they had been advised by people who were working for the Bush campaign. The allegations made by the advertisement were dubious where they were not simply wrong. Yet the media, despite their supposedly liberal, anti-Bush bias, took up the allegations without thoroughly checking them. As a result, Kerry experienced several difficult weeks trying to put the story right, and perhaps never quite recovered his image as the patriotic veteran.

Analyses of the 2008 presidential campaign suggest that, by the end of the race, Obama was running as many attack ads as was the McCain campaign, but that these ads made up a more substantial proportion of the McCain effort – probably because the Obama camp had a much larger war chest to spend on television advertising. These advertisements often tackled key issues – the developing economic crisis, the potential impact of policies on taxes, competing items on the policy agendas of the candidates. Some took a more personal approach. In the tight primary campaign between Obama and Clinton, the Clinton campaign launched an ad designed to challenge Obama's lack of experience in national security affairs. Featuring a ringing telephone, and a sleeping child, the voice over asks the viewer to consider whom they would want to answer the emergency call when the White House phone rings at 3 a.m. When advisers wanted to air ads exploiting Obama's links with the controversial preacher Jeremiah Wright, McCain vetoed this approach, but the independent National Republican Trust PAC ran such an ad, calling Obama 'Too Radical, Too Risky'. In another attempt to define Obama as too dangerous to be elected president, the McCain campaign did not hesitate to highlight Obama's alleged links to Bill Ayers, a leading 1960s radical, and later a university professor in Chicago. Barack Obama's campaign responded to these attacks, but the candidate also projected an impression of statesmanlike calm in responses to the claim of radicalism. These attacks in 2008 may have helped rally the conservative wing of the Republican voters, but could not overcome the electoral swing towards the Democrats.

Candidates versus the media

Whereas candidates can control the advertisements that are screened on behalf of their campaign, they are much more vulnerable when it comes to news coverage of elections. Here the supposedly adversarial relationship of politicians and the media comes into play. Candidates want only favourable coverage, while the media want the truth as they see it, though the truth must be packaged to meet their commercial demands.

Although the media have claimed their victims in the past, as we saw with Gary Hart above, candidates are becoming increasingly adept at manipulating the needs of the media for their own purposes. If television requires pictures, excitement and statements that can be condensed into simple language in a few sentences, then that is what politicians provide.

As a result, American elections are now governed by the 'soundbite' and the 'photo-opportunity'. In fact, campaigning amounts to creating as many opportunities as possible for the cameras to photograph the candidate in attractive settings, and to producing the telling, short phrase that will be broadcast on that evening's news programmes. Thus, in the 1996 campaign, the average length of a candidate quote on the evening news was 8.2 seconds (Just, 1997, p. 98).

Local news coverage is very important in a country the size of and as diverse as the United States, so candidates are given a manic schedule of trips to different parts of the country, spending only enough time in each to provide the media with what they need. As Christopher Arterton argued, 'If a candidate spends one hour in a city, he is likely to receive the same amount of news coverage of that visit as he would during a four-hour or eight-hour stop in the same location. Thus, modern presidential candidates are kept continually on the move by their desire for local news coverage. The scheduler's goal is to set up appearances in three or four major news markets each day' (Arterton, 1984, p. 13).

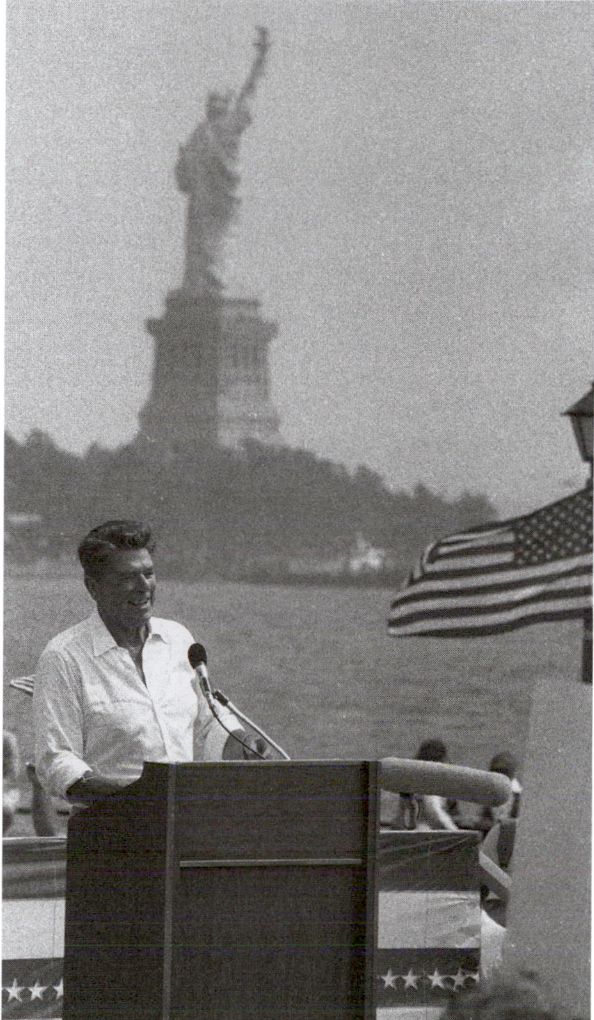

Figure 9.2 Ronald Reagan addressing a crowd against the backdrop of New York harbour and the Statue of Liberty.
Source: © Bettmann/Corbis

These appearances are carefully planned, even choreographed, to produce good visuals. Enthusiastic supporters are strategically placed to demonstrate that the candidate is popular. A site may be chosen to produce a positive response from the viewers – for example, Ronald Reagan addressing a crowd against the backdrop of New York harbour and the Statue of Liberty. Or again, the candidate might be filmed eating spaghetti at an Italian American social in order to identify himself with that particular section of the electorate. None of these images tells the voters much about the candidate's policies, but they are appealing and entertaining.

Soundbites fulfil the media's need for simplification and drama at the expense of detailed policy statements. Vice-President George H. Bush's most famous statement about his economic policies was the endlessly repeated 'Read my lips – no new taxes.' Unfortunately, this soundbite returned to haunt him as president when he *did* agree to raise taxes, but at least Bush's slogan purported to say something about policy. In 1992, the Clinton soundbite that took the media's fancy was a sentimental reference to his birthplace that was supposed to rekindle belief in the American dream: 'I still believe in a town called Hope.' Hope and Change were key words for the 2008 Obama campaign, but 'Yes, we can' was the beating mantra of the campaign and of many campaign speeches.

Candidate control of media reporting of elections was taken to extremes by Michael Deaver, Ronald Reagan's media adviser, in the 1984 election. Because Reagan was always liable to make a gaffe when questioned by reporters, Deaver permitted just one press conference with the president during the entire campaign. However, he did supply endless attractive photo-opportunities which the media felt bound to broadcast.

In 1992, the presidential candidates found new ways to bypass the rigours of media interrogation. Instead of reaching the public through interviews with 'heavyweight' political journalists, they appeared instead on popular television programmes, like the *Larry King Show*, *Phil Donahue* and *Arsenio Hall* and the rock music station MTV. Here candidates were not in danger of being confronted with difficult questions and they could also provide good photo-opportunities, as when Bill Clinton donned dark glasses and played the saxophone. Ross Perot went even further, simply buying media time to broadcast his own 30-minute specials. Jon Stewart's *The Late Show* proved a more difficult popular culture appearance for Barack Obama when, as sitting president, and attempting to help Democrats resist the tide of defeats they were facing in the 2010 mid-term elections, he opined that perhaps the 2008 slogan should have been 'Yes, we can, but. . . .'

Even when candidates cannot hide from the political media, they are not without means of trying to ensure that coverage is favourable. All campaigns employ spin doctors whose job it is to move among the media after, say, a televised debate or primary election, trying to persuade them that their candidate was the victor. Bill Clinton's team provided an excellent illustration of this in the 1992 presidential election. In the key New Hampshire primary, Clinton was beaten by Paul Tsongas. Nevertheless, the Clinton team claimed victory by arguing that because the campaign had been hit so badly by sex scandals, his second place was truly remarkable. They even persuaded the media to adopt their description of Clinton as 'the Comeback Kid'.

Moreover, for reasons that are not always clear, some candidates and politicians seem to get away with serial gaffes. President Reagan usually joked his way out of such difficulties, but President George W. Bush lacked Reagan's easy charm. Nevertheless, although he often garbled his words, creating a well-publicised list of 'Bushisms', a sufficient number of voters were willing to discount his verbal frailties and elect him president in both 2000 and 2004.

Candidates and new media

Candidates and their campaigns have always been enthusiastic users of newly developing communications. In the nineteenth century, new forms of printing, new media and new ways to deliver a campaign message included glassware, ceramics, posters, banners, medallions and the invention of the campaign button. Radio and television came in the early and mid-twentieth century, and since Sir Tim Berners-Lee's launch of the world wide web some observers have been eager to declare each election the year of the internet. It is possible that 2008 finally provided that opportunity.

In 2004, Democratic hopeful Howard Dean ran a vigorous campaign on the internet, using the web to raise money, to create supporter groups, to arrange rallies and generally to add energy and efficiency to traditional campaign activities. The Dean effort attracted attention, and elevated his campaign into strong contention, but in the end the voters did not have confidence in the candidate, and the Dean bandwagon failed. The Obama campaign and others learned a great deal from Dean's efforts, and in Obama the Democrats appeared to find a candidate of the quality to capitalise on the reach of the new media.

All candidates now have Facebook pages, websites, twitter feeds and a team fully aware of the needs of web-based media. To some extent, these become a monitor of comparative success – Obama's three million Facebook friends outnumbered McCain's by five to one. My.BarackObama.com became a social network unmatched by any of the other candidates. YouTube provided another fruitful outlet, and Obama's Flickr stream was so popular that the site temporarily crashed.

The 2008 election saw a continuation of earlier decline in newspaper use, balanced against a sharp increase in internet use, with more than half of over-18-year-olds using the internet to participate in or find news of the campaign (Smith, 2009, p. 3). While the Obama campaign used the internet most effectively, supporters of McCain were slightly more likely to be internet users. This is probably because Republicans and internet users both tend to have higher income and education levels, and points to the possibility of a degree of 'democratic deficit' in the new media. The 2008 campaign suggests that the quality of the candidate has the potential to generate interest and activity to counter any modest inbuilt disadvantage, and the steady spread of new social media is also likely to level the playing field at the same time as increasing the significance of this sector.

Chapter summary

Ideally, the media should communicate the kind of political information that the electorate needs in order to make rational voting decisions. Voters should know what policies the candidates propose and what the effect of those policies is likely to be. Voters should also be informed about the past record of politicians and the kind of government they propose to run.

Clearly, however, current media presentation of politics falls far short of these goals. Politicians seem increasingly able to package themselves for television in ways that make them attractive figures, without revealing much about their true selves or their policies. Media personnel may try to penetrate the politicians' veneer but, even when successful, they provide mostly a simplistic, trivial and perhaps distorted picture.

It is not clear, however, how much of the blame for this should be laid at the door of the media, for any citizen who wishes to be well informed can find newspapers, magazines and television programmes that provide serious and detailed coverage of politics. If the average voter wanted such coverage, then popular print and broadcast media would provide it – for commercial reasons, if nothing else. Most Americans, however, appear to value entertainment more than real politics and that, therefore, is what both politicians and the media seek to give them.

Discussion points

1. Does media coverage of politics give viewers the information they need?
2. How biased is media coverage of politics?
3. How important is 'image' in elections?
4. Is negative advertising harmful to the political process?

Further reading

An excellent introduction to this subject is Doris Graber, *Mass Media and American Politics* (8th edn, Washington, DC: CQ Press, 2009). See also Graber's *Media Power in Politics* (5th edn, Washington, DC: CQ Press, 2006). A good discussion of the impact of television on the political process is Robert Entman, *Democracy Without Citizens: Media and the Decay of American Politics* (New York: Oxford University Press, 1989). Darrell West takes a close look at campaign advertising in *Air Wars: Television Advertising in Election Campaigns, 1952–2008* (5th edn, Washington, DC: CQ Press, 2009). A useful chapter on the structure of

American media can be found in Thomas Dye, *Who's Running America?* (6th edn, Englewood Cliffs, NJ: Prentice Hall, 1995). For an analysis of the media campaign in the 2000 election, see G. Pomper *et al.*, *The Elections of 2000: Reports and Interpretations* (Chatham, NJ: Chatham House, 2001); for the 2004 and 2008 elections see M. Nelson, *The Elections of 2004* (Washington, DC: CQ Press, 2005) and *The Elections of 2008* (Washington, DC: CQ Press, 2009). For a sophisticated analysis of the power of the media in politics, see Daniel Hallin, *The 'Uncensored War': The Media and Vietnam* (New York: Oxford University Press, 1986).

References

Arterton, F. (1984) *Media Politics* (Lexington: Lexington Books).

Davies, P. (1992) *Elections USA* (Manchester: Manchester University Press).

Diamond, E. (1980) *Good News, Bad News* (Cambridge, Mass.: MIT Press).

Dye, T. (1995) *Who's Running America?* (6th edn, Englewood Cliffs, NJ: Prentice Hall).

Elegant, R. (1981) 'How to lose a war', *Encounter*, August, pp. 73–90.

Entman, R. (1989) *Democracy Without Citizens: Media and the Decay of American Politics* (New York: Oxford University Press).

Graber, D. (1989) *Mass Media and American Politics* (3rd edn, Washington, DC: CQ Press).

Graber, D. (2002) *Mass Media and American Politics* (6th edn, Washington, DC: CQ Press).

Hallin, D. (1986) *The 'Uncensored War': The Media and Vietnam* (New York: Oxford University Press).

Just, M. (1997) 'Candidate strategies and the media campaign' in Pomper, G. *et al. The Elections of 1996: Reports and Interpretation* (Chatham, NJ: Chatham House).

Pew Research Center for the People and the Press (2008a) 'The color of news: how different media have covered the election', http://pewresearch.org/pubs/1011/color-of-news-coverage

Pew Research Center for the People and the Press (2008b) 'Internet now major source of campaign news', http://pewresearch.org/pubs/1017/internet-now-major-source-of-campaign-news

Rees, L. (1992) *We Have Ways of Making You Think* (BBC2, broadcast 1992).

Smith, Aaron (2009) 'The internet's role in campaign 2008', Pew Internet and American Life Project, http://www.pewinternet.org/Reports/2009/6-The-Internets-Role-in-Campaign-2008.aspx

Spero, R. (1980) *The Duping of the American Voter: Dishonesty and Deception in Presidential Television Advertising* (New York: Lippincott & Crowell).

White, T. and McCarthy, L. (1985) *Television and the Presidency* (BBC2, broadcast 1985).

Chapter 10

Political parties

Political parties are a universal and essential feature of western democratic systems. Although often the target of cynical comment, parties are usually recognised as providing a vital link between the government and the governed. At first glance, American parties occupy the same place in the politics of the United States as do their European counterparts in their own countries. Thus, for well over one hundred years, national and local elections have been dominated by the Democratic party and the Republican party. On closer inspection, however, American parties differ significantly from those in Europe. Moreover, America's always relatively weak parties have been in yet further decline over recent decades, despite occasional evidence of strengthening in some respects. As a result, it is appropriate to ask whether parties in the United States any longer play a major role in politics and government.

Origins and history of American political parties

Anti-party feeling and the Constitution

The Founding Fathers took a dim view of political parties. They regarded parties as selfish factions which sought to use governmental power to satisfy their own desires, while neglecting the legitimate interests of other citizens. If such a faction commanded the support of a majority of citizens, a political party might even institute tyranny. In short, parties were viewed as divisive at a time when the country's greatest need was unity.

In *The Federalist* (no. 10) James Madison made clear both his negative view of factions and the ways in which the Constitution was designed to keep them in check. Yet despite his best attempts to create what has been described as a 'Constitution against party' (Hofstadter,

1969, p. 40), it was soon clear that Madison had failed. By the end of George Washington's presidency in 1797, the United States possessed its first party system, pitching the Federalists against the Jeffersonian Republicans. In his farewell address, Washington warned the country against 'the spirit of faction' that had arisen, but to no avail. In 1800, there occurred the first presidential election fought along clear party lines. What then were the forces which compelled the emergence of political parties?

The first party system

First, and by far the most important, was the simple fact that Americans were divided by their own self-interests and the public policies linked to them. Although free of the extreme class and ideological divisions of Europe, the United States was not without economic, sectional and political rivalries. Thus, economic activity in the South consisted mainly of agriculture, while that of the Northeast was geared to shipping, banking and commerce. From these differences arose competing views of what constituted good government.

The independent farmers of the South had little need for an active federal government to support their agricultural economy and, therefore, tended to take the view that 'the government governs best that governs least'. Those engaged in commerce, however, required the national government to introduce protective tariffs for American manufacturing and to help establish the creditworthiness of American business. Logically enough, these interests called for an expansive role for the federal government.

Given the fundamental nature of these issues, it comes as no surprise that they quickly emerged as political conflicts. President Washington's Treasury secretary, Alexander Hamilton, presented Congress with a set of proposals in 1790–91 designed to promote commerce and, along with it, the power of the federal government. Those who supported him were dubbed the 'Federalists', the name that had first been used to describe the proponents of the Constitution of 1787.

Ironically, the opposition to Hamilton's policies in Congress was led by James Madison, a former Federalist himself and, of course, the opponent of party politics. Along with Thomas Jefferson and others, he saw in Hamilton's policies the threat of a return to autocratic, even monarchic, government as a centralising authority sought to promote the interests of the rich at the expense of 'the common man'. Seeing themselves as the guardians of the American republic, they took the name 'Republicans'. As they increasingly gathered around Jefferson's presidential efforts, they became known as Jeffersonian Republicans.

The split between Federalists and Jeffersonian Republicans was not solely the product of economic self-interest and domestic policy. Political philosophy and foreign affairs intervened in respect of American policy towards the Anglo–French war of the 1790s, which followed the French Revolution of 1789. The more aristocratic Federalists supported the British, while the Republicans leaned towards the French.

The second main reason for the rise of political parties in the United States was that which is common to all democracies: the need to organise for competitive elections. While the Jeffersonian Republican party began as a Congressional opposition to a Federalist presidency, the aim of the movement quickly became the capture of the presidency itself. This required organisation not merely in Congress, but also in the country at large.

Republican congressmen therefore began to form Republican clubs at the state and district level. For the election of 1800, Jefferson drew up a party platform designed not merely to ensure his own election to the presidency, but also to produce a Republican majority in Congress.

This brings us to a third reason for the rise and persistence of parties in the United States. The very separation of powers which was designed to inhibit the growth of parties paradoxically makes them a necessity. Fragmentation of political power invites an organisational network which can bring institutions together for the purpose of advancing particular policies. The best way of producing such institutional coalitions is a party which can offer candidates for each of the institutions in question. Party, then, can supply the glue which holds a fragmented political system together.

This is not to say that the 'Constitution against party' has wholly failed in its goal. For as we shall see, while it did not succeed in containing the spirit of faction, it has helped to ensure that American political parties are weak.

Changes in party systems

The Democratic party

The first party system did not last long, but since the brief 'Era of Good Feelings', when party politics dissipated, the United States has experienced a series of party systems. Parties have come and gone and, equally importantly, parties which have not changed their name have nevertheless mutated in ways that defy their origins.

Both the emergence of new parties and the transformation of established ones have been brought about principally by developments in the fundamental issue agenda of American politics. Such developments have often been accompanied by the rise of new interests and groupings in the American electorate.

Andrew Jackson and the Democratic party

The Democratic party arose in 1828 in conjunction with the presidential candidacy of General Andrew Jackson, the military hero who had defeated the British at the Battle of New Orleans in 1815. The Democratic campaign concentrated heavily on promoting Jackson as a personality. However, it tapped important new sources of electoral support, such as recently enfranchised lower-class voters, particularly in the West, and Irish and German immigrant voters in the cities of the North.

These voters resented what they saw as their opponents' bias towards the interests of the rich, the banks and the corporations, and they enthusiastically bought the image of Jackson as the champion of 'the common man'. The Democrats eventually succeeded in building the first mass, popular party in the United States. However, unlike today, the Democrats at that time believed that the interests of lower-class Americans were best served by opposing the growth of governmental power, especially federal governmental power. They feared that the wealthy were intent on using the federal government not merely to enrich themselves at the expense of other Americans, but also to encroach upon the autonomy of the states' governments.

This fear was famously illustrated when President Jackson fought a running battle with his congressional opponents over their attempt to renew the charter of the National Bank. Jackson saw the bank as the epitome of centralised power in the hands of the rich, and in 1832 he vetoed the re-charter bill passed by Congress. In his message accompanying the veto, Jackson proclaimed an egalitarian philosophy. Accepting that some distinctions of wealth were inevitable and natural, he continued, '. . . but when the laws undertake to add to these natural and just advantages artificial distinctions, to grant titles, gratuities, and exclusive privileges, to make the rich richer and the potent more powerful, the humble members of society – the farmers, mechanics and labourers – who have neither the time nor the means

Box 10.1

Party systems in American history

1793–1816	*Federalist* v. *Jeffersonian Republican*
1816–1828	No party system: 'Era of Good Feelings'
1828–1856	*Democrat* v. *National Republican/Whig*
1856–1932	*Democrat* v. *Republican: pre-New Deal system*
1932–present day	*Democrat* v. *Republican: New Deal system*

of securing like favours to themselves, have a right to complain of the injustice of their government' (Rozwenc, 1963, pp. 88–9).

This philosophy of Jacksonian Democracy embodied themes which have been an ever-present feature of party politics in the United States. In particular, the philosophy is *populist* in its distrust of the combination of federal government power and the economic power of the banks, corporations and the rich. It is *egalitarian* in its belief not in equality, but in equality of opportunity – the right of the 'have-nots' to improve themselves without having to battle against artificial barriers designed to keep them in their place. Its *anti-elitism* is not radical in the sense that it is anti-capitalist: rather, it celebrates the form of capitalism represented in the American dream, a capitalism which creates individual wealth but does not entrench privilege.

The Democrats' opponents struggled to put together a party which could capture the presidency. Eventually settling on the name of 'the Whigs', they did succeed in electing two presidents: William Henry Harrison and Zachary Taylor. However, these victories followed economic downturns and represented a rejection of the incumbent Democrat, rather than a triumph for Whig principles.

Anti-slavery and the Republican party

Nevertheless, the Whig belief in promoting national economic development through federal government activity attracted the support of many whose economic self-interest was bound up with manufacturing. Most importantly, this included the growing number of white labourers in the country. Unlike farmers, their prosperity was enhanced by tariffs which protected American manufacturing from its overseas competitors. Unlike southerners, they also had good reason to oppose the spread of slavery throughout the country. Since slave labour was inevitably cheaper than free labour, slavery, if allowed to spread, would undercut the opportunities available to white workers in the North and West. Thus, when the slavery issue came to the fore in the 1850s, it created new electoral possibilities for the Federalist/Whig belief in promoting the national economy.

Slavery was a sectional issue which divided the country along geopolitical lines. As such, the increasing bitterness over the issue split the national parties asunder. The Democrats, whose core was in the agricultural South, gradually became the pro-slavery party; northern Democrats tried desperately to promote a compromise on slavery that would keep the party together. In 1860, however, the Democrat presidential nominating convention broke up on sectional lines, with southerners nominating John C. Breckinridge of Kentucky and northerners nominating Stephen A. Douglas of Illinois.

Anti-slavery sentiment found its expression in a number of third parties, such as the Liberty party, the Free Soil party, and the American party or 'Know Nothing party'. However, it was the Republican party, founded in 1854, which was able to combine anti-slavery with other policies and produce a viable electoral alternative to the Democrats.

The Republicans' anti-slavery policy should not be confused with abolitionism or a belief in racial equality. The Republicans did not propose to end slavery in the United States, but rather to confine it to the states where it already existed. Moreover, most Republicans did not believe in equality of the races. While many accepted that slavery was morally wrong, few advocated racial integration. Indeed, where Republicans acquired sufficient power, as in Kansas, they banned all blacks, free or slave, from entering the state.

The Republicans' anti-slavery position thus married a moral principle with the self-interest of northern and western white labourers. And the more the Democrats thundered about slave-owners' rights and 'states' rights', the more the Republicans benefited from pro-Union sentiment and resentment of 'southern arrogance' in the North and West.

However, the Republicans were not a single-issue party. They campaigned for the protective tariff and free homesteads in the West for white settlers. Moreover, in nominating Abraham Lincoln for the presidency in 1860, the party chose a moderate on the slavery issue and a westerner, rather than a northern radical, such as Senator William H. Seward from New York. The aim was to appeal to the northern and western labourers, without frightening them with radical racial policies. It worked:

without capturing a single electoral college vote in the South, or even campaigning there, Lincoln won the presidency with just 39 per cent of the popular vote. As Wilfred Binkley said, 'The successful drive to capture the labor vote was the key to Lincoln's election' (Binkley, 1947, p. 230).

As the Democrats had done earlier, the Republicans had built a successful political party by combining a moral and political vision with the self-interest of a large section of lower-class Americans. Indeed, this progressive aspect appears to be an essential ingredient of successful party politics in the United States. As has been pointed out, 'In its origins, the Republican party, like all the other dominant major parties [Jeffersonians, Jacksonians and New Deal Democrats], was if anything a party of the left, not of the right' (McSweeney and Zvesper, 1991, p. 24).

Two-party politics since the Civil War

Outwardly, the party system has not changed since the Civil War (1861–65). The Democrats and Republicans have remained the only parties with a realistic chance of capturing the Congress or the presidency, although there have been occasional serious third-party candidates. As we saw in Chapter 8, third parties are inhibited by the electoral system. Equally important in perpetuating the Democratic/Republican rivalry, however, has been the flexibility of these two parties. Although both have been at times closely identified with particular principles, these have rarely been permitted to stand in the way of policy reorientations deemed necessary for electoral success. In other words, the Democratic and Republican parties have survived because they have been willing to change in response to a changing society. Two features of the parties have greatly facilitated this flexibility: ideological pragmatism and coalition politics.

Ideology and party

The two major American political parties occupy a very narrow ideological space. Both are (and always have been) utterly committed to the preservation of capitalism and constitutional democracy, as indeed have most parties which have appeared on the American scene. Thus, the United States differs strikingly from European democracies in its failure to produce a major political party committed to some form of socialism or of authoritarianism.

There have been a number of socialist parties in the United States, but they have enjoyed little electoral success. At the presidential level, the high point came in 1912 when Eugene Debs, the candidate of the Socialist Party of America (SPA), took 6 per cent of the popular vote. This is puzzling since, in many respects, the factors which promoted socialism in Europe – industrialisation, ruthless exploitation of the working class, demands for socio-economic reforms – were equally present in the United States. Many writers have sought to explain the peculiar weakness of American socialism and have pointed to a combination of causal factors. These range from the underdevelopment of working-class consciousness, owing to ethnic divisions, and the relative affluence of the American working class compared with its European counterparts, to state repression of radical movements, as typified by the Red Scare after the First World War and McCarthyism after the Second World War.

A contributing factor to socialism's electoral failure has been the readiness of Democrats and Republicans to steal the thunder of radicals by adopting at least some of their policies and even co-opting some of the radicals' leaders. For example, in the 1890s, distressed farmers organised the Populist party. The Populists attacked the banks and corporations for their exploitation of farmers and labourers, especially by their adherence to 'hard money': this was a policy of restricting the amount of money in circulation in line with the available supply of gold. Farmers wanted a 'Greenback policy': the printing of sufficient paper money to reduce the need for credit and high interest rates. While the Republicans stood firm behind hard money, in 1896 the Democrats moved to incorporate the Populists by proposing the expansion of the money supply by allowing the free coinage of silver. The Democrats still lost the election, but the Populists disappeared altogether.

The Progressive era

During the Progressive era (1900–17), the clamour for the reform of industrial urban society became so great that *both* Republicans and Democrats moved to adopt Progressive policies. Each party succeeded in capturing the presidency with a Progressive nominee – Theodore Roosevelt (Republican, 1901–9) and Woodrow Wilson (Democrat, 1913–21).

Progressive Democrats and Republicans were responsible for enacting valuable reforms at the federal and state level. However, their leadership of their respective parties lasted only as long as the public mood demanded reform. In the 1920s, both parties reverted to conservatism, leaving their Progressive wings isolated. The two main parties had thus ridden the Progressive wave while it was electorally expedient to do so, but had not become radicalised in the process. Yet during this critical period, they had become sufficiently reformist to persuade the electorate that a genuinely radical third party was unnecessary. This flexibility within an ideologically conservative framework has allowed both Democratic and Republican parties to marginalise radical and third-party movements.

The New Deal Democratic party

The greatest success of such flexibility undoubtedly came with the New Deal of the 1930s. An unprecedented seven-year period of economic expansion and prosperity had come to an abrupt, catastrophic end with the Wall Street Crash of October 1929. President Herbert Hoover responded to the collapse of the stock market and the ensuing loss of business confidence with orthodox economic measures, including cutting government spending and raising taxes. This only made matters worse and helped to cause the Great Depression. By the time of the next presidential election, in November 1932, the economy and social fabric of the country were in deep crisis. Unemployment nationally had reached 25 per cent, but in many cities it was 50 per cent or higher.

Worse still, there was little or no welfare provision for the unemployed and their families. Some states did offer support, but even the most generous states could not begin to cope with the scale of social distress. President Hoover refused to countenance any provision of welfare by the federal government. He had once referred to Britain's dole system as 'the English disease', believing that welfare would undermine the American tradition of economic self-reliance.

Furthermore, Hoover was opposed to almost all proposals to stimulate the economy which involved direct action by the federal government, such as government building projects that would create thousands of jobs. Hoover believed that there was no alternative to individualism and free-enterprise capitalism that would not, in the long term, seriously damage the American economic system. Such was his ideological conviction that he led the Republican party into the election promising four more years of the same policies.

The Democratic candidate in 1932, Governor Franklin D. Roosevelt of New York, was also generally orthodox in his economic faith in American capitalism. However, unlike Hoover, he was a pragmatist rather than an ideologue and was prepared to experiment with ways to restore the American economy to health. Moreover, if he was to become only the second Democrat president in the last 40 years, he needed to offer the electorate something different from Hoover's rigidity.

Roosevelt therefore turned flexibility and pragmatism into the main planks of his electoral platform. In one speech, for example, he said, 'The country needs, and unless I mistake its temper, demands bold, persistent experimentation. It is sensible to take a method and try it. If it fails, admit it frankly and try another. But above all, try something.'

Roosevelt won the election by a large majority. Having won the election on a promise of flexibility and pragmatism, he proceeded to govern accordingly. Eschewing Hoover's restraint, he threw the energies of the federal government into attempts to solve the major problems of the Great Depression. Moreover, he cared little for whether policy solutions came from the left or the right of the political spectrum, for rather than search for ideological consistency, Roosevelt sought to provide practical help for those who needed it. Roosevelt's 'New Deal' was aimed primarily at helping the underdog – the unemployed, the impoverished farmer, the homeless – but it did so by strengthening banking, manufacturing and landowning interests as well.

So successful was this new philosophy of governmental activism that Roosevelt was re-elected by a landslide in 1936 and went on to win two further elections. Equally important, his party had discovered a new recipe for electoral success. As we noted above, the Democrats had always been the party of limited government and states' rights. With the electoral triumph of the New Deal, however, the Democrats became the party of federal government activism. From now on, the Democrats would argue that the federal government must take responsibility for the economic health of the country and the social well-being of its people. Government regulation of the economy, expansion of the welfare state and continuing social reform became the paramount policies of the 'new' Democratic party.

This transformation of the Democratic party left the Republicans electorally stranded for decades. Since its inception in 1854, the Republican party had identified itself with promotion of the national economy, prosperity and social improvement. However, by allowing the Democrats to seize the initiative during the Great Depression, the Republicans were left with the choice of either opposing the new Democratic creed or adopting a 'me-too' approach. Thus, for years to come, the Republicans found themselves offering the electorate either an unacceptable alternative to New Deal liberalism or no real alternative at all.

Coalition politics

Roosevelt's brand of pragmatic politics was greatly aided by the fact that American political parties have never been ideologically based. That is to say that, although parties have advanced particular principles, it is not necessarily those principles which unite the different elements within parties. Thus, in the second half of the nineteenth century, for example, the Democrats' main electoral bases were southerners and the immigrants of the northern cities. These two groups had little in common other than their dislike of the Republican party. Southerners disliked the Republicans because of the Civil War; many immigrants, particularly Catholics, disliked the nativist and pietist tendencies of the Republicans. In that sense, party coalitions were based upon the principle that 'the enemy of my enemy is my friend'. Different groups came together under a party banner in order to share the spoils of victory and to deny those spoils to the common enemy.

In a country as heterogeneous as the United States, attempts to enforce ideological conformity on the party usually end in electoral disaster or worse, as the southern Democrats discovered when they tried to impose a pro-slavery policy on the party before the Civil War. The secret of a successful governing party coalition, then, is to be able to reward one element of the party without causing too much offence to another.

This strategem generally works best when the party concentrates upon sharing out material benefits to coalition members and playing down the importance of ideological, moral or symbolic issues. Roosevelt was the practitioner par excellence of this strategem. Thus, he won the support of farmers by introducing agricultural subsidies; of the unemployed by creating jobs; of industrial workers by raising wages and supporting trade unions; of the elderly and the infirm by instituting social security; and of black Americans by not excluding them from these benefits. This coalition was new in that it broke previous voting patterns. For example, blacks had, until 1936, generally supported the Republican party since it had been responsible for the abolition of slavery.

At the same time, the new Democratic coalition had to keep the lid on issues which could divide the party. The southern wing of the party, for example, had little sympathy with labour unions, liberal social policies and, above all, the civil rights demands of blacks. It is something of a political miracle that for 30 years the Democrats were able to count among their leaders and supporters both those who believed in racial segregation and those who were working for a civil rights revolution. What kept them together for so long were the material benefits in terms of government largesse that such an unholy alliance could bring.

Party realignment

The New Deal enabled the Democrats to initiate what political scientists call 'a partisan realignment'. The notion of partisan realignment views American electoral history in cyclical terms. It argues that one party dominates elections for both the presidency and the Congress – and often state elections, too – for several decades. It dominates the political agenda and normally can rely upon a majority of the electorate to support it. Then, because new issues arise that cut across previous party loyalties, a *critical election* occurs which transfers dominance to the opposition party.

Box 10.2

Critical elections and partisan realignment

1. **Election of Andrew Jackson (D) as president, 1828**

   Dominance of Democratic party, 1828–60
   Years in control of:

Presidency	24
Senate	28
House	24

2. **Election of William McKinley (R) as president, 1896**

   Dominance of Republican party, 1896–1932
   Years in control of:

Presidency	28
Senate	30
House	26

3. **Election of Franklin D. Roosevelt (D) as president, 1932**

   Dominance of Democratic party, 1932–68
   Years in control of:

Presidency	28
Senate	32
House	32

Until the contemporary electoral era cast doubt upon it, realignment theory seemed a useful way of understanding changes in the fortunes of the main political parties.

Party dealignment since 1968

In the period since 1968, the cyclical pattern described above has become less clear. While the Democrat ascendancy has come to an end, it is still not certain that a Republican ascendancy has replaced it. The potential for Richard Nixon's election in 1968 to serve as a platform for a period of Republican dominance was fatally undermined when Nixon became the only president to resign, in the wake of the Watergate scandal. The 1980 election of Ronald Reagan, accompanied by Republican victories in the US Senate, gave the party new hope of a delayed realignment, but in spite of holding the presidency for 12 years, the party did not establish firm control of the legislature, and 1992 saw the start of Bill Clinton's Democratic presidency.

Some Democrats hoped that this signalled the end of a period of uncertainty, with a return to Democrat dominance, but only two years later large Republican legislative gains returned the inter-party combat to Washington's branches of government. To be sure, President George W. Bush won two successive elections in 2000 and 2004 and the Republican party captured the Congress, too. However, the margins of victory in both presidential elections were so narrow that it is unconvincing to describe them as constituting a realignment. Furthermore, the Bush presidency faltered, the Democrats regained legislative strength, and in 2008 the presidency returned to the Democrats with the election of Barack Obama.

In control of the executive and both chambers of Congress, some Democrats again thought this might signal the beginning of a Democratic realignment. However, once again, only two years later, the party suffered huge legislative electoral defeats and lost control of the House of Representatives. The past generation, uniquely in American history, has been one of close competition and divided party government. At the presidential level, the

Republican party has had a slight but persistent edge over the Democratic party, but most of the time the two parties have each had some bastion in Washington through control of the executive or at least one chamber of Congress, and have competed, compromised and sometimes cooperated from this position.

While it is always possible that the pattern of partisan realignment will reassert itself in the future, some political scientists have identified factors which may prevent this from happening. Byron Shafer, for example, has expounded the idea of 'electoral order' as an alternative to realignment theory. Shafer suggests that electoral periods involve a more complex and differentiated relationship between issues, parties and government institutions than realignment theory can cope with.

Thus, since the 1960s, there have been three grand issue areas in American politics: economic and social welfare, moral and cultural values, and foreign policy. A majority of the American public are conservative (or traditionalist) on moral issues and foreign policy, but liberal on social welfare. When these majorities come to vote, they respond according to which institution is involved.

The presidency occupies itself more with foreign policy and cultural values, and hence the public majorities on these issues tend to prefer the conservative Republican party for this office. On the other hand, the Congress (and particularly the House) occupies itself predominantly with social welfare policies. Since the public majority is liberal on such issues, it tends to choose the more liberal Democratic party to run this institution (Shafer, 1991).

Shafer's notion of an electoral order worked well in the period from 1968 to 1992, but is challenged by the electoral outcomes since 1994. The Republican capture of both the House and Senate in 1994 might have been dismissed as a 'rogue election' had the House, in particular, returned to the Democratic fold in 1996. However, the Republicans retained control of both the House and the Senate, even though a Democrat was elected president in 1996. Divided government disappeared after the 2000 election, with Republican President George W. Bush faced with a Republican-controlled US House and Senate. But the electorate was still evenly divided and after the elections of 2006 George W. Bush faced Democrat majorities in the US House of Representatives and the US Senate. The Democrats consolidated their hold when President Barack Obama took the presidency in 2008, but the Republicans struck back quickly, taking the majority of seats in the US House of Representatives in 2010. In this continuing phase of divided party government, both parties hope that they can establish themselves in the dominant role.

An alternative explanation of the post-1994 election era is that of the 'no majority realignment', proposed by Everett Ladd. He argues that the old realignment theory still works as far as its philosophical/political dimensions are concerned. In other words, a philosophical realignment has indeed taken place since 1968, just as it has done with each major realignment. In this case, the philosophical realignment consists of a marked shift to the right, based upon a growing scepticism about the effectiveness of centralised government (Ladd, 1997, p. 5).

This philosophical realignment, however, has not been matched by a party realignment. When the 1994 elections seemed to threaten one, President Clinton and many other Democrats moved their own positions significantly to the right. Thus President Clinton proclaimed in his 1996 State of the Union address that 'the era of Big Government is over'.

However, an alternative, though not incompatible explanation, exists, according to Ladd: 'the chief reason no party has majority status is that large segments of the electorate are abandoning firm partisan ties' (Ladd, 1997, p. 13). Traditional realignment presupposes the existence of parties which are strong enough to exert comprehensive control of the electoral environment. Yet, in recent decades, the argument goes, American parties have actually been in decline in this respect, losing their grip on voters and politicians alike. This view, however, has been challenged by what appears to be the continuing attraction of party identification for a substantial majority of voters.

Party decline?

Until the 1990s there was wide agreement that political parties were of declining significance in American politics. Since the 1960s, social, technological and institutional changes had undermined the importance of parties in their two main spheres of operation: elections and government.

Prior to the 1960s, parties could fairly claim to represent the views and interests of the great mass of Americans. As a result, parties not only dominated the electoral process, but they provided a reasonably effective means of ensuring cooperation between different offices of government. There then followed a sharp decline in many aspects of party influence, leading many analysts to write the obituary for the American party system. However, parties have made a determined effort to regain some of their lost influence. While this has not been successful in all respects, parties are no longer in danger of extinction and they play a significant, though not dominant, role in both the electoral process and government.

Partisan identification

Whether partisan identification in the United States is in decline depends in part upon how it is measured. The most common method is to ask voters whether they consider themselves to be Democrats, Republicans or Independents. Some studies also distinguish between 'strong' and 'weak' Democrats and Republicans (McSweeney and Zvesper, 1991, p. 143).

The general picture obtained by such data suggests that, after a marked dip in the 1970s, partisan identification made something of a recovery. This is especially true when those who describe themselves as leaning towards one party or the other are counted as party identifiers.

These figures tell us only how people think of themselves, rather than how they actually vote. A more reliable guide to party loyalty may be obtained by comparing the figures on self-identification with the actual votes cast by these identifiers in elections. By measuring the number of 'deserters' or split-ticket voters, we can see how much hold the party label has on voting behaviour. Studies indicate that split-ticket voting surged in the period 1956–84, but has since decreased. Thus whereas in 1984, 43.9 per cent of congressional districts were carried by the presidential candidate of one party but the House candidate of the other party, this figure fell to 25.5 per cent in 1996 and to 20.0 per cent in 2000 (Keefe and Hetherington, 2003, p. 225) and remained at similar levels through 2008.

The number of people who identify themselves as independent of party identification varies in the short term in response to disaffection with government policies or economic conditions, but in general we can say that about one-quarter to one-third of the American electorate do not choose, unprompted, to identify themselves with one of the two main parties. Moreover, even among those who do

Table 10.1 Party identification, selected presidential years: 1952–2000

Party identification	1952 %	1964 %	1980 %	1992 %	1996 %	2000 %	2004 %	2008 %
Strong Democrat	23	27	18	18	18	19	17	19
Weak Democrat	26	25	23	17	19	15	16	15
Independent Democrat	10	9	11	14	14	15	17	17
Independent-Independent	5	8	15	13	10	13	10	11
Independent Republican	8	6	10	12	12	13	12	12
Weak Republican	14	14	14	14	15	12	12	13
Strong Republican	14	11	9	11	12	12	16	13

Note: Columns may not add to 100 because of rounding
Source: Center for Political Studies, University of Michigan

identify, from one-fifth to one-quarter do not stay loyal to their party. As a result, there is a large body of voters for whom party is a weak or meaningless influence. This group may switch votes from one election to the next, making sustained periods of electoral dominance difficult to achieve.

Nevertheless, the puzzle remains as to why, after a period of decline, party identification stabilised. After all, as we shall see below, campaigns remain candidate-centred and primary elections rather than party officials still dominate the candidate-selection process. The answer, according to many, lies in the increased ideological polarisation of the political parties from the 1980s onwards. As the Republican party in Washington became more uniformly conservative and the Democrat party more uniformly liberal, partisan conflict in Congress sharpened. And 'in a world characterized by significant cleavages between the parties, who wins and who loses matters a great deal. In short, greater partisan differences in Washington have created a more partisan public' (Keefe and Hetherington, 2003, p. 180).

Nominating candidates

As noted in Chapter 8, the proliferation of primary elections has all but ended party influence in the selection of candidates for office. All those who call themselves a Democrat (or a Republican) are entitled to enter a party primary, provided the technical requirements have been fulfilled. And given that candidates these days are largely independent of the party in terms of finance and organisation, they are free to pursue their own electoral strategy regardless of party wishes.

It is even possible for successful primary candidates to be so at odds with the party that the party feels obliged to disown them. Such was the case with David Duke, a former Grand Wizard of the Ku Klux Klan, who won the Republican Senate primary in Louisiana in 1990. President George H. Bush and the National Republican Party urged voters not to support Duke in the primary and publicly denied that Duke was a 'real' Republican.

More recently, the Tea Party movement made a strong showing in the 2010 mid-term elections. While the Republican party did not wish to disown this energetic force in conservative politics, it certainly faced difficulties in managing its impact in a year when disaffection was a driving force in US politics. Tea Party-supported candidates won a substantial number of Republican primaries – including some cases where they unseated incumbents, and others where candidates likely to be more appealing to the party hierarchy were defeated. In Alaska, Lisa Murkowski, the Republican incumbent who lost in the primary, brought the tension into high relief, going on to win the general election with a write-in campaign. The Tea Party claimed the credit for bringing seats into the Republican column in an election year when the party performed extraordinarily well, but some of their nominees appear to have had the opposite effect. Sharron Angle (Nevada), Christine O'Donnell (Delaware) and Ken Buck (Colorado) all won Republican nominations for the US Senate with Tea Party support, but did not meet the same enthusiasm from the general electorate, losing in the general election to Democrats in states that had been reasonable Republican targets.

Financing elections

There were important reforms in the laws governing campaign finance in the 1970s (see Chapter 11). These laws introduced limits on the amounts of money that parties, groups and individuals could contribute to a candidate's election campaign. In the case of presidential elections, public funding of campaigns was also introduced.

One result of these reforms was to eliminate parties as a significant source of direct campaign donations. The national parties in 2011 could give only $43,100 (index linked) to each Senate candidate, with state parties being allowed to donate a further $5,000. For the House the figure was also $5,000.

Thus, in the 1980 congressional elections, the percentage of campaign donations by the parties to their candidates was just 4 per cent for the House and 2 per cent for the Senate (Malbin, 1984, p. 39). In the presidential election that year, Reagan and Carter received approximately $29 million of government money each, compared with $4 million from the national parties (Malbin, 1984, p. 20). Candidates clearly did not rely upon the parties for donations and thus owed them little loyalty or deference.

However, in the wake of further amendments to the campaign finance laws in 1979, parties were given a new lease of life by being permitted to raise and spend so-called soft money. This allowed the parties to raise and spend funds independent of particular candidates – for example, on voter registration and turnout drives or campaign buttons and bumper stickers. In 1992, 1996 and 2000 the parties exploited the possibilities of using soft money for generic advertisements at both the federal and state level. In fact, for many, soft money came to be seen as a legal method of evading the spirit, if not the letter, of the campaign finance laws of the 1970s. This impression was compounded by the fact that the 'fat cat' contributors to the parties were back on the scene in force and because there were allegations that the Democratic National Committee, in particular, had sought and received soft money contributions from non-Americans (Corrado, 'Financing the 1996 Elections', in Pomper *et al.*, 1997, pp. 152–4). This in turn led to a public demand after the 1996 election for a clean-up of the campaign finance legislation that would eliminate the loopholes being exploited by soft money. Reform was finally achieved with the passage of the Bipartisan Campaign Reform Act of 2002.

Soft money expenditures soared in the 1990s, rising from some $80 million in the 1992 elections to $300 million in 2000 (Magleby and Monson, 2004, p. 45). Yet there is a debate over whether greater soft money expenditures actually translated into stronger parties. Thus only a relatively small part of these expenditures went on party-building activity, while a high percentage was spent on campaign advertisements with no long-term party-strengthening results. One study found that the phenomenon of soft money strengthened *national* parties, but only by weakening *state* parties: 'Soft money has both strengthened and weakened parties. National party organizations are strengthened through having money to spend on targeted races . . . With the additional funds has come increased power for those who allocate the money, notably the national party committees and their leadership. Party committees clearly exercise substantial control over soft money, even when it is transferred to the state parties' (Magleby and Monson, 2004, p. 56).

What, then, of the effect of the Bipartisan Campaign Reform Act which was intended to substantially reduce the role of soft money? The 2004 elections were the first to be conducted under the new rules. Yet most observers believe that the parties managed quite quickly to find ways to circumvent the legislation. In particular, the creation of so-called '527 groups', named after the tax code which exempts them from the 2002 contribution limits, enabled soft money expenditures to continue. As we shall see in the next chapter, 527s raised and spent hundreds of millions of dollars on the 2004 elections. The leading spender was America Coming Together, a group launched to defeat President Bush, and sponsored by the billionaire George Soros. According to Federal Election Commission records, by January 2005 America Coming Together had registered expenditures of $76,270,931. The infamous Swift Boat Veterans & POWs for Truth, which launched advertisements attacking Senator John Kerry's Vietnam War record, spent $22,424,420. It is not totally clear how much direct influence the parties had over the 527s, but it is clear that the expenditures were mostly for highly partisan purposes. These committees continued to be effective in 2008, but the record-breaking fund-raising by the candidate campaigns, especially the Obama campaign, at least temporarily overshadowed these independent committee efforts.

Campaign services and organisation

In addition to their partially revitalised role in funding elections, the parties have also become more energetic in providing their candidates with various services. Thus, 'along with increased funding, the national parties have provided help for their candidates in campaign planning, polling, and the production of campaign advertisements, including experiments in generic national ads for congressional candidates' (Caesar, 1990, p. 121).

Nevertheless, campaigns are resolutely candidate-centred and candidate-controlled. Candidates have their own strategists, media consultants, pollsters and managers. Moreover, not only has the rise in non-party sources of finance stimulated this independence, but the development of the electronic media has eliminated much of the parties' previous role in communicating with the voters.

Thus the revitalisation of the parties in the electoral process since the 1980s should not be exaggerated. Links between candidates and parties are stronger than they were in the 1970s, but in the key elements of nominations, finance, organisation and communication, parties play, at best, a secondary role.

Party government

We noted above that one reason why parties developed in the United States was the need to coordinate the activities of different office-holders. There are two particularly important facets to this function today: coordination between different members of Congress, and coordination between Congress and the president. An examination of both these relationships yields yet further evidence of the problematic nature of party unity.

Party unity in Congress

Members of Congress are much more independent of party control than, say, their British counterparts. In the first place, since senators and representatives do not owe their election to the party whose label they wear, they do not feel bound to follow party policy. This is particularly true where the party line is unpopular with the member's constituents.

Secondly, and largely as a result of members' electoral independence, party discipline in Congress is weak. There *are* designated party leaders in Congress, including whips; Congress is also organised on party lines and party members do meet in caucus to try to develop strategies and policies that will unite the party. Nevertheless, there is little the party can do to force unwilling members to conform to party wishes. Parties do not possess the power of ultimate sanction – deselection of disloyal members. Moreover, members of Congress value their own independence and are therefore content to allow a similar autonomy to their colleagues. Leaders in Congress can offer inducements to members to support the party line, such as help in getting the best committee assignments, but they have less to mete out as punishment. As Senator Tom Daschle (D – South Dakota), the former co-chair of the Senate Democratic Policy Committee, put it, a Senate leader trying to influence a colleague's vote has 'a bushel full of carrots and a few twigs' (*CQ Almanac*, 1992, p. 22-B).

Thirdly, as noted above, American political parties are broad coalitions of diverse interests. As a result, one wing of a party may be fiercely opposed on certain policies to another wing. This produced a situation in the twentieth century whereby the conservative southern wing of the Democratic party formed an informal coalition with the Republicans to defeat certain legislation proposed by their northern Democrat colleagues. This so-called 'Conservative Coalition' was, for example, responsible for defeating all meaningful attempts at civil rights reform in the 1950s and was invaluable to President Reagan in his efforts to foster a 'conservative revolution' in the early 1980s (Keefe and Ogul, 1993, p. 292).

As the South has largely realigned and become a Republican stronghold, the Conservative Coalition is no longer as significant as it once was. Nevertheless, it may still play an important role on occasion. Thus, when Bill Clinton's very presidency was on the line in August 1993 over his budget proposals, the Coalition almost defeated him. Despite a Democratic majority of 82 in the House, the president's proposals were approved by a margin of just two votes, and a Senate Democratic majority of 8 resulted in a tie in the Senate, with the budget being passed only on the casting vote of the speaker, Vice-President Al Gore. In short, conservative members of the Democratic party were not only prepared to defeat Clinton's budget, but also willing to see their votes cripple, even destroy, his presidency. And in 2004, retiring Georgia Democratic Senator Zell Miller demonstrated his loyalty to the party by appearing on the platform of the Republican nominating convention and endorsing George W. Bush.

Even aside from the Conservative Coalition, then, party unity has generally been low in the Congress, compared with, say, parliamentary parties in Britain. Take, for example, the frequency of party unity votes in the Congress. The definition of such votes is hardly a stringent one – simply it is when the majority of one party in the House or Senate votes against a majority of the other party. Although the number of such votes rose significantly in the 1990s to levels of 65 per cent, they fell back again in the first two years of George W. Bush's presidency to below 50 per cent (Keefe and Hetherington, 2003, p. 148). In short, while most members of Congress prefer to vote in line with their party, they do not feel obliged to do so. Thus, while the Republican leadership in Congress opposed the Bipartisan Campaign Reform Act of 2002, many Republicans voted in favour of it simply because it was popular with their constituents.

Party unity: Congress and president

A second measure of party unity in government can be gained by examining the frequency with which members of Congress vote in support of a president of their own party. Since the 1950s, presidents have, on average, been able to count on the support of their fellow party members in 72 per cent of House votes and 76 per cent of Senate votes (McSweeney and Zvesper, 1991, p. 168; *Congressional Quarterly*, various years). Thus, in the 1997 session of Congress, the average House Democrat backed President Clinton in 71 per cent of the votes on which he took a clear position. This was about the same as in the previous year. By contrast, the average House Republican supported Democrat President Clinton in 30 per cent of votes, down from 38 per cent the previous year (*Congressional Quarterly*, 3 January 1997, p. 17). President George W. Bush achieved a very high success rate in his first two years in office, showing that party presidential support can be very strong when members of Congress so wish. However, as the historical variations in support for the president demonstrate, such unity can never be taken for granted.

Examples of party unity and disunity were starkly evident in the aftermath of President Obama's election. The unity of the Republican party in opposing President Obama on major issues was remarkably strong. The success with which Obama pressed legislation through Congress in his first two years was nevertheless very high. The proportion of representatives and senators voting with their party on party unity votes remained at the high levels steadily reached over the past generation, and these votes took place in a Congress that appeared increasingly ideologically polarised. The Democrats found that the boost to their support brought by President Obama in the 2008 presidential election could not be transferred to the 2010 congressional elections. The Republicans found that an emerging form of radicalism in their own ranks, the Tea Party movement, could be both energising and threatening to the GOP.

Within days of President Obama taking office, the Republicans in Congress showed unusual unity in casting not one vote for the administration's economic recovery plan, an item of legislation that one might have expected to have some bipartisan support in the face of the economic problems that faced the USA when President George W. Bush left office. This signalled a Republican strategy of unified opposition that gained traction as it appeared to energise the Republican core electorate at the same time as catching the Democrats unprepared for such an approach. High-profile battles on health care and automobile industry support gave the opportunity for the Republicans to repeat this strategy, to the Democrats' discomfort. The legislative success rate of the Obama administration was overshadowed by the Republican ability to generate a sense of controversy and suspicion.

In 2009, Democrats in both House and Senate voted in agreement with their own party members 91 per cent of the time in party unity votes. On the same votes, Republicans voted with their party members 87 per cent of the time. These figures have been fairly consistent in the current century, but were a little lower in the 1990s, about 10 per cent lower in the 1980s, and 15 to 20 per cent lower in the 1970s. In part, this indicates the declining importance of the Conservative Coalition. The liberal wing of the Republican party, formerly a fixture of northeastern politics, has declined almost to invisibility. At the same time, many southern conservatives have found themselves increasingly comfortable within the Republican party. The winning electorates in Republican conservative constituencies and the winning electorates in Democratic progressive constituencies are also very different from each other in terms of ideology. So at the same time as becoming more partisan, Congress's partisanship has become more ideologically coherent, more contested, and put in place by representatives and senators supported by identifiably ideologically different sets of voters. This context has developed over the past generation of US politics, but there can still be strong pressures for legislators to vote outside their normal party boundaries. Democrats did so poorly in the 2010 mid-term elections that some legislators felt that President Obama and his agenda were a liability to their own re-election chances, leading to members of his own party joining the Republicans to erode gains that had been made only a couple of years earlier.

While the 2010 mid-terms brought substantial losses to the Democrats, the gains made by the Republicans came with the potential liability of the emergence of the Tea Party movement. The Tea Party built on electoral disaffection with the lack of success of the administration's attempts to tackle the economic malaise inherited from the Bush administration, and on public concern that these weak responses were nevertheless examples of more 'big government' in the USA. The Tea Party also attracted support from the small but intense sector of the electorate that suspected the first African-American president of not being fully committed to the nation or its dominant religious culture, and doubted that he was actually born in the USA. The Tea Party had the attraction of an insurgent and energetic political group wishing to bring change to US politics, and if they fell more naturally within the conservative wing of the Republican party than in any part of the Democratic party, this was a group with a rhetoric that challenged the established forces of politics. They did not consider the Republican party to have been doing a very good job either. For all its outsider appeal, many of the Tea Party candidates had held office previously, and it is likely that the Republican party leadership hoped to meld the newcomers steadily into the party's mainstream. However, in 2010, Minnesota Congress woman Michele Bachmann became chair of the newly established Tea Party caucus in Congress, providing the group with funds, staff and a base from which to operate. By early 2011, Bachmann had also announced her intention to run for the Republican 2012 presidential nomination.

The historical data suggest that party policy and party discipline are important, but not necessarily controlling, factors in congressional behaviour. In fact, negotiation and compromise in pursuit of consensus across party lines remains a notable feature of Congress. This is true despite attempts by both parties to develop clearer party positions and coherence. Increased partisanship may please more ideologically pure politicians and voters but it may turn the mass of general election voters off. In an era when the control of government in Washington has been divided and shared between the two major parties, the public appears generally to expect the president and Congress to overcome partisan differences and work together for the good of the country. This, of course, is precisely what the constitutional scheme of separation of powers and checks and balances was intended to promote. As Representative David Skaggs (D – Colorado) commented in 1997, 'We all have to go back to school on a regular basis to remember that this is not a parliamentary system, and the Constitution essentially drives a consensus approach to government in the country' (*Congressional Quarterly*, 3 January 1997, p. 18).

In the next chapter, we will see that politicians in the United States are not simply faced with a choice of pleasing public or party. Moreover, voters themselves do not rely solely, or even mainly, on parties to represent their interests in government. Political parties, therefore, have a major rival for their claims on voters and politicians alike – interest groups.

Chapter summary

Although the framers of the Constitution considered political parties harmful to the political process, the United States quickly developed a two-party system. This was because parties performed useful tasks, such as representing interests, organising elections and coordinating government within and between Congress and the presidency. However, because of the great size and diversity of the nation, parties have been based as much on coalitions of interest as they have been on ideology. This has been a factor in weakening party discipline, as has the more recent advent of media coverage of elections and interest-group funding of elections. Elections in America are candidate-centred, rather than party-centred – something which applies as much to voters as it does to candidates themselves. Although the strength of party ties has grown since the 1990s, it still remains the case that politicians and voters alike will break with their party when reasons to do so present themselves. The Bush and Obama terms have thrown up more examples of the tensions within and between parties, both when a single party dominates, and when control of Washington's institutions is divided.

Discussion points

1. To what extent and why are political parties in decline?
2. What are the advantages and disadvantages of weak party discipline in the federal government?
3. Why has there been party dealignment, but not realignment, since 1968?
4. What are the main differences today between the Democratic party and the Republican party?

Further reading

One of the most accessible but authoritative books on this subject is W. Keefe and J. Hetherington, *Parties, Politics and Public Policy in America* (9th edn, Washington, DC: CQ Press, 2003). Another which encompasses the relationship of parties to interest groups is R. Benedict, M. Burbank and J. Hrebenar, *Political Parties, Interest Groups and Political Campaigns* (Boulder, Col.: Westview, 1999). Another useful text is J. Green and D. Shea (eds), *The State of the Parties: The Changing Role of Contemporary American Parties* (3rd edn, Lanham, Md.: Rowman & Littlefield, 1999). On the issue of the alleged decline of parties, see J. Cohen, R. Fleisher and P. Kantor, *American Political Parties: Decline or Resurgence?* (Washington, DC: CQ Press, 2001). For a thoughtful reflection on the issue of party realignment, see E. Ladd, '1996 elections: the "no majority" realignment continues', *Political Science Quarterly* (Spring 1997, pp. 1–28). On the connection between parties and campaign finance, see P. Kobrak, *Cozy Politics: Political Parties, Campaign Finance and Compromised governance* (Boulder, Col.: Lynne Rienner, 2002).

Websites

http://www.democrats.org
http://www.rnc.org
http://www.politics1.com/parties.htm
http://www.fec.gov

References

Binkley, W. (1947) *American Political Parties: Their Natural History* (New York: Knopf).

Caesar, J. (1990) 'Political parties – declining, stabilizing, or resurging?', in King, A. (ed.) *The New American Political System* (2nd version, Washington, DC: American Enterprise Institute).

Hofstadter, R. (1969) *The Idea of a Party System* (Berkeley: University of California Press).

Keefe, W. and Hetherington, J. (2003) *Parties, Politics and Public Policy in America* (9th edn, Washington, DC: CQ Press).

Keefe, W. and Ogul, M. (1993) *The American Legislative Process* (8th edn, Hemel Hempstead: Prentice Hall).

Ladd, E. (1997) '1996 elections: the "no majority" realignment continues', *Political Science Quarterly*, Spring, 1–28.

Magleby, D. and Monson, J. (eds) (2004) *The Last Hurrah: Soft Money and Issue Advocacy in the 2002 Congressional Elections* (Washington, DC: Brookings Institution).

Malbin, M. (ed.) (1984) *Money and Politics in the United States: Financing Elections in the 1980s* (Chatham, NJ: Chatham House).

McSweeney, D. and Zvesper, J. (1991) *American Political Parties* (London: Routledge).

Pomper, G., Burnham, W., Corrado, A., Hershey, M., Just, M., Keefer, S., McWilliams, W. and Mayer, W. (1997) *The Elections of 1996: Reports and Interpretations* (Chatham, NJ: Chatham House).

Rozwenc, E. (ed.) (1963) *The Meaning of Jacksonian Democracy* (Boston: D.C. Heath).

Shafer, B. (ed.) (1991) *The End of Realignment? Interpreting American Electoral Eras* (Madison: University of Wisconsin Press).

Chapter 11

Interest groups, political committees and campaigns

Whereas parties in American politics have always had their weaknesses, interest groups (or pressure groups) have always been strong. The diversity of American society has encouraged Americans to make full use of their freedom to petition the government, a right guaranteed by the First Amendment to the Constitution. With the huge growth in governmental activity since the New Deal of the 1930s, the importance of representing one's group interests in politics has become paramount. Nevertheless, interest-group activity is the subject of considerable controversy. On the one hand, it is argued that such groups perform a legitimate and valuable representative function. On the other, it is alleged that interest groups subvert democracy by making government the pawn of the rich and well organised.

Interest groups

Definitions and origins

An interest or pressure group is an association of individuals or organisations who band together to defend or advance the particular interests they have in common. Those may range from shared business interests and professional status, through common ethnic origins and religion, to shared public policy and ideological convictions. There are literally thousands of interest groups in the United States. While they can be categorised as shown in Table 11.1, it is worth remembering that a group might well encompass the attributes of more than one category. Many, if not most, for example, have an ideological orientation, even if their principal goal is representing the particular interests of a profession or advancing a particular issue.

Table 11.1 Typology of interest groups

Business/Trade	Agriculture	Unions	Professional	Single issue	Ideological	Group rights	Public interest
American Business Conference National Association of Manufacturers National Automobile Dealers Association	American Farm Bureau Federation National Farmers Union Associated Milk Producers, Inc.	American Federation of Labor–Congress of Industrial Organisations (AFL–CIO) United Auto Workers International Association of Machinists and Aerospace Workers	American Medical Association National Education Association Association of American Universities	National Abortion and Reproductive Rights Action League Mothers Against Drunk Driving National Rifle Association	American Conservative Union People for the American Way Christian Voice American Civil Liberties Union	National Association for the Advancement of Colored People (NAACP) National Organization for Women American Association of Retired Persons	Common Cause Friends of the Earth Children's Defense Fund

The United States has always been fertile soil for interest group formation. In 1835, the great French observer of American politics, Alexis de Tocqueville, wrote: 'Americans of all ages, all conditions, and all dispositions constantly form associations. Wherever at the head of some new undertaking you see the government in France, or a man of rank in England, in the United States you will be sure to find an association' (Tocqueville, 1956, p. 198).

The prevalence of interest groups in American political life is due to four broad factors. First, the sheer diversity of American society has spawned numerous ethnic, social, economic and issue groups. Secondly, as we have already seen, weak parties have failed to fulfil the representative needs of the American people. Thirdly, the fragmented and decentralised structure of American government means that there are numerous points of access to the policy-making process that groups can readily exploit. Fourthly, and particularly true since the 1930s, the rapid expansion of governmental activity means that more and more groups have found their interests affected by public policy.

More recently, the 1960s and 1970s witnessed an 'advocacy explosion' (Berry, 1989, p. 42). Several particular factors contributed to this. Among the most important were the new burst of government programmes associated with President Lyndon B. Johnson's Great Society; the rise of many new divisive political issues (such as race and gender, the Vietnam War and lifestyle issues); and the simple fact that, as some interest groups became prominent, other groups formed in imitation (Cigler and Loomis, 1991).

Furthermore, a little-known variant of the interest group – the political action committee (PAC) – proliferated astonishingly in the 1970s and 1980s, stimulated by new campaign finance laws (see below). Another example of the energetic way in which interests respond to a changing environment was provided by the explosion of '527 groups' in the wake of the Bipartisan Campaign Reform Act of 2002, and the interest in '502 (c)(4) groups' in the run-up to the 2012 election. These methods of channelling funds into public debate existed previously within the US tax code, but were increasingly exploited as orthodox donation routes became more regulated.

Not surprisingly, the exponential growth of interest groups since the 1960s appeared to eclipse the representative functions of political parties. Moreover, because interest groups conduct much of their activity away from the public view, in the corridors of Congress or the federal bureaucracy, there developed a heightened anxiety over whether representation by interest group was good for American democracy.

Interest group functions

There are, it is said, five principal functions of interest groups: representation, citizen participation, public education, agenda building and programme monitoring (Berry, 1989, pp. 4–5). The last four, however, are really aspects of the central task of self-interest representation.

Interest groups, like parties, are representative institutions, but their aims and methods are not the same. Most importantly, interest groups do not put forward candidates for elected office. Although some interest groups do try to influence electoral outcomes, most concentrate on representing their members' interests in the policy-making process. This means lobbying not only elected politicians but also those who wield power in the bureaucracy and the judiciary.

Interest group methods

Public campaigning

Interest groups operate in a variety of ways. One means of influencing the policy-making process is to stir up public opinion, in the hope that this will put legislators under pressure. One of the oldest forms of interest-group activity in this respect is the public march. This can be very successful, as when a host of civil rights groups got together to organise the 1963 'March on Washington'. The march, coming after almost a decade of public campaigning to end racial segregation, was designed to put pressure on President Kennedy and Congress to take action on the pending Civil Rights Bill. Whatever the precise role of the march in producing the Civil Rights Act of 1964, there can be little doubt that it was a moving spectacle that won converts to the cause.

Public demonstrations can, however, prove counter-productive. Thus, anti-abortion groups organise an annual protest outside the Supreme Court to commemorate the day of the historic 1973 *Roe* decision, which announced a new constitutional right to abortion. When that right seemed threatened in the 1980s, pro-abortion groups began holding counter-demonstrations on the same day.

Another related form of public campaigning is direct action. Here, too, anti-abortion groups have been prominent. For example, Operation Rescue specialises in trying to block access to clinics where abortions are performed. Its members hope that their activities – and their frequent arrest by the police – will stimulate the conscience of judges, legislators and the public and result in a ban on abortions.

Other forms of public campaigning include newspaper and television advertising. In the early 1990s, for example, the National Rifle Association (NRA) produced television advertisements featuring the veteran Hollywood star Charlton Heston as part of its ultimately unsuccessful campaign against the Brady Bill. The legislation aimed only to improve checks on would-be gun purchasers, but the NRA opposes virtually all gun legislation.

Less spectacular, but potentially effective nevertheless, is direct mailing of group members and likely sympathisers. Taking advantage of computerised mailing systems, interest groups learned quickly how to identify and mobilise members on behalf of a particular campaign. During the intense fight over ratification of the Panama Canal Treaties in 1978, conservative groups mailed an estimated 7–9 million letters to members of the public (Berry, 1989, p. 60). Social networking platforms, such as Facebook and Twitter, have proved valuable both to established groups and to new ones, such as those associated with the Tea Party movement.

However, although the above strategems for mobilising members and the general public are often employed, the oldest and still the most effective activity of interest groups is lobbying.

Lobbying and lobbyists

The most desirable method of influencing policymakers is through direct contact with them. For that reason, the more affluent and powerful interest groups maintain a permanent office in Washington and employ professional lobbyists to act on their behalf.

These lobbyists may be committed activists in the groups they represent, but these days are increasingly likely to be neutral 'guns for hire' – experts

Box 11.1

A day in the life of a lobbyist

This is how the Washington lobbyist for a professional association describes his typical day:

'I am one of those people who gets to work no later than 7.45. The first hour is spent reading the papers – the *Washington Post*, *Wall Street Journal*, and *New York Times*, trade association publications, and the *Congressional Record* from the prior day. Each of these plays into my need to plan the activities for the current day. The next activity is meeting with the staff for a brief period to check the work plans for any changes. There is then one or more hearings on the Hill in the morning. After lunch, I usually meet with committee staff or use that time to lobby specific members of Congress. I'm usually back by 4.00 to meet with the staff to check on what's happened while I was gone and if we are on top of the work planned for the day. About 5.30 I usually go to some reception or fund-raiser to represent our group. These settings give me an opportunity to swap stories and position with members and other lobbyists who are concerned with the same issues as we are. I usually get home for dinner about 8.00.'

Source: Extract from Berry, 1989, pp. 77–8

in the legislative process, who sell their skills to those who can afford them. Thus, in 1993, the top lobbying firm of Patton, Boggs and Blow was working to obtain government money to save jobs at Chrysler, supporting a bill to make it easier for the homeless to vote, and fighting a constitutional amendment that would ban flag-burning. In the past, it had also represented Baby Doc Duvalier, the Haitian dictator, and the scandal-ridden Bank of Credit and Commerce International. The firm's most prominent lobbyist, Tommy Boggs, once said: 'We basically pick our customers by taking the first one who comes in the door' (*The Economist*, 27 February 1993, p. 56). The typical working day of a professional lobbyist is described in Box 11.1.

Lobbyists have often acquired their detailed knowledge of the policy-making process from having worked in the federal government – as legislators or legislative assistants, bureaucrats or presidential advisers. Such experience can be invaluable, not merely for the expertise acquired but also for the personal contacts and relationships established over the years. Thus, when Senators Russell Long and Paul Laxalt retired in 1986, their services were sought by many Washington law firms which represent clients before government agencies. Both eventually joined Finley, Kumble at salaries of $800,000 a year (Berry, 1989, p. 86).

This so-called revolving door phenomenon has been criticised as unethical, and measures have been taken to try to limit it. In 1978, Congress passed the Ethics in Government Act, which forbade certain former executive branch officials from lobbying their previous government agencies within a year of leaving them. In 1989, Congress applied a similar restriction on former legislators and legislative staff. Nevertheless, continuing scandals did little to reassure the public that these measures were sufficient. When President Clinton took office in 1993, therefore, his first executive order extended the one-year limit to five years on all top executive branch officials, and banned them from lobbying on behalf of foreign governments and parties for ever.

The revolving door problem is just one of several aspects of lobbying that have been addressed over the years. For example, the first attempt to monitor the activity of lobbyists came with the Regulation of Lobbying Act of 1946. Under this, all people hired principally for the task of lobbying Congress were required to register with the House or Senate. Its terms, however, were easily evaded. More recent moves towards regulated transparency and accountability in the Washington lobbying process have been seen with the Lobbying and Disclosure Act of 1995 and the Honest Leadership and Open Government Act of 2007. This legislation sought to increase public disclosure of lobbying activity and expenditure, to limit the ease of moving from government posts to lucrative jobs in lobbying and to tighten up the House and Senate rules relevant to activities involving lobbyists. President Obama has signalled his interest with a number of executive orders and presidential memoranda on the topic, as well as proposals for further legislation.

The American League of Lobbyists (ALL) responded robustly to President Obama's interest in lobbying with a letter from its president, Howard Marlowe, to President Obama published on the ALL website in May 2011. The letter opposed the idea for an executive order 'requiring companies and their representatives who apply for federal contracts to disclose their political contributions'. The argument put was essentially a free speech position, defending 'the ability to voice a political position using financial resources', but the letter went on to encapsulate a vision of the value and virtue of lobbying. 'Lobbyists play an important role in the legislative process, serving as educators to elected officials. It is in the best interest of government to have informed individuals who serve as experts in every area of public policy. Our ability to access and navigate the legislative process and push issues forward through a bureaucratic cluster is a vital service to the nation' (Marlowe, 2011).

If all that lobbyists did was to act as the eyes and ears of their organisations and try to convert policy-makers to their members' point of view, their activities would be largely uncontroversial. However, what transforms the perspective on interest groups is money – the money they give to legislators in the form of electoral campaign donations. Immediately, then, the suspicion arises that lobbying Congress involves a form of bribery: interest groups enable legislators to get re-elected by financing their campaigns, and legislators in return listen to the pleadings of interest groups and advance their interests through the nation's policy. This suspicion is at the heart of the controversy over interest groups in American politics.

Campaign finance

Interest groups, and particularly business corporations, have always tried to buy favours from legislators by giving them money: hence Will Rogers' satirical comment that 'Our Congress is the best that money can buy!' Bribery and corruption were especially rife in the late nineteenth century and the first attempt at reform came with the passage of the Tillman Act in 1907. This banned business corporations from making direct contributions to federal election campaigns.

Nevertheless, the flow of illegal funds continued and it was only when the Watergate scandal broke in 1973, with its revelations of slush funds, huge personal donations and laundered money, that more determined action was taken (Sabato, 1985, p. 4). In 1974, Congress amended the Federal Election Campaign Act (FECA) of 1971 in ways that were to transform, but not necessarily improve, the funding of federal elections.

In an attempt to lower the cost of elections and to reduce the power of rich individuals and organisations, Congress enacted three major reforms. First, it provided public funds for presidential elections. Secondly, it set strict ceilings on the amount of money that any person or group could give to a candidate for the presidency or Congress. Thirdly, it limited the overall amount of money that could be spent on congressional elections.

The limits on spending were quickly challenged in the courts as an unconstitutional restriction on free speech. In *Buckley* v. *Valeo* (1976), the Supreme Court upheld the restrictions on personal and group donations to candidates, but struck down those which limited expenditures independent of particular candidates and the amount that candidates could spend out of their own pockets, except for presidential candidates who accepted public funds.

Presidential elections

The campaign finance reform legislation of the 1970s largely ended the controversy over donations direct to the campaigns of presidential candidates from rich individuals and interest groups. In the pre-nomination phase, candidates may seek donations from both, though these are strictly limited. Such limits do not prevent huge sums being raised and spent.

The modern presidential candidate is a political entrepreneur in a highly competitive environment. The political parties manage a nomination system that draws hopefuls into intra-party combat to become the official candidate. The primary season consists of a series of state-level contests taking the competition to party loyalists around the nation, but that, in its turn, is a political and logistic challenge so considerable that the pre-primary period of planning and activities has become very extended in recent elections.

Given the fixed timetable of US elections, hopefuls for office have a firm, if skeletal, structure on which to hang alternative strategic plans. Campaign planning is said to start the day after any election, as those ambitious to be the next, or even the next but one, in the White House consult with their closest supporters about the potential opportunities in four or more years, and the way in which their career might map to fit. Developing that cadre of close support into an election-winning network is one important part of the process.

The official contest to gain the nomination to run for president as the general election candidate of a major political party most obviously starts early in election year with the first state-level caucuses and primaries. In order to be considered in some of these contests, hopefuls for the nomination will have had to register some months before, in the autumn of the previous year, and the most well-organised and better-funded contestants will have been making appearances and placing some paid advertising in these critical early states for some time. For recent presidential elections, campaign activity has been noted on the ground in the early states from the early summer of the year before the election, while the run-up to the 2008 election was longer than ever, with both major parties' hopefuls engaging in advertising, campaigning and televised debates on a scale not previously seen before the election year itself.

The first official primary season contests, the Iowa caucuses and the New Hampshire primary, attract international media coverage. In spite of the fact that these states are not representative samples of the US electorate, the results there can have massive significance, at least in winnowing the field of candidates, if not necessarily in pinpointing the eventual victors. It is important in such high-profile times to manage public expectations well.

In 2008, preconceptions that the nomination races would be decided quickly were not fulfilled, but, with close contests taking longer than expected, the early predictions that this campaign would be the most expensive ever proved accurate. The Center for Responsive Politics calculated that, by the end of July 2008, the Obama campaign had already spent over $323 million and the McCain campaign over $141 million. Some of the hopefuls had also spent heavily: Clinton over $234 million; Romney over $107 million; Edwards and Giuliani over $114 million between them. That aggregated to almost $1,100 million for all the presidential hopefuls together, even before the costs of the party conventions and the general election were incurred.

Spending at that rate requires a businesslike, even industrial, approach, but it is not difficult to understand. The USA has a population exceeding 300 million, spread over 50 states, some of which are thousands of miles apart. The campaigns need not only to communicate with their voters, but to make sure that they are registered to vote (a substantial proportion of the eligible electorate is not) and that they turn out to vote in their different states, in both primary and general elections. The main means of communication is the electronic media. The internet is playing an increasingly important part, and attracting appropriate campaign investment, but thousands of television advertisements are still used as the campaigns try to get their message across, in competition not only with other political campaigns, but with all the other well-financed corporate advertising that fills the American airwaves. Campaigning in the US context is a big operation and demands heavy investment.

The campaigns are, therefore, faced with a huge fund-raising requirement, and there is a rigid legal context for this effort. The basic shape of current federal campaign finance law was set in the 1970s, and adapted most recently by the Bipartisan Campaign Reform Act of 2002. Over the years it has also been shaped by court decisions on individual cases. Candidates and political parties can only raise money from individuals or from specified categories of political committees. The vast majority of presidential campaign money comes from individual donors. In 2008, federal campaign finance law restricted individual donations to no more than $2,300 to a candidate for any election, a limit that rises with the rate of inflation. Up to the end of June 2008, over one-half of Obama's funding had been raised in contributions of less than $200 each. To raise the totals that current presidential campaigns demand in this way requires hundreds of thousands of donations to be made to major candidates, totalling millions of separate contributions for all candidates.

Hopefuls in the primary season may also call on the federal government for funding. Those who raise a threshold amount of $100,000 by collecting $5,000 in 20 different states in amounts no greater than $250 can apply for matching funds from the federal government. Most candidate campaigns have done this since the possibility was first introduced in 1976. However, accepting federal matching funds also involves contracting to limit primary spending to a figure that in 2008 was $50.5 million. Increasingly, the major contestants have felt that the acceptance of the spending limit was too great a handicap and have opted instead to raise all their own funds. In 2008, five Democrats, two Republicans and the Independent Ralph Nader accepted a total of $21.7 million in primary matching funds. This was $6.7 million less than four years previously, and indicates the strong shift away from federal funding by the leading candidates. Neither Obama nor Clinton used primary matching funds, and McCain, who initially declared that he would, changed his mind. John Edwards, accepting $12.9 million, was the biggest user of the fund, with Democrats Biden and Dodd and Republican Tancredo accepting about $2 million each.

The primary season culminates in the national conventions, generally held at the end of the summer of election year. Once quadrennial meetings where regional and ideological factions within the parties would thrash out compromises on policy and candidacies, these have increasingly become vehicles for showcasing a nominee whose victory is already clear. They also present one of the few opportunities for direct corporate and union expenditure on the campaigns. In 2008, the federal government granted nearly $17 million to each of the two major political parties to support the conventions, but private donors were estimated by the Campaign Finance Institute to be donating in excess of $118 million, 80 per cent of which was given in donations of between $250,000 and $3 million. The Institute also calculated that 187 organisational donors to the conventions' costs had made over $273 million in federal election contributions since 2005 and had incurred over $1,600 million in federal lobbying expenditures over the same period.

After the conventions the campaigns are back on the streets and back in the states. The multi-state context of the general election has many similarities to that of the primary season, but while the primaries are spread over months, the general election takes place in all the states on the same day. The financing of this stage of the campaign is even more extreme than that of the nomination process. The federal government offers the nominees of the two major parties a grant that in 2008 was $84.1 million, on condition that the candidate campaigns accept no private donations to their general election fund and observe federal campaign expenditure limits. In 2008, Obama became the first candidate since the 1976 introduction of this grant to refuse the federal funds, preferring instead to raise his own money and to run a campaign unfettered by federal limits on his campaign spending.

Obama's rejection of the federal election grant and of the attached spending limits has almost certainly changed fundamentally the campaign finance strategies of major candidates for the office. The Democratic campaign was more successful at raising funds than any campaign in US history, raising around $745 million, over twice as much as the McCain campaign's final total of $368 million. In this, as in other aspects of the campaign, the Obama team appeared to find a way of melding traditional and cutting-edge campaign methods. More large donations were attracted to the campaign once its bandwagon was firmly rolling along, but the unusual reliance of this campaign on small donations was nevertheless retained. According to the Campaign for Responsive Politics, donations of $200 or less provided 54 per cent of the Obama campaign's donations. This compares with 34 per cent for the McCain campaign. Figures over 50 per cent are generally associated with small, grass roots, minor party campaigns, and would seem to indicate the resonance of the 2008 Obama campaign with a wider demographic than is commonly associated with a presidential candidacy. Many of these small donors also turned out to be repeat donors, but, even when this is taken into account, Obama received substantially more support from relatively small donors than his opponents, or than the leading candidates of either major party in recent presidential elections.

The internet has become a major tool for fundraising and campaigning in recent years, and the Obama team used this very effectively. They used it to maintain contact with donors who might be persuaded to increase their financial commitment, and generally to rally those who had expressed an interest in the campaign. YouTube and Facebook were among the other web-based outlets that the Obama campaign used to maintain contact with millions of potential supporters, and the campaign's own site was an effective web presence. This leadership in the most modern techniques was, at times, merged with traditional campaigning. In important marginal states, the campaign put a considerable effort into door-to-door canvassing, recruiting many volunteers through the internet and directing them to their target location with internet-generated maps and directions. The Obama campaign may have broken the mould of a pattern of presidential campaign finance that has lasted for a generation, but it appeared simultaneously to generate a grass roots strategy that was a throwback to earlier times. Early reports of the 2012 campaign indicated that the Obama fundraising effort had a target of raising another $750 million, but, with him as an incumbent not expecting any primary challenges, this time it would be possible to concentrate the whole war chest on the general election campaign.

Campaign finance law of the past generation has tended to push presidential candidates increasingly to rely on the construction of fundraising machines capable of attracting donations from individuals. While the role of the interest groups in presidential campaigns moderated, it did not disappear. Independent spending through committees established for the purpose has grown, and operates supposedly without influence from the candidate campaigns. Furthermore, it has been predicted that the Supreme Court's 2010 decisions in *Citizens United* v. *Federal Election Commission*, which allows corporations and unions to fund directly their own independently produced political broadcasts, and in *SpeechNow.org* v. *Federal Election Commission*, which allows independent expenditure committees to raise and spend unlimited funds in support of or opposition to candidates, created new routes into the electoral process for interest group monies.

Congressional elections

Unlike for presidential elections, the reforms of the 1970s failed to provide public funding for congressional elections. Several reasons lie behind this and subsequent refusals to introduce public funding. Republicans, in particular, tend to believe that using so much taxpayers' money is simply wrong.

Nevertheless, the subject keeps forcing itself back onto the agenda for one simple reason: the widespread public belief that interest-group donations to congressional candidates mean that Congress represents interest groups rather than the public. This situation was, if anything, exacerbated by the 1970s reforms. As with presidential elections, individual and group donations to candidates were subjected to limits. Individuals could donate up to $1,000 for each phase of an election, with a maximum to all candidates of $25,000 per campaign cycle. Groups could give up to $5,000 to one candidate for each phase of an election, with no overall maximum. Later legislation amended these limits, index-linking some of them. In 2011–12, individuals were allowed to donate $2,500 each to a candidate campaign, to a maximum of $46,200 to all candidates over a two-year campaign cycle. Group limits remained limited to $5,000 per candidate campaign, with no overall limit on donations. The key to raising campaign funds became soliciting money from as many groups and individuals as possible. It was in this context that political action committees (PACs) came into their own.

Political action committees

Political action committees are a form of interest group which exists for the sole purpose of raising and channelling campaign funds. Although they have been in existence since the 1940s, they were rare before the passage of the 1974 FECA amendments. Thus, in 1972, there were just 113 PACs registered with the government. The 1974 amendments, however, stimulated a rapid growth in their number, with the total settling down in the 1990s at around 4,500. Although each PAC was limited in how much it could give to a candidate, there was no limit on how many PACs could make a donation. Logically enough, then, the number of groups proliferated.

Most of the early growth in PACs was driven by business corporations: in 1995 there were 1,670 corporate PACs, compared with 334 labour union PACs and 804 PACs sponsored by trade and professional associations (Hrebener, 1997, p. 198). Moreover, although labour unions are prominent in the list of the biggest donors, collectively business easily outspends labour and other groups in campaign donations. In the 2009/10 election cycle, labour PACs donated $63.7 million to candidates,

Table 11.2 Growth of political action committees, selected years, 1974–2010

Year	Corporate	Labour	Trade, membership, health	Independent	Cooperative	Corporation without stock	Total
1974	89	201	318				608
1976	433	224	489				1,146
1978	785	217	453	162	12	24	1,653
1980	1,206	297	576	374	42	56	2,551
1982	1,469	380	649	723	47	103	3,371
1984	1,682	394	698	1,053	52	130	4,009
1986	1,744	384	745	1,077	56	151	4,157
1988	1,816	351	786	1,115	59	138	4,268
1990	1,795	346	774	1,062	59	136	4,172
1992	1,735	347	770	1,145	56	142	4,195
1994	1,660	333	792	980	53	136	3,954
1996	1,642	332	838	1,103	41	123	4,079
1998	1,567	321	821	935	39	115	3,798
2000	1,545	317	860	1,026	41	118	3,907
2002	1,528	320	975	1,055	39	110	4,027
2004	1,622	306	900	1,223	34	99	4,184
2006	1,582	273	937	1,254	37	100	4,183
2008	1,598	272	995	1,594	49	103	4,611
2010	1,683	283	1,004	1,747	39	103	4,859

Note: For 1974 and 1976 the data for trade, membership, and health PACs include independent, cooperative, and corporation-without-stock PACs. On November 24, 1975, the FEC issued its 'SUNPAC' advisory opinion. On May 11, 1976, FECA (Public Law 94–283) was enacted. All data are from the end of the year indicated

Source: Federal Election Commission, January, 2011, http://www.fec.gov/press/summaries/2011/2011paccount.shtml

Table 11.3 Highest spenders in congressional elections, 2008

House candidates	Amount spent ($)	Senate candidates	Amount spent ($)
Polis, Jared (D)+ (Colorado District 2)	7,323,502	McConnell, Mitch (R)*+ (Kentucky)	21,306,296
Treadwell, Sandy (R) (New York District 20)	7,038,552	Franken, Al (D)+ (Minnesota)	21,066,834
Kirk, Mark (R)*+ (Illinois District 10)	5,449,409	Coleman, Norm (R)* (Minnesota)	19,011,108
Boehner, John (R)*+ (Ohio District 8)	5,345,276	Dole, Elizabeth (R)* (North Carolina)	17,468,134
Honeycutt, Deborah (R) (Georgia District 13)	5,204,670	Cornyn, John (R)*+ (Texas)	16,454,518
Oberweis, James (R) (Illinois District 14)	5,084,489	Chambliss, Saxby (R)*+ (Georgia)	15,692,294
Foster, Bill (D)*+ (Illinois District 14)	5,047,518	Udall, Mark (D)+ (Colorado)	12,987,562
Gillibrand, Kirsten (D)*+ (New York District 20)	4,489,381	Warner, Mark (D)+ (Virginia)	12,515,479
Burner, Darcy (D) (Washington District 8)	4,462,884	Kerry, John (D)*+ (Massachusetts)	12,279,425
Buchanan, Vernon (R)*+ (Florida District 13)	4,345,554	Smith, Gordon (R)* (Oregon)	11,372,481

All of those listed were candidates in the 2008 general election.
* Incumbents running for re-election in 2008. + Winner in this election.
Source: Federal Election Commission: http://www.fec.gov/press/press2009/2009Dec29Cong/17hsedisb08.pdf; http://www.fec.gov/press/press2009/2009Dec29Cong/11sendisb08.pdf

a figure almost matched by the $62.9 million from the finance, insurance and real estate industry alone. With a further $21.2 million from transportation industries, $54.6 million from health businesses, $15.5 million from the construction industry, $23 million from agribusiness and $25 million from electronics and communications businesses, it is clear that the aggregate spending by business exceeds union spending by a substantial margin. PAC growth in recent years has been driven almost entirely by expansion in the 'independent' PAC sector, a category that includes those ideological and single-issue PACS that contributed $60.3 million during the 2010 campaigns (Center for Responsive Politics website, http://www.crp.org/, 2011).

A further spur to PAC growth has been the rapidly rising cost of running an election campaign for Congress. In particular, the increasing use of expensive television slots contributed to the escalation. By 2004, the total cost of congressional elections was a staggering $1 billion and it has continued to increase, with a total of $1.8 billion spent by all candidates and hopefuls in the 2010 congressional elections. There is a considerable variation in the costs of individual elections. A notable case was the Senate race in South Dakota, where the Republicans mounted a successful bid to defeat the Democrat Senate leader, Tom Daschle. Together, the two main candidates spent some $36 million dollars on an election in which fewer than 400,000 votes were cast, deciding the Senate seat of one of the least populous states in the Union. In 2008, the leading candidates in the very close race for the US Senate seat for Minnesota spent $40 million.

The 2010 elections stimulated spending at a high level as the Republicans recognised the opportunity for their party at a time of low approval of the administration, Democratic incumbents fought hard to hang on to their seats, and the Tea Party movement energised part of the electorate. High spending did not always result in victory. Tea Party-supported Linda McMahon (Connecticut) spent $50 million of her own money, and Sharron Angle (Nevada) spent $28 million without taking these Senate seats. Alan Grayson (D – Florida District 8) was the Democrat Representative who spent most ($5.5 million) unsuccessfully defending his seat.

Soft money

The 1990s witnessed an explosion of so-called 'soft-money' donations. These evaded the campaign finance laws by giving money to parties for general expenditures not directly associated with particular candidates. The result was that soft money accounted for 48 per cent of funds raised by the parties in 2001, compared with just 17 per cent ten years earlier. They were widely viewed as subverting the purposes of the original campaign for finance reform and there was an irresistible call for soft-money donations to be brought under control. In 2002, Congress passed the Bipartisan Campaign Reform Act (or McCain–Feingold Act, as it was frequently referred to). The Act banned soft-money donations but permitted an increase in hard-money donations from $1,000 per federal candidate to a figure of $2,000 that would rise automatically with the rate of inflation. Many interest groups and some politicians opposed the new restrictions and mounted a constitutional challenge. In the case of *McConnell* v. *FEC* (2003), however, the Supreme Court upheld the main portions of the legislation, but the erosion of the legislative limits continued in various ways.

Interest groups and PACs have shown themselves to be adept at getting ever-increasing sums of money to politicians they wish to influence, and the switch to more intense and effective hard-money fundraising was evident as soon as the new legislation was in place. The regulations also continued to be contested in court. On the whole, the limits on soft-money donations to campaigns held up, but other politically interested committees and groups have been given increased liberty to spend money directly on activities which appear, at least to the lay observer, to have an impact on electoral politics.

527 and 501(c) groups

The 2004 elections witnessed the rise to prominence of so-called '527 groups', named after the Internal Revenue Service code relating to their tax-exempt status. While they were recognised as existing to influence elections and public appointments, because they were not explicitly linked to particular candidates or parties, they were able to raise and spend millions of dollars during the election. Most of the major 527s were liberal groups, such as America Coming Together (ACT), an organisation backed by billionaire George Soros, which set out to defeat George W. Bush. ACT spent over $76 million on the election. The group which probably received the most attention, however, was Swiftboat Veterans and POWs for Truth. The group was dedicated to attacking the Democratic candidate, John Kerry, who, they alleged, had misrepresented his own war service in Vietnam and falsely accused other US servicemen of war crimes. They spent over $22 million on this cause and most commentators believe they did serious damage to their target. In December 2006, the Federal Elections Commission reported that three 527s, including Swiftboat Veterans and POWs for Truth, had paid fines of $630,000, having been judged to be acting as political committees in ways not protected from regulation by their 527 status. While these fines indicate a willingness by the FEC to attempt to prevent breaches of the boundaries of campaign regulation, they have the disadvantage of coming well after the activity has had its intended political impact.

The growth destination for unlimited soft-money donations in 2008 was among 501(c) groups. These are social welfare, labour union, and business league groups which may pursue similar political objectives to those of 527s, and engage in certain categories of campaign spending, as long as these activities are not their primary objectives. Since less than 50 per cent of their effort is spent directly on election-influencing activity, these groups fall outside the regulatory remit of the FEC. Their political activities are therefore less transparent than those of political action committees, and they constitute an attractive conduit into politics for donors of soft money. Research by the Campaign Finance Institute suggests that 501(c) political expenditure tripled to more than $200 million between 2004 and 2008. While the development of 527s favoured the Democratic campaign war chest, early 501(c) activity contributed more to the Republican campaign effort (Campaign Finance Institute, 2009). In April 2011, the *New York Times* reported that leading liberals had formed Priorities USA Action, a super PAC, and Priorities USA, a 501(c)(4) to allow supporters of President Obama the opportunity to channel unlimited funds into the Democratic effort for 2012. These developments suggest that the amount of unlimited independent money in campaigns is set to continue to increase. President Obama has maintained his opposition to anonymous money in campaigns, but the existence of such efforts drives him, and all

Table 11.4 Congressional election campaign contributions and expenditures, 2008

Party	No. of candidates	Total raised $	Total from PACs $	Total from individuals $
House:				
All	2,096	983,776,750	300,655,706	528,814,319
Dem.	863	539,584,022	184,057,175	289,953,963
Rep.	810	440,759,677	116,557,215	236,849,823
Senate:				
All	286	436,237,242	79,317,440	270,059,610
Dem.	116	239,545,296	34,098,484	150,769,895
Rep.	95	196,026,120	45,214,656	118,929,477

Based on data released by the FEC on Tuesday, 29 December 2009

candidate campaigns, to raise even more money in order to maintain control of the political agenda in their own campaigns.

Influence of interest groups, PACs and super PACs

Closer examination of campaign contributions to congressional candidates sheds considerable light on the motivations behind them.

The first point to note is that not all interest groups have as their primary aim the election of a candidate who shares their political viewpoint. True, ideological groups give overwhelmingly to candidates who champion their preferred policies; and labour unions give funds almost exclusively to Democrats. Thus, in the 2009–10 cycle, one of the largest union donors, the International Brotherhood of Electrical Workers, gave a total of $3.4 million, 97 per cent of which went to Democrats. During the same election cycle, Associated Builders and Contractors, a trade association, gave 100 per cent of its $1.3 million donations to Republicans. The American Medical Association (AMA) gave around 60 per cent of its donations to Republicans in the 20 years up to the 2010 election, but in 2009–10 gave just over half of its $1.5 million donations to Democrats. Koch Industries gave 94 per cent of its $1.7 million donations to Republicans. The billionaire brothers David and Charles Koch have long been associated with conservative political groups – most recently, the Tea Party movement. Other groups take a more pragmatic approach. They want to influence whichever party or candidate succeeds and they spread their money accordingly. Thus, the National Association of Realtors split their $4 million in donations 55 per cent to Democrats and 45 per cent to Republicans. The American Dental Association split their $1.8 million 50 per cent to Democrats and 50 per cent to Republicans.

A second notable feature of PAC donations is that they are not necessarily intended to affect the outcome of the elections concerned. Large amounts of money are given to candidates whose victory is a foregone conclusion, but whose position makes them enormously powerful. Take, for example, the Republican Speaker of the House, John Boehner, who represents the 8th district in Ohio. Boehner won his 2008 race with 68 per cent of the vote. Nevertheless, in 2010 he still received $2.6 million in PAC donations, 96 per cent of it from business groups. Boehner was re-elected with 66 per cent of the vote. Then House Majority Leader Steny Hoyer (Democrat, Maryland's 5th District) retained his seat in 2008 with 74 per cent of the vote. He was attractive enough to gather $2.9 million from PACs, 85 per cent from business groups. He was re-elected with a comfortable majority (Center for Responsive Politics). Quite simply, many recipients of PAC largesse do not need the money in order to win.

What most PACs – especially corporate PACs – want, therefore, is less to influence elections than to cultivate and influence those who make policy between elections. This is reinforced by the fact that, on average, those with most influence in policy-making – committee chairpersons – get 20 per cent more in PAC donations than ordinary House members (Stern, 1988, pp. 5–6). Further support for this view comes from the fact that PACs target their money on incumbents who sit on the committees that deal with legislation most likely to affect their group.

PACs are still limited by regulation of the money they can receive and donate. Individuals can only give $5,000 a year to PACs; PACs are limited to contributions of $5,000 to candidate campaigns and $15,000 to party committees, and all donors are identified. Super PACs, or 'independent-expenditure only committees', on the other hand, may channel unlimited anonymous donations into election activities on behalf of candidates. This change has come after the Supreme Court's decision in *Citizens United* v. *Federal Election Commission (2010)* overturned limits in the Bipartisan Campaign Finance Act of 2002 that had been designed to limit the potential impact of outsider spending in the late stages of election campaigns. The first election to take place under this new regime is in 2012, an election season of considerable import to the future of both major political parties, and therefore a context in which new campaign spending opportunities for lobbying groups are likely to be heavily exploited.

Access or votes?

Lobbyists for interest groups readily concede that they expect something in return for their money, but categorically deny that they are engaged in simple vote-buying. Instead, they hope to obtain access to those who write the nation's legislation. In this way, they are at least assured that policy-makers listen to their side of a policy debate before any action is taken. Lobbyists are aware that legislators are kept extremely busy by the demands of their job and that they have only a limited amount of time to devote to any one issue. If lobbyists get the opportunity to present a legislator with information and a point of view on the issue, there is a good chance that this will influence his thinking. As one lobbyist put it, 'I know what it means to put in a call to a legislator and get a call back and not to get a call back. And if that $500 is going to increase my chances of getting a call back, that is a heck of a lot, because frequently all it takes is the opportunity to talk to a legislator 10 or 15 minutes to make your case. He may not have 10 or 15 minutes to hear the other side' (Sabato, 1985, p. 127).

If a lobbyist can build up a long-term working relationship with a legislator, by providing expert and accurate information, he can acquire the status of a valued and trusted adviser. It may even reach the point where, when a relevant issue arises, it is the legislator who contacts the lobbyist to request information (Berry, 1989, p. 84).

The essence of this view of pressure-group activity is that influence is only exerted where the legislator receives an informed briefing by a lobbyist and is convinced by it. Donations to campaign funds facilitate the likelihood of that briefing taking place, but they do not buy, or even attempt to buy, legislators' votes.

Although this argument may raise eyebrows, given the large sums of money involved, there is evidence to support it. In the first place, even a generous PAC is only one factor in determining a legislator's vote. Party loyalty or personal ideology may be pulling in a contrary direction. Above all, however, a member of Congress will pay the closest attention to what her constituents think on a subject. She is unlikely to risk alienating her voters in order to please a PAC who gave her $5,000.

Moreover, a number of academic studies tend to support the view that legislators do not sell their votes to generous interest groups. By comparing legislators' votes on bills with the campaign donations received from interested groups, the studies have concluded that while money certainly does buy access, at best it only influences votes at the margins – when legislators have no strong inclinations or contrary pressures being exerted on them (Wright, 1990; Evans, 'PAC Contributions and Roll-call voting: Conditional Power', in Cigler and Loomis, 1991).

It is also important to remember that a mere correlation of votes with donations does not establish an unambiguous relationship of cause and effect.

Quite sensibly, interest groups try to reinforce the position of those whom they know are already sympathetic to their views. In other words, money may follow the voting inclinations and behaviour of legislators, rather than determine them.

Nevertheless, there is other evidence that contradicts this limited view of the influence of campaign finance. In the first place, some members of Congress openly acknowledge that it is difficult to resist the pressure to vote in line with groups who have contributed money. As Representative John Bryant said, 'Anytime someone, whether a person or a PAC, gives you a large sum of money, you can't help but feel the need to give them extra attention, whether it is access to your time or, subconsciously, the obligation to vote with them.' Representative (now Senator) Barbara Mikulski put it less gently: 'I fear we could become a coin-operated Congress. Instead of two bits, you put in $2,500 and pull out a vote' (Sabato, 1985, p. 126).

While it is members of the House of Representatives who are often seen as most vulnerable to the temptations of PAC money, the Senate is by no means immune. One of the greatest scandals of recent times was the case of the so-called Keating Five. In the 1980s, five senators – Cranston, Riegle, Deconcini, Glenn, McCain – had repeatedly intervened with federal regulators on behalf of Charles Keating's Lincoln Savings and Loan Association. The Savings and Loan eventually collapsed in 1989 because of financial irregularities. The ensuing inquiry revealed that the senators who represented Keating during the investigations had received a total of $1.5 million in donations from him. Moreover, the inquiry found that 'In numerous instances – especially in the cases of Cranston, Riegle and Deconcini – Keating's donations coincided in time with official actions taken by the senators on his behalf' (*CQ Almanac*, 1991, p. 27). Equally worrying, however, Senator Cranston responded to an official reprimand by the Senate Ethics Committee by telling his fellow senators that he had done nothing unusual: 'My behavior did not violate established norms. Here, but for the Grace of God, stand you' (ibid., p. 26).

In January 2006, lobbyist Jack Abramoff agreed to plead guilty on three criminal charges connected to his lobbying activities: conspiracy to defraud clients and to bribe public officials; mail fraud of a public official; and tax evasion. Abramoff also agreed to cooperate with prosecutors investigating the range and nature of corrupt political practices in Washington DC. Abramoff was given a sentence of 5 years and 10 months, but it was his extensive links with and donations to a range of politicians that caused consternation. His contacts reached into the office of Tom DeLay, Republican House Majority Leader, whose connections with the scandal forced him to step down from that office in September 2005, and influenced his decision not to stand for re-election in 2006. DeLay's leadership role in his party was firm, he was known as 'The Hammer', and had launched the 'K Street Project' designed to tie favoured lobbyists closely to his Republican colleagues. The energetic Republican-leaning lobbyist Jack Abramoff was the perfect companion for DeLay, but the combination of such enthusiastic political players created an atmosphere in which breaches of the law were more easily overlooked. As well as Abramoff, several others pleaded or were found guilty, including Michael Scanlon, former communications director for Tom DeLay, and Tony Rudy, former lobbyist and DeLay staffer. In January 2011, DeLay announced his intention to appeal a 3-year prison sentence for money laundering handed down by a Texas court. Former Representative Bob Ney served 17 months of a longer sentence in connection with political business he had undertaken with Abramoff. The Abramoff scandal had long tentacles, but not all scandals resulted from his activities. In 2006, former Congressman Randy Cunningham was sentenced to more than 8 years for charges related to receiving bribes. Nor did all cases involve Republicans. William Jefferson, who had the distinction of being Louisiana's first black congressman since the post-Civil War Reconstruction, went on to receive a 13-year sentence on charges related to bribery in November 2009.

We noted above that a mere correlation between votes and campaign donations is not enough to establish a clear causal relationship. Nevertheless, some analyses of voting and donations do produce the strong implication that money has sometimes

Table 11.5 Campaign donations and the 'lemon law' vote in the House of Representatives, 1982

Amount received from NADA PAC, 1979–82	Percentage of House members voting against the 'lemon law' in 1982
More than $4,000	90.2
$1,000–3,000	88.3
$1–1,000	68
Zero	34.2

Source: Stern, 1988, p. 45

determined votes. Philip Stern's analysis of the lobbying campaign by the National Automobile Dealers Association (NADA) to defeat the 'lemon law' is a case in point. The lemon law was a regulation issued by the Federal Trade Commission requiring second-hand car dealers to inform prospective customers of any flaws in a car of which they were aware. In the early 1980s, NADA campaigned to have Congress veto the regulation. This campaign included making donations totalling over $1 million to over half the members of Congress. The larger the donation, the more likely a member was to vote against the lemon law.

Even such figures as these cannot prove conclusively that NADA bought votes in the House. Nevertheless, episodes such as this, the Savings and Loan and Abramoff scandals and other individual cases ensure that campaign donations by interest groups will remain a controversial topic.

Interest groups and the public good

Policy

It may be argued that, on balance, interest groups make a valuable contribution to the development of good public policies. As a powerful representative force, their activities help to keep politicians in touch with the needs and demands of different social groups. If one measure of good public policy is its responsiveness and acceptability to the people at large, then interest groups may plausibly be said to be a positive element in the political system.

Yet there are many who claim that interest groups distort the policy-making process and are a prime cause of many of the policy problems which the United States has faced in recent years.

Iron triangles

One such line of criticism is that interest groups have formed a mutually regarding and mutually rewarding relationship with two other political institutions: congressional committees and subcommittees, and the bureaucratic agencies which correspond to the same policy areas. These three-way relationships are known as iron triangles.

The most famous (or infamous) of these iron triangles has been that concerned with national defence. As far back as 1961, President Eisenhower took the opportunity of his farewell address to warn the country of the dangers posed by what he termed 'the military–industrial complex'. The three points of the triangle here are arms manufacturers, the government defence establishment, including the armed forces and Defense Department, and members of Congress who represent constituencies whose economies are defence-oriented. All three have a vested interest in ever-larger defence expenditures. The arms manufacturers reap profits from such outlays, the government defence establishment acquires more power, and members of Congress earn the votes of constituents who gain jobs in the defence plants.

What is missing, as Eisenhower tried to point out, is any concept of the national interest. And the danger is that the iron triangle will cause greater expenditure on arms than the nation needs or can afford. Although the military–industrial complex provides a dramatic example of an iron triangle, similar relationships can be seen to exist right across the range of policy areas (Levine and Thurber, 'Reagan and the Intergovernmental Lobby' in Cigler and Loomis, 1991).

Indeed, in his farewell address in 1989, President Reagan blamed 'special interests' and iron triangles for America's massive annual budget deficits. They prevented their favourite expenditures from being cut and effectively shut off debate on alternative policies that might be harmful to them, although beneficial to the nation.

Democracy

Finally we come to the most fundamental question of all: are interest groups compatible with democracy? As with most aspects of the interest group debate, opinion remains divided on this.

We have already noted that interest groups can be seen as performing a valuable and legitimate representative function. Indeed, at one time, so-called 'pluralist' political theorists argued that interest groups positively advanced democratic values. They believed that, since all interests in society could be organised into groups, and because these groups would compete with each other and then compromise, the end-product of interest group activity would mirror the nation's demands as a whole (Truman, 1971).

Pluralist theorists acknowledged the fact that not all interest groups were equal, with corporate groups, for example, having far greater financial resources than others. Nevertheless, it was argued that interest group resources were not cumulative: that is, no one type of group possessed an advantage in all resources. Thus, while corporate groups had an advantage in money, labour or civil rights groups had an advantage in numbers (Dahl, 1961).

The principal critics of the pluralist view have been elite theorists on both the political left and right (Mills, 1956; Dye, 1995). They stress the cooperation that occurs between privileged interest groups, especially those from the corporate sector, and

Figure 11.1 The military–industrial complex: US military power defending the oil industry rather than the national interest.
Source: © Kirk Anderson

other government elites. They deny that this political network is equally open to all comers, especially groups that lack the financial clout to 'buy themselves a seat at the table'.

Those who defend the role of interest groups today concede some of the arguments made by the critics. Not only is there a real inequality among interest groups in terms of resources, but they are not even internally democratic. They tend to be run by a handful of full-time leaders who rarely consult their members on policy issues (Berry, 1989, p. 66).

Nevertheless, the sheer number of interest groups tends to support the view that they perform a valuable representative function. They are a vehicle for putting new issues on the public agenda and for encouraging Americans to participate in a small way in their own government. And for all that Americans lambaste the power of special interests in general, they tend to value the role of the groups that represent *them* (Berry, 1989, p. 8).

For both good and ill, therefore, interest groups will remain a powerful force in American politics. They will continue to organise and represent significant sections of the community, and to provide the financial fuel for congressional elections. This in turn means that they will continue to have a privileged claim on the attention of policy-makers and a privileged opportunity to place private interest at the heart of public policy.

Chapter summary

The heterogeneous nature of American society has given rise to an impulse to form interest groups. This was encouraged by the constitutional protection of the rights to assemble and to petition government. As government has grown in its responsibilities, the activities of interest groups have expanded, especially as the fragmented system of government gives numerous points of access to the policy-making process. Interest group activity is, however, highly controversial, owing mainly to the fact that the groups provide candidates for office with a large percentage of their campaign funds. This has led to the popular belief that Congress is in the grip of rich 'special interests' who put their own needs before those of the nation. While there is contradictory evidence on this issue, there is no doubt that the ability of certain interest groups to gain access to the nation's top policy-makers gives them a very powerful position in the American political process.

Discussion points

1. Why are interest groups so numerous in the United States?
2. How did the Federal Election Campaign Acts of the 1970s affect the role of interest groups?
3. How plausible is the argument that interest group money buys access but not votes?
4. What are the differences between interest group participation in presidential and congressional elections?
5. Do interest groups impair or enhance American representative democracy?

Further reading

Excellent introductions to this subject include R. Shaiko *et al.*, *The Interest Group Connection: Electioneering, Lobbying and Policymaking in Washington* (2nd edn, Washington, DC: CQ Press, 2004); R. Hrebener, *Interest Group Politics in America* (3rd edn, New York: Sharpe, 1997); A. Cigler and B. Loomis, *Interest Group Politics* (6th edn, Washington, DC: CQ Press, 2002) and J. Berry, *The Interest Group Society* (2nd edn, Glenview, Ill.: Scott, Foresman/Little, Brown, 1989). On PACs in particular, see L. Sabato, *PAC Power: Inside the World of Political Action Committees* (New York: Norton, 1985). On finance laws, see M. Malbin, *Parties, Interest Groups and Campaign Finance Laws* (Washington, DC: American Enterprise Institute, 1993).

Useful websites are http://www.opensecrets.org; http://www.cfinst.org.

References

Berry, J. (1989) *The Interest Group Society* (2nd edn, Glenview, Ill.: Scott, Foresman/Little, Brown).

Campaign Finance Institute (2009) http://www.cfinst.org/Press/PReleases/09-02-25/Soft_Money_Political_Spending_by_Nonprofits_Tripled_in_2008.aspx

Cigler, A. and Loomis, B. (1991) *Interest Group Politics* (3rd edn, Washington, DC: CQ Press).

Dahl, R. (1961) *Who Governs?* (New Haven: Yale University Press).

Dye, T. (1995) *Who's Running America? The Clinton Years* (6th edn, Englewood Cliffs, NJ: Prentice Hall).

Hrebener, R. (1997) *Interest Group Politics in America* (3rd edn, New York: Sharpe).

Marlowe, H. (2011) http://www.alldc.org/press/Letter_to_the_President_Draft_EO.pdf

Mills, C. (1956) *The Power Elite* (Oxford: Oxford University Press).

Sabato, L. (1985) *PAC Power: Inside the world of Political Action Committees* (New York: Norton).

Stern, P. (1988) *The Best Congress Money Can Buy* (New York: Pantheon Books).

Tocqueville, A. de (1835) *Democracy in America* (Reprinted 1956, New York: Mentor).

Truman, D. (1971) *The Governmental Process* (2nd edn, New York: Knopf).

Wright, J. (1990) 'Contributions, lobbying and committee voting in the United States House of Representatives', *American Political Science Review*, vol. 84, pp. 417–38.

Part 4
The executive process

The executive branch of American government includes the most visible part of that government – the presidency – and one of its least visible parts – the executive bureaucracy.

The constitutional ambiguity of the extent of the executive power of the presidency, coupled with the fact that the office is held by one person alone, has meant that the presidential role in the political system has depended heavily on the electoral needs and administrative capacities of individual presidents.

However, presidents are by no means alone in exercising their powers. They are surrounded by assistants, and they preside over a large number of federal employees. Although this federal bureaucracy resides within the executive branch, and therefore might appear at first glance to be subordinate to the president, in reality it is better to see the federal bureaucracy as something of a battlefield between presidents and other forces in American politics, both those already examined in Part 3 (voters, parties, media and pressure groups) and those we shall be looking at in Parts 5 and 6 (Congress and the courts).

Contents

Chapter 12
Presidential power

The presidency of the United States is often referred to as the most powerful office in the world. At election times, citizens in more than one other country may joke that selection to so significant a political office should be seen as too important to leave to American voters alone. In truth, the executive is but one branch in American constitutional government, and the presidents who occupy the leading office in this branch face considerable complications in turning their executive agenda into deliverable policy. The Constitution provides the president with the tools of office, and the office-holders use these tools with differing skills, and in differing contexts. The office has certainly taken a central role in national and international perceptions of American government, and this perception itself adds to the authority that it has gained over the centuries. The president still faces a complex situation, having at all times to negotiate major initiatives with the members of the US Congress. The authority that the executive takes into these negotiations still reflects the cautious debate and final decisions undertaken in composing the Constitution.

The constitutional debate

The members of the US Constitutional Convention debated long and hard about the form that the nation's executive should take. Many felt that the policy failures of George III and his immediate advisers lay at the core of American colonial grievances; that the intransigence of these English politicians led by the King led inexorably to the War for Independence; and that the inadequate royal leadership of the war had contributed to American success. England's monarch, with his strong and unchecked executive powers, had managed to lay the foundations for war, promote the war, and then lose the war.

The authors of the US Constitution could take a number of lessons from this experience. Strong and unchecked executive leaders clearly could damage their country. Ill-advised and distant leaders could become out of touch with their countrymen. These perceptions were aired in the discussions at the 1787 Philadelphia Convention. There was little enthusiasm for a system that might replace George III with a home-grown executive in similar mould.

There were concerns, nevertheless, that the new nation should have an executive leadership capable of acting decisively in the nation's interest when necessary. In the earliest years of the USA, its leaders had first an interim form of government, then designed the Articles of Confederation as the basis for their national government. Central to the system was a Continental Congress, and the nearest thing to a national executive was the presiding officer of this body. This office was primarily ceremonial, carrying little authority, which may have contributed to the fact that these presidents of the Continental Congress served on average for less than a year, even before a one-year term was written into the Articles.

The Philadelphia delegates could also observe the various forms of state governorship that emerged in the early years of independence. Most states limited their governors to one-year terms, and few used direct popular election, but there were exceptions that allowed comparison, and startling similarities emerged, in spite of the different approaches. The practical result within the variety of systems adopted was that most states chose stability in their executive leadership. Governors were often re-elected where this was an option. Change of leadership happened, but rarely was this an annual event. The new states provided examples of executive leadership that was more responsible and checked than the English model, and with more potential and dynamism than the early US national model.

In a study of the origins of the American presidency, Thomas Cronin (1989) points out that at least 60 votes were taken by the authors of the US Constitution on the method of election of the executive, eligibility to hold the office, and the length and number of terms of office. These issues impacted upon each other as the delegates searched for a form that would produce a relatively autonomous and energetic executive. It should be not too dependent on, or in league with, the legislature, but checked from having absolute power; connected to the consent of the governed, but without the potential to rule through the mob; and should have the qualities that would be respected in an executive.

Terms of office were considered ranging from two years to life, with eligibility for re-election and without, with appointment by the legislature or through popular election. On more than one occasion, the decision appeared to be final – only to be reopened. The final form was agreed only days before the Convention ended. The president of the United States would serve for four years, would be eligible for re-election, and would be selected through a new invention – the electoral college.

The electoral college

The electoral college has not always given the nation a smooth ride on the way to choosing its president. As recently as 2000, the result was not decided for five weeks after polling day. Even after the position had been declared in all the other states, the election result in Florida remained very close. Things were finely balanced nationally, and the winner in Florida would also be the next president. Legal battles over the vote counting and recounts eventually reached the US Supreme Court, and its decision effectively confirmed George W. Bush as the winner in Florida, and therefore as the president elect of the United States. Elections anywhere in the world can be close, and may need recounts or result in battles in court. The difference that made this race compelling for onlookers worldwide was that a win in the extraordinarily tight Florida race would give Bush victory in the electoral college, even though he would not have a lead in the popular vote. In the national popular vote, George Bush had received more than half a million fewer votes than his Democratic opponent, Al Gore, but in the electoral college Bush had won. The electoral structure that produced this apparently contradictory outcome is written into the US Constitution.

The authors of the US Constitution heard arguments for various forms of presidential selection.

Direct popular election of the president was considered, as well as various forms of appointment of the president by the national legislature. Through much of the debate, appointment of the president by the national legislature seemed the most likely outcome. Delegates were not convinced that the ordinary citizens in America's original 13 states would have the broad knowledge of national affairs and personalities required to make an informed personal choice between presidential candidates, while their state office-holders would have greater knowledge and a broader background for making such a decision. But serious objections to appointment by legislature prevented these eighteenth-century thinkers from making a hasty decision on the presidential selection structure.

Appointment by legislature would threaten to make the presidency too much a creature of the US Congress, and to weaken its independence and authority within the system. In addition, the individual states, and especially the small states, had reservations about an executive elected either directly, or by the national legislature. In either case, the process might ignore and erode the identity of individual states. Small states in particular ran the risk of having their interests overlooked in any presidential election process that did not include a specific role for states.

The electoral college attempted to address some of these concerns. Electors, chosen by the states, would in their turn choose the president. The number of electors would be equal to the total congressional representation of each state. Originally, state legislatures were allowed to decide the method of choosing the electors. Popular voting for electors had become the norm in most states by the 1830s, with all states using this method after the Civil War. The electors meet and cast their votes in the various state capitals, the votes then being carried to Washington DC for the final count. This system, which has remained fundamentally the same for over two centuries, expressly recognises the place of the states in American national government.

The number of electors is equal to the number of US representatives (a distribution based on population), plus the number of US senators (two per state). By the Twenty-third Amendment to the Constitution, in 1961, the federal district of Washington DC (which is not part of any state) was allocated three electoral college votes, the same number as the least populous states. The inclusion of two votes per state, regardless of size, has the most impact on the states with small populations. For example, Vermont and South Dakota would each have only one electoral college vote based on population alone, but the two votes per state 'bonus' trebles their electoral votes to a total of three. In a heavily populated state such as California, with 53 US representatives, this 'bonus' has less impact.

The total number of electoral college votes nationwide is 538. Victory in the presidential election requires a candidate to collect an absolute majority, or at least 270, of these votes. If no candidate receives an absolute majority, the Constitution describes a method for the House of Representatives to choose from the leading candidates.

The idea that electoral college members would exercise strong individual choice eroded fairly quickly in the nation's political history. From a very early stage in US political development, party political organisations began to marshal electoral college voters into blocs committed to particular candidates. As popular voting became widespread in presidential elections, any sense that electoral college members were independent decision-makers eroded further, but in spite of hundreds of alternative proposals having been made over the past two centuries, the electoral college still functions as the way of choosing the president.

All the states except Maine and Nebraska have adopted the practice of awarding all of their electoral college votes to the candidate who leads in the state's popular vote. This maximises the impact of an individual state's electoral college votes in the final election tally. In the 2008 election, Nebraska's electoral college vote was split, when voters in Omaha gave their support, and one electoral vote, to the Democratic candidate, Barack Obama, while the other four of the state's electoral college votes went to Republican John McCain. The effect was that the state gave a net gain of three votes to McCain, while the practice of most states would have resulted in McCain gaining all five of the state's votes.

This structure has generally resulted in the electoral college inflating the leading candidate's margin of victory. In 1996, for example, Democrat Bill Clinton received over 49 per cent of the popular vote; his leading Republican opponent, Bob Dole, received just under 41 per cent; and Reform party candidate Ross Perot, putting on a remarkably good show for a minor party, had over 8 per cent of the more than 96 million votes cast nationwide. Interpreted through the electoral college, the result appeared even more clear cut. Perot won no states, and therefore had no electoral college votes. Dole's victories in 19, mainly small, states gave him 159 votes in the electoral college. Clinton's sweep of the rest of the states resulted in 379 votes, or over 70 per cent of the total available in the electoral college. In 2008, Barack Obama's 53 per cent of the popular vote converted into 68 per cent of the electoral college vote.

However, when public support for the leading candidates is very close, there is potential for the electoral college results, totalled from all the states, not to favour the candidate who has been supported by most individual voters. This is what happened in 2000. George W. Bush took many more of the small states than Al Gore. In all, Bush took 30 states, to Gore's 20 states (plus Washington DC). The popular vote favoured Gore by about 0.5 per cent of the total. But Bush's support was distributed between enough states to give him 271 electoral college votes – just exceeding the necessary absolute majority in the electoral college, enough to make him the next president of the United States. There have been only a few elections in US history when the victor in the electoral college has not also had a popular majority lead, though there have been other elections, such as 1960, 1968 and 2004, where it came close. The American electorate is perfectly aware of this possibility, and generally seems content to live with it. The result in 2000 caused controversy and some bitterness, but most of that was concentrated on the technical problems of counting a close vote accurately in the state of Florida, not on the existence of a voting system that confirms the importance of the states, as well as the people, in selecting the nation's leader.

Figure 12.1 Barak Obama 2008 campaign poster.
Source: © Alamy Images/flab

A national office

The presidency holds a special place with American citizens, whose respect for the office often provides the foundation for admiration of the office-holder (see Box 12.1). Does this well-documented and steady admiration indicate that the president is a particularly powerful person? Certainly, the president and vice-president are the only office-holders in the US government that are elected nationally. While the contemporary electoral college is built firmly on the eighteenth-century constitutional foundations of the USA, the presidential election process has adapted to the contemporary context of the twenty-first century.

Figure 12.2 The annual State of the Union address is just one of the responsibilities that put the president at the centre of the public's perception of politics. . . .
Source: © Hicks

The choice of the national executive leadership is one political event in which every eligible citizen of the United States can take part.

The presidential election process becomes visible at the beginning of the very public processes that the political parties use to choose their candidates. A series of primary elections, caucus meetings, and conventions are organised all across the nation, beginning in January of election year in the sparsely populated states of Iowa and New Hampshire. From then until the general election, on the Tuesday after the first Monday in November, the public battle to become president is an almost continuous lead story in the news. Given that the candidates' campaigns for the nomination have to be active well in advance of January, the presidential election is an event that can engage interested voters for a full year.

The election process appears to put the president at the centre of the national political process, and the modern media coverage of elections, and of the policy process, often gives the same impression, but it is not clear that the Constitution was written with this aim in mind.

The US Constitution does not make the executive branch its first concern. It moves on to this branch in Article II, after devoting the first Article of the Constitution to the legislative branch. It may be that the authors of the Constitution felt that the legislature, and especially the US House of Representatives, which was in the early days the only directly elected part of the national government, would be the most dynamic element of national government. In fact, it was clear quite quickly that the presidency had great potential to establish a clear leadership role in national government.

Box 12.1

The most admired American

For over 50 years the Gallup organisation has conducted an end-of-year poll, asking Americans, 'What man that you have heard or read about, living today in any part of the world, do you admire most?' On the eve of 2009, Gallup announced that 32 per cent of Americans mentioned President-elect Barack Obama as the man they admire most in the world. President George W. Bush, only a month from leaving office, took second place in the poll, with 5 per cent, and presidential candidate John McCain placed third.

For the previous seven consecutive years, President Bush had held the top position in this poll. In other words, for almost the complete time that he had held the office of President of the United States of America, that country's citizens had annually chosen him as their most admired man in the world. The terrorist attacks on New York City and Washington in September 2001 undoubtedly had some bearing on these results. Americans naturally rallied in support of their nation and its leaders in the face of such aggression. The later difficulties of Bush's Republican administration also had an effect, and Bush's lead in this poll gradually declined, but it did not disappear until Obama had been elected to take over that office.

Bill Clinton continued to feature in the poll, placing fourth in 2008. Though he had left presidential office in January 2001, former President Clinton had by 2008 never slipped outside the top four places. Former presidents Jimmy Carter and George H.W. Bush were not far outside the 2008 top ten, respectively 28 and 16 years after they had left the White House.

A parallel poll found the most admired woman to be Hillary Clinton. She had occupied this position for 13 of the 16 years from when she entered the White House as Bill Clinton's First Lady to her own challenge for the presidency.

Throughout the entire period that the question has been asked by the Gallup polling organisation, the president currently in office has generally taken first place, and living former presidents have often achieved top ten placings. The last time that a president-elect displaced the president for the top slot was in 1952, when the popular Dwight Eisenhower was waiting to take over from President Truman, another executive who lost a great deal of public support towards the end of his administration. President Obama's popularity also declined in office, but as 2012 arrived he was still the nation's most admired man. The Gallup results indicate that US citizens see their president as a touchstone for admiration and have done so consistently for as long as this measure has been available.

'The executive power shall be vested in a President'

After opening with this unambiguous statement, Article II of the Constitution moves on to list and describe elements of the president's office. The second section of this Article determines that the president is the sole commander-in-chief of the nation's armed forces, and of the state militias when they are called into national duty. The president is also given the power to require responses from the principal officers in each constituent department of the executive.

The same section of the Constitution describes the president's powers to make treaties, to appoint ambassadors and judges of the Supreme Court, and to make other senior national appointments. But the Constitution of the United States is at all times careful to limit the threat of concentrating too much power in one part of the governmental structure. In all of these cases presidential power to act and to appoint is checked and balanced by the institutionalised intervention of one of the other branches of federal government. In particular, presidential treaty-making and appointment powers are subject to the advice and consent of the US Senate.

Article II, Section 2 also gives the president, in his turn, a checking and balancing role in US government, with the assertion of the executive power to grant reprieves and pardons, thereby providing a political counterbalance to scrutinise judicial decision-making.

Section 3 of the executive Article goes on to provide that the president 'shall from time to time give to the Congress information of the state of the union, and recommend to their consideration such measures as he shall judge necessary and expedient'. This has developed into the State of the Union address, now delivered annually in January or early February. Given by the president before a joint meeting of both chambers of Congress, and now one of the most watched political events to be covered by television, the State of the Union address acts as a showcase for the president to outline the administration's achievements and goals, to present a blueprint of the administration's current legislative targets and to challenge the US Congress to meet them.

While it is generally expected that the US Congress has the autonomy to organise itself, Article II, Section 3 gives the president the authority to convene special sessions of Congress, and to adjourn Congress if the two chambers cannot agree a time of adjournment. Presidential intervention in the legislative process is even more clear in the granting of the veto power. Article I, Section 7 of the Constitution declares that all legislation must be presented to the president for approval. The president has the authority at this stage to veto a bill, usually by returning it to Congress with his objections. This check on the legislature's authority can, in its turn, be overridden, but only if two-thirds of both chambers of Congress vote to defeat the president's blocking manoeuvre.

The position of the president as chief executive is also firmly supported by other statements in the Constitution – for example, that the president will 'faithfully execute the office of the President', 'preserve, protect and defend the Constitution', and 'take care that the laws be faithfully executed'.

Presidential centrality: commander-in-chief

The constitutional grants of power and authority to the president have been said by some analysts to give the appearance of establishing a set of institutionalised presidential 'chiefdoms' putting the president at the centre of US government. The most clearly mentioned of these constitutional roles is commander-in-chief of the armed forces. The army, navy and state militias that made up America's forces in the late eighteenth century were crucially important. After all, this was a country born out of war, and still unconvinced that its international competitors were ready to allow it to fulfil its national destiny. National self-preservation was very important.

The significance of the commander-in-chief role is never more evident than in times of international stress, and has a clear and strong relevance at the beginning of the twenty-first century. The president's commander-in-chief powers have been most tested during major combats, such as the War of 1812, the American Civil War, the world wars, the Vietnam War, the Gulf War, and most recently the post-11 September 2001 engagements with Afghanistan and Iraq.

Through much of the second half of the twentieth century, the USA and the USSR were seen as superpowers maintaining an uneasy international balance. The implosion of the USSR has left just one international superpower, and while Russian defence spending still leaves it in the same league as the United Kingdom, Japan, France or Germany, none of them comes close to the USA, where the annual defence budget is now double that of all these other countries combined.

As commander-in-chief, the president leads an armed force of almost 1.5 million. There are also many civilian personnel involved, and the Department of Defense is the largest executive department, with almost 700,000 employees. These non-uniformed government defence workers make up about 40 per cent of the total government employment in all 15 executive departments within the executive branch.

The commander-in-chief power is not without controversy. During the American Civil War, for example, President Abraham Lincoln announced the suspension of habeas corpus, and ordered the use of military courts for some cases. In *Ex parte Milligan*, a case conveniently left undecided until after the conflict was finished, the Supreme Court ruled against the late president's actions. The court's decision liberated Lambdin Milligan from prison, and established precedent aimed to protect citizens' civil liberties in wartime.

A century after the *Milligan* case, the USA was again at war, this time against communist foes in Southeast Asia. The conduct of the war by successive administrations disturbed the US Congress enough that in 1973 it overrode the veto of President Richard Nixon to pass the War Powers Resolution, requiring consultation with Congress on troop deployments. While presidents have, on occasion, taken the debate on military actions to Congress, they have generally indicated their willingness to ignore the apparent limitations of war power legislation, citing the need for effective and decisive executive action in times of crisis.

The significance of these issues has re-emerged at the start of the twenty-first century, as President George W. Bush led the United States into what he termed a 'war on terror'. Reacting after the September 2001 terrorist outrages on the United States, President Bush led his country, and some allies, into attacks on Afghanistan and Iraq. The United States chose to hold captives taken in Afghanistan at a detention camp in Guantanamo, Cuba and indicated that it saw these prisoners as outside the scope of the Geneva Convention, and as subject to US military law. Domestically, a new executive department of Homeland Security was established, and actions taken which some criticised as contrary to American traditions of individual rights. The legal and practical repercussions have been long-lasting. The federal courts system has been the theatre for a number of cases concerning some of those held at Guantanamo and challenging the authority of the USA to seize, hold, and process them in the ways initiated by the former commander-in-chief, George Bush. Only two days after his inauguration, President Obama signed an Executive Order to close the Guantanamo Bay detention centre by January 2010. However, the logistics of finding suitable locations for those who are still considered a risk, and who have been held without trial for nearly a decade, made this project very difficult. Obama eventually conceded that Guantanamo could not be closed.

Presidential centrality: chief diplomat

The diplomatic centrality of the president appears quite clear in the Constitution. The president receives ambassadors, thereby recognising other nations and their leaders, and, with the advice and consent of the US Senate, the president appoints ambassadors from the United States, and makes treaties with foreign nations.

The constraint of being checked by a legislative chamber, though, is not inconsiderable, especially as treaties have to be agreed by a two-thirds majority of senators. Perhaps the executive calamity most recalled is that afforded to President Woodrow Wilson after the First World War. Welcomed in Europe as a saviour, Wilson led the negotiations for a post-war League of Nations, only to find on his return to Washington that he could not negotiate his own international plan through the US Senate.

Presidents may reinterpret existing treaties to suit their administration's strategic aims more closely, and they can end treaties without congressional sanction, but they must find a way to work with Senate in order to establish new treaties. Executive agreements, though, do provide one alternative mechanism for a more independent conduct of some diplomacy. Actions based on the broad constitutional statement of the president's executive power, and on interpretations of existing legislation, have been used by many presidents. These are usually, though not always, quite tightly constrained agreements.

In spite of repeated congressional attempts to limit presidential use of the executive agreement, it has become a substantial tool for any administration wishing to use the president's centrality in foreign and diplomatic policy to its full extent. The president is head of state, and this is exhibited most clearly in the conduct of foreign affairs, where the executive can make strategic use of the office's diplomatic and commander-in-chief powers with international consequences. As the post-Cold War USA has emerged to occupy a position without international equal in terms of power and authority, the president's foreign affairs leadership roles have acquired ever-increasing significance, both internationally and in terms of the domestic prestige associated with the position of world leadership.

Presidential centrality: chief legislator

It is perhaps stretching a point to claim this title for the president, but it cannot be ignored that the office brings with it a defined legislative role. The State of the Union address has become a key annual feature of any administration, giving the president a clear and unchallenged opportunity to present the administration's achievements in the best possible light, as well as the chance to recommend to the Congress those measures which the administration would like to see enacted.

Skilfully used, the State of the Union address can act as an important part of the agenda-setting that any ambitious president will want to see as part of the administration's activity. Passing this executive wish list into legislation, however, will still take a great deal more than sending a presidential message.

Congress is the legislative branch, and its members guard that privilege jealously. Even when Congress is controlled by members of the president's own political party, they cannot be relied on to respond unquestioningly to the executive prompt. The executive branch has to liaise carefully with members of Congress to make sure that the major elements of its legislative agenda pass relatively unhindered through the system. Congress will take account of many cues. For example, a president with a substantial and recent election mandate is likely to have an advantage in dealing with Congress; a president with skilful liaison aides and whose message is clear and accompanied by helpful evidence and documentation will have improved chances for success.

Negotiation with Congress takes many forms, and probably the most used constitutional legislative power afforded to the president is the power to veto legislation. In fact, very little legislation is vetoed, and both the executive and Congress recognise this as a heavy-handed tool in the process, but the threat of presidential veto can have the effect of concentrating the minds of everyone interested in passing legislation, thereby contributing to compromise legislation being designed.

Certainly, the president is a serious player in the legislative process, even if the institutional structure limits and encumbers the executive's freedom as a player in the law-making process.

Limited powers and presidential personality

While the institutional 'chiefdoms' that make up the role of chief executive are solidly founded in the Constitution, the powers granted are not huge, and it is clear that the accompanying checks and balances constrain even further the power of the presidency. Still, it is not uncommon for the presidency of the USA to be referred to as the most powerful political office not just in America but in the world. There are clearly elements other than the defined constitutional parameters of the office that contribute to the perception of the presidency as having such potential for power.

One of the most influential analyses of the presidency, by the late Richard Neustadt, was based originally on his first-hand observations of the presidencies of the mid-twentieth century. Neustadt (1990) concluded that the limited and constrained authority granted to the president in the Constitution did not aggregate to very much presidential power. Other resources for presidential power exist, said Neustadt, and the personal political skills of the president in mobilising these resources go a long way to accounting for the success or failure of a particular administration.

Key to Neustadt's perception of presidential potential were the forces of modernisation in twentieth-century America. In part, the shift was a reflection of the course of history. It had been observed before that in times of crisis, such as war, the nation demanded centralised leadership, and that the president was the natural focus of national authority from which the citizenry expected that leadership to emanate. Two world wars, the Great Depression, the Cold War, the war in Southeast Asia, the collapse of the communist hegemony, together put a series of intense demands on the federal executive through most of the twentieth century. The policy leadership provided was not uncontested, but always placed the executive at the very centre of the action and the debate.

Presidential centrality: the media

The death of former President Ronald Reagan, in June 2004, prompted a host of commentators to recall the impact of his 1981–89 occupancy of the White House. Repeated through much of this coverage was reference to Reagan's reputation as the 'Great Communicator', a shared term of commemoration that emphasised the way the growth of electronic media has transformed the public and political relations role of the president. The relaxed and calmly confident style that Barack Obama brought to his campaign suggested that he might be a president more capable than most of taking advantage of this media centrality. Certainly, President Obama is well aware of the value of communication. In one interview, explaining why he especially admires Abraham Lincoln, he pointed to the Civil War president's ability to listen and to communicate: 'Lincoln just found a way to shape public opinion and shape people around him and lead them and guide them . . . [through his] way of helping to illuminate the truth. I just find that to be a compelling style of leadership' (Balz and Johnson, 2009).

President Obama's communications skills remained evident when he reached office, but, as the fierce debate on health care reform in the first year of his administration showed, the president is an important actor who operates in a system that demands negotiation and compromise. Interests compete to influence public opinion, especially on issues that generate strongly held positions, and even a Congress of the same party as the president will reflect the resulting range of opinions in their policy debates with the executive.

Administrations have taken media relations seriously for many years. Well before the advent of the electronic media, successive presidential administrations had occasionally suffered from adversarial press coverage, and benefited from supportive reporting. President Theodore Roosevelt was an active campaigner for his policies, and believed that press dissemination of his energetic and well-constructed speeches could act to maintain his proposals high on the public agenda, even to the extent of appealing directly to the public in an attempt to influence congressional receptiveness to presidential initiatives. Roosevelt's belief that the presidency was a 'bully pulpit' for ideas has become one of the received wisdoms of executive life.

In the twentieth century, radio, and then television, became the major sources of public news consumption. Some elements of the press remained important, however, with a few major newspapers finding new roles through investigative and in-depth reporting that could influence the news agenda of the other news formats. President Woodrow Wilson was the first to use occasional formal press conferences as a way of channelling and guiding media coverage of the presidency, but the electronic news media had an immediacy that forced administrations into a much more continuous, varied and active media management style by the twenty-first century.

Within the White House, the Press Office and the Office of Communications work constantly with representatives from all the reporting media in an effort to gain favourable coverage of the administration, and to limit the damage caused by negative coverage. A level of activity has developed that might previously have been expected only in election years, as presidents have moved towards adopting a strategy of 'permanent campaign' to maintain political and public engagement with their agenda, and to minimise the diversions that might be caused by political scandal or criticism.

Certainly, presidents appear to have some genuine advantages in their attempt to manage their position in the mediation of American politics. The executive, led by a single figure and with concentrated resources, is easier to cover than the legislature. The presidential election campaign provides a foundation of knowledge about the administration that has been projected through a high-expenditure media-based campaign. The presidency has an iconic place in US politics that gives its occupants a media advantage – it is just more likely that what a president does can be classified as news. There is, nonetheless, a tension in the relationship between commentators and those being commented on. The journalists want access to potential stories to be as free as possible, while the subjects of the limelight would prefer to have as much control as possible over the message that will be projected to the public. Therefore, while the presidency may have an advantage in attracting attention, it also applies considerable resources to 'spin' that attention to its greatest advantage.

While the president is a central actor in American political reporting and campaigning, not all analysts

Box 12.2

Controversy: President Bush lands on the USS *Abraham Lincoln*

On 1 May 2003, President George W. Bush arrived on the deck of the aircraft carrier USS *Abraham Lincoln*, flying in the co-pilot's seat of a Navy S-3B Viking. The plane was marked *Navy-1*, and 'George W. Bush Commander-in-Chief' had been painted below the cockpit window. The landing was covered live on television, and the president posed for the cameras in his flight suit with sailors and pilots. Later on the same day, President Bush delivered a nationally televised speech from the deck of the ship, saying, 'Major combat operations in Iraq have ended. In the battle of Iraq, the United States and our allies have prevailed.' A banner saying 'Mission Accomplished' hung behind the president.

Critics argued that the White House was manipulating the president's authority as commander-in-chief, and misusing taxpayer-funded resources to create a media event that would enhance his own position with the public, and potentially provide positive images moving into the 2004 election campaign.

The Bush administration responded that the speech was primarily about thanking the armed forces; that the 'Mission Accomplished' sign was put up independently by the ship's crew; and that the president's glamorous arrival by jet had been necessary because the carrier's distance from shore made the more usual helicopter ride unfeasible. After repeated questioning over some months, it was announced that the White House had funded and arranged for the printing and placement of the banner, and that no operational reason prevented the use of a helicopter for the journey.

The events on the USS *Abraham Lincoln* brought together the president's role as commander-in-chief, chief executive and media focus. The division of opinion as to whether this was a legitimate use of executive authority to announce and celebrate American military success, or a cynical campaign stunt financed out of the public purse is unlikely to be resolved. The image created was certainly powerful, and if it helped at all in the 2004 election, it also dogged the administration as a symbol of its over-confidence and complacency as the American presence in Iraq extended to many years, at the expense of lives and injuries to American service personnel as well as high budgetary costs to US taxpayers.

agree that this translates automatically into communications success. George C. Edwards III (2004) argues that even President Reagan had little effect in changing public attitudes, but points out that presidential communication strategies can still help facilitate political success. Presidential intervention may help a policy campaign that is already going in the right direction, and leadership that appears to move public opinion a few points on any closely fought issue is going to be significant. Successes of this kind can prove a valuable asset in the longer term by enhancing an administration's reputation for influencing public opinion and political outcomes. Despite all the work that goes into maintaining and developing the president's media centrality, this cannot be counted on always to offer the same potential, and there are indications that media coverage of hard news, political news, and of the presidency itself, has declined in recent years.

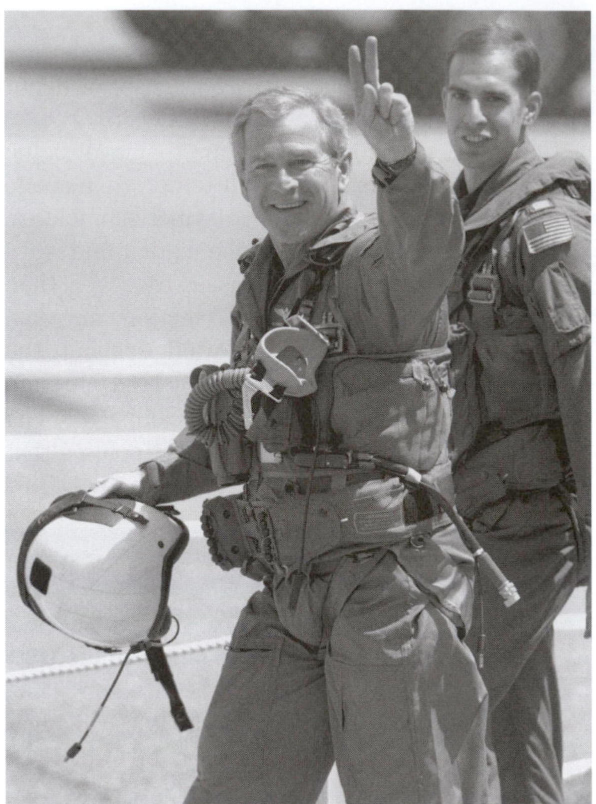

Figure 12.3 President Bush's helicopter landing on the USS *Abraham Lincoln* attracted considerable coverage in the mass media. Source: © Reuters/Corbis

Presidential centrality: the party

In spite of the fact that two major political parties occupy almost all the elected partisan offices in the USA, the nation is often referred to as having a weak party political system. The weakness lies not in the abilities of Democrats and Republicans to dominate the election process, but in the relatively loose ideological affiliations that exist under the umbrellas offered by these two parties, and in the absence of sanctions with which party managers may exert authority over their elected colleagues. In effect, the electoral strengths and the internal weaknesses of US political parties are opposite sides of the same coin. In such a large and diverse nation it is unlikely that two parties could dominate electoral politics so well if they did not allow for considerable internal variation, dissent and independence of action.

While the role of party leader does not necessarily appear to offer a huge resource, party loyalty may offer a president some leverage, especially if the incumbent is associated with other indications of success. A large, or surprising, electoral victory, a perceived skill in using the media to communicate with the electorate, and skill in managing legislative initiatives can all consolidate party loyalty and enhance the advantages of party leadership. But even at its weakest, party leadership still gives the president an advantage. One can really speak only of the incumbent party as having a leader at all, since there is no clearly identifiable single political leader of the party that is not in the White House.

Presidential centrality: the offices of persuasion

Presidents use formal and informal management techniques in the attempt to give their priorities an advantage in the Washington policy process. The Executive Office of the President has grown substantially since it was established in 1939, and now includes a dozen separate units, including such important elements as the National Security

Council, the Council of Economic Advisors, the Domestic Policy Council, the National Economic Council, the Office of Science and Technology Policy and other small groups of key advisers on major policy areas. A major unit within the Executive Office is the Office of Management and Budget, a large body of officials dedicated to producing annually the budget that the president will send to Congress, and which the administration hopes will dominate and set the parameters for the policy-making agenda.

Within the Executive Office, the White House Office is especially critical to the president, and his choice of White House Chief of Staff is considered an important indicator of an administration's style and direction. On taking office, President Obama appointed Rahm Emanuel. Emanuel had been a senior adviser in the Clinton White House, after which he had entered Congress as representative for Illinois' 5th District. As chair of the Democratic Congressional Campaign Committee, Emanuel gained considerable credit for his party's successes in the 2006 election, and after this became Chair of the Democratic Caucus in the House. With close connections to the Clintons, Emanuel did not endorse Obama until the presidential primaries were over and Senator Clinton's failure to obtain the nomination was clear. Emanuel brought to the office a range of high-level experience, extensive political networks and a reputation for strong leadership and successful pursuit of targets. The White House Chief of Staff is an important appointment, but only one of around 2,000 employees in the Executive Office. All of the units that they staff have a role in bringing together expertise to help and support efficient administration-led policy-making and implementation.

The federal bureaucracy of the USA is covered separately in this volume, a fact which helps alert us to the reality that even the president's relationship with large, cabinet-led departments has to be negotiated. The expertise within the Executive Office and within the White House staff is closely connected to the president, and is dedicated to helping the president present a convincing policy agenda. This concentration of skills is impressive – however, presidential strategy cannot depend solely on the weight of argument and conviction that comes from these bodies of advisers. The White House must also be able to create and take advantage of policy opportunities.

The transition period from the election of a new president in November into the early days of the new administration, almost three months later, is a critical period in which the ground can be laid for a successful term of office. A speedy and well-ordered transition, in which the new administration lines up its major appointments, enters into constructive liaison with Congress and moves rapidly towards establishing policy priorities, gives the impression that the president is hitting the ground running. In a system where relations between branches of government, between major departments, and even within the political party, are subject to constant negotiation and potential re-definition, there is also a role for an etiquette that displays awareness of, and respect for, the political forces in the nation's capital. Any president should recognise that authority lies in many places in Washington DC, and that bargaining will be part of any administration. Telephone calls, invitations and courtesies that recognise those in whose hands some share of authority lies will establish a foundation on which communications and negotiation can be built.

The White House Office, in particular, will maintain the effort to bolster the president's potential in the system. Work specifically designed to promote the president's programme in Washington DC will include public opinion polling and the identification and nurturing of political allies, especially if the programme faces hard challenges in the legislative process. From the transition stage onwards, the presidency will be engaged in the active pursuit of its political ends, but the value of the office-holder as an asset in this continuous process necessarily declines. All other things being equal, a president near the end of his term has less clout than one with a full term ahead, and the Twenty-second Amendment to the Constitution, imposing a two-term limit on holding the office, means that a president's second term is hampered by the certain knowledge that someone else will be taking office at its end.

Persuasion may not be everything

Neustadt's analysis is central to the scholarship of the presidency, but it is not universally accepted. Among the dissenters, Charles O. Jones (1994) similarly accepts that the president's authority as rooted in the US Constitution is limited, but Jones is unconvinced by Neustadt's argument that the resources exist whereby the system can in practice be adapted to become presidency-centred.

This alternative to the Neustadt view points out that the president's media centrality is a result of recent developments in the communications industry, rather than the consequence of presidential actions, and argues that focusing on the president as the pivot of American government ignores the more complex reality of how American government operates. Analysing the Jones perspective, Tim Hames (2000) also points out that the different political contexts within which presidential administrations operate and the electoral advantages with which an administration starts provide an individual framework of constraint on the presidential ability to persuade. This individual level of constraint on a presidency is, in its turn, a manifestation of the general limitations of a system that was designed with a healthy respect for leadership from Congress, as well as from the executive.

Meeting twenty-first century challenges

The presidential centrality explored in this chapter suggests that attention will inevitably concentrate on the occupant of the White House, but the opening decade of the new century has been a period when the examination has seemed even more acute than usual. The three presidential elections of the new century have been conducted in a febrile atmosphere of close competition, with both parties at times feeling they had the chance of short-term victory and long-term success, with contextual circumstances changing dramatically, and with historic implications.

As mentioned earlier in this chapter, the 2000 presidential election race was so close it was decided in the courts. Democrat Al Gore led in the national popular vote, but George W. Bush became the 43rd president of the United States with a lead in the Electoral College. It was not clear that the new president could claim any kind of mandate and, under the circumstances, it is not surprising that the new administration would come under particular scrutiny.

Given the paper-thin Republican majorities in the US Senate and House of Representatives, Bush appeared to be taking a politically risky path, constructing an administration that drew deeply on Republicans with previous experience, and pitching his message into the Republican heartland. Analyses of the early period of George Bush's presidency were often not generous, the defection from the Republican party of Vermont's Senator Jim Jeffords put the Senate back in Democrat hands only months after the 2000 election, and the Bush administration did not appear strong.

The attacks on New York and Washington DC of 11 September 2001 changed the context for the Bush administration, and the effect will continue to be felt for the foreseeable future. In the immediate aftermath of the attacks, an already weak stock market plunged, wiping out years of recent gains. The Bush administration launched attacks on Afghanistan, hideout of those who had launched the 11 September attacks, and on Iraq, perceived by the USA as a threat. The broad international sympathy that was felt for the first of these military reactions was not generally evident for the second. As commander-in-chief, Bush led the country on the international stage, firmly on his own terms.

Typically in American history, the presidency has gained authority when the nation is defending itself. In the case of the Bush administration's post-2001 War on Terror, the lack of an enemy defined by geographical position or national status created unusual difficulties in the conduct of the war, the identification of the enemy, and the ability to define what constitutes victory and conclusion. The Bush administration appears to have expanded the president's foreign policy authority, at least initially with the general support of the American public.

Figure 12.4 Family and Flag are important icons in the American political process.
Source: © Getty Images/*NY Daily News*

On the domestic front, a series of budget surpluses that had been projected for the early years of the century rapidly disappeared under the pressure especially of increased security and defence expenditure. The administration's commitment to cut taxes did not waver, and the USA once again was in the counter-intuitive position of having a Republican president lead it through a period of deficit spending and increased national debt. The 2004 election result was evidence of mixed opinion on the administration of President Bush. He defeated his opponent clearly, but without the level of endorsement that a war-time incumbent might expect. However, he led the Republican party to the best position it had held in nearly 80 years in terms of Senate and House seats. The party leadership was beginning to talk of this presidency as the foundation of a new generation of Republican party success.

Two years later, growing disquiet with the conduct of foreign policy, concern about the administration's stumbling reaction to the devastation and problems caused by Hurricane Katrina and worries about the economy contributed to major Republican congressional losses in the 2006 mid-term elections. By 2008, concerns over economic policy had increased markedly, especially with the collapse of Lehman Brothers in September of that year. Anxiety about presidential leadership in foreign affairs had not been assuaged and, as America's commitments in Iraq and Afghanistan became more extended and increasingly costly, President Bush's public approval rating declined to rival the lowest ever recorded. The Democrats took the White House and consolidated their control of both chambers of the US Congress. It took just the four years of President Bush's second term for his reputation as one of the greatest party builders to lead the Republican party to corrode irreparably.

The Barack Obama campaign presented their candidate as the voice and embodiment of change. The Democrats who nominated him as their candidate for the White House found it difficult to choose between Obama – an African-American – and Hillary Clinton – a woman. Either way, this nomination was going to be an historic first. In the face of the perceived presidential failure of George W. Bush, the message of change appealed strongly to the electorate, and 2008 saw the USA elect for the first time an African-American to its executive office.

Obama indicated that he was indeed in office to implement change right from the outset. Two days into his term, he signed an executive order that plans be made for the closure of the Guantanamo Bay internment camp, and another within six weeks of taking office pledged to support stem cell research, reversing the previous administration's position. Obama used his persuasive power and his party's majority in both chambers to pass a huge economic stimulus bill. He attempted to capitalise on the momentum his administration had developed with a proposal for major health care reform. Executive confidence was clear in this willingness to tackle what has always been a difficult topic in the USA. The solid opposition of Republicans, the major public campaign by health care interests both for and against the proposals, and the rifts in his own party in the ensuing debate were clear evidence of the strong and competing positions held by Americans on this topic. Nevertheless, after a process of negotiation and compromise, Obama secured the passage of the Patient Protection and Affordable Care Act of 2010.

The beginning of the twenty-first century has seen a presidential election that almost ended in stand-off; an almost unimaginable terrorist attack that demanded rapid and authoritative presidential leadership; a devastating hurricane on the Gulf coast that exposed the presidency to criticism for the weakness of its response; a president that led his party to great gains and then even larger losses and an election in which it became clear that the presidency is no longer the preserve of white men. These are very significant events and developments, but in this century, as before, the continuing power of America's presidency will rely on the ability of successive administrations simultaneously to engage with the demands of domestic and foreign policy-making in a changing political environment, to maintain public understanding of, and support for, its actions, and to negotiate successfully with political institutions that have their own long heritage and expectations of authority.

Chapter summary

The Founding Fathers may have expected the legislature to be the primary driving force in US politics. They made the legislature the subject of the US Constitution's first Article, relegating the presidency to Article II. Over time, the executive has emerged as a clear and central focus within the separated, checked and balanced federal system.

The presidency and vice-presidency are the only offices in America to be elected nationally. The electoral college process can occasionally result in apparently confusing results, but was invented to meld the influences of the popular vote and the demands of the federal system. It was tested severely in 2000, but appears unlikely to be reformed in the near future. It does maintain the position of the president as central in the nation's electoral and political structure.

The centrality of the presidency has emerged in a number of parallel and mutually supporting ways. The constitutional roles assigned to the president in international affairs, legislative development and passage, and as commander-in-chief, have been developed and expanded over time, as a result both of presidential actions and the growth of the USA as a world military and economic power. Other roles outside constitutional definition – for example, as a focus of national and international media attention, and as the only leader of a political party in the United States – have acted to bolster the president's central position in the American political system.

Notwithstanding the potential afforded to the executive by its constitutional and unconstitutional roles, the way in which this is operationalised has varied considerably between different presidential administrations. Presidential scholars have sought to explain the operation of presidential authority in terms of context, governmental structure and personal skills. President Truman's comment to presidential scholar Richard Neustadt that the key to presidential power lies in the ability to persuade has generated much of the contemporary debate on the presidency.

The early twenty-first century, with one presidential election decided in the US Supreme Court, an international and domestic agenda shifted dramatically by the attacks of 11 September 2001, a second election decided by a clear but narrow majority, and a period of one-party leadership in the legislature and executive unusual in recent decades, presented a context of both challenges and opportunities for the presidency. The public loss of faith in the Bush presidency, and the banking crisis beginning in 2008, contributed to a public enthusiasm for change, and for credible candidacies by non-white and non-male contenders for the White House. The end of the first decade of the new century saw the USA breaking new ground with the election of President Obama.

Discussion points

1. The president may be potentially the most powerful individual in American government, but is the executive necessarily the most powerful branch?

2. Is there a particular advantage for the presidency in the growing importance and immediacy of the national and international media?
3. Does persuasion really lie at the core of presidential power?
4. How would you measure the impact of presidential character on executive authority?
5. Presidential administrations have to respond to circumstances that are continually changing. Examine the success of the current administration in establishing its authority.
6. How could the presidential administration most effectively try to ensure that it had impact that lasted beyond the end of its term of office?

Further reading

Presidential scholars offer many structures for the discussion of the presidency. Fred I. Greenstein's *The Presidential Difference: Leadership Style from FDR to George W. Bush* (2nd edn, Princeton: Princeton University Press, 2004) offers a range of six qualities that bear on presidential leadership. This list includes public communication, organisational capacity, political skill, policy vision, cognitive style, and emotional intelligence. Individual presidential qualities are also significant in James P. Pfiffner's *The Character Factor: How We Judge America's Presidents* (College Station, Tex.: Texas A&M Press, 2004), which examines the centrality of truthfulness and lying to crises that have faced the modern presidency. An older study, James David Barber's *The Presidential Character: Predicting Performance in the White House* (4th edn, Englewood Cliffs, NJ: Prentice-Hall, 1992), divides presidents into four categories based on broad character patterns.

The Center for Congressional and Presidential Studies can be found at http://www.american.edu/ccps, while the White House's own site is http://www.whitehouse.gov. Individual presidencies provide the case studies for any generalisations on the executive branch. Fred Greenstein's *The Hidden-Hand Presidency: Eisenhower as Leader* (New York: Basic Books, 1982) re-examined one presidency in a way that changed views both of the Eisenhower years and of the way that the executive might be researched. David Mervin, in *Ronald Reagan and the American Presidency* (London: Longman, 1990), and in *George Bush and the Guardianship Presidency* (London: Macmillan, 1996) examines successive and very different presidencies. While these books do not directly comment on whether President George W. Bush brought into the twenty-first century presidency more influences from his father, the 41st president, or from the apparently more bold and successful 40th president, Ronald Reagan, it is worth bearing this question in mind while reading them. Preparedness is a key feature of the presidency, and perhaps this has become even more important in the rapidly changing world of the new century. James P. Pfiffner's *The Strategic Presidency: Hitting the Ground Running* (2nd edn, Lawrence: University Press of Kansas, 1996) examines carefully the urgent need for an administration to get control of government, and the strategies that can be adopted to do this.

The author also found the following useful when considering the relationship of the presidency to elections and political communications: Sidney Blumenthal, *The Permanent Campaign* (New York: Simon and Schuster, 1982); Patricia Heidotting Conley, *Presidential Mandates: How Elections Shape the National Agenda* (Chicago: University of Chicago Press, 2001) and John Maltese, *Spin Control* (2nd edn, Chapel Hill: University of North Carolina Press, 1994). The special place of the president in public opinion was addressed through the data of the Gallup organisation on http://www.gallup.com. Varying approaches to the structure, organisation and management of the executive branch were evident in the following works: Stephen Hess, *Organizing the Presidency* (3rd edn, Washington, DC: Brookings Institution, 2002); Louis W. Koenig, *The Chief Executive* (6th edn, Fort Worth, Tex.: Harcourt Brace, 1996); James P. Pfiffner and Roger H. Davidson, *Understanding the Presidency* (3rd edn, New York: Longman, 2003) and Shirley Anne Warshaw, *The Keys to Power: Managing the Presidency* (New York: Longman, 2000).

References

Balz, Dan and Johnson, Haynes (2009) *The Battle for America 2008: The Story of an Extraordinary Election* (New York: Viking).

Cronin, Thomas E. (ed.) (1989) *Inventing the American Presidency* (Lawrence: University Press of Kansas).

Edwards III, George C. and Davies, Philip John (eds) (2004) *New Challenges for the American Presidency* (New York: Pearson Longman).

Hames, Tim (2000) 'Presidential power and the Clinton presidency', in Grant, A. (ed.) *American Politics: 2000 and Beyond* (Aldershot: Ashgate).

Jones, Charles O. (1994) *The Presidency in a Separated System* (Washington, DC: Brookings Institution).

Neustadt, Richard E. (1990) *Presidential Power and the Modern Presidents: The Politics of Leadership from Roosevelt to Reagan* (New York: The Free Press).

Chapter 13

The federal bureaucracy

The executive branch of the federal government includes a vast array of experts organised into departments and agencies. Their purpose is to serve the government, and especially the president, by providing specialist knowledge to policy-makers and by administering national laws and policies. However, some argue that the civil service has an uneasy and sometimes hostile relationship with the president and that it constitutes an unelected and independent source of government power. In this chapter, we examine how the federal bureaucracy came to occupy such a controversial position in American government and whether its critics are right.

The executive branch of the US government employs almost 2.9 million men and women, that is, approximately one in 50 of all Americans in work (US Bureau of the Census, 2012). While a large civil service is common to most modern societies, this is a remarkable number of government employees for a nation which prides itself on its individualism and its belief in limited government. Nevertheless, the phenomenal growth in the size and range of the federal bureaucracy since 1789 is no aberration. Rather, it has been a logical response to the increasing complexity of American society and the unrelenting growth in federal government responsibilities.

Main elements of the federal bureaucracy

The cabinet

Even in 1789, when George Washington became the first president of the United States, there was a clear recognition of the need for specialist departments within the executive branch. Washington's cabinet consisted of three department heads – state, treasury and war – and an attorney-general. Along with the postal service, these constituted the executive branch establishment.

In 2009, there were 15 departments and their heads, or secretaries, form the core of the president's cabinet. As the number of employees in the departments indicates, cabinet secretaries are responsible for a wide number and variety of policy programmes. Indeed, along with the independent agencies and commissions (see below), the department secretaries administer some 1,400 federal programmes.

Beneath the department secretary is an under-secretary and several assistant secretaries. These top officials and other senior appointees, about 3,300 in total, are nominated by the president but require Senate confirmation (DiClerico, 1995, p. 165). While the president can usually rely upon getting his nominees confirmed, the Senate has developed a marked tendency in recent years to seize opportunities to reject nominees. Thus, President George H. Bush fought a losing battle to have former Senator John Tower confirmed as secretary of defense. The Senate was ostensibly concerned about Tower's alleged history of heavy drinking and womanising, but some observers believed that the Senate was simply engaged in a power play to undermine the president. In his first term, President Clinton had to withdraw his first two nominations for attorney-general because the nominees ran into serious trouble in the Senate over their failure to make social security payments for their domestic employees. President George W. Bush faced concerted opposition to his nomination of Alberto Gonzalez as attorney-general in 2005.

Table 13.1 Government departments under President Obama, 2009

Department	Number of civilian employees
State	36,762
Treasury	110,686
Defense	714,483
Justice	111,214
Interior	71,536
Agriculture	97,803
Commerce	74,305
Labor	16,316
Health and human services	65,389
Homeland security	177,428
Housing and urban development	9,636
Transportation	56,310
Energy	15,613
Education	4,097
Veterans' affairs	289,335

Source: Statistical Abstract of the United States, 2011

Presidential selection of cabinet secretaries

Presidents are free to nominate whoever they wish to cabinet posts. Most cabinet appointees either have strong political ties to the president's party or are respected for skills and expertise displayed outside the political arena. A president may well also take into account the likely reaction to an appointment from the main groups that deal with a particular department. Thus, the president may appoint to the Treasury Department someone who is trusted and respected by bankers and the business community and to the Labor Department someone who is similarly appealing to unions. This would certainly explain President Clinton's first-term appointments of the economically conservative Lloyd Bentsen at Treasury and the economically liberal Robert Reich at Labor. In these appointments, Clinton was trying to reassure the respective 'clients' of Treasury and Labor that the administration would be sympathetic to their interests and views.

President Clinton had yet another criterion in making his cabinet appointments. In an effort to consolidate his support among diverse sections of the community, he wanted a cabinet that 'looked like America'. This translated into a policy that became known as EGG – ethnicity, gender and geography. Clinton kept his promise by appointing more women and members of ethnic minorities to his cabinet than any president before him. In his second administration, four cabinet posts went to women: Madeleine Albright as secretary of state; Janet Reno as attorney-general (Justice Department); Alexis Herman as secretary of labor; and Donna Shalala as secretary of health and human resources.

Clinton also appointed the first Puerto Rican-born American to a position of cabinet rank when Aida Alvarez became head of the Small Business Administration. President George W. Bush continued the diversity theme. In 2005, for example, he appointed the first Asian-American woman to the Cabinet, Elaine Chao, as secretary of labor. Similarly, Alberto Gonzalez became the first Hispanic attorney-general.

While there appeared to be no general theme to explain President Obama's cabinet nominations, there was clearly an attempt to demonstrate both continuity and change in the area of foreign and defence policy. Thus, Obama asked President George W. Bush's secretary of defense, Robert Gates, to remain in office. On the other hand, when it came to selecting his CIA director, President Obama was so keen to break with controversial practices of the agency under Bush that he chose Leon Panetta, a man with no background or expertise in intelligence matters. The other eye-catching nomination was that of Hillary Clinton as secretary of state. Clinton had vied closely with Obama for the Democratic nomination in 2008 and the nomination may have been inspired in part by a desire to bring the two wings of the Democratic party back together.

When making cabinet appointments, then, the president combines political and practical criteria. Ideally, his appointees will obtain Senate confirmation with ease, earn the respect of those who deal with particular departments and also satisfy the president's supporters and the public at large. Of course, the president also wants his cabinet secretaries to further his goals and policies, in as far as he has any. As we shall see below, this can prove quite difficult.

The cabinet in operation

The American cabinet is a weak body in that it meets solely at the president's discretion and discusses only those topics that the president chooses to put before it. Furthermore, it has no collective responsibility for the administration's policy. Thus, as Louis Koenig writes: 'The cabinet . . . has rarely been a source of advice upon which the president continuously relies. It exists by custom and functions by presidential initiative and is therefore largely what the chief executive chooses to make of it' (Koenig, 1996, p. 188).

President Kennedy actually only held six cabinet meetings in three years, while President Nixon was of the view that 'No [president] in his right mind submits anything to his cabinet' (Pious, 1996, p. 277). Consequently, the cabinet exists collectively only to serve goals of secondary importance, such as acting as a sounding board for new and possibly controversial ideas or for trying to coordinate public pronouncements on administration policy.

Individually, however, department secretaries can wield considerable influence over policy in their own area of competence and perhaps outside of it as well. This is likely to be the case when the secretary heads one of the more prestigious departments, such as State, Defense or the Treasury, or when he is a particularly valued adviser to the president.

Finally, some presidents have used sub-groups of the cabinet as important policy-makers on particular clusters of issues. Thus the Reagan administration created 'cabinet councils', each with 6–11 cabinet members, to advise in areas such as economic affairs, natural resources and environment, and food and agriculture (Whicker, 1990, p. 57). Some of these worked well, while others met infrequently and produced little of any value. Much of their effectiveness depends upon the ability of different cabinet members to cooperate without allowing 'turf fights' and egos to get in the way.

Ultimately, however, the cabinet amounts to far less than the sum of its individual parts. Department secretaries are highly important members of the executive branch, not because they collectively devise administration policy, but because individually they are responsible for carrying out administration policy on vital matters. In that sense, they are the real heads of the federal bureaucracy.

Independent agencies and commissions

While there are only 15 departments, there are dozens of agencies and commissions within the federal bureaucracy – 136 of them in 2005. Some of these play an enormously important role in implementing government policy and regulating key areas of public business. Thus the Equal Employment Opportunity Commission (EEOC) has developed many of the policy guidelines which attack race and sex discrimination in employment; the Federal Reserve Board (the Fed) is a major influence in economic policy through its power to set interest rates; and the Federal Communications Commission (FCC) oversees broadcasting policy and sets national standards. Others are far more obscure, such as the Advisory Council on Historic Preservation and the Postal Regulatory Commission.

Like department secretaries, the chairpersons of these agencies are appointed by the president. However, while secretaries can be sacked at will by the president, agency heads are usually appointed for a set term of office, something which gives them greater autonomy from the White House. As we shall see below, agency heads can thwart or even defy the president on policy by exploiting their independence and status.

Career civil service

The great mass of the federal bureaucracy consists of career civil servants. Their numbers grew steadily in the nineteenth century: while there were some 20,000 federal employees in the 1830s, this had more than doubled by the end of the Civil War to 53,000 and then reached 131,000 by 1884 (Garraty, 1968, p. 253). Moreover, serious problems had emerged regarding the professionalism of these employees.

Patronage and professionalism in the civil service

It had always been understood that the main role of the federal bureaucracy was to serve the president. For that reason, the president was given the power to appoint civil servants, even though the most senior of them, such as cabinet secretaries, were subject to Senate approval. However, under the presidency of Andrew Jackson (1829–37), the right to appoint civil servants became a crude power of patronage, with appointees receiving their public posts as rewards for political service rather than for their administrative skills or expert knowledge. This, in turn, led to a civil service that was often both inefficient and corrupt.

This deterioration in the quality of the federal bureaucracy reached its lowest point in the late nineteenth century. By this time, appointments were so thoroughly in the hands of corrupt party bosses that President Benjamin Harrison (1889–93) found himself unable even to select his own department secretaries. All the cabinet posts had literally been sold by the party bosses to pay the election expenses.

At a lower level of the federal bureaucracy, steps had already been taken to end corruption and cronyism. In 1881, President James Garfield had been assassinated by a disappointed office-seeker, creating an irresistible demand for civil service reform as a consequence. In 1883, the Pendleton Act (or Civil Service Reform Act) was passed. This 'classified' certain positions within the federal bureaucracy, subjecting applicants to competitive examination. The Act also created the Civil Service Commission to oversee recruitment, thus further undermining corrupt political control. Finally, the president was empowered to place further posts within the classified category, with the result that by the end of the century, roughly half of all federal employees were in classified positions (Garraty, 1968, pp. 257–8). The Pendleton Act may therefore be seen as the foundation stone of the modern American civil service, bringing genuine specialist knowledge and administrative skill to prominence within the federal bureaucracy.

The qualities of bureaucracy

As in most countries, there are unflattering stereotypes of civil servants in the United States. Sometimes they are viewed as slow and obstructive, sometimes as interfering and unappreciative of the needs of the 'real world'. Yet bureaucracy and civil servants bring valuable, even vital, qualities to American government. As theorists of bureaucracy from Hegel onwards have pointed out, these negative and positive attributes of bureaucrats are actually two sides of the same coin, so it is difficult to have the advantages of modern bureaucracy without the disadvantages.

The 'permanent government'

Unlike politicians who come and go, the federal bureaucracy brings a sense of permanence and continuity to American government. Many policy programmes transcend the terms of office of presidents and members of Congress and it is clearly important for those affected by a programme to know that its operation is not dependent upon the whim, inexperience or ignorance of incoming politicians.

Moreover, career civil servants constitute a government store of knowledge about issues, problems and programmes. No new presidential administration, however radical in intent, would wish or be able to redesign all the federal government's major policies. And even the most ambitious of administrations would still depend to a considerable degree upon the advice and assistance of the bureaucracy in formulating and, above all, implementing new policy.

Bureaucratic creativity and administrative law

The federal bureaucracy is no mere passive repository of expertise and experience. Frequently, it plays a major part in legislating by filling in the details of congressional legislation. It is very common for Congress to write legislation in broad terms, leaving detailed 'guidelines' for the implementation of the bill to departments and agencies. This has created a mass of so-called 'administrative law' (as opposed to the statutory law of Congress).

Administrative law can be highly creative. For example, when Congress passed the Civil Rights Act of 1964, it failed to define what it meant by 'discrimination' on grounds of race or sex. It was therefore left to the federal bureaucracy to determine exactly what constituted discrimination and what kinds of evidence would demonstrate its existence in any particular context. In the field of race discrimination in employment, it was the Department of Labor, through its Office of Federal Contract Compliance (OFCC), that initiated a policy of affirmative action to fulfil the aims of the 1964 Act. In 1968 and 1971, the OFCC issued guidelines which established numerical goals and timetables for the greater employment of minority group members in certain jobs, and then decided that a disproportionately low employment rate of such members in any occupation was proof of discrimination. Whether this was a good policy or not, it was undoubtedly a radical development from what Congress had in mind when it passed the basic legislation in 1964.

Bureaucratic rationalism and neutrality

As well as bringing collective knowledge and experience to bear on problems, the federal bureaucracy is also presumed to be rational in proposing solutions. More precisely, civil servants are supposed to discount political and partisan considerations and to give advice which is politically objective. Elected politicians rarely have the luxury of being able to avoid the demands of interest groups or public opinion, but, sheltered as they are from such political pressures, civil servants are expected to give their political masters neutral advice.

This expectation stems, of course, from the basic assumption that the federal bureaucracy is willing and able to serve political masters of differing political complexion. Even when the change from one administration to the next is unusually sharp, as when President Reagan replaced President Carter in 1981, the federal bureaucracy is supposed to serve the new as faithfully as it served the old. We shall see below, however, that this bureaucratic ideal of political neutrality is viewed with considerable scepticism by politicians, who see political motivations in the resistance to administration policy that they frequently encounter. For the moment, it is sufficient to note that there is solid evidence to suggest that Democrats greatly outnumber Republicans in the career civil service. Moreover, even those bureaucrats who define themselves as Independents have political attitudes that are far closer to Democratic than to Republican philosophy (DiClerico, 1995, p. 166).

These statistics are not especially surprising, given the fact that the Democratic party has traditionally favoured governmental activism, while the Republican party has often attacked it. It is only logical that those who harbour a belief in governmental activism should be more likely to seek government employment than those who do not.

Controlling the federal bureaucracy

Having described the basic contours of the federal bureaucracy, it is now necessary to analyse the power that it wields: for if the ideal of the bureaucracy is of a body of disinterested experts, advising the president on policy matters and faithfully carrying out his wishes, the reality is significantly different.

Figure 13.1 Bureaucratic rivalry: the FBI and CIA pull in opposite directions trying to promote homeland security after 9/11. Source: © Steve Sack

Presidential control of the bureaucracy

Most presidents have found dealing with the bureaucracy to be one of the most frustrating aspects of their job. President Truman (1945–53) once commented: 'I thought I was the president, but when it comes to these bureaucracies, I can't make them do a damn thing.' Years later, President Carter indicated that things had not changed much: 'Before I became president, I realized and was warned that dealing with the federal bureaucracy would be one of the worst problems I would have to face. It has been even worse than I had anticipated' (DiClerico, 1995, pp. 163–4).

Bearing in mind that these were Democratic presidents experiencing difficulty in controlling the bureaucracy, it is safe to assume that Republican presidents must expend even more effort if they wish to tame the bureaucracy.

President Reagan entered office determined to do something to bring the bureaucracy under his control. He started at the top, making sure that his cabinet secretaries were ideologically sympathetic to his conservative goals. Then, instead of leaving the secretaries to select their own sub-cabinet top officials, the Reagan White House took control. They insisted that all secondary and tertiary positions in the departments were given only to those who had voted for Reagan, who were known Republicans and who were known conservatives (DiClerico, 1995, pp. 189–90). Moreover, President Reagan insisted that both cabinet and sub-cabinet appointees be briefed not by the permanent civil servants, but rather by White House staff indisputably loyal to the president.

Reagan had other plans for the career bureaucrats. The president had campaigned for office proclaiming, 'Government isn't the solution: government is the problem.' Strongly opposed to 'big government' and what he considered to be intrusive bureaucracy, President Reagan quickly set about reducing both the number of civil servants in domestic policy agencies and departments and the number of federal regulations. He also made extensive use of the powers given to the president under the Civil Service Reform Act of 1978. This allowed him to reassign senior career bureaucrats who were classified as part of the senior executive service. Needless to say, some of these reassignments were made to undermine the power and influence

Box 13.1

President Clinton and the Federal Reserve Board

Early in his presidency, Bill Clinton learned the power of the bureaucracy of which he was the titular head. His Republican predecessor, George Bush, reappointed his fellow Republican, Alan Greenspan, to a second term as chairman of the Federal Reserve Board in March, 1992. Because the chairman of the Fed served for four years and could not be sacked for political reasons, President Clinton was obliged to work with Greenspan for at least most of his first administration. Clinton wanted to see a lowering of long-term interest rates, since this would help to fulfil his much-publicised promise to reinvigorate the economy and create new jobs. However, it is the chairman of the Fed, not the president of the United States, who determines interest-rate policy. Clinton's advisers told him that Greenspan would only lower interest rates if the president introduced budget cuts, because only if the budget deficit were reduced would the stock exchange dealers in government bonds feel safe in lowering their rates. On hearing this,

> Clinton's face turned red with anger and disbelief. 'You mean to tell me that the success of the programme and my re-election hinges on the Federal Reserve and a bunch of (expletive) bond dealers?'

Source: Extract from Woodward, 1994, p. 84

of those deemed insufficiently supportive of the president's agenda.

President Reagan certainly gained increased control of the bureaucracy through making ideological sympathy and personal loyalty determining factors in appointments. In other respects though, the degree of change he wanted was limited by the fact that his appointees necessarily were often lacking in experience and competence in administration (DiClerico, 1995, p. 192).

'Presidentialising' the bureaucracy

President Reagan was merely raising to a new level the process of 'presidentialising' the bureaucracy: that is, using his appointment power to try to bring the bureaucracy under closer political control (Rourke, 1991). Why should presidents have to work so hard to ensure the loyalty of the members of their cabinet and of the sub-cabinet and permanent civil servants?

Going native

As far as political appointees are concerned, there is always the fear in the White House that they will 'go native'. This means that, instead of imposing the president's agenda on the permanent bureaucracy, they come to share the bureaucracy's outlook and start to resist the White House. This can happen where the cabinet secretary or deputy secretary disagrees with presidential policy or simply believes that the civil service has a better policy. Or going native can occur simply as a result of the fact that political appointees to the bureaucracy spend far more time in the company of civil servants than they do with senior White House personnel. Little by little, the appointee becomes socialised by the culture of the department or agency.

The president may use the appointments process to try to minimise this, but he may also try to increase the involvement of White House staff in the departments and agencies. This can cause serious friction between presidential aides and civil servants, who resent interference from those they consider to lack the requisite knowledge and experience to make sound decisions.

Politicising the bureaucracy

There is a very fine line between strengthening presidential control of the bureaucracy and politicising the bureaucracy. It is possible to see President Reagan's actions as either an attempt to force the bureaucracy to follow his legitimate requests as its chief, or an attempt to persuade the bureaucracy to become part of an ideological or partisan crusade. There is no clear line that separates policy-making from policy implementation. Equally, it is difficult to identify the line between loyally serving an administration and abandoning the virtues of bureaucratic neutrality and professionalism. As is so often the case in US politics, there is a trade-off to be made between following the democratic imperative and searching for rational and effective policy.

Political versus bureaucratic values

Disputes between presidents and bureaucrats have their roots in one basic factor: the two have real differences in outlook. Presidents and their White House assistants see themselves as bearers of a democratic mandate. The president, as candidate, has presented his policies to the people and received their approval. He is therefore fully entitled to implement the policies he chooses. Even where there was no firm policy commitment during the election, the president has a mandate to use the power the people have given him to do as he thinks best for the nation.

As democracy's champion, the president embodies what some see as the core values of democracy: responsiveness, direction and revitalisation. The values of the modern administrative state, however, are different; here the emphasis is upon continuity, professionalism, expertise and effectiveness. All of these values may be desirable, but they are not always compatible. Thus a president will, quite reasonably, wish to demonstrate to his supporters that the government can respond to their needs and can be made to perform more economically. Bureaucrats, however, may not see the drive to satisfy a particular section of the electorate as a factor in producing a rational policy response to a problem, or a reduction in their capacity as a means to more effective administration.

Moreover, if presidents and other politicians are most likely to believe that their loyalty lies with the electorate, bureaucrats will tend to identify with their department or even with a particular programme operated by their department. It is not uncommon for senior civil servants to spend 25 or 30 years working within the same policy area. During that time, they may acquire not merely a knowledge of the subject that greatly surpasses that of politicians, but also a belief that their programmes must continue for the good of the people. In that sense, politicians and bureaucrats can have quite different visions of what constitutes 'good' public policy.

Bureaucratic political resources

The differences of values that produce tensions between the president and the bureaucracy can, as we have seen, lead to a struggle between them for control of policy. The president can use his appointment powers and his White House staff as instruments of control. The bureaucracy, however, is by no means without its own resources in these power struggles.

The first and most obvious weapon of the recalcitrant bureaucrat is delay. This is particularly the case in the United States, where the president may serve only four or, at most, eight years in office. Simply by refusing to follow the spirit of the president's orders or by throwing up seemingly endless objections to proposed changes, civil servants may succeed in a waiting game with the White House.

Iron triangles

Beyond that, however, lies the fact that bureaucrats can and do build alliances with other political actors. Most notably, they form mutually beneficial relationships with committees in Congress and with interest groups. These 'iron triangles' are based upon the fact that all three elements have a common interest in a particular policy area or programme.

Congress and the bureaucracy

Throughout this chapter, we have looked at the bureaucracy as if it were simply under the aegis of the president. Yet it is important to understand that Congress, as well as the president, has a significant measure of control over the bureaucracy. This means that the bureaucracy must seek to satisfy its congressional master, as well as the White House.

The principal instruments of congressional control of the bureaucracy are its general legislative power and its appropriations power – the 'power of the purse'. Congress uses its legislative power to create, abolish or merge departments, to inaugurate new programmes and agencies, and to fix terms of appointment and other structural details. It is true that Congress has ceded the initiative to undertake such reorganisations to the president in recent decades, but it retains the power to veto presidential reorganisation plans and to institute its own. Following the terrorist attacks of 11 September 2001, President George W. Bush wanted to establish a Department of Homeland Security. While he eventually got his way, it was only after considerable discussion and compromise with members of Congress.

Congress uses its appropriations power to fund departments, agencies, programmes and, not least, civil servants. Since money is the oil that makes the machinery of government turn, the federal bureaucracy cannot afford to alienate its source in Congress.

Congress therefore establishes the structural and financial parameters of the federal bureaucracy, and presidential control must be exercised within those constraints. From the perspective of those who work for the federal bureaucracy, this makes the presidency their day-to-day manager, but it makes the Congress the manager upon whom they are ultimately dependent for their sheer existence.

Figure 13.2 Creating new bureaucratic structures may reassure the public that something is being done, but may prove ineffective if too complex. Source: © Steve Sack

Congress also has another major instrument of control over the federal bureaucracy: oversight. This is the right to investigate the operation of any part of the executive branch, and will normally include holding hearings and calling executive branch personnel to testify before a congressional committee. Depending on the outcome of the investigation, Congress may reward certain departments or programmes with better finance or more staff, or it may shut them down altogether.

There is, however, a two-way relationship between Congress and the bureaucracy. Bureaucrats seek funding, enlargement, programmes and discretion from the congressional committees with which they deal most closely. For the bureaucracy, discretion comes in the form of statutory language that is simply broad or unclear. Either way, it gives bureau chiefs discretionary power to make important decisions.

Members of congressional committees also stand to gain from their relationship with the bureaucracy. Most importantly, they wish to ensure that programmes administered by bureaux bring benefits to their constituents back home. Most members of Congress seek membership of committees that deal with matters closest to the heart of their electorate. Thus those members who represent agricultural constituencies will want, first, membership of the Agriculture Committee and, second, membership of sub-committees that deal with the particular branches of agriculture most important to the constituency's economy. Thus, if a bureau is responsible for distributing subsidies to dairy farmers, then members of Congress with a lot of dairy farmers in their electorate will want to ensure, first, that the subsidies are large enough and, second, that 'their' dairy farmers get them.

We can see here the basis for a mutually supportive and beneficial relationship between members of Congress and the bureaucracy. In this example, both have an interest in maintaining and enhancing dairy subsidisation programmes, even if the president, in the interests of, say, budget deficit reduction, would like to reduce or eliminate them.

The third element in the 'iron triangles' is the interest groups and their paid lobbyists. With regard to the bureaucracy, lobbyists seek access to and influence over decisions made within the civil service. This can involve participation in the writing of administrative law or even in the appointment of particular individuals to key posts. In return, lobbyists will work to enhance the power and prestige of the bureau by testifying before Congress that it is doing a fine and important job, and by lobbying the president to the same effect.

As we saw in Chapter 11, interest groups and Congress have a strong relationship based on the need of lobbyists to gain access to those who legislate in their areas of concern and the need of members of Congress to obtain election campaign funds from interest groups and their political action committees. Thus, bureaux, congressional committees and interest groups have tight bonds of mutual self-interest that can unite them against a president who wishes to make unwelcome changes. To put it another way, any president who tries to exercise total control over 'his' bureaucracy may soon discover a wall of resistance which is at times impossible to break down.

Issue networks

Iron triangles are accompanied by what Hugh Heclo (1978) has called issue networks. These characterise the way that policies are debated in certain areas of economic regulation, especially in cases where federal agencies (for example, the Environmental Protection Agency) have economy-wide purview rather than being restricted to a certain segment of the economy (for example, farming). Issue networks are, in one sense, more democratic than iron triangles: they are more open and can involve many more participants. One becomes part of an issue network simply by becoming recognised as an expert in the field, somebody who needs to be consulted. Compared with iron triangles, issue networks are more amorphous, more complex, less predictable and less amenable to control. They are less reliable as building blocks of durable coalitions. They can be better at prolonging debate than at reaching decisions. So their appearance on the scene has complicated an already complex policy-making system.

Bureaucratic agencies involved in issue networks are subject to many pressures and for that reason are, if anything, even less likely to be decisively influenced by either presidents or Congress. This newer pattern of policy-making thus underlines many of the doubts that had already been raised about the role of bureaucracy in the American political system.

This is not to say that policy-making always goes badly wrong, and that considerations of the long-term public interest are always left out of the equation. Indeed, the phenomenon of issue networks can be seen as a sign that ideas do matter in public policy (Reich, 1990), but the tendency towards short-term electoral bias in members of Congress, coupled with the equally self-interested behaviour and the limited outlook of bureaucrats, does make any upbeat portraits of the policy-making process somewhat optimistic.

Bureaucracy and effective government

We saw in the previous chapter that the president of the United States has many demands made upon him, but inadequate means of ensuring that he satisfies them. One might think that, as chief executive, he could at least count upon the federal bureaucracy to carry out his wishes, but this is simply not the case. Just as the president must struggle to exert influence over Congress, so too he must treat the bureaucracy as a potential rival rather than a willing partner.

At first glance, this may seem a wholly regrettable state of affairs. How can the United States have good government if its chief political officer is thwarted even by those whose supposed reason for existence is to assist him? Nevertheless, there is another side to this situation. Koenig writes that:

> It is good for democracy but bad for an effective presidency – though by no means always for either – that the chief executive possesses a highly imperfect capacity to induce the vast officialdom of the executive branch to abide by his purposes and follow his directives.
>
> Koenig, 1996, p. 181

What Koenig has in mind here is that total presidential control of the bureaucracy could and sometimes does lead to presidential abuse of that power. President Nixon, for example, put pressure upon the Internal Revenue Service (IRS) and the Federal Bureau of Investigation (FBI) to aid him in his attempts to destroy those he considered his political enemies. A civil service that believed it had no means of resisting such unconstitutional demands could easily be turned into a weapon that undermined or even destroyed democracy.

As in other aspects of American politics, then, we must look at the bureaucracy through the perspective of the separation of powers and checks and balances. Effective government and democratic responsibility require that the president should be able to direct the bureaucracy and have it co-operate with his legitimate policy initiatives. On the other hand, effective government and democratic values also require that the bureaucracy should not be left wholly vulnerable to a president animated by crass and even unconstitutional motivations.

In short, the fact that the federal bureaucracy in the United States possesses a measure of autonomous power is neither surprising nor unwarranted. However, the fact that its self-interest sometimes defeats the national interest as embodied in presidential policy is a genuine cause for concern. President Obama came to the conclusion that the

Box 13.2

President Obama on the reform of the federal bureaucracy
State of the Union address 2011

'We shouldn't just give our people a government that's more affordable. We should give them a government that's more competent and more efficient. We can't win the future with a government of the past.

We live and do business in the Information Age, but the last major reorganization of the government happened in the age of black-and-white TV. There are 12 different agencies that deal with exports. There are at least five different agencies that deal with housing policy. Then there's my favorite example: the Interior Department is in charge of salmon while they're in fresh water, but the Commerce Department handles them when they're in saltwater. I hear it gets even more complicated once they're smoked.

Now, we've made great strides over the last two years in using technology and getting rid of waste. Veterans can now download their electronic medical records with a click of the mouse. We're selling acres of federal office space that hasn't been used in years, and we'll cut through red tape to get rid of more. But we need to think bigger. In the coming months, my administration will develop a proposal to merge, consolidate, and reorganize the federal government in a way that best serves the goal of a more competitive America. I will submit that proposal to Congress for a vote – and we will push to get it passed.'

entire structure of the federal bureaucracy was in urgent need of reform and modernisation.

The president's proposals reveal an enduring truth about the federal bureaucracy. It has a vital role to play in the government of the United States, but it will also be a constant target for criticism from those who want quick political action.

Chapter summary

We have seen that, despite its ideological opposition to 'big government', the United States has developed a vast federal bureaucracy. This bureaucracy brings considerable virtues to American government, especially expertise, experience, professionalism, political neutrality and continuity. However, the very size and authority of the federal bureaucracy make it difficult for the president, the supposed head of the executive branch, to control it. This is exacerbated by the ability of the bureaucracy to form alliances against the president with other political actors. The tensions that exist between the president and the bureaucracy give rise to conflicting and seemingly insoluble concerns about an ineffective presidency and an overpoliticised bureaucracy.

Discussion points

1. When is the bureaucracy justified in resisting presidential leadership?
2. Is bureaucratic professionalism compatible with democratic principles?
3. Are iron triangles a positive feature of American politics?
4. Is the federal bureaucracy too powerful?

Further reading

There are few books devoted solely to the bureaucracy which are appropriate at this level, but the best is Francis E. Rourke, *Bureaucracy, Politics and Public Policy* (Boston: Little, Brown, 1984). A useful collection of short essays about presidential/bureaucratic issues is James Pfiffner (ed.), *The Managerial Presidency* (Pacific Grove: Brooks/Cole, 1991). Three books which deal more generally with the presidency have excellent sections on the bureaucracy: Louis Koenig, *The Chief Executive* (6th edn, Fort Worth, Tex.: Harcourt Brace, 1996); Richard Pious, *The Presidency* (Boston: Allyn & Bacon, 1996) and Richard DiClerico, *The American President* (4th edn, Englewood Cliffs, NJ: Prentice Hall, 1995). On the cabinet, see Anthony Bennett, *The American President's Cabinet: From Kennedy to Bush* (Basingstoke: Macmillan, 1996).

References

DiClerico, R. (1995) *The American President* (4th edn, Englewood Cliffs, NJ: Prentice Hall).

Garraty, J. (1968) *The New Commonwealth* (New York: Harper & Row).

Heclo, H. (1978) 'Issue networks and the executive establishment', in King, A. (ed.) *The New American Political System* (Washington, DC: American Enterprise Institute).

Koenig, L. (1996) *The Chief Executive* (6th edn, Fort Worth, Tex.: Harcourt Brace).

Pious, R. (1996) *The Presidency* (Boston: Allyn & Bacon).

Reich, R., ed. (1990) *The Power of Public Ideas* (Cambridge, Mass.: Harvard University Press).

Rourke, F. (1991) 'Presidentializing the bureaucracy: from Kennedy to Reagan', Pfiffner, J. (ed.) *The Managerial Presidency* (Pacific Grove: Brooks/Cole).

US Bureau of the Census (2005) *Statistical Abstract of the United States* (Washington, DC).

Whicker, M. (1990) 'Managing and organising the Reagan White House', in Hill, D., Moore R. and Williams, P. (eds) *The Reagan Presidency* (Basingstoke: Macmillan).

Woodward, B. (1994) *The Agenda: Inside the Clinton White House* (New York: Simon & Schuster).

Part 5

The legislative process

As we saw in Part 4, the office of the presidency looms large in the legislative process. Yet for all the importance of the presidency in proposing and drafting legislation, it is a basic fact of political life in the United States that only Congress can pass national laws. This means that the legislative efforts of the president, interest groups and, indeed, all political actors at the national level, must ultimately focus on the Congress.

In Part 5, therefore, we examine the legislative power and role of Congress, especially in relation to the presidency (Chapter 14). We also examine the way Congress is organised and the impact that its internal structural and processes have on its legislative and other governmental functions (Chapter 15).

Contents

Chapter 14

Congress and the president

Congress and the president are rivals for political power generally, and legislative power in particular. To a considerable extent, this rivalry is a 'zero-sum' game: any increase in the power of one player inevitably means a corresponding loss of power for the other. Nevertheless, as a responsible national legislature, Congress cannot simply devote itself to institutional self-preservation. It must pass laws to advance the national interest and, to do this, it needs to cooperate with the president. In this chapter, we trace the origins and development of this ambiguous relationship with the presidency and assess the contemporary balance of power between the two. We also ask whether Congress is any longer either willing or able to provide legislative leadership for the country.

Legislative power: the constitutional design

Legislative power is the power to pass laws. It lies, therefore, at the heart of the policy-making process and, indeed, is a central attribute of what we more generally call political power. Although the framers of the Constitution were concerned that no single institution should accrue too much political power, it is clear that they entrusted legislative power mainly to the Congress. True, the president was also given a role in the legislative process, but it was not until the twentieth century that he began to expand this role at the expense of Congress and to assume legislative leadership.

Legislative powers of Congress

Article I of the Constitution begins by stating that 'All legislative powers herein granted shall be vested in a Congress of the United States, which shall consist of a Senate and House

Box 14.1

Functions of Congress

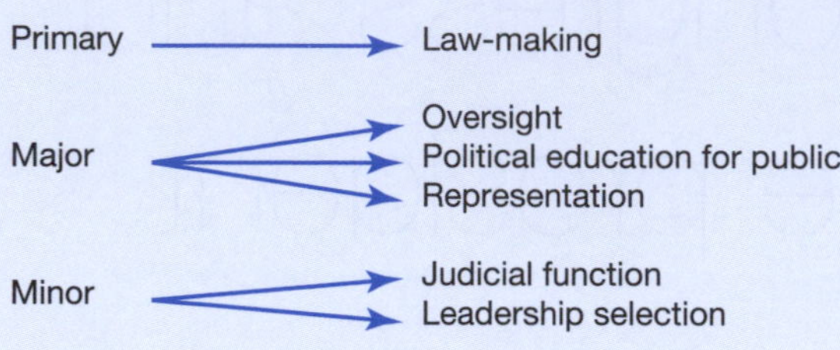

These are six functions of Congress, categorised by their importance (Keefe and Ogul, 1993, p. 16). The primary and major functions are discussed in this chapter. The minor functions can be briefly summarised: the judicial function consists mainly of the role of Congress in the process of impeachment. This procedure allows for the removal of presidents and federal judges from office for 'high crimes and misdemeanors'. Rarely used, but dramatic when it is, the most significant instance of impeachment came in 1974, when President Nixon resigned after the House Judiciary Committee investigating the Watergate scandal voted to indict him on three counts. Had Nixon not resigned at that point, the Senate would have acted as the 'jury' in his impeachment trial. In December 1998, President Bill Clinton was impeached by the House of Representatives, but he was acquitted by the Senate in February 1999. His impeachment sparked a bitter debate about whether the president's opponents were abusing the impeachment power for partisan ends.

The leadership function is an unwritten but important contribution to political life: it allows politicians to develop their skills and reputations, with the Senate in particular often providing a launch pad for the presidency. President Obama was previously a senator from Illinois and his vice-president, Joseph Biden, was previously a senator from Delaware. While none of President Obama's five most recent predecessors (George W. Bush, Bill Clinton, George Bush, Ronald Reagan and Jimmy Carter) had served in the Senate, three of their vice-presidents had done so (Al Gore, Dan Quayle and Walter Mondale).

of Representatives'. Section 8 of Article I goes on to specify the particular powers which the framers wished to transfer from state legislatures to the federal legislature. Among the most important of these *enumerated powers* are the power to levy taxes; the power to regulate both international and interstate commerce; and the power to declare war.

The framers did not intend that the new Constitution signify a general transfer of legislative power from the states to the Congress, hence the detailed specification of the matters on which Congress was entitled to pass laws. The Tenth Amendment to the Constitution (1791) reinforced the fact that the legislative ambit of Congress was strictly limited by stating that 'The powers not delegated to the United States by the Constitution . . . are reserved to the States respectively, or to the people.'

Nevertheless, the legislative range of Congress *did* expand, thanks in particular to the doctrine of *implied powers*. The seeds of this were sown in the last paragraph of Article I, Section 8 of the Constitution. This entitled Congress 'to make all laws which shall be necessary and proper for carrying into execution the foregoing powers'. This was intended merely to enable Congress to use its enumerated powers, rather than to provide it with an additional, general grant of power. However, expansive interpretation of the 'necessary and proper clause' by the Supreme Court has allowed Congress to legislate on virtually any matter it wishes.

The key Supreme Court decision came early, in *McCulloch* v. *Maryland* (1819). Here the Court decided that 'necessary and proper' meant convenient, rather than indispensable, to the exercise of an enumerated power. Subsequent Court decisions, such as those legitimating the New Deal legislation of the 1930s, recognised the political reality that national problems required national solutions, even if this meant allowing Congress to encroach upon state legislative power as conceived by the framers in 1787. Consequently, 'Nowadays, so long as Congress's actions do not violate specific constitutional rights of individuals or interfere with Constitutional powers delegated by the Constitution to the president or federal courts, there is little that Congress wants to do that it lacks constitutional authority to do' (Peltason, 1988, p. 36).

Legislative powers of the president

As we have seen, Article I of the Constitution stated that Congress was endowed with *all* legislative power. This, however, is not quite true. Congress is indeed legislatively supreme to the extent that it alone can pass a law, yet the president was given a certain degree of both influence and actual power in the legislative process.

The power given to the president was negative power, in the form of the veto, for Article I, Section 7 of the Constitution requires that all bills

Box 14.2

The impeachment of President Clinton

President Bill Clinton (1993–2001) was the third president to be impeached by the House of Representatives. In 1868, President Andrew Johnson was impeached, largely for political reasons, by those in Congress who wanted a more radical reconstruction policy after the Civil War. The vote in the Senate was 35–19, meaning that Johnson survived by one vote, since the Constitution specifies that a two-thirds majority is required to convict. In 1974, President Richard Nixon was impeached in a more bipartisan manner as a result of evidence suggesting he had organised a cover-up of the Watergate scandal. Nixon resigned before the Senate trial could be held, but he almost certainly would have become the only president to be removed from office by the impeachment mechanism.

President Clinton's impeachment in 1998/99 was for perjury and obstruction of justice, but was almost wholly motivated by partisan political considerations. The Constitution allows for impeachment where it can be shown that the president is guilty of 'high crimes and misdemeanors'. That phrase is vague, but is generally taken to refer to official rather than personal wrongdoing. Clinton had been hounded by arch-conservative opponents from the start of his presidency: first, for alleged corrupt financial dealings when governor of Arkansas (the Whitewater scandal) and then for alleged sexual harassment (the Paula Jones scandal). The president was wholly cleared of wrongdoing in Whitewater and the Jones scandal was going nowhere until her lawyers learned of Clinton's relationship with a young White House employee, Monica Lewinsky. It emerged that the president had lied about his relationship with Lewinsky in a grand jury statement in the Jones investigation. It was this and associated efforts to keep his affair with Lewinsky secret that led to his impeachment.

The vote in the House was overwhelmingly partisan and public opinion polls showed that some two-thirds of Americans believed that the impeachment was driven by politics rather than law. The president was easily acquitted in the Senate: the two articles of impeachment were defeated 45–55 and 50–50.

passed by Congress must be signed by the president before they can become law. Moreover, it explicitly states that the president need not sign a bill if he has objections to it: instead, he can simply return the bill unsigned to Congress, stating the reasons for his veto. Congress can only override that veto by a two-thirds majority of both the Senate and the House. Mustering such a majority of both chambers is no easy matter and thus the presidential veto is a formidable weapon with which to counter the legislative power of Congress.

As well as this negative power, the president was invited by the Constitution to influence the legislative agenda of Congress. Article II, Section 3 instructs him as follows: 'He shall from time to time give to the Congress information of the state of the Union, and recommend to their consideration such measures as he shall judge necessary and expedient . . .' As the wording of the clause suggests, it was not intended that the president recommend legislation to Congress on a routine basis. Nevertheless, it does indicate an awareness on the part of the framers that Congress might not always be capable of providing the legislative leadership that the country needs.

These avenues of presidential intrusion into the legislature's domain are, of course, applications of the principle of checks and balances. Yet while the framers intended the president to be able to check congressional legislative power, they did not intend that he should be able to usurp it, for that would have violated that other cardinal principle of the Constitution, the separation of powers. Thus, the balance struck by the Constitution was one weighted heavily in favour of congressional dominance in the legislative field: 'It is clear that the original design was intended to give Congress the legislative authority that was, in fact, the power to determine national policy' (Wayne, 1978, p. 7).

Today, however, that balance of power has been largely reversed. To be sure, the constitutional framework has barely been altered with respect to legislative power. However, historical forces, interacting with institutional capacities, have engendered a transfer of substantial legislative power from Capitol Hill to the White House.

The changing balance of legislative power

In the eighteenth and nineteenth centuries, Congress dominated the legislative process. From time to time, a strong president such as Jefferson, Jackson or Lincoln might challenge that supremacy, but most presidents readily conceded that legislation was, in essence, a matter for the Congress. Furthermore, demand for national legislation was limited during this period and Congress had little need to seek help from the presidency in accomplishing its constitutional duties. In the post-Civil War era, the presidency came close to being eclipsed altogether by a powerful and confident Congress.

Ironically, it was precisely at this zenith of congressional power that the socio-economic changes that were to undermine it were sweeping the nation. The Industrial Revolution eventually brought forth an unprecedented demand for national legislation. The federal government was asked to legislate on such matters as the regulation of the new giant corporations; the conditions of work in factories; the problems of small farmers; public health and safety; child labour; trade union rights and a host of other pressing issues.

By the end of the Progressive era (1900–17), not only had a new legislative activism been generated, but the presidency had moved to centre stage of the legislative process. President Theodore Roosevelt declared his office a 'bully pulpit' from which he could spur Congress into action. The other major Progressive president, Woodrow Wilson, became the first since John Adams to deliver his State of the Union address personally before the Congress. Moreover, he personally lobbied for bills on Capitol Hill and sometimes provided his supporters there with draft legislation (Wayne, 1978, p. 15).

What the Progressive period had demonstrated was that an activist federal government required a new level of presidential energy and initiative. Not only could the president personally dramatise legislative issues in a way that a collective body like Congress could not match, but, more important still, much of the new legislation required technical expertise that members of Congress simply did not possess. This was to be found rather in the federal bureaucracy, located within the executive branch.

These indications of an emerging new balance of legislative power between Congress and president became unmistakable – and irreversible – during the Great Depression of the 1930s. With the exception of the Civil War, the Depression was the greatest domestic crisis in American history. Industry and agriculture had all but collapsed, unemployment reached 50 per cent in some areas, and welfare provision was wholly inadequate. After enduring this misery for some three years under President Herbert Hoover, the country turned to Franklin D. Roosevelt for remedial action.

Roosevelt's first 100 days in office are rightly famous for the flood of major legislation which he sent to Congress. What is particularly striking, however, is not merely the energy and ingenuity of the president and his advisers, but the reception given by Congress to this legislative bombardment. A body which had hitherto had the reputation of moving at a snail's pace approved radical new proposals by huge majorities in a matter of days or, sometimes, hours. On some occasions, members had not even received copies of the legislation before voting for it. Moreover, when such legislation proved inadequate to the country's needs, members demanded still further legislative initiatives from the executive branch.

Roosevelt's New Deal saw more than mere legislative initiative pass from Congress to president. Many new bureaucratic agencies were created by the legislation – bodies such as the Securities and Exchange Commission, the National Labor Relations Board and the Social Security Administration. Having been set up with broad grants of power, these agencies proceeded to make detailed policy decisions on a routine basis. Such decisions amounted to the substantive exercise of legislative power, yet the agencies were located within the executive, not legislative, branch of government. The great expansion in bureaucratic structures and responsibilities under Roosevelt thus entailed a significant diminution in the legislative power of Congress relative to that of the presidency.

The New Deal years witnessed a transformation in the expectations of the presidency. Henceforth, the nation, including Congress, would look to the president and his advisers for the solution to the problems it faced. After Roosevelt, presidents would be measured by their ability to generate legislative proposals and support for them in Congress. For its part, the legislative role of Congress now was in essence to approve, amend or disapprove the president's proposals. It is almost as if the constitutional roles have been reversed: the role of Congress is to check and balance the president's legislative power by 'vetoing' legislation it thinks unwise or undesirable. While such negative legislative power is important, it provides no basis for Congress to supplant the presidency in legislative leadership.

Events since the 1930s have generally had the effect of enhancing the legislative dominance of the presidency. Most importantly, the emergence of the United States as a world superpower has maximised the foreign policy powers inherent in the presidency. However, in the field of domestic affairs too, the sheer volume of legislation, combined with an ever-greater need for technical expertise, has also made presidential leadership the central feature of the legislative process.

This presidential aggrandisement begs the question of how Congress has responded to the erosion of its power and what role it is left to play in the legislative process today. Above all, we need to examine the reasons for its decline and the likelihood of Congress ever recapturing its former pre-eminence.

Congress today: mandate and the legislative agenda

In the early autumn of 1993, the *Congressional Quarterly* looked forward to the legislative battles ahead. It noted that President Clinton was in an inherently weak position, having been elected the previous November by a plurality rather than a majority of the voters. Yet, it reported,

this fall's legislative calendar is a reminder of Clinton's power to determine what Congress fights over – even if he lacks the clout to control the outcome. Congress's agenda for the rest of the year is jammed with White House proposals on trade, health care and other domestic policies.

CQ Weekly Report, 4 September 1993, p. 2295

Even a relatively weak president, then, sets the legislative agenda of Congress. In his first term, President George W. Bush had an even weaker mandate than President Clinton, since he had actually won fewer votes than his main opponent. Nevertheless, Bush acted as if he had a mandate to lead and the Congress generally accepted this. In January 2009, when President Obama took office, the economy was in a downward spiral and America was mired in wars in Iraq and Afghanistan. All eyes were on the president, not the Congress, to take the initiative in dealing with these crises. Congress was perceived as having neither the capacity nor the will to undertake the necessary action. Among the reasons why it was incapable of taking the lead are the electoral characteristics of Congress.

Electoral factors in congressional decline

While Congress contains members from all parts of the nation, it is not, in important respects, a truly national body. Each member of Congress is elected by a discrete, local electorate. Even the two senators elected from the same state are usually chosen in different years, when issues and political moods may well be quite distinct. Moreover, those seeking election to Congress are not normally bound by a common set of policies or manifesto, or, indeed, by strong party or ideological loyalties. An attempt to overcome this weakness occurred in 1994, when most Republican candidates for the House of Representatives signed up to the Contract with America. It was ultimately unsuccessful, however, either in attracting the attention of the public, as opposed to the media, or in legislative achievement.

All this means that congressional elections are, in essence, local elections, fought on local issues, with candidates offering themselves as representatives and guardians of local interests. As a result, when those elected on such a basis gather in Washington, they can scarcely claim to represent a national constituency or be in possession of a national mandate. In this sense, Congress as a whole is not much greater than the sum of its parts.

This is not to suggest that members of Congress have no concern with national issues or no idea of the national interest; nor, indeed, does it mean that Congress cannot influence the legislative agenda or take important legislative initiatives. Yet, in the end, members of Congress owe their election – and re-election – to their ability to represent their local constituents' interests, rather than those of the nation, and local and state interests are not only different from the national interest, they may actually conflict with it. For example, members from tobacco-growing areas may well feel bound to oppose proposed limitations on cigarette advertising, even while they concede that a reduction in smoking would be in the national interest. A concrete example of this phenomenon occurred under President George W. Bush in 2007. Congress had passed the Water Development Resources Act, which authorised flood control and other environmental projects in various parts of the country. President Bush vetoed the Act, arguing that it was financially irresponsible. For the first time in his presidency, Congress overrode his veto, with only 12 Republican senators siding with the president. The reason was straightforward: the Act promised money for projects in many states and few members of Congress could resist the temptation to put local priorities above national ones.

In short, Congress stands accused of *parochialism*, a narrowness of vision and a self-interest which gives priority to local concerns over those of the nation. This parochialism may lead Congress to behave in a frankly irresponsible manner. In 1985, for example, it passed the Gramm–Rudman–Hollings Act, which proposed to eliminate the national budget deficit by 1991. Such a rapid elimination of the deficit necessitated some very tough choices on spending cuts. Knowing its own limitations, Congress provided that, where cuts could not be agreed among its members, the comptroller general should make across-the-board cuts. When this procedure was later declared unconstitutional by the Supreme Court, Congress amended the Act to give the responsibility for making the cuts to the Office of Management and Budget. Why was Congress so willing to yield its power to others? 'No mystery surrounded the rationale for this provision. By opting for automatic, across-the-board cuts, thus relinquishing its budgetary authority, Congress sought to protect its members from having to go on the record by voting for painful spending cuts that were sure to be felt in the constituencies' (Keefe and Ogul, 1993, p. 10).

This parochialism contrasts with the national outlook, standing and responsibility of the president. He is chosen by a national constituency, all voting on the same day and on the same set of contemporary issues. Even a president who does not gain a majority of the votes cast in his election, such as Bill Clinton in 1992 and George W. Bush in 2000, can claim a mandate because he is the nation's choice to provide national leadership. Quite simply, he has a mandate from the nation which Congress cannot rival. Along with this mandate comes a responsibility which cannot easily be shirked. He is therefore entitled to establish the legislative agenda and take the initiative in drafting legislation. It should be emphasised, however, that while the president has a mandate and the initiative to propose legislation, this is no guarantee that Congress will actually enact his legislative agenda.

Institutional factors in congressional decline

In relation to the presidency, Congress has serious institutional weaknesses which inhibit its ability to provide legislative leadership. These weaknesses stem from disadvantages in both organisation and capacity.

Bicameralism

The internal organisation of Congress leads to a fragmentation of power that makes legislative coherence extremely difficult. In one basic respect, this fragmentation has its roots in the Constitution. The framers decided that Congress should be a bicameral body, composed of two chambers with more or less equal legislative power. By stipulating that all bills must be approved by both chambers in identical form, they established the possibility that one house could negate the legislative initiatives of the other. This potential for inter-chamber conflict was made all the greater by designing different electoral bases for the House of Representatives and the Senate. Even after the passage of the Seventeenth Amendment in 1913, when the Senate joined the House in being directly elected, the different electoral cycles and types of constituency represented by the two ensured that they would often have distinctive or opposed priorities.

This constitutionally ordered fragmentation of the Congress contrasts with the unitary design of the presidency. Furthermore, Congress established internal structures which only exacerbate the problem.

Committee power

One of the conditions for providing leadership *outside* of Congress is effective leadership *within*, yet the committee structure of Congress makes coherent, unified policy leadership difficult to achieve. As we shall see in detail in the next chapter, Congress carries out its legislative tasks by delegating substantial authority to specialist committees. Although each chamber as a whole must approve any bill, that approval is often a formality, a largely unproblematic ratification of the decisions taken by the committee. Moreover, power is fragmented still further by the fact that committees, in turn, delegate considerable power to their subcommittees. The practical result is that, on most occasions, the subcommittee recommendation is accepted by the full committee and the full committee recommendation is accepted by the chamber as a whole.

Unsurprisingly, then, congressional committees and subcommittees are frequently spoken of as 'little legislatures'. As long ago as the late nineteenth century, Woodrow Wilson observed that 'Congress in session is Congress on public exhibition, whilst Congress in its committee rooms is Congress at work' (Bailey, 1989, p. 103).

From the very beginning, members of Congress were aware that the use of committees threatened to disperse and undermine the power of Congress as a whole. They sought, therefore, to limit the lifetime and autonomy of committees. However, as the nineteenth century wore on, an increasing legislative workload, combined with an increasing membership of both chambers, made division of labour a necessity (Smith and Deering, 1990, p. 28). Thus, for mainly practical reasons, the structure of legislative power became more fragmented than had originally been deemed desirable.

Leadership and party weakness

At one time, this fragmentation of power to committees was offset by strong party leadership, particularly in the House of Representatives. The key figure here was the speaker. At first little more than a formal presiding officer, the speaker, chosen by the majority party, gradually accumulated important powers. The most significant of these was control over appointments to committees, including the committee chairs. Moreover, the speaker personally chaired the House Rules Committee, which effectively determined which bills would progress and which would not. The speaker was thus in a position to make or break a legislator's career, by determining both his committee service and the fate of his (and his constituents') legislative preferences. 'By the turn of the twentieth century, the Speakers' powers were almost complete, their hegemony virtually unchallenged' (Keefe and Ogul, 1993, p. 275). In short, there was a centralised authority in the House.

Eventually, however, members rebelled against this control of their interests and careers. A series of decisions in 1910–11 stripped the speaker of some of his most important powers, including his right to make committee assignments and his position on the Rules Committee. This inevitably resulted in a fragmentation of authority, which persists to this day.

As for the Senate, it has never experienced the kind of centralised power that the House once knew. It has been noted that 'senators tend to regard themselves as unregimented ambassadors from their states' (Bailey, 1989, p. 154). They are, therefore, most reluctant to subordinate themselves to others and expect to be treated as a co-equal by those at the head of the party.

Although there has been some strengthening of party discipline in recent years, party leaders have little control over members who wish to go their own way. Both the House and the Senate have a hierarchy of party leaders and whips (see Chapter 15) but, as former senator Alan Cranston put it: 'A lot of leadership is just housekeeping now. Occasionally you have the opportunity to provide leadership, but not that often. The weapons to keep people in line just aren't there' (Keefe and Ogul, 1993, p. 272).

Without an effective and coherent internal leadership, Congress is simply incapable of either putting together a legislative agenda or ensuring that an agenda is acted upon. Such leadership as Congress recognises, therefore, must come from outside and that means, first and foremost, the presidency.

A further disadvantage of the Congress is its relative lack of specialised knowledge compared with the presidency. As we saw in the previous chapter, the president is the head of a vast federal bureaucracy, employing thousands of specialists on every aspect of likely legislation. Whenever a problem arises, then, the president is well placed to ascertain its origins and scope and to draw up legislative proposals accordingly.

Members of Congress are, in essence, amateurs in policy matters, although they may have a measure of expertise in one or two areas, thanks to previous careers or service on specialist committees. Nevertheless, they can rarely match the bureaucratic experts.

Since the 1970s, Congress has taken steps to establish its own bank of policy specialists in an attempt to reduce its dependence upon executive branch expertise. It established new specialist support agencies, such as the Office of Technology Assessment (1972) and the Congressional Budget Office (1974), and doubled the staff of existing agencies like the Congressional Research Service and the Government Accounting Office. Furthermore, between 1970 and 1986, the number of committee

Box 14.3

Legislative and presidential power

Presidential advantages

- Can recommend laws
- Veto
- National constituency
- National mandate
- National perspective
- Unitary structure
- Unitary authority
- Bureaucratic expertise

Congressional advantages

- Exclusive right to pass laws
- Veto override

Presidential disadvantages

- No power to pass laws

Congressional disadvantages

- Local constituencies
- Local mandates
- Parochialism
- Weak internal authority
- Fragmented committee power
- Bicameral division

staff increased by 250 per cent and the personal staff of members by 60 per cent (Mezey, 1989, p. 133).

While these changes have undoubtedly provided Congress with an independent source of expertise and information, it is by no means clear that they have enabled it to perform its legislative tasks any better. Critics have argued, for example, that increased support personnel means that legislators spend more time on managing their staff than deliberating on public policy. Moreover, it is the staff who, in effect, perform many of the legislative tasks previously done by members. Thus, 'A recurrent complaint is that staffs have encroached on the members' role in policymaking' (Keefe and Ogul, 1993, p. 201).

Other critics argue that the Congress has proved incapable of making good use of the information now available to it. Most notably, Congress tends to ignore information which suggests policies that might conflict with political considerations, such as constituency interests (Mezey, 1989, p. 134).

It would be a mistake to think that the president is wholly free of these electoral and institutional weaknesses that bedevil congressional leadership. Nevertheless, whatever its own failings, the presidency is more unified, better resourced and more nationally focused than the Congress. The cumulative impact of these advantages, at a time when more – and more complex – national legislation is deemed desirable, is that the president must lead. Consequently, Congress is left only with what Arthur Maas has called 'leadership reserve'. Congress may still exercise leadership, but only when the president chooses not to lead himself. Such leadership reserve can only be exercised episodically, says Maas, because Congress lacks the will and capacity to do so on a regular basis. 'Furthermore, the president is free at any time to include any subject in his programme and thereby to be the leader. The Executive always has the resources for this. As a general rule, whenever the president is disposed toward leadership, it is his to be had' (Maas, 1983, p. 14).

However, the fact that the president may choose to lead at any time does not mean that the Congress is bound to follow.

Congressional cooperation and resistance

It is worth emphasising that this fundamental shift in legislative power from the Congress to the presidency was accomplished without any significant formal change in the constitutional structure. The president is now expected to do far more than in 1787, but there has been no constitutional recognition of the fact. Congress, then, retains 'all legislative power'.

Many have recognised what Godfrey Hodgson called this 'paradox of presidential power'. In terms of practical politics, it means that the president is powerless to command Congress to act. All he can do is urge, bully, cajole, woo and induce legislators to pass his proposals. In the famous phrase of Richard Neustadt, presidential power is 'the power to persuade' (Neustadt, 1960). If so, then the legislative power of Congress can be described as 'the power to refuse'. For in the final analysis, Congress, or even just one of its chambers, retains the autonomy to refuse the president outright or to amend his proposals out of all recognition.

For any legislation to pass, therefore, Congress and the president must cooperate. Yet cooperation is not easily achieved. As we have already noted, the president and members of Congress operate on different electoral cycles and are answerable to different constituencies. In other words, over and above any policy differences, they do not necessarily share the same legislative interests in terms of political survival.

Congressional–presidential liaison

Congressional liaison is one of the most important aspects of the modern presidency. To a significant extent, a president's legislative success or failure turns upon the skill of his liaison staff in operating the politics of persuasion. As John Hart put it:

> **The congressional relations staff act as the president's eyes and ears on Capitol Hill, as lobbyists, as providers of vital services to members of Congress, and sometimes as policy advisers inside the White House.**
>
> Hart, 1987, p. 111

This last point can be crucial, since Congress will usually take more notice of White House liaison staff who are able to speak for the president.

Be this as it may, neither liaison staff nor members of Congress have any illusions about the extent to which their real differences of interest can be ignored. Larry O'Brien, chief of congressional liaison under Presidents Kennedy and Johnson, and one of the most skilful practitioners of his art, put it this way: 'I never expected any member to commit political suicide in order to help the President, no matter how noble our cause. I expected politicians to be concerned with their own interests; I only hoped to convince them our interests were often the same' (Wayne, 1978, p. 155).

President Obama chose Phil Schiliro as his senior congressional liaison on the grounds that he had long experience of working for Democratic legislators. This experience paid off handsomely as Schiliro played a vital role in securing passage of some major bills in Obama's early years, including the 2009 economic stimulus package and the 2010 health care bill. One of the secrets of Schiliro's success was his quiet, self-effacing approach when dealing with Congress. He fully understood that trying to command members of Congress to do something was likely to prove counterproductive.

Party ties

In many political systems, party is the mechanism which links the executive to the legislature, but, as we saw in Chapter 10, parties in the United States are relatively weak. Presidents cannot simply assume that members of their own party in Congress will support them, as President Carter discovered. Although there was a clear Democratic majority in both houses of Congress, the Carter administration proved inept at mobilising party support there. As a result, some of his most important legislation, such as his energy bill, was badly delayed, significantly amended or, quite simply, dumped.

Weak parties do present some advantages to the president. Most obviously, a president whose party is in the minority in one or both chambers of the Congress can make an ideological or pragmatic appeal to members of the other party. President Reagan was able to do this in 1981 in persuading the House of Representatives to pass his tax and budget proposals. Although the Republicans were in the minority, enough conservative Democrats supported the president to ensure his success.

Nevertheless, party *is* one of the levers a president has in trying to persuade Congress to act, and so he will, if wise, make a considerable effort to liaise with his party's congressional leadership. For their part, party leaders in Congress do generally see one of their most important duties as maximising support for (or opposition to) the president's legislation. The speaker of the House of Representatives and the majority and minority leaders and whips in both chambers are right in the middle of executive–legislative relations. If of the same party as the president, they will represent his wishes to fellow party members. In turn, however, the members also expect their leaders to represent their views to the president. Party leaders are thus engaged in a fine balancing act. They must avoid being seen as those who fail to defend the interests of the institution and membership to which they themselves belong (Keefe and Ogul, 1993, pp. 270–1).

Even if they wished to do so, party leaders have little power to compel members to follow the party line. Party leaders can be helpful to a member in her daily work, providing information or useful contacts, even assisting her to get a desired committee assignment or legislative favour. In principle, therefore, they could withdraw such assistance. In practice, however, they are not likely to push her too hard if she has good grounds for opposing the party line. As former majority leader (and later, speaker) Jim Wright put it: 'The majority leader is a conciliator, a mediator, a peacemaker. Even when patching together a tenuous majority, he must respect the right of honest dissent, conscious of the limits of his claims upon others' (Keefe and Ogul, 1993, p. 269). As always with members of Congress, those with the strongest claim are the constituents whose votes sent her to Washington.

On some occasions, constituents' claims are so strong that even the party leaders do not follow the party line. President Clinton experienced this in 1993, when he was trying to secure passage of the North American Free Trade Agreement (NAFTA). This eliminated trade restrictions between the United States, Canada and Mexico. Its opponents believed that, whatever economic benefits it might bring, it would certainly entail the loss of manufacturing jobs in the United States, since companies would move to Mexico in pursuit of cheap labour.

Among those leading the fight against NAFTA were House Majority Leader Richard Gephardt (Missouri) and House Majority Whip David Bonior (Michigan). Thus the two House Democrats who ranked behind only the speaker in the party's congressional hierarchy found the pull of constituency interests to be greater than loyalty to their party's president.

It is not altogether surprising, then, that presidents are by no means guaranteed passage of their legislative proposals, even when they have given a clear lead and their party controls both houses of Congress. However, presidents whose party does not control Congress are at a disadvantage, as are those in their second term of office and therefore in the process of becoming 'lame ducks'. President Obama achieved a spectacular success rate in his first year in office, largely because nearly all the major factors were in his favour. His party had clear majorities in both houses of Congress; politics was also highly partisan following the divisive Bush years, which encouraged the Democrats to cohere; and Obama was benefiting from the political honeymoon often conferred on a new president. However, it was also important that the president chose his legislative battles carefully. For example, according to *Congressional Quarterly*, Obama took a clear position on only about one-fifth of all Senate votes in 2009. President Obama also tended to take a pragmatic approach to getting legislation passed and was willing to make small but important concessions to legislators in order to win their votes. In the lead-up to the vote on his health care bill, for

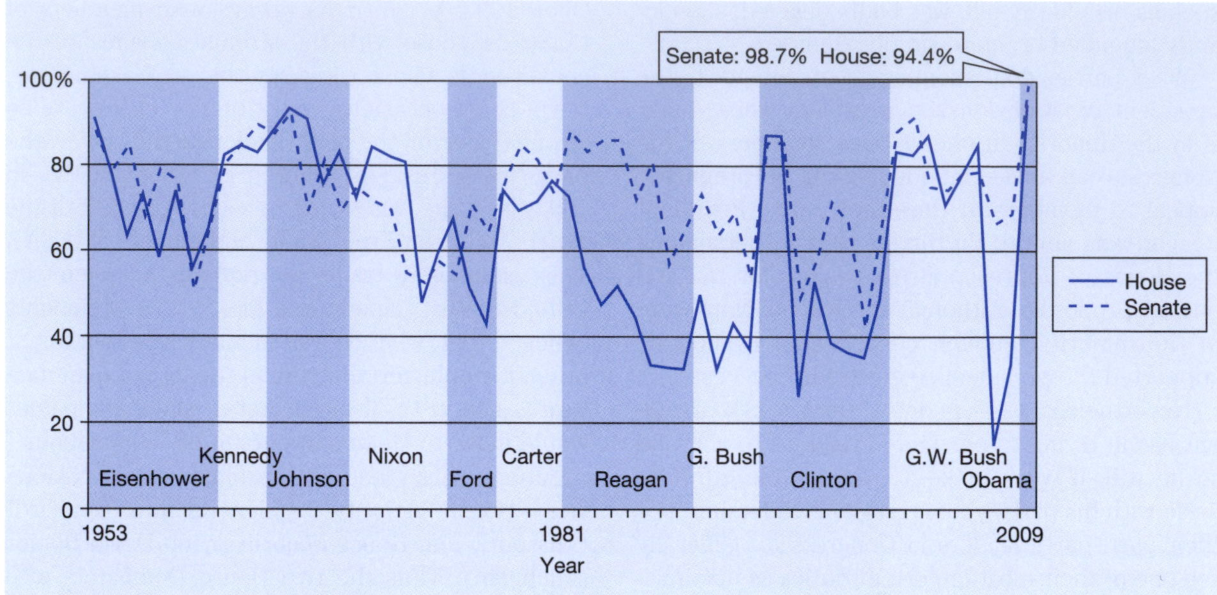

Figure 14.1 Presidential success on legislative votes: 1953–2009.

Source: *Congressional Quarterly*, 12 January 2010

example, Obama reassured House Democrats who took a pro-life position on abortion by publicly declaring that the new legislation would not apply to health care in connection with abortions.

Congressional support for presidents

Many factors help to explain why Congress supports some presidents more than others. Most obviously, a majority of members will support a president when they believe that his proposals are likely to solve a particular problem in an appropriate and successful manner. In these instances, Congress and president are of the same mind and there is relatively little need for either to draw upon its 'heavy guns'.

What about those instances where there is no easy agreement to be reached? This is often the case when controversial or difficult legislation has been proposed. What are the factors that come into play when members of Congress are reluctant to support the president, but he is determined to secure passage of his legislation? What induces members to vote for legislation when appeals to ideology, party and the public interest have failed?

As with most aspects of the congressional process, the electoral connection is vital here. The president has a number of carrots and sticks with which he can win over recalcitrant members by supporting or threatening their chances of re-election.

Where a bill involves the expenditure of money, the most powerful inducement a president can offer is to ensure that some of it will be spent in the member's district or state. This will benefit the member's constituents by providing them with jobs or services and make them more disposed to re-elect the member who secured these benefits.

If no direct material benefit is available, a president can confer prestige upon a member. Thus, in order to win the crucial support of Representative Marjorie Margolies-Mezvinsky (D – Pennsylvania) for his 1993 deficit-reduction bill, President Clinton promised to hold an important conference in her district in order to help overcome any constituent backlash against her support for the president. In this case, it did not work, and Margolies-Mezvinsky lost her seat in 1994.

Presidents can also grant access to the White House to a member and, perhaps, some of her constituents. The visit can be publicised back home, as can a photograph of the event, signed by the president. All of this can be used to convey the impression that the member is an important and influential player in national politics.

As well as being able to confer material benefits and prestige, a president can also offer his services during the member's re-election campaign. A member facing a strong challenge at the next election is grateful to a president who can use his influence to ensure a successful campaign. It appears that the vote of Senator Dennis DeConcini (D – Arizona) on the 1993 budget bill was won by an offer to swing the Democratic National Committee (DNC) behind the senator in his 1994 primary battle. DeConcini believed that the support among Democrats that the president and the DNC could mobilise outweighed any damage that might be caused by reversing his previous pledge to oppose tax increases.

A president can also refuse to provide such services as those discussed above, thereby turning carrots into sticks. In addition, however, he can bring pressure to bear directly by appealing over the heads of members to their constituents. President Reagan used this tactic to considerable effect. The basic method was to appear on television, present his proposals and then ask all the viewers who wanted to see them passed to call or write to their members of Congress to urge them to support the president. Members who were subsequently inundated with tens of thousands of letters and calls would thus feel the electoral heat and perhaps think twice about defying a popular president. In other words, a president on occasion will challenge members for the loyalty and support of their constituents.

The legislative power of Congress, then, is severely constrained by institutional weaknesses and outside political pressures. Initiative and leadership have passed to the executive branch. As we saw in Chapter 11, pressure groups and PACs contribute vital funds to members at election time and make legislative demands on the back of them. The president expects support for the policies for which he believes he has an electoral mandate. Party leaders expect solidarity. Above all, constituents expect members to serve their interests. A member of Congress has to steer her way through all these often conflicting pressures, try to produce effective legislation and secure her own re-election.

The balance of evidence suggests that it is the constituency service/electoral needs axis which generally determines congressional behaviour. What suffers as a result is the performance and reputation of Congress as a deliberative body, legislating for the national good. Thus, it is frequently observed that there is a marked difference between the attitudes of voters, on the one hand, to Congress as a whole and, on the other hand, to their particular representatives and senators. A Gallup Poll taken in October 2009 showed that a mere 21 per cent of respondents approved of the job that Congress was doing, while 72 per cent disapproved.

These figures contrast noticeably with much higher approval ratings for individual members of Congress, usually around 70–75 per cent. It seems, therefore, that the American public tends to believe that the main purpose of Congress is to represent in a narrow sense the interests of members' constituents, leaving it primarily to the president to represent and lead the nation. This supposition was, however, challenged by the so-called Republican Revolution of 1994.

The Republican 'Revolution' of 1994

In 1994, the Republican party captured the House of Representatives for the first time since 1952. It also captured a majority in the Senate. Even more impressively, the Republicans held on to the House (and the Senate) in 1996, thus winning consecutive House majorities for the first time since 1928.

Under the aggressive leadership of Newt Gingrich (R – Georgia), the House Republicans fought the 1994 elections in a manner that sought to remedy some of the long-standing weaknesses in congressional power described above. Thus, they attempted to overcome the parochialism of both congressional elections and congressional legislative activity by 'nationalising' their approach.

The Contract with America

Gingrich was determined that the House Republicans should fight the 1994 elections on the basis of a common manifesto which, if successful, would provide a mandate for party unity and legislation in the 104th Congress (1995/96). A media event was staged on the steps of the Capitol in which some 30 Republican candidates for the House signed a pledge to act on a series of key legislative items within a year.

In some respects, the Contract with America was a gimmick. Although House Republicans may genuinely have intended to act in united and determined fashion on an agreed agenda of measures, this could by no means guarantee that those measures would become law. First, the Republicans in the Senate made no commitment either to support the House legislative agenda or to heighten party unity. Secondly, even if the two chambers of Congress could produce an agreed bill, there was every possibility that the Democrat in the White House would veto it. In short, the Contract with America stood little chance of performing the functions of a manifesto and legislative agenda in any real sense.

Nor did the contract have much of an impact upon the American electorate. A survey undertaken at the time of the 1994 election revealed that 71 per cent of voters had never heard of it. Indeed, while 7 per cent said the contract made them more likely to vote Republican, 5 per cent said it made them less likely to do so (Jacobson, 1996, p. 209). On the other hand, although voters may not have been able to recall the contract itself, it is possible that it helped Republicans to establish their campaign themes more clearly in the public's mind (Hershey, 1997, p. 208).

Moreover, the contract did have an effect on House Republicans, making them more willing to act in unified fashion and more amenable to strong party leadership from the new speaker, Newt Gingrich. However, to a significant degree, this proved unsustainable. While stronger partisanship and greater ideological coherence enabled House Republicans to fulfil the contract pledge in so far as they brought their main legislative proposals to a vote in the House, none, with the exception of major welfare reforms, had been enacted into law as the 1996 elections approached. In part, this was because traditional factors inhibiting the effectiveness of Congress reasserted themselves to a greater or lesser extent.

First, the conservative ideological drive of the majority of House Republicans tended to alienate the small but potentially important moderate wing of the party, especially on items that were not in the contract. For example, in 1995, the Republican leadership attempted to undermine existing environmental protection laws, but thereby caused a sufficient number of moderate Republicans to vote with the Democrats to defeat their party's proposals (Hershey, 1997, p. 212).

Predictably enough, the Senate Republicans declined to follow the lead of their House colleagues. As we shall see in the next chapter, senators are far less willing to submit to party discipline or centralised leadership than members of the House. Therefore, while House Republicans rejected traditional bargaining and compromise with those who disagreed with them, Senate Republicans were more realistic.

The real war was, of course, with Democrat President Clinton and the climactic battle came with the struggle over the 1995 budget. The House rejected Clinton's budget, pushing instead for cuts in expenditure that would produce a balanced budget. In turn, the president refused to sign the congressional budget bill, because it threatened important programmes such as Medicare and education. The new fiscal year came into force on 1 October 1995, with the impasse still in place. In the past, Congress had dealt with this by authorising temporary funds to keep the wheels of government in motion. With Gingrich to the fore, however, the Republicans refused to do this, which, in turn, led to the shutdown of many government offices and government-run tourist attractions.

This tactic rebounded badly on Gingrich and the Republicans. Cleverly exploiting his role as the nation's leader, President Clinton was able to portray his opponents as irresponsible extremists. When public opinion polls decisively pinned the blame for the crisis on the Republicans, they were forced to back down. Indeed, only when, in the summer of 1996, House Republicans decided to revert to the time-honoured strategy of compromise with the president and Senate on a number of important issues, did they succeed in putting onto the statute books any elements of the Contract with America (Hershey, 1997, p. 216).

As noted above, the Republicans retained control of the House (and Senate) in 1996, but with a reduced majority and, therefore, with even less chance to force through a partisan agenda. While conservative Republicans pushed their cherished items again in 1997, they 'failed to muster enough votes to overcome either bipartisan opposition or the prospect of a presidential veto' (*Congressional Quarterly*, 20 December 1997, p. 3103). Moreover, Speaker Gingrich faced two serious attempts to unseat him, and committee chairs reasserted their power against the party leadership (see next chapter). Finally, leadership of the congressional Republican party slipped from the House to the Senate in the form of the more pragmatic Senate majority leader, Trent Lott of Mississippi.

The Republican Revolution of 1994 was a failure. A bold attempt at party government foundered on the rocks of the Constitution's structures and the political and legislative constraints they impose. Even though supported by a public mood favourable to Republican ideology and a majority in both chambers of Congress, it proved impossible to govern from Capitol Hill.

Of course, President Clinton found it difficult to govern from the White House, even when Democrats controlled Congress, but when bargaining and compromise failed, it was the president who emerged the victor from the struggle with Congress. It is also significant that once the House Republicans had one of their own in the White House, in the form of George W. Bush, they were happy to cede leadership to him and to play a supportive role. In that sense, the Republican Revolution was perhaps never much more than a 'second-best' option, born, in part, of the failure to capture the natural home of political leadership in the United States – the presidency.

The same is true of Republican discipline in opposing the Obama administration. There is a powerful feeling in Republican congressional circles that they must do everything they can to stop the Obama administration achieving its political agenda. However, this does not mean that there is the same desire to supplant presidential leadership with congressional leadership. An interesting illustration of this occurred in 2011, when Obama and the Republicans were struggling over the terms that would accompany the raising of the US debt ceiling. Basically, Obama wanted tax increases for wealthier Americans and some spending cuts, while the Republican leadership wanted huge spending cuts and no tax increases. Many conservative Republicans, especially in the House, resurrected an old favourite of theirs, an amendment to the US Constitution that would require a balanced budget. Yet when Republicans controlled both the House and the Senate under President George W. Bush, they never voted for an actual balanced budget, never mind a constitutional requirement to achieve one. In short, when the congressional parties have one of their own in the White House, they are content to allow presidential leadership in most policy areas.

The inability of Congress to perform successfully the legislative leadership role as originally conceived by the framers has led some commentators to emphasise the value of other aspects of the legislature's duties. Louis Fisher, for example, believes that one of the most important tasks of Congress is 'the daily grind of overseeing administration policies' (Fisher, 1985, p. 334). This brings us, then, to a consideration of the function known as 'congressional oversight'

Congressional oversight

You will search the Constitution in vain for an explicit reference to the oversight function of Congress, yet the very notion of 'checks and balances' invites Congress to ensure that the executive branch does not abuse its power.

Moreover, there are clauses of the Constitution which do explicitly give Congress the right to constrain executive power. For example, the president is required to obtain the support of two-thirds of the Senate before any treaty he has negotiated can become law (Article II, Section 2(ii)). The same clause requires a simple majority of the Senate to approve presidential nominations for the Supreme Court, ambassadorships, cabinet secretaries and, indeed, all federal officials save those exempted by Congress itself. Congress may also exploit the 'power of the purse' given to it by the Constitution: for the exercise of executive power depends to a considerable extent on the willingness of the legislature to vote the necessary funds.

To these constitutional controls, Congress itself added the right to hold public investigations into the activities of the executive branch. This has been described as an 'inherited power' of Congress, because it follows from the British Parliament's practice of conducting investigations for the purpose of gathering information with a view to legislation (Peltason, 1988, p. 74). It has not been restricted to the generation of new legislation, but also includes the right to investigate whether the executive branch is properly administering existing legislation.

Congressional oversight, then, involves both substantive powers and investigative authority over the executive branch. Yet there is still no common succinct definition of what it is. Indeed, Congress itself has employed different terms at different times. Thus, the Legislative Reorganization Act of 1946 referred to 'continuous watchfulness', whereas the Legislative Reorganization Act of 1970 mentioned 'legislative review' (Hart, 1987, p. 140). Part of the difficulty arises from the fact that Congress tries to accomplish more than one objective through oversight.

In the first place, as the term 'oversight' suggests, Congress tries to ensure that the executive branch faithfully administers programmes and legislation as Congress intended. This is, in essence, a retrospective form of oversight. It may involve, for example, examining policy guidelines drawn up by a bureaucratic agency or monitoring expenditures to see that they are in line with congressional intentions. At the level of personnel, oversight may seek to establish whether individual bureaucrats are performing their duties satisfactorily.

Secondly, oversight more generally can be seen as part of the legislative–executive struggle over policy. In this aspect, oversight capacity may be used prospectively to establish future policy. For example, when the Senate rejected President Reagan's nomination of Robert Bork to the Supreme Court in 1987, it purported to have doubts about his temperament and judicial qualifications for the job. In fact, the underlying reason for rejecting Bork was simply that he was too right-wing and would indubitably strengthen the radical conservative bloc on the Court. This was use of the oversight power not to monitor the executive branch, but rather to undermine its will.

Thirdly, there are more narrowly self-interested motivations and purposes behind some exercises in oversight. Thus, 'the ostensible goal of legislative oversight is to promote rationality, efficiency and responsibility in the bureaucracy. Although some legislators have high regard for this goal, they are also concerned with promoting their own careers and causes' (Keefe and Ogul, 1993, p. 407). This may take the form of interceding with the bureaucracy on behalf of a constituent or interest group, or, more spectacularly, using the power of investigation for self-promotion, as Senator Joe McCarthy did so notoriously in the 1950s.

Box 14.4

Instruments of congressional oversight

- Hearings/investigations
- Legislative veto
- Appointments
- 'Power of the purse'
- Required reports
- Sunset legislation*
- Informal contact

* Acts which cease to exist after a specified date

Congressional oversight, therefore, is best seen as a series of practices by which Congress can project its power into the executive branch. The purpose of oversight *may* be to ensure bureaucratic efficiency and responsibility, but it may also be exercised in pursuit of institutional and individual aggrandisement.

Effectiveness of oversight

There is a broad consensus among scholars that Congress does not perform its oversight functions very well. Peter Woll concluded, for example, that 'effective oversight performance is at best sporadic' (Woll, 1985, p. 145). Thus, from time to time, there are spectacular congressional hearings which have a major impact: the Watergate hearings which led to the resignation of President Nixon in 1974 are the most obvious example. Other hearings, however, produce meagre results, even when considerable time and effort are expended on them by Congress. For all the publicity and drama of the Iran–Contra hearings of 1987, little effective action was taken against members of the Reagan administration who had breached both law and government policy in selling arms to Iran and channelling the proceeds to the counter-revolutionary forces in Nicaragua. Even more serious, the 9/11 Commission criticised the ineffective process and structures of congressional oversight of intelligence and homeland security policy. Despite such criticism, the initial response of Congress was not impressive, as members seemed reluctant to give up their vested interest in the existing system.

The Senate exercises oversight in the form of its power to confirm or reject presidential nominees to federal posts. However, with one important exception, the Senate confirmation of these nominees is usually routine and perfunctory. Thus, in 1990, for example, President George H. Bush sent some 2,443 nominations to federal posts to the Senate. Of these, 2,145 (87.8 per cent) were approved, 11 were withdrawn and 287 (11.7 per cent) were not confirmed (Keefe and Ogul, 1993, p. 400).

Box 14.5

Oversight of anti-terrorism policy v. interests of members of Congress

The independent 9/11 Commission report of 2004 concluded that 'Congressional oversight for intelligence – and counterterrorism – is dysfunctional.' What explains the failure of Congress to put its house in order some three years after the traumatic attacks of 11 September 2001? The answer lies in a familiar tale of 'turf wars' and 'pork barrel' politics. And the problem pre-dates 9/11. According to one account, responsibility for intelligence oversight rests with 'at least 17 committees' *(New York Times,* 23 August 2004) and according to another, '88 separate committees and sub-committees' (Newsday.com, 23 August 2004). Despite numerous attempts since the 1970s to consolidate intelligence oversight and make the process more coherent, there has been no effective action. Part of the reason is that members of the various committees are reluctant to give up their power – 'turf'. More important still, members are reluctant to lose their ability to channel homeland security funds into their districts – 'pork barrel'. In the three years following 9/11, Congress had some $23 billion to distribute for enhanced homeland security. Rather than giving this money to the areas most at risk of terrorist attack, however, it was divided up to give each state a share. This may help members of Congress to get re-elected, but it is not an effective way to improve homeland security. As a result, the 9/11 Commission recommended either the creation of a joint Senate–House committee with sole responsibility for intelligence and security, or perhaps one permanent committee with sole responsibility in each chamber. The 9/11 Commission also recommended major changes in the intelligence and security structures of the executive branch. However, as Senator Susan Collins (R – Maine) commented: 'It's extraordinarily difficult to reorganize the executive branch, but that is going to be a piece of cake compared to reorganizing Congress' *(Washington Post,* 23 August 2004).

The rejection of presidential nominees to the most important posts is an embarrassing blow to any president, as when President Bush's first nominee as defense secretary, John Tower, was rejected in 1989, or when President Clinton had to withdraw his first two nominees as attorney-general, Zoe Baird and Kimba Wood, in 1993. Generally, such failures are due to perceived personal weaknesses on the part of the individual nominee concerned – in these cases, Tower's alleged excessive drinking and womanising, and Baird's and Wood's failure to pay social security taxes for domestic staff. When the president selects nominees without such personal vulnerabilities, the Senate rarely denies him his choice.

These are legitimate exercises of oversight power by the Senate, particularly if one considers the peccadillos of nominees to be relevant to their ability to perform the duties in question. On the other hand, the Senate frequently approves the appointment of federal office-holders who are not obviously qualified for the post and whose main asset appears to be a record of political support for the president. Likewise, some of those rejected, including the three mentioned above, *are* eminently qualified in terms of experience and knowledge. Thus, it is difficult to make the case that Senate confirmation powers constitute an effective exercise of oversight.

The exception mentioned above concerns nominees to federal judgeships. Until quite recently, nominations to the federal district and appeals courts were routinely confirmed. However, during President Clinton's second term, the Republican majority in the Senate began delaying consideration of nominated judges whom they considered to be too liberal. The Senate Democrats responded in kind under President George W. Bush. Nevertheless, although the judicial confirmation process is less automatic than before, this does not necessarily constitute good use of the oversight power. Judges should be confirmed mainly on their fitness for office, in terms of skills, experience and temperament, rather than upon their political ideology. When a tit-for-tat, partisan war breaks out, as it did under Presidents Clinton and George W. Bush, it results in many judgeships being left vacant and thus a more inefficient federal judiciary.

Nevertheless, while public, formal oversight by Congress may produce little tangible evidence of effectiveness, it may be that informal oversight is more productive. By definition, the effect of informal oversight is impossible to measure. Yet, it seems logical, at least, to assume that the daily, routine contacts which members of Congress have with federal bureaucrats attune the executive branch to the preferences, interests and objections of the legislative branch. Bureaucrats, therefore, will try to anticipate the views of legislators and, if possible, accommodate those views when devising and implementing policy (Keefe and Ogul, 1993, pp. 411–12).

Political education for the public

The legislative and investigative functions of Congress involve informed, public debate on the major political issues confronting the nation. As a result, Congress may be said to have an important role to play in educating the public. It may further be argued that an increasing tendency in recent years to allow hearings, floor debates and even committee sessions to be televised has enhanced the importance of this function of Congress.

While political elites, including the media, may take advantage of congressional activity to inform themselves on political issues, it is rare that the public takes much notice of what Congress does. As we have already seen (Chapter 9), the public gets most of its political information from television, and television coverage of politics is generally brief and superficial. Certainly, it excludes detailed coverage of congressional debates or hearings, unless something quite sensational is involved. Thus, while detailed coverage of Congress is available on the C-Span cable channel, this is not part of the viewing habits of the vast majority of the American public.

The significance of the educative function of Congress, therefore, is not that the public actually pays attention to what Congress is saying, but that congressional activities provide a major source of political information for those who wish to know what government is doing. In this respect, Congress plays an important part in ensuring an open system of government.

Congress is, in many regards, an institution under attack. In terms of its major functions, it seems to have lost the will or capacity to perform them to the public's satisfaction. As we saw above, public opinion polls indicate that it is held in relatively low esteem. As a consequence, many states have introduced term limits in an attempt to improve congressional performance.

Yet Congress should not have to shoulder all the blame for its failings. Most democracies experienced a drift of power from the legislative to the executive in the twentieth century. Moreover, for historical and cultural reasons, Congress does not have strong political parties to help it perform effectively. On the other hand, there is little doubt that the internal structures and processes of Congress also play their part in hampering legislative performance. The next chapter examines those in detail.

Chapter summary

Although Congress retains its exclusive power to enact laws, much of the initiative in legislation has passed to the presidency. This is due largely to the institutional advantages enjoyed by a unitary executive compared with a fragmented legislative branch. Another major cause is the tendency of members of Congress towards parochialism and the desire to serve their constituents in order to enhance their prospects of re-election. This does not mean, however, either that Congress has yielded all rights to initiate legislation or that it passively accepts what the president puts before it. While the Republican Revolution of 1994 may not have succeeded in restoring congressional pre-eminence in the field of legislation, it was a powerful reminder of the fact that the president and the Congress remain rivals for legislative power and that cooperation between the two is essential if laws are to be enacted.

Discussion points

1. What explains the shift in legislative initiative from the Congress to the presidency in the twentieth century?
2. What are the principal purposes of 'legislative oversight' and how effective is Congress in pursuing them?
3. How accurate is the view that Congress is a fundamentally parochial institution?
4. Under what conditions might Congress regain its old pre-eminence in the field of legislation?

Further reading

A useful introductory text is R. English, *The United States Congress* (Manchester: Manchester University Press, 2003). Two comprehensive and authoritative works on Congress are R. Davidson and W. Oleszek, *Congress and Its Members* (13th edn, Washington, DC: CQ Press, 2011) and L. Dodd and B. Oppenheimer (eds) *Congress Reconsidered* (9th edn, Washington, DC: CQ Press, 2008). An interesting sociological approach to changes in Congress is taken in N. Polsby, *How Congress Evolves: Social Bases of Institutional Change* (Oxford: Oxford University Press, 2004). For an analysis of congressional elections see M. Nelson (ed.) *The Elections of 2008* (Washington, DC: CQ Press, 2009). If you are fortunate enough to have access to it, *Congressional Quarterly* is a marvellous source of up-to-date information and analysis.

Websites

http://thomas.loc.gov
http://www.house.gov
http://www.senate.gov

References

Bailey, C. (1989) *The US Congress* (Oxford: Basil Blackwell).

Fisher, L. (1985) *Constitutional Conflicts between Congress and the President* (Princeton: Princeton University Press).

Hart, J. (1987) *The Presidential Branch* (Chatham, NJ: Chatham House).

Hershey, M. (1997) 'The congressional elections', in G. Pomper *et al.* (eds) *The Elections of 1996: Reports and Interpretations* (Chatham, NJ: Chatham House).

Hodgson, G. (1980) *All Things to All Men* (New York: Simon & Schuster).

Jacobson, G. (1996) 'The 1994 House elections in perspective', *Political Science Quarterly*, vol. 111, no. 2, pp. 203–23.

Keefe, W. and Hetherington, J. (2003) *Parties, Politics and Public Policy in America* (9th edn, Washington, DC: CQ Press).

Keefe, W. and Ogul, M. (1993) *The American Legislative Process: Congress and the States* (8th edn, Englewood Cliffs, NJ: Prentice Hall).

Maas, A. (1983) *Congress and the Common Good* (New York: Basic Books).

Mezey, M. (1989) *Congress, the President and Public Policy* (Boulder, Col.: Westview).

Neustadt, R. (1960) *Presidential Power* (New York: Wiley).

Peltason, J. (1988) *Corwin and Peltason's Understanding the Constitution* (11th edn, New York: Holt, Rinehart & Winston).

Smith, S. and Deering, C. (1990) *Committees in Congress* (2nd edn, Washington, DC: CQ Press).

Wayne, S. (1978) *The Legislative Presidency* (New York: Harper & Row).

Woll, P. (1985) *Congress* (Boston: Little, Brown).

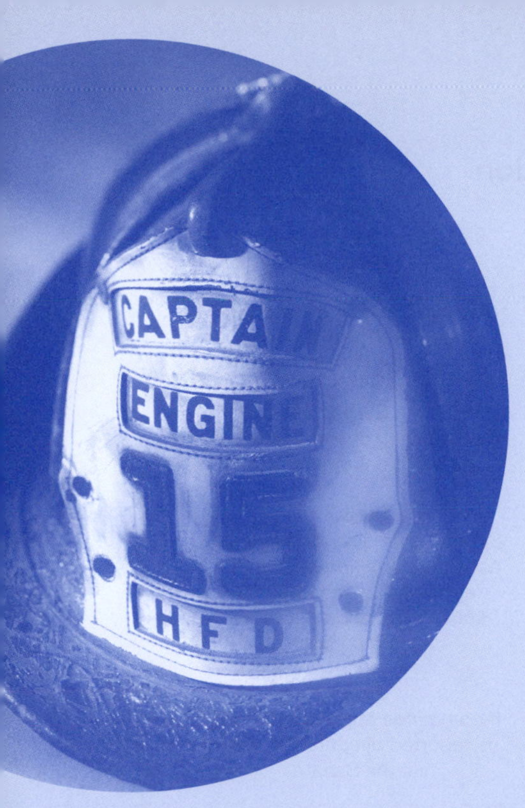

Chapter 15

Congressional structures and processes

Like most legislatures, Congress has its own distinctive set of structures, processes and institutional norms. We saw in the previous chapter how some of these can help or hinder Congress in the performance of its major tasks. In this chapter, we take a closer look at congressional practices in order to understand how the legislative process works. We also examine the members of Congress themselves – what kinds of people they are, and what their methods of work and their career aspirations are.

A bill becomes law

There are many bills introduced into Congress every session, but very few become law. Many bills are introduced without any serious expectation that they will be passed. However, even the most earnestly and widely supported bills have to struggle to overcome the many obstacles and opportunities for sabotage and derailment that await them. As we saw in the previous chapter, the parochialism and fragmentation of power within Congress, combined with the absence of strong party loyalties and disciplines, makes the path of legislation unusually incoherent and uncertain.

In formal terms, all bills follow more or less the same route. The complexity of the legislative process stems from the fact that problems may arise at any step along the path. For example, the requirements of bicameralism mean that separate bills must be introduced into both House and Senate. However, not only may the two chambers pass different amendments, but the two bills may be different from the outset, depending on the distinctive goals and strategies of the bills' sponsors. The wording of a bill is vital if its sponsor has a strong preference for a particular committee to take jurisdiction of it. Thus seeking a 'friendly' home

The path of legislation
House of Representatives
Senate
Step 1
A bill is introduced by a member, and is assigned to the appropriate *standing committee*
Bills may not be identical
Step 1
A bill is introduced by a member, and is assigned to the appropriate *standing committee*
Step 2
The *standing committee* refers the bill to a subcommittee
Step 2
The *standing committee* refers the bill to a subcommittee
Step 3
Subcommittee holds hearings, considers amendments and, if approved by members in some form, returns it to the *standing committee*
Bills emerge with different amendments
Step 3
Subcommittee holds hearings, considers amendments and, if approved by members in some form, returns it to the *standing committee*
Step 4
If *committee* approves, the bill is reported, via the *Rules Committee*, to the *floor* of the House
Step 4
If *committee* approves, the bill is reported direct to the *floor* of the Senate
Step 5
Floor action – debate and further amendments
Bills in different forms
Step 5
Floor action – debate and further amendments
Step 6
If both chambers approve bill, but in different forms, a *conference committee* drawn from both chambers meets to reconcile the two versions
Step 7
Full House votes on *conference committee* bill
Bills now identical
Step 7
Full Senate votes on *conference committee* bill
Step 8
If passed by both chambers, the bill is sent to the *president* for signature or veto

in each of the two chambers may require differences in the initial House and Senate bills.

Committees and legislation

The main legislative work begins when the standing committee which takes jurisdiction of a bill when it is introduced assigns it to one of its subcommittees, for it is at the subcommittee stage that there are hearings, proposed amendments and the first major vote.

Committee hearings

Hearings involve the calling of witnesses to appear in public before the subcommittee. Such witnesses are typically from the executive branch or from interest groups, although independent experts and constituents may also appear. Witnesses are expected to supply information about a problem in which they have an interest or of which they have experience. The formal purpose of hearings, then, is to inform Congress so that it may take appropriate legislative action.

In theory, those who testify before congressional subcommittees may be supportive, hostile or neutral towards the bill concerned. In practice, it is often the case that the chairs of the subcommittees and their staff carefully select witnesses who will support their own position. Indeed, the very purpose of hearings may be less to acquire information otherwise unavailable, than to allow committee members to perform in the limelight (Woll, 1985, pp. 114–15).

Nevertheless, whether intended for information-gathering, personal advancement or symbolic reassurance to the public that Congress is open and democratic, the fact is that hearings rarely make any direct difference to the content of legislation. Quite simply, witnesses are unlikely to provide significant information of which Congress is not already aware. On the other hand, hearings may help to generate or solidify a coalition behind the bill (Smith and Deering, 1990, p. 142). Committee hearings can focus the attention of Congress and the country on an issue and, by parading the evidence of witnesses, mobilise support for legislation that has already been drawn up.

There are several types of committee in Congress. The basic type is the *standing committee* and its *subcommittees*. These are permanent committees. This means that they automatically continue in existence from one Congress to the next, unless Congress decides to abolish or amalgamate them. Perhaps the most important feature of standing committees and subcommittees is that they have legislative jurisdiction over one or more policy areas. Thus, in the Senate, the Armed Services Committee deals with defence-related issues only. On the other hand, the Banking, Housing and Urban Affairs Committee deals with different policy areas that are not directly related to each other. Senate and House committees do not necessarily have precisely parallel jurisdictions. Thus, the issues dealt with by the Senate Labor and Human Services Committee are handled in the House by the Appropriations Committee. The fact that the House has 435 members, compared with just 100 senators, means that the House has greater scope for both more and larger committees and subcommittees.

The second type of committee is the *select* or *special committee*. These are not formally permanent, nor do they have legislative authority. Their main task is to investigate or highlight particular issues or problems. The most famous of such committees are those which investigate scandals, such as the Watergate Committee or the Iran–Contra Committee.

Select committees can, however, become standing committees or, at least, acquire the same permanence and legislative status as the latter possess. The infamous House Committee on Un-American Activities, which investigated alleged communist subversives in the 1940s and 1950s, was made permanent in 1945, though it had existed as a select committee since 1938. More recently, the Intelligence Committees of both houses have become permanent, even though they are not listed as standing committees in the rules of the two chambers. Normally, select and special committees are established with specified time limits on their existence, but in the case of the Intelligence Committees these limits have been dropped (Smith and Deering, 1990, pp. 5–6).

The third major type of committee is the *conference committee*, made up of members of both the Senate and the House. These have the vital task of harmonising, or *reconciling*, the House and Senate versions of the same bill. In order to accomplish their task, members of a conference committee must necessarily devise amendments to the bills as passed by the two chambers. They can, therefore, wield substantial legislative power. Of course, the conference committee bill must be approved by both House and Senate, but faced with a choice of that bill or no legislation at all, the conference committee version is usually adopted.

The fourth type is the *joint committee*. Currently there are four of these. Composed of members of

Box 15.1

Committees in the 112th Congress (2011/12)

Senate

- Agriculture, Nutrition and Forestry
- Appropriations
- Armed Services
- Banking, Housing and Urban Affairs
- Budget
- Commerce, Science and Transportation
- Energy and Natural Resources
- Environment and Public Works
- Finance
- Foreign Relations
- Health, Education, Labor and Pensions
- Homeland Security and Governmental Affairs
- Judiciary
- Rules and Administration
- Small Business and Entrepreneurship
- Veterans Affairs

House

- Agriculture
- Appropriations
- Armed Services
- Budget
- Education and the Workforce
- Energy and Commerce
- Ethics
- Financial Services
- Foreign Affairs
- Homeland Security
- House Administration
- Judiciary
- Natural Resources
- Oversight and Government Reform
- Rules
- Science, Space and Technology
- Small Business
- Transportation and Infrastructure
- Veterans Affairs
- Ways and Means
- Intelligence (Select)
- Joint Economic Committee (with Senate)
- Joint Committee on Taxation (with Senate)

both House and Senate, they are non-legislative committees, but some do make significant contributions to policy-making. For example, the Joint Committee on Taxation has a large staff of experts and its work services the two legislative taxation committees, the House Ways and Means Committee and the Senate Finance Committee.

Mark-up sessions

When any hearing on a bill has been completed, the subcommittee will 'mark up' the legislation: that is, it takes the initial bill and amends it through additions and deletions. This mark-up process usually involves an attempt by the chairperson of the subcommittee to produce a broad consensus among the members. Thus mark-up sessions may involve intense political bargaining between individual members of the committee and between members of the majority and minority parties. Bargaining and compromise are desirable because a bill with broad support stands a much better chance of surviving the later stages of the legislative process than one which is divisive and likely to attract hostile actions (Woll, 1985, p. 117).

The subcommittee stage of a bill's progress is usually the most important. Although not the final stage, it is at this point that the real specialist members of Congress, together with their even more specialised staff, have the opportunity to define the basic shape of the bill. Other members not on the subcommittee tend to defer to the expertise of those who are, unless they have a particular reason for opposing them. This is especially true of the House, whose large membership encourages legislative specialisation. Senators, owing to their much smaller numbers, are obliged to sit on more subcommittees and committees and are therefore somewhat less specialised and less deferential.

'Subcommittee Bill of Rights'

In the 1970s, several important reforms enhanced the power and prestige of subcommittees. The reforms had two main goals: first, to free subcommittees from the control of full committee chairpersons, and, secondly, to disperse power more widely among members. House Democrats set the ball rolling in 1971 when they limited each member to the chair of no more than one legislative subcommittee. Until this reform, the chairs of full committees dominated subcommittees by heading several subcommittees themselves. The new limitation automatically gave more members the opportunity to chair subcommittees, thus dispersing and democratising power. In its first year of operation, the rule change brought in 16 new subcommittee chairpersons, most of whom were younger and less conservative than their predecessors (Vogler, 1983, p. 151).

In 1973 came the 'Subcommittee Bill of Rights'. This transferred significant power over subcommittees from full committee chairpersons to the Democratic group, or *caucus*, on each committee. Henceforth, the caucus would decide who would chair the subcommittees and also ensure that all members were given a major subcommittee assignment. Other reforms ended full committee chairpersons' control over the referral of legislation to subcommittees: they had previously used their position either to block referral completely, thus preventing any progress on a bill, or to refer it to a subcommittee under their personal control. Now referral would be automatic and subcommittee jurisdictions strictly delineated.

The reforms continued in 1974, when the number of subcommittees was increased by a new rule requiring all full committees with more than 20 members to establish at least four subcommittees. This was aimed squarely at Wilbur Mills, the chairman of the key Ways and Means Committee, which deals with taxation. Mills had kept control of policy for over 15 years by refusing to establish any subcommittees at all (Vogler, 1983, p. 152).

Still more changes followed, all with the same aim of increasing the power and autonomy of subcommittees. As David Vogler wrote: 'The greatest effect of these reforms was to shift the site of most congressional lawmaking from the full committee to the subcommittee level. . . . It is clear that subcommittees in the House have come into their own as new centres of power' (Vogler, 1983, p. 154).

Power in the Senate had always been more decentralised than in the House, but in 1977 it, too, reorganised its committee and subcommittee structures. The number of committees was reduced by one-fifth and subcommittees by one-third. Each senator would also now be limited to service on no more than three committees and eight subcommittees. Furthermore, no senator could chair more than three committees and subcommittees.

Whatever benefits the subcommittee reforms produced, they also exacerbated the problem of fragmentation within Congress. Congress has itself recognised this and there were attempts to modify some of the measures of the 1970s. These attempts failed, however, largely because, for most members, the admitted loss in institutional coherence was outweighed by the gain in the power and autonomy of subcommittee members. Subcommittees give

Box 15.2

A typical committee/subcommittee structure: The Senate Foreign Relations Committee 112th Congress (2011/12)

Subcommittees

International Operations and Organisations, Human Rights, Democracy and Global Women's Issues	African Affairs
East Asian and Pacific Affairs	European Affairs
Near Eastern and South and Central Asian Affairs	Western Hemisphere, Peace Corps and Global Narcotics Affairs
International Development and Foreign Assistance, Economic Affairs, and International Environmental Protection	

members their best chance to make their mark in the legislature and, consequently, with the voters back home. Too many of them are therefore simply unwilling to forgo the opportunities the strengthened subcommittees offer them.

The 1994 Republican Revolution

As noted in the previous chapter, however, the remarkable Republican victory in the 1994 elections led to an attempt to instil stronger party government into the House of Representatives. The new speaker of the House, Newt Gingrich, fully appreciated that such a change must inevitably involve a reduction in the decentralising force of committee and subcommittee autonomy and set about reforming committee structures accordingly. The House Republican Conference authorised Gingrich to select committee chairs and to ignore claims of seniority where deemed appropriate. In addition, the tenure of committee and subcommittee chairpersons was limited to a maximum of six years. The speaker was also given greater influence over committee assignments and the choice of committee to which bills are referred. Moreover, three committees and 31 subcommittees were abolished altogether (Foley and Owens, 1996, p. 36).

Yet by the beginning of the 105th Congress (1997–98), much of the revolution had been undone. As with other aspects of the Republican Revolution of 1994, the roots of this return to traditional arrangements lie in the failure of the House Republicans to secure passage of their key legislative priorities by pure partisanship. Forced in 1996 to compromise in order to get action on welfare reform and other items, the House Republicans found that committees were the best forum for bargaining and making deals across party lines (*Congressional Quarterly*, 22 March 1997, p. 9).

For similar reasons, committee chairs have regained much of their power to initiate and control legislative initiatives; where bipartisanship is essential to enacting legislation, committee leaders are better placed than party leaders to assess and manage the potential for acceptable compromise.

Reporting bills

Many bills fail to progress beyond the subcommittee stage. If, however, the subcommittee can agree and approve a version of the bill, then it is sent back to the full committee for consideration. The full committee may choose to hold further hearings and mark-up sessions, though on the whole it will accept the recommendations of the subcommittee. At this point, if the committee approves the bill, it is reported to the floor for consideration by the full chamber. The vast majority of bills are never reported: one count in the mid-1980s revealed that only 12 per cent of House bills and 24 per cent of Senate bills survived the committee stages of the legislative process (Bailey, 1989, p. 98).

House rules

At this point, the House and Senate processes diverge. In the House, the reported bill must go to the *Rules Committee* where it will be given a 'rule' determining the conditions of debate and the extent to which amendments may be offered. If the majority party is united on the bill and wishes to protect it, the committee can give it a rule which forbids amendments altogether. In the Senate, however, this is possible only where there is a unanimous vote to limit debate or amendment. Given that a single senator can prevent such limitation, Senate bills are more vulnerable to hostile amendment on the floor than House bills.

Floor action

Floor action refers to the activities of the whole chamber when a bill is reported to it. In essence, this means debate, amendments (unless a 'rule' determines otherwise) and the final vote.

As noted above, the extent of such activities may be restricted in the House, but the Senate has a rule of unlimited debate. Because senators may talk for as long as they like, they can exploit this to try to exact further concessions from the bill's supporters or even to kill the legislation altogether. When organised with real determination, this is known as a filibuster. The filibuster is at its most effective when several senators combine to keep debate going. One such effort in 1893, designed to prevent repeal of the Silver Purchase Act, lasted for 46 days (Woll, 1985, p. 55).

However, precisely because the filibuster is a method by which a minority can block the wishes of even a clear majority of senators, considerations of both democracy and efficiency have led to attempts to restrict its force. In 1917, the Senate approved a cloture rule, otherwise known as Rule 22. This allowed debate to be ended if two-thirds of the Senate voted to do so. Cloture was significantly strengthened as a weapon against the filibuster in 1975, when the number of votes required to end debate was reduced to 60 members. This more than doubled the number of successful cloture votes to over 50 per cent of those attempted (Woll, 1985, p. 57).

During the presidency of George W. Bush, the minority Democrats in the Senate employed the filibuster to block some of the president's more conservative judicial nominees. This led Senate Republican leaders to threaten to restrict the uses of the filibuster, something which made even some other Republicans very anxious. The fact is that the filibuster is not merely a traditional power of senators, but one valued by members of both parties. Although it cannot be used as a matter of routine, it does serve a useful purpose by forcing a choice between consensus or inaction on issues where passions run high.

Conference

If both the Senate and the House pass a bill, it goes to a *conference committee*. A conference committee is composed of a delegation of members from both the House and the Senate. Their task is to take the two versions of the bill passed by the Senate and the House and reconcile them: that is, produce a common version of the bill. This may involve both removing clauses from the original versions and adding completely new clauses. An agreed version, known as the Committee Report, is accepted once it has been signed by a majority of each chamber's delegation. It is then sent back to the House and Senate for a final vote.

The conference stage of a bill can be of enormous importance. In the first place, it is rare for a conference report to be defeated in the Senate or House. Equally important, no amendments to a Committee Report are permitted. Senators and representatives are therefore confronted with what is called a straight 'up or down' vote – a simple choice between approving or disapproving the report as it stands. Whatever is agreed in the conference committee, therefore, will almost certainly be what becomes law.

The membership of conference committee delegations is usually dominated by those who serve on the standing committees and subcommittees. They tend to use the conference stage to remove floor amendments of which they disapprove and, as a result, the conference committee tends to be yet one more instrument by which the specialised committees of Congress dominate the legislative process.

Bargaining and compromise in the legislative process

The legislative process as outlined above offers a series of points at which a bill may be fundamentally altered or defeated altogether. Each stage provides individual members of Congress, interest groups and representatives of the executive branch with a point of access to the legislative process. Combined with a set of detailed and complex rules governing legislative procedure, this makes negative legislative action far easier than positive legislative action. In simple terms, it is easier to prevent than to secure the passage of a bill.

Given the difficulty of operating on partisan lines, the best method for securing the passage of a bill is to ensure that it serves the interests and needs of as many individual members as possible. This means that, for each new bill, its sponsors must try to build a coalition which will support it through the difficult process which lies ahead. However, since the specific interests and needs of individual members may vary considerably, this inevitably entails bargaining and compromise on the details of the legislation. If a bill involves a distributive policy – that is, one which involves the allocation of funds or other benefits – then the simplest method of building a successful coalition is to make sure that enough members' constituencies benefit from the expenditure. If little or no money is involved, as with a civil rights bill, then bargaining and compromising will revolve around the terms and language of the legislation: some members may seek to strengthen the bill, while others try to dilute it.

In either case, the effect on the original bill can be very significant. Ensuring the passage of a distributive bill may simply necessitate spending more money than the nation's financial position makes desirable. This could contribute to a budget deficit or to other programmes being starved of vital finance. Diluting the terms and language of legislation may render it less effective or even completely worthless. An interesting example of this is the Civil Rights Act of 1960. Congress responded to the mounting pressure of the civil rights movement by trying to ensure greater compliance with existing laws. In order to gain the necessary support from southern members, however, the enforcement provisions of the 1960 Act were so watered down that the legislation could not possibly achieve its original goals. As the leading civil rights activist (and later Supreme Court justice) Thurgood Marshall observed, 'The 1960 Civil Rights Act isn't worth the paper it's written on.' The *New York Times* apparently agreed, since it did not bother to report the passage of the Act on its front page. Congress had thus wasted considerable time and energy on a bill rendered worthless by the need for bargaining and compromise; consequently, it was very quickly obliged to take up consideration of a new civil rights bill.

In short, the need to bargain, compromise and make deals may well undermine the achievement of good public policy. Nevertheless, it continues to be a central feature of the congressional process because there is no other, more effective method of aggregating the interests of individual members in a fragmented legislative body.

Members of Congress

Although Congress is a representative institution, its members are not at all typical of the population at large. They are disproportionately old, male, white and wealthy compared with those who elect them.

Table 15.1 Portrait of the 111th Congress (2009/10)

	Senate	House
Average age	63.10	57.20
Women in Congress	17	76
Minorities		
Black	1	41
Hispanic	1	28
Asian	2	8
American Indian	0	1
Career background		
Law	51	152
Public service	33	182
Business	27	175

Source: Congressional Research Service

Some of these imbalances are less worrying than others. For example, the predominance of lawyers is hardly surprising, given that politics is all about the making of laws. The gender and ethnic imbalances, on the other hand, indicate that there remain considerable barriers preventing members of historically disadvantaged groups from entering the corridors of power. Nevertheless, there are more women members of Congress today than there have ever been. There has also been progress in the number of members who come from ethnic minorities.

For minority candidates, it is clearly easier to get elected to the House than to the Senate. This reflects two main factors. First, because House districts are smaller than those for the Senate, they may contain concentrations of minority voters who constitute a relatively high percentage of the district's electorate. This factor was given added impetus in the early 1990s, when the Justice Department put pressure upon states to create 'majority-minority districts'. However, a series of Supreme Court decisions, beginning with *Shaw* v. *Reno* (1993), has ruled many of these districts unconstitutional as racial gerrymanders.

The second, and closely related, factor which makes it difficult for minority candidates to get elected to the Senate is that many white voters seem very reluctant to support them. Since whites constitute a large majority in all states, the state-wide electoral constituency of senators militates against the success of minority candidates. As a result, unless there is a marked change of attitude on the part of white voters, minority membership of the House may already be close to its maximum possible level. It is likewise difficult to imagine much further progress being made in the Senate. Nonetheless, the 2004 Senate race in Illinois produced the unprecedented phenomenon of both major party candidates being black.

Congressional careers

Once elected to Congress, however, members from all backgrounds face a similar career structure. Apart from their own talents and ambitions, the main determinant of their success is committee work. As we have seen, it is in committee that the main legislative work of Congress is done, and so it is also here that members have a chance to make their name. They want to demonstrate to their party leaders, colleagues and the media that they are able and intelligent; but most of all they want to demonstrate to the voters back home that they have the skills and power to secure major benefits for their district or state. This is because the first goal of all members of Congress is to win re-election – that is the precondition of any other goals, such as making public policy or gaining influence and prestige within Congress (Mayhew, 1974, p. 16). The first aim of a new member of Congress, then, is to secure a seat on the most electorally advantageous committee.

Committee assignment

All committees and subcommittees are organised along party lines. That is to say, the party which has an overall majority in the chamber as a whole is entitled to have a majority of the seats on every committee and subcommittee. Logically enough, then, it is the two parties that allocate their members to committees. Each party in each chamber has a committee on committees, although their official names vary somewhat. In the Senate, there are the Democratic Steering Committee and the Republican Committee on Committees. In the House, there are

Box 15.3

Committee preferences

Although some of the categories below overlap to a considerable extent, they do indicate the main motivations expressed by members when seeking particular committee assignments.

Prestige committees

Attract members primarily because of the status they confer. Examples:

House Appropriations Committee
House Ways and Means Committee
House Rules Committee
Senate Appropriations Committee
Senate Armed Services Committee
Senate Foreign Relations Committee

Policy committees

Attract members primarily because of the opportunity to influence policies of personal interest and national importance. Examples:

House Financial Services Committee
House Education and the Workforce Committee
House Judiciary Committee
Senate Armed Services Committee
Senate Finance Committee
Senate Small Business and Entrepreneurship Committee

Constituency committees

Attract members primarily because of the opportunity to service the needs of a particularly important section of voters. Examples:

House Agriculture Committee
House Resources Committee
House Science Committee
Senate Agriculture, Nutrition and Forestry Committee
Senate Energy and Natural Resources Committee
Senate Environment and Public Works Committee

Unrequested committees

Fail to attract members because they offer few career or electoral benefits. Examples:

House Standards of Official Conduct Committee
Senate Rules and Administration Committee

Source: Adapted from Smith and Deering, 1990, pp. 87, 101

the Democratic Steering and Policy Committee and the Republican Steering Committee (Foley and Owens, 1996, pp. 116–18).

Although the precise manner of choosing members of the committees is different in each case, all involve some balance of party leaders and members elected by the caucus. This reflects the need for harmony between party leaders and rank-and-file members if the two groups are going to work together effectively in the forthcoming sessions. Party leaders will want to ensure that committees are filled with those who will work well towards party goals, while rank-and-file members require assignment to their preferred committee. On the whole, it is the committee preferences of rank-and-file members which dominate the assignment process, subject to availability.

In order to share membership of committees on a reasonably fair basis, Senate committees are divided into A, B and C classes and no senator may be a member of more than two A class and one B class committees.

Members' committee preferences differ according to their personal interests and how they choose to attempt to advance their careers. From this perspective, committees can be divided into four groups: prestige committees, policy committees, constituency committees and unrequested committees (Smith and Deering, 1990). A member bent on building up his power within the House might well aim for the House Rules Committee since this has considerable sway over the progress of most legislation. On the other hand, a member from a mainly rural area might request a place on the Agriculture Committee in order to ensure that she can protect the interests of the farming communities in her constituency. Then again, a senator with presidential aspirations might seek a place on the Foreign Affairs Committee in order to acquire and demonstrate expertise in matters that preoccupy most residents of the White House.

The seniority principle

Once on a committee and subcommittees, members will almost invariably rise through the ranks, largely on the basis of seniority. Seniority is acquired by years of continuous service on a committee. Thus, a member who has served 12 years continuously on the same committee outranks one who has served only 10 years.

The seniority system has certain advantages for members of Congress. First, those with most legislative experience of the issues dealt with by a committee will also be its highest-ranking and most influential members. Secondly, it guarantees all members 'promotion' on a neutral basis: a member knows she need only wait her turn to rise to the top, probably to become chairperson of a subcommittee or even full committee. This also helps to avoid recriminations and feuds between members over promotions.

There are disadvantages to the seniority system, however. For example, it promotes the longest-serving committee members regardless of their talent, diligence or loyalty to party and colleagues. Seniority thus also frustrates more able but junior members of Congress. It was for reasons such as these that Congress gradually abandoned the absolute application of the seniority rule in the 1970s. A series of changes gave the party caucuses the ultimate power to overturn the assignment of committee chairs based on seniority.

This was used in 1975 to unseat three incumbent committee chairpersons who owed their position to seniority. The next major departure from seniority did not occur until 1985. In that year, the seventh-ranking member of the House Armed Services Committee, Les Aspin, campaigned successfully for the chair against the incumbent chairman and senior member, David Price. Price was considered by Democrats to be too supportive of President Reagan's policies and also suffered from ill health. Aspin promised more effective opposition to administration policies and duly won in a vote of House Democrats. More recently, in 1995, House Speaker Newt Gingrich, backed by the Republican caucus, ignored seniority in regard to the chairs of three committees.

Despite these exceptions, however, seniority remains the dominant principle in determining who shall rise to become chairpersons of congressional committees. To a considerable extent, this is because it avoids the problem of finding a better method of appointment: 'Reliance on seniority, unless there is an overwhelming reason to oppose the most senior member, resolves the question of choosing between the alternatives and minimises internal party strife' (Smith and Deering, 1990, p. 134).

Party leadership

Apart from the power that comes through committee service, members of Congress may also seek to become party leaders. As we saw in the previous chapter, party leaders do not have the disciplinary powers that would enable them to control party members. This is particularly true when party policy conflicts with members' constituency interests. Nevertheless, party leaders in Congress are in a position to command the respect, if not the absolute loyalty, of fellow party members. Although there are no formal rules governing who may occupy these top-level party positions, it is usually those who have served in Congress for some considerable time who are chosen. A second key factor is their personality and style. As befits an institution in which party is a significant, though not dominant, feature of members' behaviour, prospective party leaders must be seen as people who can energetically pursue party goals whilst simultaneously respecting individual legislators' autonomy. Tact, persuasion and goodwill towards colleagues are usually among the required qualities of party leaders.

Box 15.4

Party leadership in Congress
Main office-holders in the 111th Congress (2011/12)

Republicans	**Democrats**
House	**House**
Speaker John Boenher (Ohio)	– –
Majority leader Eric Cantor (Virginia)	*Minority leader* Nancy Pelosi (California)
Majority whip Kevin McCarthy (California)	*Democratic whip* Steny Hoyer (Maryland)
Senate	**Senate**
Minority leader Mitch McConnell (Kentucky)	*Majority leader* Harry Reid (Nevada)
Minority whip Jon Kyl (Arizona)	*Majority whip* Dick Durbin (Illinois)

Speaker of the House

Speaker of the House is the most important party position in either chamber of Congress. This is partly because it is the only leadership position created by the Constitution. Originally intended as a nonpartisan presiding officer, the speaker is today the leader of the majority party in the House. All members take part in the election of the speaker at the beginning of each new Congress. However, the vote is normally strictly partisan.

The speaker possesses important powers which help him lead his party and the House. He is influential in determining the committee assignments of members of his party, who are therefore mindful of his opinion of them. He can influence the outcome of legislation through his power to choose the committee to which a bill is assigned, and he largely controls appointments to the Rules Committee, which determines how a bill will be handled on the floor of the House.

When the president is of a different party, the speaker can also take on the role of unofficial 'leader of the opposition'. Speaker Tip O'Neill tried to do just this during the first six years of the Reagan administration. Even so, O'Neill was not able to hold his party together in opposition to President Reagan's tax and budget proposals, thus underlining once again the limits of party authority in Congress. Speaker Newt Gingrich sought to go beyond oppositional status in the 1990s and tried to wrest national political leadership from President Bill Clinton. However, this failed and Gingrich succeeded only in lowering his standing in public opinion polls, as respondents saw him as aggressive and extreme.

In 1997, Gingrich's bid for power was further reined in when there were two attempts by some House Republicans to unseat him as speaker. Although both failed, the fact that they were in part caused by resentment of Gingrich's increasing power served as a salutary reminder to the speaker that his tenure in office cannot be taken for granted. As a result, Gingrich's power was significantly reduced. Finally, as a result of the poor showing by Republican House candidates in the 1998 mid-term elections, Gingrich was obliged to step down as speaker. Gingrich was succeeded by Dennis Hastert, who showed himself to be more conciliatory and collegial than his predecessor – and was all the more popular for it. Ultimately, therefore, the speaker's power is dependent upon the will of the party caucus in the House. If it wants a strong leader, it will have one; but if it prefers to devolve power to committee chairs, there is little he can do about it.

House majority and minority leaders and whips

House majority and minority leaders and whips are chosen in intra-party elections. The majority leader's principal task is to support the work of the speaker. He also has a distinct advantage on the floor of the House, because he is always first to be recognised by the speaker. The minority leader, by definition, has no supportive relationship with the speaker. He does, however, carry out similar functions to those of the majority leader – liaising between party members, gathering intelligence and trying to persuade them to follow party policy. If the president is of the same party, then the minority leader will have an additional important task of liaising with the White House.

The main function of the majority and minority whips is to advise party members about important votes that are coming up and finding out their members' voting intentions. In this they are assisted by an elaborate network of junior whips. However, despite the large number of whips in the House, their influence over members' voting behaviour is limited. Despite the significantly increased activities of party leaders in the 1990s (Foley and Owens, 1996, p. 153), the fact remains that representatives are not dependent upon their party for either nomination or election to Congress. This means that party leaders lack the decisive weapon enjoyed by their counterparts in many other political systems: the power to deprive a member of his or her seat.

House caucus and conference chairpersons

The Democratic caucus and the Republican conference consist of all the members of the respective parties. If members wished it, the chairpersons of these two groups could wield considerable power, even more than that of the speaker and majority and minority leaders. Since the caucus or conference chooses all other party leaders, it has the potential to define the hierarchy of party leadership.

In practice, members who do not accept binding party discipline see little need for powerful caucus or conference leaders. Nevertheless, chairing the caucus can be a useful step on the political ladder for an ambitious member of Congress.

Senate party leaders

There is no equivalent position to that of the speaker in the Senate. The presiding officer stipulated in the Constitution is an outsider, namely the vice-president of the United States.

This means that the majority and minority leaders take on the mantle of party leaders. The majority leader, for example, has some of the same responsibilities as the speaker, including scheduling legislation, organising the chamber and acting as a focal point for party unity. The minority leader, when the president is of the other party, may also try to emulate the speaker by assuming the role of 'leader of the opposition'.

However, owing to the differences in culture between the two chambers, these positions are of less importance in the Senate than they are in the

House. Senators are more individualistic and less deferential than members of the House. This means that leadership in the Senate must be even more collegial in nature. Gone are the days of the 1950s when Lyndon B. Johnson, with the aid of a few senior senators, could cajole or even bully members into compliance. The Senate is much more a body of equals than it was then, and party leaders are expected to work in a cooperative rather than a hierarchical manner. Combined with the fact that they have no formal, constitutional basis for their power, they have little choice but to do so.

Congressional staffs

Senators and representatives are clearly the most prominent members of the Congress, but they are not the only important group in the legislature. Increasingly, the staff who support congressional committees and the individual members themselves are being seen as vital participants in the legislative process. Indeed, these congressional staff have been characterised as 'the invisible force in American lawmaking' (Fox and Hammond, 1977).

The number of these personal and committee aides has grown rapidly in the past 50 years, as well as the number of those working for congressional support agencies. Between 1967 and 1977, the number of staff working in the offices of members of Congress in Washington almost doubled, from 5,804 to 10,486. In the case of senators, in 1967 they had an average of 17.5 staff per member, including those working back at the offices in the state; by 1991, the average was 57 per member. Committee staff also grew rapidly in number, from a total of 1,337 in 1970 to 3,231 in 1991. When those working for support agencies, such as the Congressional Research Service, were included, it made for a total of some 24,000 staff working for Congress in the early 2000s (Davidson and Oleszek, 2004, p. 28). Although the levels stabilised at the end of the 1970s, owing mainly to financial constraints, and were then cut by the Republicans when they captured Congress in 1994, the thousands of congressional staff who remain must clearly fulfil important functions.

Committee staff

The rapid growth of committee staff began with the Legislative Reorganization Act of 1946. This permitted each standing committee to employ up to 4 professional staff and 6 clerical aides. The number was increased in 1970, and then in 1974 the House raised its number to 18 professional assistants and 12 clerical aides (Smith and Deering, 1990, p. 149). A variety of factors accounts for the increase. In the first place, Congress simply has to cope with more legislative work than before – this reflects the general growth in governmental activity in the United States since the Second World War.

Secondly, the marked upsurge in the 1970s was stimulated by the attempt to reassert congressional power vis-à-vis the presidency. Congressional laxity was seen as partly responsible for the Vietnam and Watergate episodes, and increasing staff was considered one means of strengthening both the legislative and oversight functions of Congress.

Thirdly, the subcommittee revolution of the 1970s also played a part, particularly in the House of Representatives. Between 1970 and 1990, the share of staff in the House attached to subcommittees, as opposed to full committees, rose from 23.2 per cent to 45.2 per cent (Smith and Deering, 1990, p. 152). Altogether, there are now some 2,000 staff attached to congressional committees and subcommittees (Schneider, 2003, p. 3).

Committee staff, and many personal staff, are thus closely involved in all the main functions of Congress. They organise hearings, draft legislation, meet interest groups and negotiate between members on details of policy and votes. Critics argue that they have become more influential than the elected legislators themselves, or that, rather than help deal with the congressional workload, they actually increase it unnecessarily in order to justify their existence.

Certainly, even major bills, such as the Budget and Impoundment Control Act of 1974, are marked up, given initial consideration and redrafted by staff (Fox and Hammond, 1977, p. 143). While the ultimate approval of such legislation remains with members themselves, there can be little doubt that the duties of congressional staff afford them considerable opportunities for influencing the content of national legislation.

Personal staff

As already noted, some of the staff attached personally to members of Congress carry out legislative and oversight functions. There is evidence to suggest, however, that most of the work done by personal staff is connected to the representative roles of members (Vogler, 1983, p. 130). Employed either in Washington, DC or in offices back in the state or district, they deal with constituents' complaints and problems, schedule meetings and personal appearances for the member and try to ensure a flow of good publicity. They also conduct frequent polls in order to try to keep their member in tune with political developments and moods among their constituents.

As usual with members of Congress, the electoral connection here is all too apparent. The ultimate task of personal staff engaged in representative work is to provide the high level of constituency service and political intelligence that will ensure their member's re-election. Given today's incumbency re-election success rates of better than 90 per cent, the creation of large personal staffs seems to have paid off.

Chapter summary

The central feature of legislative activity in Congress is the committee. Although the precise amount of power wielded by committees and their chairpersons varies over time, committees remain central because it is in committee that the details of legislation are hammered out. Committees are also important because they are the principal instrument of career progression for members. This is both because they offer the best opportunity for members to service their constituents' interests, thus enhancing their electoral prospects, and because service on a committee over time usually brings a steady increase in power and prestige with colleagues.

Party is also a significant factor in the organisation of Congress, because it brings coherence and discipline to legislative activity. Ultimately, however, members of Congress remain individualists who will come together with party colleagues when it appears to be in their interest, but will not hesitate to exploit the fragmented structures and processes to serve the needs of their constituents and their own careers. Legislating in Congress is therefore a complex and difficult process. It requires considerable bargaining and compromise in order to accommodate the diverse interests of members, for without such accommodation, it is relatively easy for a minority of members to block the legislative process.

Discussion points

1. Why is the committee system central to the legislative process in Congress?
2. Why is it so difficult to centralise authority within Congress?
3. What are the most important differences between the Senate and the House of Representatives?
4. What are the advantages and disadvantages of a national legislature that finds it difficult to legislate?

Further reading

See suggestions at the end of Chapter 14.

References

Bailey, C. (1989) *The US Congress* (Oxford: Basil Blackwell).

Davidson, R. and Oleszek, W. (2004) *Congress and Its Members* (9th edn, Washington, DC: CQ Press).

Foley, M. and Owens, J. (1996) *Congress and the Presidency: Institutional Politics in a Separated System* (Manchester: Manchester University Press).

Fox, H. and Hammond, S. (1977) *Congressional Staffs: The Invisible Force in American Lawmaking* (New York: Free Press).

Mayhew, D. (1974) *Congress: The Electoral Connection* (New Haven: Yale University Press).

Schneider, J. (2003) 'The Committee System in the US Congress' (Washington, DC: Congressional Research Service).

Smith, S. and Deering, C. (1990) *Committees in Congress* (2nd edn, Washington, DC: CQ Press).

Vogler, D. (1983) *The Politics of Congress* (4th edn, Boston: Allyn & Bacon).

Woll, P. (1985) *Congress* (Boston: Little, Brown).

Part 6

The judicial process

'We are under a Constitution, but the Constitution is what the judges say it is.' So said Charles Evan Hughes, politician and jurist, and later to become chief justice of the United States Supreme Court. His perceptive remark succinctly identifies the vital connection between the American political system and the American judiciary. As we saw in Part 1, American politics is conducted within the framework of a written Constitution which establishes the powers of different branches of government, as well as many of the fundamental rights and liberties of American citizens.

The Constitution, however, is a brief document, written mostly in broad, even vague language. Its precise meaning in any particular situation is rarely self-evident. Consequently, the application of constitutional law requires constitutional interpretation, and that has become the primary function of the federal judiciary, especially the United States Supreme Court.

In Part 6, we examine first the origins of the Supreme Court's role as the authoritative interpreter of the Constitution, and the procedures and processes through which it plays that role (Chapter 16). We then go on to analyse how and why the Supreme Court transcends its judicial role and is, in many ways, a political body. We assess, too, its overall importance and its impact upon American politics and society (Chapter 17).

Contents

Chapter 16

The Supreme Court and judicial review

The key to understanding the Supreme Court is to appreciate that it is both a judicial and a political body. This means that its formal structures and procedures are, in essence, those of a court of law, while its agenda, its interpretation of the Constitution and its impact are inescapably political. In this chapter, we focus primarily upon the legal and judicial aspects of the Court, although, as befits the dual nature of the institution, even here it is impossible to avoid a political dimension.

Article III of the Constitution deals with the judicial power of the American system of government and it makes the United States Supreme Court the nation's highest judicial body. Most importantly, this is the final court of appeal from the lower federal courts and the court systems of the 50 states in all cases involving the Constitution or federal laws.

In line with the principle of separation of powers, the framers of the Constitution wanted to ensure that the judges, or *justices*, of the Supreme Court would be truly independent of both the executive and legislative branches. They also wanted the Court to be beyond the control of the electorate. For these reasons, justices of the Supreme Court are appointed, not elected, and they are appointed for life, so that their tenure of office does not depend on pleasing either the people or their political representatives. There is no doubt, therefore, that the framers wanted a genuinely independent Supreme Court that would settle legal disputes without fear or favour.

Article III, however, says nothing about a political role for the Court. In particular, it does not say that the Supreme Court has the power to declare legislation or executive branch policies unconstitutional. Yet it is precisely this power over federal and state legislation that has changed the Court from being a mere judicial body into a major political force in the American system of government. Let us examine how and why this came about.

Judicial review

The foundation of the Supreme Court's legal and political power is the American version of the doctrine of *judicial review*. This empowers the Court to declare any law or action of a governmental institution to be unconstitutional. This entails a majority of the nine justices deciding that a challenged law or administrative action violates one or more clauses of the Constitution. When a law is declared unconstitutional by the Court, it is null and void. The power of judicial review extends beyond *constitutional interpretation*, however. The Supreme Court also adjudicates alleged violations of federal laws by state laws or by the actions of private organisations. This is known as *statutory interpretation*.

There is, however, a crucial difference between constitutional interpretation and statutory interpretation. If the Supreme Court interprets a federal statute in a way that offends Congress, then the legislators can simply amend the law to nullify the Court's decision. If, on the other hand, a Court decision is based upon constitutional interpretation, then Congress has no power to overturn it. True, it can initiate the process of constitutional amendment, but this is extremely difficult to bring to a successful conclusion. In virtually all cases, then, a decision of the Supreme Court based upon constitutional interpretation is final, unless the Court can be persuaded to change its mind.

The power of judicial review, therefore, has serious implications for the operation of American democracy. Since, in principle, all government policies can be challenged in the federal courts as unconstitutional, it can be argued that the Supreme Court, as the final court of appeal, is superior to both the Congress and the president in matters of legislation and public policy. Indeed, critics of the Court have sometimes alleged that the United States has 'government by judiciary'.

In fact, such charges are a gross exaggeration. As we shall see, there are many practical restrictions on the power of judicial review. Nevertheless, because the Supreme Court is recognised as the authoritative interpreter of the Constitution, it has a stature and role in American government that makes it a political force to be reckoned with. Remarkably, however, it is not at all clear that the framers of the Constitution intended the Court to play such an important role.

Inventing the Supreme Court

As noted above, Article III of the Constitution clearly created a *court* when it opened with the words 'The judicial power of the United States shall be vested in one Supreme Court, and in such inferior courts as the Congress may from time to time ordain and establish.'

As many scholars have pointed out, however, Article III makes no mention of judicial review or of the power of the Supreme Court to declare legislation unconstitutional. Nor does the Judiciary Act of 1789, by which Congress created the first federal court system. In other words, both the Constitution and the first congressional legislation on the matter are silent on the very power that today makes the Supreme Court a major actor in American politics.

The explanation for this silence is not entirely clear. Some argue that it was simply *assumed* by the constitutional framers that the Court would exercise judicial review and be able to strike down state and congressional laws. This is implausible, given that the framers spelled out the basic powers of the executive and legislative branches with varying levels of precision, even where they were uncontroversial. A more likely explanation is that getting agreement on judicial review, especially in respect of acts of Congress, was too difficult to achieve in the time available. While some framers supported judicial review, others did not: the latter believed it was simply undemocratic and would be employed on behalf of conservative policies. Those who favoured it argued that fears of judicial autocracy were fanciful, though they did hope that judicial review would act as a brake on the 'democratic excesses' of the electorate. No agreement was reached at Philadelphia and, accordingly, the wording of Article III was left vague.

The proponents of judicial review, however, continued their campaign. In the course of the public debates over ratification of the new Constitution,

Alexander Hamilton established their basic case in a three-step argument in *The Federalist* (no. 78). First, he pointed out that, since the Constitution was the supreme law of the United States, legislative Acts which conflicted with it must be illegitimate. Secondly, in the event that such a conflict was alleged to exist, some body or another must be empowered to interpret the Constitution in order to arbitrate the dispute. Thirdly, Hamilton argued that the Supreme Court was the logical institution to play this role: after all, courts had traditionally performed the task of interpreting other forms of law. Moreover, to allow legislative bodies to exercise review, as some suggested, would create the unsatisfactory situation in which legislators would sit in judgement on the constitutionality of their own actions. To say the least, this would raise doubts about their impartiality in the matter.

Hamilton made one further argument of great importance: he denied that giving the Court the power to strike down Acts of Congress and state legislatures would make the federal judiciary the most powerful branch of government. On the contrary, he famously predicted that a Supreme Court endowed with judicial review would prove 'the least dangerous branch' of the government, because it possessed 'neither Force nor Will, but only judgment'. By this, he meant that the Court was inherently weaker than either the Congress or the presidency. Those two branches controlled both expenditure and law enforcement and without these the Court was in no position to implement its decisions. It would have to rely on the cooperation of Congress and the president. Furthermore, Congress and the president were driven by the will and desires of the population, something which

Box 16.1

Marbury v. *Madison* (1803) and the creation of judicial review

Chief Justice Marshall headed a thoroughly Federalist Supreme Court when the *Marbury* case came before it. Yet the politics of the issues involved were most delicate. Towards the end of the outgoing Federalist administration of President John Adams (1797–1801), several new justices of the peace were appointed, all staunch Federalists, but their commissions were not delivered before the new administration of President Thomas Jefferson (1801–9) took over. Given the bitter rivalry between Federalists and Jeffersonians, the new secretary of state, James Madison, refused to complete delivery of the commissions, one of which was destined for William Marbury. Marbury went to court, claiming that Section 13 of the Judiciary Act of 1789 empowered the Supreme Court to order Madison to complete delivery of his commission.

The Court sympathised with Marbury, but knew that a decision in his favour would invoke the wrath – and disobedience – of the Jefferson administration. Since this would damage the Court's prestige and, therefore, its potential use as an instrument of Federalist power, the Marshall Court ruled in favour of Madison. However, it did so in a manner that made the Court a vital player in the future of American politics. Marshall argued that he could not order Madison to complete Marbury's commission because Section 13 of the Judiciary Act violated the Constitution by enlarging the Court's power of *Original Jurisdiction*; and that such an enlargement could only be achieved by constitutional amendment, and not by federal statute. Many scholars doubt the validity of Marshall's argument. However, it was politically adroit. Mollified by their immediate victory, the Jeffersonians denounced the chief justice and his concept of judicial review, but did nothing substantial to negate the Court's claim to possess the power to declare an act of Congress unconstitutional.

could lead to rash actions. The justices of the Supreme Court, on the other hand, would not be ideological partisans: they would be impartial legal technicians – judges – who merely established the facts of whether a given law conflicted with a given clause of the Constitution.

Plausible as it was, Hamilton's argument did not yet convince the country. As a result, the early years of the Supreme Court were exceedingly dull and uneventful. Without the power of judicial review, the Court lacked stature compared with the Congress, the presidency or even the higher offices of state government. As a consequence, it proved difficult to persuade people of high standing to serve on the Court and it appeared destined to play only a minor part in the nation's government.

Marbury v. *Madison*: a political coup

The transformation in the role and power of the Supreme Court came in 1803, as a direct result of the bitterly fought presidential election of 1800. The more conservative Federalist party, having lost that election to the Jeffersonians, sought to use their remaining months in office to make the unelected judiciary a bastion of Federalist power. Most significantly, the outgoing Federalist secretary of state, John Marshall, was appointed chief justice of the Supreme Court.

In the case of *Marbury* v. *Madison* (1803), Marshall and his colleagues staged a political coup by claiming the power to declare an Act of Congress unconstitutional. With consummate skill, Marshall avoided a political war with the Jeffersonians – a war the Court was bound to lose – yet simultaneously won implicit acceptance of the power of judicial review. To Chief Justice John Marshall, then, goes the ultimate credit for making judicial review of legislation a significant reality of American political life.

We will examine in the next chapter how the Marshall Court and its successors used the power it had awarded itself. First, though, it is important to understand how the process of judicial review works. For this reminds us that, no matter how embroiled it becomes in politics, the Supreme Court operates in a completely different manner from other political institutions. Quite simply, it is a *court*, and therefore its procedures are those of a court.

Stages of judicial review

Initiating a case

There are several formal steps through which any Supreme Court case proceeds. The first is that an individual, organisation or government body must decide to *litigate*: that is, to bring a lawsuit in a lower federal court or a state court. These litigants must do more than merely allege that someone has violated the Constitution: they must show that they have personally suffered some concrete harm as a result of the violation.

In theory, this first stage means that litigation cannot be used simply as a forum for political debate or controversy. For example, the requirement that the litigants must have a real stake in the case aims to prevent people from challenging laws simply because they oppose them on political grounds.

It is also important to note that the judiciary cannot take the initiative on an issue, unlike the president or the Congress. Rather, it must wait until the issue is placed before the courts in the form of a lawsuit. Moreover, it is not usually possible to take a case straight to the Supreme Court: litigants must work their way up through the hierarchy of lower courts and so a case may take several years before the justices settle the question definitively.

These constraints on the Court's freedom of manoeuvre are in line with the language of Article III of the Constitution, which says that the Court's power extends to all 'cases and controversies' arising under the Constitution. Cases must be real legal disputes, not merely hypothetical or political arguments.

Interest group intervention

In practice, litigation today is frequently initiated by specialist interest groups whose strategies are legal but whose mission is entirely political. These groups seek out individuals who have real cases

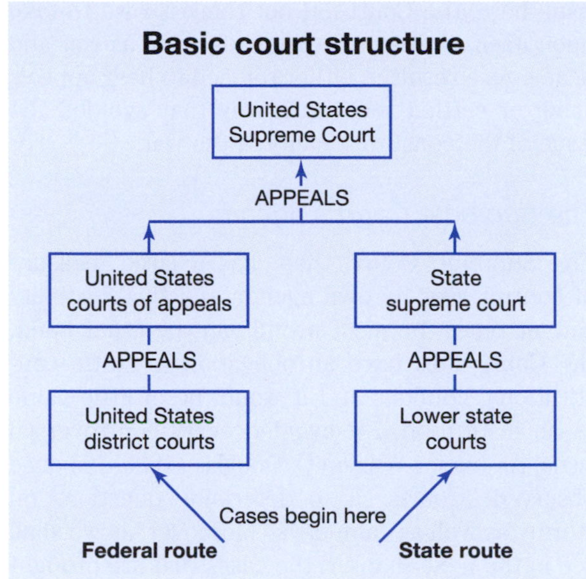

and effectively take them over. They provide individual litigants with the legal and financial resources to take their case through the expensive minefield of preparing and arguing cases in the judicial system – if necessary, going through one or more appeals to get to the Supreme Court. These organisations hope that, by winning a concrete case for the individual, they will simultaneously win a constitutional ruling that will benefit others. In short, these interest groups sponsor or manufacture test cases which they hope will have wide social and political significance.

Perhaps the most famous example of the successful use of the courts to bring about political reforms is that by the National Association for the Advancement of Colored People (NAACP). This group sponsored some of the main cases in the racial segregation controversies of the 1950s and 1960s and became a role model for other litigation groups.

The American Civil Liberties Union (ACLU) is another group which frequently sponsors litigation on behalf of liberal political causes. In the 1970s, for example, it created a specialist branch, the Women's Rights Project, which proved successful in persuading the Supreme Court that the Constitution should be interpreted to ban most of the legal distinctions between men and women.

Class-action suits

An important legal device which greatly aids the political use of the courts by interest groups is the so-called class-action suit. This means that an individual who brings a case may do so not merely on her own behalf, but also for all those similarly situated. An example would be that of an African-American parent whose children are denied entry to a school because of their race. As well as suing to have her own children admitted, a class action enables her to sue on behalf of all African-American parents throughout the entire country whose children are similar victims of racial discrimination. Class actions, then, combined with the activities of litigation interest groups, ensure that major political issues are frequently brought to the courts, albeit in the guise of lawsuits.

Appeals

As noted above, the first round of a constitutional case takes place in a federal district court or a state court. (The only exceptions are the one or two cases each year which come direct to the Court under its *Original Jurisdiction*.) When the decision is announced in the lower court, the loser may appeal to either a federal appeals court or a state's highest court. These courts may affirm or reverse the lower court's decision but, either way, the loser may then try an appeal to the Supreme Court.

At this point, however, we come to a most important feature of the Supreme Court. It is not obliged to hear any appeal. Originally, there were a considerable number of appeals that the Court was obliged to hear. Owing to the Court's increasingly heavy workload, however, Congress has removed virtually all mandatory appeals and has left the Court with full discretion over its docket. Thus, the justices receive thousands of petitions for appeal each year, mostly in the form of petitions for review called *writs of certiorari* – however, the Court frequently accepts fewer than one hundred of these for full consideration: that is, cases accepted and decided with written opinions (see Table 16.1).

The Court is not obliged to give any reason for its refusal to hear the thousands of appeals it rejects

Table 16.1 The Supreme Court's discretionary control: cases granted review

Term	Review granted	Petitions considered	% granted
2008/09	87	7868	1.1%
2007/08	95	8374	1.1%
2006/07	77	8922	0.9%
2005/06	78	8236	0.9%
2004/05	80	7542	1.1%

Source: Annual statistical review of the Supreme Court, *Harvard Law Review*, various years

each year, which means that the justices can avoid involvement in an issue if they wish. A prime example of this occurred during the Vietnam War, when anti-war activists wanted the Court to pronounce the war unconstitutional because President Johnson had never asked Congress for a formal declaration of war. Although there was a clear constitutional issue here, the Court did not think it wise to take upon itself such a momentous decision as war and peace. As a result, it either refused to hear appeals at all or settled them in a way that avoided the issue of the constitutionality of the war.

The Supreme Court's agenda

The Supreme Court, then, has a large measure of control over its own agenda and this flexibility can, at times, be most useful. On the other hand, the Court does have an obligation to settle constitutional conflicts and it would be of little value as an institution if it avoided every controversial issue. As Justice William O. Douglas (1939–75) once observed: 'Courts sit to determine questions on stormy as well as calm days.' Moreover, as we shall see in the next chapter, the cases that are brought before the Court are often precisely those which are politically controversial. So, as the nineteenth-century commentator Alexis de Tocqueville famously

Figure 16.1 Supreme Court decisions on the separation of Church and State suggest that even the Pledge of Allegiance may be declared unconstitutional due to its mention of God.
Source: © Bob Gorrell

said (admittedly with a measure of exaggeration): 'Scarcely any political question arises in the United States that is not resolved, sooner or later, into a judicial question.'

Judicial decision-making: the formal procedures

The basic procedures that the justices of the Supreme Court follow in deciding a case are relatively straightforward. First comes the decision whether or not to take an appeal at all: five votes are formally needed to grant judicial review of a case, but the custom is that the 'rule of four' applies. Thus if four justices favour review, a fifth justice will supply the additional vote.

Next, the Court schedules a date for *oral argument*. This is when lawyers for each party to the case will appear before the justices and in public to present the arguments for their clients. Normally, each side is allowed 30 minutes to speak, but the lawyers may be frequently interrupted by questions from the justices. The record suggests that the justices are rarely swayed by the oral arguments, and the questions they put to the lawyers are intended mainly to draw attention to a point which they have already decided is dispositive, one way or the other.

This is in part because, before oral argument, the lawyers will have submitted detailed, written *briefs* stating their arguments in full. Furthermore, interest groups also frequently submit briefs at this stage. Although not always a party to the case, an interest group is allowed to participate as an amicus curiae (literally, friend of the court). In its amicus brief, the interest group will hope to place before the justices evidence or arguments that they may find persuasive. Some briefs rely on the special expertise of the group concerned. For example, in cases concerning abortion rights, the American Medical Association submitted briefs which addressed the specifically medical aspects of the abortion issue. Other groups may offer innovative legal arguments or, like the National Organization for Women, hope to impress the justices with the fact that their large membership deems abortion rights to be fundamental to their lives.

Another significant participant at this point may be the federal government, in the form of the solicitor-general. Coming below the attorney-general, the solicitor-general is the second-ranking member of the Department of Justice. The solicitor-general frequently appears before the Court, either because the United States is itself a party to the case, or because it has a particular view to articulate as an amicus curiae.

For much of the period since 1870, when the office was created, the solicitor-general was regarded by the justices as a valued source of neutral, legal expertise. Because of this, the solicitor-general was often referred to as 'the tenth justice'. However, like virtually every other aspect of the Court's environment, the office has recently become much more politicised. Under President Reagan, for example, the solicitor-general was sent to the Court as the standard-bearer of the administration's crusade against abortion rights and affirmative action. As a consequence, the office lost some of the respect previously shown to it by the justices.

Case conference

After reading the briefs and hearing the oral arguments, the justices meet in a *case conference* to discuss and to take preliminary votes. About one-third of cases are decided unanimously, but most involve at least one dissenting justice (see Table 16.2).

In theory, a 5–4 decision is as authoritative as a unanimous decision. In practice, however, the former is far more vulnerable to attack than the latter. First, a 5–4 split indicates that there may be good constitutional reasons for believing the case to have been decided wrongly. Secondly, a 5–4 decision can easily be reversed when one of the majority justices leaves the Court and a new one is appointed. A unanimous decision, on the other hand, is well-nigh unassailable. In the major cases where it is possible, therefore, the justices work hard to produce unanimity, including making compromises over the wording and scope of the opinion. This will help to sustain a decision which is likely to meet with resistance in some quarters. Unanimity was an important feature, for example, of the

Table 16.2 Unanimity rates on the Court: decisions with full opinions

Term	Unanimous decisions	With concurring opinions	With dissenting opinions
2008/09	19 (24.4%)	6 (7.7%)	53 (67.9%)
2007/08	21 (28%)	5 (6.7%)	49 (65.3%)
2006/07	21 (28.8%)	5 (6.8%)	47 (64.4%)
2005/06	36 (44.4%)	8 (9.9%)	37 (45.7%)
2004/05	24 (30.4%)	6 (7.6%)	49 (62.0%)

Source: Annual statistical review of the Supreme Court, *Harvard Law Review*, various years

Court's desegregation decision, *Brown* v. *Board of Education* (1954), and also of its decision ordering President Nixon to release the 'Watergate tapes' (*US* v. *Nixon*, 1974).

After the vote, the chief justice, provided he is with the majority, assigns himself or another member of the majority the task of producing a formal, written *opinion* explaining the Court's decision. If, however, the chief justice is in the minority, then the most senior associate justice in the majority assigns the opinion. Those justices in the minority may well decide to write a *dissenting opinion*, explaining why they disagree with the majority. Yet a third type of opinion is the *concurrence*, in which a justice usually explains that he agrees with the majority's decision but for different reasons than those given in the Court's opinion.

Before the Court's decision is formally announced, draft versions of these opinions are circulated among the justices for their comment and may well be amended as a result. Votes may even be switched at this stage. Eventually, the Court announces its decision and the opinion(s) are published.

Although few people outside of politics, the law schools and the media actually read Supreme Court opinions, they are nevertheless very important. The opinion of the Court is both an explanation and a justification of the Court's decision. An opinion which fails to convince those who read it will give ammunition to those who disapprove of the result.

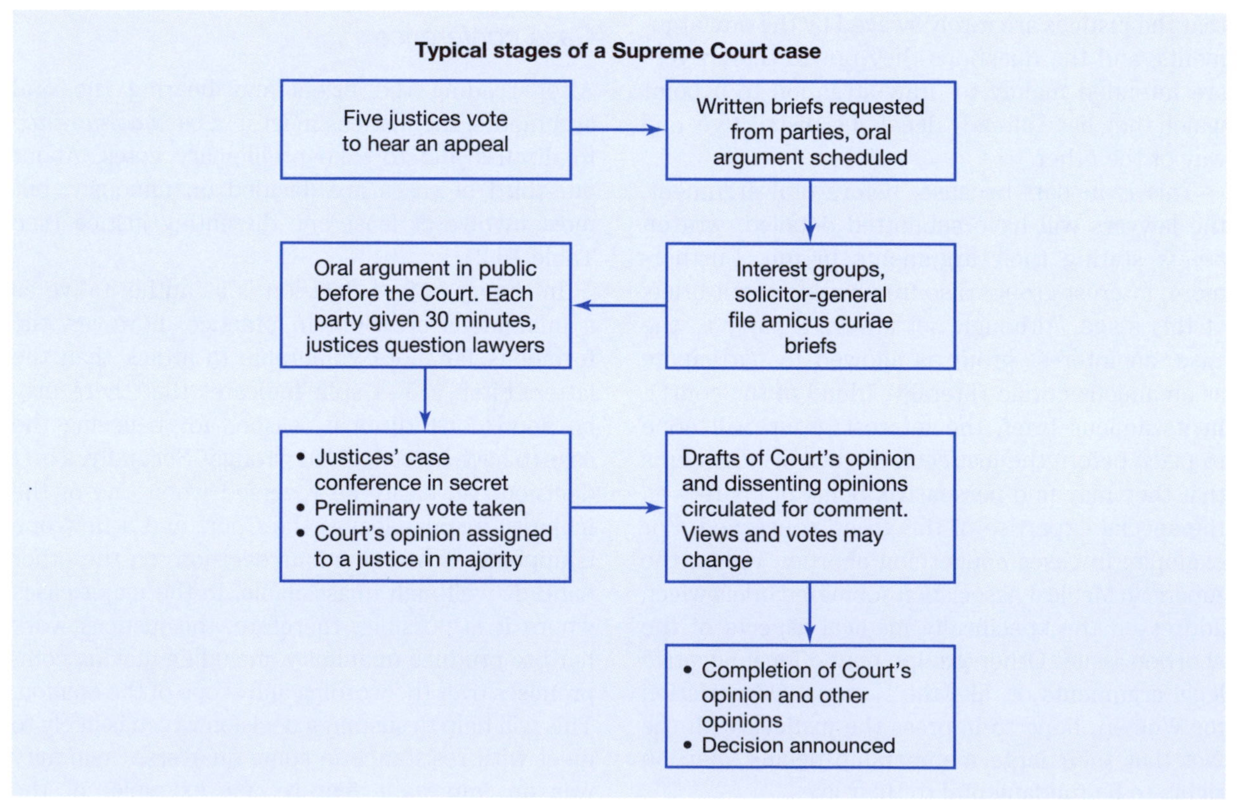
Typical stages of a Supreme Court case
Five justices vote to hear an appeal
Written briefs requested from parties, oral argument scheduled
Interest groups, solicitor-general file amicus curiae briefs
Oral argument in public before the Court. Each party given 30 minutes, justices question lawyers
• Justices' case conference in secret
• Preliminary vote taken
• Court's opinion assigned to a justice in majority
Drafts of Court's opinion and dissenting opinions circulated for comment. Views and votes may change
• Completion of Court's opinion and other opinions
• Decision announced

For example, the opinion of the Court in *Roe* v. *Wade* (1973), which announced a new right to abortion, was deemed seriously flawed, even by some who support abortion rights. This has strengthened the hand of pro-life activists who wish to see *Roe* overturned.

Judicial reasoning and politics

The procedures outlined above are those of a court, not those of what we traditionally think of as a political institution. Moreover, as we saw from Alexander Hamilton's defence of judicial review, Supreme Court justices were expected to eschew politics and to carry out their duties in a politically neutral manner. Yet today there are many judicial scholars who argue that it is neither possible nor even desirable for the justices to escape from their own political, philosophical or moral values. Others, however, believe that the Court can usually make decisions that are politically neutral and that it should at least always attempt to do so. Let us examine each of these arguments in turn.

Judicial traditionalism

Until the twentieth century, the notion of politically neutral, or value-free, Supreme Court justices was largely accepted. At the heart of this concept was the belief that, when a justice struck down a law as unconstitutional, he was not enforcing his own values but rather the values enshrined in the Constitution by the framers. The justice merely used his legal knowledge and skills to discover what the will, or intention, of the framers actually was and how it should be applied in the particular case before the Court.

Justice Owen Roberts expressed this view of judicial neutrality in 1936 in the case of *US* v. *Butler*. The decision in *Butler* was one of a series in which the Court struck down some key elements of President Franklin D. Roosevelt's New Deal. Many people thought the justices were simply motivated by their ideological conservatism. Roberts, however, rejected this accusation:

> It is sometimes said that the Court assumes the power to overrule or control the action of the people's representatives. This is a misconception. The Constitution is the supreme law of the land ordained and established by the people. All legislation must conform to the principles it lays down. When an Act of Congress is appropriately challenged in the courts as not conforming to the constitutional mandate, the judicial branch of government has only one duty – to lay the article of the Constitution which is invoked beside the statute which is challenged and to decide whether the latter squares with the former. All the Court does or can do is to announce its considered judgment upon the question. The only power it has, if such it may be called, is the power of judgment. This Court neither approves nor condemns any legislative policy.

Roberts sought to make a vital distinction between the *political result* of a Supreme Court decision and the *process* by which that decision was made. Thus, although the decision in *Butler* had great political significance because it scuppered President Roosevelt's policy for agricultural recovery, that did not mean that the Court's decision was motivated by a desire to defeat that policy. All Roberts and his colleagues had done, he maintained, was judge that the policy was at odds with the design of the Constitution. That was a quite separate question from whether the policy was good for the country.

Today, judicial traditionalists emphasise that the justices of the Supreme Court must follow the original intentions of those who framed the Constitution. They argue that the doctrine of *original intent* prevents justices from inflicting their personal policy preferences on the country. In turn, this secures the legitimacy of judicial review in a democracy. For if, on the contrary, the justices abandon original intent and substitute their own or some other set of values for those intended by the framers, then unelected judges are, in effect, selecting the values and policies that govern the country. Such a situation, they claim, is more akin to judicial autocracy than representative democracy.

As we shall see shortly, many doubt whether judicial neutrality is really possible. However, there

Box 16.2

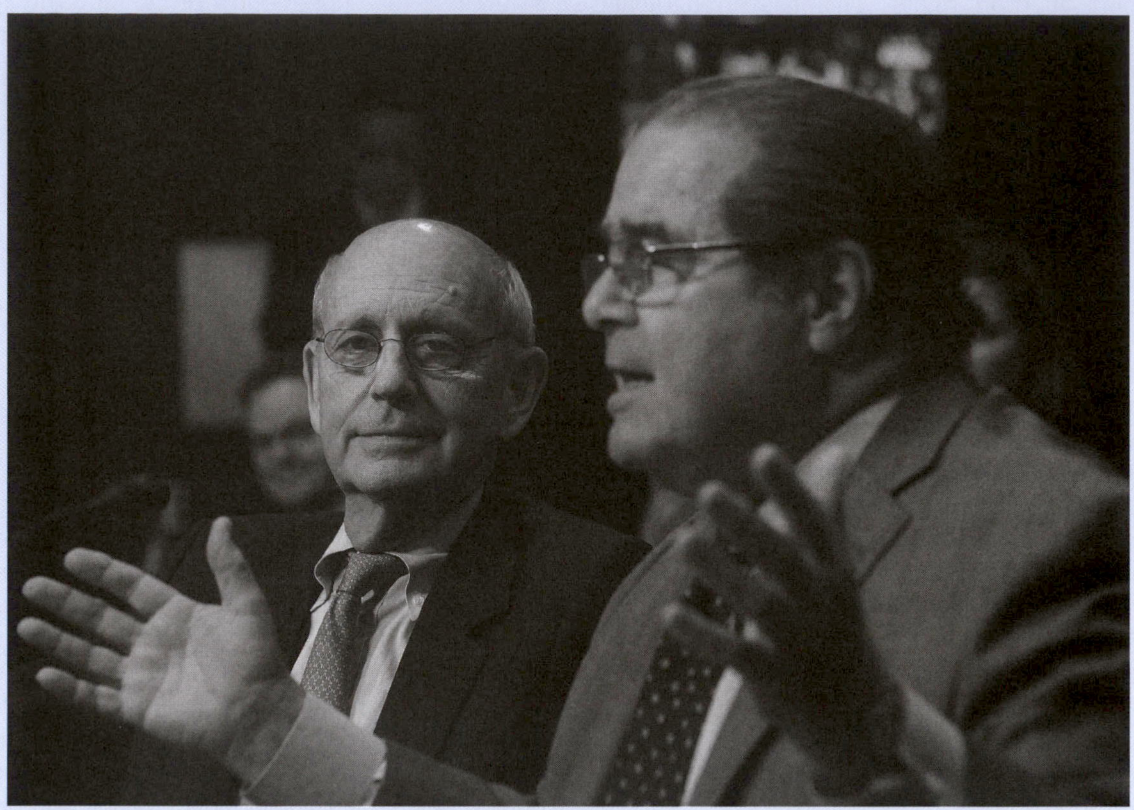

On the contemporary Supreme Court, Justices Antonin Scalia (right) and Stephen Breyer (left) take opposing views on how the Constitution should be interpreted and both have written books to explain their ideas. For Scalia, the Court must follow the original intent of those who wrote the Constitution. It must understand and interpret constitutional language as it would have been understood and interpreted at the time it was originally written. Breyer, on the other hand, believes that those who wrote the Constitution did not intend to tie the hands of future generations in the manner that originalists suggest. Rather, the Court should look to the broad purpose behind constitutional language and apply it within a contemporary framework of understanding and social needs.

Source: © Getty Images/Jewel Samad

are plenty of instances in which justices of the Supreme Court have clearly voted in line with what they see as the command of the Constitution, even though this meant going against their own personal values. For example, in the 1972 case of *Furman* v. *Georgia*, Justice Harry Blackmun declared himself to be personally opposed to capital punishment, yet he voted to uphold the constitutionality of various state death penalty laws. And in 1989, in the highly emotive decision in *Texas* v. *Johnson*, Justice Anthony Kennedy voted to uphold the right to burn the American flag as a political protest, even though he expressed his distaste for that activity. He ruefully noted that 'The hard fact is that sometimes we must make decisions we do not like. We make them because they are right, right in the sense that the law and the Constitution, as we see them, compel the result.'

Judicial modernists

Other justices and scholars see many problems in the doctrine of original intent. In the first place, it is by no means always easy to establish exactly what the framers did intend. We have already seen that they left Article III unclear on the role and powers of the Supreme Court and the same lack of precision characterises many other clauses of the Constitution. What is an 'unreasonable search and seizure' (Fourth Amendment) or a 'cruel and unusual punishment' (Eighth Amendment)? Traditionalists argue that, where the text of the Constitution is unclear, the historical record surrounding it will help. Not so, say the modernists: evidence such as debates in Congress may simply reveal that politicians who supported a particular constitutional clause did so for different reasons and with different understandings of what was intended.

However, modernists believe that, even if the original meaning of a clause is clear, it does not follow that the justices should be bound by it. After all, they argue, much of the Constitution was written in 1787 and those who drafted it could not possibly foresee the needs and values of American society in future centuries. Chief Justice Marshall, the architect of judicial review, identified this dilemma early on. In 1819, in *McCulloch* v. *Maryland*, he wrote that the Constitution was 'intended to endure for ages to come, and, consequently, to be adapted to the various crises of human affairs'. Marshall thus created the concept of the *living Constitution*. In this view, the Constitution is an organism which must grow and adapt as society develops. It is the duty of the Court to interpret it flexibly, so that the country is not oppressed by the dead hand of the past.

In effect, this power to reinterpret the Constitution in the light of changing societal needs can amount to the power to amend the Constitution. For this reason, Woodrow Wilson once famously wrote, 'The Supreme Court is a constitutional convention in continuous session.' Of course, the original Constitution did provide for a process of amendment in Article V, but this is too cumbersome to be invoked on every occasion when a significant innovation is required. Many scholars and, indeed, judges believe that, while the Supreme Court must be faithful to the spirit of the original Constitution, it must define that spirit by reference to contemporary values. As Justice William Brennan said in 1985 in response to traditionalist criticisms: 'We current justices read the Constitution in the only way that we can: as twentieth-century Americans.'

Virtually all justices today accept that their task of interpreting the Constitution involves some measure of 'updating'. A clear example is the current interpretation of the Eighth Amendment's ban on 'cruel and unusual punishments': even those who most admire intentionalism agree that ear-clipping, branding and other punishments familiar to the framers in 1787 are no longer permissible.

What divides the justices, then, is the degree of creativity they allow themselves in applying the Constitution. At one end of the spectrum is the 'intentionalist' or 'strict interpretivist', whose ideal it is to follow closely the will of the framers. At the opposite end are the 'non-interpretivists', who not only pay little or no heed to the original meaning of the Constitution, but are also willing to create new rights on subjects that the framers had never even contemplated. Between these two extremes are those justices, probably a majority, who take a pragmatic approach, trying to harmonise fidelity to original meaning with the demands of contemporary realities.

Judicial role

We can see from the above discussion that the concept of 'judicial role' is an important one in understanding how the Court works. Unlike others involved in making decisions that determine public policy, most Supreme Court justices do not believe that they can simply vote for their own political preferences. Even the most non-interpretivist of justices will at least argue in his written opinion that his vote is explained by his understanding of what the Constitution requires, rather than his personal notions of good public policy. As the traditionalist scholar and failed Supreme Court

Box 16.3

Approaches to constitutional interpretation

Traditionalist	Pragmatist	Modernist
Strict interpretivism or 'Strict Construction'	Balances traditionalist concerns against those of modernists	*Non-interpretivism or 'Broad Construction'*
Follows the original intent of the framers		Disregards original intent, creative in applying contemporary values to interpret the Constitution

nominee, Robert Bork, once commented with acid humour: 'The way an institution advertises tells you what it thinks its customers demand.' For the fact is that the public *does* expect the justices of the Supreme Court to behave like judges, and not like politicians. Moreover, much of the authority and prestige which the Court possesses depends upon its being perceived as, if not totally above politics, then at least different from 'politics as usual'.

Box 16.4

Politics, statesmanship and the Court: *Bush* v. *Gore* (2000)

No other modern Supreme Court case has provoked such accusations of political decision-making by the justices as *Bush* v. *Gore*. The case arose out of the close and confused presidential election in Florida. Victory in Florida was originally awarded to George W. Bush, but the margin was extremely narrow – the first official figure was 1,784 (out of almost 6 million votes cast), but this was to fluctuate over the following weeks. The Democratic candidate, Al Gore, challenged the result, arguing that some ballot papers had not been counted, even though it was possible to see in them a clear intention to vote for a candidate. This was the issue of the 'hanging chads' – ballot papers which the voting machines had failed to punch a clear hole through. The Gore campaign asked several counties to undertake a manual re-count, with a view to including those previously rejected ballots. The Constitution assigns the supervision of presidential elections to each of the states and their judicial systems. The pro-Bush Florida secretary of state, Katherine Harris, insisted that any re-counts had to be finished within one week of the election. There then began a series of cases in the Florida courts over what deadlines should be imposed on the re-counts. As the weeks passed, and re-counts were started and stopped and then restarted, the situation became even more confused. Eventually, the Bush campaign asked the Supreme Court to intervene, arguing that the re-counts in the various counties were using different criteria to assess the intention of the voter and that this violated the Equal Protection clause of the Fourteenth Amendment.

In a 5–4 vote, the most conservative justices stopped the re-counts and effectively handed victory to George W. Bush, while the four more liberal members would have left the issue with the Florida courts, with the possibility that Al Gore might eventually take the state and the presidency.

Most observers believed the justices had all decided the case on the basis of who they wanted to see elected president. The accusation was all the more serious because whoever won the election would nominate the replacement justice for any who retired in the next four years. To many, this was an inexcusable and unacceptable violation of the separation of powers. However, there is another possible explanation. The Court may, with some justification, have decided that the wrangle over Florida needed to be brought to an end. The election had taken place on 7 November and over a month had passed by the time the Court issued its decision on 12 December. There was also the distinct possibility that the wrangle would continue well into the future. If Gore had been declared the winner, the Bush camp would certainly have challenged *that* result in the courts. Moreover, there was the suspicion that Florida judges, as well as its politicians, were engaged in a partisan struggle to ensure their preferred candidate became president. It is plausible, therefore, to think that the nation needed an end to the Florida wrangling and needed to know who would be president in January. In short, while the Court may have intervened when it was not constitutionally required to, it acted in a diplomatic fashion by bringing a political crisis to an end. A majority of the public approved of the Court's decision, even though, of course, a majority had not voted for George W. Bush. The episode shows that the Court is held in high esteem by the public and is trusted to settle disputes in a manner that the other branches of government are not.

The Supreme Court therefore has a delicate role to perform in American politics. On the one hand, it is expected to be a judicial body which is politically impartial, and which must attempt to transcend passing political passions and uphold the eternal values of the Constitution. On the other hand, it is expected to resolve the sometimes highly charged political controversies which come before it in the form of lawsuits, with the inevitable result that its decisions will have a profound political impact and be attacked vehemently by whichever party has lost the case. Moreover, these judicial decisions are often made under considerable political pressure, since the presidency, the Congress, interest groups, legal scholars, the media and the public may all seek to influence the Court in its decision.

In the next chapter, we examine how well the Court has performed this delicate balancing act. We will see that the Court has become increasingly politicised in all its aspects, including the process by which new Supreme Court justices are appointed. Finally, we shall assess whether, for all the controversies that surround the Court, its power to make public policies has been exaggerated.

Chapter summary

The Supreme Court was established as a judicial body and thus its formal structures and processes are those of a court of law. However, the acquisition of the power of judicial review transformed the Court. Authorised now to declare legislation and executive decisions unconstitutional, the Court necessarily became involved in the policy-making process. Moreover, because constitutional interpretation often requires the justices to define vague and highly political concepts, such as equality and liberty, it is an inherently political process. The Supreme Court therefore has a dual nature, part judicial and part political. Its decisions can have a major impact on public policy and its judicial decision-making processes require an infusion of political, moral and philosophical reasoning.

Discussion points

1. What grounds are there for doubting that the framers of the Constitution intended the Supreme Court to exercise the power of judicial review?
2. To what extent is constitutional interpretation an inherently political exercise?
3. How, if at all, do the Supreme Court's legal structures and processes restrict its political power?
4. What is the significance of interest group participation in the Supreme Court's decision-making process?
5. Is it acceptable from the point of view of democratic principles that the Supreme Court can 'update' the Constitution?

Further reading

Two very useful reference works on the Supreme Court are: Kermit L. Hall (ed.) *The Oxford Companion to the Supreme Court of the United States* (2nd edn, Oxford: Oxford University Press, 2005) and Lee Epstein *et al.* (eds) *The Supreme Court Compendium: Data, Decisions and Developments* (4th edn, Washington, DC: CQ Press, 2007). A basic introductory book on the Supreme Court is Kenneth Jost (ed.), *The Supreme Court A–Z* (Washington, DC: CQ Press, 2003). A more sophisticated but very accessible discussion of the interaction between politics and law and the policy-making role of the Court is David M. O'Brien's *Storm Centre: The Supreme Court in American Politics* (8th edn, New York: Norton, 2008). A very readable account of the contemporary Court is Jeffrey Toobin's *The Nine: Inside the Secret World of the Supreme Court* (New York: Anchor Books, 2008). On the appointment process, the most comprehensive work is Henry Abraham's *Justices and Presidents* (5th edn, Lanham, Md.: Rowman & Littlefield, 2008). See also Robert J. McKeever, 'Presidential Strategies in the New Politics of Supreme Court Appointments', in George Edwards and Philip Davies (eds) *New Challenges for the American Presidency* (London: Pearson, 2004).

Websites

http://www.supremecourtus.gov
This is the official website of the US Supreme Court and contains much valuable information about the Court and the Justices. It also has all the Court's Opinions, even the most recent ones.

http://www.oyez.org
This is a great website for Supreme Court enthusiasts, created by Professor Jerry Goldman of Northwestern University. Among other things, it contains audio-visual materials, including recordings of oral arguments before the Supreme Court.

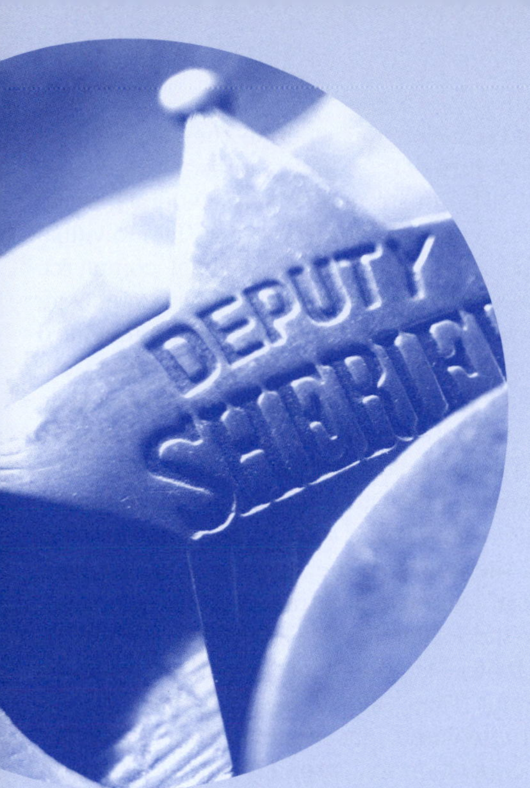

Chapter 17

The Supreme Court and American politics

We saw in the previous chapter that the Supreme Court's power of judicial review makes it a potentially powerful player in American politics. In this chapter, we examine how the Court has used this power in different historical periods. We also analyse the constraints upon the political role and power of the Court and assess its overall significance in the political system. Finally, we examine the men and women who wield the power of judicial review – the justices of the Supreme Court – and the nature of the process by which they are appointed.

The Supreme Court's role as the authoritative interpreter of the Constitution has been applied to two broad areas of government and politics. First, the Supreme Court defines the powers of other government offices established by the Constitution. Thus it settles disputes over the relative powers of Congress and the presidency, and over the relative powers of the federal government and the governments of the 50 states. In other words, the Court interprets the Constitution to determine exactly what is required by the separation of powers and by the principle of federalism. Thus, in *Clinton* v. *New York* (1998), the Court declared unconstitutional the congressional grant of a line-item veto to the president. The Court reasoned that the Constitution empowered the president to veto only an entire bill, rather than a part of one, and therefore that the only way he could acquire a line-item veto was through the process of constitutional amendment.

Secondly, the Supreme Court settles disputes over the constitutional legitimacy of particular legislative acts or other policy decisions. Of course, sometimes both these kinds of dispute are involved in the same case. However, it is useful to bear this distinction in mind when considering the controversies that have arisen over the Court's decisions, for, generally speaking, decisions on the precise parameters of the powers of the president or Congress do not generate much public excitement. When a case involves the legitimacy of particular policies, however, that is when the Court is likely to occupy the public limelight, simply because such policies tend directly to affect the daily lives of individuals, interest groups and various sections of the community. This does not mean that decisions regarding federalism and separation of powers are not important: they unquestionably are since they can have significant implications for the operation of government throughout the United States. However, as we now go on to examine the uses of judicial review in American history, we will find that, on the whole, the power of the Court becomes controversial when it decides cases that involve controversial policy decisions.

Judicial activism and judicial self-restraint, 1789–1954

The prominence and power of the Court has varied over the years. In some eras, the Court has practised *judicial activism*: this means that the Court has asserted its power, even when faced with hostile challenges from the Congress, the president or the public. Such periods of activism are indicated by the unusually large number of federal or state laws which the Court has struck down as unconstitutional. They may also be characterised by innovations in constitutional interpretation and the suspicion that the justices are motivated by their own political viewpoints. As a result, judicial activism has usually been controversial.

In contrast to judicial activism stands *judicial self-restraint*. When the Court practises restraint, it is cautious, passive and, above all, shows great deference to the elected branches of government. The Court seeks to avoid making controversial decisions and rarely declares an Act unconstitutional. It also tends to avoid innovations in constitutional interpretation and instead follows precedent: that is, the principles announced in past decisions.

We have already noted that, after a quiet start, the Supreme Court became a dynamic institution under the leadership of Chief Justice John Marshall. After the Marshall Court (1801–35) had established the legitimacy of judicial review in *Marbury* v. *Madison*, it proceeded to make bold decisions which had a major impact upon the political and economic future of the United States. In particular, the Marshall Court strengthened the federal government at the expense of the power of the individual states and also ensured that national commerce and capitalism were given free rein. For example, in *McCulloch* v. *Maryland* (1819), Marshall announced the doctrine of 'implied powers' which gave Congress broader control over commercial policy than had been indicated on the face of the Constitution. Furthermore, in cases such as *Dartmouth College* v. *Woodward* (1819), *Gibbons* v. *Ogden* (1824) and *Brown* v. *Maryland* (1827), the Marshall Court curtailed the power of the states to interfere with commercial contracts and trade.

Under the leadership of Chief Justice Roger B. Taney (1836–64), the Court generally practised self-restraint. Taney, like President Andrew Jackson who had appointed him, was associated with the political opposition to a strong federal government and was therefore disinclined to follow Marshall's line. Typical of the Taney Court's restraint was the decision in *Luther* v. *Borden* (1849). The case involved the state of Rhode Island, where two rival governments each proclaimed their legitimacy. The Court refused to resolve the dispute, inventing the doctrine of 'political questions'. A 'political question' was said to be one the resolution of which had been consigned by the Constitution to the elected branches of government. In fact, then as now, the doctrine of political questions is little more than a device by which the Court can avoid politically delicate decisions.

Unfortunately for the Taney Court, it is remembered less for its characteristic restraint than it is for its lone, disastrous foray into judicial activism. In *Dred Scott* v. *Sanford* (1857), the Court helped precipitate the Civil War (1861–5). Giving a much broader ruling than was required by the facts of the case, the southern-dominated Court declared that the Missouri Compromise on slavery, worked out by Congress, was unconstitutional. This meant not only that the westward expansion of slavery could continue, but also that Congress could not fashion a compromise between pro-slavery and anti-slavery forces.

It should be noted, however, that under both Marshall and Taney, it was rare for a law to be declared unconstitutional. Between 1800 and 1860, just two federal laws and 35 State laws suffered this fate. To a great extent, these figures reflect the fact that levels of legislative activity were still low at this stage in the nation's history.

This situation began to change drastically with the onset of industrialisation in the last quarter of the nineteenth century. As government tried to regulate the explosion in economic activity and cure the social ills which accompanied it, the Supreme Court established itself as the last bastion of laissez-faire economics. While it did permit some economic regulation and some social reform, the Court increasingly interpreted the Constitution's guarantees of liberty to protect the economic rights of individuals and corporations against interference from both federal and state government. For example, in *Adair* v. *United States* (1905) the Court struck down a congressional Act outlawing 'yellow-dog contracts'. These obliged workers to agree not to join a union as a condition of employment. The justices reasoned that the Act violated the constitutionally guaranteed freedom of contract of both employer and employee to make any agreement they wished.

In the same year, the Court decided in *Lochner* v. *New York* (1905) that freedom of contract also prevented the state from restricting the maximum hours of work of bakery workers to 60 a week; and in yet another infamous case, *Hammer* v. *Dagenhart* (1918), the Court ruled that Congress had no power to prohibit factories from using child labour.

Although these decisions were by no means without constitutional basis, they were activist and controversial. The Constitution makes no mention of freedom of contract, for example. Rather, the justices interpreted the general guarantee of liberty in the Fifth and Fourteenth Amendments to include freedom of contract, and then exalted that right above the general power of government to provide for the public welfare. In simple political terms, however, the Court was imposing a set of values and policies upon the country which the electorate and their chosen representatives no longer supported.

Table 17.1 Federal and state laws declared unconstitutional by the Supreme Court, 1790–2002

Decade	Federal laws	State laws
1790–1799	0	0
1800–1809	1	1
1810–1819	0	7
1820–1829	0	8
1830–1839	0	3
1840–1849	0	9
1850–1859	1	7
1860–1869	4	24
1870–1879	7	36
1880–1889	5	46
1890–1899	5	36
1900–1909	9	41
1910–1919	6	112
1920–1929	8	131
1930–1939	14	84
1940–1949	2	58
1950–1959	5	59
1960–1969	19	123
1970–1979	20	181
1980–1989	16	161
1990–2002	30	57

Source: adapted from Epstein *et al*., 2003, pp. 163–93

The Court in political crisis

This ongoing crisis came to a head during the Great Depression of the 1930s. In the presidential elections of 1932 and 1936, the nation gave impressive victories to the Democratic party candidate, Franklin D. Roosevelt. He had promised the voters a 'New Deal'. Together with a large Democratic majority in Congress, Roosevelt experimented with various forms of government intervention in an attempt to alleviate the economic and social catastrophe that had befallen the country. The Supreme Court, however, declared some of his most important policies unconstitutional. The National Industrial Recovery Act of 1933 was struck down in *Schechter* v. *United States* (1935) and the Agriculture Adjustment Act of 1933 in *US* v. *Butler* (1936).

Roosevelt's response was to do battle with the Court. In 1937, he proposed a bill that purported to aim at helping the ageing justices to cope with their workload. For each justice over the age of 70, the president would be empowered to appoint an additional member of the Court. As it so happened, six of the nine current justices were over 70, so at one fell swoop, Roosevelt would be able to make six new appointments to the Court. Assuming he would appoint only those known to support the New Deal, this would bring an end to the Court's resistance. It was clear to all that this was a crude attempt to bring the Court to heel and the proposal became known as the Court-packing plan.

There was considerable opposition to the Court-packing plan, even among Roosevelt's regular supporters in Congress. They feared that, if passed, it would violate the principle of the separation of powers and create a dangerously dominant presidency. Before Congress had to vote, however, the Court itself rendered the bill politically unnecessary. In *West Coast Hotel* v. *Parrish* (1937), the Court surprised everyone by upholding the constitutionality of a minimum-wage law of a type that it had previously struck down. Moreover, language in the Court's opinion suggested that, henceforth, economic liberties would take second place to government's view of what was required by the public welfare. And so it proved. Since 1937, the Supreme Court has virtually abandoned the field of economic regulation to the Congress, the president and the states.

Political lessons of the Court-packing plan: the Supreme Court and the political majority

Although debate continues over the precise reasons for the Court's change of direction in 1937, there is no doubt that it was a severe political setback for the Court. It had engendered considerable public hostility over the previous decades and had lost much of its prestige. The justices were viewed by many as political reactionaries rather than impartial interpreters of the Constitution.

The Court's strategic error in the 1930s was in overestimating the degree to which the Supreme Court can resist an insistent political tide. Ultimately, the power of the Court rests upon the respect it can command. It can rely upon a degree of automatic respect because of its constitutional position. Beyond that, however, it must continuously nurture and renew its status as the guardian of the nation's fundamental values, as expressed in the Constitution. In order to do that, it must convince the nation that its decisions as a whole are in the country's long-term interests. In this sense, the justices do have a 'constituency', like other political actors. In the 1950s, a leading political scientist, Robert Dahl, advanced the argument that the Court never remains out of step with the national political majority for very long (Dahl, 1957).

This, in turn, highlights a very important aspect of the Court's role in American government: it acts as a legitimator of political change. The New Deal involved a marked break with American traditions of politics and government responsibility yet, by eventually conferring its constitutional blessing upon this shift, the Court signalled that it was an acceptable addition to the fundamental political values and practices of the nation.

More recently, a study of the Court's decisions in relation to public opinion tended to support this view that the Supreme Court is, in essence, a majoritarian institution (Marshall, 1989). The fact is that if the Court becomes isolated from all major exterior sources of support – Congress, the presidency and the public – it has insufficient independent resources to withstand a concerted attack. In short, if the Court is to embark upon controversial, activist decisions, it must have strong allies among the elected branches of government.

The Supreme Court crisis of the 1930s was, however, an extreme example of judicial extravagance. It paid dearly for its intransigence by losing virtually all of its power over socio-economic legislation. Nevertheless, because the precise role of the Court is not fixed in the Constitution, or anywhere else, it has the potential to construct a new agenda for itself. Before the Civil War, it worked to strengthen the national government and national commerce. From the onset of industrialisation until 1937, its self-assigned task was to nurture laissez-faire economics. In the 1950s, after a period of passivity and self-restraint, it emerged in yet another new guise: defender of civil liberties and the interests of subordinate social groups.

The Supreme Court since 1954

In hindsight, the year 1954 can be recognised as a watershed in the history of the Supreme Court. For it was then that the Court took on not just a new agenda of issues, but a significantly different method of constitutional interpretation.

Brown v. *Board of Education* (1954)

The catalyst for these changes was a decision ordering an end to racial segregation in the nation's school systems. It had long been the practice – particularly, but not exclusively, in the southern and border states – to require black and white children to attend separate schools. The Supreme Court had validated this and other forms of racial segregation in *Plessy* v. *Ferguson* (1896). There the Court ruled that, providing facilities were 'separate but equal', racial segregation did not violate the Fourteenth Amendment's guarantee of equal protection of the laws.

In *Brown* v. *Board of Education* (1954), the Court unanimously voted to reverse its *Plessy* decision. Under the leadership of its new chief justice, Earl Warren (1953–69), it argued that separate facilities were inherently unequal: the mere desire to segregate by race implied the inferiority of one of the races compared with the other. Therefore, racial segregation did indeed violate the Fourteenth Amendment's command that the states must give all persons the 'equal protection of the laws'.

Although unarguably the right moral decision, *Brown* was rather unconvincing in terms of constitutional interpretation, as even sympathetic scholars acknowledged. The decision could not be justified by original intent, as the historical record made clear. In fact, the members of Congress who approved the Fourteenth Amendment in 1866 lived and worked in Washington, DC, which itself operated a racially segregated school system. There was not the slightest indication that they intended to put an end to that system.

In *Brown*, therefore, the Court ignored history and judicial precedent, and relied instead upon some rather flimsy social science evidence purporting to show that black children suffered psychological damage as a result of segregated schooling. The Court's reasoning, however, was regarded as secondary to the overwhelming moral rightness of the decision. Legal scholars, in spite of their misgivings, applauded the decision. This encouraged the Warren Court along a new path of using constitutional interpretation as a means of promoting what many Americans considered to be benign social reforms. The *Brown* decision thus illustrates the fact that the Court can sometimes get away with decisions the constitutional underpinnings of which are shaky, provided they are viewed as just and desirable by other politicians and the public.

The Warren Court became increasingly bold, activist and, eventually, bitterly controversial. After *Brown*, a series of decisions swept away every law which required racial segregation. However, the Court also turned its activist guns onto other targets. In *Baker* v. *Carr* (1962), the Court reversed a relatively recent precedent, *Colegrove* v. *Green* (1946), and ordered the state of Tennessee to reapportion its legislative districts. The population in some counties was much greater than in others, with the result that counties containing two-thirds of the state population chose only one-third of the members of the state legislature.

Once again, the political case for the Court's decision was overwhelming, but the constitutional basis was less convincing. Most importantly, the *Colegrove* decision had held that the Court had no power to adjudicate reapportionment cases: these fell into the category of 'political questions', the resolution of which had been consigned by the Constitution to other branches of government. Now the Warren Court rejected that restraint and narrowed the range of 'political questions'.

More controversy followed over reapportionment as a result of *Gray* v. *Sanders* (1963), *Wesberry* v. *Sanders* (1964) and *Reynolds* v. *Sims* (1964). Here the Warren Court not only ordered legislative reapportionment, but actually prescribed the apportionment formula to be applied throughout the country: 'one man, one vote'. (In later cases, this was rephrased as 'one person, one vote'.) At first glance, this may appear reasonable and fair. However, it is simply not a formula required by the Constitution. Most obviously, the United States Senate itself is not based upon one person, one vote, but rather two senators per state, regardless of population. If the Constitution permits the Senate to be grossly malapportioned because there are deemed to be other benefits resulting from the scheme, upon what basis can the Court declare that the Constitution finds such malapportionment intolerable elsewhere?

Once again, however, the fact that the Court reached a manifestly just result in other respects overcame objections that it was not so much interpreting the Constitution as reading into it the justices' own notions of what was good for the country. This type of judicial decision-making came to be known as results-oriented jurisprudence: this means that Supreme Court decisions are determined (and evaluated) by the social and moral good that they achieve, rather than by what the Constitution mandates. Moreover, the reapportionment cases illustrated another important change in the nature of judicial review. For much of its history, the Court's activism had been predominantly negative, telling government what it could *not* do. The Warren Court's activism now developed a positive aspect, telling government what it *must* do and also *how* to do it.

In cases such as *Brown* and *Baker*, where there is a wide consensus on what actually *is* the social and moral good, the Court's decisions prove politically acceptable when they are in accord with that consensus. However, in cases involving such issues as abortion, homosexuality, pornography, and government-sponsored religion, no such consensus exists. It is over just these types of cases that the contemporary Supreme Court has claimed authority and caused a backlash against its power and role in the political system.

In 1969, President Nixon appointed Warren Burger as chief justice. By 1975, Nixon and his Republican successor, Gerald Ford, had appointed a further four new justices. They had been appointed to practise judicial self-restraint, and many expected the Burger Court (1969–86) to launch a counter-revolution against the Warren Court's liberal activism. However, with a few exceptions, this failed to materialise. Indeed, in many respects, the Burger Court was even more activist than the Warren Court. Many scholars took this as a sign that the Court's role in the political system had undergone a fundamental change. No longer would there be cycles of activism and restraint: the Court would now be more or less permanently activist. Judicial review, it seemed, had become the means through which policy on socio-moral issues would be made in the United States.

The Burger Court's decisions certainly gave ammunition to this theory. It announced innovations in constitutional interpretation by holding that the Fourteenth Amendment banned traditional gender classifications (*Reed* v. *Reed*, 1971); that the Eighth Amendment banned all existing state death penalty laws (*Furman* v. *Georgia*, 1972); that women had a constitutional right to terminate pregnancies by abortion (*Roe* v. *Wade*, 1973) and that the Constitution's requirement of race equality in the law did not disbar affirmative action policies that avoided 'quotas' but which were intended to give racial minorities certain advantages in college applications (*Regents of the University of California* v. *Bakke*, 1978).

Decisions such as these provoked considerable anger among conservatives and, at both the state and federal levels of government, there were determined and partially successful attempts both to reverse them and to force the Court to abandon its activism. This backlash revealed once again that, when it provokes significant opposition, the Court's decisions can suddenly take on the appearance of great vulnerability.

The Burger Court was succeeded by the Rehnquist Court (1986–2005). During this period, the conservative effort to roll back the judicial liberalism of the Warren and Burger Courts reached new heights. Strengthened by the appointment to the Court of staunch conservatives, such as Antonin Scalia and Clarence Thomas, many expected to see a widespread counter-revolution and the overthrow of major precedents. Yet although there was a discernible shift to the right under Chief Justice Rehnquist, a combination of liberal and moderate-conservative justices defeated attempts to overturn key decisions, such as *Roe* v. *Wade* (1973). The same political dynamics govern the Roberts Court to date (2005–). Indeed, many point out that the Roberts Court is actually the Kennedy Court,

Box 17.1

The Supreme Court, gay rights and same-sex marriage: *Lawrence* v. *Texas* (2003)

The capacity of the Supreme Court to set off a political firestorm was illustrated by this case dealing with privacy rights under the Constitution. Texas law criminalised certain sexual acts when practised by homosexuals. Two men convicted under the statute appealed to the Supreme Court, arguing that the 'liberty' to which they were entitled under the Constitution was violated by the Texas legislation. The Supreme Court had dealt with this issue before, in *Bowers* v. *Hardwick* (1986). The Court had ruled in a 5–4 vote that the US Constitution did not protect the right claimed by homosexuals and that it was up to each state legislature to decide for itself whether these homosexual acts should be legal or not. The *Bowers* decision had been roundly condemned in many quarters for its insensitivity to personal privacy rights and it came as no surprise when, in *Lawrence*, the Court overruled *Bowers* by a 6–3 vote. Since the earlier decision, changes in Court personnel and the progress made by gay and lesbian groups in fighting discrimination had significantly altered attitudes to homosexuality. However, *Lawrence* proved controversial because one of the dissenting justices, Antonin Scalia, suggested the decision could lead a later Court to rule that gay marriage was also protected by the Constitution. Certain religious and conservative groups went into immediate action and tried to pass an amendment to the US Constitution declaring that marriage could only be between a man and a woman. Although it failed, over 40 states have banned same-sex marriage under their own statutes or constitutions and the issue was much debated in the presidential election of 2004. In the face of such political pressure, the Supreme Court will surely tread cautiously if the issue of gay marriage comes before it. On the other hand, its decision in *Lawrence* shows once again that the Court plays a vital role in defending the rights of minorities.

because Justice Anthony Kennedy is the swing voter who often decides whether the liberal or conservative wing triumphs in 5–4 decisions.

The history of the Burger, Rehnquist and early Roberts Courts demonstrates an important fact about the Supreme Court: it is extremely difficult to bring about a fundamental change of direction by the Supreme Court. Change does of course happen, but it is more likely to be gradual and incremental than sudden and radical.

Supreme Court decisions: implementation and resistance

There are several formal means at the disposal of other branches of government if they wish to reverse a constitutional decision by the Court. Most obviously, they can attempt to pass a constitutional amendment. However, this is a difficult, time-consuming and uncertain device. As a result, it has been employed successfully on only four occasions in American history. The Eleventh Amendment overturned *Chisholm* v. *Georgia* (1793); the first part of the Fourteenth Amendment overturned *Dred Scott* v. *Sanford* (1857); the Sixteenth Amendment reversed *Pollock* v. *Farmers' Loan and Trust Co.* (1895); and the Twenty-sixth Amendment reversed *Oregon* v. *Mitchell* (1970).

Nevertheless, despite the slim prospects of success, members of Congress often introduce constitutional amendments as a symbolic gesture to express their hostility to the Court. Thus, for example, within 18 months of the Court's decision banning school prayer (*Engel* v. *Vitale*, 1962), no fewer than 146 constitutional amendments to reverse it were introduced into Congress.

An even worse success rate characterises a second device to overturn a Court decision: *withdrawal of appellate jurisdiction*. The Constitution allows Congress to vary the kinds of case which may be taken on appeal to the Supreme Court. If Congress dislikes the Court's decisions on, say, abortion, it can simply remove the Court's right to hear appeals in cases involving abortion. In fact, such withdrawal of appellate jurisdiction has happened on only one occasion: just after the Civil War, Congress removed the Court's right to hear appeals involving convictions for sedition by a military commission. In 1958 the Jenner–Butler bill, designed to withdraw the Court's jurisdiction over certain national security issues, failed to pass the Senate by just one vote. On the whole, however, proposals for the withdrawal of appellate jurisdiction, like constitutional amendment, are in essence symbolic. They are not an effective means of actually reversing the Court's decision, but they do fire a warning shot across the Court's bows.

In 2005, the arch-conservative Republican leader in the House of Representatives, Tom Delay, attacked federal judges for their handling of the Terri Schiavo case. Schiavo had been kept alive for years only by life-support mechanisms and her family was divided over whether these mechanisms should be switched off. The case went through several courts, including the Supreme Court, with the end result that Schiavo was allowed to die. Delay launched a broadside against the federal judiciary, threatening to impeach certain justices and remove federal court jurisdiction over these kinds of issues. The reaction, even within his own party, was to criticise Delay for seeking to undermine the independence of the judiciary and he was forced to apologise.

The failure of so many proposals to reverse the Court by withdrawing appellate jurisdiction or amending the Constitution reveals something important about the Court's power. No matter how much the justices may anger Congress by particular decisions, a majority of its members are deeply reluctant to inflict permanent, structural damage upon the Court. Frequent surgery upon the Court with such blunt instruments would soon leave it incapable of truly independent decision-making – and it is that independence which makes the Court so valuable in settling constitutional conflicts.

In the previous chapter, however, we noted Alexander Hamilton's observation that the Court was inherently weak because it had to rely on others to implement its decisions. The history of the Court bears this out. An early illustration came in *Worcester* v. *Georgia* (1832), when the Marshall Court offended anti-Indian sentiment by telling the state it could not make laws for the local Cherokee nation. Not only did Georgia refuse to obey the order, but President Andrew Jackson is reputed to have said: 'John Marshall has made his decision. Now let *him* enforce it.' Three years after the Court's decision, most of the Cherokees were forcibly removed from the state.

In modern times, non-compliance with Court decisions is fairly common. The most famous example concerns the 'massive resistance' to the *Brown* school desegregation decision, organised by southerners. Ten years after the Court made its order, hardly any black children in the Deep South were attending integrated schools. Southern governors such as George Wallace (Alabama) and Orval Faubus (Arkansas) openly led the resistance. As a result of the latter's activities, President Eisenhower was obliged to use federal troops in order to allow black children to enter Little Rock High School in 1957.

Even then, however, Arkansas, like the rest of the South, did not implement desegregation. As one analyst wrote:

> The statistics from the Southern states are truly amazing. For ten years, 1954–64, virtually nothing happened. Ten years after *Brown* only 1.2 percent of black schoolchildren in the South attended school with whites. . . . Despite the unanimity and forcefulness of the *Brown* decision, the Supreme Court's reiteration of its position and its steadfast refusal to yield, its decree was flagrantly disobeyed.
>
> Rosenberg, 1991, p. 52

It is obvious that the mere fact that the Court ordered states to desegregate their schools was wholly insufficient to bring about any significant change. Compliance with *Brown* came only in the

Table 17.2 Black children in desegregated southern elementary and secondary schools

	1954/55		1959/60		1964/65	
	%	No.	%	No.	%	No.
Alabama	0	0	0	0	0.03	101
Arkansas	0	0	0.09	98	0.81	930
Georgia	0	0	0	0	0.40	1,337
Louisiana	0	0	0	0	1.1	3,581
Mississippi	0	0	0	0	0.02	57
South Carolina	0	0	0	0	0.10	265

Source: Adapted from Rosenberg, 1991, pp. 345–6

late 1960s, after Congress and President Johnson combined to produce legislation which allowed stricter enforcement and which provided financial 'carrots and sticks' for state school systems. Particularly important were the Civil Rights Act of 1964 and the Elementary and Secondary Education Act of 1965. Table 17.3 indicates the impact of the increase in federal funds for southern state school systems on the pace of desegregation.

Non-compliance with *Brown* was simply illegal. On the issue of the Court's death penalty decisions, however, many states used a more legitimate means of resistance. In *Furman* v. *Georgia* (1972), the Court had not ruled that capital punishment was, in itself, unconstitutional. Rather it said that current laws were so infrequently, randomly and capriciously applied that they amounted to 'cruel and unusual punishment' in violation of the Eighth Amendment. Nevertheless, most observers agreed that the Court had accomplished the effective abolition of capital punishment. A majority of states, however, simply refused to accept that result. Some 35 of them passed new death penalty laws, including 15 who dealt with the issue of arbitrariness by making the death sentence mandatory for certain offences. Faced with this evidence of continuing support for capital punishment, the Court backed away from its near-abolitionist position. In *Gregg* v. *Georgia* (1976), Justice Stewart conceded that 'It is now evident that a large proportion of American society continues to regard the death penalty as an appropriate and necessary criminal sanction.'

Table 17.3 Impact of the increase in federal funds on the pace of desegregation in southern schools

	Federal funds as percentage of state education budget		Percentage of black children in integrated schools	
	1963/64	1971/72	1964/65	1972/73
Alabama	7.6	21.5	0.03	83.5
Arkansas	11.1	21.2	0.81	98.1
Georgia	7.1	15.7	0.40	86.8
Louisiana	4.8	14.6	1.1	82.9
Mississippi	8.1	27.8	0.02	91.5
South Carolina	7.5	18.7	0.10	93.9

Source: Adapted from Rosenberg, 1991, p. 99

The Court's 1973 abortion decision produced several forms of resistance. States which favoured illiberal abortion statutes placed many obstacles in the path of women seeking terminations. Many refused to allow abortions to be performed in public hospitals, leaving women reliant upon private clinics which might be located hundreds of miles away. Others introduced cumbersome administrative procedures which required women to attend the abortion facility more than once. A favourite strategy, emulated by Congress in 1976 with the passage of the Hyde Amendment, was to withdraw public funds for poor women seeking abortions, even though funds were available for childbirth expenses and, indeed, all other types of medical treatment. In the first full year of the operation of the Hyde Amendment, the number of Medicaid (publicly funded) abortions fell from 200,000 to fewer than 2,000. The Reagan administration also joined the attack by banning any federally funded pregnancy counselling service from providing advice or information on abortion. On several occasions, President Reagan's solicitor-general also intervened as amicus curiae, urging the Court to reverse its decision in *Roe*.

The Court had thus ruled that states could not ban abortions, but the response of many states and the other branches of the federal government was to do their utmost to undermine that policy. The result was that, although women retained a theoretical right to abortion, many experienced some difficulty in turning that right into a practical reality. The constraints upon the Court, then, are less the formal ones of reversal by constitutional amendment or withdrawal of appellate jurisdiction; rather, they are the pressures and indirect restrictions which arise from the unwillingness of the elected branches to implement the Court's decisions. In short, the main constraint upon the Court is the political hostility that its decisions engender.

There is, however, yet one other major way in which Supreme Court decisions may be changed by the actions of elected politicians. That is through the appointment process.

Supreme Court appointments

The power to appoint Supreme Court justices is shared by the president and the Senate. Article II, Section 2(ii) of the Constitution stipulates that the president shall nominate new justices 'with the advice and consent of the Senate'. In other words, the Senate has the power to confirm or reject the president's nominees. Here again, the constitutional system of checks and balances provides the executive and legislative branches with an 'invitation to struggle'. Yet the president usually has the upper hand in such struggles, simply because the Constitution gives him the initiative in the appointment process. The Senate can reject the president's nominee, but it knows it cannot replace that nominee with its own preferred candidate. It must always calculate, therefore, whether the rejection of one nominee will lead to the appointment of a better one. Nevertheless, in recent decades, the Senate has become a lot more assertive in the appointment process than in the first two-thirds of the twentieth century.

Presidential nominations to the Court

Presidents have no power over how many nominations they can make to the Court. With justices being appointed for life, presidents must wait until a member of the Court either resigns or dies. Some presidents are luckier in this respect than others. Most obviously, President Carter had no opportunity at all to nominate a justice during his single term, while President George H. Bush made two nominations during his single term; and while Presidents Johnson and Nixon served for similar lengths of time, the latter filled twice as many vacancies as the former. President George W. Bush had no vacancies to fill in his first term, but two arose early in his second term.

Presidents rightly cherish their opportunities to make nominations to the Court. In the short term, it allows them to place political allies and sympathisers in another branch of the federal government. In the long term, those justices and their political viewpoints will still be influencing government long after the presidents themselves have left office.

Take the case of Justice William O. Douglas, nominated by Franklin D. Roosevelt in 1939. Roosevelt died in office in 1945, but Douglas did not retire from the Court until 1975, some 30 years after Roosevelt died. In fact, while no president may serve more than 8 years (up to 10 years exceptionally), the average length of service of justices appointed since 1937 is 15 years (excluding those still serving). Moreover, of those 22 justices, 3 served more than 30 years, a further 3 more than 20 years, and a further 8 more than 15 years. The longest-serving of the modern Court was Chief Justice William Rehnquist. Appointed as an associate justice in 1971,

Table 17.4 Number of Supreme Court vacancies per president since 1945

President	Years in office	Number of vacancies
Truman	1945–53	4
Eisenhower	1953–61	5
Kennedy	1961–63	2
Johnson	1963–69	2
Nixon	1969–74	4
Ford	1974–77	1
Carter	1977–81	0
Reagan	1981–89	3
Bush (41)	1989–93	2
Clinton	1993–2001	2
Bush (43)	2001–09	2
Obama	2009–11	2

Rehnquist served on the Court for 34 years – that is, some 28 years more than the length of time his appointing president, Richard Nixon, occupied the White House.

Criteria for nomination

There are no formal requirements for those who serve on the Court. While it is convention that nominees should possess a law degree, they are not required to have practised law, never mind have experience as a judge. Many of the justices considered to be outstanding had no judicial experience prior to their nomination: thus, Chief Justice Warren had been governor of California and an unsuccessful Republican vice-presidential candidate. Justice Hugo Black (1937–71) had been a senator and Justice Felix Frankfurter (1939–62) a law professor and adviser to President Franklin D. Roosevelt.

There would appear to be no connection between prior judicial experience and greatness on the Court, perhaps because the functions of the Court require political and philosophical skills, as much as they require purely legal skills. However, recent Republican presidents, all striving to appoint strict constructionists, have nominated only those with at least some judicial experience. The thinking is that those with personal experience of judging, as opposed to politics, will behave more 'judicially' and less 'politically' once they are on the Court.

Since the 1950s, it has been the custom of presidents to submit the names of potential nominees to the Committee on the Federal Judiciary of the American Bar Association. The committee ranks potential nominees to the Court according to their perceived competence, integrity and judicial temperament. Although the committee has no formal powers with respect to nominations, its ratings may influence the Senate's decision whether or not to confirm a nominee. For example, in 1987, Robert Bork was given the highest ranking of 'well qualified', but the fact that the vote was not unanimous added fuel to the political fire which eventually engulfed the nominee.

Some conservatives alleged that the ABA committee was politically biased in favour of liberal nominees and presidents. This perception persuaded President George W. Bush to try to limit the influence of the ABA. He ceased consulting the ABA on potential nominees and only submitted for evaluation the names of those who had formally been nominated. This snub to the legal profession did not appear to have much impact either way. However, President Obama resumed the practice of consulting the ABA on potential nominees, suggesting that most presidents think it is important to have the profession's approval for any nomination they may make.

The overwhelming criterion for nomination is political compatibility with the president. This can be identified in a number of ways. Most obviously, presidents usually nominate those affiliated with their own party. Of the 112 justices who have served on the Court up to 2011, only 13 have not been members of the nominating president's party. Even then, such cross-party nominees have usually been known to share the president's ideology.

Another way the president may try to ensure that the nominee is compatible with his own views is to nominate a friend or political ally. President Lyndon B. Johnson went to great lengths in 1965 to put his long-time friend and adviser Abe Fortas on the Court. First, he manufactured a vacancy by persuading Justice Arthur Goldberg to accept the bait of becoming ambassador to the United Nations. Then he successfully nominated Fortas to the Court. Three years later, when Earl Warren expressed his wish to retire, Johnson tried to elevate Fortas to the chief justiceship. This failed, in part precisely because Fortas was known to be so close to the president and so the nomination smacked of cronyism.

It was President Reagan, however, who established the most elaborate method of screening nominees for political compatibility. During his administration, all potential candidates for nomination to the Supreme Court, or lower federal courts, were vetted by a President's Committee on Federal Judicial Selection. This committee analysed all the published writings and statements of those being considered for nomination. Candidates would be interviewed and asked their views on issues about which the administration felt strongly. Indeed, under Presidents Reagan and Bush, it was widely perceived that the 'litmus test' for any nominee to the Court was opposition to the *Roe* v. *Wade* (1973) abortion decision, although both administrations denied this. Republican Presidents George H. Bush and George W. Bush continued with the Committee, suggesting it is an effective means of identifying potential judges who are compatible with the president's own ideology.

Beyond political compatibility, the president may have a variety of secondary, and in essence symbolic, criteria for nomination. Until the early twentieth century, presidents considered the nominee's home state to be important, because it was thought desirable that the Court should reflect the country's regional diversity. In the twentieth century, a desire for ethnic diversity was a factor. In 1916, Louis Brandeis became the first Jew to be appointed to the Court and the tradition of a 'Jewish seat' continued until the retirement of Abe Fortas in 1969. In 1967, Thurgood Marshall became the first black Supreme Court justice. When he retired, President George H. Bush nominated another black, Clarence Thomas, to fill his seat.

Such nominations are not free of political calculation. The president will hope to reap electoral rewards for his actions by showing his symbolic support for the group concerned. This was certainly a factor for President George H. Bush in nominating Justice Thomas. Bush was widely perceived as unsympathetic to the cause of racial equality and the nomination gave him the opportunity to curry favour with African-American voters. Similar considerations lay behind President Reagan's 1981 nomination of the first woman Supreme Court justice, Sandra Day O'Connor. Reagan was not noted for his enthusiasm for gender equality and, in the 1980 election, he had received a lower percentage of the votes of women than of men. The nomination of Justice O'Connor was a means of countering this 'gender gap'. President Barack Obama used his first Supreme Court vacancy to nominate Justice Sonia Sotomayor, who duly became the first Hispanic-American to sit on the highest court in the land, and only the third woman.

However, these secondary criteria should not obscure the overriding importance of political considerations. Thus, for example, President Reagan made sure he appointed a *conservative* woman, President George H. Bush made sure he appointed a *conservative* African-American and President Obama selected a *liberal* Hispanic-American. Quite simply, the political stakes are too high in Supreme Court nominations to make it otherwise.

Senate confirmation and rejection

The president has sole prerogative over who is *nominated* to the Court, but the Senate has equally sole prerogative over who is *confirmed*. Historically, about one in five presidential nominees to the Court fails to be confirmed by the Senate. Sometimes they are rejected outright by Senate vote; sometimes their nominations are withdrawn before a vote because of the certainty of defeat.

The historical frequency of Senate rejections of presidential nominees to the Court is not, however, even, and a marked change in that respect took place at the end of the 1960s.

Two facts stand out in the confirmation statistics. First, in the earlier period, all 22 nominees were confirmed, while in the later period, 6 out of 22 failed to make the Court.

Secondly, in only 7 of the 22 earlier nominations did the Senate bother to record a vote: even then, not one of the recorded votes indicated substantial opposition to the nominee. In the second period, however, all nominations were subject to a recorded vote, save those which were withdrawn. Moreover, those votes show that, as well as the three rejections, there was a serious attempt to deny confirmation on several further occasions, most notably in the case of Clarence Thomas. The votes on the Alito, Sotomayor and Kagan nominations suggest that pure partisanship is increasingly a major factor in Supreme Court nominations. None of the nominees had anything significant against them, except for their ideology, and the votes were very much along party lines. In the Alito case, only one Republican voted against him and only 4 Democrats voted for him. In Sotomayor's case, no Democrat voted against her, while only 9 Republicans voted for her. And in Kagan's case, only one Democrat voted against her, while only 5 Republicans voted for her.

Table 17.5 Senate confirmation/rejection of Supreme Court nominees, 1937–2009

1937–67			1967–2009		
Nominee (year of Senate action)	**Result**	**Vote**	**Nominee (year of Senate action)**	**Result**	**Vote**
Hugo Black (1937)	Con.	63–16	Abe Fortas[a] (1968)	With.	–
Stanley Reed (1938)	Con.	–	Warren Burger (1969)	Con.	74–3
Felix Frankfurter (1939)	Con.	–	Clement Haynsworth (1969)	Rej.	45–55
William Douglas (1939)	Con.	62–4	G. Harrold Carswell (1970)	Rej.	45–51
Frank Murphy (1940)	Con.	–	Harry Blackmun (1970)	Con.	94–0
Harlan Stone[a] (1941)	Con.	–	Lewis Powell (1971)	Con.	89–1
James Byrnes (1941)	Con.	–	William Rehnquist (1971)	Con.	68–26
Robert Jackson (1941)	Con.	–	John Paul Stevens (1975)	Con.	98–0
Wiley Rutledge (1943)	Con.	–	Sandra Day O'Connor (1981)	Con.	99–0
Harold Burton (1945)	Con.	–	William Rehnquist[a] (1986)	Con.	65–33
Fred Vinson (1946)	Con.	–	Antonin Scalia (1986)	Con.	98–0
Tom Clark (1949)	Con.	73–8	Robert Bork (1987)	Rej.	42–58
Sherman Minton (1949)	Con.	48–16	Douglas Ginsberg (1987)	With.	–
Earl Warren (1954)	Con.	–	Anthony Kennedy (1988)	Con.	97–0
John Harlan (1955)	Con.	71–11	David Souter (1990)	Con.	90–9
William Brennan (1957)	Con.	–	Clarence Thomas (1991)	Con.	52–48
Charles Whittaker (1957)	Con.	–	Ruth Bader Ginsberg (1993)	Con.	96–3
Potter Stewart (1959)	Con.	70–17	Stephen G. Breyer (1994)	Con.	87–9
Byron White (1962)	Con.	–	John G. Roberts (2005)	Con.	78–22
Arthur Goldberg (1962)	Con.	–	Harriet Miers (2005)	With.	–
Abe Fortas (1965)	Con.	–	Samuel Alito (2006)	Con.	58–42
Thurgood Marshall (1967)	Con.	69–11	Sonia Sotomayor (2009)	Con.	68–31
			Elena Kagan (2010)	Con.	63–37

Con. = Confirmed Rej. = Rejected With. = Withdrawn
[a] Sitting associate justice nominated to the chief justiceship

In short, between 1937 and 1967, there were 22 almost wholly problem-free Senate confirmations of presidential nominees to the Court. Since 1967, however, half of the 22 presidential nominations have met substantial opposition in the Senate (and elsewhere). Clearly then, the appointment of Supreme Court justices has become a major political battleground, with far less certainty of presidential success than before. Why has this happened?

The fundamental reasons have to do with the increasing realisation since the 1960s of the political nature and importance of the Court in the policy-making process. As we noted above, the Warren Court engaged in results-oriented decision-making and thereby initiated some strikingly liberal policies. By 1968, a conservative backlash against the Court was under way, and Republican presidents such as Nixon, Reagan, George H. Bush and George W. Bush were determined to place new justices on the Court who would halt or even reverse the liberal advances. Thus, because the Court behaved in an explicitly political manner, presidential nominations took on a more explicitly political aspect.

A second source of increased friction between the Senate and the president was the emergence of divided government, in which one party controls the Congress and the other the White House. This deprives the president of the crutch of a partisan majority in the Senate. Nevertheless, divided government is by no means the whole story. President Eisenhower, for example, had 4 of his 5 successful nominees confirmed by a Senate with a Democratic majority, and Justices Souter and Kennedy of the present Court won easy confirmation by Democratic Senates, despite having been nominated by Republican presidents.

What has changed, then, along with the politicisation of both the Court's role and the criteria for presidential choice of nominees, is the way the Senate views its role in the appointment process. According to Laurence Tribe, there has until recently been a tendency for Americans to believe in 'the myth of the Spineless Senate' (Tribe, 1985). This myth argues that Supreme Court appointments are the prerogative of the president, and that the Senate should confine itself (and it usually has) to the rejection of nominees who are not qualified for the job. Above all, the Senate should not reject nominees because of their political ideology or judicial philosophy. By and large, says the myth, the president is entitled to place on the Court whomsoever he wishes.

The rejection of one in 5 nominees would seem to support Tribe's view that such an understanding of the appointments process is indeed mythical. Yet, upon closer inspection, the myth would appear to merit greater credence. One study suggests that only a handful of the pre-1968 rejected nominees were voted down for their political views and only one for what might be termed his judicial philosophy (Vieira and Gross, 1990). In the former category, we find, for example, the first rejected nominee, John Rutledge, nominated as chief justice by President Washington in 1795. His political crime was to have denounced the Jay Treaty with England; the treaty's Senate supporters decided to punish him by rejecting his nomination.

Prior to the modern period, the sole candidate rejected because of his judicial philosophy was John Parker, nominated in 1930 by President Hoover. Parker was certainly well qualified and was supported by the legal community. He was rejected, however, largely because of his anti-union record. Parker was the last nominee to be rejected until Abe Fortas in 1968. For almost 40 years and through 24 nominations, then, the myth seems to have applied. However, whether a new phenomenon or a new phase in an old phenomenon, the contemporary struggles over Supreme Court appointments are an important feature of American politics.

Senate confirmation battles

When the president and the Senate do battle over a Supreme Court nominee, they are fighting for a major political prize: influence over the future direction of a co-equal branch of the federal government. The more political the Court's decisions, the more both president and Senate want that influence.

Take, for example, the historically unprecedented rejection of two successive nominees under President Nixon. During the 1968 presidential election campaign, Nixon had attacked the Warren Court for a number of its liberal-activist decisions. He promised to appoint new justices who would practise strict construction. The president also had a second political goal: to appoint a southerner to the Court. Nixon believed, rightly, that the traditionally Democratic, but conservative South was potentially a Republican stronghold. The appointment of a southerner, Clement Haynsworth of South Carolina, was therefore part of Nixon's plan to woo the region away from the Democrats.

Haynsworth was undoubtedly qualified for the office, but Democrats seized upon an alleged minor breach of judicial ethics as an excuse for rejecting him. Nixon's response was to nominate G. Harrold Carswell of Florida, a federal judge with a background of racial bigotry and incompetence. Nixon wanted to punish the Senate for the rejection of Haynsworth by obliging them to accept someone far worse. Nixon falsely assumed that the Senate would not dare reject two successive nominees. However, he made it easy for the Democrats by nominating a man who was clearly unsuitable. Senator Roman Hruska unintentionally damned Carswell with faint praise when he famously remarked of the nominee: 'Even if he is mediocre, there are a lot of mediocre judges and people and lawyers. They are entitled to a little representation, aren't they?'

The politics of appointment reached new heights of intensity with the nominations of Robert Bork and Clarence Thomas. On each occasion, the nomination was believed to be more than usually important because the other justices were more or less evenly divided on many of the big issues. The appointment of one new justice could swing the Court one way or the other on abortion rights, for example. As a result, both president and Senate went all-out for victory against the backdrop of a massive lobbying campaign by interest groups on both sides. Senate hearings were televised live and the whole nation became absorbed in the fate of a Supreme Court nominee.

Robert Bork was a noted judicial scholar and a judge of some considerable experience. What led to his defeat was the fact that he had been the nation's foremost critic of the modern Court's failure to follow the doctrine of original intent. As such, he was portrayed by his opponents as being 'outside the judicial mainstream' and therefore lacking in 'judicial temperament'. This was untrue, but Bork *was* a controversial figure and President Reagan nominated him precisely because he was a high-profile scourge of liberal judicial activism. Certainly Bork's own fidelity to original intent would undoubtedly lead him to conservative decisions in most cases. In nominating Bork, therefore, the president deliberately issued a challenge to the Senate Democrats, apparently in the belief that they could not prevent him from shifting the Court decisively to the right.

Many liberal interest groups joined in the battle, raising huge sums of money to persuade Senators and the public that Bork was an extremist. According to one estimate, groups such as the National Abortion Rights Action League (NARAL), the National Organization for Women (NOW) and People for the American Way spent around $15 million on their anti-Bork campaign (Hodder-Williams, 1988, p. 628). Conservative groups such as the National Right to Life Committee (NRLC) and the National Conservative Political Action Committee (NCPAC) mounted a counter-campaign, though not quite on the same scale. Robert Bork himself appeared before the Senate Judiciary Committee to answer questions on his judicial views for over 30 hours.

The final vote against Bork was almost, but not quite, strictly partisan. Only two Democrats voted for Bork, while six Republicans voted against him. Ultimately, the rejection of Robert Bork was political and partisan. It was significant, however, that senators professed that they rejected Bork because he did not possess 'judicial temperament', rather than admitting that they simply did not like the way he would vote once seated on the Court.

A similar legitimating device was used to cloak the essentially political reasons that almost led to the rejection of Clarence Thomas in 1991. President George H. Bush had wrong-footed Senate Democrats by nominating a conservative who was also black. It was difficult for liberals to oppose the appointment of only the second African-American justice in the Court's history. Nevertheless, liberals wanted to defeat the nomination because Thomas's record indicated he would tip the balance of the Court further, perhaps decisively, to the right. However, Thomas was not the kind of antagonistic figure who could unite the liberal opposition.

The anti-Thomas campaign was therefore foundering until one of his former colleagues, Professor Anita Hill, alleged that Thomas had sexually harassed her some 10 years before. Thomas denied the allegations and there was an absence of corroborative evidence to determine which of the two was the more credible. Despite this, liberals now had a 'legitimate' and 'non-political' reason for doubting Thomas's fitness for a seat on the Court. As a result, the anti-Thomas campaign gathered sudden momentum and only fell short of securing his rejection by three votes.

Thomas survived because, although there was again a strong partisan aspect to the Senate vote, this was qualified by other political considerations for some senators. Only 2 Republicans voted against Thomas, but 11 Democrats voted for him. Of these, 8 were from the South and were particularly dependent for election upon the support of black voters. When polls told them that, in spite of Professor Hill's allegations, these voters believed Thomas should be confirmed, they cast their votes in line with constituency opinion. Thus, even though the Thomas vote was not simply partisan, it was wholly political.

The history of recent Supreme Court appointments suggests that the conditions for presidential success have changed. The Senate is still reluctant to be *seen* as opposing a nominee on purely political grounds. Thus, Antonin Scalia and Anthony Kennedy were unanimously confirmed, even though their judicial views (and votes) were close to those of Bork and Thomas. In this sense, the president still has the upper hand in the appointment process.

However, if the president makes a mistake in selecting his nominee, either by going out of his way to provoke the Senate (Carswell, Bork), or by picking someone with a possible skeleton in the cupboard (Douglas Ginsburg's admitted marijuana smoking, Thomas's alleged sexual harassment), he thereby gives politically motivated opponents the 'judicial' legitimation and momentum they need to reject the nominee.

On the evidence of his nominations of Ruth Bader Ginsburg (1993) and Stephen G. Breyer (1994), President Clinton appeared to absorb these lessons of recent bitter nomination battles. While both the nominees were chosen because they broadly shared the president's political philosophy, he was also careful to select candidates who were well respected by the Republican opposition in the Senate. Thus both Ginsburg and Breyer had an easy ride to confirmation.

The evidence of the Alito and Sotomayor nominations may suggest that even such caution as President Clinton exercised is no longer any guarantee of a smooth passage through the Senate. While it was patently clear that the two nominees were conservative and liberal, respectively, neither was unduly provocative like Robert Bork, or had an alleged stain on their character, such as Justice Thomas. Nevertheless, as noted above, both attracted considerable opposition of an almost wholly partisan nature. Moreover, during the Bill Clinton and George W. Bush presidencies, fierce partisan battles took place even over presidential nominations to the lower federal courts. It would seem, therefore, that political control over the federal judiciary is now deemed a prize worth a long and costly partisan war.

Post-appointment performance: do presidents get what they wanted?

Nothing guarantees that a president's successful nominee will vote as anticipated once on the Court. Justices of the Supreme Court are answerable to no one for their decisions, and it may be that their behaviour on the Court departs significantly from what their pre-Court record suggested. President Eisenhower expected Chief Justice Warren to be a moderate conservative, just like himself. Instead, Warren led the Court in a liberal-activist direction, causing Eisenhower to comment later that nominating Warren was 'the biggest damned-fool mistake I ever made'. President Nixon nominated Justice Blackmun as a strict constructionist, but on abortion and many other issues Blackmun voted with the liberal non-interpretivists. Likewise, current justice David Souter, nominated by President Bush, has turned out to be much more liberal than many Republicans expected.

These, however, are the exceptions that prove the rule. By and large, justices *do* turn out the way their nominating president had hoped. Thus, if the president gets the chance to fill sufficient vacancies, he can change the Court's direction altogether. Although President Franklin D. Roosevelt's Court-packing plan was never passed by Congress, his eventual nominees to the Court ensured that New Deal-type legislation was deemed acceptable under the Constitution. The more recent Reagan–Bush (41)–Bush (43) campaign to shift the Court in a more conservative direction also paid off in many ways, though not as decisively as conservative Republicans had hoped: abortion rights have been significantly undermined, affirmative action policies much more difficult to pursue and convicted murderers more likely to be executed.

At the same time, on particular issues or in particular cases, justices do not necessarily do what their nominating presidents desire. Thus, although Justices O'Connor, Kennedy and Souter have undermined the Court's 1973 abortion decision, they have not squarely reversed it, as both presidents Reagan and George H. Bush urged. In part, at least, this is owing to the fact that most justices of the Supreme Court are not simply politicians in disguise. They cannot escape their political environment entirely, but there are also judicial imperatives that may constrain them. Law, even constitutional law, requires a good measure of stability and consistency of principle. If the Court simply tacks with every change in the prevailing political winds, it risks losing the very character that makes it distinctive and authoritative in American politics. As the three Justices wrote when refusing to reverse *Roe* v. *Wade*:

The Court must take care to speak and act in ways that allow people to accept its decisions on the terms the Court claims for them, as grounded truly in principle, not as compromises with social and political pressures having no bearing on the principled choices that the Court is obliged to make. Thus, the Court's legitimacy depends on making legally principled decisions under circumstances in which their principled character is sufficiently plausible to be accepted by the Nation.

Joint opinion of Justices O'Connor, Kennedy and Souter, *Planned Parenthood of Southeastern Pennsylvania* v. *Casey*, 1992

It is no accident that the word 'principle' appears four times in just two sentences, for it goes to the very heart of the notion of having a written constitution, the principles of which are superior and more enduring than the views of the latest legislative majority. The Supreme Court is the guardian of the Constitution and is therefore duty-bound to resist political pressures that conflict with the principles it contains. In the long run, the appointment process will ensure that the Supreme Court falls into line with the political majority on most issues. In the meantime, the Court provides a valuable, if imperfect, insurance against legislative and executive abuse.

Chapter summary

Throughout American history, the Supreme Court has oscillated between judicial activism and judicial self-restraint. When the Court has been activist, opponents have charged that the supremacy of the Constitution has been perverted to create the supremacy of the Supreme Court in the American political system. In fact, there are enough formal and informal constraints upon the Supreme Court's power to ensure that this does not happen and, in the long term, the Court usually does comply with the wishes of the majority. Nevertheless, precisely because the Supreme Court is a judicial body endowed with significant political power, presidents go to considerable lengths in the appointment process to shape the direction and decisions that the Court will take.

Discussion points

1. What are the distinguishing features of the concepts of *judicial activism* and *judicial restraint*?
2. How powerful is the Supreme Court?
3. Should we regard the Supreme Court as in essence a legal or a political body?
4. What does a president look for in a Supreme Court nominee?
5. Why are some Supreme Court nominations so controversial?

Further reading

See suggestions at the end of Chapter 16.

References

Dahl, R. (1957) 'Decision-making in a democracy: the Supreme Court as a national policy-maker', *Journal of Public Law*, vol. VI, pp. 279–95.

Epstein, L. *et al.* (2003) *The Supreme Court Compendium: Data, Decisions and Developments* (3rd edn, Washington, DC: CQ Press).

Hodder-Williams, R. (1988) 'The strange story of Judge Robert Bork and a vacancy on the United States Supreme Court', *Political Studies*, vol. XXXVI, pp. 613–37.

Marshall, T. (1989) *Public Opinion and the Supreme Court* (Boston: Unwin Hyman).

Rosenberg, G. (1991) *The Hollow Hope: Can Courts Bring About Social Change?* (Chicago: University of Chicago Press).

Tribe, L. (1985) *God Save This Honorable Court* (New York: Mentor).

Vieira, N. and Gross, L. (1990) 'The appointments clause: Judge Bork and the role of ideology in judicial confirmations', *Journal of Legal History*, vol. XI, pp. 311–52.

Part 7

The policy process

In this final part of the book, we examine the policy-making process in the context of major issues on the agenda of American politics. While there are some significant differences between policy-making on domestic issues and the making of foreign policy, there are also striking similarities. This holds true even in the exceptional context of the 'War on Terror'. Policy-making on all issues in the United States is conducted within a constitutional framework that encourages the participation of multiple players in multiple fora – a fragmentation that can create serious problems in the generation of coherent and effective policy. Each of the chapters also pays considerable attention to the historical and ideological contexts of the issues concerned, since these are crucial factors which make some policy outcomes much more likely than others.

Contents

Chapter 18

Serving the people: government and domestic policy

One explanation given by some non-voters of their lack of engagement is the complaint that it makes no difference who is elected, that politics goes on in much the same way. Adding to this impression, observers have sometimes pointed to the United States as a nation where the two major political parties have much in common. For example, Democrats and Republicans do not differ in their fundamental commitment to the capitalist, private-enterprise market system. Certainly, policies can sometimes draw bipartisan support, and American legislators feel free to vote with their party political opponents when pressures from their constituency, from convincing lobbyists, or their personal moral positions seem more compelling. In domestic policy especially, however, one can see the different forces impelling the competing politicians of the USA. The presidency of George W. Bush launched the new century with the pursuit of a forceful policy agenda rooted in the president's conception of a 'compassionate conservatism'. After eight years, the electorate responded positively to the Obama campaign's invitation to 'Vote for Change', but while the balance of power in Washington shifted, the partisan battles over policy became no less vigorous. Fewer than two years into the Obama administration, the Republicans made major gains in the mid-term elections, taking control of the US House of Representatives. Many areas of domestic policy are the subject of fierce argument and negotiation between America's politicians and, according to some observers, the early twenty-first century has seen an increasingly confrontational style in American politics. In this highly contested political theatre, the administrations of the early twenty-first century have not always found it easy to turn their policy proposals into legislation.

The twenty-first century policy debate

When President Barack Obama took office in January 2009, he spoke in his inaugural address of the United States being a nation 'in the midst of crisis'. He had come to office after his election campaign had projected images and words of hope, change and empowerment in response to a widespread sense that the USA had become an embattled nation, challenged by difficulties at home and abroad to which its government had shown a less than sure-footed response.

Even before the Obama campaign was underway, there was already a growing sense of doubt evident in the public's opinions on Bush administration policies. The Bush White House, in reaction to its perception of the threat from international terrorism, pursued a robust foreign policy that initially garnered widespread support. Over time, the human and financial costs of these policies had a domestic impact; questions arose about the effectiveness of the strategies adopted, and support for the policies waned. Some voters were beginning to question the administration's competence. In August 2005, Hurricane Katrina devastated parts of the Gulf coast, severely damaging the iconic city of New Orleans. The less-than-dynamic reaction by government agencies to this very public and obsessively reported domestic crisis accelerated the decline of faith in the government's abilities.

In the 2006 mid-term elections, President Bush saw his fellow Republicans lose control of both chambers of the US Congress, adding a partisan hurdle to the institutional checks that are already built in to the legislative process. In late 2008, it became clear that the US financial sector was at the heart of an international banking crisis. The evidence of these difficulties increased during the last couple of months of that year's presidential election campaign. In such circumstances, it is not surprising that the administration's successful domestic initiatives trickled almost to a stop. But the US legislative process is a rough and tumble exercise in negotiation and compromise between the branches of government and the political parties and interests operating within them. Over its eight-year term the Bush administration did have significant domestic policy achievements. The roots of some of this success pre-dated the election of George Bush, and lay in the robust actions of the Republican legislature during the Clinton presidency. The Obama administration, in its turn, faced difficulties harnessing the enthusiasm of an election victory into a force that could deliver key policy accomplishments, and found that even having a party political majority did not automatically turn the legislature into a biddable partner on all policies.

While the appeal of change helped the Democrats to victory in 2008, only four years previously, the Republicans had dared to hope that they might be starting a substantial period of party domination. When President George W. Bush took office for his second term, in January 2005, it was the first occasion since the 1920s that the Republicans had held the presidency and simultaneously had a Republican-majority Senate and a Republican-majority House of Representatives. The second half of the twentieth century was characterised by a period of 'divided government', during which, more often than not, control of the elected branches and chambers of government was divided between the two major political parties. By the end of the 1900s, national authority in terms of control of elective office was very finely balanced between Democrats and Republicans. When opinion is so evenly matched, it takes only a slight shift in the public's voting patterns to tip the scales. The election result of 2004 suggested a small, but telling change, moving the Republican policy agenda firmly to centre stage for the opening years of the twenty-first century.

The domestic policy agenda that set the tone for the Bush administration concerned matters that have been central to American political debate for many years: the role of government in supporting individual Americans; the extent of government involvement in guiding social policy; and the cost to Americans of implementing these policies.

The first Bush administration saw the passage in 2001, 2002 and 2003 of legislation selectively reducing taxes. Some of these cuts were time-limited. A debate over national welfare provision continued in the context of discussions over the long-term shape that the existing Temporary Assistance for

Needy Families (TANF) programme should take. The health care system was modified, with altered prescription benefits for Medicare recipients. The federal role in education provision increased, with the passage of the No Child Left Behind Act.

This Republican agenda, together with the increased foreign policy spending prompted by the administration's increased defence and security activities in the wake of 11 September 2001, contributed to a considerable increase in the national debt, and an apparent change of attitude to deficit spending since the 1990s. The policies of the first Bush term were based on the thinnest of presidential election victories. With a clear margin of public as well as electoral college support, the second Bush term opened with commitments to continue on the same path, with proposals for income tax and Social Security reform, permanent tax cuts, and more education initiatives. All of these fit into the historic debates of American domestic policies over the years.

The Bush administration's fortunes slipped to the point where, in 2008, the vast majority of the electorate voted for change. Even those voting for Republican candidate John McCain did so in the overwhelming expectation that he would take a different direction from that defined by Bush's policy leadership. In a political atmosphere where change itself has such a strong appeal, it is easier for challengers to avoid detailed policy outlines. Nevertheless, Obama's campaign included commitments in a range of domestic areas, including aims on taxation, ethics in government, the economy, health care, education and science research.

America's public support policies

Competing philosophies of the American welfare state

There has been historically a strong tendency to avoid US federal intervention in areas of social policy. The proponents of this position consider that American beliefs in federalism, and in individual self-reliance, both underpin their case.

The Tenth Amendment of the US Constitution reserves to the states and the people those powers not particularly delegated in the body of that document. The eighteenth- and nineteenth-century development of US politics saw federalism observed as a division in which the vast majority of domestic policy was decided and implemented at the state level, and often delegated by states to local governments. While the division of authority between governments at national and state level was never entirely clear-cut, the tradition that decisions about the level of provision and allocation of costs for social policies such as education and welfare should be taken at the state level – close to constituencies that are affected – is well established and respected in the United States.

The Declaration of Independence speaks of all Americans' unalienable rights to 'Life, Liberty and the Pursuit of Happiness'; the US Constitution mentions the aim 'to promote the general welfare, and to secure the blessings of liberty', and goes on to include specific rights and protections in its amendments, but nowhere does it guarantee a particular standard of living. Some would interpret the role of American government to include the protection of its citizenry against individual misfortunes such as poverty and deprivation. Others, however, are firm in the belief that if life, liberty and rights are properly protected, then citizens have the responsibility to avail themselves of the opportunities that American society offers.

The provision of any social goods, whether roads, health facilities, educational opportunities or public welfare, inevitably throws up the issue of cost. Questions of how much provision should be provided on the public purse involve consideration both of what is an adequate level of service, and of how much can be afforded. A community facing the question of what services to provide is inevitably faced with the parallel question of what taxes will be needed to pay for them. In spite of having used income tax to collect revenue in the Civil War era, an attempt in 1894 to introduce a more permanent income tax was declared unconstitutional by the Supreme Court (*Pollock* v. *Farmers Loan and Trust Company*), and it took the passage of the Sixteenth Amendment to the Constitution in 1913 before the federal government had the opportunity to use this flexible tax resource – probably an essential tool of modern social welfare.

The debate over social policy adapts according to changing definitions of need and adequate provision, but the competing schools of thought have developed relatively consistent approaches.

On the one hand, there is the position that the freedom and liberty of the American polity and economy also imply an obligation and responsibility to make the best use of opportunity. In this scenario, citizens and their families should make adequate provision for their own long-term needs. In case of difficulties, people should be relied on to remedy social problems, acting individually or through charitable or other community organisations. Government intervention, according to this school of thought, will lead to higher taxes, which undermines individual opportunities to act in a civically responsible manner. Furthermore, government will expand, if it is required to make increased provision for social policy, and large agencies become wasteful, inefficient and distanced from the ordinary citizen.

This position on policy is often reinforced by a commitment to the devolution of policy decision-making and delivery to states and localities. The advocates of this approach argue that locally taken decisions are most likely to reflect local opinion and to be most appropriate to local policy needs. Furthermore, devolved decision-making keeps spending choices closer to those capable of assessing, and committed to working with, appropriate levels of local resources.

In contrast to this is the position that, while the freedom and liberty of American society may create much opportunity, equality of opportunity cannot be assumed to arise for absolutely everyone in contemporary American society. Not all citizens will have the same chance to succeed. Opportunity has to be underpinned by service provision, and government has an obligation to ensure that appropriate provision exists to support its citizens adequately in their pursuit of their target lifestyles and standards of living. Furthermore, some individuals and families will still fail to provide for themselves, and society has the obligation to ensure guaranteed standards of support for all of its citizens.

This more interventionist position is often accompanied by a more centralist approach to government activity. The proponents of this argument are unconvinced that social policy-making benefits from a piecemeal regional approach. They support the establishment of national standards to underpin these areas of policy. They suggest that states and localities are not always willing to address problems, but that the social welfare of the population is too important to leave without the imposition of national minimum standards.

There are many subtle variations on these positions. There are, for example, spectrums of opinion regarding which public services should be considered a broad public right, and which should not. And there are divisions of opinion regarding whether some parts of the population are more or less deserving of public service support. The roots of these debates sometimes lie in the early history of particular social service provision.

Early social welfare policy

Debates over the nature and extent of provision have been nowhere more vigorous than in the area of welfare. Many community practices in the early United States were continuations of colonial practices that, in their turn, had been imported from England. Welfare provision was no exception. Based on ideas that were codified in Elizabethan England, the relief of the poor was considered a local community responsibility. Persons in poverty might be given charitable help, or, in some places, they might be accommodated temporarily in the less than welcoming, purpose-built, local workhouse.

These imported traditions underpinned a restricted idea of general welfare. The stress was on the rights and responsibilities of the individual in a land of opportunity and resources. The idea of general welfare was restricted to limited public goods, such as the provision of roads and some system of public order. Limited individual relief was directed to those considered deserving – for example, those frail with age, or disabled – with an assumed obligation on private individuals and their charity. However, some researchers into modern US welfare consider it to be a twentieth-century innovation, sharing many conceptual foundations with poor relief, but emerging more directly from a concern to support poor mothers and their children, especially those in single-parent households.

After the stock market crash of 1929, the US economy slumped into a period that is now recalled as the Great Depression. Employment opportunities collapsed, throwing millions out of work, and putting unprecedented demands on the jigsaw of welfare provision made by the states at that time. In a nation hit so hard by economic conditions beyond any individual's control, it was hard to distinguish between those poor who were deserving, and those who could be thought of as undeserving. The body of opinion that supported universal standards for all gained strength in the face of the Depression's reality. While this did not result in the establishment of a European-style welfare state, some government projects did emerge. Among these, the models provided by various state initiatives to give limited support through 'mother's pensions' were drawn on in the creation of a national system of aid within the Social Security Act of 1935.

From New Deal to War on Poverty

Democratic President Franklin D. Roosevelt took office in 1933 with a mandate to tackle the problems of what appeared to be a national economic and social crisis. The Republican party's faith in the economic system to correct itself with very limited intervention had apparently failed. It has been estimated that up to 50 million Americans were in desperate poverty when Roosevelt became president. There followed a period of energetic expansion of the federal government's role in domestic policy as the administration used legislation proactively in a range of initiatives designed to combat the crisis.

The Civilian Conservation Corps (CCC) and the Civil Works Administration (CWA) were used to provide work relief, while the Federal Emergency Relief Act (FERA) made direct grants to the poor as well as providing funding through grants to state and local governments. The government sought directly to create jobs through such initiatives as the Works Progress Administration (WPA) and the Public Works Administration (PWA), which funded a huge range of building projects from modest local post office buildings to vast hydro-engineering projects. The government sought to lift and protect rural incomes through price supports and production controls in laws such as the Agricultural Adjustment Act (AAA). This New Deal alphabet of legislation signalled an extension of federal government activity into domestic social policy, and the Social Security Act was a very significant element.

Over time, the term Social Security has increasingly been applied solely to the system of benefits and pensions to which retired or disabled persons and their families are entitled, which were established by the Act. The original Social Security Act also contained other critically important sections setting up a system of unemployment benefits, and creating the programme that was to become the bedrock of federally funded poverty relief, Aid to Families with Dependent Children (AFDC).

All of these programmes had a long-term effect on the social and economic security of American workers. In particular, many of the elderly have been protected by their Social Security pension – a federal entitlement that does not depend on state-level intervention – from descending into poverty once their working lives are completed. Others have found periods of temporary unemployment easier, receiving support as of right, though these benefits do vary between states. By the end of the twentieth century Social Security entitlements accounted for 22 per cent of federal budgetary expenditure.

From an early stage, there was a clear distinction between the entitlement programmes within the Social Security Act, and AFDC. The latter, a means-tested welfare programme, was a regular source of controversy. There were certainly voices within the administration of the new welfare system that supported the idea that the needy should have simple and universal access to support, but there was resistance to this too. By definition, AFDC appeared to deem mothers and their children as more clearly deserving of support than other poverty-hit groups in society, and the administration of the welfare system seemed to its critics to emphasise the grudging and selective nature of welfare support.

States used residency laws to cut the costs of help for poor people. People who had migrated across state borders were in some states refused support until they had been resident in the state for long periods. Some states required up to five years' residence. States on occasion attempted to restrict the freedom of women on welfare to form sexual relationships, or imposed other regulations on recipients' behaviour. In some states, welfare applicants were threatened with home inspections that could result in children being taken into care. In few states did welfare payments come close even to the US government's own definition of the poverty income level. There was also a steady shift from a position that saw welfare support, however limited, as a right to enable poor women to stay at home with their children, towards one that perceived the working mother as a virtuous model, towards which welfare recipients should be guided.

These complex and adapting regulations, predominantly imposed by the states which were obliged to administer this federal programme, helped maintain a debate about the fairness of America's web of welfare provision. Arguments over the success of welfare support were themselves complicated by differing definitions of how success should be measured. Nevertheless, the US Congress, where the US House of Representatives especially was dominated by the Democratic party with only very brief interruption for more than half a century beginning in the 1930s, acted to make AFDC available to more categories of Americans – for example, in 1954 expanding it to include agricultural workers, who had previously been excluded.

During this period, two very different visions of AFDC emerged. On the one hand, the poor and their advocates were conscious of a welfare system that varied considerably, almost capriciously, between states, and within which some states supported the nation's poor at an unbearably low standard of living. While addressing health, education, training or child care needs might help some recipients change their circumstances, programmes were limited and underfunded. These critics felt, furthermore, that regulation of the system was at times conducted in a punitive fashion, and regulatory impositions such as those on sexual partners could be positively destructive to the family.

A very different perspective was held by those who criticised the system as becoming too unwieldy and expensive, and who accused it of 'featherbedding' unworthy recipients. Certainly, the expense of the system was growing apace. There was a twofold increase in those eligible for AFDC in the 15 years from 1950 as Congress expanded coverage, and as demographic and social changes in the USA led to a growth of households headed by females. Regardless of state-level restrictions, the overall cost to the taxpayer of welfare was growing steadily. Perceptions grew of a welfare population that chose dependency, of a system that was inefficient and corrupt in its operation, and of a programme that shifted resources from middle-class white taxpayers to unemployed black welfare recipients. However mistaken, these images of the welfare system in operation took firm root.

Research consistently found little fraud in American welfare provision, identified the vast majority of welfare recipients as genuinely needy, and pointed out that the number of white poor and welfare beneficiaries exceeded the number of blacks on the rolls. It found that almost all recipients had ambitions to improve their lot, and were willing to make the most of the limited opportunities available. In spite of the understandable anxiety expressed by American taxpayers that welfare was helping to drive an expansion of provision, and feeding a tendency towards 'big government', the 1960s was also a period which saw an expanded belief in the effectiveness of government as a positive force for change, which could reach out through its agencies to identify and solve social problems with interventionist legislation.

There was a brief period of enhanced government activism in social policy. Some older politicians may have felt that extended and supportive social policies were a natural heritage of the New Deal. A younger generation of politicians looked to research and experimental work on poverty and urban sociology, which appeared to indicate new approaches to long-lasting problems.

The proposals of the War on Poverty, and of Lyndon Johnson's Great Society programme emerged out of this political and conceptual coalition. The mid-1960s produced a range of legislation that affected social welfare support in various areas of policy, including the US Civil Rights Act, the introduction of food stamps, and the critically important Economic Opportunity Act, all in 1964, and the legislation introducing Medicare and Medicaid, the Elementary and Secondary Education Act and the Higher Education Act in 1965. Johnson asserted that his target was an end to poverty in America. In order to achieve this, his administration adopted the approach that poverty is the sum of many parts. While income support is a major element of an anti-poverty strategy, such matters as health care, jobs training, education and skills development, and motivation cannot be ignored.

Food stamps aimed to help the poor purchase food; the Education Acts included elements intended to provide targeted support to improve schools in poor areas. Related legislation provided breakfast programmes in schools, and the Headstart programme funded extra tuition for children from deprived areas. The federal support for benefits available under AFDC was expanded, and the numbers on the public welfare rolls grew by about 4 million between the mid-1960s and 1970. This period also saw a reduction in poverty among the sharpest ever measured, from 22 per cent to 13 per cent in the decade to 1970.

A small, but widely noted element of the anti-poverty strategy was to encourage client participation in local decision-making. This was prompted by research indicating that people who engaged with local issues with some chance of solving problems not only benefited their community, but also gained skills and self-confidence that could help their personal development. To the embarrassment of the federal government, some community action was so energetic that city, state and local governments felt threatened by the emergence of communities ready to make challenge against existing centres of power.

In health care Medicare provided some health insurance benefits for the elderly, while Medicaid was a parallel programme designed to help the poor. These programmes of health care support repeated the distinction made between Social Security and AFDC, a generation earlier. Medicare, like Social Security, was introduced as a federal government-funded programme paid to recipients as a matter of right. Eligibility for Medicaid, however, as for AFDC, has to be established through fulfilling various criteria, and both eligibility requirements and degree of coverage are set variously and locally by the states, through which the federal government channels the funds for these programmes. These programmes helped increase government spending considerably and, especially in view of very substantial rises in the fiscal demands made in other areas of policy, maintained the heated debate over government policies on taxing and spending.

From Nixon's plan to Newt's contract

Levels of direct economic aid to the poor remained low even in the most generous states, and ancillary programmes were often underfunded and bureaucratically complex, given their broad social aims. Nonetheless, the broader range of programmes and of eligibility increased the total cost to the taxpayer.

President Richard Nixon's administration saw a shift away from the vision of government as a problem-solving and interventionist force, and towards an interpretation of social welfare policy as a major cost on American taxpayers. Setting themes that have resonated in American government ever since, the Nixon White House launched a vigorous attack on high-tax, high-spending, big government policies that were portrayed as the heritage of a generation of Democratic party political dominance. At the core of Nixon's response was a proposal for welfare reform, a theme taken up by successive presidents for the rest of the twentieth century. Nixon's proposal, the Family Assistance Programme, including a minimum wage that would be guaranteed to employed persons through both regulation and payments made through the taxation system, was not wholly antagonistic to centralised social welfare policies, but was defeated by an unusual coalition of the right, who felt the programme too expensive for the taxpayer, and the left, who felt it too inadequate for the recipients' needs.

The big cost increases for social welfare were in Social Security and Medicare, those policies that could be expected automatically to deliver benefits to most of the population. Nevertheless, it was means-tested benefits that generally came under attack. President Ronald Reagan employed anti-welfare rhetoric in his campaigns, and his administration tightened eligibility requirements, increased state-level flexibility on regulation and increased work requirements.

The growing influence of conservative interest groups gave new validation to the old distinctions between those more or less deserving of public support through social policies. A debate on 'family values' that was to continue to influence American politics into the twenty-first century emerged strongly under Reagan. Conservative critics of welfare and other forms of public support argued that these policies generated a condition of social dependency that undermined both the American individual and the traditional structure of the family. In spite of actual support levels being very low, this school of thought argues that the nation's network of support offers the choice to be unemployed, and to indulge in creation of families of illegitimate children.

The shift in the late twentieth century was such that its last president, Bill Clinton, a Democrat, pledged an end both to big government, and to 'welfare as we know it'. Any doubt that substantial change would be achieved was eradicated when the Republicans took control of the US Congress after the 1994 elections. The new Speaker of the House, Newt Gingrich, had placed his Contract with America at the centre of the election campaign that had brought the Republicans victory, and he took this list of proposals as his agenda for the foundation of a new political approach for the new century.

The Contract with America continued the attack on big government, and the political engagement with concepts of family values. Among the contract's proposals were that funding would shift from social programmes to prison building; welfare spending would be cut; under-age welfare mothers would lose benefits; welfare mothers with new illegitimate children would receive no benefits for the new children; welfare periods would be limited; work requirements would be increased; and job creation would be encouraged through benefits to business. The contract was not passed in full, but formed part of a contest between the Republican Congress and President Clinton's Democratic White House that produced the 1996 Personal Responsibility and Work Opportunity Reconciliation Act.

The debates and legislation of the turn of the century continue to underpin the social support system on which the Bush and Obama administrations of the twenty-first century have since made their mark. Welfare, education, health care and pensions are so important that a presidential administration will inevitably address at least some of these areas of social policy. President Bush made education reform a core issue in his first presidential campaign, his administration initiated some health care reforms, and it proposed adaptations to the new welfare system. The Bush second term began with targets to reform Social Security. For a long time in the early part of the Obama administration, press coverage gave the misleading impression that health care was almost the only item on the political agenda. All of this social policy activity is constrained by the financial context. America's politicians are very aware of their public's general resistance to tax increases. The banking and financial crisis that began in the later stages of the Bush presidency made unusually stark and expensive policy demands on American government.

Items from a twenty-first century agenda

Temporary Aid for Needy Families (TANF)

When President Clinton signed the Personal Responsibility and Work Opportunity Act into law at a high-profile ceremony held on the White House lawn in the run-up to the 1996 Democratic National Convention, it signalled the end, after 60 years, of AFDC at the centre of welfare policy, and its replacement by TANF. While Clinton skilfully co-opted this legislation as a credential for his claim to be a welfare reformer, the new law clearly bears the imprint of the Republican congressional vision of the direction that should be taken in the new century.

The US government's stated core objectives for TANF are that the programme provides assistance to families with children or where there is a pregnant woman. The legislation establishing this programme sets itself firmly against what conservative critics perceived as the dependency culture infecting the welfare system. The legislation concentrates on job preparation and employment. Furthermore, the TANF vision puts a high value on the importance of the family unit. Promoting marriage, reducing illegitimacy and encouraging two-parent families are seen as proper elements of this twenty-first century policy.

Federal funds distributed to the states underpin the finances of the new welfare system. Within parameters set by the federal legislation, the individual states have some discretion regarding the regulation of eligibility and participation. The states also contribute some matching funds from their own resources, and may fund additional public welfare initiatives of their own. The shift from welfare based on the principle that recipients should have some basic level of income, however minimal, to a programme stressing the centrality of work, is especially evident in the funding limitations and reporting requirements that are contained within the legislation.

States receive federal block grants under TANF, which means that they are required to design their own individual plans to achieve the targets set by the federal government. Funding penalties are threatened if states fail to meet targets without acceptable explanation. Among the targets set are minimum employment participation rates by the recipients.

Sensitive to the criticism that welfare might be an incentive for single parents to stay home and bring up children, TANF may allow a period of home-based child care, but requires that, after a maximum of 24 months, parents in families receiving TANF must be engaged in work activities. States have the discretion to tighten this requirement, and about a quarter of the states demand immediate work activity from their TANF recipients. States are also free, within limits, to define what they mean by work activity. It may be staged from active and evident job-seeking, through participation in education and job training programmes, to community service and various categories of part-time and full-time employment.

Employment requirements on the individual vary from 20 hours per week for the single parent of a child under the age of 6, to a work requirement of 55 hours shared between the two parents if both are present, neither is disabled, and federal child care is available. The requirements on the states are that 50 per cent of all families and 90 per cent of two-parent families on TANF must be participating in work activities. Discretion exists to vary these bench-marks in special conditions – for example, in case of a severe economic recession in a region, or if a state has been able significantly to reduce its aggregate welfare caseload.

This was a landscape for welfare provision with which the Bush administration felt comfortable, claiming that nearly 3 million families had left welfare by 2002, with over 2 million families remaining on the rolls. The administration's aim continued to be the redeployment of welfare recipients out of welfare provision and into work. Academic research on poverty confirms that the number of people on welfare in the USA fell by about 60 per cent in the first few years that the new system was in operation. It is not entirely clear what all of these people found on leaving welfare, but certainly the employment rates among single mothers and other affected groups rose significantly.

Other forms of aid, such as Medicaid and food stamps, continued to form part of the welfare support system, and a Clinton initiative, the Earned Income Tax Credit, helped reduce the tax burden on low-income groups. While engagement with the workforce and the employment pool are generally seen as positive, there is concern among some observers that the current welfare system is promoting these features at the expense of providing a guaranteed and humane standard of living. Poverty and the associated need for welfare support are not always associated with unemployment. The poor in America are more typified by those who work in minimum-wage, or low-paying, and often very hard

Box 18.1

Goals and methods of TANF

The four purposes of TANF

- Assisting needy families so that children can be cared for in their own homes
- Reducing dependency of needy parents by promoting job preparation, work and marriage
- Preventing out-of-wedlock pregnancies
- Encouraging the formation and maintenance of two-parent families

Selected highlights of TANF

- Recipients (with few exceptions) must work as soon as they are job-ready or no later than two years after coming on assistance.
- Failure to participate in work requirements can result in a reduction or termination of benefits.
- Families with an adult who has received federally funded assistance for a total of five years (or less at state option) are not eligible for cash aid under the TANF programme.
- States [may] create jobs by taking money that is now used for welfare payments and using it to create community service jobs, provide income subsidies, or provide hiring incentives for potential employers.

Source: <http://www.acf.hhs.gov/opa/fact_sheets/tanf_factsheet.html>, US Department of Health and Human Services, Administration for Children and Families Office of Public Affairs Fact Sheet

jobs, and who nevertheless do not earn enough to break out of poverty. A system that increasingly forces welfare recipients into the low-wage job market may, in some states, benefit some former welfare cases, persuading them of their skills, helping them with job training, and even adding child care to ease their entry to the job market. In other states, the support systems may be meagre, and the results may look more like pushing an unskilled and unwaged group of people off welfare to create a labour pool that will help maintain low wages in parts of the employment sector.

Poverty rates fell dramatically in the second half of the twentieth century, but, while people have been leaving the welfare system, there has been no significant fall in poverty rates since the 1990s, and the economic slump starting in the last year of the Bush administration saw poverty rates rise above 13 per cent in 2008, the highest rates in more than a decade. Neither the Bush nor the Obama administrations have seen this as a reason to move away from the TANF approach. During debates on the future of TANF, the Bush administration affirmed its belief in the programme, listing as key aims promoting work, strengthening families, devolving authority to the states and localities, and denying access to most welfare benefits to immigrants until they have been in the USA for five years. A key difference during the Obama administration has not so much been a change of aims, as a $5 billion boost to TANF funds contained in the February 2009 economic stimulus bill that the new administration sponsored as a response to the recession that it inherited. All of this extra money was drawn on by the states before the end of 2010.

While the economic conditions at the end of the first decade of the new century led to an increase in the number of those seeking help from TANF and other welfare services, such as the Food Stamps Program, it did not significantly change the nature of the US debate over such support. Liberal voices subscribed to a narrative where the low-income employed and the unemployed found it difficult to qualify for the aid that might help them progress from dependency to productivity. What might be seen as a compassionate conservative analysis welcomed the economic flexibility that allowed TANF to increase its work in response to the needs of a recession-hit population while continuing to stress the primary objective of the programme as guiding and prompting people into income-generating employment. Those with a more strongly conservative view retained their opinion that TANF, along with many other income support and welfare provisions, acts as a subsidy to low-income populations, reducing incentives and interfering with the free operation of the labour market. They were concerned that any temporary extension of support prompted by recession might solidify into a more permanent liberalisation of the system. These debates continue within the context of a welfare programme that must be seen as having had considerable long-term impact.

No Child Left Behind

Presidents often bring to their administration ideas coming from their earlier experience in other offices or fields of endeavour. One policy that George Bush brought from his governorship of Texas was his active promotion of standards in education. Texas, with over 7,500 schools, nearly 300,000 schoolteachers, and well over 4 million school students, has the second-largest state education system (after California), and is responsible for almost 9 per cent of all America's school students. In the late twentieth century, however, there were concerns that educational standards were failing the clients of Texan schools.

Moves to improve matters in Texas pre-dated the Bush governorship. Future independent presidential candidate H. Ross Perot cut his political teeth leading a commission calling for improvements in the state's delivery of education. The call for educational improvements supported by some system of public accountability appealed to a wide cross-section of the public, gained bipartisan support, and was taken up at the national campaigning level. The Bush administration tightened the regime of school-based tests in reading and mathematics, and operated vigorously the Texas Assessment of Academic Skills (TAAS) tests which students had to pass in order to fulfil their high school completion requirements. The aggregate student performance on these standardised tests also fed into the assessment of schoolteacher and school management performance, providing a loop that connected student success or failure with the fate of educational personnel and institutions.

The importance that the Bush presidential administration attached to this domestic policy, and perhaps their eagerness to prove that faith in Republican domestic policy was not misplaced, was indicated when the new administration issued a full legislative proposal only three days after taking office in January 2000. After some negotiation, the bill attracted bipartisan support, with the late Senator Ted Kennedy as a sponsor, and the new legislation, replacing the previous Elementary and Secondary Education Act, was passed in December 2001.

Some Republicans were worried that the Bush proposals indicated a level of federal intervention in state affairs that went beyond the normally conservative approach espoused by that party. Primary and secondary education, above almost all other policy areas, was one where the traditional federal approach of devolving important local decisions to state and local governments had been well entrenched throughout American history. The establishment of a federal Department of Education had been achieved over the opposition of many Republicans. To some in the GOP, the Bush education policy seemed to be precisely the kind of big government they opposed, interfering in its regulation, expensive in its provision, and with the potential to expand.

It is nonetheless difficult for any government to remain entirely distant from a social policy area that delivers services to a shifting population of about 50 million school students, and which impacts not just on those clients, but on their parents, their family, and their future employees and colleagues. The Bush administration could also project the policy as part of its support both for work-oriented policies, and of the poor through improving their opportunities to create their own wealth, and ultimately reducing the numbers who would be claiming welfare through lack of preparation for the job market. These targets are encapsulated well in the political rhetoric of the legislation's name: 'The No Child Left Behind Act'.

As passed, the legislation requires annual state-imposed tests on all children in grades 3 (about age 9) to 8 (about age 14), with another test for school students during their final couple of years at school. The test results are made public, and, as well as being subject to scrutiny through the publication of these results, schools are required to meet target overall standards, as well as to achieve standards within substantial ethnic minority groups represented in the school. Schools can be identified as failing, parents have the right to move children between schools on the basis of results, and failing schools and school districts may be restructured by state authorities. The legislation also allows considerable state-level discretion over high school graduation requirements, and variation in methods of tallying, tracking and reporting results.

There has been much debate over the ability of this legislation to deliver the results it promised, and suspicion that some states have used the variability allowed for in the legislation to set their standards lower and thereby inflate the apparent quality of their education systems. Nevertheless, while some voices have called for repeal, the educational policy debate has generally proceeded in a way that has accepted the premise of the legislation and its key place in the federal role in this policy area. The Obama economic stimulus package of 2009 included $4.35 billion for the US Department of Education to pass to states with innovative ideas in education. In the pursuit of these funds, at least ten states passed legislation in 2009 to address the US Department of Education's concerns on the details of educational testing, the evaluation of teachers and the innovative management of schools.

Between 1991 and 2005, the federal government share of national spending on education rose from 5.7 per cent to 8.3 per cent. The recession at the end of the new century's first decade has left all levels of government struggling with budgets, but the states generally have less flexibility than the federal government to respond, and this gives an opportunity for Washington to increase its minority share of education funding. When funding is tight, even small percentages of new money can have considerable leveraging power when it comes to influencing policy and the Obama administration recognised this opportunity, proposing a real-terms increase in federal education funding in return for reforms. President Obama spent a substantial part of his January 2011 State of the Union address speaking of education, including a commitment to replace the No Child Left Behind Act with other educational reform. Some will see this as the natural continuation of the longstanding inter-party debates over education policy. Others will be concerned that a policy area traditionally reserved for state and local governments is being increasingly centralised. And those Republicans who worried that George Bush was too much a 'big government' Republican may identify education policy as being an area where Republican reform became a hostage to fortune in the hands of a subsequent Democrat administration.

Taxation and Social Security

The Bush administration placed tax cuts at its centre, in a way reminiscent of Ronald Reagan's focus on tax reductions just 20 years before. The argument had similarities, too. If big government is starved of funds, then it must necessarily shrink, and if people have more money left in their pockets, they will be more economically active, and generate more wealth. As more wealth circulates, continues this logic, jobs are created, and some of the costs of big government, such as welfare and social support policies, decrease, completing the circle. Among its first acts, the administration demanded tax cuts in excess of $1.6 trillion, and, on the basis of strong partisan support in Congress, managed to come close to this target in its 2001 tax reduction efforts. Further cuts were enacted in 2003.

The last years of the Clinton administration had been unusual in that the annual government budget had been in surplus. This situation reversed sharply early in the new century. Spending demands on the US government were growing very quickly. The attacks of 11 September 2001 prompted a vigorous response in terms of security-related legislation. Active military engagements were undertaken in Afghanistan and Iraq. The labour needs of the new policies added considerably to the government's wage bill. The hardware costs were also high, in terms both of the equipment needed to maintain a domestic security operation – for example, in airport security – and of the military equipment committed to the engagements overseas. The recession that started towards the end of the Bush term did not help the public finances. The US gross national debt of $5.6 trillion in 2000 had increased by 2010 to just under $13.5 trillion, and from 58 per cent of GDP to over 93 per cent of GDP. Reacting in part to these figures, the financial agency Standard and Poor downgraded to 'negative' the USA's credit rating in April 2011. While this will have no immediate impact on the US economy, it is one indication of the concern that has developed within the financial world that long-term economic stability has become a problem for even the strongest economies to address.

The prospect of increased deficit spending did not appear to check the Bush administration's enthusiasm for tax cuts, and the public resistance to tax increases severely limited the Obama administration's ability to manoeuvre. The Obama campaign had made much of its commitment to protect the middle-income groups and, in particular, not to increase the tax burden on any family earning less than $250,000. There was also strong pressure to make the earlier Bush tax cuts permanent when they came up for renewal. This was in spite of a huge surge in government expenditure in response to the banking and recessionary crises that affected the USA from around 2007. The government banking bailout and the economic stimulus legislation were hugely expensive projects that added to the national debt. The government's requirement to borrow in the face of these difficulties has been projected to remain at levels around 100 per cent for several years, facing administrations of any political stripe with very difficult economic decisions.

One area of public funding that has helped cover some of the US debt has been the Social Security fund, or those annual taxes paid by Americans to support the pensions system. The surplus of income over payments has meant that Social Security has been an asset to the annual debt in recent years. This is projected to change around 2016, when the impact of a gradually ageing population will mean that Social Security payments exceed the taxes collected, a deficit that is projected to increase steadily thereafter.

Social Security, like taxes, is a hard policy area for any administration to navigate. Taxpayers and pensioners are among those groups most likely to vote, and office-holders are careful not to antagonise such groups, if at all possible. It was therefore bold of George W. Bush to enter his second term expressing a wish to part-privatise the US Social Security system. Bush recognised the sensitivity of the issue, but felt that his high public opinion standing at that time gave him an opportunity to risk some of his popularity in the pursuit of what he felt was a necessary revision of the system. Social Security pays out on a non-means-tested basis, as of right. A threat to Social Security is not just a threat to poor people, but a threat to all potential American pensioners. The promise not to mess with Social Security has been a touchstone of American politics for more than a generation, and launching into a public debate around the topic was a bold move.

The Bush reform proposals were, in themselves, quite modest. Only a small proportion of wages would potentially be diverted from social security taxes into private investments but, as Bush's head of Strategic Initiatives Peter Wehner wrote at the time: 'the Social Security battle is one we can win – and in doing so we can help transform the political and philosophical landscape of the country'. However, in spite of widespread concern about the financial state of the Social Security system, this policy terraforming did not take place. Pensioner groups were not convinced; unions were resistant; Republican legislators were not convinced they wanted to campaign on the issue. Bush's first step towards reform would, at least initially, have cost money rather than saved it, and Bush's approval ratings, part of the capital being expended on this policy effort, began to fall sharply in his second term.

Pensions provision in the face of growing government deficits and a declining proportion of the population in work may not be an intractable problem, but is clearly both difficult in real terms and sensitive politically. President Bush felt that high public standing and a re-election victory gave him the potential to have a serious long-term impact in this policy area. Some analysts feel that the second term of an administration is already too late to tackle such a deeply embedded policy area and its attached interests, and consider instead that most presidents need to move early in their first term if they have tough targets in their sights. This was probably the thinking behind the timing of President Obama's health policy proposals.

Health care

Current health care provision in the USA reflects the complexity found in all areas of the nation's social support policies. In the main, US health care is funded from private, rather than public or government sources. In 2007, total health expenditure in the USA exceeded $2.24 trillion. Between 2000 and 2007, health spending rose by 66 per cent, and further growth of 81 per cent was projected for the next decade. Less than half of this total, or just over $1 trillion, was public expenditure, primarily paid through Medicare and Medicaid. Most of the rest of America's health expenditure came from its citizens through their health insurance premiums ($775 billion) and their direct out-of-pocket cash expenditure on health services and supplies ($269 billion).

Most Americans are covered by health insurance, either through private purchase, as an employee benefit, or through coverage by one of the government programmes for the elderly, disabled or poor. The nation has historically preferred to approach health care as an insurance-based provision, rather than as a public service akin to police protection. Those covered by insurance – public, private, or employer-based – may have access to very high-quality services and some cutting-edge health technology. Not all health insurance policies cover all eventualities, however, leaving part of the population under-insured. Typically, during the first decade of the twenty-first century, over 15 per cent of the US population had no health insurance at all, and the impact of economic recession was seen when this figure rose as high as 16.6 per cent in May 2009. Especially low rates of insurance are experienced by Hispanics, people in less affluent families, young adults (especially those under 30 years of age) and the black population.

The Medicare programme provides benefits to the elderly and to certain categories of disabled persons specified in the legislation. The core provision, an entitlement to certain hospital care, is funded from federal taxes on workers, with extra Medicare benefits covering physicians' fees available through a federally sponsored contributory insurance programme. The number enrolled on Medicare exceeded 45 million persons in 2008. At the same time, there were also around 40 million on the Medicaid programme. Targeted at the poor, this programme is supported by federal grants to state health authorities, and varies in its coverage according to the level of added state support and state regulation. As with all welfare-oriented programmes, Medicaid can be controversial, but government spending on its Medicaid recipients was lower than on the similar number entitled to Medicare. While the 2006 cost of the entitlement programme, Medicare, was $380 billion, payments under the public assistance Medicaid programme amounted to $270 billion.

Inflation in medical costs has affected the whole range of health provision. Health care costs exceeded 16 per cent of US gross domestic product by 2008, a figure well ahead of other developed countries, and the US percentage was projected to continue growing. At state level, Medicaid programmes have faced repeated examination for savings opportunities, continuing a long tradition of rationing social support provision for the poor.

Dealing with a broader and more affluent population, private insurers in America have attempted to protect themselves by regulating closely the procedures for which they provide coverage. The threat that cost limitations imposed by insurers may extend some elements of health care rationing beyond the poor to the majority of Americans, has prompted calls for a 'Patients' Bill of Rights' placing obligations on the insurers.

Costs did not prevent President Bush succeeding in late 2003 in getting a Medicare prescription drug benefit passed through Congress, which is the largest single expansion in Medicare expenditure in the 40 years since it was founded. The benefit, met critically by some who felt it did not go far enough and was too complex in its operation, was nonetheless a burden on government finances at a time when other pressures – most notably the combination of expensive foreign and defence policies and a commitment to tax cutting – were producing a substantial national deficit. Not all conservative Republicans were happy with their president's enthusiasm for further Medicare provision and expenditure, which might be interpreted as another example of 'big government' Republicanism. That said, the retired population which benefits most from Medicare has a high election turnout rate, and is a prime target for the Republican party.

Health care policy in the USA is a topic that generates strong feelings. The effort to maintain clinical excellence while limiting expanding costs, to guarantee access while avoiding a welfare-driven approach, and all the time working within an insurance-based model has ensured this policy area a place on the policy agenda of many presidential administrations. President Clinton famously failed to persuade Congress to enact the substantial health reform proposed when he was first in office, a failure that contributed to the heavy defeats for his Democratic colleagues in Congress in the mid-term elections of 1994. Health care remained a very live issue, and President Obama again proposed reform when his administration took office in 2008.

The progress of President Obama's health care legislation illustrates well the difficulties faced by attempts to pass landmark domestic policies. The legislative process in the USA has been envisaged by some analysts as a corridor punctuated by many doors. For proponents to traverse the corridor successfully, they need to open all the doors in their path. Opponents only need to keep one door closed to ensure the journey fails. The early signs for Obama's health proposals were quite positive when, only two weeks into his term of office, he signed into law an update of the Child Health Insurance Program (S-CHIP) which expanded its coverage from 7 million to 11 million children. This legislation gained almost unanimous Democratic support in Congress, and attracted bipartisan approval from a number of Republicans.

Bipartisanship was not evident on other key matters at this time. For example, the American Recovery and Reinvestment Act, responding to the recession, attracted no Republican support in the House and only 3 Republican votes in Senate. The reduced number of Republicans in the first Congress faced by Obama tended to reflect the more conservative positions from the party's political spectrum. The unexpected success of the Democrats in temporarily reaching the filibuster-proof figure of 60 supporters in the US Senate appeared to prompt the Republicans into a more united and determined opposition to the administration than has often been the case. The Democratic majorities in House and Senate were the best the party had achieved for many years, but the Democrat majorities included conservatives who had concerns about some aspects of the health care reform proposals – especially in terms of cost control and increased government intervention.

In March 2009, President Obama demonstrated his administration's investment in health care reform with a White House Forum on Health Care Reform which brought together opinion leaders from Congress, business, communities and a range of organisations. By early April, he had established a White House Office of Health Reform to coordinate the administration's efforts, though, in an attempt to avoid some of the problems faced when President Clinton presented a large and complex bill to Congress, Obama adopted a more hands-off approach, encouraging Congress to develop the initiatives. A large item of this kind may not fall within the remit of a single congressional committee.

In the House, the three Committees on Ways and Means, Energy and Commerce, and Education and Labor were all directly concerned with the legislation and, in the other chamber, the Senate Finance Committee and the Senate Committee on Health, Education, Labor and Pensions each had a say. The three House committees jointly released a bill on June 19, thereafter holding separate hearings. In July, largely on party lines, each of these committees voted in favour of reform. The last of these votes, by the House Energy and Commerce Committee, came after negotiations led to concessions in the draft legislation to the concerns of conservative Democrats. The Senate committees worked separately on their drafts of the legislation, and conciliation of the various drafts remained incomplete as the 2009 congressional summer recess started.

The recess saw a period of increased and vigorous public debate on health care, with interests expressing strong opinions on all aspects of reform. The Republican minority appeared increasingly united in its opposition to the overall reform effort. In the House, provisions for a government-run 'public option' in the proposed health reform were watered down, and restrictions on abortions tightened in order to maintain enough support from conservative Democrats. In the Senate, where the support of 60 of the 100 Senators is needed to force a vote on legislation, wavering supporters of the Democratic party's proposals had especially high leverage. The public option was dropped from the Senate version to ensure support from Independent Senator Joe Lieberman (CT), and Democrat Senator Ben Nelson (NB) gained abortion restrictions and particular benefits for his state. The House passed its version of a health bill on 19 November, and the Senate on 24 December.

In order to keep clear the corridor from proposal to legislation, the supporters of health reform had guided their bills through 5 congressional committees, engaged in a vigorous public debate, and made compromises and adjusted the proposals to maintain a large enough majority in both chambers of Congress. All of this effort had delivered a tight, 5-vote, majority in the House, and the bare 60-vote 'supermajority' required in Senate. The next stage was expected to involve careful negotiation between the House and Senate towards the creation of common wording that could be presented to both chambers with a reasonable chance of successful passage. It was at this point, on 20 January 2010, that Republican Scott Brown unexpectedly won the special election held in Massachusetts to fill the seat previously held by Democrat and staunch health reform supporter Senator Edward Kennedy. The Democrat expectation of 60 relatively reliable votes in Senate collapsed with this loss, and the party had to look to redesigning its strategy. Within days, President Obama signalled a shift to an increased focus on economic and employment issues, moving health care away from the centre of attention, and, in an attempt to keep the door from closing on his reform efforts, he called a bipartisan summit on health care. Almost exactly a year after President Obama's White House forum to launch his administration's health care effort, the theatre for the debate returned to the same place.

Democratic party leaders were divided over the appropriate course to take on the legislation, but President Obama opted to move forward quickly. The Patient Protection and Affordable Care Act, based on the legislation passed in Senate on 24 December 2009, with some rapidly negotiated adaptations, was signed into law in March 2010. In parallel with the Health Care and Education Reconciliation Act, this constituted the content of the Obama health care reforms. The Obama administration delivered health care reform in line with its campaign promises, but did not receive wholehearted plaudits as a result. Early polls suggested that, while over 40 per cent of the electorate supported the reforms, more than half the respondents did not. To add more complexity, about two-thirds of opponents felt the reforms went too far, but almost one-third of them thought they had not gone far enough.

The health care battle provoked fierce opposition from a substantial minority of the US population. It dominated the first year of the Obama administration and provided a clear and tangible topic around which opposition could organise. The need to compromise for victory undermined the strength and loyalty of support. Once again, while health care had been identified by the electorate as one of the major issues to be tackled, an administration has found only electoral punishment in doing so.

The context and the future

An administration must expect considerable challenges if it attempts to reform some aspect of the nation's core domestic policy structures. When an issue lies at the centre of party political, or even national, political philosophy, an administration will have to be ready to try to maintain unanimity in its own party and to woo potential support from factions in the other party. The political arena for these debates may stretch beyond the chambers of government, into the media, and to grass roots activity when proposals prompt many and varied interests into reaction.

The reputations of administrations are very influenced by the success or failure of such high-profile issues, but there is not always a perfect fit between successful pursuit of these policies and consistent progress on the broad range of initiatives that are the responsibility of any administration.

President Bush ended his term with exceptionally low public opinion approval. His flagship foreign policies had lost public support, and his plans to reform Social Security never gained any traction. Nevertheless, domestic policy had been remodelled in a way consistent with the stated aims of Ronald Reagan – a president much admired by George W. Bush. Tax cuts had been made and retained through the term of the administration, reducing the government funds available for domestic policy initiatives. An unintended consequence of the administration's 'War on Terror' was that budgetary flexibility in domestic policy was further reduced. On the domestic policy scene, at least, one could argue that a conservative vision had been fairly successfully achieved during the Bush presidency.

President Obama's first years in office saw setbacks as the Democrats lost important gubernatorial elections in New Jersey and Virginia, as well as the loss of the Senate seat in Massachusetts which eliminated the 60-seat 'supermajority' that his party had come to depend on in the legislative battle over health care reform. The president's public opinion approval ratings had fallen faster than those of any recently elected president in their first year in office. Nevertheless, the Obama White House had shown considerable skill in its legislative work. By choosing his issues carefully, compromising when necessary, and adopting a clear leadership role when appropriate, he gained a notable success rate in promoting legislation through Congress. On issues where the president took a position in his first year of office, he achieved a 98.7 per cent success rate in the Senate, and 94.5 per cent in the House – the highest scores since this calculation was first made in the 1950s. That legislative success does not necessarily turn into political success was shown in the 2010 mid-term elections, when an administration that had initiated health care reforms, passed anti-recession legislation and had foreign policy successes lost heavily in the competition for House and Senate seats. The strategic skills made evident by the Obama administration's legislative successes are still only likely to gain public recognition if relatively high-profile policies are deemed at least to be a medium-term success.

Chapter summary

Debate on American social and domestic policy provision has always contained the strands of two arguments in addition to the content of the policy. One of these strands has been the ever-present tension over state versus federal authority in the provision of domestic policies. The other is the continuing debate over the proper reliance that should be made on public as opposed to private spending in these policy areas.

While never embracing European models of state provision, for much of the twentieth century, successive American administrations created a complex welfare state providing health, education, welfare and other supports.

The Bush administrations of the early twenty-first century continued with Clinton's aim to 'end welfare as we know it', and pursued domestic strategies through tax cuts. They also showed willingness to challenge their own ideological right wing at times, and to be interventionist – for example, in education and Medicare – in order to achieve their policy aims. Nevertheless, the policy debate has steadily shifted from one based on a conception of a right to particular standards of social and welfare support, to one based on taxpayers' rights and the obligation of the state-supported population to undertake work activities, and to take responsibility for themselves.

The recession that started in the later stages of the Bush administration, together with the banking crisis in the final months of that presidency, presented the Obama administration with a changed political context, immense inherited challenges, and some opportunities. The presidents of the twenty-first century have been bold in their attempts to remould the political landscape, but it will be some time before it is clear which vision has the most impact.

Discussion points

1. Has the turn of the twenty-first century brought a distinctively different form to the American welfare state?
2. Is welfare and human support policy in the USA typified more by forward planning, or by response to crisis?
3. Whose interests are best served in the operation of the American welfare state?
4. Is the expansion of federal involvement in the field of education likely to be paralleled by growing federal engagement with other domestic policy areas?
5. Why are some parts of the spectrum of social support policies more subject to change than others?
6. Is the American health care debate more about costs than it is about coverage?

Further reading

Beyond the purely academic approaches to America's domestic condition, Barbara Ehrenreich's *Nickel and Dimed: On Not Getting By in America* (New York: Henry Holt/Owl Books, 2002) is a vividly lived and vividly written participant observation study of being among the working poor in America. Gwendolyn Mink and Rickie Solinger (eds), in *Welfare: A Documentary History of US Policy and Politics* (New York: New York University Press, 2003), provide nearly 1,000 pages of documentation from scores of sources, and some valuable commentary, especially covering the century up to TANF re-authorisation.

In *No Child Left Behind? The Politics and Practice of School Accountability* (Washington, DC: Brookings Institution, 2003), editors Paul E. Peterson and Martin R. West provide valuable insights into both the politics and the educational theory behind the federal government's expanded education role. Any attempt substantially to revamp the pensions element of Social Security is likely to lead to fierce debate in the quality news media and in political campaigns, but the story so far can be found in Sylvester Schieber and John Schoven's *The Real Deal: The History and Future of Social Security* (New Haven: Yale University Press, 2000).

The Bureau of the Census (www.census.gov) provides data on many aspects of American social policy and information on the progress of legislation can be found on a special site at the Library of Congress (http://thomas.loc.gov). Recent debates on policy can be followed in major news sources such as the *New York Times* (http://www.nytimes.com) and the *Washington Post* (http://www.washingtonpost.com).

Simon P. Newman, *Embodied History: The Lives of the Poor in Early Philadelphia* (Philadelphia: University of Pennsylvania Press, 2003) provides an insight into the experience of the poor in the earliest years of American independence. Michael J. Heale, in *Twentieth Century America: Politics and Power in the United States, 1900–2000* (London: Arnold Publishers, 2004) and *The Sixties in America: History, Politics and Protest*

(Edinburgh: Edinburgh University Press, 2001), looks at the battles over social policy in the USA in the century and in an important decade. A useful contemporary overview of two significant policy areas is provided by John Iceland, *Poverty in America* (Berkeley: University of California Press, 2003). Shirley Anne Warshaw's *The Co-Presidency of Bush and Cheney* (Stanford: Stanford University Press, 2009) gives a good overview of approaches to policy and policy-making in the Bush White House, John Kenneth White's *Barack Obama's America: How New Conceptions of Race, Family and Religion Ended the Reagan Era* (Ann Arbor: University of Michigan Press, 2009) gives an early analysis of the cultural tensions that underly the policy battles of the early twenty-first century, and Gary C. Jacobson's 'Legislative success and political failure' *Presidential Studies Quarterly* vol. 41, no. 2 (June 2011), 220–43, does the same looking back from the Democratic failures in the mid-term elections.

Chapter 19

Abortion

This chapter examines what has undoubtedly been the most controversial social issue in the United States over the past three decades or so. As well as being interesting and important in its own right, abortion politics provides an illuminating case study of the policy-making process. It brings into dramatic light the operation of the core constitutional principles of federalism, the separation of powers, and checks and balances. It also reveals the conflict that can arise over policy-making between different government institutions and between different interest groups.

In August 1994, Dr John Britton was shot and killed as he was leaving his clinic in Pensacola, Florida. It came as no surprise to learn that the man arrested for his murder, Paul Hill, was a militant anti-abortion activist. A similar murder had taken place the previous year and groups such as the Army of God had been bombing clinics for some time. What made Dr Britton a target was the fact that his clinic performed abortions. While this was perfectly legal, it was also dangerous, given the rise in anti-abortion violence. Indeed, Dr Britton had adopted the practice of wearing a bullet-proof vest to work, but even this could not save him.

The murder of John Britton came after some 25 years of acrimonious political conflict, during which the political system of the United States struggled to establish a policy on abortion that could satisfy, or at least placate, different points of view and demands. The fact that it has failed to do so is partly owing to the highly emotive character of the abortion issue. It also reflects, however, the unusual degree to which different institutions of American government can pursue and enforce different and contradictory policies on the same issue.

The rise of the abortion issue: state legislation

As recently as the early 1960s, abortion policy was not an issue at all in American politics. In the first place, abortion was one of many policy areas that the constitutional principle of federalism had assigned to the individual states. Thus, abortion was not an issue on which the national government was expected to have a policy. Secondly, most states had determined their abortion policies in the second half of the nineteenth century and there had been little reconsideration of them since. Those nineteenth-century abortion laws were generally very restrictive, usually only permitting abortion when the mother's life would otherwise be endangered.

Nothing much changed until the 1960s when two distinct, but mutually reinforcing developments occurred. The first concerned abortion as a *medical issue*. In 1962, the pregnancy of Sherri Finkbine, a resident of California, became national news. Finkbine had been taking tablets containing the drug thalidomide, which soon became infamous for causing severe foetal deformities. Finkbine's doctors initially recommended that she have her pregnancy terminated, but the hospital stalled because it was not clear whether the abortion would be legal under Californian law. Finkbine then flew to Sweden for the abortion. The foetus was, indeed, badly deformed and would not have lived, according to the Swedish doctors.

Shortly after, there was an epidemic of rubella (German measles) in California. It was well known that the foetuses of pregnant women who contracted rubella were often seriously deformed. Yet doctors who wished to perform abortions on such women were again uncertain whether the state's nineteenth-century law made these abortions illegal.

As a result of the Finkbine case, the rubella epidemic and a long-standing concern over the evils of illegal 'back-street' abortions, the medical profession in the United States began to campaign for liberalised abortion laws. What they sought were laws which allowed abortions where doctors considered there was danger not merely to the mother's life, but also to her physical and psychological well-being. These medical factors, then, lay at the heart of the drive for abortion reform in the 1960s.

Towards the end of that decade, the second development occurred. This was the movement for women's liberation or gender equality (see Chapter 6). Along with other radical movements that arose in the 1960s, the women's movement was determined to challenge the established political, social and economic order. However, the movement quickly came to the conclusion that, unless women had control over their reproductive capacities, all other reforms would be undermined. How, for example, could women compete with men on an equal basis in the workplace if they could suddenly be incapacitated by an unwanted pregnancy? While easy access to contraception had gone a long way in mitigating such problems, the women's movement believed that women would never have true reproductive freedom, and therefore equality with men, unless they had the right to abortion. In the words of one feminist writer, abortion was 'a condition of women's liberation' and 'a paradigmatic feminist demand' (Petchesky, 1981, p. 210).

In 1967, the National Organization for Women (NOW) made reproductive freedom, including abortion, part of its Women's Bill of Rights. This was clear evidence that the movement for liberalised abortion had now transcended its purely medical parameters. While groups such as NOW were certainly concerned with women's health, they were equally convinced that women's freedom involved the right to choose abortion regardless of whether there were medical problems or not. They wanted 'abortion on demand' as a fundamental political right. In time, this would significantly alter the public perception of the abortion issue. Instead of being seen primarily as a serious health matter, on which deference was due to the medical profession, it became perceived by many as a controversial political issue, associated with a radical, feminist agenda for widespread social change.

Until the early 1970s, the medical image of the abortion issue predominated, and health care professionals led successful movements for liberalised abortion in a number of states. For example, the legislatures of California, Colorado and North Carolina all passed reform bills in 1967. These new laws, although widening access to abortion, placed the emphasis upon health (or *therapeutic*) grounds for abortion. As a result, doctors rather than pregnant women themselves took the ultimate decision over whether an abortion would take place. This failed to satisfy the women's movement, which wanted women to be empowered to make the decision. They also wanted abortion legalised, even for *non-therapeutic* reasons.

The first such radical success came in New York in 1970. Following a campaign, which for the first time included significant activities by women's groups, the state legislature passed a new law which, in effect, permitted abortion on demand during the first three months of pregnancy (Tribe, 1990, p. 141). Unlike the earlier reform campaigns in California, North Carolina and Colorado, the debate over the New York law was highly charged and acrimonious. Indeed, no sooner had it been passed than anti-abortion groups began to campaign for its repeal. In 1972, the state legislature voted to do just that, only for Governor Nelson Rockefeller to thwart them by using his veto.

By 1972, a majority of states had considered reforming their nineteenth-century abortion laws. Some had actually passed new laws; others had rejected them. Although the issue was beginning to take on the character of a fundamental ideological conflict between pro-choice and pro-life pressure groups, its explosiveness was diluted by the fact that a different battle was being fought in each of the 50 states. Moreover, this federalism aspect allowed different outcomes in different states, so that each side to the conflict could count some victories, as well as defeats. However, that was about to change with the intervention of the Supreme Court.

The Supreme Court and *Roe* v. *Wade* (1973)

As we saw in Part VI, the Supreme Court has a policy-making role in American politics. Through its power of judicial review, the Court can order any branch of American government, federal or state, to change its policies if those policies are deemed to violate the Constitution. Of course, there are relatively few policy areas addressed by the Constitution and accordingly, the Court intervenes only infrequently in the policy-making process. On the other hand, since the 1950s, the Court has shown a marked appetite for asserting the civil liberties of individuals against government regulation: and in 1973, the Court decided to extend its liberal judicial activism to the issue of abortion.

The campaign for the reform of abortion laws had not confined itself to the arena of state legislatures. Some pro-abortion activists were hopeful that they could convince the judiciary that abortion rights were so fundamental to women's freedom that they should be recognised as constitutionally protected. They were encouraged in this by a Supreme Court decision of 1965, *Griswold* v. *Connecticut*. In that case, the justices had upheld the right of married couples to use contraceptives in the face of a state ban. They concluded that the Constitution protected certain privacy rights of citizens, including the right to choose whether to beget children. In 1972, the same right was extended to non-married couples (*Eisenstadt* v. *Baird*).

There were, however, significant obstacles to a Court decision upholding abortion rights against restrictive state laws. First, the 'right to privacy' announced in *Griswold* was rather tenuous: no such right is mentioned in the Constitution and many legal scholars were unconvinced by the rationale for declaring its existence as an 'unenumerated right'. Secondly, even if the right to privacy was sound, it was not obvious that it could be applied to abortion: a termination of pregnancy not only took place in a public facility, it also involved the elimination of a 'living' entity – the embryo or foetus. Thirdly, abortion policy had always been considered the province of the states and not the federal government, including the Supreme Court.

Nevertheless, to the surprise of even pro-abortion activists, the Court not only found that the right to abortion was constitutionally protected, but also devised a very liberal framework within which that right could be exercised. In essence, a woman in the first six months of pregnancy, and having consulted a physician, could not be prevented by government from having an abortion; even in the last three months of pregnancy she had the right to an abortion if there was otherwise a threat to her life or health.

The *Roe* decision did not give pro-choice activists everything they wanted. It did not, for example, allow abortion on demand at all stages of pregnancy and the medical profession still had considerable influence over a woman's decision. Nevertheless, it was so liberal that every state law except New York's was rendered unconstitutional. In effect, the Supreme Court had constitutionalised and nationalised abortion rights, leaving the states with little control over this area of social policy.

Box 19.1

The *Roe* v. *Wade* case (1973)

In this landmark case, the Supreme Court voted 7–2 to hold that the Constitution, through its unenumerated right to privacy, protected a woman's right to choose to terminate a pregnancy by abortion. The justices also recognised that states had certain legitimate interests in abortion decisions – preserving maternal health and protecting potential life. The Court therefore sought to balance the competing interests of the mother's right to abortion against the states' interests within the following chronological framework:

First trimester (first three months of pregnancy)

In consultation with her physician, a woman is free to choose to have an abortion. The state may not interfere with this decision. As abortion is medically safer than continuing pregnancy during this period, the state has no reason to prevent the abortion to protect maternal health. As the embryo/foetus is not capable of life outside the womb at this stage, the state has no reason to prevent the abortion in order to preserve potential life.

Second trimester (second three months of pregnancy)

A woman is still free to choose an abortion, in consultation with her doctor, but because abortion now poses a greater medical risk to her than continuing the pregnancy, the state's interest in preserving maternal health becomes operative. It can therefore regulate the conditions under which terminations take place, such as the kinds of hospital and clinic which may perform them. However, since the foetus is still not capable of life outside the womb, the state has no right to prevent the abortion pursuant to its interest in protecting potential life.

Third trimester (final three months of pregnancy)

At about the end of the second trimester, the foetus becomes 'viable': that is, it is capable of living outside the mother's womb, with or without artificial means of support. The state's interest in protecting potential life is thus relevant to this stage of the pregnancy. In addition to regulating the conditions under which abortion may take place, therefore, it can now ban them altogether, but with one major exception: if her doctors agree that continuing the pregnancy poses a threat to her life or health, the mother may still choose an abortion.

Box 19.2

Who has an abortion in the United States?

The data below make clear that, in about 80 per cent of cases, women who have abortions are unmarried, in their twenties or early thirties and less than 11 weeks pregnant.

Number of abortions performed, selected years, 1972–2008

	No. of abortions
1972	587,000
1975	1,034,000
1978	1,410,000
1982	1,574,000
1992	1,529,000
2000	1,313,000
2008	1,210,000

Abortions, by selected characteristics, 2008

	Percentage of all abortions
Age	
Under 15 years	0.4
15–19 years	17.2
20–24 years	33.4
25–29 years	24.4
30–34 years	13.5
35–39 years	8.2
Over 40 years	2.9
Race	
White	36.1
Black	29.6
Hispanic	24.9
Other	9.4
Marital status	
Married	14.8
Co-habiting	29.2
Never married, not co-habiting	45.0
Previously married, not co-habiting	11.0
Weeks of gestation (2006)	
Less than 9 weeks	61.8
9–10 weeks	17.1
11–12 weeks	9.1
13–20 weeks	10.4
Over 20 weeks	1.5

Source: Jones, Rachel K, Finer, Lawrence B. and Singh, Susheela, ***Characteristics of US Abortion Patients 2008***, Guttmacher Institute, 2010; ***Facts on Induced Abortion in the United States***, Guttmacher Institute (May, 2011)

While *Roe* was welcomed as a great victory by pro-choice activists, it simultaneously caused deep offence to two distinct elements in the country. First, it antagonised state legislatures who had been deprived of their policy-making powers. Secondly, it disturbed, if not outraged, many who considered that abortion would now be undertaken 'lightly': that is, without any medical justification. In his dissenting opinion in *Roe*, Justice Byron White alleged that the Court had approved abortion 'on the whim or caprice' of pregnant women. Those who disagreed with the Court, therefore, set out to reassert the states' powers and to reverse the abortion policy of *Roe* v. *Wade*.

Pressure groups and abortion policy

In the late 1960s, groups campaigning for women's equality, like NOW, began to address the issue of abortion as part of their concept of reproductive freedom. They were supported to a greater or lesser extent by a wide variety of other interest groups. Some were dedicated to the abortion issue and related reproductive matters. These included NARAL, the National Association for the Repeal of Abortion Laws, founded in 1969. (While keeping the same acronym, NARAL has changed its name twice. After *Roe*, it became the National Abortion Rights Action League, and in 1994 it changed again to the National Abortion and Reproductive Rights Action League.) Another major campaigner for abortion rights was the Planned Parenthood Federation of America (PPFA). In addition to these policy groups, many professional organisations backed at least therapeutic abortions: these included the American Medical Association (AMA), the American Psychiatric Association (APA) and the American Public Health Association (APHA). There were also ethnic and religious groups which supported abortion rights, including the American Jewish Congress (AJC). In short, the abortion rights campaign was quite well advanced in that most crucial feature of contemporary American politics, interest group activity.

Until the *Roe* decision, anti-abortion activism was confined largely to the Catholic Church, although the defeat of an abortion reform referendum in Michigan in 1972 was brought about partly by the founder of the National Right to Life Committee (NRLC), John C. Willke (McKeever, 1993, p. 82).

Such was the shock of *Roe*, however, that it galvanised the anti-abortion movement. The Catholic Church was still central, particularly its Pastoral Plan for Pro-Life Activities, launched in 1975, but opposition to *Roe* went beyond traditional Catholic dogma. Many social conservatives, particularly in the middle and lower-middle classes, felt not merely that abortion involved the taking of innocent life, but that it was part of a broader threat to traditional family values (Conover and Gray, 1983). They swelled the ranks of groups such as the NRLC, the League for Infants, Fetuses and the Elderly (LIFE) and the Christian Coalition. In the 1980s, more militant anti-abortion groups emerged, such as Operation Rescue.

A fierce conflict soon developed between pro-choice and pro-life groups, as they preferred to call themselves. Pro-choice groups adopted a defensive posture, seeking to preserve the gains made in *Roe*. Pro-life groups went on the attack. They prompted sympathetic politicians to introduce pro-life measures into Congress and state and local legislatures; they supported these measures in the courts through amicus curiae briefs; and they launched public campaigns, including an annual March For Life outside the Supreme Court in Washington on the anniversary of the *Roe* decision (22 January). All this activity quickly paid dividends.

Congress and abortion policy

Abortion is the kind of divisive policy issue of which many legislators prefer to steer clear, for whatever they may gain in votes and campaign donations from supporting one side, they are likely to lose as much, if not more, by alienating the other. Before *Roe*, members of Congress could avoid taking a stand on abortion by arguing that it fell within the exclusive jurisdiction of state legislatures. Once *Roe* had nationalised abortion rights, however, they were put under pressure to take a public position by pro-life legislative proposals. These included constitutional amendments to outlaw virtually all abortions; statutory measures declaring the foetus to be a legal person and therefore having all the same rights to life and liberty as American citizens; and bills that would remove the right of the Supreme Court to hear cases involving abortion. All of these failed. In part, this was because of opposition by pro-choice legislators, but it was also because they were such drastic measures and, in effect, embodied a frontal assault on the Supreme Court and its authority in interpreting the Constitution.

The Hyde Amendment

Many members of Congress were ready, however, to do something to placate the rising anger of the pro-life movement. In 1976, they passed the Hyde Amendment. The pro-life representative Henry Hyde (R – Illinois) introduced a rider to the Health, Education and Welfare Appropriations bill, that cut off Medicaid funds for virtually all abortions. Medicaid is the federally funded health care programme for America's poor. The Hyde Amendment continued to permit Medicaid funds to be used for all health care associated with pregnancy. However, not even therapeutic abortions (medically necessary) would henceforth be covered unless the mother's life was otherwise endangered. In subsequent years, other exceptions to the amendment's ban were included: thus the measure passed in 1993 allowed Medicaid funds for abortion where pregnancy had resulted from rape or incest.

Nevertheless, the Hyde Amendment achieved its main goal of eliminating virtually all Medicaid abortions. In 1978, its first full year of operation, the number of such abortions fell from 295,000 in the previous year to just 2,000 (Petersen, 1984, p. 170). While it did not affect the abortion rights of the great majority of women who were not eligible for Medicaid health care, it certainly made it very difficult for poor women to exercise their constitutional rights as declared in *Roe*.

Congress had thus shied away from a direct attack on *Roe*, but had undoubtedly undermined the new abortion right by the indirect method of refusing public funds to facilitate its exercise. The same tactic lay behind the Adolescent Family Life Act of 1981. This Act gave grants to organisations to promote chastity among teenagers, but no organisation giving contraception or abortion counselling was eligible for funds (McKeever, 1993, p. 259). In effect, then, Congress used its control of the public purse to adopt a compromise position in the pro-choice/pro-life conflict.

Presidential abortion policy

Views on abortion transcend party lines in the United States. For the most part, however, the pro-choice movement has made its home in the Democratic party, and the pro-life movement in the Republican party. Given the ascendancy of Republicans in the White House since the *Roe* decision, it comes as no surprise to learn that the executive branch has opposed the judicial branch over abortion. This was particularly true of presidents Reagan and Bush.

Despite the fact that both presidents regularly called for a constitutional amendment, they lacked the means directly to overturn the Supreme Court's decision in *Roe*. They did, however, possess a number of powers that could, like Congress, attack it indirectly. They employed three such powers in particular. First, they used executive orders and administrative guidelines to cut any kind of support for abortion counselling. Most notably, President Reagan issued a 'gag rule' in 1988, forbidding anyone employed on a federally funded health programme from even discussing the subject of abortion with a patient.

Secondly, the Reagan and Bush administrations instructed the solicitor-general to intervene in abortion cases before the Supreme Court and to urge the justices to reverse their decision in *Roe*.

Thirdly, and most controversial of all, President Reagan employed presidential powers of appointment to pack the federal judiciary with judges antagonistic to *Roe*. Through the newly created President's Committee on Federal Judicial Selection, the Reagan administration sought to appoint only those judges with a conservative judicial philosophy. Such a philosophy usually entails opposition to the *Roe* decision and the administration was widely perceived by its opponents as operating a 'litmus test' for judicial nominees: did they oppose the constitutional right to abortion?

At the Supreme Court level, President Reagan's plan worked well enough until he attempted to appoint Robert Bork in 1987. Bork was a knowledgeable but controversial constitutional theorist and judge. He was deeply hostile to the Court's reasoning in *Roe* and, indeed, in many other modern cases. His nomination also came at a time when the Court was thought to be evenly balanced on the merits of *Roe* and hence Bork was regarded as a certain fifth and decisive vote to overturn it (Hodder-Williams, 1988). A massive movement was mounted to persuade the Senate to reject Bork's nomination. At the heart of it were the leading pro-choice interest groups, as well as others concerned with the preservation of the civil rights gains of the past 25 years (Bronner, 1989). Together, they assured Bork's defeat.

Nevertheless, President Reagan appointed three new members of the Court: Sandra Day O'Connor, Antonin Scalia and Anthony Kennedy. President Bush appointed two further justices: David Souter and Clarence Thomas. Gradually, these changes were to place the survival of *Roe* in great jeopardy. They combined with congressional actions to cast abortion policy at the federal level of government into turmoil. The Supreme Court had, in effect, established a policy which said that women were free to have an abortion for any reason during the first six months of pregnancy and thereafter for serious health reasons. Congress made clear its distaste for that policy by banning the use of federal money to fund it, thereby effectively discriminating against America's poorest women; and Presidents Reagan and Bush were doing all they could to get the Supreme Court to reverse itself on abortion, while also making it as difficult as possible for women to receive advice and information on their constitutional rights.

State responses to *Roe*

Some states welcomed the new liberal abortion policy announced by the Supreme Court. Others, however, either refused to comply with it or sought to undermine it by adopting regulations which were clearly intended to make it difficult in practice for women to obtain abortions. Rhode Island, for example, responded by passing a law stating that life begins at conception, that a foetus was a legal person and that physicians performing abortions not necessary to save the mother's life would be liable to criminal prosecution. Pennsylvania and Missouri enacted laws requiring a woman wishing to have an abortion to obtain her husband's consent. Other states simply surrounded the abortion decision with a maze of regulatory and administrative procedures designed to deprive women of a real choice (Ford, 1983). Still others banned abortions from being performed in public hospitals, leaving women reliant upon private clinics. While this posed no great problem in the country's major metropolitan centres, women in rural areas and smaller towns often had to travel hundreds of miles to obtain abortion services, sometimes having to go to another state. In short, many states observed what they took to be the letter of *Roe* v. *Wade*, while doing everything possible to violate its spirit.

Public opinion on abortion

While interest groups, the Supreme Court, president, Congress and states all vied with one another for control of abortion policy in America, each naturally sought to influence public opinion. Yet, despite the raging political battle in the corridors of government and, indeed, in the streets of America, public opinion has settled into a stable pattern. In particular, the rival sets of interest groups have both been unable to shift majority public opinion away from its middle-of-the-road position. That said, the 'pure' pro-choice position receives significantly greater support than the 'pure' pro-life position.

Table 19.1 Public opinion on abortion, 2011

Issue: A woman should have the right to decide to terminate a pregnancy in the first few months of her pregnancy

Strongly agree/Agree **%**	**Strongly disagree/Disagree** **%**
64	35

Question: With respect to the abortion issue, would you consider yourself to be pro-choice or pro-life?

Pro-choice **%**	**Pro-life** **%**
49	45

Sources: *Time* Poll, June, 2011; Gallup Poll, May, 2011

Most analyses show that a majority of Americans favours liberal access to abortion services for health reasons, but disapproves of non-therapeutic abortions. Moreover, the majority does not believe that public funds should be available for abortions for any reason. In political terms, a majority of the public rejects the Christian Right's goal of banning or severely restricting abortion rights.

In other words, both the Supreme Court's *Roe* decision and the policy preferences of pro-choice groups would appear to be to the left of public opinion. In 2005, this was implicit in Senator Hillary Clinton's public statements on abortion, where she emphasised the undesirability of abortion while still defending it as a constitutional right. Presidential policy under recent Republican administrations and the position of pro-life groups appear to be sharply to the right of public opinion. As always, however, one must treat public opinion surveys with some caution. For example, while a majority of the public disapproves of non-therapeutic abortions, some polls show a majority simultaneously claiming to support the Court's decision in *Roe*.

Whether these incompatible majorities reflect the different wording of the questions asked, or the ignorance or indecisiveness of many Americans, is not clear. What is more certain, however, is that public opinion is more supportive of a compromise on abortion policy than are the activists on both sides of the conflict.

The Supreme Court revisits *Roe* v. *Wade*

The *Roe* decision was by no means the Supreme Court's last word on abortion policy. In the first place, the decision established a policy framework for the competing claims of women and government, rather than a detailed policy covering all aspects of abortion. Secondly, as we have seen, many simply did not accept the decision and sought to thwart its implementation. Inevitably, many of these state and federal responses to *Roe* were challenged as unconstitutional and found their way to the Supreme Court. In a series of cases continuing to the present day, therefore, the justices had the opportunity to flesh out the policy framework of *Roe* in greater detail, and, if they wished, to incorporate some of the objections to their original decision. Naturally, the arrival of newly appointed justices at the Court would play a large part in any such reconsiderations.

As noted above, *Roe* was approved by a majority of 7–2 of the justices. Gradually, however, that majority was whittled away. In 1976, in *Planned Parenthood* v. *Danforth*, a 6–3 majority struck down Missouri's spousal consent law. In 1977, the Court actually upheld Connecticut's law cutting off public funds for non-therapeutic abortions (*Maher* v. *Roe*), and three years later, the Court upheld the Hyde Amendment, cutting off funds for both non-therapeutic and therapeutic abortions (*Harris* v. *McRae*). These cases did not involve a challenge to the basic right to choose an abortion, but many commentators suspected they indicated waning enthusiasm on the Court for defending *Roe* v. *Wade*.

Those suspicions were further raised by the Court's decisions in *Akron* v. *Akron Center for Reproductive Health* (1983) and *Thornburgh* v. *American College of Obstetricians* (1986). In both these cases, legislatures adopted 'regulations' which were, in fact, a transparent attempt to put pressure on women not to have abortions at all. For example, the Akron ordinance, written by a lawyer for the Ohio Right to Life Society, contained an 'informed consent' provision, requiring that certain information be given to a woman before she could have an abortion. The information in question was blatant pro-life propaganda designed to make the woman believe that the embryo/foetus was a person and that abortion was a major medical procedure. Writing for the Court, Justice Lewis Powell described this information as a 'parade of horribles' intended 'not to inform the woman's consent but rather to persuade her to withhold it altogether'.

The law at issue in *Thornburgh* contained similar provisions, and Justice Harry Blackmun's majority opinion sharply rebuked Pennsylvania, commenting that 'the States are not free, under the guise of protecting maternal health . . . to intimidate women into continuing pregnancies'. It was worrying for pro-choice activists, however, that the 6–3 majority of *Akron* was now reduced to 5–4 in *Thornburgh*. In other words, one more switch in the vote in a future case and not only would anti-abortion regulations like those enacted by Akron and Pennsylvania become constitutional, but the basic right to have an abortion might also disappear.

It was after the *Thornburgh* decision that President Reagan made his ill-advised and unsuccessful attempt to put Robert Bork on the Supreme Court. The campaign to defeat the Bork nomination had the effect of reinvigorating the pro-choice movement. Having become somewhat complacent after *Roe*, and relying too much on the Court to fight off the assault of pro-life groups and the Reagan administration, the battle over the Bork nomination made the pro-choice movement realise how close it was to losing the constitutional right to an abortion. If the Court ever allowed *Roe* to be reversed, either wholesale or in part, then the conflict over abortion rights would be returned to the states and, possibly, Congress. In short, abortion policy would be determined once again by legislatures.

It was precisely that outcome that many predicted for the Court's next major consideration of the abortion issue in 1989, in *Webster* v. *Reproductive Health Services*. Again, a number of unmistakably anti-abortion 'regulations' were at issue in the statute from Missouri. These included a preamble declaring that life begins at conception and a foetal viability examination in the second trimester – even though *Roe*'s framework had said

Box 19.3

Leading abortion cases in the Supreme Court since *Roe*

***Planned Parenthood* v. *Danforth*, 1976**

A 6–3 majority declares unconstitutional a Missouri law requiring a woman to obtain her husband's consent for an abortion.

***Maher* v. *Roe*, 1977**

A 6–3 majority *upholds* the constitutionality of a Connecticut law cutting off Medicaid funds for non-therapeutic abortions.

***Harris* v. *McRae*, 1980**

A 5–4 majority *upholds* the Hyde Amendment passed by Congress, which cut off Medicaid funds for non-therapeutic *and* therapeutic abortions, except where necessary to save the mother's life.

***Akron* v. *Akron Center for Reproductive Health*, 1983**

A 6–3 majority declares unconstitutional an Akron (Ohio) ordinance placing various conditions upon a woman's right to choose an abortion. These included an 'informed consent' provision, a 24-hour delay between signing the consent form and having the operation, and a requirement that the foetal remains be disposed of 'in a humane and sanitary manner'.

***Thornburgh* v. *American College of Obstetricians*, 1986**

A 5–4 majority *strikes down* several provisions of a Pennsylvania statute similar to those in *Akron.*

***Webster* v. *Reproductive Health Services*, 1989**

A 5–4 majority *upholds* provisions of a Missouri abortion law, even though at least one appears to violate the trimester system established in *Roe* v. *Wade*. Of the majority justices, only Justice O'Connor seems unwilling squarely to reverse *Roe*. Chief Justice Rehnquist declares *Roe* to be 'modified'.

***Planned Parenthood* v. *Casey*, 1992**

A 5–4 majority *upholds* several provisions of a Pennsylvania statute similar to those declared unconstitutional in *Akron* and *Thornburgh*. The trimester system of *Roe* is abolished. However, to the surprise of many, 5 justices nevertheless vote to sustain the basic constitutional right to choose an abortion.

***Stenberg* v. *Carhart*, 2000**

A 5–4 majority *strikes down* a Nebraska state law banning the use of the partial-birth abortion technique. The majority insists that any such law must contain an exception where there is a threat to the life or health of the woman.

***Gonzales* v. *Carhart*, 2007**

A different 5–4 majority effectively reverses the *Stenberg* decision and upholds the federal Partial-Birth Abortion Act of 2003. The switch is explained by the replacement of Justice O'Connor by Justice Alito in the intervening period.

that states could not act on their interest in protecting potential life until the third trimester. More openly, both the state and the Bush administration urged the Court to overrule *Roe*.

The pro-choice movement was as pessimistic as the pro-life movement was optimistic. After all, the Court now contained not only the two original dissenting justices in *Roe* (Rehnquist and White), but three justices appointed by President Reagan (O'Connor, Scalia and Kennedy). There was, then, a likely majority for abandoning *Roe* v. *Wade*. Fearing the worst, the pro-choice movement put on a show of political strength by organising a demonstration of some 300,000 people outside the Court on the day the case was argued.

There was, however, no clear-cut decision in *Webster*. This was due principally to the tightrope walked by Justice O'Connor. On the one hand, she agreed with Rehnquist, White, Scalia and Kennedy, that all the provisions of the Missouri statute were permissible, but on the other hand, she alone insisted that this was not incompatible with *Roe*. As a result, it was not possible to muster a majority to overturn *Roe* and Chief Justice Rehnquist was obliged to say that it was modified and narrowed, but its basis left undisturbed.

If *Webster* resolved little in the abortion conflict, its tolerance of the Missouri regulations was an invitation to states to pass similar laws and even to test further the limits of the Court's increasing willingness to allow them to regulate the constitutional right to abortion. As Justice Blackmun wrote in dissent, the Court's opinion was 'filled with winks, nods, and knowing glances to those who would do away with *Roe* explicitly'.

The fundamental issue left hanging in *Webster* was whether the Supreme Court still held to the view that there was a right contained in the Constitution that allowed a woman to have an abortion, even when her state legislature was vehemently opposed. By the time the next major case came along in 1992, it seemed certain that that issue would be resolved, for in the years since *Webster*, President Bush had been able to replace two of *Roe*'s staunchest champions on the Court – Justices William Brennan and Thurgood Marshall – with two nominees of his own – David Souter and Clarence Thomas. In fact, of the original majority of seven justices in *Roe*, only Harry Blackmun remained. The constitutional right to abortion seemed doomed.

In *Planned Parenthood* v. *Casey* (1992), however, the Court reaffirmed *Roe* in a manner which secured the basic constitutional right while allowing still further state regulation. The Pennsylvania law under review contained, among others, a 24-hour waiting period and informed consent provision reminiscent of those declared unconstitutional in *Akron* and *Thornburgh*; it also contained a provision requiring a woman intending to have an abortion to notify her husband of the fact. In yet another complicated voting line-up, a bloc of seven justices upheld the waiting period and informed consent provisions, thereby in effect overruling *Akron* and *Thornburgh*. Moreover, the trimester system was explicitly abandoned and states could henceforth adopt regulations that applied at any stage of pregnancy, provided they did not put an 'undue burden' on the woman's right to choose.

A different bloc of five justices, however, declared the spousal notification provision unconstitutional. Much more important still, the same bloc reaffirmed the basic constitutional right to abortion. The key group of justices in *Casey* consisted of Sandra Day O'Connor, Anthony Kennedy and David Souter. In their joint opinion upholding the fundamental element of *Roe*, the three justices emphasised the importance of stability in the law. First, they said, some stability in abortion law was due to women who needed it and had grown used to it:

> **For two decades of economic and social developments, people have organized intimate relationships and made choices that define their view of themselves and their places in society, in reliance on the availability of abortion in the event that contraception should fail. The ability of women to participate equally in the economic and social life of the Nation has been facilitated by their ability to control their reproductive lives.**

Secondly, the three justices emphasised the importance of stability for the concept of a society governed by laws and for the Supreme Court as the interpreter of the Constitution. While they implied that they did not necessarily agree with the *Roe* decision as originally made, they argued that to overrule it now would create the impression that they had retreated in the face of the political pressure applied by the pro-life movement. Such an impression would seriously diminish respect for both the law and the Court itself. Without absolutely compelling evidence that *Roe* had been wrongly decided, therefore, they would not overturn it while 'under fire' or 'surrender to political pressure'.

Abortion policy today

Political developments since *Casey* have consolidated the abortion policy established there. Most important was the election of Bill Clinton, the first pro-choice president since 1976. Clinton reversed the administrative orders put in place by presidents Reagan and Bush, including the 'gag order'.

Moreover, in his first 18 months in the White House he had the opportunity to appoint two new Supreme Court justices. In 1993, Justice Byron White, one of the original dissenters in *Roe*, announced his retirement and was replaced by Judge Ruth Bader Ginsburg. As a lawyer, Ginsburg had worked on many of the key gender equality cases of the 1970s and, although somewhat critical of the legal reasoning in *Roe*, she is known to support the constitutional right to abortion. In 1994, the author of the Court's opinion in *Roe*, Harry Blackmun, also retired, to be replaced by Judge Stephen Breyer. Although his record on the issue is limited, he too is thought to support the essence of *Roe* v. *Wade*. As far as the Supreme Court is concerned, therefore, the basic constitutional right to an abortion looks set to remain in the foreseeable future. At the end of its 1997 term, the Court had only three justices – Rehnquist, Scalia and Thomas – who would reverse it altogether. This explains the fact that the Supreme Court has not decided any major case on the fundamental right to abortion since *Casey*.

Of course, abortion policy is more complicated than the basic constitutional issue. Beyond the right to have an abortion is the problem of obtaining an abortion in practice. We saw above how the Hyde Amendment cut off federal funds for abortion for poor women, and this shows no sign of changing – all attempts to overturn the ban have been easily defeated in both the House and Senate.

States are free to use their own funds to pay for abortions for indigent women, but only a few do this. For most American women, therefore, the right to an abortion depends partly on their ability to pay. Poverty is compounded by the fact that, following the decisions in *Webster* and *Casey*, some states have clamped down on abortions being performed in public hospitals. Many women therefore have to travel long distances to private abortion clinics; and the costs involved are further increased by the waiting period provisions of many state laws, which may necessitate an overnight stay in a hotel.

It is not merely public hospitals which are performing fewer abortions: fewer doctors and clinics are offering abortion services. According to one count, in 1992, 18 per cent fewer clinics provided abortion services compared with ten years earlier (*The Economist*, 16 July 1994). This may be due to the intimidatory tactics of extreme anti-abortion groups like the Army of God and Operation Rescue. As well as murderous bombings and attacks on clinics and doctors, some groups have become effective at physically blocking access to clinics that provide abortions. Here, however, there is now some sign of policy cohesion at the federal level. In 1994, Congress passed the Freedom of Access to Clinic Entrances Act (FACE), making it a federal criminal offence to blockade abortion clinics or threaten those who wish to enter them. Also in 1994, the Supreme Court decided unanimously that the Racketeer Influenced and Corrupt Organizations Act (RICO) could be used to prosecute those conspiring to organise such clinic blockades (*National Organization for Women* v. *Scheidler*). Further cases will be needed, however, to clarify just how far government can go in stopping clinic protests, without violating the First Amendment free speech rights of anti-abortion protesters.

If the pro-choice movement achieved a congressional success with FACE, it also suffered a major setback in 1993 when Congress abandoned consideration of the Freedom of Choice Act. This was an attempt to codify the abortion rights of *Roe* v. *Wade* into federal law, thus contradicting many of the state law provisions permitted by the Court in *Webster* and *Casey*. It was originally introduced during the presidency of George Bush and the hope was that the arrival of the pro-choice Bill Clinton in the White House would ensure its passage. However, when it proved impossible to obtain a consensus on what restrictions the Act should contain, legislators decided not to proceed (*National Journal*, 5 March 1994).

The conflict over abortion continues, then, but has reached a stalemate for the foreseeable future. The Supreme Court looks set to defend the basic right to abortion, a right of which some 1.3 million women avail themselves every year. Since this represents over a quarter of all pregnancies, it is clear that the pro-choice movement is driven as much by social need as by ideology.

Meanwhile the pro-life movement continues to campaign for the abolition of that right. It searches for new tactics and issues by which to maintain the pressure on abortion rights. Thus it seized on the rarely practised procedure known as 'partial-birth abortion' to advance its case that abortion involves the killing of an innocent life. Such was the success of this campaign that the Republican-controlled Congress outlawed it. As is typical of the abortion issue, however, this was immediately countered by the actions of a different political institution – President Clinton vetoed the ban in 1997. And in 2000, in a 5–4 vote in *Stenberg* v. *Carhart*, the US Supreme Court struck down a Nebraska state statute that banned the procedure.

Pro-life forces were reinvigorated by the election of George W. Bush in 2000, with the result that Congress re-passed the Partial-Birth Abortion Ban Act in 2003. By the time the issue came back to the Supreme Court in 2007, President Bush had replaced Justice O'Connor with Justice Alito, with the result that the Stenberg decision was effectively reversed.

However, the fight over partial-birth abortion was really just a skirmish, while the main protagonists await the main battle: a renewed attempt to overturn *Roe* v. *Wade*. Pro-life forces were stymied by the election of the pro-choice Barack Obama as president in 2008. His subsequent nomination of two pro-choice justices, Sonia Sotomayor and Elena Kagan, meant that a five-justice majority still supported *Roe* v. *Wade* – Justices Kennedy, Ginsburg and Breyer, plus the two Obama nominees. Much may depend on whether or not President Obama wins a second term in office and whether or not he has new opportunities to make nominations to the Supreme Court.

Chapter summary

Since the Supreme Court's intervention in *Roe* v. *Wade* in 1973, abortion has been the most intractable of all policy issues in the United States. The policy-making process has struggled to contain it. In part, this is because the opposing factions do not merely disagree over policy, but also have fundamentally different sets of values about individual freedom and social values. The conflict is also fuelled, however, by the fact that the fragmented nature of the American policy-making process, characterised by numerous access points and forums, always seems to offer determined protagonists another chance of turning defeat into victory. It is hardly surprising, therefore, that political activists who are dealing with matters of life and death take full advantage of what the system has to offer.

Discussion points

1. Why is abortion such a divisive issue in the United States?
2. Should judges or elected politicians make national policy on abortion?
3. Why has the pro-life movement failed to reverse the Supreme Court's decision in *Roe* v. *Wade*?
4. Is abortion policy better made at the state level than at the federal level?

Further reading

Two classic works on the politics of abortion are K. Luker, *Abortion and the Politics of Motherhood* (Berkeley: University of California Press, 1984) and P. Conover and V. Gray, *Feminism and the New Right: Conflict Over the American Family* (New York: Praeger, 1983). The story of *Roe* v. *Wade* is told in accessible fashion by M. Faux, *Roe* v. *Wade*: *The Untold Story of the Landmark Decision that Made Abortion Legal* (rev. edn, Lanham, Md.: Rowman & Littlefield, 2001). For a subtle analysis of the limitations on abortion rights, see W. Saletan, *Bearing Right: How Conservatives Won the Abortion War* (Berkeley: University of California Press, 2003). For a comprehensive legal account of the abortion controversy, see N. Hull *et al.* (eds), *The Abortion Rights Controversy in the United States: A Legal Reader* (Chapel Hill: University of North Carolina Press, 2004). For a recent overview of the subject, see Dorothy E. McBride, *Abortion in the United States* (Oxford: ABC-Clio, 2008).

References

Bronner, E. (1989) *Battle for Justice* (New York: Doubleday).

Conover, P. and Gray, V. (1983) *Feminism and the New Right: Conflict Over the American Family* (New York: Praeger).

Ford, N. (1983) 'The evolution of a constitutional right to an abortion', *Journal of Legal Medicine*, IV, pp. 271–322.

Hodder-Williams, R. (1988) 'The strange story of Judge Robert Bork and a vacancy on the United States Supreme Court', *Political Studies*, vol. XXXVI, pp. 613–37.

McKeever, R. (1993) *Raw Judicial Power? The Supreme Court and American Society* (Manchester: Manchester University Press).

Petchesky, R. (1981) 'Antiabortion, antifeminism, and the rise of the new right', *Feminist Studies*, vol. VII, pp. 206–46.

Petersen, K. (1984) 'The public funding of abortion services', *International and Comparative Law Quarterly*, vol. XXXIII, pp. 158–80.

Tribe, L. (1990) *Abortion: The Clash of Absolutes* (New York: Norton).

US Bureau of the Census (2005) *Statistical Abstract of the United States* (Washington, DC).

Chapter 20

Foreign policy

The history and role of the United States in the international system is undoubtedly a remarkable one. From a loose association of 13 former colonies perched on the Atlantic seaboard in 1776, the USA became the world's only superpower by the end of the Cold War in 1989. This chapter charts that rise and, equally importantly, examines the debates that have long surrounded the nature and goals of US foreign policy. In particular, it analyses the claim that the United States is an 'exceptional' state in the international system. The argument for 'American exceptionalism' is essentially that the founding values of the United States led it to behave quite differently from other states in the international system. Whereas 'Old World' European states had developed out of rivalries between absolutist monarchies bent on maximising their wealth and power, the United States developed out of the 'New World' and was based upon republican values of liberty, constitutionalism and national self-determination.

The United States and international relations theory

The behaviour and motivations of states in the international system is a hotly debated subject. Until comparatively recently, most scholars accepted the validity of the theory of 'classical realism'. This holds that the international system is essentially anarchic in that there are no international laws that a state is ultimately obliged to observe, nor any international institutions that can effectively enforce such international laws as do exist. This means that each state is compelled to act according to its own interests and in a manner best suited to serving those interests. According to classical realists, states therefore seek to maximise their power in order to protect their interests and use that power against other states, even to the point of waging war.

Realist theories of international relations are challenged by idealist theories. These take various forms but two which are frequently cited in explaining American foreign policy are liberalism and constructivism. For some, liberalism and US foreign policy are synonymous. In many ways, the theory of liberalism was developed precisely to explain how and why the United States behaved differently from other states in the international system. From the very start, the liberal argument goes, the United States sought to break away from the Old World practice of international relations. For example, the country declared itself opposed to military alliances that, sooner or later, dragged nations into war. America viewed itself as different from other nations and these differences were to be reflected in its foreign policy. Because the United States was a liberal, republican nation, American foreign policy was also liberal and republican. Thus, just as the United States sought national self-determination from the British in the War of Independence, so too did it support the right to national self-determination for others. The United States was opposed to empire-building.

An interesting more recent theory of international relations is constructivism. This emphasises the identity and self-image of a people as a determinant of foreign policy. Whereas realism is based on material self-interest and liberalism on political ideas, constructivism argues that foreign policy at any given time will reflect how a nation sees itself and particularly how it distinguishes itself from other peoples and nations.

If we apply these theories to American foreign policy during the Cold War, realism would suggest that the USA was seeking to maximise its power and defend its economic and security interests in the face of a military threat from the Soviet Union and its allies. Liberalism would emphasise that the United States was defending freedom and democracy and the right of nations to self-determination. Constructivists would emphasise that America at this time came to see itself as a 'global policeman' whose role and duty was to ensure a peaceful world order.

These and other theories of American foreign policy should not be viewed as mutually exclusive. In a matter as complex as foreign policy, it is almost certain that material self-interest, political ideas and ideals and national identity will come into play. Similarly, foreign policy is likely to be affected by factors both external and internal to the nation. The task then, for students of the United States, is less to validate one theory or the other, than to understand what each theory can contribute to an explanation of American foreign policy at any given point in its history.

Nature of foreign policy

Foreign policy is a broad term, covering many different spheres of policy and action. Its concerns include defence and national security, overseas trade and commerce, global stability and conflict, and the values and rules which govern relations between states. The instruments for carrying out foreign policy are equally varied: economics, diplomacy and military action each offer a wide range of means of pursuing foreign policy goals.

The goals themselves are innumerable in a complex and interdependent world, but may broadly be subsumed under three headings: security, economic prosperity and ideology. In its pursuit of economic prosperity and national security, the foreign policy of the United States resembles that of other nations: these are, after all, the basic necessities that all countries seek in their dealings with other nations. As such, they loom large in the *realist* school of foreign policy which holds, for example, that the United States should only intervene militarily in international conflicts when there is a clear and substantial American economic or security interest at stake.

The ideological content of American foreign policy is, however, more distinctive. It has its roots in the earliest years of the American colonies, when settlers from Europe set out to build a newer and better society than those they had left behind. Inspired by religious idealism, they eschewed the corruption and strife of Europe. They saw themselves as pilgrims in a land that God had reserved for a special destiny: the creation of a society morally, socially and politically superior to any that had gone before. Unsurprisingly, therefore, they also believed that their new society would serve as a model for the future progress of the human race. As John Winthrop, the leader of those who established the Massachusetts Bay Colony in 1630, told his group: 'We must consider that we shall be as a city upon a hill, the eyes of all people are upon us.'

Thus, from their earliest days, Americans developed a sense of *mission* and almost inevitably this found its way into American foreign policy. After all, a belief in one's distinctiveness and superiority as a nation is bound to colour one's relations with other nations not so blessed. Yet this 'myth of superiority', as Henry Steele Commager called it, did not demand an inflexible policy in dealing with the outside world. On the contrary, it justified both remaining aloof from international politics and leading crusades for a better world. Thus, whether discussing nineteenth-century isolationism or twentieth-century globalism, we quickly encounter the idealistic underpinnings of American foreign policy.

Some believe that such American idealism is little more than rhetoric, designed to cloak the presence of the baser motivations of national self-interest. Indeed, it would be foolish to argue that politicians do not attempt to dignify their policies, foreign or domestic, with the language of higher moral purpose. On the other hand, as Michael Hunt has pointed out, such rhetoric only works and continues to be employed because it taps into deep-seated beliefs in American culture:

> **In the United States, foreign-policy rhetoric has been peppered with widely understood codewords. References in speeches, school texts, newspaper editorials, and songs to liberty, providential blessings, destiny, and service to mankind have been fraught with meaning shared by author and audience. Precisely because of their explanatory power and popular appeal, such simple but resonant notions become essential to the formulation and practical conduct of international policy.**
>
> Hunt, 1987, p. 16

This does not mean that we must accept that American foreign policy actually *is* more moral than that of other nations. Rather, it means that we must seriously consider the possibility that American foreign policy-makers – and the American public at large – do conceive of their foreign policy as something more than the mere pursuit of national self-interest.

This tradition of *idealism* in American foreign policy is often said to be at odds with the tradition of realism, noted above. As we shall see, 'They compete with each other as conceptions of how the United States ought to define its foreign policy objectives, even while they coexist with one another. While one tradition may predominate over the other at any single point in time . . . neither has managed to obliterate the influence of the other' (Kegley and Wittkopf, 1987, p. 78).

US foreign policy, 1783–1941

Victory in the War of Independence (1776–83) brought the end of British colonial rule. Now the United States of America had to face up to the challenge of being a new nation in the international system. Inevitably, the country found itself having to balance its ideals and identity against the demands of the political and military context in which it found itself. In short, a measure of pragmatism and realism were required.

The early republic

It is sometimes thought that, before the Second World War, American foreign policy was generally isolationist. This, however, is misleading. The fact that the United States showed reluctance to join the great European powers in vying for international supremacy does not mean that it shunned contact with them. Indeed, both geopolitical factors and economic self-interest demanded that the United States devote great care and attention to its relations with the likes of Great Britain, France, Spain and Russia.

Box 20.1

American neutrality in foreign affairs

Presidents George Washington and Thomas Jefferson made a strong stand in favour of neutrality in international politics, fearing in particular that joining permanent alliances with other nations would inevitably drag the United States into wars that were not in its interests. Furthermore, they believed that adherence to such neutrality placed the United States upon superior moral ground.

Extract from George Washington's farewell address, 1796

'Observe good faith and justice toward all nations. Cultivate peace and harmony with all . . . It will be worthy of a free, enlightened and at no distant period a great nation to give to mankind the magnanimous and too novel example of a people always guided by an exalted justice and benevolence . . .

The great rule of conduct for us in regard to foreign nations is, in extending our commercial interests, to have with them as little political connection as possible . . .

Europe has a set of primary interests which to us have none or a very remote relation. Hence she must be engaged in frequent controversies, the causes of which are essentially foreign to our concerns. Hence, therefore, it must be unwise in us to implicate ourselves by artificial ties in the ordinary vicissitudes of her politics or the ordinary combinations and collisions of her friendships or enmities.'

Extract from Thomas Jefferson's first inaugural address, 1801

'About to enter, fellow citizens, on the exercise of duties which comprehend everything dear and valuable to you, it is proper you should understand what I deem to be the essential principles of our Government . . . Equal and exact justice to all men, of whatever state or persuasion, religious or political; peace, commerce, and honest friendship with all nations, entangling alliances with none . . .'

At the very moment when the United States secured its independence from Britain, it was surrounded by European colonial powers. Not only were these powers potential or actual rivals to the commercial and territorial interests of the United States, but their incessant bellicosity towards each other threatened to engulf the new nation. American diplomacy was thus confronted with the difficult task of maintaining good relations with all of these bitter enemies.

Geopolitical considerations were made more complex by the fact that the health of the early American economy was dependent upon international commerce. American exports increased greatly in value in the years following independence. Even more important was the income generated by US shipping, which carried goods across both the Atlantic and Pacific oceans.

These issues of national self-interest also, however, intersected with ideological positions. These revolved around the political conflicts generated by the French Revolution of 1789 and which fuelled the Napoleonic wars until 1815. Many Americans, most notably Thomas Jefferson, sympathised with the republican radicalism of the French, with whom they identified as fellow revolutionaries. More conservative Americans, including George Washington and his Federalist supporters, were shocked by the excesses of the French Revolution. Moreover, as substantially products of English culture and tradition themselves, they were drawn towards the side of the mother country.

Thus, while the idealism embodied in the notion of American exceptionalism might otherwise have persuaded the United States to adopt a truly isolationist position from the start, less noble but more immediate considerations demanded an active foreign policy.

The foreign policy of the Washington administration was thus more akin to 'active neutrality' than isolationism. Seeking to avoid becoming embroiled in war, the president issued the Neutrality Proclamation in 1793. Two years later, and in spite of British attacks on American shipping, he signed the Jay Treaty with Britain. Although many Americans denounced the treaty as a surrender to British naval muscle, Washington was motivated by the need to avoid a costly, perhaps suicidal, war with Britain.

Also in 1795, Washington signed the Pinckney Treaty with Spain, which allowed Americans tax-free use of New Orleans. This Spanish port lay at the mouth of the Mississippi River and was thus vital to American traders in the West.

Given that friendly relations had been secured with Britain and Spain, it was not surprising that relations with France deteriorated. French attacks on American shipping increased dramatically in the last years of the eighteenth century, and the possibility of war arose. Once again, however, the United States avoided military conflict: the Convention of 1800 made financial concessions to France in return for recognition of America's trading rights as a neutral country.

The United States had thus established the central principles of its foreign policy very quickly. These were, first, to pursue honest and open relations with all countries: this was not only morally right, but would allow Americans to trade freely. Secondly, the United States must avoid becoming involved in conflicts originating in the corrupt Old World of Europe. Once again, this stance blended moral principle with economic and defence needs: the United States would indulge neither in intrigue nor war, simultaneously ensuring that no nation felt compelled to invade American territory or attack American commerce.

However, these principles could not totally be preserved in the face of the recurring pressures caused by the Napoleonic wars. In 1807, the Jefferson administration faced increasing restrictions on American shipping from both Britain and France. Sticking to its principle of non-involvement, the US government passed the Embargo Act, which closed American ports and banned exports. The problem was that this idealistic stand did great harm to the country's own economy. Before he left office in 1809, Jefferson bowed to domestic economic pressures and reopened the country's ports. The ban on British and French ships remained, but this brought no change in their hostile behaviour.

The War of 1812

American resentment at foreign restrictions on their shipping came to focus principally on Britain, which had also been in league with native Americans who were resisting the attempts of the US government to take over yet more of their land. Eventually, President James Madison decided that war against Britain was the only solution and, in 1812, obtained a declaration of war from Congress.

This was no mere war of self-defence, however. Madison hoped to seize Canada, just as in the previous year he had seized western Florida from Spain. American forces also took the opportunity to push native Americans still further to the west. In short, the United States sought to expand its territory through war, making its foreign policy uncomfortably similar to those of the corrupt Old World.

The War of 1812 came perilously close to being a humiliating disaster for the United States. The British navy was far too powerful and soon controlled the Atlantic coast. British troops landed in Washington in 1814 and set fire to the city, forcing the US government to flee. On Christmas Eve 1814, the United States signed the Treaty of Ghent with Britain, which simply restored pre-war boundaries and gave the United States nothing on the crucial issue of neutrals' shipping rights. It could have been far worse had the British not wished to concentrate their resources on bringing the Napoleonic wars to an end in Europe, rather than on the difficult task of conquering the United States.

However, what saved the war for the United States was the fact that news of the Treaty of

Ghent was slow in crossing the Atlantic. Thus, in January 1815, General Andrew Jackson defeated a British invasion at New Orleans, not only establishing his own reputation as a great American hero, but also transforming the war from an American catastrophe into a phenomenal victory over the world's greatest military power.

It is clear, then, that the period 1789–1815 was far from being one of American isolationism in foreign

Box 20.2

Key dates in American territorial expansion

1803 **The Louisiana purchase**
President Thomas Jefferson buys the Louisiana territory from France for $15 million. The new territory, stretching from the Mississippi River to the Rocky Mountains, doubles the size of the United States and eventually is made into 13 new states.

1819 **The Transcontinental Treaty**
Spain cedes Florida to the United States after an American threat to take it by force. In return, the United States recognises Spain's claim to Texas (but see the Treaty of Guadelupe–Hidalgo below).

1830–35 **Expulsion of native Americans**
The Choctaw, Chickasaw, Creek and Cherokee nations are forcibly removed from the south to the Oklahoma Indian Territory across the Mississippi River. Likewise, the Fox and Sauk are removed from the north to Oklahoma.

1846 **Buchanan–Pakenham Treaty**
Having threatened war, President James K. Polk agrees to divide the disputed Oregon Territory with Great Britain. This pushes the north-west American boundary to the 49th Parallel.

1848 **Treaty of Guadelupe–Hidalgo**
Following the annexation of Texas from Mexico in 1845, the United States goes to war with Mexico. It gains the California Territory, running from Texas to California, thereby increasing the US landmass by some 50 per cent.

1853 **The Gadsden purchase**
The United States purchases a small but significant piece of land from Mexico, extending the southern borders of what were to become the states of Arizona and New Mexico. Its great value is that it permits the completion of a southern transcontinental railroad.

1867 **The Alaska purchase**
For the sum of $7.2 million, Russia sells the United States Alaska – a territory over twice the size of Texas.

1862–90 **Indian wars in the west**
A series of wars against native American nations, resulting in their mass annihilation and the removal of those left alive from their territories to reservations.

policy. Moreover, while successive administrations espoused idealistic sentiments, the period demonstrated that the United States was willing to employ both the means and the ends of foreign policy that it condemned in other nations. This was confirmed over the next one hundred years. For although a century of peace in Europe released the United States from entanglement in Old World conflicts, Americans turned their energies to acquiring vast swathes of new territory in the New World.

Territorial expansion and conquest in the nineteenth century

In the period before the American Civil War (1861–65), the United States grew from an eastern seaboard nation to a vast continental power. This was achieved by a combination of war and shrewd diplomacy. After the Civil War, considerable effort was spent in 'taming' the great western territories, a process that included the near-genocide of those native Americans who resisted the loss of the land that had been promised to them in perpetuity by the US government. Once the continental United States was consolidated, there began the first major attempt to extend American power overseas. Once again, therefore, it is something of a misnomer to characterise this era as one of isolationism. Rather, it was a period when the United States' foreign policy paid scant attention to European politics and concentrated upon relations with other nations in the New World.

Manifest destiny

Whether it concerned war, diplomacy or land purchase, American foreign policy was impelled by the notion of what became known as 'manifest destiny'. Coined in the 1840s, the term denoted the belief that the whole of the New World was destined by God to be owned and run by the people of the United States. Although territorial expansion was eventually limited, there were many who believed that Canada, Mexico, Central America, the Caribbean and perhaps South America would all one day become part of the United States – and by military conquest, if necessary (LaFeber, 1989, p. 134). Indeed, as early as 1823, the government had announced officially that it viewed the New World as a place where the political and social values of the United States were destined to hold sway. Thus the concept of manifest destiny and the policies it stimulated can be seen as a phenomenon that the theory of constructivism helps to explain.

The Monroe Doctrine of 1823

The original intention behind President James Monroe's address to Congress in 1823 was to warn the European powers that they should cease to regard New World territories as targets for inclusion in their empires. Although he made no threats against existing European colonies, Monroe decreed that the political and social future of nations in the Americas would be constructed along the democratic and republican lines of the United States itself.

In its original form, therefore, the Monroe Doctrine was not so much an attempt to lay claim to the territories of the Americas, as a warning to the Old World not to impede the 'natural' development of societies in the New. Such development, of course, coincided with the economic and security interests of the United States in the Americas.

As the nineteenth century progressed, however, American expansionism saw the Monroe Doctrine transformed into a rationalisation of the New World as a United States' sphere of influence. Moreover, the United States went to war to acquire what were, in effect, colonial possessions.

The Spanish–American War of 1898

The war of 1898 arose from rebellions by the remnants of the Spanish empire in the Caribbean and the Pacific to achieve independence. On the pretext of a Spanish attack upon the USS *Maine*, the United States entered the conflict on the side of the rebels in Cuba. Victory over Spain was achieved quickly, but Cuban independence was not the outcome. Rather, Cuba became a US 'protectorate'. The 1903 treaty settlement allowed the Cubans to determine their own internal laws, but Senator Orville Platt's amendment to the original version gave the United States ultimate control. In particular, the Platt Amendment gave the United States

Box 20.3

The Monroe Doctrine, 1823

In his seventh annual message to Congress, President James Monroe alluded to recent discussions with Russia and Great Britain about rival claims in the north-west of the American continent, and to continuing warfare in Europe. He then asserted the principle:

'that the American continents, by the free and independent condition which they have assumed and maintain, are henceforth not to be considered as subjects for future colonization by any European powers . . .

In the wars of the European powers in matters relating to themselves we have never taken any part, nor does it comport with our policy to do so. It is only when our rights are invaded or seriously menaced that we resent injuries or make preparation for our defense. With the movements in this hemisphere we are of necessity more politically connected, and by causes which must be obvious to all enlightened and impartial observers . . . We owe it therefore, to candor and to the amicable relations existing between the United States and those powers to declare that we should consider any attempt on their part to extend their system to any portion of this hemisphere as dangerous to our peace and safety . . .

Our policy in regard to Europe . . . is not to interfere in the internal concerns of any of its powers; to consider the government *de facto* as the legitimate government for us; to cultivate friendly relations with it, and to preserve those relations by a frank, firm, and manly policy, meeting in all instances the just claims of every power, submitting to injuries from none.'

the right to intervene militarily in Cuba 'to protect its independence'; and granted the United States a 99-year lease on a naval base at Guantanamo Bay.

The war also saw the United States annexe the Philippines, Puerto Rico and Hawaii. The Filipinos, who had originally welcomed the Americans as allies against Spain, fought a bloody but unsuccessful guerrilla war against the American occupying forces for three years. It eventually required some 120,000 US troops to subdue the Filipinos, whose deaths from the fighting, starvation and the American concentration camps may have reached 200,000 (LaFeber, 1989, p. 202).

In the wake of the war, it was clear that the United States was now behaving as an imperial power, much like the nations of Europe. Moreover, the American empire was founded not merely on economic and territorial ambition, but on the notion of a racial hierarchy. Just as Europeans justified colonialism in terms of 'the white man's burden', most Americans deemed Latins, orientals and blacks to be so far inferior to Anglo-Saxons that they could not be entrusted with self-rule.

An oft-repeated, though apocryphal, story reveals how Americans rationalised their imperialism at the end of the nineteenth century. The story has President McKinley telling an audience of churchmen how he had prayed late into the night for divine guidance on what to do with the Philippines after the Spanish had been defeated:

And one night it came to me in this way – We could not give the Philippines back to Spain: that would be cowardly and dishonorable. We could not turn them over to France and Germany, our commercial rivals in the Orient: that would be bad business. There was nothing left to do but take them all, and educate the Filipinos, and uplift and civilise them,

and by God's grace do the very best by them as our fellow men for whom Christ also died. And then I went to bed, and went to sleep and slept soundly.

LaFeber, 1989, p. 200

The hard realities of the new American imperialism were, however, easy enough to discern. In 1903, when Colombia refused the United States permission to construct a canal from the Atlantic to the Pacific on its territory, the administration of President Theodore Roosevelt sponsored a local revolution which led to the creation of the state of Panama. The Panama Canal was duly constructed and placed under American control.

The following year, the president placed the official seal on the new American hegemony in the western hemisphere. In the Roosevelt Corollary to the Monroe Doctrine, he announced that the United States was assuming responsibility for maintaining stability and order in the Americas. Henceforth, when nations in the region behaved irresponsibly, the United States would intervene, with armed force if necessary, to correct the situation.

In the years around the turn of the century, then, the United States appeared ready to assume the global role to which its economic wealth, large population and dynamic expansionism were so suited. That, however, did not happen for another 50 years. The principal reason is that a countertendency in American ideology reasserted itself: isolationism, or more precisely, the desire to avoid entanglement in European conflicts.

Box 20.4

The Roosevelt Corollary, 1904

'It is not true that the United States feels any land hunger or entertains any projects as regards the other nations of the Western Hemisphere save such as are for their welfare. All that this country desires is to see the neighboring countries stable, orderly, and prosperous. Chronic wrongdoing, or impotence which results in a general loosening of the ties of civilized society, may . . . ultimately require intervention by some civilized nation, and in the Western Hemisphere the adherence of the United States to the Monroe Doctrine may force the United States, however reluctantly, in flagrant cases of such wrongdoing or impotence, to the exercise of the international police power.'

The First World War and the inter-war years

President Theodore Roosevelt's successors did not share his enthusiasm for military action, but they were convinced that the United States must pursue an activist international policy. They were fully aware that the American economy depended more than ever on overseas markets, a fact which led the United States to adopt an 'open door' policy with regard to international trade. This would allow American business to have access to markets and raw materials on the same terms as other nations. The administration of President Taft (1909–13) thought this could best be achieved through 'dollar diplomacy', whereby American capital investment in other nations would guarantee the United States both economic access and political influence.

Along with economic self-interest went a desire to export liberal or 'American values': republicanism, democracy, free enterprise and individualism. Under President Woodrow Wilson (1913–21), liberalism in foreign policy reached new heights, culminating in Wilson's attempt to create a new framework for the conduct of politics between nations.

On the outbreak of the First World War in Europe in 1914, the familiar combination of economic self-interest and American values persuaded Wilson to remain neutral. This permitted American business to make huge profits from selling to both sides of the conflict, while simultaneously refusing to descend to the levels of European power politics.

Gradually, however, the war encroached unbearably on American freedom to trade – particularly German U-boat attacks upon American merchant ships. By 1917, Wilson realised that the United States must become a belligerent if it wished to protect its economic interests. Moreover, Wilson understood that, if the United States was to influence the post-war settlement and international order, it would have to negotiate as a victor.

In April 1917, Wilson sought and obtained a declaration of war from Congress. Declaring that neutrality was no longer feasible or desirable, Wilson proclaimed a crusade to make the 'world safe for democracy'. The president continued in idealistic vein in his 'Fourteen Points' speech to Congress, in January 1918. Although it played to the economic interests of the United States, with its advocacy of absolute freedom of navigation and the open door in trade, the speech also envisaged self-determination for all nations and international peace based upon collective security. This latter idea would relieve nations of the need to engage in balance-of-power politics and arms races to protect themselves. Instead, the pooled force of what shortly became the League of Nations would deter and punish aggressor nations. In a sense, therefore, a liberal international order would replace a realist one.

Whatever initial enthusiasm Americans may have had for Wilson's idealistic proposals, the experience of war and its aftermath left them severely disillusioned. It became evident during the negotiations over the peace settlement that America's European allies did not share Wilson's vision of a new world order. Rather, they seemed intent upon conducting business as usual as they sought only to serve their own national interests.

When Wilson proved unable to change European habits, Americans turned inwards. Ironically, the president, by raising exaggerated hopes and then failing, helped to bring about a new phase of isolationism. In effect, American participation in the First World War served only to confirm the view that the United States could and should avoid entanglement in Europe. The most important immediate consequence of this disillusionment was the Senate's rejection of United States membership in the League of Nations. In the longer term, it led the United States to retreat ever deeper into isolationist behaviour, even in the face of blatant aggression by Nazi Germany in the 1930s.

The Second World War

Wilsonian internationalism still had its supporters in the United States in the inter-war years, particularly among the makers of foreign policy. However, isolationism was strong in the Congress. Many Progressive politicians from the Midwest and western states were principled opponents of what they saw as the threat to American virtue stemming from involvements in Europe. Senators such as William Borah of Idaho and Gerald Nye of North Dakota argued fiercely against any repetition of First World War engagements. In the 1930s they were joined by demagogic populists, such as Senator Huey Long of Louisiana and the publisher William Randolph Hearst. Between them, they managed to defeat President Franklin D. Roosevelt's 1935 proposal for the United States to join the World Court of the League of Nations. They followed this by passing three separate Neutrality Acts in the period 1935–7.

Thus, even after Roosevelt had begun helping the British and, indeed, the Soviet Union, to fight against Germany, he admitted to the British prime minister, Winston Churchill, that isolationist opposition in Congress prevented him from declaring war.

Roosevelt's dilemma was solved by the decision of Hitler's ally, Japan, to attack the American Pacific Fleet at Pearl Harbor, Hawaii, on 7 December 1941. In the light of such aggression, Roosevelt had no difficulty persuading Congress to declare war on Japan. Germany responded by declaring war on the United States. Thus the Americans, who had spent the past 20 years desperately trying to avoid military entanglements, now found themselves at war across both the Atlantic and the Pacific.

The United States emerged from those conflicts as the world's dominant economic and military power. During the war years, the American economy had recovered fully from the Great Depression. While the American economy boomed, the major European powers, whether in victory or defeat, had suffered economic devastation. Consequently, the end of the Second World War saw the United States uniquely positioned to lead the world out of the economic chaos of the previous two decades.

Moreover, economic dominance translated ineluctably now into political and military dominance. The United States needed a thriving capitalist world economy if its own businesses were to prosper. However, the world capitalist economy could only recover if stable and supportive political conditions existed – and the sole country with the power to assure such conditions was the United States. American policy-makers recognised this and moved their country towards a position in international politics that, in effect, reversed some 150 years of foreign policy tradition. Unsurprisingly, that change in policy also necessitated a transformation in the structures and processes of American foreign policy-making.

The Cold War

Historians disagree about the origins of the Cold War – that permanent state of crisis and tension between, principally, the United States and the Soviet Union, which lasted from the late 1940s to the late 1980s. The liberal school of western scholars blames the aggressive, expansionist actions and rhetoric of the Soviets, particularly in eastern Europe, for provoking the conflict. For, between 1945 and 1948, the Soviet Union gradually installed puppet regimes in East Germany, Poland, Hungary, Czechoslovakia and Bulgaria. Moreover, with the spread of communism to other countries, including Rumania, Yugoslavia and, in 1949, China, many in the West perceived a Moscow-directed plan to conquer the world for communism.

Revisionist historians, however, point to American political and economic aggression, backed by the threat of military force. Certainly, the United States was determined to create a post-war economic order that would serve its own interests. In 1944, the United States called an international meeting at Bretton Woods, New Hampshire. The outcome of that meeting was that while the United States would promote economic growth through the loan and investment of billions of American dollars, the world, including the British Empire, would have to open itself to US trade.

The Bretton Woods agreement created two new powerful instruments for American economic domination: the International Bank for Reconstruction and Development – or the World Bank, as it is often called – and the International Monetary Fund (IMF). Primed with American finance and dominated by American administrators, these two institutions would help to ensure that the world would provide the United States with necessary export markets and outlets for capital investment.

Although many countries stood to gain from increased American investment, they were aware that the price to be paid was economic subordination to the United States. Thus, the British prime minister, Winston Churchill, resisted American terms at Bretton Woods: 'US officials, however, simply steamrolled over London's objections' (LaFeber, 1989, p. 411).

If a close ally, such as Great Britain, was fearful of the consequences of the new American economic domination, it is not surprising that the Soviet Union was deeply suspicious. Although the Soviet Union and United States had been allies during the Second World War, this had been a marriage of convenience. Even as the United States entered the war, Senator (later, President) Harry Truman said the Soviets were as 'untrustworthy as Hitler and Al Capone' (Hunt, 1987, p. 156). Soviet communism and American capitalism lay at opposite ideological poles and each viewed the progress of the other as a threat to its own existence. Thus, while President Franklin D. Roosevelt had hoped that the wartime collaboration with the Soviet leader, Josef Stalin, might continue after the war, the old mutual suspicions quickly reemerged.

To the Soviet Union, the United States represented not merely an economic threat, but a military danger as well. This danger was most dramatically embodied by America's exclusive possession of the atomic bomb. When the United States had used the bomb to end the war with Japan, it had done so, in part, to save the lives of thousands of American troops who would surely have been killed in the course of a traditional invasion. Yet the atomic devastation of Hiroshima and Nagasaki was also intended 'to make clear to the world that the United States was ruthless enough to drop the bomb on live targets' (McCormick, 1989, p. 45).

Thus, American foreign policy-makers hoped that they could exploit their atomic monopoly and practise 'atomic diplomacy' upon the Soviets. Unfortunately, the Soviets reacted to these pressures in ways that only heightened tensions: 'atomic diplomacy reinforced Russia's security fears, strengthened its disposition to control its Eastern European buffer zone more tightly, undermined soft-liners on German policy, and led Soviet leaders to create a crash atomic bomb project of their own' (McCormick, 1989, p. 45).

Containment

Wherever the responsibility for the Cold War should lie, the fact is that, in the years following the Second World War, relations between the United States and the Soviet Union deteriorated rapidly. Rightly or wrongly, from the American viewpoint, the Soviet Union was an aggressive, expansionist state, armed with a messianic ideology that saw war with international capitalism as inevitable. This was the prism through which American policy-makers viewed not merely Soviet conquests in eastern Europe, but the activities of all communists throughout the world.

The decisive episode for US foreign policy came in 1947 and arose from the civil war taking place in Greece between local communists and royalists. Up to this point, Britain had been backing the royalists in an attempt to prevent the emergence of the first communist government in western Europe. Britain, however, was bankrupt and informed the United States that it could no longer sustain its effort. It also had to withdraw support from Turkey, which was coming under pressure from its Soviet neighbour.

President Truman, and his secretary of state, Dean Acheson, decided that the time had come to confront the Soviet threat. They had been primed for a new policy by the ideas of an American diplomat in Moscow, George Kennan. In February 1946, Kennan had sent a long, secret telegram to Washington, giving his analysis of the nature of Soviet aggression. The following year, Kennan, using the pseudonym 'X', published his views in an article entitled 'The sources of Soviet Conduct'. Kennan believed that the Soviet Union was inherently aggressive for a number of reasons, including its ideology and its sense of national insecurity. Although he did not believe that the Soviets had any immediate plans to go to war with the West, they would, he argued, try to exert pressure whenever and wherever the opportunity presented itself. They must, therefore, 'be contained by the adroit and vigilant application of counterforce at a series of constantly shifting geographical and political points'. Thus, the policy of containment was born. Truman decided in 1947 that Greece and Turkey were the places to begin application of the doctrine.

The Truman administration was ready to transform the United States into the 'world's policeman', yet such a change, involving global responsibilities and entanglements, went against the grain of a century and a half of American foreign policy tradition. The president therefore faced the task of convincing the American people and a Congress controlled by the opposition Republican party, that such a new departure was necessary and in the best interests of the United States. At a meeting with congressional leaders in February 1947, Truman and Acheson argued that it was imperative to stop communism in Greece and Turkey, before the 'infection' spread through the entire Middle East and Europe. The leading Republican foreign policy spokesman, Senator Arthur Vanderberg, agreed, but reportedly told Truman that if he wanted to get aid for Greece and Turkey from Congress, he would have to 'scare hell out of the American people'.

In his speech before Congress on 12 March 1947, President Truman tried to do just that. Describing the sources of world tensions and conflict in simplistic but stirring terms, Truman declared: 'I believe that it must be the policy of the United States to support free peoples who are resisting attempted subjugation by armed minorities or by outside pressures.' While Truman was only asking for $400 million to help Greece and Turkey, his speech placed no geographical limits on his pledge to resist communism. Containment in Greece and Turkey, then, was merely the first step toward a policy of global containment.

As we saw in Part 2, a broad consensus quickly developed behind the policy of containment – or 'the Truman Doctrine', as it was sometimes called. Despite disagreements over specific aspects of policy, the politicians, media and people of the United States shared the belief, first, that Soviet communism and its allies posed a mortal threat to the non-communist world, including the United States, and, secondly, that this justified American intervention in all corners of the globe, no matter how distant from the United States or how costly in American resources. Even after the reassessment that followed the defeat in Vietnam, it was only a few years before many in America believed that a new or second cold war was necessary to preserve American values, security and influence.

President Ronald Reagan (1981–9) shared many of the views of the Soviet Union held by President Truman. Along with many others, he viewed the period known as Détente in the 1970s as one in which attempts to negotiate with Soviets had only encouraged them to seek to expand their power. Moreover, the Soviets failed to honour the commitments they made in agreements such as the Helsinki Accords of 1975, in which they promised to improve their human rights record.

As a result, President Reagan embarked upon a major increase in US military expenditures and supported anti-Soviet forces who were fighting Soviet-backed regimes in places such as Afghanistan and Nicaragua. At the same time that the Reagan administration was exerting greater pressure on the Soviet Union, the Soviets themselves were beginning to acknowledge the economic and, to a lesser extent, political failures of their form of communism. However, attempts to reform Soviet communism failed and the Soviet Union was dissolved in 1991. By that time, virtually all of the communist governments in Eastern Europe had also collapsed. In perhaps simplistic terms, the United States had won the Cold War and now stood as the world's only superpower.

Unsurprisingly, the four decades of political, economic and military commitment to global anti-communism had a considerable impact upon the way in which American foreign policy was formulated. We now turn, therefore, to an examination of how foreign policy has been made in the United States, particularly since the end of the Second World War.

Box 20.5

The separation of powers in foreign policy

Constitutional powers of the president

- To act as commander-in-chief of the armed forces
- To make treaties
- To nominate ambassadors and top foreign policy-makers, e.g. the secretary of state
- To 'receive' representatives of foreign governments

Constitutional powers of the Congress

- To declare war
- To ratify or reject treaties
- To confirm or reject ambassadorial and government nominees
- To 'raise and support' armies

The foreign policy-making process

The transformation in US foreign policy wrought by the onset of the Cold War called into being the modern foreign policy-making process. The Constitution of 1787 had indicated the broad powers of the president and Congress in this field. It was, however, only when foreign policy assumed the scale and importance that it did in the Cold War, that a massive and elaborate set of arrangements was needed to serve the nation's new global crusade.

The constitutional framework

In keeping with its overall strategy, the Constitution of 1787 divided the power to make foreign policy between the president and the Congress. Thus, while the president was made responsible for the negotiation of treaties with foreign nations, they must be approved by a two-thirds majority of the Senate (Article II, Section 2(ii)). And while the president is commander-in-chief of the armed forces, only Congress has the power to declare war (Article II, Section 2(i) and Article I, Section 8(i), respectively). Thus, the great constitutional scholar Edward Corwin described this sharing of power as 'an invitation to struggle for the privilege of directing American foreign policy' (1957, p. 171).

Growth of presidential power in foreign policy

It is clear beyond doubt that, today, the president has predominant power in the foreign policy-making process. This does not mean that the president's power is absolute or that its pre-eminence is bound to continue. Indeed, as we shall see, the end of the Cold War and other global developments have undoubtedly diminished the power of the presidency in foreign affairs.

Nevertheless, the presidency has distinct advantages over other policy-makers, especially Congress, and some of these are traceable to the original constitutional design. For example, the president (and vice-president), as the only office-holder chosen by a national electorate, can lay claim to be the main political embodiment of the nation. Moreover, arising from his explicit powers to conduct day-to-day relations with other nations, and his more general status as chief executive, the president was clearly intended to perform the role that we now call 'head of state'.

It is also the case that the different structures of the presidency and Congress make the White House, rather than Capitol Hill, the more natural home for foreign policy-making. Foreign policy decisions often require a measure of secrecy, specialised knowledge, cohesion and the ability to act decisively. All these characteristics play to the strengths of the executive branch rather than a Congress composed of 535 autonomous and often parochial individuals, whose deliberations are conducted largely in public. If, as is often asserted, foreign policy-making is inherently authoritarian, then the presidency is the American government institution that comes closest to fitting the bill. However, as we shall see, it would be unwise to overstate the abilities of the presidency in this respect. The point here is that the presidency is *relatively* superior to the Congress in its ability to conduct foreign policy.

Nevertheless, the modern predominance of the presidency in foreign policy owes more to historical developments than it does to constitutional logic. In particular, the onset of the Cold War transformed both the quantitative and qualitative dimensions of American foreign policy-making.

Table 20.1 US armed forces, selected years, 1950–2008

	Thousand personnel				
Year	**Army**	**Navy**	**Marines**	**Air Force**	**Total**
1950	593	381	74	411	1,459
1955	1,109	661	205	960	2,935
1960	873	617	171	815	2,475
1968	1,570	764	307	905	3,546
1975	784	535	196	613	2,128
1980	777	527	188	558	2,051
1985	781	571	198	602	2,151
1990	732	579	197	535	2,044
2000	482	332	173	356	1,384
2008	544	382	199	327	1,402

Source: Statistical Abstract of the United States, 2010

Quantitatively, the Cold War, with its commitment to global containment, simply required a vast increase in the foreign policy- and war-making capacity of the US government. As well as generating an enormous growth in the foreign policy-making establishment, it also called into existence a permanent standing army of unprecedented proportions, peaking in 1968 at the height of the Vietnam War.

Given the president's roles as chief executive and commander-in-chief, both these developments occurred within the executive branch of government, with a concomitant increase in presidential power. In other words, the Cold War enhanced the constitutional powers of the president by bringing to the fore his responsibilities as commander-in-chief and head of the foreign policy-making bureaucracy.

The Cold War as crisis

The Cold War was a permanent crisis in American foreign policy because it constituted a continuing threat to national security. It was, moreover, a crisis that could lead to nuclear war at any given moment. In such a climate of fear and danger, American foreign policy underwent a *qualitative*, as well as quantitative, change. Now it became unwise, perhaps even foolhardy and unpatriotic, to challenge presidential predominance in foreign policy. This did not mean that presidential conduct of foreign policy was beyond criticism, but at no point until the failure in Vietnam did Congress attempt to wrest a significant measure of foreign policy-making power from the president.

This was true even when explicit powers of Congress were involved. For example, although Congress alone possesses the power to declare war, it was content to allow the president to initiate wars, as well as less significant military actions, without its approval. Thus, neither President Truman (Korea) nor President Johnson (Vietnam) sought or obtained a declaration of war from Congress.

By the early 1970s, some believed that such developments in foreign policy-making powers had helped to create an 'imperial presidency' (Schlesinger, 1973). According to this view, presidential power was now more akin to that wielded by an emperor than an elected chief executive in a democracy. If so, however, it must be said that Congress had willingly acceded to the surrender of much of the substance of its constitutional powers. In the climate of the Cold War and the foreign policy consensus it produced, Congress was content to trust to the superior resources and judgement of the president in matters of foreign policy.

As we saw in Part 2, the Vietnam War did mark something of a turning point in presidential–congressional relations in foreign policy-making. Nevertheless, it remains the case today that there is simply no alternative to presidential leadership in conducting foreign affairs. Congress may take a closer interest in foreign policy and frustrate the president more than before; interest groups and public opinion may also be more influential as a result of the increase in 'intermestic issues' (see below). The president, however, is uniquely able to give direction and vigour to US foreign policy. To a considerable extent, this is because he sits at the apex of a vast network of foreign policy-making bureaucracies.

The foreign policy-making establishment

Until the Cold War, the US government had made do with relatively few foreign policy-making institutions and personnel. The State Department, whose main responsibility is diplomacy, was created in the early days of the new Constitution in 1789, as was the Department of War. In 1798, a Department of the Navy was added, but there was no further growth in specifically foreign policy-making institutions until the Cold War.

In 1947, Congress passed the National Security Act. This created a Department of Defense, combining the previous War and Navy departments and adding a new military service, the Air Force, the National Security Council and the Central Intelligence Agency (CIA). Together with the State Department and the president himself, these three institutional products of the Cold War have dominated American foreign policy-making over the past half-century.

Let us look briefly at each of these five main players.

The president

The character and interests of the individual president can go a long way in explaining the substance and management of American foreign policy in any given period. Some presidents are far more interested in foreign policy than domestic policy. In recent times, Presidents Nixon and Bush stand out as 'foreign policy presidents', while Presidents Johnson and Clinton at least attempted to devote their main energies to domestic rather than foreign policy. One of the results of Nixon's deep interest in international politics was that he took personal charge of foreign policy, deliberately appointing 'weak' secretaries of state and defense and relying instead for advice on his national security adviser, Henry Kissinger.

Other factors than the president's predilections may determine the extent to which he concentrates upon foreign policy. Up to a point, for example, it is true that Republican presidents may have a greater propensity to concentrate upon foreign policy than Democrats, because they do not share the latter's commitment to the creative use of government power to improve society at home. This was particularly true of President Bush, for example.

On the other hand, Democratic presidents have often been forced by circumstances beyond their control to devote considerable time to foreign policy, as was the case with President Truman and the Cold War, and President Johnson and Vietnam. Even President Clinton, elected in part because of a backlash against his predecessor's perceived neglect of domestic policy, quickly found himself under attack for devoting insufficient time to America's world role.

It has also been argued that presidents have been drawn into greater involvement in foreign policy because they are less constrained by Congress here than in domestic policy. This gives presidents more scope for initiative and action and, hence, a better chance of attaining their policy objectives (Wildavsky, 1975). To some extent, however, this explanation has been undermined by a more assertive Congress in the wake of the disastrous 'presidential war' in Vietnam.

Furthermore, in an increasingly interdependent world, the dividing line between domestic and foreign policy has become blurred. For example, when President Carter imposed a ban on grain sales to the Soviet Union, as punishment for the latter's 1979 invasion of Afghanistan, he did not foresee the impact this would have on America's grain farmers. So badly hit were they by the loss of income from these sales, that they prevailed upon the arch anticommunist Ronald Reagan to drop the ban when he replaced Carter in the White House.

Thus, it has become common today to talk of 'intermestic' issues and policies – issues with significant implications for both international and domestic politics. As we saw in Chapter 14, Congress will always try to assert its power against the president when the domestic – and therefore intermestic – policy at issue is concerned with the immediate self-interest of the American electorate.

Such is the importance of foreign policy to the United States today, that no president can afford to neglect or delegate responsibility for it to others without running great risks, for not only are American economic and security interests closely bound up with events in the wider world, but American prestige is easily tarnished by foreign policy mishaps. In varying degrees, the presidencies of Lyndon B. Johnson (Vietnam), Jimmy Carter (the Iran hostage crisis), Ronald Reagan (the Iran–Contra scandal) and Bill Clinton (the failed intervention in Somalia) were all damaged by foreign policy failures.

The State Department

Of all the agencies and federal bureaucracies engaged in foreign policy-making, the State Department is, in principle at least, the first among equals (Kegley and Wittkopf, 1987, p. 372). It was created in 1789 for the purpose of conducting US foreign relations. This means, among other things, representing the United States through its embassies and consulates throughout the world; negotiating treaties with other nations; acting as a repository of specialised knowledge about other nations and developments in international politics; and drawing up policy recommendations for the president and then, perhaps, implementing them.

It also houses bodies with specialised functions, such as the Agency for International Development (AID), the Arms Control and Disarmament Agency (ACDA) and the United States Information Agency (USIA).

Apart from the relatively small number of top political appointees to the State Department, its thousands of employees are true bureaucrats: that is, career specialists who tend to spend their whole working life in the department. The State Department can therefore reasonably claim to be the most authoritative and wide-ranging source of information and perspective upon the world outside the United States.

For all that, the State Department is not only a much-criticised body, but some presidents have regarded it as untrustworthy and consequently have preferred to rely on others as their principal source of policy advice. There are various reasons for this distrust, although in many ways they all relate to the same point: that the president and his personal advisers believe that State Department personnel are out of tune with domestic political perspectives and demands. For example, the State Department is variously accused of being elitist, arrogant and indecisive, with a marked tendency to 'go native' when stationed abroad.

There is undoubtedly something in all of these criticisms. For example, there is a 'subculture' within the State Department that leads Foreign Service officers to believe that outsiders cannot understand the subtleties of their craft and should, therefore, bow to their superiors (Kegley and Wittkopf, 1987, p. 376).

It is also true that the State Department can appear indecisive and prone to fudging issues. Within Washington, it has few natural allies to help buttress a strong position on any given issue: it lacks the Defense Department's enthusiastic backing by the arms industry, the CIA's patriotic appeal or the president's electoral support. Outside the United States, the State Department has to maintain good relations with a couple of hundred nations and international bodies. Compromise may often be the best way forward, given that a decisive stand may win friends only at the cost of making enemies (Hilsman, 1990, p. 194).

Nevertheless, these accusations are usually brought to bear when the White House fears that the State Department will not be sufficiently supportive of the administration's position, or when other policy-makers wish to undermine the department in order to advance their own policy agenda. Thus Republicans, in or out of office, tend to distrust Foggy Bottom (the area of Washington where the State Department is located), because they see it as dominated by the East Coast liberal establishment. In the 1950s, the populist demagogue senator Joe McCarthy made accusations of State Department sympathy with communism central to his more general witch-hunt for subversives. As noted above, President Nixon quite deliberately subordinated the State Department to his national security adviser, Henry Kissinger, because he assumed from the start that the department was likely to view his administration with something less than enthusiasm. Yet even liberal Democrats have been critical of the State Department and unwilling to rely on it: President Kennedy once described it as 'a bowl of jelly' because of its inability to be decisive and dynamic (Hilsman, 1990, p. 194). Even John Kenneth Galbraith, a quintessential member of the East Coast liberal establishment, complained to Kennedy that the ethos at the State Department was 'that God had ordained some individuals to make foreign policy without undue interference from presidents and politicians' (Kegley and Wittkopf, 1987, p. 381).

Ultimately, the bureaucrats of Foggy Bottom are too independent in their judgements and too distant from the White House inner circle to dominate, or even lead, foreign policy-making.

The Department of Defense

Often referred to as the Pentagon, because of the shape of the building in which it is housed, the Department of Defense is a powerful player in the foreign policy-making process. It has the vital task of ensuring that the United States is militarily capable of defending the nation and its interests, both at home and abroad. This responsibility immediately confers great power and influence upon the Pentagon, particularly during a prolonged period of international crisis, such as the Cold War.

However, there is more to the power of the Defense Department than its formal role, important though that is. The key to Pentagon power in Washington is the enormous defence budget.

The massive expenditures by the Defense Department attract two major sources of support: arms manufacturers and the Congress. The arms industry is eager to support Pentagon requests for increasingly large and more sophisticated military hardware, since it stands to gain massive profits from supplying these weapons. Arms industry interest groups therefore have a strong incentive to lobby both Congress and the president for the increased militarisation of US foreign policy. Worse still, it is sometimes alleged, the Defense Department and the arms industry deliberately exaggerate the threat posed to the United States by foreign countries in order to justify ever higher expenditure on armaments.

The second group which has a strong interest in sustaining high defence expenditures is Congress – or, more specifically, those members of Congress whose districts and states benefit from arms industry employment and the presence of military bases and installations. By voting for military programmes and distributing the benefits among their constituents, members of key congressional appropriations and armed services committees can obtain a substantial boost to their chances of re-election.

Table 20.2 Federal expenditures on national defence, selected years, 1960–2010

Year	Total expenditure $bn	Percentage of federal outlays	Percentage of GDP
1960	53.5	52.2	9.5
1965	56.3	42.8	7.5
1970	90.4	41.8	8.3
1975	103.1	26.0	5.7
1980	155.2	22.7	5.1
1985	279.0	26.7	6.4
1990	328.4	23.9	5.5
2000	341.6	16.4	3.0
2010 (est.)	821.8	19.9	4.8

Source: Statistical Abstract of the United States, 2010

By the late 1950s, there was increasing concern about this relationship between the Defense Department and the arms industry and its implications for both foreign policy and the nation's budget. In his farewell address of 1961, President Eisenhower felt moved to warn the country about the military–industrial complex.

Box 20.6

The military–industrial complex

Extract from President Eisenhower's farewell address, 1961

'This conjunction of an immense Military Establishment and a large arms industry is new in the American experience. The total influence – economic, political, even spiritual – is felt in every city, every statehouse, every office of the Federal Government. We recognize the imperative need for this development. Yet we must not fail to comprehend its grave implications. Our toil, resources, and livelihood are all involved. So is the very structure of our society.

In the councils of government we must guard against the acquisition of unwarranted influence, whether sought or unsought, by the military–industrial complex. The potential for the disastrous rise of misplaced power exists and will persist.

We must never let the weight of this combination endanger our liberties or democratic processes . . .'

Eisenhower's address inspired a debate, which continues to this day, over the validity of the 'military–industrial complex thesis'. While the more extravagant notions of a conspiracy by the military–industrial complex to control foreign policy lack convincing proof, there is considerable evidence to support the essence of the thesis. Kegley and Wittkopf, for example, writing from the perspective of the mid-1980s, listed seven basic reasons for lending it 'substantial credibility':

1. Employment in America is significantly dependent upon military expenditures: one in ten jobs is directly or indirectly linked to such expenditures.
2. Congress has at times gone beyond presidential requests in voting defence appropriations. It is argued, for example, that Congress was responsible for increasing expenditures on the MX missile from roughly $150 million to $600 million per missile in the 1980s.
3. Profits in the defence industries are higher than those in most other manufacturing sectors. This is owing in no small measure to the generous manner in which the Pentagon treats defence contractors: for example, handing out millions of dollars in grants and interest-free loans, repaying the costs of even unsuccessful bids, and allowing tax deferments on profits.
4. Sheer extravagance, waste and fraud: for example, the Lockheed corporation was paid $640 for an aeroplane toilet seat.
5. Universities, which should keep a critical eye on the military–industrial complex, have in fact been seduced by it: they accept millions of dollars' worth of research contracts connected to defence expenditures.
6. Defence industry consulting firms and think-tanks have mushroomed over the years. Most employ former members of the Defense Department and the Armed Forces, and their advice to their former employers usually supports the wishes of the military–industrial complex.
7. Defence expenditures have remained a priority, even during times of massive budget deficits (Kegley and Wittkopf, 1987, pp. 271–4).

In some respects, this evidence is not at all surprising. American politics generally gives considerable scope to coalitions of interests – bureaucracies, legislators, pressure groups – to work for public policies that reward themselves in various ways. In other words, we should expect the military–industrial complex to be self-promoting in the same way that farmers, the Department of Agriculture and members of Congress from farm states are self-promoting over agriculture policy. However, given the huge sums of money involved and the absolutely critical nature of defence policy, such comparisons are of limited validity.

It should be noted that the evidence above does not suggest that the military–industrial complex routinely advocates war as a solution to foreign policy problems. While the rhetoric of some may be hawkish or worse, neither the civilians who head the Defense Department nor the military commanders they manage are always the strongest proponents of war. For example, it was General Matthew Ridgeway who did most to persuade President Eisenhower not to intervene in Vietnam in 1954. Thus,

> **In general the military–industrial complex favours a high degree of preparedness and 'tough' foreign policies, but they shy away from entering wars, especially limited ones. Once committed to fighting, however, the military will usually oppose any settlement short of victory.**
>
> Hilsman, 1990, pp. 310–11

The power of the Defense Department (and its allies) to assert itself in the foreign policy-making process is then considerable, though by no means absolute. And, as with all the players in this particular game, it must compete with others for influence over policy.

The National Security Council

The National Security Council (NSC) was created by Congress in 1947 to 'advise the President with respect to the integration of domestic, foreign, and military policies relating to national security' (Kegley and Wittkopf, 1987, p. 345). In other words, the creation of the NSC was recognition of the fact that, with the advent of the Cold War, the United States needed better coordination of foreign policy. In line with these objectives, Congress required that the president, vice-president, secretaries of state and defense, the chairman of the joint chiefs of staff and the director of the CIA must all be members of the NSC. It also created a new post of 'special assistant to the president for national security affairs', often referred to more briefly as the national security adviser (NSA). From time to time, different presidents have added others to the membership of the NSC – for example, the Treasury secretary and the attorney-general.

In its early years, the NSC made some important contributions to American foreign policy, none more so than National Security Council Memorandum 68 (NSC-68) of 1950. This review of US global strategy in the light of the Soviet acquisition of the atomic bomb and the Chinese communist revolution in 1949 established the broad thrust of American Cold War policy for the next 20 years. Most importantly, NSC-68 instigated a massive militarisation of US global strategy, involving an increase in the military budget from $14 billion in 1950 to $53 billion in 1952 (McCormick, 1989, p. 94).

Yet it took some time before the NSC and, in particular, the national security adviser achieved top status in the foreign policy-making establishment. As part of the Executive Office of the President, the precise role and influence of the NSC and NSA is left to the discretion of the president. Truman, for example, originally did not attend NSC meetings and during both his and Eisenhower's administrations the national security adviser was little more than 'a glorified clerk-secretary to the NSC, overseeing its agenda and following up the president's decisions' (Hilsman, 1990, p. 134).

Moreover, under Eisenhower, the NSC was heavily criticised for failing to produce rational policy choices for the president, owing to its tendency to promote incoherent compromises between the preferences of the Council's members (Kegley and Wittkopf, 1987, p. 347). While Kennedy put the NSC and NSA to better use by requiring clear policy alternatives to be submitted to him, it was not until the Nixon administration that they achieved great prominence. This was owing mostly to Nixon's determination to reduce the power of the foreign policy-making bureaucracy, particularly the State Department, and to his appointment of Henry Kissinger as national security adviser.

Kissinger increased the number of professional staff on the NSC to about 150, compared with a dozen or so under Kennedy (Hilsman, 1990, p. 137). This allowed him to produce policy recommendations that rivalled those of the Departments of State and Defense. Combined with the fact that President Nixon simply placed greater trust in Kissinger than in any other adviser, this ensured that the NSC and Kissinger became the principal source of foreign policy advice to the president.

President Carter's NSA, Zbigniew Brzezinksi, was also a principal presidential adviser. Even if he never achieved the prominence of Henry Kissinger, Brzezinski was a rival for influence with Secretary of State Cyrus Vance. Indeed, when the NSA and the secretary of state clashed once again in 1980 over the plan to use commandos to release the American hostages held in Iran, it was Vance, not Brzezinski, who resigned his office.

Since the Carter years, the roles of the NSC and NSA have changed again. President Reagan had no fewer than six different national security advisers during his eight years in office. Reagan also adopted a 'hands-off' approach to the operation of the NSC, something which helped to allow the Iran–Contra scandal to develop.

Using the NSC as their base, Reagan's third and fourth NSAs, Robert McFarlane and John Poindexter, together with a marine officer attached to the NSC, Colonel Oliver North, employed illegal methods in an attempt to solve two of the president's major foreign policy problems. The first was to secure the release of American hostages being held by Iranian-backed groups in Lebanon. The second was to provide money for the American-backed counter-revolutionaries in Nicaragua, the Contras. Congress had cut off all funds for the Contras in 1984, but the Reagan administration was determined to find ways of keeping them supplied.

North secured approval from his NSC superiors to sell arms to Iran in the hope that they, in turn, would use their influence to secure the release of the hostages in Lebanon. This was done, in spite of the administration's oft-stated policy of not selling arms to Iran. The profits from the sales were then illegally diverted to the Contras, in defiance of the congressional ban.

Such activity was far from what Congress had in mind when it created the NSC in 1947. Thus, the Iran–Contra scandal demonstrates that the NSC can play whatever role the president wishes or allows it to. Equally, the role of the national security adviser may vary from glorified clerk, to chief architect of foreign policy, to overseer of covert policy operations.

The Central Intelligence Agency

The mere mention of covert activities immediately calls to mind the CIA. Yet although the CIA has rightly become synonymous with American espionage and secret operations in foreign countries, it was not created with these in mind. Rather, as its name suggests, it was founded in 1947 to provide better intelligence about the world that the United States was now seeking to lead. In particular, there was a perceived need to coordinate the intelligence gathered by the different intelligence agencies of various government departments. It was made responsible to the NSC and thereby to the president.

Almost immediately after its creation, however, the CIA acquired responsibility for covert operations. This was prompted by the communist coup in Czechoslovakia in 1948, after which President Truman authorised the CIA to undertake sabotage and subversion in such a way that, if these operations were discovered, the US government could plausibly deny responsibility for them (LaFeber, 1989, p. 459).

Since then, the CIA has become the most notorious and controversial institution in American government. It has claimed, or been charged with, responsibility for such acts as interfering in Italian elections since 1948 in order to ensure victory for the Christian Democrats against their communist opponents; installing the Shah on the Iranian throne in 1953; planning and executing the bungled Bay of Pigs invasion of Cuba in 1961; devising Operation Mongoose, a series of assassination attempts on President Fidel Castro of Cuba in the 1960s; running a secret army and war in Laos during President Johnson's administration; helping to organise the murder and overthrow of the elected Marxist president of Chile, Salvador Allende, in 1973; blowing up oil terminals and other targets in Nicaragua during the Reagan administration and, of course, carrying on a continuous campaign of espionage and clandestine operations against the Soviet Union and its eastern European allies.

However, the notoriety of the CIA and the extensiveness of its activities should not be confused with the question of its power in the foreign policy-making process. True, the CIA has some of the characteristics of a 'state within a state' (Hilsman, 1990, p. 201). Its need for secrecy, in both intelligence gathering and covert operations, has meant that it is left largely free of normal outside scrutiny and accountability. The 1970s witnessed several attempts to make the CIA more accountable: for example, the Hughes–Ryan Amendment of 1974 required covert operations to be reported to certain congressional committees, and new Senate and House Intelligence Committees were established to exercise more systematic oversight.

On the whole, however, these reforms have made little significant difference to the secrecy which shrouds the CIA. The simple fact is that, once the need for an organisation such as the CIA is accepted, it is somewhat counterproductive to expose its activities to a Congress where secrets are difficult to keep, still less to the public, media and other nations. Indeed, even Congress recognised this overriding need for secrecy, by partially reversing its earlier reforms in the 1980s (Dumbrell, 1990, pp. 150–1).

On the other hand, it must be remembered that the CIA is responsible to and under the control of the president. For all the mythology of the CIA as a 'cowboy operation', engaging in reckless and unauthorised secret operations, it is more accurate to see it as a highly professional bureaucratic agency acting at the behest of the president or the NSC. Indeed, this was the conclusion reached by the Pike

Committee of the House of Representatives, after it had examined CIA covert operations between 1965 and 1975: 'the CIA, far from being out of control, has been utterly responsible to the instructions of the President and the Special Assistant to the President for National Security Affairs' (Dumbrell, 1990, p. 153). Or again, the 1987 Tower Commission investigation into the Iran–Contra scandal concluded that: 'The Central Intelligence Agency acted as a willing accomplice, but the NSC called the shots' (Ragsdale, 1993, p. 17). Thus, while the accountability of the CIA is a legitimate source of concern in a democracy, condemnation of its 'objectionable' activities is more properly addressed to the White House.

Other administration influences

The State Department, the Pentagon, the National Security Council and the CIA – these are the major bodies within the administration which are specifically dedicated to helping the president to decide American foreign policy. There are, however, others who wield influence in this sphere, particularly where the economic interests of the United States loom large on the horizon.

The Department of the Treasury is an influential force in foreign policy-making, particularly in relation to factors which affect the value of the US dollar. Specific responsibilities include exchange rates, tariffs and the balance of trade. The Treasury secretary also acts as the US governor of the International Monetary Fund (IMF), the World Bank and other regional international financial agencies.

Situated within the White House, the Office of the United States Trade Representative has a growing influence, in line with the increasing economic interdependence of the United States and the outside world. The major responsibility of the US trade representative is to negotiate trading agreements with other nations, most famously the General Agreement on Tariffs and Trade (GATT).

Other bodies which can influence foreign policy include the Department of Commerce, whose main responsibilities lie in implementing trade policy, and the Departments of Agriculture and Labor, whose domestic 'clients' find themselves increasingly affected by the impact of international events and agreements.

Bureaucratic politics

It can be seen, then, that the president is not short of advice on foreign policy from within his administration. Yet such an array of potential influences can be a problem, as well as a source of strength. Ideally, the American foreign policy-making bureaucracies should produce rational and effective decisions. Together, they should be able to gather and interpret information stemming from the outside world, analyse and discuss different policy alternatives in response to it and decide upon and implement the policy that maximises the chances of fulfilling the broad goals of US foreign policy. In this 'rational actor' model of policy-making, specialised bureaucracies are dedicated to providing the president with all he needs to make the correct decision, as defined by American national interests.

No policy-making machinery works perfectly and we should not expect all American foreign policies to be wholly rational, in either conception or implementation. Nevertheless, many scholars view rationality-centred models as fundamentally flawed. Instead, they posit theories of foreign policy-making that emphasise self-serving competition between the different bureaucratic organisations that have some say in the formulation and execution of foreign policy (Dumbrell, 1990, chapter 2; Kegley and Wittkopf, 1987, chapter 13; Hilsman, 1990, part 1). For the sake of simplicity, these theories will be subsumed here under the heading 'bureaucratic politics'.

Bureaucratic politics sees the president less as someone who commands the agencies created to serve him and more as someone who struggles to manage and contain their separate wills. Each organisation is parochial in outlook and reluctant to entertain novel or rival ideas; it also seeks to expand its own influence and range of responsibilities. These characteristics have several negative consequences. Organisations compete rather than cooperate with each other, which, in turn, leads to dogmatic and exaggerated viewpoints being expressed, in the hope of maximising the organisation's power when the inevitable bargaining begins between different agencies. As a result, foreign policy decisions are often incremental and insufficiently responsive to new circumstances, as well as being a 'fudge'.

Perhaps worse still, agencies which have substantially lost out when the president finally makes a decision will quite deliberately seek to thwart its implementation. Probably the most famous example of this emerged during the Cuban Missile Crisis of 1962. The previous year, President Kennedy had ordered the State Department to remove American Jupiter missiles from Turkey. The missiles were not only obsolete, but placed so close to the border with the Soviet Union that they were unnecessarily provocative. The Turkish government, however, wanted the missiles to remain and the State Department, therefore, thought it best to ignore Kennedy's order and leave the missiles in place. Thus, at the height of the missile crisis the following year, Kennedy was surprised and angry to find the Soviets able to make the reasonable point that Soviet missiles in Cuba were no more threatening than American missiles in Turkey.

Presidents, then, cannot simply assume that 'their' bureaucracy will be cooperative. They must act forcefully, decisively and even punitively when dealing with the bureaucracy if they wish to see their foreign policy goals achieved.

Non-governmental influences

Public opinion

It is generally agreed that public opinion is much less influential in the making of foreign policy than it is in domestic policy. From the perspective of most members of the public, foreign policy is figuratively and literally distant from their everyday lives. Unlike the core domestic issues of employment, the cost of living and education, for example, most foreign policy issues make little impact upon the consciousness of the average American.

This general indifference to foreign policy issues leads to low levels of knowledge about them. Time and again, studies have shown the American public to be woefully ignorant of contemporary and recent foreign affairs, even those which have received considerable coverage in the media. Thus, in 1985, only 63 per cent of those surveyed knew that the United States had supported *South* Vietnam during the Vietnam War; 44 per cent did not know that the United States and the Soviet Union were allies during the Second World War, with 28 per cent believing the two had been at war with each other; and in 1983, 47 per cent did not know whether the Reagan administration supported or opposed the Sandinista government of Nicaragua (Kegley and Wittkopf, 1987, p. 288).

This public lack of concern has some significant consequences for the foreign policy-making process. Most importantly, it helps to make that process one dominated by elites, thereby reinforcing its intrinsically authoritarian nature. In this respect, foreign affairs provides a major exception to the democratic openness of the general American policy-making process.

The combination of public ignorance and elite control and secrecy makes public opinion on foreign policy malleable, if not downright manipulable, and the main beneficiary of this is unquestionably the president. As the personification of the national identity and pride, the president is generally trusted by the public to act in the nation's best interest. This frequently means that the public accepts whatever policy decisions the president makes and supports them enthusiastically. In times of crisis, this is termed the 'rally round the flag' phenomenon. In short, most of the time, presidents lead, rather than follow, public opinion on foreign policy.

However, none of the above should be read as meaning that public opinion is irrelevant to foreign policy. In the first place, presidents do pay considerable attention to public opinion poll data on foreign affairs. Any politically astute president will wish to know 'the outer limits of consent' of the American public, if only in order to gauge the possible repercussions of any decision he takes.

Secondly, under certain circumstances, the public *does* take a strong interest in foreign policy and may have clear policy preferences. This is particularly true where US military action is being contemplated and has become more critical in the wake of the defeat in Vietnam (see Part 2). Although the precise role of American public opinion in the Vietnam War is still hotly debated, there is no doubt that the slowly dwindling public support for the war did limit the options of both Presidents Johnson and Nixon. The dominant issue for the public was less the morality of US intervention in Vietnam, than its human costs in terms of US casualties (Mueller, 1971).

Thus, since Vietnam, presidents have been wary of adopting policies that might lead to intensive and prolonged military engagement. Moreover, presidents are now less willing to intervene militarily unless they have overwhelming evidence that success is probable. The American public is still very tolerant of presidential policies it deems successful, as the invasions of Grenada (1983) and Panama (1991) demonstrate. On the other hand, so concerned are presidents now about hostile public reaction to US war casualties, that they tend to disengage quickly when losses are incurred. This was the prime reason for the withdrawal of US troops from the Lebanon under President Reagan in 1984 and from Somalia under President Clinton in 1994.

Public opinion can also be aroused by other issues which connect close to home, such as trade agreements or immigration policy. In addition, media portrayal of human suffering caused by war can put pressure on government to act.

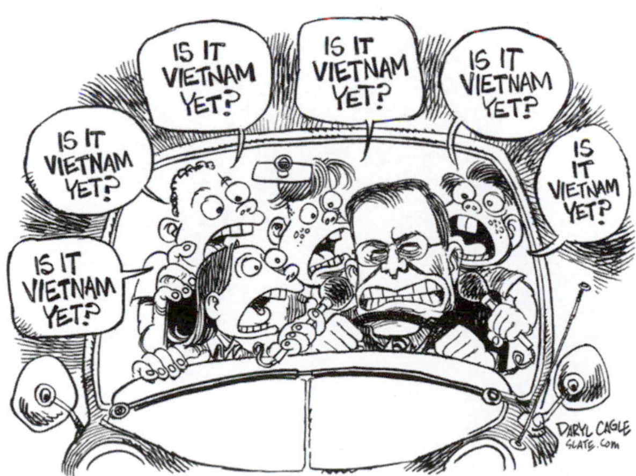

Figure 20.1 Ghost of Vietnam haunts Secretary of Defense Donald Rumsfeld during the war in Iraq.
Source: © Daryl Cagle

Nevertheless, it remains the case that, exceptions aside, the American public knows or cares little about foreign policy, rarely determines its votes in elections by reference to foreign affairs and rarely makes irresistible demands on either the Congress or the president over foreign policy issues.

Pressure groups

Unlike the general public, certain pressure groups know and care about foreign policy. For example, both business and labour groups take a close interest in trade policy because it directly affects the profits and jobs of their members. Thus, business groups lobbied strongly in favour of President Clinton's decisions in 1994 to lift the trade embargo on Vietnam and to renew China's 'most favoured nation' trading status. In both cases, American business saw great opportunities for investments and profits in these former enemy nations, and hence countered pressures from those who wished to punish China for its human rights abuses and Vietnam for its alleged foot-dragging over the fate of US prisoners of war.

As well as groups motivated primarily by economic interests, there are those which can be termed 'ethnic lobbies' (Dumbrell, 1990, p. 176). Among the most prominent of these are the American–Israeli Public Affairs Committee (AIPAC) and the Irish Northern Aid Committee (NORAID).

AIPAC is often credited with a major role in maintaining strong American commitment to Israel and, indeed, there is some evidence to support that (Dumbrell, 1990, p. 176). On the other hand, it is easy to overestimate AIPAC's influence. First, it is often the case that AIPAC is pushing at an open door: the United States has had important ideological and strategic interests in sustaining a strong Israel and its policy might well have been the same without the lobbying by AIPAC. Moreover, the US government has ignored AIPAC when its interests have so dictated: for example, in 1983, President Reagan pushed ahead with his policy of selling advanced warning aircraft (AWACs) to Saudi Arabia, despite a considerable lobbying effort against it by AIPAC.

Other ethnic lobbies have far less influence than AIPAC. Although presidents may pay lip-service to such groups, and offer them symbolic victories in the hope of cultivating their electoral support, they would not allow ethnic pressure groups to determine the nation's policy. Thus, while NORAID and the wider Irish lobby may have been instrumental in persuading President Clinton to allow Gerry Adams of Sinn Fein into the country in 1994, the Clinton administration continued to support the broad approach of the British government on the status of Ulster.

As with public opinion, then, the influence of pressure groups over foreign policy is more limited than in the domestic sphere. Thus, 'Interest groups may be effective on certain special issues. More often, however, it would appear that the foreign policy process is relatively immune from direct pressure by interest groups' (Kegley and Wittkopf, 1987, p. 280).

Foreign policy in the 1990s

We have seen that, in the era of the Cold War, the United States developed a new international grand strategy – containment – and a new foreign policy establishment – the National Security Council. But what of these two pillars of American foreign policy when the Cold War which engendered them disappeared?

It is difficult to exaggerate the fundamental changes in international politics represented by the end of the Cold War. Gone was the rigid, bipolar confrontation that sucked in virtually every nation on earth and threatened them with nuclear annihilation. Gone was the conflict that obliged the United States to maintain a massive standing army and a network of alliances all around the globe. Gone was the need to engage in proxy wars

Figure 20.2 President Ronald Reagan and Soviet leader Mikhail Gorbachev were equally pleased to bring the Cold War to an end.
Source: © Miroslav Zajic/Corbis

in places like Korea, Vietnam, Afghanistan, the Horn of Africa and Central America. Above all, gone was the great superpower rival, the Soviet Union, with its ideology and economy in ruins. Truly, the end of the Cold War was an occasion for rejoicing in the United States. As the sole remaining superpower, the United States regained the unequalled military status that it enjoyed briefly at the end of the Second World War.

For all its peerless military power, however, the United States struggled somewhat to define its role and ambitions in the post-Cold War era. Partly this was an inevitable consequence of the uncertainties that followed from the collapse of the Cold War system. For all its terrible aspects, the Cold War provided a relatively stable and predictable framework in which to formulate American foreign policy; and not least, the Cold War produced an unusually long period of peace between the two major powers, when compared with earlier eras in international relations (Kegley, 1991). The United States now had to deal with a world in which it had no major enemy and no simple yardstick for evaluating and responding to the challenges and conflicts in the outside world. To a considerable extent, therefore, the United States found itself in uncharted waters and it is understandable that it needed time to set its compass.

However, there was more to America's international dilemmas than the novelty of the situation it found itself in. Calculations of what international strategy the United States *should* adopt cannot be made without a simultaneous consideration of what role it is *capable* of adopting – and here we come to the question of the *relative decline* of the United States.

It has been apparent since the 1970s that the United States has been in relative economic decline: that is, while still the world's greatest economy, the United States has been losing ground to other countries in matters such as its economic productivity and its share of world trade. Nothing symbolises this more than the fact that, since the 1980s, the United States has had a trade deficit with Japan averaging around $50 billion a year. Moreover, during the same period, the United States passed from being the world's greatest *creditor* nation to the world's greatest *debtor* nation. Although the years of the Clinton presidency witnessed a sustained recovery in the economy, the fact remains that the United States has to fight harder than ever before to maintain its economic status.

This relative decline of American economic power inevitably had repercussions for its global political and military strategies. Indeed, it was even being considered possible that the United States might go the way of previous hegemonic nations by falling prey to 'imperial overstretch': this occurs when a nation's global interests and obligations are too great for its economy to sustain (Kennedy, 1988, p. 515). Just as Great Britain and others before it failed to reconcile the gap between overseas demands and domestic capacity, so too the United States might lose its hegemonic status. As we saw in Part 2, there were already signs of such imperial overstretch during the Vietnam War.

Furthermore, in the years after Vietnam, other domestic issues increasingly came to demand attention. While the long-standing problem of an annual federal budget deficit averaging well over $200 billion was solved, it helped to generate a continuing preoccupation with low taxation and lean government expenditures. In addition, with the disappearance of the international communist threat, the public tended to believe that domestic programmes should be given priority over at least some kinds of foreign policy expenditures. In short, there were far fewer funds available in the 1990s for defence and foreign affairs than there were during the Cold War. Indeed, the 1997 congressional appropriation for international affairs was less than half what it was in 1984, in part because 'the cold war used to provide a fiscal fig-leaf for what would now be immediately denounced as profligacy' (Naim, 1997/98, p. 38).

In short, as the world's sole superpower, the United States had greater opportunities, choices and responsibilities as a result of the end of the Cold War. Simultaneously, however, the resources available to be devoted to this international agenda were diminishing as a result of relative economic decline and the rival claim to resources of domestic crises. Thus it is ironic that 'as the external environment has widened the range of choices for the

United States, its domestic situation has narrowed them' (Art and Brown, 1993, p. 2).

The phenomenon of globalisation also brought additional problems for American foreign policy-makers. The opening up of international trade and competition has created greater freedom for non-governmental organisations (NGOs). These include multinational corporations with agendas that may differ from that of the US government. Moreover, such corporations may have direct access to foreign governments eager for inward investment and thus the US government may simply be bypassed (Naim, 1997/98, p. 39).

In the light of these new challenges and constraints, it is hardly surprising that the first post-Cold War administrations of Presidents Bush and Clinton struggled to articulate a new vision of America's role in the world.

The new world order

For a brief period in the early 1990s, it seemed that the United States had found the solution to its foreign policy dilemmas. President Bush, flushed with the success of the American-led multinational force in expelling Iraq from Kuwait, announced the arrival of a new world order. He and other foreign policy-makers set out a vision of a global order in which the United States continued to offer leadership, but other nations assumed a greater responsibility for the human and economic costs of keeping the peace and maintaining stability.

For President Bush, the new world order was founded upon 'universal' values of capitalism, liberal democracy, free trade and the renunciation of aggression as an instrument of foreign policy. Nations which transgressed the new order by using force should expect to be met by the collective force of the international community, especially the United Nations. The United States would offer military leadership to the international community, but would not attempt to turn this into a *Pax Americana*.

The Bush concept of a new world order struck some familiar themes in American foreign policy. Thus, American values were, in fact, universal values and the United States a political and social model to which other nations aspire. The idealist tradition in American foreign policy also appears in the advocacy of collective security and the implicit assertion that US policy is geared to the good of the international community as a whole, rather than the entrenchment of American power.

However, 'Even the most favourable reading of the diplomacy and rhetoric of the "new world order" project could not fail to ignore its central affirmation of the primacy of American global power' (McGrew, 1994, p. 220). Yet if the new world order suggested an America still hankering to play the role of policing the world, US foreign policy under President Clinton had a significantly different emphasis.

The Clinton administration came in for sustained criticism for its alleged failure to define a coherent agenda and strategy for US foreign policy (Haas, 1997; Naim, 1997/98). While such critics acknowledge that President Clinton had to contend with new constraints, they underestimate the extent to which he did, in fact, possess both a vision and a foreign policy for the changed world of the 1990s. As Michael Cox has argued:

> Clinton (like Ronald Reagan) assumed office with a fairly clear view of the world and the sort of policies he would have to pursue in order to enhance American power. Of course, unlike his neo-conservative predecessor, his main interest was not in the evil empire but in the world economy; and the principal means he hoped to use to mobilize Americans behind his policies was not anti-communism but raw economic self-interest.
>
> Cox, 1995, pp. 22–3

Logically enough, therefore, Clinton's emphasis was upon strengthening American power through restoring its economic competiveness. This, in turn, involved both domestic policy, such as bringing the budget deficit under control, and foreign policy, such as the formation of a free-trade zone in the western hemisphere in the form of the North American Free Trade Agreement Treaty (NAFTA) of 1993.

Box 20.7

The new world order

'You see, as the Cold War drew to an end we saw the possibilities of a new order in which nations worked together to promote peace and prosperity. I'm not talking here of a blueprint that will govern the conduct of nations or some supernational structure or institution. The new world order does not mean surrendering our national sovereignty or forfeiting our interests. It really describes a responsibility imposed by our successes. It refers to new ways of working with other nations to deter aggression and to achieve stability, to achieve prosperity and, above all, to achieve peace.

It springs from hopes for a world based on a shared commitment among nations large and small, to a set of principles that undergird our relations. Peaceful settlements of disputes, solidarity against aggression, reduced and controlled arsenals, and just treatment of all peoples.

This order, this ability to work together got its first real test in the Gulf war. For the first time, a regional conflict – the aggression against Kuwait – did not serve as a proxy for superpower confrontation. For the first time, the UN Security Council, free from the clash of Cold War ideologies, functioned as its designers intended – a force for conflict resolution and collective security . . .

The new world order really is a tool for addressing a new world of possibilities. The order gains its mission and shape not just from shared interests, but from shared ideals. And the ideals that [have] spawned new freedoms throughout the world have received their boldest and clearest expression in our great country, the United States. Never before has the world looked more to the American example. Never before have so many millions drawn hope from the American idea. And the reason is simple: unlike any other nation in the world, as Americans, we enjoy profound and mysterious bonds of affection and idealism. We feel our deep connections to community, to family, to our faiths.

But what defines this nation? What makes us Americans is not our ties to a piece of territory, or bonds of blood. What makes us Americans is our allegiance to an idea that all people everywhere must be free. This idea is as old and enduring as this nation itself – as deeply rooted, and what we are as a promise implicit to all the world in the words of our own Declaration of Independence.'

President George Bush, Remarks at Maxwell Air Force Base War College, Alabama, 13 April 1991

'Twice before in this century after world wars, US presidents have led efforts to create an international mechanism for collective resistance to aggression – first, President Wilson and the League of Nations and then President Roosevelt and the United Nations. Yet, now, with the end of the Cold War, in the Persian Gulf for the first time an international body – the UN – has played the role dreamed of by its founders – orchestrating and sanctioning collective resistance to an aggressor. The potential for the UN to continue to play this role, and the new willingness of many nations to contribute money and military units, are the foundation stones of a new era of international security – a new world order characterized by a growing consensus that force cannot be used to settle disputes and that when the consensus is broken, the burdens and responsibilities are shared by many nations.

The new world order is neither a *Pax Americana* nor a euphemism for the US as a world policeman. It is simply an attempt to deter aggression – and to resist if necessary – through the collective and voluntary action of the international community.'

Robert Gates, Deputy National Security Adviser, Address to the American Newspaper Publishers' Association, Vancouver, 7 May 1991

It is important to stress, however, that this new emphasis on geopolitics does not entail a wholesale retreat from American military leadership. As events in the former Yugoslavia demonstrated in the 1990s, even an economically powerful European Union possessed neither the will nor the means to promote and sustain a resolution to civil war. The Dayton Agreement on Bosnia could never have worked without American leadership. Furthermore, the renewed crisis with Iraq in 1998 over its alleged store of weapons of mass destruction produced a convincing demonstration of America's readiness to use its military might to impose its will, even when most of its allies in the Gulf War refused to support its stand.

It is true that the United States did not develop a comprehensive global strategy to replace containment, but then there was no clear agreement that one was necessary. The precise direction of American foreign policy in the post-Cold War context was still a matter of debate. Three basic schools of thought can be discerned: American primacy, neo-isolationism and new internationalism (McGrew, 1994, pp. 226–34).

Those who advocate American primacy are motivated by a mixture of realism and idealism. They believe that the United States must maintain and enhance its preponderance of power in the world in order to shape it in ways that favour American economic interests and political values. To do otherwise risks allowing a hostile world environment to develop, perhaps forcing the United States once again to rely upon military might to secure its prosperity, and even its democracy, at home. Along with these powerful elements of realism goes the belief that it is America's historic mission to universalise its political and economic values.

Neo-isolationists also blend realism with idealism in their desire to return to the foreign policy principles and practices of the early republic. They advocate 'selective engagement' with the outside world, guided in this by economic self-interest. They saw the end of the Cold War as an opportunity to focus attention once again on domestic matters, rebuilding a strong, prosperous and stable society at home.

New internationalism views neither neo-isolationism nor primacy as a realistic option. On the one hand, nations are too interdependent to permit successful partial withdrawal from the world, and power is too fragmented to allow the United States to reassert its primacy for very long. Instead, the United States must pursue multilateralism, offering leadership to, but not attempting to dominate, institutions such as the United Nations. Within the global framework of peace and stability delivered by such multilateralism, the United States can concentrate on renewing its economic strength. With military force no longer a viable means of achieving international ends, and economic power widely dispersed, the new internationalism in effect calls for an end to any American pretence to be a superpower. Instead, the new internationalism envisions the United States as one of many nations enjoying peace, security and free trade and offering international leadership based on economic strength and moral standing.

There are clearly areas of overlap between these three schools of thought. Most importantly, perhaps, they all stress the need to strengthen America's economic position. However, it is still not clear which blend of realism and idealism the United States will take forward as its foreign policy for the twenty-first century. The terrorist attacks of 11 September 2001 forced the United States, temporarily at least, to put this debate to one side and instead adopt a strategy for action. As we shall see in the next chapter, President George W. Bush adopted a policy of rebuilding America's military might, committing it to a long-term 'War on Terror' and taking unilateral decisions where other governments or institutions failed to follow America's lead. If and when the crisis of terrorism is significantly diminished, however, there can be little doubt that the United States will once again turn its attention to its traditional foreign policy debate. For in the oft-quoted words of the American revolutionary, Thomas Paine, the United States still considers itself to be 'the last best hope of mankind', and reluctantly or otherwise, many nations still look to the United States for leadership in a world where order is a fragile commodity.

Chapter summary

American foreign policy has always been a blend of realism and idealism and of internationalist and isolationist tendencies. Nevertheless, there has been an almost inexorable rise of the United States to the status of world power and then lone superpower. Parallel with this has occurred a gradual rise in the importance of the presidency within the foreign policy-making process. While both the presidency and the United States seemed weakened and uncertain in the 1990s, the aftermath of 9/11 makes clear that, in times of crisis, there is still no rival to American power and no rival to the presidency in providing leadership.

Discussion points

1. Which international relations theory best explains the development of US foreign policy?
2. Why did the United States rise to become a superpower?
3. What are the major constraints upon presidential power in foreign policy-making?
4. What are the main foreign policy dilemmas facing the United States today?
5. Is isolationism a myth in the history of American foreign policy?

Further reading

There are many useful introductory texts on the making of American foreign policy, but among the best are J.A. Rosati and J.M. Scott, *The Politics of United States Foreign Policy* (5th edn, Boston: Wadsworth, 2010) and B. Jentleson, *American Foreign Policy: The Dynamics of Choice in the 21st Century* (4th edn, New York: Norton, 2010). A more specialised but comprehensive volume is M. Cox and D. Stokes, *US Foreign* Policy (2nd edn, Oxford: OUP, 2011). A very readable and balanced history of US foreign policy is W. LaFeber, *The American Age: US Foreign Policy at Home and Abroad Since 1750* (2nd edn, New York: Norton, 1994).

References

Art, R. and Brown, S. (1993) *US Foreign Policy: The Search for a New Role* (Basingstoke: Macmillan).

Commager, H. (1974) 'Myths and realities in American foreign policy', in Commager, H. (ed.) *Defeat of America: Presidential Power and the National Character* (New York: Touchstone).

Corwin, E. (1957) *The President: Office and Powers* (New York: New York University Press).

Cox, M. (1995) *US Foreign Policy after the Cold War: Superpower Without a Mission?* (London: Pinter).

Dumbrell, J. (1990) *The Making of US Foreign Policy* (Manchester: Manchester University Press).

Graebner, N. (1984) *America as a World Power: A Realist Appraisal from Wilson to Reagan* (Wilmington: Scholarly Resources).

Haas, R. (1997) 'Fatal distraction: Bill Clinton's foreign policy', *Foreign Policy*, vol. 108, Fall, pp. 112–23.

Hilsman, R. (1990) *Politics of Policy Making in Defence and Foreign Affairs* (2nd edn, Hemel Hempstead: Prentice Hall).

Hunt, M. (1987) *Ideology and US Foreign Policy* (New Haven: Yale University Press).

Kegley, C. (ed.) (1991) *The Long Postwar Peace* (London: HarperCollins).

Kegley, C. and Wittkopf, E. (1987) *American Foreign Policy: Pattern and Process* (5th edn, Basingstoke: Macmillan).

Kennedy, P. (1988) *The Rise and Fall of the Great Powers* (London: Unwin Hyman).

LaFeber, W. (1989) *The American Age: United States Foreign Policy at Home and Abroad Since 1750* (London: Norton).

McCormick, T. (1989) *America's Half-century: United States Foreign Policy in the Cold War* (Baltimore: The Johns Hopkins University Press).

McGrew, A. (1994) 'The end of the American century?', in McGrew, A. (ed.) *The United States in the Twentieth Century: Empire* (London: Hodder & Stoughton).

Mueller, J. (1971) 'Trends in popular support for the wars in Korea and Vietnam', *American Political Science Review*, vol. 65, pp. 358–75.

Naim, M. (1997/98) 'Clinton's foreign policy: a victim of globalization?', *Foreign Policy*, vol. 109, Winter, pp. 34–45.

Ragsdale, L. (1993) *Presidential Politics* (Boston: Houghton Mifflin).

Schlesinger, A. (1973) *The Imperial Presidency* (Boston: Houghton Mifflin).

US Bureau of the Census (2005) *Statistical Abstract of the United States* (Washington, DC).

Wildavsky, A. (1975) 'The two presidencies', in Wildavsky, A. (ed.) *Perspectives on the Presidency* (Boston: Little, Brown).

Chapter 21

Contemporary US foreign policy

Andrew D. Moran

At the beginning of the twenty-first century, many American foreign policy analysts believed that the world was living in a unipolar moment, with the USA as a sole superpower, dominant economically, politically, and culturally. Within ten years, the debate had dramatically shifted to whether America was now a power in decline. Much was made of America's failure to bring peace and security to Iraq and Afghanistan, whilst the credit crunch of 2008 was viewed as originating from weaknesses in the American economy. A great deal of the criticism was directed at the controversial presidency of George W. Bush. But even the remarkable election victory of Barack Obama, and the hope that this generated, both in America and around the world, could not stop questions about America's future. As other powers jockeyed for position – most notably, the burgeoning economies of Brazil, Russia, India and China – commentators began to consider whether America would simply become one power amongst many, or even whether it was now in terminal decline.

Context

The 1990s were a confusing decade for many Americans. Though America had triumphed in the Cold War, many were left asking exactly what this victory meant and what actually had been 'won'. A common criticism of the Clinton administration (1993–2001) was that it had failed to articulate a new grand strategy of America's national interest and foreign policy direction in the post-Cold War era. Furthermore, though Clinton could claim success in securing peace agreements, notably the Dayton Accords ending the war in Bosnia, and support for the rapid spread of democratisation and liberal capitalism around the world, problems remained with America's globalisation agenda.

With the ending of the Cold War, it appeared that the American model of liberal capitalism had triumphed. Former communist states rushed to embrace economic freedom and market-based reforms, whilst technological and transportational developments brought the developing world into an international market which promised global prosperity. Clinton spoke of a 'train of globalization' that 'cannot be reversed', pulled by the engine of America's economic success, which, he believed, would 'lift hundreds of millions of people out of poverty' (Clinton, 2000).

Though economic globalisation would improve living conditions for many around the world, some states were left behind, failing to attract foreign investment or to find new markets for their goods. As a result, by the end of the decade Clinton would warn that globalisation needed 'a more human face' that addressed an increasing list of problems, which included: the growing gap between the world's rich and poor; perceived exploitation of workers by multinational companies; increased global pollution; the promotion of consumerism over cultural diversity; and the global AIDs crisis. A significant number of critics of globalisation identified America as a major source of these difficulties because most of the world's corporations were based there and its government had played a central role in promoting economic globalisation. The anger that these critics felt would develop into a growing anti-globalisation movement that would express itself violently at the World Trade Organization meeting in Seattle in 1999, and then at subsequent international economic meetings around the world. The anti-Americanism that came with these protests took many Americans by surprise. Then came the attacks of 9/11.

It is difficult to underestimate the impact of the events of 11 September 2001 on the American psyche. In a single day, nearly 3,000 people were killed by 19 men armed with box cutter knives who hijacked four planes and smashed them into the symbols of American power – the first two hit the World Trade Centre (economic), the third the Pentagon (military), and the fourth, brought down in a field in Pennsylvania, would most likely have hit the White House or Capitol Hill (political). More Americans died that day than on any since the bloodiest days of the American Civil War of 1861–5. It was the first attack on the capital, Washington DC, since the British burnt down the White House in 1812. 'U.S. ATTACKED', screamed the *New York Times* headline the next day, detailing a 'hellish storm of ash, glass, smoke and leaping victims' as the World Trade Center towers collapsed, televised by global media to billions around the world (Schmemann, 2001, p. A1). Even the French newspaper, *Le Monde*, a frequent critic of American foreign policy, declared, 'We are all Americans.' America's response would be to launch a 'war on terror' that would see it take the fight outside the United States, to Afghanistan and Iraq, and covertly to countries such as Pakistan and Yemen, led by a president, George W. Bush, whose controversial defeat of incumbent Vice-President Al Gore in the election in 2000 had divided the nation.

The presidency of George W. Bush

When Bush became the 43rd president of the United States in 2001, there was little to suggest that he would be remembered for his foreign policy. In fact, in the 2000 election, foreign policy had played little part. Bush had run on a domestic agenda that appealed to the Republican Party base of conservatives and the Christian Right. What criticism he had made of Bill Clinton's foreign policy centred on an accusation that he had a tendency towards interventionism and 'overambition'. This was reflected by an electorate that focused primarily on domestic issues and appeared generally unconcerned that Bush had little knowledge or experience of foreign policy.

Bush reassured voters that he would be 'surrounded by good, strong, capable, smart people who understand the mission of the United States to lead the world to peace' (Mann, 2004, p. 255). In fact, he chose skilled, experienced political players who knew the machinations of foreign policy inside out. Vice-President Dick Cheney had served in Congress, been White House Chief of Staff (for

Figure 21.1 The moment George W. Bush was told that a second plane had hit the World Trade Center, 11 September 2011.
Source: © Corbis/Reuters/Win McNamee

President Gerald Ford), and defense secretary for Bush's father, George H. W. Bush. Secretary of State Colin Powell had also served in his father's administration, as Chairman of the Joint Chiefs of Staff. National Security Adviser Condoleezza Rice had been a National Security Council staff specialist on the Soviet Union, whilst Secretary of Defense Donald Rumsfeld had been United States Permanent Representative to NATO under Nixon, and Chief of Staff and Secretary of Defense for President Ford.

They were all well known to the foreign policy community and most shared the view that Charles Krauthammer had expressed at the end of the Cold War that America had entered a unipolar moment that would begin an era of American dominance which would last 30–40 years. It was the world's sole superpower, preponderant both economically and militarily (Krauthammer, 1990/91, pp. 23–33 and 2002–03, p. 17). This belief was reflected by the Bush administration adopting a more unilateralist position than its predecessor, combined with an aggressive diplomatic style, both demonstrated by a rejection of the Kyoto Protocol on climate change, a refusal to sign up to the International Criminal Court, and opposition to the international ban on landmines.

This new approach was influenced by the so-called 'neo-conservatives'. Originating predominantly from disillusioned liberals and left-wingers who had been critical of the liberalism of the Great Society in the 1960s and détente in the 1970s, neo-conservatives believed that Clinton had squandered the unipolar moment that victory in the Cold War had created, and had missed a crucial opportunity for America to shape the world in its own image and in favour of America's interests.

A key think-tank promoting this message, and one which sought to influence the Bush administration in the 2000 election and beyond, was the Project for the New American Century, several members of which took up key policy positions within the administration, notably Paul Wolfowitz. They advocated 'unchallenged American global leadership and the expansion of the American empire of liberty, democracy, and free markets backed up by a mighty military machine' (Williams, 2005, and Nuruzzaman, 2006, p. 248). It was the projection of what Krauthammer called 'democratic globalism' (Krauthammer, 2004a). The initial response to the 9/11 attacks would be dominated by neo-conservative thinking, with the pursuit of power, freedom and liberty as the cornerstones of a new grand strategy known as the 'Bush Doctrine'.

The 'war on terror'

The response of the Bush administration to 9/11 was to declare a 'war on terror'. In the immediate aftermath of the attacks, Bush warned, 'We will pursue nations that provide aid or safe haven to terrorism. Every nation, in every region, now has a decision to make. Either you are with us or you are with the terrorists.' Furthermore, the United States would 'make no distinction between the terrorists who committed these acts and those who harbour them' (Bush, 2001).

The terrorist group al-Qaeda, led by Osama bin Laden, was quickly identified as the perpetrator of 9/11. Emerging out of the Afghan war in the 1980s, and opposition to America's increasing role in the Middle East in the aftermath of Iraq's failed invasion of Kuwait in 1990–91, it had already been responsible for a number of attacks on the USA overseas, including the August 1998 bombings of the American embassies in Kenya and Tanzania and the October 2000 bombing on the USS *Cole* in a harbour in Yemen. Bin Laden had warned the USA of his intentions in an interview with Peter Arnett on *CNN*, in March 1997, when he proclaimed, 'We declared jihad against the US government, because the US government is unjust, criminal, and tyrannical. . . . The whole Muslim world is the victim of international terrorism, engineered by America at the United Nations' (Arnett, 1997).

Though the Clinton administration had viewed terrorism as a problem, and even considered targeting bin Laden, this had not been considered a priority security issue. Bush continued this approach, rarely mentioning terrorism or al-Qaeda during his 2000 campaign. In fact, as Stephen Walt notes, at the beginning of his administration, National Security Adviser Condoleezza Rice downgraded the status of the national coordinator for counter-terrorism, Richard Clarke, and little attention was paid to the intelligence that warned the White House of an impending attack. Deputy Secretary of Defense Paul Wolfowitz went as far as to tell Clarke that he was 'giv[ing] bin Laden too much credit' (Walt, 2010).

Arguably, the 'war on terror' would give bin Laden the status he craved. Instead of being labelled an international criminal, he was now the symbol of defiance against the world's sole superpower. Bush's strategy also implied that terrorism was a military problem, within a realist framework of power, rather than one that could be won through patient intelligence, domestic security measures, and cooperation between governments, security and law-enforcement agencies.

The 'war on terror' formed the cornerstone of what became known as the 'Bush Doctrine'. First articulated in his State of the Union message on 2002, it was reinforced by his speech to the West Point Military Academy on 1 June 2002 and in the administration's national security strategy of 2002.

The doctrine had a number of key elements. First was the defensive strategy of pre-emptive war – the right to strike an enemy who posed an imminent threat before they attacked first. Though

America has long reserved the right to act preemptively as a means of self-defence, never before had this been so explicitly stated, or codified. It also meant a rejection of the Cold War doctrines of deterrence and containment. (See Box 21.1)

Second was a belief in regime change and the promotion of democracy. In his State of the Union message in the aftermath of 9/11, Bush declared that states such as Iraq, Iran and North Korea were part of an 'axis of evil', which sought to aid terrorists, 'aiming to threaten the peace of the world'. They were 'rogue states' that needed to be challenged and the leadership replaced, by force if necessary (Bush, 2002a). The Middle East would be the starting place.

The administration set this radical approach within a moral framework, harking back to its exceptionalism and frequently using terms such as 'good', 'evil', 'democracy', 'liberty' and 'freedom', whilst calling bin Laden and other terrorists 'evildoers'.

The administration argued that, if America was to achieve these goals, the defence budget of the

Box 21.1

The beginnings of the Bush Doctrine

On 1 June, 2002, President Bush delivered a speech to graduates at the US Military Academy at West Point. In it he laid the foundations for what would become known as the Bush Doctrine.

'For much of the last century, America's defense relied on the Cold War doctrines of deterrence and containment. In some cases, those strategies still apply. But new threats also require new thinking. Deterrence – the promise of massive retaliation against nations – means nothing against shadowy terrorist networks with no nation or citizens to defend. Containment is not possible when unbalanced dictators with weapons of mass destruction can deliver those weapons on missiles or secretly provide them to terrorist allies.

We cannot defend America and our friends by hoping for the best. We cannot put our faith in the word of tyrants, who solemnly sign non-proliferation treaties, and then systemically break them. If we wait for threats to fully materialize, we will have waited too long.

. . . The war on terror will not be won on the defensive. We must take the battle to the enemy, disrupt his plans, and confront the worst threats before they emerge. In the world we have entered, the only path to safety is the path of action. And this nation will act.

. . . Our security will require transforming the military you will lead – a military that must be ready to strike at a moment's notice in any dark corner of the world. And our security will require all Americans to be forward-looking and resolute, to be ready for preemptive action when necessary to defend our liberty and to defend our lives. . . .

Because the war on terror will require resolve and patience, it will also require firm moral purpose. In this way our struggle is similar to the Cold War. . . .

Some worry that it is somehow undiplomatic or impolite to speak the language of right and wrong. I disagree. Different circumstances require different methods, but not different moralities. Moral truth is the same in every culture, in every time, and in every place. . . . There can be no neutrality between justice and cruelty, between the innocent and the guilty. We are in a conflict between good and evil, and America will call evil by its name. By confronting evil and lawless regimes, we do not create a problem, we reveal a problem. And we will lead the world in opposing it.'

http://georgewbush-whitehouse.archives.gov/news/releases/2002/06/print/20020601-3.html, accessed 1 July 2011

USA must be rapidly expanded to meet the new threats it faced. Within five years of the 9/11 attacks, the defence budget would almost double, reaching $604 billion in 2006 – at that time, a figure equal to 45 per cent of all the world's defence spending.

This militarisation of the 'war on terror' included the development of the controversial National Missile Defense System which would involve the development of anti-ballistic missiles designed to shoot down any incoming missiles fired at the USA from rogue states. Not surprisingly, when Bush announced that these missiles, and their early warning systems, would be stationed in the Czech Republic and Poland, this was met with unease from Russia. Relations between the two were not helped when, to enable this to happen, Bush unilaterally withdrew the USA from the Anti-Ballistic Missile treaties of the early 1970s with Russia. Those treaties had been designed to hinder the development of ABMs for fear that they might tempt one side to launch a first-strike attack against the other, knowing they could knock out their opponent's retaliatory weapons. Bush's proposal for NMD was widely criticised – it increased tensions with the Russians, was expensive (the Congressional Budget Office put the estimated cost over 15–25 years at $238 billion), and it would not have stopped the 9/11 attacks.

The Bush Doctrine suggested a more unilateralist foreign policy, centred on American preponderance and primacy, with America asserting its power for the good of the world – by force, if necessary. As Bush put it: 'America will never seek a permission slip to defend the security of our country' (Bush, 2004).

What many Americans perceived as self-confidence grounded in the nation's own exceptional values was, however, viewed in a negative light by others. Harvard political scientist Stanley Hoffman was extremely critical, suggesting that 'the Bush Doctrine proclaims the emancipation of a colossus from international constraints (including from the restraints that the United States itself enshrined in networks of international and regional organizations after World War II). In context, it amounts to a doctrine of global domination' (Hoffman, 2003). The fear that many countries would later express was that the USA was becoming a unilateral, imperialist state.

Afghanistan

The first application of the Bush Doctrine was, arguably, the invasion of Afghanistan in 2001. Here, the United States took the fight to the enemy, intervening against the Taliban government that had harboured bin Laden and his al-Qaeda network. As Jentleson notes, to begin with the war was 'as internationally consensual as wars get' (Jentleson, 2010, p. 411). The USA could justify its actions in terms of self-defence, whilst the Taliban government itself had been denied its seat at the UN, with only two countries in the world granting it diplomatic recognition, and it had one of the worst records on human rights – particularly women's rights – in the world.

Though the extraordinary power of America's military might quickly removed the Taliban from power, many of the Taliban leadership and members of al-Qaeda, including bin Laden himself, were able to escape and America very quickly found itself bogged down in a security operation where it was unclear who the enemy were. This was made worse by a number of factors: an Afghan army whose capabilities remain questionable; a slow pace of economic reconstruction and development, reflecting, in part, an unwillingness by other countries to become involved; and a political elite, led by Hamid Karzai, which was perceived as being corrupt and incapable. Even today, despite the best efforts of the occupying forces, opium production remains one of the few growth areas of the Afghan economy, fuelling the illegal drug trade in Russia and the West. As Bush would discover, it is easier to overthrow a regime than it is to stabilise a country in its aftermath and build a democratic society and government. By the end of the Bush presidency, though a rudimentary democracy was in place, there was little security outside of Kabul, and the Taliban had returned, carrying out attacks against civilian and military targets.

A common criticism of the Bush administration's approach to Afghanistan was that it broadened the 'war against terror' to include Iraq too soon, before the war had actually been won. Though America's forces were stretched thin across the vast, unwelcoming terrain of Afghanistan, the US took the decision to fight a second war, in the process drawing troops away from one war zone to another. This would prove to be a significant tactical mistake.

Iraq

According to the journalist Bob Woodward, Bush had asked Donald Rumsfeld very soon after 9/11 about the status of military planning for a possible invasion of Iraq (Woodward, 2002). This had been a particular source of interest, and influence, for neo-conservatives who argued that Saddam Hussein's replacement by a democratic regime would inspire democratic revolutions throughout the Middle East. According to David Rothkopf, 'The neocons saw their opportunity to assert their case that diplomatic balancing acts in the Middle East had created danger for the United States, and the time had come for stronger measures, whatever the costs' (Rothkopf, 2005, p. 39). Like Bush, Krauthammer even went so far as to equate the 'war on terror' with the Cold War, writing 'The existential enemy then was Soviet communism. Today, it is Arab/Islamic radicalism' (Krauthammer, 2004b, p. 17). Krauthammer hoped that the Middle East would be transformed by the Bush administration, as, he argued, the Soviet Union had been as a result of the Reagan presidency.

Unlike the war in Afghanistan, the invasion of Iraq in March 2003 divided the United Nations, NATO allies, and the American public. Initially, it was justified on security grounds which required the removal of a dictator, Saddam Hussein, who abused his own people and threatened stability in the Middle East and beyond. This would be linked to Hussein's alleged development of weapons of mass destruction and his encouragement of terrorism, with the Bush administration making frequent links between Iraq and the 9/11 attacks. Both would prove to be unfounded. Weapons of mass destruction were never found and, much to the astonishment of the American public, media and politicians, Bush would later deny he had ever suggested Hussein was in league with bin Laden. In fact, bin Laden had frequently criticised Hussein for the apparent secularism of Iraq, calling him an 'infidel'. It is not surprising that, given Iraq's large oil reserves, many argued the war was driven by a need to acquire this valuable resource (America being the world's leader in oil usage) whilst some wondered if it was an act of revenge, completing the failed attempt to remove Hussein after the first Gulf War of 1990–91.

The swift military victory in Iraq, using 'shock and awe' tactics, at first enhanced the credibility of American power within the region, and did enough to persuade Colonel Gaddafi in Libya that he should abandon his nuclear proliferation programme in fear that he would be next. By May 2003, Bush felt able to announce on board the USS *Abraham Lincoln* that combat missions had ended, a sign behind him proudly proclaiming 'Mission Accomplished'. The euphoria proved short-lived. The removal of Hussein would be followed by widespread violence and bloodshed. In line with Rumsfeld's view that US war-making abilities should be transformed, with fewer, but more potent battalions using state-of-the-art technology, only 200,000 troops were deployed in Iraq – far fewer than the half a million who had removed Hussein's forces from Kuwait in 1990–91. The disbanding of the Iraqi security forces and Ministry of the Interior, putting almost 700,000 unemployed Iraqis on the street, helped fuel an insurgency which was exacerbated by jihadists from across the Middle East crossing Iraq's unprotected borders and a near-all-out civil war between Iraq's rival Muslim sects – Shiites and Sunnis. The occupying forces soon found themselves victims of hit-and-run attacks whilst Iraqis fought each other. To date, the dead number 4,000 Americans and over 100,000 Iraqis, with a further 30,000 Americans wounded and several million Iraqis refugees. In financial terms, the costs were enormous. But the wider costs have been much greater.

The world's richest and most powerful country found itself isolated, unable to impose its will overseas, with an international community opposing the invasion and refusing to finance the subsequent state-building programme, whilst a strategy designed to produce US-friendly democracies in the Middle East instead resulted in an emboldened Iran.

At home, opposition to the war would see Bush sacrifice his Secretary of Defense, Donald Rumsfeld, in the aftermath of the disastrous mid-term election results of 2006 which saw Democrats regain control of Congress, in what was widely seen as a rejection of Bush's failing foreign policy.

Academics and writers, both realist and liberal, also criticised the war. The failure to prepare for reconstruction in Iraq and the difficulties in providing internal security led foreign policy specialist John Ikenberry to brand it 'the end of the neo-conservative moment' (2004, pp. 7–22). Realists John Mearsheimer and Steven Walt labelled Iraq an 'unnecessary war' which would sap America's power rather than strengthen it (Mearsheimer and Walt, 2003). Liberals argued the invasion lacked legitimacy as it was not sanctioned by the UN, would isolate the USA, and would weaken the structures of global cooperation that had helped create stability since the end of World War II. Political economist Clyde Prestowitz went so far as to describe the USA as a 'rogue nation', suggesting that its actions had gone beyond the norms of international behaviour (Prestowitz, 2003).

The moment of almost universal support for the USA in the wake of the 9/11 attacks proved to be short-lived, with the Iraq invasion marking a new low in relations between the USA and UN, and the Bush Doctrine raising fears of open-ended American military operations around the world. By January 2007, a BBC survey of 24 countries found that nearly three-quarters of citizens disapproved of US actions in Iraq, whilst a majority viewed US influence in the world as 'mostly negative' (BBC, 2007).

In the USA, the pursuit of the 'war on terror' led to accusations that the Bush team had been distracted from other problems, failing to stop North Korea's detonation of its first nuclear bomb in 2006, and preventing concerns growing over Iran's ongoing enrichment of nuclear fuel, possibly to develop their own nuclear weapon, and raising fears of an arms race in the Middle East. America's own non-proliferation agenda was deemed hypocritical, weakened by its continued support for Israel, which already had weapons of mass destruction, and an agreement to trade in nuclear technology with India. Though the latter was widely seen as Bush's attempt to develop relations with India as a counterbalance to growing Chinese influence in Asia, it left many feeling that there was one rule for America and another for the rest. Iran faced economic sanctions and military threats, whilst India did not.

The Bush years would also see a resurgence of Russian nationalism under Putin, who, in a stark warning, challenged America's claim to unipolarity in a speech in Munich in 2006. Russia opposed the invasion of Iraq, and increasingly threatened the developing democracies of Ukraine and Georgia, leading to a brief war with the latter. Russia also weakened American resolutions on Iran and North Korea in the UN Security Council, and opposed the installation of the National Missile Defense shield. Putin forcefully pursued an agenda that placed Russia as an active contradictory player to America.

Meanwhile in Latin America, a region that America dominated for over a century, and which it traditionally regarded as its own backyard, anti-Americanism flourished, led by the formidable and well-resourced Hugo Chávez of Venezuela. The Bush administration proved ineffective at halting its growing isolation in the region and the apparent onward march of the political left.

Bush and the imperial presidency

From the outset, the circumstances surrounding the election of George W. Bush in 2000 raised questions about his legitimacy as president. These concerns were only overcome in the wake of the traumatic events of 9/11, which strengthened his position as commander-in-chief. From 2002–3, his Gallup approval ratings would consistently be in the 60–75 per cent range.

In 2002, the administration skilfully used the mid-term elections as a referendum on Bush's leadership of the 'war on terror', resulting in an increase in Republican seats. Questioning the concept of the separation of powers, and the existence of checks and balances during a wartime situation, Bush claimed to be accountable only to the American people, not the other branches of government. 'I am the decider', he said in 2006, 'and I decide what is best' (Bush, 2006). Dick Cheney would support this view, arguing that, if the 'war on terror' was to be successful, 'It can only be directed by a strong executive who alone is not subject to the conflicting pressures that legislators or judges face' (Pfiffner, 2007).

In part, this reflected Bush's personality as president. According to Woodward (2002), Bush 'described himself at various points as "fiery", "impatient", "a gut player" who liked to "provoke" people around him'. Thomas and Wolfe argued that disagreement in the Bush White House was 'often equated with disloyalty . . . In subtle ways, Bush [did] not encourage truth-telling or at least a full exploration of all that could go wrong' (Thomas and Wolfe, 2005, pp. 33–37). This extended to Bush's closest advisers, Fukuyama arguing that Cheney and Rumsfeld were 'excessively distrustful of anyone who did not share their views, a distrust that extended to Secretary of State Colin Powell and much of the intelligence community'. According to Fukuyama, who would later disown the Bush administration after initially supporting the 'war on terror', 'Team loyalty trumped open-minded discussion, and was directly responsible for the administration's failure to plan adequately for the period after the end of active combat [in Iraq]' (Fukuyama, 2006, p. 61).

Not surprisingly, this led to accusations of a rebirth of the imperial presidency. As presidential scholar James Pfiffner notes, this concern was compounded in the years 2001–6, during which Bush issued over 800 so-called 'signing statements' that challenged or reinterpreted acts of Congress, arguing that they conflicted with his responsibilities as commander-in-chief. This compared with fewer than 600 signing statements from all previous presidents combined (Pfiffner, 2008).

If this showed disregard for the notion of checks and balances and the principle of a separation of powers, Walt argues the Bush administration enforced a set of practices that 'are normally associated with brutal military dictatorships' (Walt, 2010). In pursing the 'war on terror', Walt notes that the administration authorised 'the systematic use of torture, the suspension of habeas corpus, secret renditions of suspected terrorists, targeted assassinations, and indefinite detention without trial at Guantanamo and other overseas facilities'. The photographed abuses at Abu Ghraib caused international outrage, as did Dick Cheney's assertion that 'waterboarding' was little more than an 'enhanced interrogation technique', whilst the American classification of prisoners at Guantanamo Bay as 'unlawful enemy combatants' was seen as nothing more than an attempt by the USA to circumvent the Geneva Convention. To this could be added the PATRIOT Act, Bush authorising wiretaps of US citizens without warrants (breaching the Foreign Intelligence Surveillance Act of 1977) and establishing military tribunals within the executive to try suspected terrorists without due process.

In part, Bush was aided by congressional and Republican willingness, along with the media, to support the commander-in-chief at a time of conflict – to do otherwise, the Bush administration suggested, would be unpatriotic. This changed gradually as the wars in Afghanistan and Iraq failed to reach a conclusion. After the Republicans lost control of Congress in the 2006 mid-term elections, Bush found himself a considerably weakened, lame duck president. By 2008, his popularity had declined so far that few, if any, Republican candidates were prepared to be photographed with the president. Domestic dissatisfaction with his handling of the Hurricane Katrina disaster in New Orleans and growing economic uncertainty, combined with a questioning of America's role in Iraq and Afghanistan, would see Bush's approval rates plummet from over 80 per cent in the immediate aftermath of 9/11 to below 30 per cent for the last year and a half of his presidency – as low as Nixon during the Watergate scandal (Jentleson, 2010, p. 43).

The Bush legacy

The presidency of George W. Bush remains one of the most controversial in recent American history. John Lewis Gaddis considered it to be the most significant redesign of American foreign policy since Franklin Roosevelt, arguing 'The President and his advisers [seemed] to have concluded that the shock the United States suffered on September 11 required that the shocks be administered in return, not just to the part of the world from which the attack came, but to the international system as a whole. Old ways of doing things no longer worked. The status quo everywhere needed shaking up. Once that happened, the pieces would realign themselves in patterns favourable to U.S. interests. . . .' This was misguided, he suggests, squandering 'the moral advantage the United States possessed after September 11 and should have retained' (Gaddis, 2005, pp. 2–15).

In contrast, some analysts, such as Melvyn Leffler (2004), argue that the Bush administration actually represented continuity, rather than discontinuity, with America's past and its foreign policy traditions – that pre-emption was not unusual, and the administration's pursuit of democracy promotion had been a mainstay of America's exceptionalism.

Bush himself compared his presidency to that of Harry S. Truman, believing that history would eventually judge him positively. Before he left office, he would argue that his policies had been effective, noting that there were no further successful terrorist

Box 21.2

Hard, soft and smart power

Since he first proposed the theory of 'hard' and 'soft' power in 1990, Joseph's Nye theory has become one of the most influential when examining the nature of American power. Considering the 'war on terror', Nye had this to say:

'Power is the ability to alter the behavior of others to get what you want. There are basically three ways to do that: coercion (sticks), payments (carrots), and attraction (soft power). . . . Whether power resources produce a favorable outcome depends upon the context. . . . Having a larger tank army may produce military victory if a battle is fought in the desert, but not if it is fought in swampy jungles such as Vietnam.

A country's soft power can come from three resources: its culture (in places where it is attractive to others), its political values (when it lives up to them at home and abroad), and its foreign policies (when they are seen as legitimate and having moral authority).

. . . . [S]oft power got nowhere in luring the Taliban away from al Qaeda in the 1990s. It took American military might to do that. But other goals, such as the promotion of democracy and human rights are better achieved by soft power. Coercive democratization has its limits – as the United States has (re)discovered in Iraq. . . .

. . . . The efficiency of the initial US military invasion of Iraq in 2003 created admiration in the eyes of some foreigners, but that soft power was undercut by the subsequent inefficiency of the occupation and the scenes of mistreatment of prisoners at Abu Ghraib.

. . . the current terrorist threat is not Samuel Huntington's clash of civilizations. It is a civil war within Islam between a majority of moderates and a small minority who want to coerce others into an extremist and oversimplified version of their religion. The United States cannot win unless the moderates win. We cannot win unless the number of people the extremists are recruiting is lower than the number we are killing and deterring. . . . That equation will be very hard to balance without a strategy to win hearts and minds. Soft power is more relevant than ever.'

'Think Again: Soft Power', Joseph S. Nye Jr., *Foreign Policy*, 1 March 2006 attacks on the USA during his watch. He also developed relationships with India, accepting its regional importance as a counterweight to China and as a global economic power, and increased the aid budget to Africa well beyond any limits reached by the Clinton administration.

Perhaps the most influential assessment of Bush's foreign policy came from the American academic, Joseph Nye. In the early 1990s, Nye had reconceptualised notions of power and how it came be used in two distinct ways: 'hard power' and 'soft power'. Hard power he described as the ability to coerce others, based on a country's military and economic might. Soft power, Nye defined as 'the ability to get what you want through attraction. . . . It arises from the attractiveness of a country's culture, political ideals, and policies.' Considering America's foreign policy agenda, Nye argued that 'When our policies are seen as legitimate in the eyes of others, our soft power is enhanced' (Nye, 2004, p. x).

Nye suggests that, during the Bush years, the stunning hard power victory in Iraq was matched by a decline in America's soft power as the situation deteriorated and many feared that America was seeking to export its values by force. In effect, Bush squandered the boost in America's soft power generated in the wake of 9/11, damaging America's international standing. It was this that his successor, Barack Obama, would raise during the election campaign of 2008, and seek to put in reverse on becoming president in 2009.

The foreign policy of Barack Obama

In general, it is true to say that many around the world, particularly throughout Europe, greeted Barack Obama's election with relief that George W. Bush would no longer be president. Stanford University Professor Josef Joffe called it 'a moment of relief at having a US president who made it possible for the world to love his country again' (Joffe, 2009). Even though Obama's approval ratings may have fallen at home since becoming president, as tends to happen to any president, America's stock globally has increased as more people around the world feel more positively about the USA.

Like Bush, on becoming president Obama suffered from a lack of experience in foreign policy. To counteract this, he deliberately went on a world tour during the election campaign, visiting American troops overseas, and delivering a major speech to hundreds of thousands of people in Berlin, recalling the famous imagery of John F. Kennedy proclaiming 'Ich bin ein Berliner!' in the 1960s and Ronald Reagan demanding Russia tear down the Berlin Wall in the 1980s.

Obama also surrounded himself with experienced foreign policy practitioners. His vice-president, Joe Biden, had been chairman of the Senate Foreign Relations Committee; Secretary of State Hillary Clinton was a member of the Armed Services Committee (and had a recent ex-president as husband). Secretary of Defense Robert Gates continued in the role in which he had served under the previous president, reflecting the respect he commanded within the Pentagon and the need to ensure some continuity in policy during a period of transition. Obama also appointed Richard Holbrooke as special representative for Afghanistan and Pakistan, and Richard Armitage as special representative for the Middle East.

Obama was acutely aware that he had become president at an extraordinarily difficult moment for America. He had inherited two unpopular wars in Iraq and Afghanistan, a broader war against terrorism, and an economy that was teetering on collapse both at home and internationally. Not surprisingly, his administration's first priority was to prevent the economy slipping further into a catastrophic 1930s-style depression. In the first months of his presidency, Obama sought to restore the confidence of the credit markets through an expansive stimulus package, supported by a quantitative easing policy adopted by the Federal Reserve. Significantly, he also highlighted the need for international cooperation (through the G-20 and international institutions), arguing that the collapse was global in reach and the USA could not unilaterally address the problem, given the spread of globalisation.

This approach was indicative of how Obama would come to view foreign policy. From the outset, he deliberately linked domestic and foreign policy, stating that domestic rejuvenation was crucial for his long-term economic and foreign policy strategy. In December 2009, he stated: '[We have] failed to appreciate the connection between our national security and our economy . . . Our prosperity provides a foundation for our power. It pays for our military. It underwrites our diplomacy' (Obama, 2009b). He would consistently argue that America's strength came from its economic and technological vigour rather than its military power alone, suggesting that America faced a 'Sputnik moment' – the need to boost, amongst other things, America's education and science provision to ensure it remained in competition, both economically and militarily, with rising powers around the world (Obama, 2011).

With this came a belief that America had over-extended itself in Iraq, Afghanistan, and the more general war against terrorism. It had effectively neglected other issues and this, in turn, had damaged America's credibility around the world. In this Obama is neither a realist nor liberal idealist, but a pragmatist, signalling a more discriminating foreign

Box 21.3

The Obama Doctrine?

In his address to cadets at the US Military Academy at West Point on 22 May 2010, President Obama articulated a vision of a changing world in which America would move from the unilateralism of Bush to a more multilateral policy, based on American domestic renewal.

'Time and again, Americans have risen to meet and to shape moments of change. This is one of those moments – an era of economic transformation and individual empowerment; of ancient hatreds and new dangers; of emerging powers and new global challenges.

. . . . [W]e must first recognize that our strength and influence abroad begins with steps we take at home. We must educate our children to compete in an age where knowledge is capital, and the marketplace is global. We must develop clean energy that can power new industry and unbound [sic] us from foreign oil and preserve our planet. We have to pursue science and research that unlocks wonders as unforeseen to us today as the microchip and the surface of the moon were a century ago.

Simply put, American innovation must be the foundation of American power – because at no time in human history has a nation of diminished economic vitality maintained its military and political primacy . . .

. . . . [T]he second thing we must do is build and integrate the capabilities that can advance our interests, and the common interests of human beings around the world. . . . We will need the renewed engagement of our diplomats, from grand capitals to dangerous outposts. . . .

The burdens of this century cannot fall on our soldiers alone. It also cannot fall on American shoulders alone. Our adversaries would like to see America sap its strength by overextending our power. . . .

Yes, we are clear-eyed about the shortfalls of our international system. But America has not succeeded by stepping out of the currents of cooperation – we have succeeded by steering those currents in the direction of liberty and justice, so nations thrive by meeting their responsibilities and face consequences when they don't. . . .'

http://www.whitehouse.gov/the-press-office/remarks-president-united-states-military-academy-west-point-commencement (accessed 1 July 2011) policy that reduces America's overseas commitments and avoids the open-ended interventions of the Bush era. Or as Ben Rhodes, Obama's Deputy National Security Adviser for Strategic Vision, explained to *The New Yorker*, if the administration could boil down its foreign policy strategy to a bumper sticker, it would read: 'Wind down these two wars, reestablish American standing and leadership in the world, and focus on a broader set of priorities, from Asia to the global economy to a nuclear-nonproliferation regime' (Lizza, 2011).

In his inaugural speech, Obama announced that he would adopt a much more multilateralist position than Bush, emphasising global institutions and America's role in promoting democratic values, rather than pre-emptive war. It was not coincidental that Obama broke with tradition after his inauguration and chose to visit the State Department first rather than the Defense Department. Though this move undoubtedly reflected a need to demonstrate support for Secretary of State Hillary Clinton, whom he had defeated in the Democratic primaries in 2008, there was a broader message that Obama was seeking to re-engage in dialogue with the outside world. This was reinforced by Clinton announcing in July 2009, 'We will lead by inducing greater cooperation among a greater number of actors and reducing competition, tilting the balance away from a multipolar world and toward a multipartner world' (Clinton, 2009).

Recognising the limitations of America's abilities in the post-Bush era, Obama has pledged to shape a new 'international order' based on diplomacy and engagement. Not surprisingly, this apparently more liberal message was received positively in many parts of the world, but what is interesting is that Obama has attempted to reach beyond traditional allies to embrace the challenges posed by globalisation and the resulting shifts in economic and political power.

When he took office, he announced that he would seek to prioritise relations with rising powers, including China, India, Russia and Brazil, adopting a strategy of setting aside smaller issues as a bargaining chip to cooperate on bigger ones. A good example of this is his controversial decision to downplay human rights in his initial dealings with China. He has also made it clear that a major goal of his administration will be to develop stronger links, economically and politically, with many Asian countries to tackle a variety of issues, including nuclear proliferation, climate change, and economic instability. This reflects a growing view amongst many analysts, such as Niall Ferguson and Joseph Nye, that economic and political power is now shifting from the Atlantic to the Pacific (Ferguson, 2011 and Nye, 2010).

Obama has also made it clear that he is willing to go further than talking to America's allies, and would reach out to states that 'unclench their fists' in order to further America's interests (Obama, 2009a). Many took this to mean Iran, but it also included talking with the Taliban and North Korea, amongst others. Obama has also attempted to rebuild relations with Islamic countries. For him, there is no clash of civilisations, as Samuel Huntington once hypothesised would happen between the Christian and Islamic worlds. In his first year in office, he gave a landmark speech in Cairo, making it clear that America's relationship with the Muslim world would be based on mutual interest and respect.

Though dialogue is clearly important, Obama has not shied away from the use of force – perhaps reflecting a continuity with Bush – nor is he embarrassed by America's power. 'The American moment is not over, but it must be seized anew', wrote Obama in 2007. 'To see American power in terminal decline is to ignore America's great promise and historic purpose in the world' (Obama, 2007, p. 4). But Obama has also stressed that 'our power alone cannot protect us, nor does it entitle us to do as we please . . . Our power grows through its prudent use, our security emanates from the justness of our cause, the force of our example, the tempering qualities of our humility and restraint' (Obama, 2009a). There is what Hillary Clinton has called the application of 'smart power' – a greater reliance on its soft power (unlike Bush), but with the contingent use of its hard power when necessary. A concept first put forward by Joseph Nye and then developed by Suzanne Nossel, smart power is evident in many areas of Obama's foreign policy, such as the application of sanctions against Iran as it continues to develop its nuclear facilities, the surge in troop numbers in Afghanistan, and the use of drones in Pakistan, Yemen, and elsewhere. In short, Obama has adopted a strategy of 'using all elements of American power to keep us safe, prosperous and free', combined with a belief that 'America is strongest when we act alongside strong partners' (Obama, 2008).

In the meantime, he has not ignored America's traditional relationships. With regards to Russia, after the souring during the Bush years, Obama's response has been quite literally to announce that he was seeking to reset the relationship, something highlighted by an uncomfortably stage-managed first meeting between Hillary Clinton and her Russian counterpart in 2009, when she presented him with an actual reset button. The approach appears to be paying dividends, with Obama and President Medvedev signing the Strategic Arms Reduction Treaty in 2010 and Obama announcing that he will be abandoning the National Missile Defense as envisaged by Bush – although a scaled-down version will be developed which will be open to inspection by Russia. It is unclear, however, how this relationship will develop, particularly as Medvedev may be replaced by Putin in the next presidential elections in Russia.

With China, Obama has sought to establish a new US–China strategic and economic dialogue. This desire to create a 'G-2' reflects the administration's awareness of the challenges China represents, both politically and economically, and the importance of healthy relations between the two (particularly as China is effectively financing much of America's economic deficit, the Chinese leader being described by one commentator as 'Obama's bank manager'). To the dismay of many of Obama's supporters, one unexpected outcome of this was that Hillary Clinton announced in 2009 that human rights would not be prioritised in the administration's dealings with China. However, in July 2011, Obama met the Dalai Llama, and supported rights for Tibetans, much to the consternation of China, which publicly condemned the meeting. It is unclear where the relationship between America and China will go in the long term, particularly given the latter's willingness to ignore American pressure on economic policy to devalue its currency and slow down its export-led economy (which many feel is damaging the American economy), and China's increasing global ambitions.

It will be interesting to see whether Obama will continue to build stronger relations with India as a regional counterbalance to China. Shortly after his inaugural trip to China in 2009, Obama hosted a state visit of the Indian Prime Minister Manmohan Singh – the first of his administration and the second state visit by the Indian leader – the last being in 2005. Many took this as a significant event, designed to send a message to both the Indian government and the Chinese leadership.

The issues that dogged the Bush presidency, however, remain the thorns in the side of Obama's foreign policy. On becoming president, Obama distanced himself from the abuses of the Bush administration by ordering the closure of the prison at Guantanamo Bay and a review of detention and interrogation policy, as well as prohibiting the use of torture. Frustratingly for Obama, Guantanamo Bay remains open, in part due to the reluctance of other countries to take any of the prisoners held there, or a fear that, if they are repatriated, they may be released – something of particular concern in relation to the many prisoners from Yemen held there.

With regard to Iraq, Obama was a critic of the invasion from the very beginning and made it a major part of his campaign in 2008. He achieved his pledge to end combat missions in Iraq by 31 August 2010, with the remaining troops being withdrawn by the end of 2011. But, though the beginnings of a democracy appear to be developing in Iraq, the day-to-day security of Iraqis remains fragile, with regular suicide bombings still taking place, and major infrastructure problems remaining.

The pledge to reduce troops from Iraq also proved controversial, as many of them were simply been drawn down and redeployed to Afghanistan. It is here, arguably, that Obama's greatest problems exist. As public support for America's long war in Afghanistan has declined, it has become imperative for a political solution to be found to end the conflict. In a significant change to policy, Obama has moved from spreading democracy and promoting human rights in Afghanistan to a military mission which is now solely committed to providing security in the region, with a view to American troops eventually leaving. Central to this is an approach designed to disrupt, dismantle and defeat al-Qaeda and to prevent their return to either Afghanistan or Pakistan in the future. Indeed, Obama's policy towards Pakistan is shaped by events in Afghanistan, the fear of terrorism, and the fact that Pakistan has nuclear weapons which might fall into the wrong hands.

Though Obama inherited the war from the previous administration, he has effectively made it his own. People now talk of Afghanistan as 'Obama's war', particularly after his agreement to increase the number of troops by 30,000 in 2009 to mirror the successful surge carried out in Iraq. This decision, however, highlighted some of the tensions present in Obama's foreign policy. It took 94 days of deliberation before Obama sent in more troops, as demanded by the generals, but he counterbalanced this with a call for their withdrawal beginning in July 2011, designed to satisfy his liberal supporters. How successful this surge will be remains to be seen, particularly given Obama's announcement that troop numbers will be reduced by 2012. Cynics point out that this date is not coincidental, given that 2012 is a presidential election year.

Whatever Obama chooses to do in Afghanistan, it is clear that any solution to the war will have to include some agreement with the Taliban, even though they are isolated and would find it extremely difficult to regain control of Afghanistan. American attempts to train up Afghanistan's own military and security forces have their limitations and some degree of compromise will be necessary to bring stability to the region. It will take particular political dexterity to sell this message to the American public, who will question why the war ever took place if the Taliban remain, but it is difficult to see any other course of action that can be taken, given the costs it inflicts on American lives and the economy.

Obama was criticised for taking so long to decide to increase troop numbers in Afghanistan, but it was indicative of a different presidential style from that of George W. Bush. According to Elizabeth Drew, Obama is comfortable listening to a wide variety of arguments, encourages disagreement, and enjoys being presented with complex information. There is an emphasis on collaboration and deliberation, working for consensus and tangible achievements. It is unlikely that Obama would make a rash decision (Drew, 2009). But, it is also important for Obama that he is seen to be commander-in-chief. This was most definitely the case with the death of Osama bin Laden in May 2011, when Obama made it clear in his address to the American public on the night of the operation by America's Navy Seals that the decision to go ahead with the mission had been his and his alone and that he had been involved from the very beginning. This was also apparent in his sacking of Commander, US and NATO forces in Afghanistan, General Stanley McChrystal, after an article in *Rolling Stone* magazine in 2010 where he questioned the administration's abilities and commitment to get the job done.

In the long term, Obama wants to scale down America's commitments overseas to focus on domestic reforms, believing that oversized commitments overseas divert resources from domestic needs. This dovetails with Obama's view that the best way to promote America's mission overseas, and to spread democracy abroad, is by becoming an example of democracy at home whilst practising moderation abroad. This, in turn, is influenced by America's economic policy. The financial and economic collapse of 2008 has exacerbated the extraordinary deficits Obama inherited from Bush, such that the chairman of the joint chiefs of staff, Michael Mullen, has identified the national debt as the single largest threat to US security as America continues to fund its military through deficit spending.

Though Obama boosted troop numbers in Afghanistan, his instinct is to reduce, preferring disarmament agreements to military build-ups. This approach is evident in his handling of the Arab Spring. One adviser described the president's

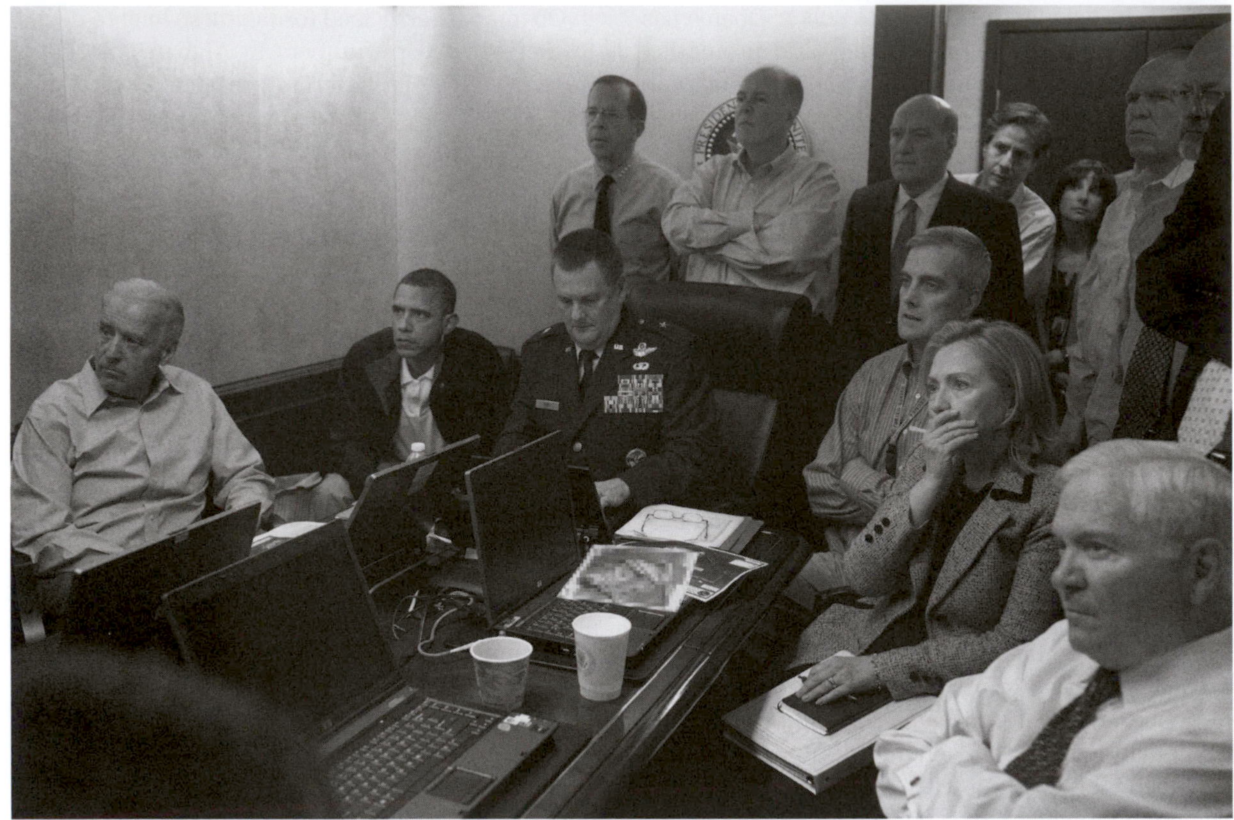

Figure 21.2 On Sunday night, 1 May 2011, President Obama announced the United States had killed Osama bin Laden, leader of al-Qaeda. That night Obama and his national security team watched events unfold live in the situation room of the White House.
Source: © Getty Images

actions in Libya as 'leading from behind', but it reflects Obama's reluctance to commit America to another war, and his desire to avoid any further damage to America's standing in the Muslim and Arab world.

Ultimately, he is seeking a world in which burdens are shared, rather than America having unilateral commitments. Within this, the United States would still remain the dominant power, but with fewer demands on its resources and a reduction in the dangers of being drawn into a new military conflict. How successful Obama will be remains to be seen, particularly as there are strong special interests in Congress which are opposed to cuts to the defence budget and altering foreign policy priorities, and are reluctant to accept that America's position in the world may be changing.

The end of the American century?

In February 1941, Henry Luce, the publisher of *Time* magazine, famously wrote that the twentieth century would be 'America's century'. At the turn of the twenty-first century, the magazine reaffirmed this conviction, suggesting the same would be true of the twenty-first century, reflected by America's victory in the Cold War and the rapid spread of liberal capitalism throughout the world. Neo-conservatives saw no reason to disagree.

The events of 11 September 2001 would shatter this illusion, unravelling America's apparent unipolar moment before it had fully begun. By 2004, America's National Intelligence Council was describing a future in which America would not be the dominant power, but simply a strong power amongst many, with a shift in power away from the United States and the West (National Intelligence Council, 2004 and 2008).

Many analysts suggest that China poses the most significant challenge to the USA: it has an economy that has been growing at an average of 9–10 per cent for three decades; is the world's leading exporter and its biggest manufacturer; and holds $2.5 trillion of foreign reserves. China has also developed strong links with many African countries, and is a major trading partner with the strongly emerging economies of Brazil and South Africa. As a result, it is expected by most economists to become the world's leading economy by the middle of the century, if not before. Goldman Sachs, for example, predicts that the Chinese economy will overtake the USA by 2027.

Not only is this challenging in economic terms, it is also creating concerns in other ways for American foreign policy makers – not least because China and the emerging powers often have foreign policy preferences at odds with those of the USA. Hence Brazil and India have sided with China on climate change talks, whilst Turkey and Brazil voted against America on sanctions against Iran. Furthermore, Fukuyama's rush to judgement that liberal capitalism had triumphed at the end of the Cold War seems even less likely now as these emerging powers have political, economic and cultural views which are not reflected in the USA. China, for example, does not consider the promotion of democracy to be an important part of its economic or foreign policy agenda.

But, as Fareed Zakaria notes, the decline may not necessarily involve the decline of the United States and the Western powers, so much as the rise of everyone else (Zakaria, 2009, p. 1). In this new world, he suggests, it will be difficult for the West or the United States to assert its preponderance – it may not even be desirable, given the experience of the Bush administration. Indeed, it is possible that the first few decades of the twenty-first century may witness what Richard Haass calls an era of 'non-polarity' or 'apolarity', with globalisation forcing an era of interdependence, particularly as America experiences chronic fiscal deficits and possible military overstretch (Haass, 2008, pp. 44–56). It would be unlikely that any other country would be able to challenge the power of the United States, even China in the short term. Optimistically, John Ikenberry suggests that 'In this new age of international order, the United States will not be able to rule. But it can still lead' (Ikenberry, 2011, pp. 56–68).

Indeed, Josef Joffe notes that the USA is still pre-eminent in economic, military, cultural and diplomatic terms, despite being involved in two wars and experiencing the worst financial crisis since the Great Depression of the 1930s. In his view, it will remain the world's dominant power because it combines its own self-interest whilst serving others, which, in turn, brings influence. It will continue to be, as a result, the world's 'default power' (Joffe, 2009).

Chapter summary

America's perceived victory in the Cold War eventually left many Americans asking what they had won. The 'war on terror' and the failure to win a clear victory in Iraq and Afghanistan, coupled with the economic collapse of 2008, have led many Americans to turn inwards. The arrogant optimism of the Bush administration has been replaced by a more realistic assessment of America's limitations. Where the unipolar moment offered clarity and purpose, now there is much uncertainty as America will be increasingly forced to do the very thing George Washington and the Founding Fathers warned against – entangling America in a series of alliances. As Joseph Nye concludes, 'The problem of American power in the twenty-first century . . . is not one of decline but what to do in light of the realization that even the largest country cannot achieve the outcomes it wants without the help of others. An increasing number of challenges will require the United States to exercise power with others as much as power over others' (Nye, 2010, p. 12). Only time will tell if America is up to the challenge of this new world order and whether the twenty-first century will be like the last – America's century.

Discussion points

1. What is meant by 'smart power' and how does its application by the Obama administration differ from the use of 'hard power' by the Bush administration?
2. How successful was the foreign policy of George W. Bush?
3. Is the USA a superpower in decline?
4. Critically assess the foreign policy of Barack Obama.

Further reading

Bob Woodward has written a number of excellent, and very readable, accounts of the foreign policies of George W. Bush and Barack Obama. They are: *Bush at War* (London: Simon and Schuster, 2002); *Plan of Attack* (New York: Simon and Schuster, 2004); *State of Denial: Bush at War, Part III* (London: Simon and Schuster) and *Obama's Wars: The Inside Story* (London: Simon and Schuster, 2010). Joseph Nye has updated his debate over the nature of power and how it might change in the twenty-first century in *The Future of Power* (New York: Public Affairs, 2011). A useful set of theoretical articles can be found in G. John Ikenberry's *American Foreign Policy: Theoretical Essays* (6th edn, Boston: Wadsworth, 2011). Three journals which offer excellent analysis of American foreign policy, both in print form and on-line, are *Foreign Affairs* at www.foreignaffairs.com, *Foreign Policy* at www.foreignpolicy.com; and *The Washington Quarterly* at www.twq.com.

References

Arnett, P. (1997) 'Interview with bin Laden', CNN, at http://edition.cnn.com/video/#/video/world/2011/05/02/video.vault.bin.laden.jihad.cnn?iref=allsearch (accessed on 1 July 2011).

British Broadcasting Corporation (2007) *World View of U.S. Role Goes from Bad to Worse*, (London: BBC).

Bush, G.W. (2001) 'Address to joint session of Congress and the American people', 20 September 2001, http://georgewbush-whitehouse.archives.gov/news/releases/2001/09/20010920-8.html (accessed on 2 July 2011).

Bush, G.W. (2002a) 'State of the Union Speech', 29 January 2002, available at http://georgewbush-whitehouse.archives.gov/news/releases/2002/01/20020129-11.html (accessed on 2 July 2011).

Bush, G.W. (2002b) 'Commencement address, US Military Academy, West Point, New York', 1 June 2002, http://georgewbush-whitehouse.archives.gov/news/releases/2002/06/20020601-3.html (accessed on 2 July 2011).

Bush, G.W. (2004) 'State of the Union Speech, 2004', http://georgewbush-whitehouse.archives.gov/stateoftheunion/2004/ (accessed on 1 July 2011).

Bush, G.W. (2006) 'President Bush nominates Rob Portman as OMB Director and Susan Schwab for USTR', 18 April 2006, at http://georgewbush-whitehouse.archives.gov/news/releases/2006/04/20060418-1.html (accessed on 1 July 2011).

Clinton, H. (2009) 'Foreign policy address at the Council on Foreign Relations', 15 July 2009, available at www.state.gov/secretary/rm/2009a/july/126071.htm (accessed on 19 July 2011).

Clinton, W. (2000) 'Speech at the University of Nebraska', 8 December 2000, *Public Papers of the Presidents: William J. Clinton 2000–2001* (Washington DC: US Government Printing Office), Vol. 3, pp. 2653–61.

Drezner, D. (2011) 'Does Obama have a grand strategy? Why we need doctrines in uncertain times', *Foreign Policy*, Vol. 90 No. 4, July/August 2011.

Drew, Elizabeth (2009) 'The thirty days of Barack Obama', *New York Review of Books*, 26 March. http://www.nybooks.com/articles/22450 (accessed on 7 July 2011).

Ferguson, N. (2011) *Civilization: The West and the Rest* (London: Penguin).

Fukuyama, F. (2006) *After the Neocons: America at the Crossroads* (London: Profile Books).

Gaddis, J.L. (2005) 'Grand strategy in the second term', *Foreign Affairs*, vol. 84, no. 1 (January/February), pp. 2–15.

Haass, R. (2008) 'The Age of Nonpolarity', *Foreign Affairs*, vol. 87, no. 3 (May/June), pp. 44–56.

Hoffman, S. (2003) 'The high and the mighty: Bush's National Security Strategy and the new American hubris', *American Prospect* 13: 28.

Ikenberry, John G. (2004) 'The end of the neo-conservative moment', *Survival* 46 (March), pp. 7–22.

Ikenberry, J. (2011) 'The future of the liberal world order: internationalism after America', *Foreign Affairs*, vol. 90, no. 3 (May/June), pp. 56–68.

Jentleson, B. (2010) *American Foreign Policy: The Dynamics of Choice in the 21st Century* (4th edn, New York: W. W. Norton).

Joffe, J. (2009) 'The default power: the false prophecy of America's decline', *Foreign Affairs*, vol. 88, no. 5 (September/October), pp. 21–35.

Krauthammer, C. (1990) 'The unipolar moment', *Foreign Affairs*, vol. 70, no. 1, pp. 23–33.

Krauthammer, C. (2002) 'The unipolar moment revisited', *The National Interest*, 70 (Winter 2002–2003), p. 17.

Krauthammer, C. (2004a) *Democratic Realism: An American Foreign Policy for a Unipolar World*, The American Enterprise Institute for Public Policy Research, http://www.aei.org/book/755 (accessed on 1 July 2011).

Krauthammer, C. (2004b) 'In defense of democratic idealism', *National Interest* 77, pp. 15–25.

Leffler, M. (2004) 'Bush's foreign policy', *Foreign Policy*, 144, pp. 22–28.

Lizza, Ryan (2011) 'The consequentialist: how the Arab Spring remade Obama's foreign policy', *The New Yorker*, 2 May 2011, available at http://www.newyorker.com/reporting/2011/05/02/110502fa_fact_lizza (accessed on 15 July 2011).

Mann, J. (2004) *The Rise of the Vulcans* (London: Penguin).

Mearsheimer, J. and Stephen Walt (2003) 'An unnecessary war', *Foreign Policy*, 134 (January/February), pp. 51–9.

National Intelligence Council (2004) 'Mapping the global future', December 2004, available at http://www.foia.cia.gov/2020/2020/pdf (accessed on 1 June 2011).

National Intelligence Council (2008) 'Global trends 2025: a world transformed', November 2008, available at http://www.dni.gov/nic/PDF_2025/2025_Global_Trends_Final_Report.pdf (accessed on 1 June 2011).

National Security Strategy, 2002 at http://georgewbush-whitehouse.archives.gov/nsc/nss/2002/index.html (accessed on 2 July 2011).

National Security Strategy, 2006 at http://georgewbush-whitehouse.archives.gov/nsc/nss/2006/ (accessed on 2 July 2006).

National Security Strategy 2010 at http://www.whitehouse.gov/sites/default/files/rss.viewer/national_security_strategy.pdf (accessed on 1 July 2011).

Nossel, S. (2004) 'Smart power', *Foreign Affairs*, March/April.

Nuruzzaman, M. (2006) 'Beyond realist theories: "neo-conservative realism" and the American invasion of Iraq', *International Studies Perspectives*, vol. 7, no. 3, pp. 239–53.

Nye, J. (2004) *Soft Power: The Means of Success in World Politics* (New York: Public Affairs).

Nye, J. (2010) 'The future of American power: dominance and decline in perspective', *Foreign Affairs*, vol. 89, no. 6 (November/December), p. 12.

Obama, B. (2007) 'Renewing American leadership', *Foreign Affairs*, vol. 4, no. 86, (July/August).

Obama, B. (2008) 'A new strategy for a new world', Washington DC, 15 July, http://my.barackobama.com/page/content/newstrategy (accessed on 1 July 2011).

Obama, B. (2009a) 'Inaugural address', 21 January 2009, http://www.whitehouse.gov/the-press-office/president-barack-obamas-inaugural-address (accessed on 1 July 2011).

Obama, B. (2009b) 'Remarks by the President in address to the nation on the way forward in Afghanistan and Pakistan', 1 December 2009, at http://www.whitehouse.gov/the-press-office/remarks-president-address-nation-way-forward-afghanistan-and-pakistan (accessed 10 July 2011).

Obama, B. (2011) 'State of the Union speech', 25 January 2011, www.whitehouse.gov/state-of-the-union-2011 (accessed on 2 July 2011).

Pfiffner, J. (2007) 'Constraining executive power: George W. Bush and the constitution', *Presidential Studies Quarterly*, vol. 38, no. 1 (March), pp. 123–43.

Pfiffner, J. (2008) *Power Play: The Bush Presidency and the Constitution* (Washington, DC: Brookings Institution Press).

Prestowitz, C. (2003) *Rogue Nation: American Unilateralism and the Failure of Good Intentions* (New York: Basic Books).

Rothkopf, David J. (2005) 'Inside the committee that runs the world', *Foreign Policy*, 147, pp. 30–40.

Schmemann, S. (2001) 'US attacked: President vows to exact punishment for "evil"', *New York Times*, 12 September, A1.

Thomas, E. and Wolfe, R. (2005) 'Bush in the bubble', *Newsweek*, 19 December, pp. 33–37.

Walt, S. (2010) 'Delusion points: don't fall for the nostalgia – George W. Bush's foreign policy really was that bad', *Foreign Policy*, 8 November 2010, at http://www.foreign policy.com/articles/2010/11/08/delusion_points (accessed on 8 July, 2011).

Williams, M. (2005) 'What is the national interest? The neoconservative challenge in I.R. theory', *European Journal of International Relations*, vol. 11, no. 3, pp. 307–37.

Woodward, B. (2002) *Bush at War: Inside the Bush White House* (London: Simon & Schuster).

Zakaria, F. (2009) *The Post-America World* (New York: W.W. Norton & Company).

Index